Rights in Exile

STUDIES IN FORCED MIGRATION
General Editors: Stephen Castles and Dawn Chatty

Volume 1
A Tamil Asylum Diaspora: Sri Lankan Migration, Settlement and Politics in Switzerland
Christopher McDowell

Volume 2
Understanding Impoverishment: The Consequences of Development-Induced Displacement
Edited by Christopher McDowell

Volume 3
Losing Place: Refugee Populations and Rural Transformations in East Africa
Johnathan B. Bascom

Volume 4
The End of the Refugee Cycle? Refugee Repatriation and Reconstruction
Edited by Richard Black and Khalid Koser

Volume 5
Engendering Forced Migration: Theory and Practice
Edited by Doreen Indra

Volume 6
Refugee Policy in Sudan, 1967–1984
Ahmed Karadawi

Volume 7
Psychosocial Wellness of Refugees: Issues in Qualitative and Quantitative Research
Edited by Frederick L. Ahearn, Jr.

Volume 8
Fear in Bongoland: Burundi Refugees in Urban Tanzania
Marc Sommers

Volume 9
Whatever Happened to Asylum in Britain? A Tale of Two Walls
Louise Pirouet

Volume 10
Conservation and Mobile Indigenous Peoples: Displacement, Forced Settlement and Sustainable Development
Edited by Dawn Chatty and Marcus Colchester

Volume 11
Tibetans in Nepal: The Dynamics of International Assistance among a Community in Exile
Anne Frechette

Volume 12
Crossing the Aegean: An Appraisal of the 1923 Compulsory Population Exchange between Greece and Turkey
Edited by Renée Hirschon

Volume 13
Refugees and the Transformation of Societies: Agency, Policies, Ethics and Politics
Edited by Philomena Essed, Georg Frerks and Joke Schrijvers

Volume 14
Children and Youth on the Front Line: Ethnography, Armed Conflict and Displacement
Edited by Jo Boyden and Joanna de Berry

Volume 15
Religion and Nation: Iranian Local and Transnational Networks in Britain
Kathryn Spellman

Volume 16
Children of Palestine: Experiencing Forced Migration in the Middle East
Edited by Dawn Chatty and Gillian Lewando Hundt

Volume 17
Rights in Exile: Janus-Faced Humanitarianism
Guglielmo Verdirame and Barbara Harrell-Bond

Rights in Exile

JANUS-FACED HUMANITARIANISM

Guglielmo Verdirame and *Barbara Harrell-Bond*

With Zachary Lomo and Hannah Garry
and a foreword by Justice Albie Sachs

Berghahn Books
New York • Oxford

First published in 2005 by
Berghahn Books
www.berghahnbooks.com

Library of Congress Cataloging-in-Publication Data

A catalog record for this book is available
from the Library of Congress.

British Library Cataloguing-in-Publication Data

A catalogue record for this book is available
from the British Library.

Printed in the United States on acid-free paper.

ISBN 1-57181-526-0 hardback

Contents

Foreword by Justice Albie Sachs   ix

Preface   xii

Acknowledgements   xix

List of Abbreviations   xxv

Introduction   1

    The setting   1

    Main movements of refugees into Kenya and Uganda   2

    Aims and objectives of the research   5

    Assumptions underlying the research   7

    Research methods   9

    Main findings   15

    A research and advocacy agenda for the future   21

1   Refugee Law and Policy in Kenya and Uganda   26

    Introduction   26

    The Legal Framework in Kenya   26

    The Legal Framework in Uganda   28

    Refugee policy in Kenya   31

    Refugee policy in Uganda   36

    Refugee law-making in fits and starts   45

    Conclusion   49

2 Getting In   55

  Introduction   55

  The influence of donor countries   55

  The OAU Convention and group recognition   57

  Admission: standards and procedures   58

  Legal hurdles to admission   59

  Ordeals of arrival   63

  New arrivals and local people   70

  Conclusion   72

**3 Status-Determination Procedures: '… and when you
go to UNHCR, pray'**   78

  Introduction   78

  Procedural standards in status determination   79

  Who is in charge?   80

  The role of NGOs   87

  Confidentiality   91

  Interpreters   92

  Advocacy   93

  Standards of evidence   94

  Decisions   96

  Exclusion   107

  Cessation   110

  Conclusion   113

4 Civil and Political Rights   120

  Introduction   120

  Non-discrimination   121

  Right to Life   130

  *Freedom from torture and from cruel, inhuman, or degrading
  treatment or punishment*   133

  Freedom from slavery and forced labour   151

  Liberty and security of the person   152

  Freedom of movement   179

  Access to courts and right to fair trial   182

  Privacy and family life   195

Freedom of expression, thought, conscience and religion, and freedom of assembly and association 198

Conclusion 201

5 Economic, Social, and Cultural Rights 214

Introduction 214

Employment 215

An adequate standard of living 225

The highest attainable standard of physical and mental health 241

Education 253

Cultural rights 260

Conclusion 263

6 Refugee Protection: What Is Going Wrong? 271

Introduction 271

Host countries 272

Donor countries 277

Resettlement 283

UNHCR 287

NGOs 312

Conclusion 324

Conclusions 332

Bibliography 340

Index 372

Foreword

Brace yourself. This is a painful book. Not only is the information in it extremely distressing; the main targets of its critique are 'the good guys'. The central argument is that the international and humanitarian organisations that are in charge of looking after refugees are responsible for extensive and avoidable violations of the rights of those dependent upon them. Considerable research was done on the life of refugees in Kenya and Uganda. The book details examples of failure to accord to such refugees respect for their human dignity. There is nothing to suggest that the treatment of refugees in these two countries was markedly inferior to the way refugees are treated elsewhere in Africa or other continents.

This is much more, however, than a denunciatory case study. It raises important questions of a general nature that go right to the heart of refugee law and practice. International organisations, NGOs, donors, and humanitarian agencies generally exercise great power over the lives of refugees. At the same time they are subjected to only minimal levels of accountability, either legal or political. In general terms, it is very rare for them to have to submit to the due process of law in national or international courts. They are seen as beneficent bodies acting to alleviate distress. While officials working on their behalf may be accountable internally to their management bodies, they are not legally or politically accountable to any external agencies. The refugees themselves, by the nature of their dislocation and lack of means, are rarely in a position to pursue legal actions against them. Not only would they have difficulty in establishing legal rights in an area where great discretion is allocated to those providing welfare; they would also be seen as biting the hand that feeds them.

Nor are these humanitarian bodies accountable to the electorate. The authors point out that in many respects they are immune to the scrutiny to which states and political parties may be subject. Political parties in office have to face criticism from political opponents, who will on occasion mobilise public opinion and activate the media to highlight governmental failure with respect to refugees. Although humanitarian organisations frequently compete for funds and sometimes over 'jurisdiction', they do not mount public campaigns against each other. Thus, as far as public opinion is concerned, humanitarian organisations are seen as wholly good. They are certainly not regarded as being responsible for abusing the rights of refugees. Indeed, the concept of rights for refugees tends to be limited in the public mind to the right to receive asylum and sufficient food and shelter to keep them alive. Their rights as human beings to take decisions for themselves, to make something of their lives, and to enjoy the ordinary pleasures of contemporary life, are simply not part of the equation. Refugee law is glacially trapped in its 1950 format when its main focus was on enabling people to flee from persecution and then simply to survive. If refugee law is to be seen as growing organically in keeping with the evolution of human rights law generally, then it needs to be given a far more expansive character, one which takes account of all the dimensions of being a human person in the world today.

Crucial to the situation is the relative powerlessness of refugees. They have little opportunity to speak for themselves in their own many voices. There are few channels available to them to make proactive proposals relating to how they should be dealt with both as communities and as individuals. Individuals may have some rights to claim classification under pre-determined categories that are favourable to them. They have little opportunity, however, to help decide what those categories should be, or to appeal to impartial tribunals against decisions made concerning them, except in the limited case where the decision relates to expulsion.

Refugees are not only voteless and voiceless; they are frequently unpopular. Often more political advantage is gained from stereotyping and denouncing them than from respecting their dignity and finding humane solutions to their situations. The focus is on who should or should not be granted asylum. This creates a climate in which scant attention is paid to the conditions under which refugees live. The authors contend that placing refugees in camps with little hope of repatriation is the source of many of the problems. They argue instead for more attention to be given to integrating refugees into local communities. This would mean looking for the skills refugees have to offer or else promoting their acquisition of skills, rather than seeing them simply as passive recipients of international welfare.

The authors write trenchantly and directly, so that no one can miss the sharpness of their critiques as academics and the strength of their indignation as human beings. Indeed, they would contend that in the area of refugee studies, intellectual enquiry must be strongly infused with human compassion. Furthermore, the compassion must not stop simply at the level of seeking to alleviate suffering. It must go on to facilitate the provision of opportunities to enable those fleeing persecution to achieve full human dignity in their new and alarming circumstances. Few could quarrel with these propositions.

Do I think the book is narrowly focused and too harsh on those that it criticises? I do. Do I think that this work pays insufficient attention to the dialectic of international responsibility for refugees? I do. The work of international organisations and humanitarian bodies has been extremely important in helping to give refugees recognised status, physical security, and at least minimal conditions of survival. Indeed, the sharp critiques made by the authors presuppose the existence of all the work, frequently arduous and thankless, done over the decades by these various institutions. Do I nevertheless think that the book must be read by anyone interested in the field of refugees and their lives? Yes I do. The very successes achieved by international humanitarian organisations in a quantitatively spectacular sense of saving people from persecution require more attention to be given to the qualitative questions of how the dignity of those affected can achieve full recognition. There is a need for devising new policies going beyond survival. There is a need for giving refugees a far more active role in deciding on their future. And there is a need for more rather than less investigative work like that done by the authors of this book. The challenges they make go well beyond polemic. They present sufficient documentary and empirically researched material to force any reader to sit up. Each one of us can make up his or her mind as to whether the characterisation of the activities of 'the good guys' is too sweeping and unduly wounding. Perhaps, not all of us would have told the story in the way that they have chosen. But this is their story, expressed in their way – openly, directly, and forcefully.

They stir the pot and the juices flow and penetrate. One hopes that those who feel that their work has been treated with unnecessary harshness will read and study this book with an appreciation of the importance of dialogue over the issues it raises. This book is a powerful voice in the debate. As I said at the beginning of this foreword, brace yourself, and read it.

Albie Sachs

Preface

Rights in Exile: Janus-Faced Humanitarianism is a sociolegal analysis of compliance with international human rights and refugee law in Kenya and Uganda. This book analyses the extent to which the rights of refugees were violated, as well as the ways in which such violations were perpetrated by a range of actors, chiefly governments and aid organisations. The findings of this book, while based on empirical research conducted in two countries, are pertinent to other host states, especially those in the 'developing world' where humanitarian organisations play the leading role in making and implementing refugee policy.[1]

The research on which this book is based constitutes the *first* long-term empirical study of violations of the full spectrum of human rights within a country with respect to a particular social group. The use of empirical methods was, in a sense, a forced choice, since there was no other way of finding out *to what extent, how,* and *by whom* the human rights of refugees were violated in Kenya and Uganda. In countries in the 'developing world', the use of traditional methods of legal research, in particular the study of judicial practice, is often severely hampered by the lack or inadequacy of case reporting. Moreover, many disputes, including criminal cases, are settled out of the court system; as far as refugee cases are concerned, an even smaller proportion is adjudicated in court.

'Experience is the life of the law',[2] and when lawyers lose touch with reality and fail to take 'experience' into account, their ability to promote the use of the law as a tool for social change is compromised. Limited by a formalist approach to legal methods, legal scholars have failed to bring attention to the *real* situation of refugees in countries in the 'developing world'. In this area, a gap of 'experience' has developed between the social sciences, where some have studied what really happens, and legal scholarship, which remains for the most part oblivious to these realities. Over fifteen years ago, *Imposing Aid: Emergency Assistance to Refugees*

(Harrell-Bond 1986) exposed the violations of economic and social rights, and the lack of physical protection and of access to justice that were suffered by refugees.[3] It showed how the methods of assistance imposed by humanitarian organisations were in themselves significant causes of many rights violations. *Imposing Aid* spawned a growth of academic critiques of humanitarianism by social scientists.[4] The first serious attempt by lawyers to follow up this evidence was reported in *African Exodus* (1996) by the Lawyers Committee for Human Rights (LCHR). This was the result of short field studies conducted in Côte d'Ivoire, Kenya, Malawi, Mozambique, Senegal, Sudan, and Zimbabwe.

The lack of attention to the many ways in which refugees' rights are violated in host countries is astonishing, if one considers that the protection of the rights of all people has been on the United Nations (UN) agenda since the adoption of the Universal Declaration of Human Rights,[5] and that refugees have formed an important part of the UN's relief work since the Second World War.[6] However, refugees have traditionally been relegated to the category of 'humanitarian' problems, the human rights dimension of their plight being generally ignored. When their problems did attract attention, this was often because it was politically convenient. The differences in treatment accorded to Haitian and Cuban refugees in the US remains one of the most obvious examples of how the identity of the persecutor can colour the reception refugees receive in countries of asylum.

Since the early 1990s refugees have been clearly put on the map of the international human rights movement, as the main international human rights organisations have begun to devote greater attention to their treatment in host countries. Nevertheless, refugees are still too often sidelined in the work of local human rights organisations in countries in the 'developing world' – partly as a function of lack of resources, but partly also as a consequence of insular attitudes and of the still prevailing belief that refugees are an 'international' and 'humanitarian' question rather than one of the key items on any national human rights agenda.

Interestingly, refugee advocates invest less of their time than environmental or development advocates trying to change existing international law. In fact, the limited attention to the human rights dimension of the treatment of refugees in host countries cannot be said to reflect legal limitations. On the contrary, although some uncertainty may persist with regard to the scope and content of particular rights, there is overall little doubt that refugees *are* legally entitled to a standard of treatment in host countries that encompasses both fundamental human rights and refugee-specific rights. The former are enshrined in international human rights law; for the latter, the 1951 Convention Relating to the Status of Refugees, which predates most human rights treaties, remains the main instrument and contains a relatively detailed enumeration of rights. In some cases the Convention requires state parties to extend to refugees the same standard of treatment as for nationals; in others[7] it obliges states to accord refugees as favourable a treatment as possible, and not less favourable than that accorded to aliens generally in the same circumstances.[8] In devising these two main yard-sticks, those who drafted the Convention clearly sought to ensure that refugees would not end up as pariahs at the margins of host societies. On the contrary, they should be treated like nationals in many cases, or, at worst, like other aliens. If the Convention were correctly applied, the situations that can be found in so many countries today in which refugees are the 'worst-treated' aliens would never obtain. The 1951 Convention also obliges state parties to issue refugees with identity papers and with documentation required for international travel, the Convention Travel Document (CTD), a prerequisite for many people to the rebuilding of their social lives and re-establishing means of livelihood.[9] It forbids discrimination on the grounds of race, religion, or country of origin,[10] and, most importantly, it protects refugees from being returned to the place where their lives and freedoms would be at risk (principle of *non-refoulement*).[11]

These provisions were set in place after the Second World War in response to the crisis of European refugees and continue to be regarded as the basis for the standards of treatment of refugees. As the sources of people fleeing wars and persecution shifted from Europe to countries in the 'developing world', the provisions of the 1951 Convention were extended globally through the 1967 Protocol, which also eliminated the temporal restrictions on eligibility for refugee status that had been limited to people fleeing events occurring before 1951. The mandate of the office of the United Nations High Commissioner for Refugees (UNHCR), set up as a temporary arm of the UN in 1950, was also expanded in 1967 to incorporate all persons seeking refuge across a border. In 1979, the General Assembly expanded UNHCR's mandate to incorporate the 1969 Convention Governing the Specific Aspects of Refugee Problems in Africa of the Organisation of African Unity (OAU Convention) (Jackson 1999: 194), which broadened the refugee definition.[12]

Any book on human rights violations is inevitably an attack on those who commit these violations or who could have prevented them. As such, this book is open to the obvious criticism of being a tirade against states, UNHCR, and humanitarian organisations. This book is intended to be, *inter alia*, an exposé, and, like most exposés, it may jolt readers with startling facts. We wrote Chapters 4 and 5 on the violations of each right, letting, as far as possible, the facts speak for themselves. We have focused on violations of human rights rather than on the instances in which human rights might have been respected, not with the aim of casting a negative light on governments or on UNHCR, but because as a matter of fact *no refugee* enjoyed his or her rights when confined to a camp/settlement; this reality is well known but continues to be ignored by those who have an interest in using relief budgets for their institutional survival. On countless occasions, when we presented our preliminary findings or during the research for this book, we were criticised for not 'discussing the whole picture' or for 'failing to talk about all the good work' of UNHCR, as if research on human rights should focus on people who are *not* arrested arbitrarily or on those whose freedom of speech is *not* interfered with. Governments, as well as any other organisation that exercises governmental functions (like UNHCR in refugee camps), ought to realise that the violation of the rights of *one* person already constitutes a breach of the law.

We have very little in common, politically or ideologically, with the views of those who criticise international organisations from a nationalist standpoint. We do not wish to see fewer or less influential international organisations. It is precisely because we believe that international organisations are important – and that, more specifically, refugees the world over *need* a system of international protection with a committed and accountable international organisation at its heart – that we want to draw attention to shortcomings in current practices and to what could appear as a tragic irony: those entrusted with the protection of refugees can, in some circumstances, become the enemies of refugee rights. We agree with Justice Albie Sachs's final remark on the focus of the book. In fact, if we could start our research from scratch, we would probably try to identify another country which could, as far as possible, be an example of 'good' practice – to convey the positive message that both governments and international organisations can get it right on refugee assistance. Nevertheless, there was hardly anything exemplary about the situation we found in Kenya and Uganda at the time of the research. The competence and commitment of various individuals, including some working for the governments and for UNHCR, did not compensate for the consequences of ill-conceived policies and flawed modus operandi. However, it is encouraging that, judging by some of the first public statements of representatives of the Kenyan government voted into power in December 2002, Kenya might well be the country offering examples of good practice on refugee rights in the near future, provided that this political will is translated into policy.

Another limitation of the book, of which we are aware, is that we pay little or no attention to the events that prompted refugees to leave their countries of origin. Until their arrival in Kenya or Uganda, their main persecutors had *not* been the host governments, let alone UNHCR or NGOs: their persecutors had been the governments, warlords, and rebel movements in their countries of origin. Yet, we wanted to write about the treatment of refugees in their countries of asylum, and this justifies our focus. At the same time, however, a complete ethnography of suffering and injustice would have to include, and indeed give prominence to, the violations of human rights committed in the countries of origin.

The Introduction to this book offers some estimates of the number and nationalities of the refugees in Kenya and Uganda at the time of the research and a brief review of the history of these two countries as hosts.

It describes the origins of the book and gives an account of the methods that were applied to collect the data. It also reviews the assumptions underpinning the study and comments on the roles of the different actors that are responsible for upholding the rights of refugees. In the Introduction, we also present our main findings.

Chapter 1, discussing the legal and policy framework for responding to refugees in both countries, begins to challenge the predominant view that power is the exclusive domain of the state. This view overlooks the complex and stratified structure of the power that derives from the interplay of various actors in a globalised environment (international organisations, foreign and local NGOs, donors, and governments). In particular, in both Kenya and Uganda, responsibility for refugee matters has been transferred from the state to humanitarian organisations – UNHCR and NGOs – which together control access to international humanitarian aid. It is argued that this transfer of power has given host states in the 'developing world' a pretext for abdicating their legal obligations vis-à-vis refugees. On the other hand, the impact that this reconfiguration of power has on the observance of human rights standards by non-state actors has also been overlooked. Through a detailed analysis of the modus operandi of humanitarian organisations, beginning in this chapter and continuing throughout the book, it is shown that, while the weakening of states and the promotion of 'powerful humanitarians' to act in their place may at first glance be viewed as emancipatory, the consolidation of power in the hands of organisations that are, in practice, unaccountable for upholding human rights represents an often underestimated threat to individual liberties (Verdirame 2001b). Indeed, a disquieting finding of the research is that some of the most glaring abuses of the rights of refugees result from the policies, actions, and omissions of the humanitarian organisations dealing with refugees.

The problems of 'getting in' to countries of asylum, discussed in Chapter 2, are drawn from the experiences of refugees who have already entered Kenya or Uganda; the numbers who never get past this first hurdle are unknown, despite the provision in the OAU Convention that equates rejection at the frontier with *refoulement* (art. 2(3)). Chapter 3 analyses the process of refugee status determination, which was characterised in both Kenya and Uganda by the anomaly of the pervasive role of UNHCR, due in part to the incorrect assumption that these countries had neither the will nor the capacity to conduct status determination themselves. We argue that assuming an adjudicative role in asylum determination compromises the protection role that UNHCR was established to fulfil.

Chapters 4 and 5 detail the violations of the full range of human rights protected under international law,[13] as well as the 1951 Convention and the OAU Convention. While emphasising the interdependence of all of these rights, these chapters go through the catalogue of civil, political, economic, cultural and social rights and identify the dynamics of the violations, elucidating the role of the different actors (host governments, UNHCR, NGOs, and refugees). We have chosen to follow the categorisation of rights to be found in human rights treaties rather than in the 1951 Convention because the human rights one is more comprehensive. Interestingly, the 1951 Convention has more to say on socio-economic rights than on civil and political rights. Moreover, in some cases the refugee standard has been superseded by a more generous human rights one. As far as primary education is concerned, the International Covenant on Economic, Social and Cultural Rights (ICESCR) provides that it shall be 'compulsory and available free to all' (art. 13(2)(a)), whereas the 1951 Convention simply stipulates that refugees are to receive the same treatment accorded to nationals (art. 22(1)). In some cases, we have subsumed refugee-specific standards under human rights. For example, state parties to the 1951 Convention 'shall not impose penalties' on refugees who 'enter or are present in their territory without authorisation' if they were 'coming directly from a territory where their life or freedom was threatened' (art. 31). We have dealt with the cases of refugees penalised in breach of this provision under liberty and security of the person, as it is a deprivation of liberty that, under international law, should not be imposed.

In Chapter 6, we attempt to answer the question 'What is going wrong with refugee protection?' A synergy of dysfunctions among the various actors dealing with refugees is identified and it is shown how this has led, among other things, to the entrenchment of segregation and encampment of refugees in countries in the 'developing world', leaving them with neither a voice nor an effective advocate. In addition, and more importantly, having arrogated powers from states, international actors constitute an exogenous apparatus that has acquired effective control over refugee policy and is not subject to the checks and balances that ordinarily constrain state bureaucracies, at least in liberal democracies.

There is a great disparity between the 'face' of humanitarian aid as it is viewed by its donors and the 'face' of that same aid as seen by its beneficiaries. Humanitarian organisations declare their commitment to respect human rights and humanitarian values, but, in practice, their 'beneficiaries' experience unfettered and unaccountable power. Given the immunity of international organisations from the jurisdiction of national courts, their actions cannot even form the object of independent and impartial adjudication. Furthermore, these international actors are shielded from local political control because of the absence of a constituency, either of nationals or refugees, with sufficient power to hold them to account. In camps, human rights violations can thus be perpetrated with impunity. The debate on solutions to the refugee 'problem' has to start from the premise that warehousing refugees in camps and respecting their human rights cannot be reconciled. The availability of resettlement to only very few and the unpredictability of repatriation make refugee integration the best solution for assistance programmes to promote.

Notes

1. *See*, e.g., these reports which identified similar problems to those analysed by us: Iranian Refugee Alliance, Inc. 1995; Sperl 2001; UNHCR 2000e; Obi and Crisp 2000; Kuhlman 2001.
2. This motto of legal pragmatism is attributed to Oliver Wendell Holmes.
3. The book is out of print, but is available at http://www.sussex.ac.uk/Units/ CDE and http://www.forcedmigration.org.
4. *See*, e.g., Keen 1992, 1994 and de Waal 1997. The *Journal of Refugee Studies*, launched in 1988, has been the major outlet for such empirical work.
5. 'You talk of refugees as though human rights did not exist which are broader and more important. Once an individual, a *human being*, becomes a refugee, it is as though he has become a member of another race, some other sub-human group' (Rizvi 1984).
6. They had also been prominent in the work of its predecessor, the League of Nations (*see* Skran 1998).
7. E.g. art. 4, religion; art. 14, artistic rights and industrial property; art. 15, right of association; art. 16, access to courts; art. 17, wage-earning employment; art. 20, rationing; art. 22(1), elementary education; art. 23, public relief; art. 24, labour legislation and social security (with certain limitations); and art. 29, fiscal charges.
8. E.g. art. 13, right to movable and immovable property; art. 18, right to self-employment; art. 19, liberal professions; art. 21, housing; art. 22(2), post-elementary education; and art. 26, freedom of movement.
9. Arts. 27–28.
10. Art. 3.
11. Art. 33.
12. The 1951 Convention defines a refugee as a person who 'owing to a well-founded fear of being persecuted for reasons of race, religion, nationality, membership of a particular social group or political opinion, is outside the country of his nationality and is unable or, owing to such fear, is unwilling to avail himself of the protection of that country; or who, not having a nationality and being outside the country of his former habitual residence as a result of such events, is unable or, owing to such fear, is unwilling to return to it' (art. 1). The OAU Convention adds that 'the term "refugee" shall also apply to every person who, owing to external aggression, occupation, foreign domination or events seriously disturbing public order in either part or the whole of his country of origin or nationality, is compelled to leave his place of habitual residence in order to seek refuge in another place outside his country of origin or nationality' (art. 1(2)).
13. These include (but are not limited to) the rights protected under: the International Covenant on Civil and Political Rights (ICCPR); the International Covenant on Economic, Social and Cultural Rights (ICESCR); the Convention on the Elimination of All Forms of Discrimination Against Women (CEDAW); the Convention on the Rights of the Child (CRC); the African Charter on Human and Peoples' Rights.

Acknowledgements

The research for *Rights in Exile: Janus-Faced Humanitarianism* was part of a collaborative and multi-disciplinary investigation into the health and welfare of refugees living in the camps and settlements of Kenya and Uganda, or outside them living among the host population. This project, entitled *Health and Welfare of Refugees* and funded by the European Union (EU),[1] was initiated by Dr Wim Van Damme, the Institute of Tropical Medicine, University of Antwerp, Belgium, and included teams of researchers from the Institute of Public Health, Makerere University, Uganda, the Centre for Refugee Studies, Moi University, Kenya, and the Refugee Studies Centre, University of Oxford, UK. Within this 'umbrella' project, field studies on refugee rights were initiated with funding from the EU, the Ford Foundation, the Norwegian Ministry of Foreign Affairs, the Nuffield Foundation, and the Rotary Foundation. The research was 'action-oriented', involving a number of projects designed to alter the status quo. Funding for two of these – the Workshop on Legal Aid held at the Fédération Internationale des Droits de l'Homme (FIDH) and courses on refugee law at the Faculty of Law at Makerere University in Kampala in which police participated – came from the EU.[2] A seminar on refugee law for judges and magistrates was funded by the Nuffield Foundation through the Faculty of Law, University of Warwick.

Startup funding for the legal aid programme for refugees in Uganda that ensued from the research, the Refugee Law Project (RLP) at Makerere University, was provided by the Amberstone Trust, later supported by the UK Department for International Development (DFID) and the Ford Foundation, Nairobi. The Friedrich Ebert Stiftung furnished the seminar room at the Makerere Institute of Social Research (MISR), providing accommodation for seminars and other regular meetings on refugee issues. A generous personal grant to Barbara Harrell-Bond from the Ford

Foundation, New York, allowed for shortfalls and for the implementation of many other projects as part of the research.

We also thank the United Nations Development Fund for Women (UNIFEM), the Lutheran World Federation (LWF), DanChurchAid, the Danish International Development Agency (DANIDA), Human Rights Watch (HRW), the Lawyers Committee for Human Rights (LCHR), and Article 19 for hiring us to undertake consultancy work that enabled us to collect other data from Kenya, Uganda, and Tanzania.

The research in Uganda had an institutional base, MISR, where Barbara Harrell-Bond was appointed visiting professor. She was involved in teaching at the Faculty of Law and in the supervision of theses. We thank all of the staff at Makerere University for their hospitality but we must especially single out Professor P.J.M. Ssebuwufu, vice-chancellor, and Professor J. Epelu-Opio, deputy vice-chancellor. At MISR special thanks are due to Professor John Munene and Dr Nakanyike Musisi, respectively acting director and director of MISR, for the use of facilities that went far beyond the flat, which became a residence and an office. Dr Nakanyike Musisi was also noticeable for the zeal with which she promoted social activities that included refugees. We want to acknowledge the assistance of Patrick Mulindwa, MISR, Dr Joseph Oloka-Onyango, dean of the Faculty of Law 1999–2002, Mr Sam Tindifa, at the time acting director and currently director, Human Rights and Peace Centre (HURIPEC), and Dr Sylvia Tamale. Special thanks go to Avitus K.M. Tibarimbasa, secretary to Council, Makerere University, who announced the decision of the 79th University Council meeting (August 1998) that henceforth refugee students would pay the same fees as Ugandan students.

Zachary Lomo and Hannah Garry were the main researchers in Uganda. Their study and work obligations did not allow them to participate in the writing of the book. However, their contribution deserves more than an ordinary acknowledgement. Both have had an opportunity to read and comment on various versions of the manuscript, and share our interpretation and analysis of the data.

In addition to the authors of this book, a number of other people in Kenya and Uganda contributed to the research: Makerere students conducting masters degree research, supervised by Barbara Harrell-Bond; individuals employed as research assistants; individuals serving as self-funded volunteer interns from many different universities who conducted in-depth research on specific issues; and various people attached to MISR as visiting fellows or students, conducting doctoral or other research for their home universities. Thanks go to Tania Kaiser, Professor Adelaida Reyes, Mauro De Lorenzo, Trine Lester, Deborah Mulumba, Neil J. Resnick, Anna Schmidt, Kate Reuer, Lucy Weir, Ellen Lammers, Cindy Horst, Mary Byrne, Alicia Samike, Magellan Kazibwe, Jessica Munson, Jude Murrison, Charles Njuguna, Justine Mwiinga, Clifton Taylor,

Sungwon Jin, Michela Machiavello, Ann Mwiriza, Christine Birabwa, Dr Gregory Elder, Ekuru Aukot, Doreen Lwanga, Ronald Kalyango, Dr Jill Craig, Dr Unni Karunakara, Patricia Kununka, Hassan Shiekh, Ibrahim Farah, Marirosi Marcellin, Julius Kayiira Lutaakome, Thomas Hertz, Elly Asiku, Paul Kapia, Thierry-Noel Mageni, Nicolas Nibikora, Willie Gisita, Cyrin Rantango, Gervais Abayeho, John Otim, Augustine Nsanze, Marie Nahimana, and Efrah Ahmed Said (who, a child herself, collected many children's testimonies). Much of their work is cited in the references. Special thanks go to Elias Lubega for managing the logistics of the research in Uganda, and to Lisa Finch and Pamela Reynell for agreeing to become the first directors of the RLP, a direct outgrowth of the research. In Cairo, where the book was written, Gina Bekker, Michael Chu, Mark Pallis, and Ahmed Siabdallah helped to organise data. Mark Pallis also helped at various stages with editing and commenting on drafts.

Other research and training activities were spawned by the EU umbrella project and it is appropriate that we acknowledge the institutions that funded them. Deborah Mulumba, funded by the Ford Foundation, Nairobi, carried out a study entitled *Towards the Integration of Health Services in Refugee Affected Areas in Uganda*. Dr Jill Craig, employed as a research assistant, began developing a project on the integration of refugee education; on her departure this was taken over by Dr Silus Oluka, Faculty of Education, Makerere University, who conducted research in Moyo and Adjumani districts. This research was funded by the International Development Research Centre (IDRC), Canada. Professor Adelaida Reyes, an ethnomusicologist whose research had until then focused on Vietnamese refugees, spent three months in Uganda and taught at the Department of Music, Dance and Drama. In 1999, a link between Makerere University and the Health and Forced Migration degree programme, Columbia School of Public Health (CSPH), Columbia University, New York, was established to provide an annual two-week course for agencies working with refugees in the health sector.[3] Funding was also obtained from IDRC to support a workshop in 1999 at Makerere University for 'stakeholders' (government officials, representatives of NGOs, and UNHCR) to identify the major policy issues requiring research. Funding from the Mellon Foundation made it possible for the hardware to be purchased to establish a computerised catalogue of library materials on human rights and forced migration at Main Library, Makerere University.[4] In 1998, funding was obtained through the Ford Foundation, the LWF, and personal sources, to allow the participation of members of the research team in the conference of the International Association for the Study of Forced Migration (IASFM) in East Jerusalem. Papers were presented by: Douglas Asiimwe, Aukot Ekuru, Gilbert Lukhoba, Deborah Mulumba, Tania Kaiser, Zachary Lomo, Kate Reur, Kenneth Porter, Anna Schmidt, Guglielmo Verdirame, and Michael

Wafula. The last session was chaired by Sam Tindifa, acting director, HURIPEC.[5]

We thank the Office of the President in Kenya and the Uganda National Council for Science and Technology for granting permission for the research. We also need to thank various government officials in both countries. In Uganda they include: John Cossy Odomel, inspector general of the police; Mr Dan Mudumba, director of training, Uganda Police Force; the Hon. Justice J.W.N. Tsekooko, justice of the supreme court and chairman of the judicial training committee; Mr Jerome Byesigwa, commissioner of prisons; Yorokamu Bamwine, acting chief registrar; the Hon. Dr Ruhakana Rugunda, minister for the presidency, Office of the President; Major Tom Butime MP and minister for disaster preparedness and refugees; Carlos Twesigomwe, deputy director for refugees (for facilitating the research in the settlements in Uganda); Douglas Asiimwe, the protection officer in the Directorate of Refugees (DoR); the late John Opio and Michael Wafula,[6] desk officers, Adjumani and Arua. In Kenya, we express our very deep appreciation to Nimrod Waweru, Arthur Andambi, Dr Kip Cheluget, Professor John Okumu, Dr Monica Kathina, Enoch Opondo, Joseph Gitari, Abi Gitari, Eugene Birrer, Sister Louise Radmeier, the Jesuit Refugee Service (JRS) staff in Kakuma in 1997, the late Chris Mulei, Ahmednassir Abdulhai, Binaifer Nowrojee, Dr Philista Onyango, Lucy Hannan, Goretty Omala, Praxidice Wekesa, Mary Ann Fitzgerald, Njoki Ndung'u, Karimi Kinothi, Father Schönecke, Bethuel Kiplagat, Jean Damascène Karara, Eroni Nakagwa, and the Sudan Women's Association in Nairobi (SWAN).

Many UNHCR staff in both Kenya and Uganda facilitated the research and we especially thank Abel Mbilinyi, Yvette Stevens, Pia Prütz Phiri, Dr Wandhe, Dr Michael Deppner, and Hans Thoolen. Many others inside UNHCR who have preferred anonymity and have not been mentioned in this book were also extremely helpful in providing documents and other information critical to our analyses. We also thank Martin Zak, head of delegation, International Federation of Red Cross and Red Crescent Societies (IFRC), the staff members of the Uganda Red Cross Society (URCS), and International Aid Sweden, an agency that worked with self-settled refugees and nationals in Moyo district. We also thank Nancy Baron of the Trans-cultural Psycho-Social Organisation (TPO) for her insightful observations at various times.

Numbers of others have helped. We thank all our colleagues at the Refugee Studies Centre, University of Oxford, but especially Belinda Allan, Sean Loughna, and Monika Porada. Professor Guy Goodwin-Gill, now at All Souls, University of Oxford, helped us devise the questionnaire for the police survey in Uganda. Colleagues who read parts or the whole of the manuscript included Michael Alexander, Rodger Haines, Mike Kagan, Dr Ken Porter, and Justice Albie Sachs. Marguerite Garling deserves special mention not only for the pivotal role she played in providing the funding for the Kenya research, but also for her comments on drafts of parts of this book and for sharing with us her insight into the situation of refugees in Kenya when we first arrived there. Sally Carpenter has carefully read and edited the first complete draft of the book, and has given us useful comments. Marion Berghahn welcomed our book proposal with enthusiasm and, together with the editors of the series, Dr Stephen Castles and Dr Dawn Chatty, took our continuous delays with considerate patience.

We want to single out Mauro De Lorenzo for special thanks. He spent a year with the research project in Uganda and quickly became a key member of the research team, conducting interviews with refugees, particularly those who spoke French, and writing a report on the situation of refugees living in Kampala. Later, we gained useful insight from discussing the concept and organisation of the book with him. In 2001–02, he gathered and wrote up some of the materials that appear in the Introduction, and was always forthcoming with details on the sociopolitical context and historical background. Last but not least, without his scanning of all the individual case files and his patient assistance with computer problems, we would have found ourselves stuck on numerous occasions.

Since the completion of the research, we have moved to different research institutions. Barbara Harrell-Bond has advised on the establishment of the Forced Migration and Refugee Studies Programme at the American University of Cairo. Cairo has been our main meeting point and workplace for writing the book. We have relied on the support of many colleagues and friends. Setting up the legal aid project in Cairo might have taken some time away from the writing, but it also acted as a constant reminder of the fundamental reasons for which we had undertaken to write this book. Guglielmo Verdirame spent three years at the London School of Economics where he wrote a doctoral thesis on UN Accountability for Human Rights Violations, which consisted of a detailed international law analysis of some of the issues raised in this book; the supervisor was Professor Christine Chinkin, whose insight and guidance were invaluable. He is also grateful to the Warden and Fellows of Merton College, Oxford, for electing him to a three-year fellowship, and to other colleagues, students, and members of staff at Merton who have helped create a most conducive and stimulating environment in which to work.

On a personal level, our families and partners supported us throughout and, on occasions too numerous to recall, they satisfied impossible demands for last-minute help on practical matters.

So many people have helped us, and we apologise if we have inadvertently omitted any of their names. The customary caveat is necessary: we alone are responsible for the contents of this book.

Notes

1. (IC18-CT96-0113 (DG 12 MUYS)).
2. (IC18-CT96-0113 (DG 12 MUYS)).
3. This course was co-sponsored by: the Institute of Public Health (IPH); the Human Rights and Peace Centre (HURIPEC), Makerere University; and African Medical Research Foundation (AMREF), an NGO, registered in Uganda, with headquarters in Nairobi. It continued under this management for three years and in 2002 it was provided independently of Columbia, the original aim.
4. At the time, Mellon also funded computers for the Legal Aid Project (LAP) and the Federación Internacional de Abogadas (FIDA), for their legal aid work with refugees.
5. Their papers may be found on http://www.gcmhp.net
6. He was also chairman of the committee drafting the refugee law and later wrote a thesis on the self-sufficiency project as conceived by UNHCR.

List of Abbreviations

AAH	Aktion Afrika Hilfe (a non-profit charitable organisation registered in 1996 in Munich, Germany. It took over the portfolio of 'Action "Africa in Need"', formed in 1990)
ACC/SCN	UN Administrative Committee on Co-ordination, Sub-Committee on Nutrition
ACF	Action contre la Faim (Action against Hunger)
ACORD	Agency for Cooperation and Research Development
ACTV	African Centre for Treatment and Rehabilitation of Torture Victims
ADF	Allied Democratic Forces (a Ugandan rebel group)
ADFER	Groupe d'Action pour la Défense des Droits de la Femme et de l'Enfant
AEF	African Education Fund (Japan)
AHA	African Humanitarian Action (an Ethiopian-based NGO that had Mrs Ogata's personal support. Employed all African staff)
AICF	Action Internationale contre la Faim
AMREF	African Medical Research Foundation (Kenya)
ANPPCAN	African Network for the Prevention and Protection against Child Abuse and Neglect
AREP	African Refugee Education Programme
AVSI	Associazione Volontari per il Servizio Internazionale (Italy)
BO	branch office (UNHCR)
CAO	chief administrative officer
CAT	Convention against Torture and Other Cruel, Inhuman or Degrading Treatment or Punishment
CC	camp commandant
CDW	community development worker

CEDAW	Convention on the Elimination of All Forms of Discrimination against Women
CHAD	Conflict and Humanitarian Affairs Department (part of DFID)
CIDA	Canadian International Development Agency
COREDA	Congolese Refugees Development Organisation (Uganda)
CRC	Convention on the Rights of the Child
CSM	community self-management
CTD	Convention Travel Document
DAFI	Deutsch-Afrikanische Frauen Initiative
DANIDA	Danish International Development Agency
DED	Deutscher Entwicklungsdienst (German Development Service)
DENIVA	Development Network of Indigenous Voluntary Associations
DFID	Department for International Development (UK)
DMO	district medical officer (Uganda)
DoR	Directorate of Refugees (Uganda)
DRC	Democratic Republic of Congo
ECOWAS	Economic Community of West African States
ECRE	European Council on Refugees and Exiles
EPRDF	Ethiopian People's Revolutionary Democratic Front
EPSR	Education Programme for Sudanese Refugees
ESO	External Security Organisation (Uganda)
EU	European Union
EXCOM	Executive Committee (of UNHCR)
FHRI	Foundation for Human Rights Initiative (Uganda)
FIDA	Federación Internacional de Abogadas (International Federation of Women Lawyers)
FIDH	Fédération Internationale des Droits de l'Homme
FONCABA	Fondation Catholique des bourses d'études pour Africains
FRC	Finnish Refugee Council
FT	*Financial Times*
GA	General Assembly
GLOBE	Global Learning Observation to Benefit the Environment
GoK	Government of Kenya
GoU	Government of Uganda
HAR	Hope after Rape
HPCT	Hugh Pilkington Charitable Trust
HRC	Human Rights Committee
HRW	Human Rights Watch
HURIPEC	Human Rights and Peace Centre (Makerere University, Uganda)
IARA	Islamic African Relief Agency

IASFM	International Association for the Study of Forced Migration
IC	individual case
ICARA II	Second International Conference on Assistance to Refugees in Africa
ICCPR	International Covenant on Civil and Political Rights
ICESCR	International Covenant on Economic, Social and Cultural Rights
ICG	International Crisis Group
ICJ	International Commission of Jurists
ICRC	International Committee of the Red Cross
ICTR	International Criminal Tribunal for Rwanda
ICVA	International Council of Voluntary Associations
IFRC	International Federation of Red Cross and Red Crescent Societies
IGO	inter-governmental organisation
ILC	International Law Commission
IMF	International Monetary Fund
INTRAC	International NGO Training and Research Centre
IOM	International Organisation for Migration
IRB	Immigration and Refugee Board of Canada
IRC	International Rescue Committee (US)
IRIN	Integrated Regional Information Network (UN)
ISO	Internal Security Organisation (Uganda)
JPO	junior protection officer (UNHCR)
JRS	Jesuit Refugee Service
JVA	Joint Voluntary Agency (US resettlement agency)
Kcal	kilocalories
KHRC	Kenyan Human Rights Commission
KSh	Kenya shillings
LAP	legal aid project (Uganda)
LC	Local Council (Uganda)
LCC	Local Council Courts (Uganda)
LCHR	Lawyers Committee for Human Rights
LRA	Lord's Resistance Army (Uganda)
LWF	Lutheran World Federation
MISR	Makerere Institute of Social Research (Uganda)
MoLG	Ministry of Local Government (Uganda)
MoU	memorandum of understanding
MRG	Minority Rights Group
MSF	Médecins sans Frontières
NCCK	National Council of Churches of Kenya
NEC	National Eligibility Committe (Kenya)
NEP	North-Eastern Province

NGO	non-governmental organisation
NRA	National Resistance Army
NRM	National Resistance Movement
NRS	National Refugee Secretariat (Kenya)
OAU	Organisation of African Unity
OC	officer-in-charge
OCHA	Office for the Coordination of Humanitarian Affairs (UN)
ODA	Overseas Development Administration (UK)
ODI	Overseas Development Institute (UK)
OLS	Operation Lifeline Sudan (UN)
OPM	Office of the Prime Minister (Uganda)
PARinAC	Partners in Action (UNHCR)
PDA	Public Defenders Association (Uganda)
PTSS	post-traumatic stress syndrome
QIP	quick impact project
RAA	refugee affected area
RCD	Rassemblement Congolais pour la Démocratie
RCK	Refugee Consortium of Kenya
RDC	resident district commissioner (Uganda)
RDR	Rally for the Return of Refugees and Democracy
REC	Refugee Eligibility Committee (Uganda)
RLP	Refugee Law Project
RPA	Rwandan Patriotic Army
RPF	Rwandan Patriotic Front
RRAP	Refugee Rights Advocacy Programme
RWC	Refugee Welfare Committee
SCF	Save the Children Fund
SHRA	Sudan Human Rights Association
SIDA	Swedish International Development Agency
SitRep	situation report
SPLA/M	Sudan People's Liberation Army/Movement
SSLS	South Sudan Law Society
SSRA	South Sudan Relief Agency
SWAN	Sudan Women's Association in Nairobi
TBA	traditional birth attendant
TPO	Transcultural Psycho-Social Organisation (Uganda)
UAM	unaccompanied minor
UDHR	Universal Declaration of Human Rights
UHRC	Uganda Human Rights Commission
UK	United Kingdom
UN	United Nations
UNAMIR	United Nations Assistance Mission in Rwanda
UNDP	United Nations Development Programme
UNFPA	UN Fund for Population

UNHCR	United Nations High Commissioner for Refugees
UNICEF	United Nations Children's Fund
UNIFEM	United Nations Development Fund for Women
UNRF II	Uganda National Rescue Front – Two
UNRWA	United Nations Relief and Works Agency
UPDF	Uganda People's Defence Forces
UPE	Universal Primary Education (Uganda)
URCS	Uganda Red Cross Society
USCR	United States Committee for Refugees
USh	Uganda shillings
WFP	World Food Programme
WHO	World Health Organisation
WNBF	West Nile Bank Front
WVV	Women Victims of Violence

Introduction

The setting

In 1997, when this research commenced, the office of the United Nations High Commissioner for Refugees (UNHCR) estimated that there were 420,300 refugees in Uganda and Kenya.[1] According to these estimates, which referred almost exclusively to encamped refugees, about 90 percent of the refugee population came from Somalia and Sudan;[2] there were smaller numbers of refugees from the Democratic Republic of Congo (DRC) (14,400), Ethiopia (8,500), Rwanda (17,900), and Burundi (100).[3] In addition, Uganda and Kenya each gave refuge to a small number of the other's citizens,[4] and received a few refugees from as far as West Africa, the Balkans, and the Middle East. Both countries witnessed internal displacement, as a result of the conflict in the north in Uganda and of the ethnic strife in various parts of the country in Kenya.[5] The majority of the refugee population in both countries consisted of people who had arrived there in the 1990s.

All of the 'assisted' refugees lived in remote rural encampments administered by UNHCR and non-governmental organisations (NGOs),[6] with the exception of an official 'urban' refugee programme for approximately 530 refugees in Kampala, Uganda.[7] In Nairobi, the Jesuit Refugee Service (JRS), contracted by UNHCR as an implementing partner, also provided some material assistance to small numbers of asylum-seekers and refugees.[8] Apart from these limited numbers of assisted refugees, Kampala and Nairobi hosted tens of thousands of refugees who lived outside the aid umbrella. Unassisted refugees could also be found in smaller towns and in rural areas. A combination of factors led these refugees away from the camps, with lack of physical security and the search for better socio-economic or educational opportunities being prominent (Kibreab 1989, 1991, 1996; Hansen 1982).[9] There was great uncertainty about their overall numbers.[10]

Main movements of refugees into Kenya and Uganda

In both Kenya and Uganda, forced migration predates independence.[11] From the 1920s to the 1950s, Rwandans and Burundians (mainly Hutus) migrated in the hundreds of thousands to Uganda and in smaller numbers to Kenya, fleeing state-imposed forced labour requirements and physical abuse, which today would qualify them for refugee status (Richards 1956; Newbury 1988). In 1936–38 alone, around 100,000 Rwandans and Burundians are believed to have entered Uganda each year; by the late 1950s their numbers were over 500,000, of whom 350,000 were Rwandan (Chrétien 1993: 277–8). Many became assimilated in the clan structure, took local names, acquired land, and married locally, and their grandchildren today may be only dimly aware of their Rwandan or Burundian ancestry. Such examples of integration of forced migrants are seldom remembered in the current climate.

The first major refugee-producing crises in the region after the Second World War began in Sudan in 1955 and in Rwanda in 1959. In 1955, the mutiny by southern Sudanese troops and the resulting seventeen-year *Anyanya* war forced many southern Sudanese to seek refuge in northern Uganda and Kenya (*see* Johnson 2002). Sudanese refugees continued to arrive in Uganda for more than fifteen years, with the main influx in 1964–65. Although the signing of a peace agreement in 1972 between Jaafar Al-Nimeiry's government and the *Anyanya* rebels paved the way for the repatriation of many Sudanese refugees (Betts 1974), in 1983 war broke out again between the forces of the Khartoum government and a new rebel group, the Sudan People's Liberation Army/Movement (SPLA/SPLM) led by Colonel John Garang. The war quickly spread to many parts of southern Sudan and, by 1986, the security situation had deteriorated to such an extent that many Sudanese fled in massive numbers to northern Uganda. In fact, they accompanied the many Ugandan refugees who had been driven out of their place of settlement in southern Sudan at the time (Harrell-Bond and Kanyeihamba 1986). More Sudanese refugees continued to arrive on a regular basis throughout the 1990s in both Uganda and Kenya – with peaks and troughs linked to the security situation in southern Sudan.

Even after independence, Rwanda remained a major refugee-producing country in the region. Although refugees from other countries have surpassed Rwandans as the largest group of exiles in Uganda, Rwandans historically played a defining role in the development of Ugandan refugee policy. Between 1959 and 1967, about 78,000 Tutsi refugees from Rwanda fled to southwestern Uganda, driving thousands of head of cattle before them.[12] They were settled in the Oruchinga valley in 1961, at Nakivale in 1962, and later in new settlements at Kahunge, Kyaka, Ibuga, and Rwamwanja in Toro (now Kabarole) district. As the crisis in Rwanda flared up again, some 20,000 refugees arrived between 1964 and 1967, and two new settlements were established at Kyangwali and Kinyara in Bunyoro (now Hoima and Masindi) districts in 1965.[13] In October 1990 a group of Rwandan refugee rebels, many of whom had served in Yoweri Museveni's National Resistance Army (NRA), crossed the border into Rwanda. Attempts to solve the conflict through peaceful means failed dramatically when on 6 April 1994 the plane carrying Presidents Habyarimana of Rwanda and Ntaryamira of Burundi was shot down as it approached Kigali airport. Within hours, a well-organised massacre began and in the following months a genocide took place, in which around 800,000 Tutsis and moderate Hutus were killed by extremists. The eventual overthrow of the Rwandan government by the Rwandan Patriotic Army (RPA) led to a massive exodus of over two million Rwandans – mainly to Zaire (now DRC) and Tanzania, but also to Kenya and Uganda (UNHCR 2000b). Unfortunately, the end of the genocide did not usher in an era of peace and stability in Rwanda. Refugees, both Hutus and Tutsis, continued to flee owing to the insecurity in parts of the country as well as political and ethnic persecution: many of these arrived in Nairobi and Kampala during our research.

The 1960–67 civil wars in the Congo and growing political repression by the Mobutu regime forced many Congolese to seek refuge in East Africa – mostly in Uganda, but also in Burundi, Tanzania, Sudan, and Kenya. Many of the estimated 33,000 Congolese were settled in camps in Achol-Pii in northern Uganda and Kyaka in western Uganda, but an unknown number of others 'self-settled' and successfully integrated into Ugandan society (Pirouet 1988: 240). Some of these 'self-settled' populations, especially the Congolese, helped their fellow nationals get settled when they fled the most recent wars in their country.

The ousting of Mobutu from power in May 1997 signalled the beginning of another chapter in the Congolese wars. In August 1998, Laurent Kabila fell out with his erstwhile allies Uganda and Rwanda, and a new wave of rebellions under different leaders, who served as proxies of Rwanda and Uganda, erupted in the now-renamed Democratic Republic of Congo (DRC), plunging the country into further turmoil and producing more refugees. After August 1998, Rwanda and Uganda openly backed the rebellion against Laurent Kabila's government in the DRC under the banner of the Rassemblement Congolais pour la Démocratie (RCD). In mid-1999, the RCD split into competing factions supported by either Uganda or Rwanda, and intensified efforts to silence human rights activists reporting atrocities under its rule (HRW 2001c).[14] Differences in strategy in the DRC wars produced serious tensions between the former allies, culminating in three separate bouts of heavy fighting in Kisangani in 1999 and 2000. Uganda backed a rebel group called Movement for the Liberation of Congo (MLC), which, led by Pierre Bemba, controlled a significant portion of territory in the east and the north of the country. The conflagration between Uganda and Rwanda in eastern DRC shifted attitudes towards the Congolese and Rwandan refugees in Uganda, although this did not necessarily increase their security.

Despite having, like its neighbour Rwanda, a constitution that was to some extent the result of an internal constitutional debate (Verdirame 2000), Burundi steadily degenerated into authoritarianism in the 1960s. After Hutu candidates obtained the majority of seats in the National Assembly in the 1965 elections, the country plunged into a state of civil war. The abandonment of the post-independence constitutional structure was sealed in 1966 when the monarchy was overthrown and Michel Micombero proclaimed himself president. The elected assembly was replaced by a Supreme Council of the Republic, which was composed of officers in the Tutsi-dominated army. The Hutu uprising in 1972 against the ethnic oligarchy that was by then in power ended in one of the worst bloodbaths in the history of the region. Educated Hutus were systematically eliminated – as many as 300,000 said to have been killed and probably more displaced. The massacre aimed to destroy the Hutu educated elite, depriving the Hutu majority of any chance to obtain power for a generation. The following two decades were in fact dominated by power struggles within the dominant Tutsi oligarchy. The 1976 coup, which brought Colonel Bagaza to power, and the 1987 coup by Major Buyoya did not signify any change for the Hutu majority, which remained oppressed and excluded from power. In 1985, for example, only four ministers out of twenty were Hutu, seventeen members of the National Assembly out of sixty-five, one ambassador out of twenty-two (Reyntjens 1994: 41). Finally, by the early 1990s, pressure to introduce a multi-party system was sufficient to lead to free and vividly contested elections in June 1993, which were won by Melchior Ndadaye, candidate of the main opposition party. Only a few months later, on 21 October 1993, President Ndadaye was murdered by members of the army, still dominated by Tutsis. Violent clashes erupted and thousands of Burundians were once again forced to seek refuge in neighbouring countries.[15] The majority sought refuge in Tanzania, but many fled also to Uganda and Kenya. Major Buyoya staged another coup in 1996, and negotiations between his government and various Hutu rebel movements took place in Tanzania, with the former Presidents of Tanzania and South Africa, Julius Nyerere and Nelson Mandela, as mediators. In April 2003, Domitien Ndayizeye, a Hutu, became president under the terms of a power-sharing agreement signed between the government and most rebel factions.

A large portion of Africa's refugees in the 1990s have come from Somalia, one of the continent's 'failed states'.[16] Somalia was created from the union of two former colonial territories, one Italian and the other, in the north, British. In 1969, Muhammad Siad Barre overthrew the government of Abdi Rashid Ali Shermarke in a coup, and, the following year, proclaimed Somalia a socialist state. The 1977–78 Ogaden war, which saw the defeat of Siad Barre's expansionist plans, accentuated internal clan divisions, and the government of Siad Barre cracked down on clans perceived to be hostile. By 1991, armed factions organised along clan lines had gained sufficient strength to topple what remained of Siad Barre's government in Mogadishu. The capital was ransacked with extreme ferocity, and the only escape route open to many was the ocean. Within weeks, Somali refugees were arriving in large numbers in Kenya's ports, particularly Mombasa,[17] and later in Uganda. In 1992–93 the Security Council authorised a peacekeeping mission in Somalia, entrusting it at one point with an essentially peace-enforcement mandate. The UN intervention ended in failure when US troops did not manage to capture warlord Muhammad Aideed. As the peacekeeping troops were withdrawn, the war in Somalia continued and various agreements between faction leaders proved precarious. After the terrorist attacks on the US on 11 September 2001, fears grew that Somalia might become a 'haven' for terrorists, and foreign aid agencies decided to scale down their presence. Meanwhile, Somaliland, the northern part of the country, declared independence unilaterally and, although it received no international recognition, it proceeded to a period of relative stability with presidential elections in April 2003.

Aims and objectives of the research

The research for this book was carried out in conjunction with a collaborative study funded by the European Union (EU) on the health and welfare of refugees in Kenya and Uganda in 1996–99.[18] The main question addressed by the EU project was whether refugees outside camps fared better than refugees in camps in terms of health and welfare. This provided a broad framework within which to investigate discrete issues in the psychosocial, legal, and policy spheres. Our project was then designed to focus on the extent to which refugees enjoyed their fundamental rights in camps/settlements, as opposed to refugees who had settled outside the aid umbrella in rural or urban areas.

The primary aim of this research was to analyse how international human rights and refugee law is implemented – in other words, how international legal protection is actually translated into the everyday life of a refugee in East Africa. The research was designed to examine refugee protection as portrayed by governments, humanitarian organisations, and by UNHCR in their official documentation, as well as to investigate their actual conduct. It was intended to act as a catalyst for the reform of law and practice in line with international human rights and refugee law, as well as for initiatives designed to promote respect for the rights of refugees in Kenya and Uganda. Other objectives of the research included:

to develop a replicable sociolegal methodology for investigation of the legal protection of refugee rights through field research and case-based methods; and to test a strategy for the dissemination of findings that could lead to greater awareness and promote reform.

It should be noted what the research did not set out to do and what, as a result, this book is *not*. Although throughout the book we do compare refugee protection in Uganda and Kenya, the research was not conceived as a comparative study per se. Rather, it was a study of the same research questions in two different settings. In some instances, comparable data were available, in others not. For example, it was possible to collect much more data on the police in Uganda than in Kenya, but on sexual violence we gathered more data in Kenya. In Uganda we made some observations on refugees who were 'self-settled' in rural areas and who were making their living through agriculture; in Kenya we did not have the opportunity to observe such groups.

This book is not a human rights report, although it is on the same subject matter. Human rights reports, written, for example, by Amnesty International or Human Rights Watch (HRW), often gather facts without extensive analysis of the systemic power relations that are at the root of certain human rights abuses. In addition, such reports are sometimes based upon short-term field visits during which there may not have been time to conduct follow-up.[19] By contrast, we aimed to gather extensive data over a prolonged period of time using a rigorous legal anthropological methodology. Although parts of this book may read like an exposé of human rights violations, we have attempted throughout to place the data in a sociolegal context. Moreover, unlike most human rights reports, our research did not deal exclusively with the actions of governments, but also examined the role of other actors in a position of power vis-à-vis refugees.

We did not dwell on the causes that prompted refugees to flee in the first place. Refugees are an 'after-the-fact' phenomenon. While knowledge of the causes within the country of origin is critical for refugee advocates in preparing cases for status determination, this information is of limited relevance to the refugees' protection needs outside their country.

This book is the result of a long-term ethnographic study of the *violations* of the catalogue of rights that refugees should enjoy, but it does not review the legal scope of each right. With a few exceptions, it is not our stated aim to further knowledge on the interpretation of particular provisions in refugee or human rights treaties. The contribution to legal scholarship that we seek to make is by illustrating and analysing the factual accounts of violations of rights – emphasising the role of perpetrators, as well as the circumstances and patterns in these violations.

There are questions that this book raises but does not examine in detail. For instance, we discuss resettlement only briefly, particularly in the context of persons who faced an imminent security risk and who should have been resettled expeditiously. We also only touch on the treatment of certain 'vulnerable groups', such as unaccompanied minors (about whom a separate book could have been written). Similarly, we have barely addressed rights associated with mental health, or the particular needs for the protection of the elderly and adolescents.

In the presentation and analysis of the research data, we have categorised cases under the main human right that was violated, with the proviso that in most cases other human rights were simultaneously being violated. For instance, interviews with headmasters and teachers on the right to education for refugees also raised issues related to labour rights, freedom of expression, and freedom of association. Another example is restriction on freedom of movement, which affected the enjoyment of virtually all other human rights to which refugees were entitled, such as physical security, access to courts, and education. Cataloguing these violations under one right was necessary for practical reasons, but this should not be regarded as a repudiation on our part of the interdependence and indivisibility of all human rights.

Five main questions were posed in order to assess the 'gaps' between law and practice. First, recognising that a multiplicity of actors (the government, UNHCR, and NGOs) are normally responsible for refugee protection in host states in the 'developing world', we sought to understand the roles played by each and their impact on refugee protection. Second, we assessed the level of protection of refugee rights in camps and settlements, as opposed to Nairobi and Kampala. Third, we examined decision making on individual asylum status-determination claims in each country. Fourth, on the premise that enjoyment of one's rights is best achieved through an *awareness* of those rights, we tried to measure the extent to which individual refugees, the host populations, the governments, and NGOs were informed about international human rights and refugee law. Finally, we examined the extent to which refugees in both countries were able to seek the enforcement of their rights. This question encompassed an analysis of the laws and policies which needed reform in order to comply with international standards.

Assumptions underlying the research

We assumed that refugee protection encompasses both general human rights and refugee-specific rights. The system of international protection originated from the need to provide refugees with an effective substitute for diplomatic protection. A group of core protection activities – including the prevention of *refoulement* and expulsion, access to status-determination procedures, grant of asylum, release from detention, identity and travel documentation, family reunion, access to educational institutions, facilitation of the right to work, solutions – can be identified on the basis of the 1950 UNHCR Statute, in conjunction with the 1951 Convention (Goodwin-Gill 1998: 230–31). With the development of human rights law, the concept of refugee protection has been expanded, as standards and procedures of universal application have evolved. 'Conditions under which they [refugees] frequently live' have to be taken into account, and, in recent years, 'added weight' has been given 'to claims for personal security, family reunion, assistance, and international efforts to achieve solutions' (ibid.: 231).

The research was based on the assumption that human rights are inter-related and indivisible. Connected to this was the premise that the welfare of refugees depends on protecting all of their rights – civil and political, as well as economic, social, and cultural. Since we assumed that respect for human rights is an intrinsically positive thing, we did not set out to subject human rights per se to a critique; nor did we question the assumption that refugee-specific rights – such as the right not to be *refouled*, or the right to obtain identity papers or travel documents – could in any way be harmful to refugees.

We agree that universality of human rights should be 'beyond dispute' (Deng 2000: 234). Hence, we did not use perceived contextual values or norms as the yardstick for gauging the situation of refugees, and were not prepared to make any justification for 'culturally acceptable' practices that constitute violations of human rights. Torture, the burning at the stake of women accused of witchcraft, and racism have all been deemed 'culturally acceptable' at some historical point: the supine defence of the cultural status quo is an ultimately reactionary position, which might appear progressive only to the ideologically confused.

We did, however, seek to benefit from 'the methodological insights' of cultural relativism (Wilson 1997: 8). It is axiomatic that the socio-economic and cultural context affects everyone, refugees and citizens alike. We recognised the importance of the social context for devising an effective strategy for research on the human rights of refugees and for understanding the nature of some obstacles to the enjoyment of rights. For example, cultural attitudes towards the stranger are an important factor in the treatment of refugees.[20]

The social context includes a multiplicity of actors, each standing in a particular relationship of power vis-à-vis the other, which the study assumed it was necessary to unravel. The organisations of UNHCR and NGOs are themselves multi-layered. We made the assumption that studying humanitarian organisations required not only examining the policy documents emanating from 'headquarters' but also the practices of regional and local offices down to the actions of individuals working at the camp level. The relative power of institutionally-based actors at different times and in various situations could not have been predicted on the basis of their mandates or public documents concerning policy. Studies of national welfare institutions have already highlighted the existence of a street-level practice which does not always operate in accordance with guidance from the management (Lipsky 1980). At every level of society there are also individuals who act as gatekeepers, empowered to control access to services. These individuals often behave in an arbitrary or discriminatory manner, even extorting money from those requiring assistance.[21] Institutional hierarchy, geographical spread, and the political, cultural, and religious biases of individuals working within humanitarian organisations constitute yet another level of complexity. Then there are the refugees themselves, some of whom acquire power over others by virtue of their military, political, religious, or economic standing.

Finally, it was assumed that international human rights and refugee law binds both states and international organisations (Verdirame 2001b). Awareness of human rights law amongst the population as a whole – including government officials, humanitarian workers, and the refugees themselves – was assumed to be a precondition for the effective protection and enjoyment of these rights. In particular, we considered UNHCR as a human rights organisation, endowed with legal personality and bound to uphold human rights law in every aspect of its work, since 'human rights standards can *define the kind of treatment refugees can expect under international protection*' (Towle 2000: 27 [emphasis added]). Not everyone is accustomed to thinking of UNHCR as a human rights organisation and the question has been raised: can UNHCR combine its 'humanitarian and non-political character' with human rights work?[22] The answer from UNHCR itself has been unequivocal: 'Placing greater reliance on human rights standards as a basis for our work does not jeopardize the humanitarian character of our activities, since international human rights law is itself non-political and non-partisan' (UNHCR 1995g: 5).[23]

Research methods

The research for this book applied social science methods, primarily anthropological, to data collection in the field. Kenya and Uganda were chosen as the site for the research for several reasons. Both were stable host countries, at least in comparison with other central and eastern African countries. In addition, previous experience and research facilitated access to the sources of data. More importantly, these two countries seemed ideal for conducting 'action research': they were in the process of reforming or introducing refugee legislation, and the research could offer a timely contribution.

In Kenya, data collection began in March 1997 with a survey of the field in Nairobi and a research trip to Kakuma refugee camp. Most data were collected between March 1997 and May 1998, with several shorter periods of research throughout the following two years. The research concentrated on refugees in Nairobi, and in the camps in Kakuma and Dadaab. In Uganda, after a short trip in April 1997, data collection began in September with the presentation of a background paper at Makerere University analysing Uganda's draft refugee bill in relation to the standards contained in Uganda's bill of rights as well as in treaties to which Uganda is a party (Garry 1998b). This presentation elicited comments and discussion among lawyers, government officials, and policy advisers on refugees in Uganda, as well as NGO staff and donors, which helped to highlight the areas on which the research should focus (Garry 1998c). Data collection continued until January 2000, and we focused on Kampala and on the refugee settlements in Moyo and Adjumani districts. Since the end of the project, we have continued to monitor the situation in both countries through the work of other researchers, and, most importantly, through the Refugee Law Project (RLP) in Kampala and the Refugee Consortium of Kenya (RCK) in Nairobi.[24]

The majority of the data were qualitative, collected through observation, unstructured conversations, in-depth interviews (some tape-recorded), and discussions with focus groups, as well as the study of documents such as court cases, government reports and records, UNHCR reports, NGO newsletters and reports, and newspaper articles. In both countries interviews were held primarily with refugees, but also with government officials (police, the judiciary, prison officers, the government's own refugee office, the immigration departments, and local administrators), UNHCR and NGOs staff, donor representatives, local lawyers, and academics. Available statistics were gathered from the Ugandan Department of Prisons and, in both countries, from courts and NGOs.

We were also able to benefit from a large number of discrete in-depth studies carried out in settlements and camps, many by volunteer interns working under our supervision, and others by Ph.D. candidates whose research complemented ours. These and other studies conducted more or less simultaneously by other scholars are cited throughout the book.

The participatory approach

Our research employed participatory methods, as distinct from the classical anthropological view of participant observation, which implies that the researcher participates in the daily lives of the 'objects' of research over an extended period of time. Our participatory approach recognised that field research is a dialogical process, which questions the subject–object polarisation typical of much anthropological research

(Horst 1999, drawing from Schrivjers 1991, 1995). It requires openness about one's research, and necessitates an actor-oriented approach. Research questions were discussed with refugees in order to help determine the best approach. Reports of work were given to various people for comment and further discussion. We wrote up interviews with agency staff and often copied them to the same staff for confirmation of our interpretation of their responses.[25]

Reconstructing the practice of law

In neither Kenya nor Uganda was there systematic law reporting. Moreover, refugee populations were usually kept in separate spaces – that is, refugee camps and settlements – where a parallel legal system operated outside the law of the host state. At times, this practice was in dramatic conflict with both national and international law.[26] Therefore, we reconstructed the practical application of the law in order to find out to what extent, by what means, and for what reasons those in charge failed to respect the rights of refugees. Reconstruction was done via observations, oral testimony, correspondence, and policy statement analysis.

Early on in the fieldwork, it became evident that it was not simply a matter of studying how the law was interpreted and applied, particularly since the domestic legal framework regulating refugee matters was either absent (Kenya) or inadequate and with lacunae (Uganda). It was at times necessary to analyse informal policy- and decision-making systems – parallel to and, at times, in conflict with provisions contained in the positive law – that had been introduced surreptitiously by the humanitarian organisations, or that reflected the customary law and the cultural norms of refugee communities as interpreted by their unelected leaders. In refugee camps/settlements, international civil servants and NGO staff rely on such systems, rather than on domestic or international legal standards, as the framework regulating their actions.

Case studies

Throughout the research, the case-study method was followed. Detailed interviews aimed to elicit the personal experiences of refugees regarding the enjoyment of particular rights, and to 'reconstruct' the facts of the case and the decisions taken by those in charge (Verdirame 1999b). For most refugees interviewed in Kampala or Nairobi, we opened individual case files containing photocopies of their documents in addition to their testimonies.[27] In camps, we could normally only take field notes, since it was not usually possible to collect documentation to the same extent.

Some questioned the reliability of the case-study method, viewing it as leading to the collection of merely anecdotal evidence. For instance, when preliminary findings were presented at a meeting of officials at UNHCR in Nairobi in September 1997, some challenged us on the need for 'statistics' – 'how many times are rights violated?' or 'what percentage of the refugee population suffered violations of a particular right?'. The mistaken assumption was that for an argument to be credibly put forward on human rights violations affecting refugees, one would need to demonstrate that such violations affect the majority, or at least a significant portion of the refugee population. However, legal materials (submissions of the parties, judgments) are often, in a sense, anecdotes – that is, narratives that summarise facts and analyse them according to legal categories and principles. A single case representing a violation of internationally agreed human rights standards suffices to justify the general statement 'Country A (or organisation B) is in breach of international law with respect to that particular standard'. Obvious as it may seem, it is necessary to emphasise that the obligation to respect a certain human right means that a state has to respect that right in *all* cases, not in the majority of them. The main research question that we addressed was not whether 'refugee rights are respected in regard to the majority of refugees' but whether 'refugee rights are respected'. Of course, a systematic pattern of abuse is more serious a breach of the law than an isolated case, and we did distinguish situations based on the incidence of the violations; such distinctions are important for developing a strategy for advocacy as well as for identifying the type of reform(s) needed for improving the situation and preventing the recurrence of abuses.

Having collected the personal testimonies of refugees, we then attempted to cross-check the facts with additional interviews, corroborating documentation, and interviews with other sources. This method was made possible in part because of the long-term nature of the study. In addition, the fact that we were providing legal assistance to many refugees for their status-determination interviews meant that we could insist that their testimonies were truthful. Some interviews relied on interpreters, but the use of them was minimised by the fact that the team included members who could speak English, French, Italian, Kiswahili, Madi, Turkana, Acholi, 'Juba' Arabic, Kakwa, Lugbara, Lingala, Runyoro, and Luganda. The only relevant languages not covered were Kinyarwanda, Kirundi, and Somali. When we used interpreters, we were aware of their potential influence: their gender, personality, skills, and actual or perceived membership of a faction, clan, or ethnic or political group might make some refugees unwilling to speak in their presence. We were also aware of the influence of others present at the interviews and attempted to ensure that all individual interviews were conducted in private, assuring full confidentiality in order to encourage as open a discourse as possible with each interviewee. However, this was not always possible; in prisons, for example, we were sometimes watched:

Aukot noticed that his interviewees seemed to be holding back information … I asked the prison warden … if maybe we could have a bit more privacy as it seemed that the refugees were not able to speak freely. The warden quickly answered that it was 'his right' as a prison warden to be present in order to 'prevent any secrets from leaving the prison' … In the end, he consulted his superior who informed him to go and talk to the remaining [refugees] waiting to be interviewed that they should 'feel free' and tell us all and not feel afraid to talk to us! … A woman warden monitored me both times [when I was in a particular prison] and I noticed that a young Dinka was very distracted by the guard and told me very little. His eyes kept averting to the warden and he acted as if he really didn't want to talk to me.[28]

Action research

The research was action-oriented. As will be shown throughout the book, we took every possible opportunity to intervene when a right was violated.[29] Many of the refugees we interviewed had problems relating to their status in Kenya and Uganda. Much of the information we collected was sensitive, having to do with torture, sexual violence, forced recruitment and defections, relationships with authorities, and all other forms of injustice and abuse. Although we did not offer material assistance, we could provide refugees with advice on their cases and, at times, refer them to others who could help.[30] By doing so, we managed to establish a relationship that was reciprocal: refugees were usually more willing to give us information because it would also be used for their own benefit.[31] Some of the more important data would not have been obtained had we not adopted this methodology. At the same time, we made certain our interviewees were aware of the larger design of the research and of the way we would use their interviews while protecting their confidentiality.

Such reciprocity was not only expedient; it also addressed some of the ethical issues of research with subjects who were victims of human rights abuses (*see* Wilson 1992). There is little doubt that our data collection, and our findings, were coloured by the role of advocates that we chose to assume. From the point of view of 'pure' social sciences, this might not be ideal, but was there any alternative? From the outset, we had envisaged that advocacy would be part of our research – for both moral and practical reasons. The situation with regard to asylum status determination, however, immediately posed a challenge to our intended methodology; the law played such a marginal role in the decision-making process that overtly assisting a refugee with his or her case could be harmful, as it might be seen as an indication that the refugee had 'dared' to seek advice outside UNHCR.[32] This capriciousness in the system, particularly in the early months of the research in Kenya, put us in a moral dilemma. We could try to help refugees within this abusive and unfair system while remaining behind the scenes. Alternatively, we could openly challenge the system with legal arguments, but run the risk of harming the individual we were seeking to help. We decided that the interests of the refugees were paramount, and we therefore did not overtly act in refugee status-determination cases, until the appointment of a new senior protection officer in August 1997 who encouraged us to intervene on behalf of asylum applicants.

In addition to advising on individual cases, in the course of the research we aimed to engage with the various actors in order to influence policy, practice, and the law-making process – in other words, to challenge the status quo. We employed a number of refugees to write reports on specific issues.[33] Whenever possible, we disseminated refugee law materials.[34] We organised courses, lectures, and seminars on refugee rights – which were open to the public – at Makerere University, Uganda and gave lectures in the Faculty of Law, Nairobi University, and at Moi University in Eldoret. We also used the press to disseminate research findings quickly (e.g., Harrell-Bond 1997b), to publicly challenge policies of the government or UNHCR (e.g., Harrell-Bond 1999b; Mwilinga 1999a, 1999c, 1999d; Lomo 1999c; Reynell 2000), and to raise awareness (e.g., Harrell-Bond 1997b, 1999c; Bouman and Harrell-Bond 1999; Mwilinga 1999e, 1999f; Taylor 1999). A group was organised to contribute to the law-making process in both Kenya and Uganda. In April 1999, a seminar on refugee law was organised at Makerere University for judges (also attended by a judge from Kenya), NGOs, government representatives, the media, and students.

We conducted a survey on knowledge of refugee law among the police, in which we interviewed some 100 police officers from five police stations in Kampala. Its primary result was awareness building. A regular relationship of consultation was established with police who began calling our office with questions on how to handle specific refugee cases according to refugee law.[35] On one occasion, when around sixty Rwandan students sought asylum in Uganda, it was a policeman from the Kampala old police station who brought a group of them to us.[36]

Our research into the level of awareness of refugee law and refugee issues among national institutions involved other actors as well. On many occasions the fact that research and activism can be coextensive and mutually supportive was confirmed. For instance, we met with members of the Uganda National Council for Children, the body responsible for coordinating all NGO and government activities vis-à-vis children. During our interview, the head admitted that refugee children were not understood to be part of their mandate and asked us to write a letter so that he could use it in promoting the Council's work in this area. More examples of actions that we took on behalf of refugees or to affect policy are discussed throughout the book.

As noted before, one of the major direct outcomes of the research in Uganda was the establishment of the Refugee Law Project (RLP) at the

Faculty of Law, Makerere University.[37] The objectives of the RLP are to provide training in refugee and human rights law for the police and other target groups (such as immigration officials), to support the development of a postgraduate course in refugee studies at Makerere, and to promote, oversee, and advise the NGOs providing legal aid services to refugees. One of the first activities of the RLP was to mount an intensive two-week course for police from refugee-affected districts. It now also offers short courses on refugee issues for NGO staff in rural areas as well as in Kampala. RLP has become the main provider of legal aid to refugees in Kampala and has extended these services to rural areas.

Action research strengthened the participatory approach: the dissemination of findings and advocacy relied on local actors to take the lead (*see* Fox and Brown 1998). Because of the paternalistic assumptions underlying them, we reject such terms as 'capacity building' or 'empowerment', which are generally employed to describe a unidirectional process in which 'insiders' benefit from 'outsiders'. To the extent that they have any relevance, these notions ought to emphasise that, in research, 'empowerment' and 'capacity building' are reciprocal. Moreover, although access to police cells, refugee camps and, sometimes, official documentation was easier for the 'outsiders' (as three of us were), advocacy cannot be entirely successful without 'insiders'. That more was accomplished in Uganda was not merely because the research extended over a three-year period, and that it had more funds available to it, but because one of the main researchers on our team was a Ugandan lawyer who knew the 'landscape', with both its pitfalls and opportunities. Throughout we tried to play on the relative strengths and weaknesses of the social and 'anthropological' position of the members of our research team.

Main findings

The model of segregated camps increases the potential for abuse rather than enhances the protection of refugee rights

The main conclusion of this book is that refugee rights cannot be protected in camps and settlements. This conclusion applied equally to the Kenyan camps and the Ugandan settlements, the latter purportedly promoting economic self-reliance. We found that in camps the law of the host country virtually ceased to be applied; camps were spaces *beyond the rule of law* in which the life of refugees was governed by an oppressive blend of customary practices and rules established by humanitarian organisations and refugees. We found evidence of violations of the full catalogue of human rights. Whether in a local camp or a settlement, refugees were effectively segregated – prevented from enjoying freedom of movement, a fundamental right upon which the exercise of other rights is contingent. Crucially, these restrictions, together with their isolation in remote areas, inhibited refugees from engaging in business and trade in order to provide for their own welfare. All of the camps and settlements in which we conducted research lacked sufficient provision for education. Although UNHCR maintained that the health services were better than those available to nationals, morbidity rates among the refugee population were generally higher than among the hosts (*see also* Porter 2001). In both Kenya and Uganda, the social make-up of camps made it impossible for refugees to enjoy the right to physical safety from internal strife and their location subjected them to rebel attacks from outside. Freedom of expression and of conscience and religion were not ensured. Many refugees were victims of discrimination, mainly on grounds of gender and membership of ethnic or religious groups.

Socio-economic integration is the best solution from the point of view of the refugees' enjoyment of their fundamental rights

In both countries, the only alternative to camps was local integration, since repatriation was not available in the foreseeable future and only small numbers could benefit from resettlement. While integration is a complex socio-economic process contingent upon several factors, a sine qua non for successful integration is the removal of legal obstacles (recognition of refugee status, identification papers, free movement and choice of residence, work permits, access to schools and universities, and so on), which result in the marginalisation of refugees. The successful situation of the refugees who had arrived in Kenya before 1991 and whose integration was not generally impeded by legal obstacles was revealing: they were generally well integrated and enjoyed a level of security from arrest and police abuse that, though far from ideal, was not worse than that of nationals. For all other refugees in both countries, however, the legal obstacles to integration were insurmountable, with the consequence of making integration in the host society unavailable as a 'durable solution'. Many refugees still chose to reside in cities like Nairobi and Kampala, where they could at least seek educational opportunities or employment in the informal sector of the economy.

UNHCR is the main authority that exercises power and effective control in camps; combined with its role in the status-determination process, this power means that UNHCR is not simply unable to promote respect for the rights of refugees, but is often responsible for the violation of these rights

While host governments may be largely responsible for the treatment of refugees in countries in the 'developed world' (*see* e.g., Nagy 2000; Helton 2000), our research found that, where UNHCR and NGOs have assumed the host state's primary obligation for status determination and control of refugee populations in camps, they may in practice bear at least an equal share of responsibility. This is despite the fact that UNHCR holds itself out to be a 'human rights organisation' and, according to the Preamble of the 1951 Convention, 'is charged with the task of supervising international conventions for the protection of refugees'. In Uganda, responsibility for the management of camps was shared between UNHCR, NGOs, and the state through the Directorate of Refugees (DoR), but the funding for this authoritarian apparatus is supplied almost entirely by UNHCR. In Kenya, UNHCR and NGOs took full responsibility for camp management. The very organisation set up to monitor the extent to which refugees enjoyed their human rights had assumed de facto sovereignty over them. Who could monitor the monitor (Wilde 1998)?

Another example of the compromise of UNHCR's mandate (Goodwin-Gill 1999, 2000) was its primary role in status-determination procedures in both countries. Rather than acting as an advocate for the asylum-seeker and monitoring a national administrative process for determining asylum status, UNHCR assumed the adjudicatory role. The process it put in place flouted minimum requirements of procedural fairness. Its power over refugees was even more conspicuous when it came to deciding whether a refugee ranked among the select few who 'qualified' to stay in urban settings or whether he or she had to live in camps to receive assistance; it was almost absolute in decisions on whose case would be submitted to the embassies for resettlement in another country.

In a highly competitive funding environment, for UNHCR and its partner NGOs, institutional survival rather than the protection of the rights of refugees became the primary determinant of policy (Walkup 1997; Kent 1987: 92, as cited in Schmidt 1998: 6). Thus, UNHCR continued to support the encampment policy because of its perceived attraction to donors, for whom the main advantage was visibility – being able to 'prove' the presence of refugees.[38] '[W]hen a tight-fisted international community says … it will provide help for refugees in camps … this evidently encourages … root[ing] out refugees who are integrated and plonk[ing] them into camps' (Malloch-Brown 1984: 9, as cited in Schmidt 1997: 28). In addition, the staff of UNHCR were often not properly informed of, nor did they consider the human rights dimension of their work. They were in denial about their role as violators of rights; they assumed that the direct violator of refugee rights was the host state.[39]

In typically bureaucratic fashion, UNHCR officials gave precedence to the implementation of internal policies, regardless of their consistency with human rights standards, with UNHCR's own mandate, or with the best interest of refugees. An example of this was the systematic withdrawal of food rations in the settlements of northern Uganda according to a schedule 'set by Geneva'. This decision was made without regard to the drought and the insecurity, which made it impossible for refugees to plant and harvest in order to have an adequate store of food to compensate for the withdrawn rations. Another vivid illustration was the destruction of Ogujebe transit centre. In the space of one week, businesses and homes were bulldozed (without always checking to see if they had been evacuated) and the army was brought in. 24,000 people were uprooted at gunpoint into large lorries with all of their life's possessions, splitting up families in the rushed process.[40] From the perspective of refugees, the demolition of Ogujebe was an extreme violation of human rights.[41] Yet the destruction of the centre was viewed as a significant achievement, even worthy of celebration, by UNHCR.[42] How could the views of refugees, ourselves, and many other onlookers be at such variance with those of UNHCR and, to a lesser extent, the NGOs?[43]

In general, rather than challenge the camps policy, UNHCR and NGOs even supported it for the perceived advantages that this concentration and isolation of the refugee population provided: administrative efficiency, the ability to control refugees, and the facilitation of the 'voluntary' repatriation of refugees (UNHCR n.d.: 136). In Kenya, for example, UNHCR admitted that the issue of local integration was never 'seriously discussed with the government' in the 1990s when Kenya moved from a laissez-faire approach to an encampment policy for refugees (UNHCR 1997a: 20).[44] In Uganda, in its comments to the Ugandan government on its draft refugee bill, UNHCR Uganda recommended: 'perhaps under this section there should be added positive powers to establish or designate specific areas as transit centre, camps or settlements where refugees will be required to stay or settle rather than just including a provision that empowers the Commissioner to specify certain areas out-of-bound for certain refugees' (UNHCR 1996j).

Host governments have abdicated their responsibilities for formulating and implementing refugee policy

Related to the previous finding is the finding that host governments have largely handed over control over refugee matters to UNHCR and to foreign humanitarian organisations. Our findings on this process of transfer of responsibilities are similar to what Karadawi found in Sudan (1999). Interestingly, Kenya and Uganda were at different stages in the process at the time of the research: the government had completely relinquished responsibility in Kenya, while in Uganda it still attempted to maintain at least the vestiges of control over refugee policy. In neither country were officials aware of the fact that, despite this 'hand-over', legally their governments remained responsible under international law for the treatment of refugees.

Governments were also responsible for some violations of refugees' human rights – especially arbitrary arrest and detention, unfairness in criminal and civil proceedings, as well as violations of economic and social rights, such as the right to work. These are detailed throughout the book.

Lack of awareness of the rights of refugees on the part of the various actors involved in refugee matters and of refugees themselves was one of the main factors that hindered respect for such rights

There was an across-the-board lack of awareness of the law and the rights to which refugees are entitled in the host state by government officials, humanitarian organisations, and refugees themselves. It was not uncommon for us to find refugees in jail cells on misinformed charges of 'lying to a police officer' or for presenting false papers to an immigration officer or on grounds of treason against the Ugandan government. Police officers in Uganda responsible for first screening asylum-seekers upon arrival would not hesitate to bar them from a status-determination interview on the grounds that they were 'economic' migrants, if, in addition to claiming persecution, they stated that they were coming to Uganda in the hope of pursuing an education or a 'better life'. Asylum-seekers themselves were often unaware of how to present their testimonies in order to meet the burden of proof necessary to be found credible as someone fleeing from persecution. Segregation in remote camps in both countries was a serious obstacle to access to courts. Even where they had access to courts, misinformation about refugees and refugee law among the judiciary hindered proper enforcement. Refugees had no voice in the political arena, or in humanitarian decision-making circles: they were stereotyped negatively and kept at a distance, and their complaints were dismissed by those in charge, whether UNHCR, NGOs, governments, or local institutions. In Uganda, we found that through simple steps such as providing training courses for the police and the judiciary, raising awareness of violations of rights through dissemination of our research, and establishing legal-aid clinics for refugees, these problems could be mitigated.

A research and advocacy agenda for the future

We did not specifically set out to test the effectiveness of different advocacy strategies for promoting respect for the rights of refugees: it would not have been possible to do this, given that in both countries one of the main problems was precisely the lack of such advocacy. However, our research was based on the assumption that it should advance refugee policy and catalyse efforts to ensure compliance with the laws and standards safeguarding the rights of refugees.

A striking feature of refugee advocacy is the lack of transnational civil society coalitions. Such groups have succeeded in promoting social change in other areas (Fox and Brown 1998). In particular, some change in international financial institutions has been accomplished by activists in affected countries liaising with lobbying groups and academics in Europe and North America. These networks have drawn attention to development programmes harmful to the environment and human rights.

We attempted to establish something akin to transnational advocacy coalitions on several occasions. For example, when refugees were deported from Belgium to Uganda on Sabena Airways, we established contact with a Belgian group of activists and members of parliament who were seeking to stop those deportations. We were in contact with researchers from Amnesty International and HRW throughout the research, especially in order to circulate information on issues such as the plight of human rights activists in the DRC or the wave of arbitrary arrests in Kenya in July 1997.

Despite some encouraging results in these instances, we were generally frustrated by the overall state of refugee advocacy. The refugees' 'protector', UNHCR, had for the most part proved to be unable to do its job properly. Because of their close partnership with UNHCR, humanitarian NGOs were reluctant to get involved in serious advocacy for refugee rights. With a few exceptions, local human rights NGOs did not usually include refugees in their activities. International human rights NGOs tended to follow a modus operandi crystallised in the 1970s: fact-finding missions followed by the publication of reports are the main tool to promote compliance with human rights organisations. Despite the utility of this method, other approaches could have been developed. For example, there was little monitoring of the actions of UNHCR or NGOs – still viewed as 'partners' against governments – and even less proactive use of local institutions, such as courts, for advancing respect for refugee rights.

What is the way forward for refugee advocacy? The establishment of effective transnational advocacy coalitions, ideally including a reformed UNHCR, would require a rethinking of the roles of all the actors, exploiting certain features of the current sociopolitical and sociolegal context. A propitious development since the 1980s has been the growth of the human rights community in many countries in the 'developing world', and the introduction of important legal and constitutional reforms. Both Kenya and Uganda could be described as having a thriving network of human rights NGOs and activists, and in both countries, albeit to a different extent, there is some room for bringing about changes through the law. Nevertheless, at the time of our research, foreign NGOs, both humanitarian and human rights ones, were too often slow to react to these developments, and seldom sought to strengthen local NGOs by, for example, mobilising funds and other resources in countries in the 'developed world' for public interest litigation on behalf of refugees.

Our research also revealed the need for more scholarly studies, in particular sociolegal ones, of human rights and refugees. Academic lawyers ought to challenge some of their deep-seated attitudes and methods. Human rights standards are universal, but power relations are contingent and the reality of refugee protection is fluid. As long as human rights and refugee lawyers do not engage with the 'field', they will remain vulnerable to accusations that the standards they propound can only work in the abstract (Morris 1999: 494).

Notes

1. *See* UNHCR (1998) 'Refugees and Others of Concern to UNHCR,' 1997 Statistical Overview, Statistical Unit, Geneva, July, at http://www.unhcr.ch.
2. Ibid.
3. Ibid. Note that according to UNHCR they were also assisting approximately 400 Mozambicans in Kenya in 1997.
4. Most of the approximately 5,500 Ugandans remaining as refugees in Kenya had gone there during the troubles in the north of the country in the 1980s, though in 1999–2000 a group of Ugandans who had escaped from the Lord's Resistance Army (LRA) in Sudan had pitched camp at Uhuru Park in Nairobi and were being screened by UNHCR. The 'Lakwena', Alice Auma – the Acholi prophetess who inspired the bloody Holy Spirit Mobile Forces rebellion against the Museveni government in 1987 – was still a recognised refugee at Dadaab camp in northeastern Kenya, where she lived in a special compound with other members, all male, of her faction (*see* Behrend 1999 for the Lakwena war). There was a group of Kenyans in Uganda in Nakivale settlement in Mbarara district, and others who had fled the clashes in the Rift Valley region during the contentious elections of 1992, and many of them were living among their hosts in Mbale district, unassisted by UNHCR. Uganda had also hosted Kenyans fleeing the British repression of the Mau Mau uprising.
5. The Akiwumi report on the ethnic violence in Kenya in the 1990s confirmed what most people suspected – that the violence was planned by various members of the ruling party.
6. These were usually called 'camps' in Kenya and 'settlements' in Uganda. Throughout this book the terms 'settlement' and 'camp' will be used interchangeably. UNHCR and the government in Uganda claimed that the settlement policy differed from encampment because refugees in settlements were given the opportunity to become 'self-sufficient'. In practice, as it will be

shown throughout this book, the difference between camps and settlements was notional.

7. UNHCR 1997 Statistical Overview *supra* note 2. Macchiavello (2001) estimates there are 14,000 refugees living in Kampala but, according to our observations, this may be an underestimate.

8. Asylum-seekers are those who have applied for asylum but have not yet been granted it; refugees, on the other hand, are already accorded status on the basis of an individualised status-determination procedure or on a prima facie basis.

9. These are normally referred to as 'self-settled' refugees, although this term is a misnomer. It would be impossible for anyone to 'settle' without the active assistance of local people, the authorities, or other refugees who had arrived previously, usually the most important source of assistance to new arrivals.

10. For example, International Aid Sweden estimated that 32,000 self-settled refugees lived along the Sudan/Uganda border in Moyo district in Uganda, but our interviews with members of the local administration, who collected taxes from them, indicated that the numbers in the district were closer to 70,000. In Kenya, there were unassisted Rwandan refugees living in Eldoret. It was also known that Somali and Oromo refugees settled among their kinfolk in Kenya.

11. Colonial appropriation of land was a cause of forced displacement in both countries, but the most violent dispossession took place in the Kenyan highlands. In Kenya, political repression of the movement for independence also took a more violent form than in Uganda: tens of thousands were displaced in the 1950s, and the internment camps built by the British during the Mau Mau rebellion were particularly brutal. In the 1940s Uganda was host to about 7,000 Polish refugees who were accommodated in camps in Masindi and Mukono districts. In addition, civilians from Axis countries who had been resident in the Middle East and Iran, were sent to Uganda and Kenya to be interned as enemy aliens for the duration of the Second World War. Nearly all of these Europeans left East Africa shortly after the end of the war (Lwanga-Luyiingo 1996). Kenya hosted Ethiopians fleeing the Italian aggression in 1935 and a small number of Europeans from the Second World War. During the war there were also camps in Kenya for prisoners of war, mainly Italians.

12. On Rwanda's history, *see* Prunier 1995, Newbury 1988, Lemarchand 1970, and Reyntjens 1994. For social aspects, *see* de Lame 1996 and Vidal 1991.

13. Kinyara was closed four years later because of 'high mortality' rates. Many of the Rwandans who lived at Kinyara had first been refugees in Zaire.

14. *See*, e.g., case nos. 064/DRC/U/98; 032/DRC/U/1999; 034/DRC/ U/1999; 037/DRC/U/1999; 044/DRC/U/1999; and 054/DRC/U/1999. These and many other young human rights activists from the DRC were finally resettled from Uganda to the US.

15. For further detail, *see* Lemarchand 1973, 1995; Prunier 1995; Reyntjens 1995, 1999. A peace accord was agreed for Burundi in 2000 in Arusha; but the main armed Hutu rebel groups did not sign, and in 2002 violence against civilians continued unabated. Meanwhile, UNHCR had made plans for repatriation (UNHCR 2000a).

16. However, after Hargeisa was sacked by the Somali army in 1988, thousands of Somalis fled to Ethiopia and Djibouti. *See* Gersony 1989. It was a prelude to what was to come.

17. For a brief treatment of Somali history, *see* Prunier 1995. For more detailed studies, *see* Lewis 1988, 1993, 1994; Cassanelli 1982; Samatar 1991.

18. Four universities (the Centre for Refugee Studies at Moi University, Kenya, the Institute of Public Health at Makerere University, Uganda, the Institute of Tropical Medicine at the University of Antwerp, Belgium, and the University of Oxford's Refugee Studies Centre, then Programme, UK) participated in the research on health and welfare of refugees.

19. For example, one of our researchers was surprised to find that the main researcher working for one international human rights organisation wrote his country report largely from his hotel room in Kampala, relying on information from other field researchers, with no time personally to gather data from the field.

20. One enormous gap in anthropological literature is information on the role of the 'stranger' in societies which host refugees (Shack et al. 1979; Elmadmad 2002). For example, in Luo society in Kenya (and no doubt among the Luo who live across its borders), there are several 'categories' of the stranger, including one which is analogous to refugee status (Opondo 1994).

21. When the stakes are so high, as in refugee status determination or resettlement, it should be anticipated that some would succumb to the temptation of selling services.

22. Sadly, it is more likely to be perceived as a welfare institution, providing humanitarian assistance that is given as charity as part of a donor government's 'largesse' (Harrell-Bond 2002).

23. Another view from outside UNHCR is that 'active involvement in human rights promotion by operational humanitarian agencies might undermine their non-political and humanitarian mandate and compromise their relation with host and donor governments' (Bayefesky 2000: ix). For other views, *see* Reilly 2000; Petrasek 2000; Towle 2000.

24. The RLP was a direct 'product' of the research, initially funded by the Amberstone Trust in 1999. Part of the Faculty of Law, Makerere University, which now offers a postgraduate diploma in refugee law and forced migration studies, the RLP provides legal aid, training for police, immigration officials, and NGO staff, and conducts research on which it bases its advocacy work. In Kenya, there had been attempts to form a refugee NGO in the early 1990s, and Guglielmo Verdirame 'kick-started' an initiative in 1997–98. RCK was founded in 2000.

25. *See* for example, Lomo's 'Notes on Meeting with Mr Hans Thoolen Representative, UNHCR, Kampala', 16 July 1998.

26. The peculiar nature of refugee camps also constitutes a legal conundrum for refugee advocates. International law cannot always be enforced domestically, and domestic legislation cannot be enforced vis-à-vis an intergovernmental organisation (IGO), which enjoys immunity. Refugees in camps are obviously entitled to respect for their basic rights, but the unavailability of a procedure for enforcing these rights in a court of law makes their actual enjoyment dependent on the 'good will' of the particular UNHCR official in charge of the camps.

27. From Kenya we have 187 individual case files; from Uganda, 232. These refugees were primarily from Burundi, Congo, Ethiopia, Eritrea, Kenya, Liberia, Rwanda, Somalia, Sudan, and Uganda, with very few from South Africa, Iraq, Senegal, and Mozambique. In this book they are cited by number, abbreviation of the country of origin, initial of the host country, and year in which the refugee was interviewed – e.g., case no. 42/Bur/K/1997. The files from Kenya are numbered by nationality with each group beginning with '1'. In Uganda, numbers were added at the end of the research and the entire group was numbered consecutively. Cases are preserved in hard copy and were scanned onto a disk. In

addition to the numbered files, notes on many more interviews with refugees appear in Garry's, Harrell-Bond's, Lomo's, and Verdirame's field notes.

28. Field notes, Hannah Garry, 7 February 1998.

29. Chapter 3 **Advocacy.**

30. We developed a list of such resources, including Ugandan medical doctors who would offer refugees services *pro bono.*

31. Moreover, the fact that the information which they were giving would be subjected to standards of 'credibility' as being applied by UNHCR, made it much easier to probe for further information so long as the relevance of the questions was explained.

32. *See* Chapter 3 **Who is in Charge?**, on advice we received from a former protection officer who was helping refugees. He did not let UNHCR know he was involved in a case and did not use legal arguments. Rather than advise on a case on the basis of refugee law, we found ourselves having to scrutinise the erratic working of an office with its internal politics and penchant for punitive actions against outspoken refugees, some of whom were punished simply because they were aware of their rights (e.g. case no. 033/DRC/U/1999).

33. For example, John Otim, a Ugandan refugee in Kenya, was employed to observe relationships between refugees and the 'gatekeepers' at the UNHCR/Jesuit Refugee Service (JRS) office in Wood Avenue, Nairobi (Otim 1998). The senior protection officer, Pia Prütz Phiri, encouraged this research and used the information he collected to introduce changes to the system.

34. For example, after our first trip to Kakuma camp in March 1997, we sent copies of the 1951 Convention and the OAU Convention to a group of Sudanese refugees with whom we had had a focus group discussion. They had 'heard' about the Conventions, but had never seen them. UNHCR in Kakuma was loath to disseminate this type of information, and it had even forcibly relocated a refugee who had organised a series of lectures on human rights, accusing him of 'subversive activities'. *See* Chapter 4 *Collective punishment in Kakuma.*

35. Members of the police force also attended a weekly seminar at Makerere University.

36. *See also* case no. 216/RWA/1999. Very early on an immigration official alerted us to the case of the Iraqi family, case no. 231/IRAQ/U/1999, who, deported to Ugandan by Swedish authorities, had been recognised under UNHCR's mandate, but no further efforts to get him resettled had been made until we were introduced to the family.

37. Seed money was obtained from the Amberstone Trust. In addition, all equipment purchased during Barbara Harrell-Bond's stay in Uganda, including a car, was donated to the RLP.

38. Interview with Eric Morris by Anna Schmidt, Geneva, September 1997, UNHCR.

39. For example, Mr Thoolen defended some of UNHCR's actions in Uganda, arguing that they were not 'direct violations of human rights' and needed to be distinguished from 'a job not properly done' (i.e. an omission to act).

40. Field notes, Hannah Garry, 17 February 1998.

41. Field notes, Hannah Garry, 17 February, 22–24 February 1998.

42. *See* Chapter 4 **Non-discrimination** and Chapter 5 *The effect of forced evictions.*

43. UNHCR and LWF justified the demotion as both 'good' and 'necessary' in order to eliminate what they saw to be corrupt usage of food rations by the refugees, who they claim were getting double or triple rations and storing or

reselling them in Ogujebe markets. It was also justified in order to comply with Uganda's settlement policy.

44. The situation changed to some extent in 1998 in Kenya when the new senior protection officer promoted some measures of integration by persuading the government to naturalise some of the pre-1991 refugees. UNHCR also agreed to the imposition of taxes on refugees, in exchange for business licences to refugee traders in camps. Nevertheless, there was no concerted effort by UNHCR to offer alternatives to the camps themselves.

1

Refugee Law and Policy in Kenya and Uganda

Introduction

Despite certain differences, a trait common to Kenya and Uganda was the influence on policy of the office of UNHCR. The countries' perceived dependence on external funding, for which UNHCR was the main conduit, was a key contributing factor in the shift in power from national to foreign actors. The disempowerment of governments and the growing dominance of the humanitarian 'internationale' (de Waal 1997) was not to the advantage of refugees. It undermined UNHCR's discharge of its function as the protector of refugees and allowed the priorities of its funders and, hence, bureaucratic interests in its own survival, to take precedence over defending the rights of refugees.

There were some important differences in the legal context in the two countries. Uganda adopted a new Constitution with a comprehensive Bill of Rights, but the 1960 Control of Alien Refugees Act (cap. 64), a draconian piece of legislation, was still in force. Kenya never enacted domestic legislation on refugees but, until 1991, its open-door laissez-faire policy was, for the most part, consistent with international refugee law. In both countries the process of introducing new refugee legislation had dragged on over the previous decade.

The legal framework in Kenya

Kenya became a party to the 1951 Convention Relating to the Status of Refugees (to which it entered no reservations) in 1966;[1] to the 1967 Protocol in 1981; and to the 1969 OAU Convention Governing the Specific

Aspects of Refugee Problems in Africa in 1993.[2] Kenya is also a party to the main human rights treaties.[3] The problem in Kenya 'is not lack of applicable refugee law on an international level, rather it is the deficiency in the implementation of the international treaties mentioned above on a domestic level' (Hyndman and Nylund 1998: 29).

The lack of enforcement also beset the Bill of Rights in the Kenyan Constitution, which is based on the 'Lancaster House' model. The Bill of Rights protects almost exclusively civil and political rights (arts. 70–86). In a series of rulings, the High Court held that the chapter on fundamental rights was not enforceable in any court of law owing to the lack of specific legislation on enforcement – thereby in practice suspending the constitutional protection of basic rights (*Maina Mbacha v. Attorney General, Kamau Kuria v. Attorney General*). Furthermore, constitutional amendments introduced in 1988–90 have eroded the independence of the judiciary (Kamau-Kuria and Vasquez 1991). As a result, the scope for successful challenges to the constitutional validity of any statutory provisions affecting rights was very limited throughout the 1990s, but in 2001 Chief Justice Chunga finally drew up the procedural rules for the enforcement of the Bill of Rights.

Despite the lack of specific legislation on refugees, certain provisions of the Immigration Act (amended in 1972) (cap. 172), the Aliens Restrictions Act 1973 (cap. 173), and the Citizenship Act 1963 (cap. 170) do affect refugees. These laws are essentially intended to ensure public order and control, without significantly distinguishing between the different categories of non-citizens. They introduce a procedure for refugees to obtain work permits, which, until 1990, was used by those whose refugee status had been recognised by the government.

The adoption of a new constitution could usher in a new era for refugee rights in Kenya. Section 52 of the draft Constitutional Bill 2002 recognises the right of asylum, enshrines the principle of *non-refoulement*, and requires the enactment of a 'law in compliance with international law and practice, governing persons who seek refuge or asylum in Kenya' (sec. 52(3)). A new bill of rights might also inject some vigour into the Kenyan judiciary, too reluctant, until now, to stand up to the executive. However, although legal protection, especially through a bill of rights, is a cardinal element for the promotion of human rights, taken alone it is not a sufficient condition (An-Na'im 2001). As recent experience in Europe shows, the constitutionalisation of fundamental rights is not an absolute guarantee against the deterioration of refugee protection. Non-legal factors, such as political culture, socio-economic relationships, civil society, or the mind-set of the judiciary, play an important and often underestimated role.

The legal framework in Uganda

Uganda is a party to the most important human rights treaties.[4] Uganda also became party to the 1951 Convention and the 1967 Protocol in 1976, and to the 1969 OAU Convention in 1987. However, it entered a number of draconian reservations to the 1951 Convention, perhaps reflecting the political climate of the period – Idi Amin was in power in 1976. Some of the reservations might even be invalid. For example, Uganda asserts the 'unfettered right to expel refugees' (in relation to article 32); the right to abridge the refugees' right to acquire property 'without recourse to courts of law or arbitral tribunals, national or international' (in relation to article 13); and the 'full freedom to withhold any or all rights' under freedom of association (in relation to article 15).[5]

The 1995 Uganda Constitution also includes a Bill of Rights, which, unlike Kenya's, enshrines not only civil and political rights, but also economic, social, and cultural rights. Rights holders are normally defined as 'all persons' or 'every person in Uganda', thereby unequivocally including refugees. An important exception is article 29(2), which provides that 'every Ugandan shall have the right to move freely throughout Uganda and to reside and settle in any part of Uganda'. In the context of a constitution that generally enshrines and strengthens human rights guaranteed under international law, this provision could be unique in abridging an internationally guaranteed right. Indeed, freedom of movement, as laid down in the international instruments to which Uganda is a party, is a right of *every person*, not only of nationals. Moreover, upon becoming a party to the International Covenant on Civil and Political Rights (ICCPR) and the 1951 Convention, Uganda did not enter a reservation to the relevant provisions on freedom of movement (articles 12 and 26 respectively). Article 286 of the Constitution provides that treaties already in force before the Constitution are not affected by it. Consequently, since Uganda cannot at this stage enter a reservation to these Conventions, it is in breach of its international commitments unless it amends article 29(2) to extend freedom of movement and of choice of the place of residence to all persons.[6] As it will be shown in Chapter 4, restrictions on their freedom of movement and choice of residence were the single most important obstacle to refugees enjoying all other rights (Beyani 2000; Lomo 1999b; Verdirame 1999b).

Other provisions in the Constitution of great importance to refugees are articles 12–13 on acquisition of citizenship by registration and by naturalisation. This provision gave rise to a long and heated debate in the Constituent Assembly and was unsatisfactorily resolved. At the heart of the debate was whether refugees should be granted Ugandan citizenship. The National Resistance Movement (NRM) government at one point seemed inclined to allow the naturalisation of refugees, describing in one document lack of provision for their naturalisation as 'one obvious flaw' that needed to be 'corrected' (GoU-MoLG 1993). In the end, the Constitution allowed aliens, including spouses of Ugandans of both sexes, to acquire citizenship either by birth, registration, or naturalisation.[7] It also identified two additional categories of non-citizens for the purposes of naturalisation: those who have 'legally and voluntarily migrated' to Uganda, for whom a period of ten years of residence is required before they can register as citizens of Uganda; and others, for whom the period is twenty years. Since refugees are, by definition, involuntary migrants, the longer period was specifically meant to make the naturalisation of refugees more difficult than for other migrants.[8] The longer period provided for refugees might reflect the resentment towards them for the role they played in Ugandan politics, especially in the 1980s.

Preceded by the Sudan Ordinance 1955, which dealt with the arrival of refugees from the *Anyanya* civil war, the Control of Alien Refugees Act, one of the earliest pieces of refugee legislation in Africa, was enacted in 1960 before independence and remains the basis of the current refugee administrative structure and policy in Uganda. As its title suggests, the act is exclusively concerned with the *control* of refugees, and not with establishing standards for their treatment. The philosophy underlying the act is that refugees are passive victims – a burden, rather than people capable of contributing to the host society. Under the act, control is achieved through five interrelated tools.

First, refugees are identified as those belonging to 'a class of aliens' that the minister declares to be such (sec. 3(1)). Refugees also have to obtain permits to remain in Uganda (sec. 6): failure to do so results in a maximum three months imprisonment (sec. 11).

Second, refugees' freedom of movement is restricted and they 'may be ordered to reside in any place in Uganda' (sec. 8) and those who 'fail forthwith to comply ... shall be guilty of an offence' (sec. 8(5)).

Third, refugees are dispossessed of some of their property. Animals 'shall be kept in such place as [the minister] shall direct, or shall be slaughtered or otherwise disposed of' (sec. 10(1)). If the animals are sold, the official is obliged to 'use his best endeavours' to ensure that the owner receives the proceeds (sec. 10(2)), while no compensation is due if the animal is slaughtered to prevent the spread of disease (sec. 10(4)). Even if precautionary measures for animals might be justifiable in order to prevent the spread of disease, there can be no justification for giving the authorities unlimited power to 'take possession of any vehicle in which refugees arrive in Uganda and ... authorise its use ... for the purpose of moving refugees or any stores or equipment' (sec. 16(1)). In case of damage to this vehicle, there is to be no liability (sec. 16(2)).

Fourth, the act creates a series of obstacles to refugee integration, most notably by making it illegal for Ugandans to 'harbour refugees' (sec. 13A).

Such conduct is a 'misdemeanour' punishable with a fine of USh 10,000 or a maximum of five years' imprisonment or both (sec. 13A(2)). A foreigner found harbouring a refugee can be deported (sec. 13A(3)). Conversely, it is an offence for a non-refugee to enter a refugee settlement without the permission of the Directorate of Refugees (DoR) or of the settlement commandant (sec. 14).[9] The act crystallised the segregation between Ugandans and refugees that was first introduced by the colonial administration. As for the right to seek employment, an indispensable condition for integration, the act vaguely states that 'Arrangement may be made to offer employment to refugees ...' (sec. 15), but 'it shall not be obligatory to pay a refugee for any employment in connection with the administration, internal arrangement or maintenance of refugee settlements'. The act also eliminates the possibility of naturalisation at the outset, since 'for the purposes of the Immigration (Control) Act and the Uganda Citizenship Act no period of time spent in Uganda as a refugee shall be deemed to be residence in Uganda' (sec. 18(2)).

Finally, the act vests unlimited powers in the administrators and makes it possible for a regime of fear to be instituted in the settlements. For example, the settlement commandant is authorised to make such arrests 'without warrant' pending the 'institution of proceedings' (sec. 22). Settlement commandants are authorised to use force, 'including firearms', in the exercise of their authority (sec. 23). If the minister is 'satisfied that any refugee is acting in a manner prejudicial to peace and good order in Uganda or is prejudicing relations between the Government and any other Government', he can order his indefinite detention (sec. 9(1)) with no stipulation as to the maximum period of time which this person, who has not been found guilty of any crime by a court of law, can serve. Indefinite detention can also be ordered by the minister if it is 'made to appear ... that it is likely' that a refugee committed a crime before coming to Uganda (sec. 19). A refugee who fails to obey a 'lawful order of the Director or of a Settlement Commandant' or who leaves the settlement without permission can be confined in a 'settlement lock-up' for thirty days or fined USh 200 (sec. 21(2)(a)). On the good side, the act prohibits *refoulement* and prevents deportations (secs. 6(2), 20).

The Control of Alien Refugees Act is in flagrant conflict with the Ugandan Constitution, as well as with other international legal obligations accepted by Uganda since 1960, and – in our view – is in urgent need of repeal. Already in the 1970s, it was observed that the act was 'never strictly enforced' and that a 'growing number [of refugees] have not obtained permits and have either not been directed to refugee settlements or have chosen not to reside in the settlements' (Holborn 1975: 1218). In 1997, the deputy director of DoR, the body in charge of refugee affairs in Uganda, maintained that this law was no longer observed, and that the 1951 Convention and the 1969 OAU Convention were applied in practice despite the lack of statutory incorporation (*see* GoU-MoLG 1993). Nevertheless, the act has established a culture of centralised control that still pervades the administration of refugee affairs and has survived the NRM government's policy of devolution of power to the district levels; it also entrenches the colonial practice of confining refugees in settlements.

Refugee policy in Kenya

Refugee policy in Kenya evolved over the decades from an open door, laissez-faire approach to a policy of control and containment in camps. In this process, the balance of power shifted from the government to UNHCR. Within the Kenyan government, the National Refugee Secretariat (NRS), based at the Ministry of Home Affairs and National Heritage in 1997, was the office responsible for refugee matters. The head of this unit reported to the permanent secretary. Different departments dealt with immigration and security, and came under the Office of the President, as did the intelligence services and the special branch. It was the Office of the President that issued the orders for the two large-scale roundups of refugees in Nairobi in July 1997 and September 1998. In these situations, UNHCR's protection officers bypassed the NRS and dealt directly with immigration officials.

Phase One: Government controls refugee policy

Until approximately 1990, the Kenyan government was in charge of refugee affairs but received little multilateral aid to support refugees. Notwithstanding the experience of the colonial government, which had encamped Ethiopian refugees (Opondo 1994), in the post-independence period Kenya operated a policy of benign neglect, allowing refugees to settle freely in towns and cities to secure their own means of livelihood as best they could (Headly 1986; Hopkins et al. 1990). Limited assistance from UNHCR was only available in Nairobi. UNHCR had a designated implementing partner, a church organisation, which dispensed meagre allowances to particular categories of people considered destitute – for example, women-headed households and physically disabled persons. UNHCR funded a modest scholarship programme and, from time to time, implemented different projects to help refugees acquire new skills and seek employment. Some assistance was also available to refugees through other church organisations and NGOs (Headly 1986).

Up to 1991, the Kenyan government conducted refugee status-determination interviews with UNHCR acting in an advisory role. The NRS administered a small, open reception centre at Thika where destitute asylum-seekers could reside during the process. At Thika they received dry rations and could cook for themselves. Those granted status were expected to move out of this reception centre and settle outside. Refusal letters advised those not granted asylum to 'find another country' within a specified period, normally three months. It is likely that few were successful in doing so and that most remained in Nairobi.

Although it took no positive action, in this period the government at least refrained from creating obstacles to local integration and to the enjoyment of such basic rights as work, education, and freedom of movement. In fact, some refugees were able to establish fairly secure livelihoods. Through self-help associations and private entrepreneurship, businesses – for example, restaurants – were established. One Ethiopian started a textile factory employing many Kenyans as well as refugees; others started transport businesses. Ugandan professionals found employment as teachers in primary and secondary schools, in Kenya's universities, and in the health sector. In fact, the departure of Ugandans after 1986 created a serious vacuum, especially in the teaching profession. A few individual refugees obtained funding for projects in the slum areas of the city where they lived, providing services – such as health and education – for both refugees and Kenyans.[10] Ugandans even started their own secondary school during the 1980s.

On the other hand, refugees experienced the economic uncertainties and general hazards of life under an authoritarian regime in the same way as Kenyan nationals. Most refugees probably lived on the edge of survival and many fell victim to police harassment, with few effective means of redress. Police competed to be stationed in the areas where refugees lived because extorting bribes in exchange for freedom from arbitrary arrest or detention became an easy way of supplementing meagre salaries. At times, such harassment was officially sanctioned. For example, in 1987, at least one instance of a large-scale *refoulement* ensued after one of President Moi's public inflammatory statements that 'Kenya was for Kenyans'. On this occasion, the police responded by rounding up large numbers of Ugandans and Rwandans and transporting them by train across the Uganda border. However, even when such crises occurred, there was an immediate response by concerned Kenyans, including church leaders and NGOs, who protested and took action to save many individuals.[11]

Phase Two: The balance of power shifts

The war in Somalia, and the subsequent arrival of some 400,000 Somali refugees in Kenya after 1990, combined with the arrival of the Sudanese – initially some 7,000 'walking boys' in the northwest – prompted the government to appeal for foreign assistance. By 1991, the situation in Thika reception centre had become 'an embarrassment'. Initially set up to house

350 refugees, its population had grown to 8,000. 'All the pit latrines are full to the brim, the flush toilets never function because the cistern tanks are broken and have never been replaced. The sewage is blocked and filthy water is overflowing all the time. The garbage dumps are full. In short, the centre is a man-made disaster' (UNHCR 1992c). The situation had deteriorated to this point because in the tug-of-war between UNHCR and the government, UNHCR, considering the government too corrupt, insisted that the management of Thika should be handed over to an NGO, sub-contracted by UNHCR, rather than to the government.

Having resisted it for so many years, the Kenyan government finally acquiesced in the encampment of refugees, agreeing to provide land, albeit for the most part in inhospitable areas.[12] UNHCR first set up camps for the Somalis around Mombasa and then in Dadaab, and, for the Ethiopians, in Mandera, in the North-Eastern Province at the border with Ethiopia. Kakuma camp, located in the Turkana district, initially set up to receive the thousands of unaccompanied minors who had fled the war in Sudan, was, in 2000, hosting a population of over 70,000. NGOs were contracted to provide specific services in these camps as UNHCR's implementing partners. Between 1995 and 1997, in response to tensions between Kenyan and Somali traders, the camps around Mombasa were closed and refugees had to choose between repatriation to Somalia or relocation to other camps in the northeast or the northwest.[13] This resulted in placing refugees where they had little or no opportunity to generate their own income in the informal sector of the economy, forcing them to be almost totally dependent on the distribution of rations made available by the World Food Programme (WFP). Since that time, all the encamped refugees have resided in either Kakuma or Dadaab – each comprising three separate camps.

Unlike the reception centre in Thika, these camps were administered by UNHCR, which established sub-offices to carry out this work. Another difference was that, once assigned to the camps, the refugees were required to reside in them. In the bureaucratic jargon of the post-1991 refugee regime in Kenya, refugees have to reside in camps 'until a durable solution is found'. The NRS, however, had no effective control over the administration of these camps; in March 1997, one senior official, Nimrod Waweru, complained that even his visits to these camps had to be negotiated with UNHCR.[14]

Already in 1991, a special office in Nairobi, 'Wood Avenue', had been set up by UNHCR and administered by the Jesuit Refugee Service (JRS) to provide certain services to a small number of refugees and to conduct refugee status-determination interviews. It was from this office that asylum-seekers received protection letters, which 'recognised' them as 'refugees' (or usually as 'persons of concern to UNHCR'), and directed them to particular camps or, in very exceptional cases, allowed them to live in Nairobi.

This letter provided no security against the ever more frequent police roundups of refugees who chose to remain in Nairobi. The insecurity in urban areas reached a peak in August/September 1998 when, following the bombing of the US embassy in Nairobi, the government suddenly and publicly confronted UNHCR, announcing in the press that UNHCR had no authority to grant refugee status in Kenya and declaring it would no longer recognise the protection letters which UNHCR had been issuing to refugees (Warigi 1998: 28).[15]

The main reason for the transfer of responsibility to UNHCR was the lack of funds and resources to enable the government to deal with an emergency. The case of Kenya is by no means unique. For example, in Sudan – on which a comprehensive study exists (Karadawi 1999) – a similar process had taken place in the 1980s, resulting in the Sudanese Commission for Refugees losing control over refugee policy (Karadawi 1999: 193). UNHCR's takeover occurred between 1980 and 1983, after the Sudanese government's initiative in 1980 to reach out to donors independently of UNHCR had failed, mainly owing to UNHCR's hostility to this initiative, which it feared would 'lead to duplication of funding and a division of authority, in practical terms over the allocation and accounting of such contributions' (Karadawi 1999: 162–214; Betts, quoted in Karadawi 1999: 175). A major difference between Kenya and Sudan is that the Kenyan government did not pose a sustained challenge to UNHCR's monopoly over donors' funds for refugees.[16] On one occasion when it tried to do so, in 1991, a serious conflict developed between the permanent secretary, home affairs, and the UNHCR representative. After Kenya had been successful in raising some funds from the EU through the Lomé IV Convention,[17] a 'Chinese whispers' campaign was started against the Kenyan official, accusing him of corruption.[18] Relations between UNHCR and government were soured by this and other recriminations. The confrontation was eventually resolved with the removal of the permanent secretary to another ministry and the replacement of the UNHCR representative.[19]

Phase Three: Eliminating the organisational problem

The third phase in the history of refugee policy in Kenya began during the period of this research. By 1996–97, with the 'emergency phase' past, the UNHCR office in Kenya came under pressure to reduce its expenditure. As Walkup (1997b: 46) has observed, when faced with financial constraints, UNHCR staff cease to see refugees as people *with* problems; instead, refugees *become* the problem. UNHCR's efforts in these situations focus 'on eliminating the organisational problem (refugees), instead of successfully performing their assigned functions by improving their effectiveness through innovation and creativity ... Unfortunately, the organisational solution often leads to increased suffering and death.'

As budget reductions made programme cuts inevitable, UNHCR justified them by claiming that refugee numbers had decreased. It conducted 'revalidation exercises' – that is, headcounts – in Kakuma and Dadaab. In Kakuma, the official number of refugees was put at 33,000 (from 50,000), and incentives (payments to refugee workers in the camps) were withdrawn with grave consequences for the nutritional status of the population (Boudreau et al. 1996).[20] Furthermore, the numbers of those who were recognised as refugees at the end of the individual status-determination process were kept low, especially through the application of the 'first country of asylum' rule (*see* Chapter 3) and through the rejection of many cases for 'lack of credibility'.

In addition to headcounts, UNHCR employed 'push factors', such as the closure of the relatively hospitable camps around Mombasa and the transfer of the refugees to Dadaab and Kakuma (Verdirame 1999b: 71). From UNHCR's point of view, the closure of these camps represented 'significant savings in staff and administrative support costs, while the consolidation of camps should ensure a more efficient use of resources and cost effectiveness in programme delivery' (UNHCR 1997a: para. 50). Many Somali refugees who had until then resided in the camps decided to survive outside the aid umbrella, since they were not willing either to be forcibly relocated to Kakuma or Dadaab or to be repatriated.

By 1998–99, therefore, having repatriated some, rejected others, and pushed many outside the aid umbrella, UNHCR could present a picture of the refugee situation in Kenya that justified its partial disengagement and the reduction of its activities, which included the closure of its offices in Mombasa. The senior protection officer, who took office in September 1997, tried to redefine UNHCR's role in relation to the government, encouraging the government to resume some of its responsibilities:

> The system currently in place must be changed since UNHCR is doing what it is really not supposed to do [determining refugee status] ... In the medium term, UNHCR has to persuade the government of Kenya to take on board refugee status determination again. UNHCR would employ two lawyers to work with them on this procedure, while another lawyer would offer legal assistance to refugees in all sorts of other areas (crime, police abuse, family cases, employment, etc.) ... We have to go back to our protection role ... We will also need to involve NGOs more.[21]

However, despite some important achievements – for example, on the naturalisation of refugees who had been recognised by the government before 1991 (UNHCR 1999e: 4.2) – the main response from the government to the senior protection officer's proposals was that 'refugees are UNHCR's problem'. This reaction should not have been surprising given that the marginalisation of the Kenyan authorities from refugee affairs had led to a loss of experience and had also created a sense of resentment on the part of officials, encouraging apathy if not outright hostility. This is exemplified by the comments of a very senior official in the Immigration Department. Having 'welcomed' us with a rhetorical question aimed at other staff ('Who has told these two to come and bother me this morning?'), he then said about UNHCR: 'We only have asylum-seekers here because only the government of Kenya can determine who is a refugee and who is not. If UNHCR people come here and talk to me about refugees instead of asylum-seekers, I kick their asses out of here immediately, but with you I am being nicer because I need to educate you.'[22]

The efforts of the senior protection officer in 1997–2000 to revert to a 'normal' situation with a healthy division of roles between UNHCR and the government did not succeed.[23] In July 2000, the Refugee Consortium of Kenya (RCK) described the situation in the following terms:

> Regarding status determination and renewal, this is the 'preserve' of UNHCR. They handle all aspects of status determination – registration, interview, recognition, rejection and appeal. Occasionally, the government would give recognition in exceptional cases. There is an Eligibility Committee set up by the government with assistance from UNHCR (about two years ago) to attend to the issues of status determination. But this committee is most ineffective. It hardly [ever] convenes to decide cases. UNHCR gives recommendations on particular cases and the committee is supposed to decide on the basis of those recommendations. For all intent and purposes, UNHCR does the status determination. (75% of all asylum application are rejected.) (Email from RCK, 13 July 2000)

The 2002 elections could signal the beginning of a new phase in refugee policy. The initial statements made by members of the new government seem promising: for example, Moody Awory, the minister for home affairs, has called for 'the entire ownership and responsibility of refugees' to go back to the government.

Refugee policy in Uganda

In Uganda, refugee policy avowedly aimed to facilitate self-sufficiency through agriculture in confined settlements. As early as 1960, land was set aside for refugees – Sudanese in the north and Rwandans in the southwest. The administrative structure comprised the settlement commandant – an employee of the DoR – the police, and the Refugee Welfare Committees (RWCs). In practice, however, the running of the settlements was in the hands of UNHCR and its sub-contracted NGOs. Refugees had never been encouraged to live in urban centres, and, after 1998, they needed to prove that they were able to support themselves in order to be authorised to live in Kampala.

Government and refugees

Over the years, responsibility for refugees has shifted between ministries. In 1987, the DoR was moved from the Ministry of Youth, Culture and Sports to the Ministry of Local Government (MoLG) (Harrell-Bond and Kanyiehamba 1986). In 1998, responsibility was transferred to the newly established Ministry of Disaster Preparedness and Refugees, in the Office of the Prime Minister. This ministry comprised two sections that operated independently: the DoR and the Office of the Assistant Commissioner for Disaster Preparedness, the latter responsible for internally displaced persons and other humanitarian crises. The directorate was headed by the deputy director (the director being the permanent secretary to the ministry);[24] an assistant deputy commissioner headed the disaster section.

The directorate also had personnel stationed in the refugee-hosting districts – 'desk officers' responsible for supervising a staff of settlement commandants and other junior officers, some of whom resided in the settlements.[25] Some members of Uganda's Internal Security Organisation (ISO) acted as deputy settlement commandants (GoU-MoLG 1993).

Notwithstanding its proclaimed pursuit of 'self-sufficiency', in practice the government did not put refugees in a position to achieve this goal. Although the environment of the settlements in Uganda was generally more hospitable than that in the Kenyan camps, in the northern districts they were under constant threat from rebel attacks. Moreover, the land allocated, 0.03 hectare per person, was insufficient and the quality of land extremely uneven: many households were allocated land unsuitable for cultivation because it was rocky, arid, or in swamps (Lester 1998). In Nakivale settlement there was no land for cultivation at all, and in Achol-Pii, the land allocated fell short of the official standard: only 100 square metres per household (AVSI 1996: 3).

UNHCR's influence over refugee policy

UNHCR's influence grew over the years until, by the late 1990s, it effectively controlled refugee policy. Although the Ugandan government, unlike Kenya, had a body responsible for refugee status determination – the Refugee Eligibility Committee (REC) – UNHCR operated its own determination process, dealing with far larger numbers than those that went through the REC.[26] Through its position as an adviser, UNHCR also had the upper hand in most of the cases submitted through the REC. In practice, therefore, it was UNHCR, and not the government, that controlled this fundamental aspect of refugee matters.

UNHCR's ability to influence refugee policy was enhanced by its practice of 'topping up' the salaries of government officials dealing with refugees. 'Topping up' is actually an understatement as, in one case,

UNHCR was paying five-sixths of the salary: the government paid the equivalent of US\$ 100, UNHCR paid US\$ 500. Unlike the DoR, the Office of the Assistant Commissioner for Disaster Preparedness had no such 'godfather'; lacking vehicles and other vital infrastructure, the staff of this section could rely only on local government salaries. The capacity of this office to respond to 'disasters' thus depended entirely on the ad hoc contributions from international sources.

It was not only through salary top-ups that UNHCR was able to pull strings. It also provided equipment – vehicles and computers – without which the directorate could not operate. The government sometimes sought to conceal the disempowering consequences of this situation and to maintain at least the vestiges of control, but it often failed to do so, as exemplified by the saga of the car licence plates. The deputy director had put government of Uganda number plates on the vehicles supplied by UNHCR as symbolic evidence that the government was in charge. UNHCR did not appreciate this. Its representative wrote to the deputy director, and, while describing the vehicles as a 'donation', reminded him that the vehicles were actually 'owned by UNHCR and temporarily seconded (on loan) to your office' (UNHCR 1999a). Until then, UNHCR had also paid for the fuel, including customs duty. However, the deputy director was informed that there 'can be no longer a budget line for duty-included fuel in the agreement' so long as the vehicles continued to display government licences. However, were the deputy director prepared to revert to UN number plates – thus giving up the symbol of government authority – his office could benefit from tax-free fuel. In UNHCR's words, the options were 'either changing the plate numbers ... and receiving duty-free fuel *or* keeping the Government plate numbers and accept to use only government coupons' (ibid.). As Landau has observed (1997), the 'visual symbolism' of power in refugee situations is an important means of asserting authority: 'flags ... fluttering like medieval standards, UNHCR labels on food and shelter', and – we can now add – licence plates, are all part of this visual array of power.

Paying for the costs of assisting refugees is one matter; accepting external support for the bureaucratic apparatus of the state that is responsible for refugee policy making is another. In a policy document, the government of Uganda acknowledged that donor agencies had 'an upper hand in the control of the activities which they sponsor' but added, perhaps betraying some insecurity on the matter, 'This ... does not mean that they control the commandants' (MoLG 1993). Certainly, the deputy director of the DoR attempted to maintain the impression that the government was in charge.

To what extent can a government really count on the loyalty of staff members who depend on UNHCR for the major part of their salaries? The experience in Sudan suggests they cannot. There, UNHCR financed the establishment and equipment of a new office for the commissioner for refugees, funded '50 per cent salary increments to the staff as well as provision for vehicles and equipment', and placed a UNHCR senior programme officer in his office to 'help with the in-service training of the staff' (Karadawi 1999: 195). As a result, 'the new commissioner, unlike his predecessor, willingly followed the guidelines established by UNHCR for the planning and management of refugee assistance' (ibid.).

Another important means through which UNHCR exercised effective control over refugee policy was the funding and establishment of parallel services such as health, education, and sanitation for the refugee population in settlements. Although the money spent on these services was much greater than that which the government could afford for its citizens, they did not result in better nutrition and health for refugees.[28] The frustration of the government at its inability to exert effective control over the management of settlements was evident. As early as 1993, the government expressed concern at the way 'refugee settlements [had become] ... islands unto themselves and the refugees regarded them as UN territories. Speaking of Kiryandongo refugee settlement, Masindi district, the ministry insisted that services provided to the refugees should be shared by the nationals as well' (MoLG 1993). In practice, however, all the settlements were located in such sparsely populated areas that very few citizens benefited from these parallel services. In addition, there was 'very little direct contact between these institutions [the Local Council system][29] and the management of the settlement, still less between them and the refugees' (Kaiser 2001: 10). Kaiser found that Masindi '... sub-county authorities are, in practice, only aware of the settlement in the vaguest way' (ibid.).

In Adjumani and Moyo districts, under pressure from politicians,[30] UNHCR made some investments *outside* the settlements,[31] especially to maintain the airstrips and to build roads, the latter necessary, not only for access to the settlements, but also to facilitate the movement of the army.[32] It is difficult to estimate to what extent UNHCR programmes were benefiting the locals in any meaningful way, mainly because of the tendency in UNHCR field reports to exaggerate achievements and sometimes take credit for what others have done.[33]

Theoretically, the DoR's desk officer, stationed in a refugee-hosting district, was responsible for liaising with district authorities, but in practice the settlements were administered by UNHCR through its implementing partners without reference to district authorities.[34] This created tensions when UNHCR took decisions that had a bearing on the surrounding area without consulting either the district authorities or the directorate.[35] An example was when UNHCR withdrew funds from Kiryandongo refugee settlement because the refugees 'were approaching self sufficiency and ... it was time for them to be absorbed completely into local government structures' (Kaiser 2001: 1). It withdrew funding from InterAid, its implementing partner administering the settlement. InterAid then withdrew all its equipment – such as vehicles, computers, filing cabinets – leaving the settlement commandant, his assistant, and a secretary sitting alone in the office with a small portable typewriter.[36]

As Kaiser notes, UNHCR had 'carefully constructed [Kiryandongo's] reputation as a model settlement', even as 'the most successful settlement in Africa' (2001: 12). Now, from UNHCR's perspective, 'to all intents and purposes, [the people in Kiryandongo had become] ... part of the Ugandan population in administrative and economic terms' (ibid.: 11). This hand-over was to mark the end of UNHCR's financial responsibility; henceforth 'the government should meet the costs of maintaining services in the settlements through budgets allocated to the districts each year' (ibid.).

Masindi district leaders refused to cooperate. 'Unauthorized to generate taxes from the refugee population', the district officials could only envisage UNHCR as the source of the extra funding it would require (Kaiser 2001: 13). It was assumed that this would have to be 'filtered to them' through the DoR. UNHCR rejected this possibility, continuing to insist that refugees should be included in the district's annual budget (ibid.).

The response of the deputy director, who heard about the handover through an InterAid leak was no less negative. He argued that although refugee administration was a central government affair, 'UNHCR went to see the District Commissioner to hand over without going to the head of MoLG. When the UNHCR finally asked if I'd participate in the "handover" I said "No" because the settlement is already the government's. UNHCR cannot just abandon its responsibility without a durable solution being found.'[37] What really infuriated the deputy director and the local authorities was the stripping of the settlement of all capital assets that had been purchased with UNHCR's money.[38] After some argument, UNHCR finally agreed to return them to Masindi.[39] UNHCR's threatened withdrawal from Adjumani, Arua, and Moyo districts, camouflaged as promoting self-sufficiency, was met with similar resistance from local authorities.

The deputy director rejected the idea that refugees in Kiryandongo should be absorbed into the Ugandan budget. From his point of view, refugees were the *sole responsibility* of the 'international community' – an attitude (echoed in Kenya) that was almost the inevitable consequence of UNHCR's steady erosion of government control over refugee policy. By then, the government believed that by allowing refugees in and creating settlements, it had fulfilled its part in the 'burden-sharing in relation to the refugee problem' (Kaiser 2001: 9).

In the end a compromise was struck with UNHCR over Kiryandongo. The temporary resolution was that a camp commandant should remain in residence in Kiryandongo and that refugee teachers and medical staff would continue to be funded by UNHCR but paid through the DoR.[40] Nevertheless, the Kiryandongo handover vividly illustrated what should have been clear throughout: UNHCR assumed the right to take the key decisions on assistance to refugees in Uganda; it decided how, to whom and how long to provide such assistance.

Eliminating the organisational problem

As in Kenya, UNHCR in Uganda came under pressure from Geneva to reduce its expenditure in 1997. Again, the solution was to 'eliminate the organizational problem – the refugees' (Walkup 1997), but this took a different form in Uganda. The government had long promoted the policy of refugee self-sufficiency in settlements, even referring to it as 'integration', and UNHCR decided to justify its financial exit in these terms.

The major thrust of the policy was to integrate services for refugees in the three districts in the north with those of the nationals and put them under the authority of the relevant departments in each district. The proclaimed objective was to bring Sudanese refugees to a level of economic self-sufficiency so that they would be no more dependent on external sources of funding than were the nationals (UNHCR-OPM 1999). In particular, the goal was:

> ... to promote the local integration of refugees to the extent that they will be able to fully support themselves within four years (1999–2002). Any further external assistance would then come solely through the government and at the same level as that provided to nationals ... Self-sufficiency means that refugees are able to:
> 1. grow or produce their own food;
> 2. pay for the cost of the health and educational services provided to them (at the same cost level as the nationals) and take care of own vulnerables;
> 3. take part in other socio-economic, in particular income-generating activities allowed by the laws of Uganda related to refugees and aliens.
> 4. be empowered to better organize and respond to issues which concern them directly (UNHCR-OPM 1998: 7).

The same policy document went on to explain that:

> Citizenship/naturalisation is **not** [sic] the goal of this long-term strategy, but in order to provide a perspective to long-residing individual cases, it would be good to clarify what the Uganda constitution stipulates on this point as there seems to be uncertainty (UNHCR-OPM 1998: 10).

The self-sufficiency policy envisaged that, at the end of the implementation of the programme in 2004, refugees would be able to access and pay for the cost of health, water and sanitation, and educational services at the same level as the nationals, and even take care of vulnerable groups on their own! One of the research assistants on our team noted:

> The implementation of this policy is planned over a four-year period, but food aid has already been withdrawn from certain settlements on the grounds that they have been established long enough for the inhabitants to

have been able to grow enough food to feed their families. It is known, however, that many refugees do not have enough land and, in many cases, what they have is of extremely poor quality. More serious, many households lack enough labour to support themselves through agriculture. Moreover, even if they could grow enough food for household consumption, all people require cash to meet their non-food needs.

In any population, there will always be destitute households that require welfare assistance ... It was found, however, that to assist vulnerable households to become economically self-sufficient, it is necessary to address the unique circumstances of each household (Lester 1998: 2–3).

The self-sufficiency programme purported to follow the refugee-affected areas approach, which had been recommended at the July 1984 Second International Conference on Assistance to Refugees in Africa (ICARA II) (Weighill 1996). The main feature of this approach was to view the presence of refugees as a catalyst for the socio-economic development of the host region. In practice, however, the Ugandan self-sufficiency policy did not have much in common with the ICARA II approach. In fact, UNHCR was simply collapsing parallel services and expecting the so-called 'cost-sharing' on the part of refugees to take up the slack. Predictably, the local districts saw no benefit in assuming responsibility for large populations of refugees with no more resources and assets than before. None of the three districts had included refugees in their planning figures. Nor had donors taken any steps to include refugees in their normal development projects; they were noticeably absent from the meeting to launch the policy. NGOs were also ambivalent towards the policy. For example, JRS announced that it was terminating its support to refugee schools in northern Uganda and that, relying on other sources of funding, it would focus its programme on southern Sudan to promote 'conditions there conducive to refugee repatriation' (UNHCR/DFID 1998). JRS's abrupt withdrawal produced a crisis because the Universal Primary Education (UPE) system in Uganda had not yet included refugees. The district education officers were reluctantly agreeing to being involved in the recruitment, training, and inspection of refugee teachers, and the issue of the 'convergence of refugee teachers and state teachers' salaries' had not yet been resolved (ibid.).[41] It was only in 2000 that Arua district voted to accept the self-reliance programme (*New Vision*, 26 January 2000: 11). As we wrote in a letter to the district, the real challenge was at that point 'to *insist* that all donors also incorporate this additional population into the projects they fund'.[42]

The leap from a situation in which local actors were ignored to one in which they were expected to take over responsibility for refugees was dramatic. Despite the obvious problems it involved, UNHCR believed that it had no option but to introduce this policy because of:

... the phenomenon of steadily increasing donor fatigue which will result anyway in diminished funds for refugee-specific programmes in Uganda and elsewhere. This demands innovative methods to do more with less money. Where refugees are becoming self-sufficient, they should cost less in food aid and other support services. Where refugees can be treated at par [*sic*] with nationals, it is also logical that donors, UN agencies and NGOs concerned with regular development [*sic*] should move in. For this reason also they are involved in the conception and implementation of this strategy. (UNHCR-OPM 1998: 4).

UNHCR envisaged that, as a result of the self-sufficiency policy, its role would 'shift from parallel implementation to advice and monitoring of field activities in addition to policy and protection matters at national level' (GoU-OPM 1999a: 5). There were protests, but UNHCR was unwavering. The implementation of the self-sufficiency policy began with the 'sensitisation' of those involved (and hitherto ignored):

> ... UNHCR field offices have already started sensitising the refugee groups (leaders, elders, women groups) to explain the long-term strategy and obtain their feedback. At the moment there is certain reluctance among the refugees themselves. While in many settlements refugees are now 'digging in' after receiving land, tools and seeds, others have shown little willingness to start their settled life in a sustainable fashion (UNHCR-OPM 1998: 5).

Many did not react well to UNHCR's 'sensitisation'. When UNHCR did power point presentations in the districts, they failed to impress their audiences of local people, and, in Adjumani district, some local participants even walked out of the meeting.

The main problem with the apparently progressive language of the self-sufficiency policy was therefore that until then, as is common in all relief situations, UNHCR and humanitarian NGOs had been investing practically nothing in strengthening the capacity of local health and education services to absorb the refugees.[43] In August 1998, as part of an evaluation of the programme of the Lutheran World Federation (LWF) in Adjumani, we organised a meeting of the local council members, NGOs, and UNHCR to discuss the self-sufficiency policy. The head of the local council chaired the meeting and locals discussed their grievances. Among their complaints was the huge investment UNHCR had made in erecting its own offices in Pakelle, which were of no use to the district because of their location. They pointed out that only one NGO, Water Aid, had worked with both refugees and locals.

The situation in Adjumani was mirrored in all other districts where UNHCR operated, and the handover process of Kiryandongo was just one illustration of UNHCR's disregard for local actors, neglecting the chance to use the presence of refugees as an opportunity for development.[44] Payne (1997) detailed the knock-on effect of the delays and premature cuts in food rations for refugees in Ikafe: refugees lost an average of up to ten days of rations every month and, in some cases, the distribution was delayed by up to forty days (ibid. 1997: 10). Desperate refugees sold their assets at very low prices in order to buy food. Agricultural production was also affected because both men and women had to seek piecework (*leja leja*) on Ugandan farms in exchange for food rather than cultivate their crops. They ate the seeds that should have been used to grow crops for the time when WFP would cut off their rations. Even those crops that were grown had to be harvested prematurely, with a significant loss. Some refugees even resorted to prostitution; malnutrition and disease soared. All this took place during Ikafe's first two years of existence in what was to be OXFAM's model settlement. Then in April 1996, the settlement was attacked by a rebel group, the West Nile Bank Front (WNBF). Mr Komba, UNHCR head of sub-office, Arua, 'blamed OXFAM for their overambitious two-year plan [to achieve self-sufficiency]. It was difficult to achieve any meaningful integration in such a short span of time.'[45]

Moreover, the legal obstacles to the integration of refugees were not addressed in the self-sufficiency policy. The right of free movement, the right to work, and the duty to pay taxes are always material to socio-economic integration. The policy of self-sufficiency has to be considered together with UNHCR's urban policy, which came into effect in the same period (UNHCR 1997b). The vision that emerges from these two policies was that refugees 'belonged' to segregated settlements, with their physical survival dependent on subsistence agriculture, disguised in official documentation as self-sufficiency.

Towards a new structure for refugee management?

The Ugandan 1995 Constitution envisaged the establishment of a Disaster Preparedness Commission, responsible for 'both natural and man-made disasters' (art. 249(1)), to be headed by a commissioner responsible for coordinating the work of line ministries and dealing with such external issues as donor funding (Kaiser 2001: 7, fn 10). In 2000, this body had not yet begun to work owing to the lack of implementing legislation, although draft legislation existed (Disaster Preparedness and Management Bill, 1998). A draft policy paper produced by the Office of the Prime Minister (GoU-OPM 1999a) laid out a comprehensive plan for government responses to all kinds of disasters, and listed the specific committees that would be established under the Commission.[46] The policy detailed in this document admitted short-term emergency relief, but the overall emphasis was on rehabilitation and development; this policy was also in line with the NRM's policy of decentralisation, giving local authorities major responsibility for early warning and monitoring as well as implementing the response to the needs of the affected populations.

This approach to organising responses to disasters is premised on a flexible structure that is integrated into local and central administration.

If implemented, this policy would eliminate the present division of responsibilities in the ministry and integrate functions within the line ministries. It would also minimise competition for funds among different offices within the government and perhaps reverse the current situation in which there is a category of civil servants who need refugees and victims of disaster for institutional survival.[47]

This proposed flexible and integrated structure is in striking contrast to the structure of the 'humanitarian international' (de Waal 1997: 3–4), the continued existence of which depends on maintaining a strict division between relief to refugees and victims of disasters on the one hand, and the rehabilitation and development of such affected populations on the other. Whether the government of Uganda will be successful in implementing this approach will depend greatly on its *independent* ability, at both national and local levels, to persuade donors to support an integrated development approach to people who have been uprooted by both natural and man-made disasters.

Refugee law-making in fits and starts

With the revival of the East African Community also came attempts to harmonise laws on migration and refugees in Kenya, Tanzania, and Uganda. On 6/7 October 1997, officials from Kenya, Uganda, and Tanzania met in Arusha to consider the development of a harmonised law on migration and refugees.[48] Other meetings followed. In the absence of a formal consultation process with interested parties and before any debate in parliament, these meetings ended up offering the main substantive input to the civil servants who were working on the drafts of the refugee bills.[49] This process might have involved some positive cross-fertilisation: for example, the Kenyan 2000 draft borrows the idea of a Refugee Trust Fund from the Ugandan one. In the event, the main consequence of the meetings was a regional consensus that refugees are a 'security' problem. The meetings were attended by security personnel and this view was soon crystallised in official documents (e.g., East African Community 1997).

Both Uganda and Kenya produced a number of draft refugee bills during the 1990s.[50] In Kenya a Refugees Bill was published by the new government in 2003. The text of this bill is different from the 2000 draft, on which the previous government was working. The bill foresees the establishment of a Refugee Status Determination Committee comprising a chairperson and representatives of various ministries (sec. 6). Despite its name, however, this Committee is only expected to 'assist' the commissioner for refugee affairs 'in matters concerning the recognition of persons as refugees' (sec. 6(2)). The commissioner would also be vested with executive functions, such as acting as a secretary to the Status Determination

Committee, coordination, formulation, and implementation of refugee policy, the issuance of identification cards, and camp management. Appeals against decisions of the Committee and of the commissioner would be considered by a Refugee Appeal Board, and the power of judicial review of the High Court against the decisions of the board is expressly mentioned (sec. 9(3)).

The policy-making process that had been envisaged under the 2000 draft appears to have been abandoned. The 2000 draft foresaw the creation of a National Council for Refugees, which would have included two representatives of civil society, the permanent secretary in the ministry responsible for the environment, and the permanent secretary in the ministry responsible for internal security. This Council was going to be responsible for the formulation of refugee policy, and could have solicited 'local and international assistance for refugee related activities in Kenya' (sec. 4(3)(d)). As we have seen, any government's ability to control refugee policy cannot be separated from its control over and access to resources; the centralisation of the refugee policy-making process in the hands of one person (the commissioner) under the Refugees Bill 2003, and the absence of any reference to fundraising are steps in the wrong direction.

Both the 2000 draft and the Refugees Bill 2003 mention 'refugee camps', although it is not clear which categories of refugees would be expected to reside in them (sec. 13(2)(b)). The bill contains a provision on 'camp managers' (sec. 16) who would be appointed in every refugee camp. If this provision means that all refugees have to reside in camps, it could hardly be reconciled with the provisions in the same bill that accord refugees all the rights under the 1951 Convention and the OAU Convention (sec. 15), including the rights of refugees to freedom of movement and choice of residence.

Like the Kenyan bill, a Ugandan draft bill was produced in 2000. Under this draft, the Refugee Eligibility Committee (REC) would have to state reasons for negative decisions. A new body, the Refugee Appeals Board, would be established to consider appeals. However, unlike its Kenyan counterpart, the Ugandan draft does not specifically mention the High Court's judicial review of the board's decisions, although the possibility to seek review would still exist as part of general administrative law. An important safeguard of independence is the fact that the chair of the board would be appointed by the Judicial Service Commission (sec. 16(2)). Appellants may be represented by an advocate (sec. 21(3)). As far as group recognition is concerned, the minister would be empowered to declare a class of persons as refugees and would publish this declaration in the *Gazette* (sec. 25).[51]

Like the Kenyan draft, the Ugandan bill assigns a wide role to security personnel. First, the directors of both the internal and the external security organisations would sit on the REC (sec. 11). Second, members of the Refugee Appeals Board are to be chosen 'from among persons having knowledge or experience in refugee law or matters relating to immigration, foreign affairs, national security and refugees generally' (sec. 16(3)). Wide powers are also given to various categories of public officials to search refugees and their property (sec. 43(4)).

If it becomes law, the 2000 draft will be exemplary in the world for its express inclusion of gender discrimination as a ground for claiming asylum (this had been advocated in Garry 1998b).[52] In addition to reproducing the refugee definition under the OAU Convention (which incorporated the 1951 Convention definition), section 4(d) spells out that a person will qualify for refugee status if 'owing to well-founded fear of persecution for failing to conform to gender discriminating practices that person is compelled to leave his or her place of habitual residence in order to seek refuge in another place outside the country of origin or nationality'.

A highly problematic aspect of the draft is that it would maintain the reservations to the 1951 Convention that Uganda had entered under Idi Amin. It provides that refugees should be entitled to their internationally recognised rights subject to, inter alia, these reservations (sec. 28).[53]

The provisions on freedom of movement are ambiguous. Section 30 of the draft entitles refugees 'to free movement in Uganda', although it goes on to enumerate a number of purposes for which such freedom of movement can *'especially'* [emphasis added] be exercised (sec. 30) – study, professional training, gainful employment, voluntary repatriation, and resettlement in other countries. Section 44 appears to leave room for the continuation of Uganda's settlement policy. The minister may designate 'transit centres' for 'temporarily' accommodating persons seeking asylum in Uganda, and 'refugee settlements'… for the purposes of … local settlement and integration of refugees' (sec. 44(1)(b)). Moreover, this section implies that refugees need to be 'authorized to stay in any place other than the designated places or areas' (sec. 44(3)). These two sections of the 2000 bill contradict each other.

Again, on the positive side, the 2000 draft reiterates the broad formula that 'every refugee is entitled to the rights and be [*sic*] subject to obligations provided in (a) the Geneva Convention, (b) the OAU Convention, and (c) any other instrument relating to the rights and obligations of refugees to which Uganda is a party' (sec. 28). The bill goes on to list specific rights to which refugees shall be entitled, 'subject to this Act, the OAU Convention and the UN Convention' (sec. 29). Courts are empowered to enforce these provisions directly, which would pave the way for the development of refugee rights in Uganda by means of judicial intervention. The draft also makes provision for the issuing of a temporary identification to all asylum-seekers (sec. 24(1)(a)) and of identity cards upon recognition (sec. 29(a)), and it recognises the refugee's right to obtain a travel document (sec. 31(1)). Another positive aspect is that section 44 (4) acknowledges the need for assistance for asylum-seekers, a departure from current practice.

As far as the right to seek employment is concerned, the draft adopts the 'most favourably treated aliens' standard in the 1951 Convention (sec. 29) – omitting, however, to exempt refugees from the application of any restrictive measures imposed on aliens for the protection of the national labour market, and without giving 'sympathetic consideration to assimilating the rights of all refugees with regard to wage-earning employment to those of nationals' (1951 Convention, art. 17(2)(3)). Consistent with international law, refugee children would be accorded 'the same treatment as nationals with respect to elementary education' (sec. 32(1)).

Concerning policy-making, the 2000 bill establishes a Department of Refugees (sec. 7), but it does not specify in which ministry this department will be based. The head of the department is the commissioner for refugees, whose broad powers include overall responsibility for refugee protection and assistance programmes, and for providing information and advice to the REC, of which he or she is also a member (sec. 9).[54] The bill does empower the commissioner to 'solicit funds for the care and welfare of refugees and the rehabilitation of refugee-affected areas' (sec. 9(3)(b)). The functions of the department are broadly defined and include: issuing of identity cards and travel documents to refugees, providing services for the welfare of refugees, undertaking projects for refugees and refugee-affected areas, and, quite importantly, obtaining the country-of-origin information that is required for refugee status determination (sec. 8). As in the case of the 1999 Kenyan draft, the explicit attribution of a fund-raising function to the commissioner for refugees could ensure the government's control over refugee policy, and is indispensable for the effective discharge of the policy-making functions.

Using international law

The failure to fully incorporate international standards in domestic legislation in both Kenya and Uganda – albeit in different manners and degrees – raises the question of the use that can be made of international law to promote the rights of refugees within the Kenyan and Ugandan legal systems. The extent to which international law is part of the internal law of a country, and can, as such, be enforced by its courts, varies in different countries (Brownlie 2003: 31–55; Denza 2003). In common law systems, like Kenya and Uganda, rules of customary international law are generally considered to be part of the law of the land, unless they are in clear conflict with a statutory provision. For treaties, on the other hand, an act of parliament is usually required. Even in the absence of such an act of parliament, however, national courts have sometimes relied on an unincorporated treaty as an aid in the construction of the terms of a statute that covered the same ground.

In neither country, as mentioned, had the provisions of the main refugee treaties been incorporated in domestic legislation. Undoubtedly, this hamstrung attempts to invoke them successfully in refugee cases before Kenyan or Ugandan courts. Nevertheless, some potential for improving respect for international refugee law standards in these circumstances existed, but it was not usually exploited by refugee lawyers and organisations. For example, legislation enacted after Kenya and Uganda became parties to refugee and human rights treaties should be interpreted, as far as possible, in accordance with these treaties, since the presumption is that, in enacting legislation, parliament could not have wished to violate the international obligations of their state. Moreover, it could have been argued that some of the principles in the 1951 Convention and in the OAU Convention are customary, and could, as such, be enforced by national courts (e.g., Goodwin-Gill 1998a: 232–5). When Kenyan immigration authorities issued refugees with 'Notice of Prohibited Immigrant', this argument could have been tested in courts, the principle of *non-refoulement* being, in fact, part of customary law (Lauterpacht and Bethlehem 2001: 71).

Conclusion

Despite differences in the constitutional and statutory framework, Kenya and Uganda bore remarkable similarity when it came to policy making. In both countries, UNHCR aimed to assume control over refugee policy, and had succeeded in doing so by the time the research started, although in Uganda national and local authorities had not fully accepted this outcome.

The funding crisis hit UNHCR programmes in the two countries at the same time. Two different exit strategies were developed. In Kenya, UNHCR argued that the size of the 'problem' – that is, refugees – had changed and that numbers of refugees had decreased. UNHCR also tried to persuade the government to take over some responsibilities, but encountered some resistance, having contributed in the previous decade to the development of an attitude among government officials and politicians that regarded refugees as 'UNHCR's problem'. In Uganda, on the other hand, the self-sufficiency policy provided the justification for UNHCR's programme cuts: some settlements were abandoned; others, like Ogujebe, were dismantled in an attempt to concentrate the refugee population and to 'rationalise' costs.

Notes

1. The UK had entered reservations to the 1951 Convention in respect of some of its overseas territories, including Kenya. However, since Kenya chose to accede to the Convention independently in 1966 and made no reference to those reservations, it would appear that they no longer stand.
2. Hereinafter referred to as the 1951 Convention and the OAU Convention.
3. These include: the International Covenant on Civil and Political Rights (ICCPR); the International Covenant on Economic, Social and Cultural Rights (ICESCR); the African Charter on Human and Peoples' Rights; the Convention on the Elimination of all Forms of Discrimination against Women (CEDAW); the Convention against Torture and Other Cruel, Inhuman or Degrading Treatment or Punishment; and the Convention on the Rights of the Child.
4. Among others, Uganda is party to: ICCPR; ICESCR; CEDAW; the Convention against Torture and Other Cruel, Inhuman or Degrading Treatment or Punishment; and the African Charter on Human and Peoples' Rights.
5. Reservations attempt to 'exclude or modify the legal effect' of a certain provision (Vienna Convention on the Law of Treaties, art. 2). Some treaties, like the Convention Relating to the Status of Refugees, identify provisions to which states can enter no reservations, or specify other rules on the validity of reservations. When the treaty is silent on reservations – like the OAU Convention, for example – the general rule under the law of treaties is that any reservation that is incompatible with the object and purpose of the treaty is invalid (Vienna Convention on the Law of Treaties, art. 19).
6. The Refugee Bill 2000 recognises the refugees' right to freedom of movement, 'especially for the purpose of study, professional training, gainful employment, voluntary repatriation and resettlement in another country' (art. 30(1)).
7. In many other countries (for example, Egypt) refugees and others who marry women who are citizens cannot be naturalised. The children of these marriages could effectively be stateless. Although in principle they may be entitled to the nationality of the father, this may not be available because he is a refugee. In some countries, these laws have been struck down as unconstitutional for example, Botswana (*Unity Dow*).
8. The Uganda Citizenship and Immigration Control Act 1999 complicated the matter by setting the period of residence in Uganda at twenty years for *anyone* to qualify for naturalisation (sec. 17(5)(a)).
9. A power which is now occasionally used to impede independent research. For a period of several months in 2001 and 2002, the Refugee Law Project (RLP) at the Faculty of Law, Makerere University, was banned from refugee settlements in northern Uganda by the Directorate of Refugees (DoR) after it had written a critical report (RLP 2001), despite having first obtained research clearance from State House via the Uganda National Council of Science and Technology.
10. For example, Eroni Nyakagwa, a Ugandan midwife who escaped Idi Amin's regime, first established a health clinic and later expanded it to offer primary education to refugees and citizens in Kawangware (Reznick 1997).
11. The Windle Trust, an educational NGO, kept photocopies of refugee papers. One of its employees, Gilbert Lukhoba, together with Fr Eugene Birrer, who was working for the Jesuit Refugee Service, were able to rescue many refugees whose papers had been destroyed by the police.

12. Encampment is always UNHCR's preferred modus operandi to assist refugees in the 'developing world'. UNHCR's Comprehensive Policy on Urban Refugees, produced from Geneva, confirms this (UNHCR 1997b). Receiving international aid is often contingent on the host government giving land for refugee camps, as was explicit, for example, in UNHCR's agreement with Zimbabwe (Interview with Claudius J. Kasere, deputy commissioner for refugees, July 1997). The complaint of UNHCR's senior protection officer in Cairo is also revealing: noting that 'The Egyptian government does not want the UNHCR to set up camps for either refugees or rejected persons [and that] UNHCR cannot do anything about this', he suggested that refugees rejected by UNHCR in Egypt should consider 'other options' which 'include going to Kenya or Uganda, where there is material assistance in camps' ('Interview', Cochetel 1999: 29).

13. *See* 'Repatriation III: Is this trip necessary?' (Waldron and Hasci 1995: 68–69).

14. Another illustration of the extent to which UNHCR, rather than the government, controlled access to camps is a note – entitled 'Movement of GK [Government of Kenya] Vehicles in the Refugee Camp' – from UNHCR's main implementing partner in Kakuma, the Lutheran World Service (LWF). It identified three licence plates of vehicles 'which have access to pass freely to and from the compound'; only one vehicle had permission to drive 'in the refugee camps by night' (Field notes: Report by security supervisor, George Otieno, LWF, Kakuma, n.d. but probably 1996).

15. It demanded that refugees hand over these papers to the Immigration Department. Many were charged with unlawful presence in the country. Depending on the magistrate who heard the case, some refugees were given notice to leave within a set period, usually a fortnight, but sometimes forty-eight hours, while others were released and referred back to UNHCR. Although arbitrary arrests of refugees had occurred before, this time refugees also bore the brunt of the frustration and resentment that Kenyan government officials felt towards UNHCR.

16. In Kenya, the 1994 initiative of local NGOs – spearheaded by the Kenya Section of the International Commission of Jurists (ICJ) – to promote refugee rights was also perceived as a threat to UNHCR's control over refugee matters (*see* Chapter 6 *PARinAC: a case-study in cooptation*).

17. The Fourth Convention between the African, Caribbean and Pacific Group of Countries (ACP) and the European Economic Community (EEC) was signed in Lomé on 15 December 1989. It aims to increase trade between the EEC and a large number of developing countries, also by making provision for some aid and development programmes and funds.

18. Information from the Ministry of Foreign Affairs.

19. Again, in Sudan a similar situation occurred (Karadawi 1999: 194–5).

20. This is not to suggest that refugees do not seek to maximise their food supply in every way possible, including fabricating numbers. The point is that not only do the rations represent an inadequate diet, they represent the only access to 'capital' to exchange for other necessities. For example, without matches to light a fire it is impossible to cook and matches must be bought with cash.

21. Interview with Pia Prütz Phiri, senior protection officer, UNHCR, Nairobi, 30 September 1997.

22. Interview with Mr Kyambo, senior immigration officer, Nairobi, 29 October 1997.

23. The Refugee Affected Area (RAA) policy, discussed below in regard to Uganda, was not generally applied in Kenya. In fact, it was only when the use of services provided for refugees by locals could not be controlled in the Dadaab camps that the agencies conceded very reluctantly to a de facto RAA approach. In Kakuma, even during the drought of 1997, food rations were not distributed to the Turkana. Turkana were allowed access to water and, when DanChurchAid, a funder, visited Kakuma in April 1998, they insisted that their future contributions be spent on projects that benefited the locals.

24. The Kampala office, at the time of the research, had a staff of fourteen: the deputy director who was also the chair of the Refugee Eligibility Committee (REC) (see below); three settlement officers, responsible for protection and education, integration, and resettlement; assistant settlement officers responsible for education, social services, accounts, and programmes; and support staff.

25. Email from DoR, 14 July 2000.

26. The complex 'division of labour' in status determination, between the government and UNHCR, is discussed in Chapter 3 **Who is in charge?**

27. Staff working in the disaster section reported having some assistance programmes for destitute *oustees*, persons uprooted by development projects.

28. *See* Chapter 5 *An adequate standard of living.*

29. 'The Local Council (LC) ... system consists of five levels of elected committees. The Local Council I is elected by all members of a single village, LC II by all members of a parish, LC III by all members of a Sub-County, LC IV by all members of a County and the Local Council V is elected at district level' (Kaiser 2000).

30. Brigadier Moses Ali played a key role, convincing the government to declare Adjumani a separate district from Moyo district, and forcing the hand of UNHCR and NGOs, such as LWF that had some of its own money, to invest in this new district.

31. It has also constructed office buildings for local officials in Adjumani town; even a modest football 'stadium' was constructed for the town.

32. In both districts, settlements suffered attacks by rebel movements. Adjumani settlements, located mainly along the border of the Kitgum and Gulu districts, were regularly subject to attacks by the Lord's Resistance Army (LRA), whereas in Moyo district, it was the West Nile Bank Front (WNBF). *See* Chapter 4 *Physical safety in camps and settlements.*

33. Chapter 6 *Image management: reporting the field.*

34. In Arua, before UNHCR built new offices and handed over the old ones it vacated to the DoR, the desk officer, Mr Michael Wafula, worked from the offices of the chief administrative officer (CAO) and, in fact, served as the deputy CAO. In Adjumani, however, the desk officer, Mr Opio, had offices in Pakelle, a village some distance from the Adjumani town headquarters where UNHCR had also built its offices. Two of his junior assistants used the office allocated to him in the district headquarters in Adjumani.

35. InterAid was originally a US NGO that came to work in Kiryandongo. It was transformed into a national NGO and had one other project in Koboko, for reaforestation.

36. An official from the DoR conducted an impromptu evaluation of the infrastructure at Kiryandongo. The stores were locked, but when they were forced open by this official, they contained not much more than a broken motorcycle. He found that insufficient cement had been used in construction everywhere, from latrine slabs that were crumbling before they were installed, to school and medical facilities, some of which were 'abandoned after poor

workmanship and … already collapsing' (Mugumya 1997: 6). He measured the road construction that was to have been 107 km and found that road opened amounted only to 45 km. The report noted that the team from Geneva that had evaluated the project did not 'bother to verify what InterAid was reporting' and that 'UNHCR had simply provided funds without verifying what was happening – but was simply fed on the notion "Kiryandongo is a success story"'. He recommended that in future the MoLG should not sign any tripartite agreement with InterAid, and that special auditors be sent to evaluate the project. InterAid should refund the money for the 'programme it never completed and where it over exaggerated work done', and 'UNHCR should provide MoLG funds to complete work on buildings to save them from collapsing' (ibid.: 9–10).

37. Interview with Carlos Twesigomwe, deputy director for refugees, 3 April 1997.
38. Others were also infuriated by such decisions because they created anti-refugee sentiments: 'Although the refugees are closely related to the locals and some of them live in the community, the attitude of locals towards the refugees would be much better if the water tanks, tents and so on would remain when the agencies leave' (Interview with Mr Tomomimbise, Kisoro camp commandant, 26 April 1997).
39. Interview with Ms Adera Tsegaye, deputy representative, UNHCR, Kampala, April 1997.
40. When Deborah Mulumba was doing her research in Kiryandongo, in March 1999, she found that teachers and medical personnel were not receiving their entire salaries.
41. *See also* Chapter 6 **Donor countries**.
42. We added: 'We fully appreciate the reasons for you and your colleagues' hesitancy, but when one considers the millions that have been wasted on relief and on creating parallel services for refugees, one could only wish that Uganda had had the courage to have said no to camp-based relief programmes long ago. True development of regions like Arua can only be enhanced by adopting a policy that releases the energies of refugees to work as part of a coherent plan into which they have been incorporated and in which they can be part and parcel' (Letter, 26 January 2000).
43. The one notable exception is the investment in roads in Adjumani, prompted, as mentioned, by the need of the army to get access to the areas which rebels were infiltrating.
44. Such ill-conceived approaches to self-sufficiency are not limited to Uganda. Another shocking example in East Africa was the complete destruction of *all* infrastructure in Ngara, Tanzania, where, less than four years after the forced repatriation of Rwandans, the entire area had been bulldozed leaving hardly any sign that this area had been the second largest urban agglomeration in Tanzania, host to several hundreds of thousands of refugees. UNHCR, in that case as in others, did not want to leave anything 'standing' because it feared that this could entice refugees back.
45. Notes of the interview with Mr Tamba Komba, head of sub-office, UNHCR, Arua, by Deborah Mulumba, 28 March 1998.
46. These committees would address such specific aspects of disasters as chemical and industrial accidents, pollution, or the release and dispersion of toxic chemicals. One committee would be a 'Refugee and War Management Committee (RWMC), specifically responsible for disasters involving human

displacement (that include people displaced internally as a result of natural disasters, conflict, and development projects) and refugees'.

47. The Sudanese Commission for Refugees attempted to promote the same approach. Had the Refugee Fund Act 1982 been implemented, 'all funds and property related to refugee services would have been pooled in this fund' (Karadawi 1999: 176). In addition to UNHCR's vigorous opposition, other events interfered. In particular, the government response to the famine of the mid-1980s was to establish a completely separate department for 'Disasters' located in a different ministry, destroying any possibility of an integrated response.

48. No NGOs were included in this meeting, but Nimrod Waweru, head of Kenya's National Refugee Secretariat (NRS), made special efforts to ensure the presence of Professor John Okumu, director of the Centre for Refugee Studies, Moi University, who played an important role in bringing a perspective not centred on security. Dr Bonaventure Rutinwa, Centre for the Study of Forced Migration at the Faculty of Law, Dar es Salaam University, also attended. Although Dr Joseph Oloka-Onyango, Faculty of Law, Makerere University, is an authority on refugee law and human rights, the Ugandans made no similar efforts to include such independent academic input. As Nimrod Waweru put it in a meeting in Nairobi, 'The group is at a loss as to who is acting as the focal point for such matters in Uganda' (Letter to B. Harrell-Bond, 5 October 1997).

49. Unlike Kenya and Uganda, Tanzania adopted a new piece of legislation in the late 1990s: the Tanzania Refugee Act 1998, a particularly restrictive piece of legislation, was hurriedly passed through Parliament around the time when the harmonisation process began.

50. As part of our action approach, in both countries the research team initiated meetings to debate the drafts and make recommendations to government.

51. *See* Jackson 1999.

52. South Africa and Canada are other examples of 'best practice' on the recognition of gender persecution. The South African Refugees Act 1998, specifies that 'social group' in the refugee definition 'includes, among others, a group of persons of particular gender, sexual orientation, disability, class or caste' (art. 1). In Canada, despite the absence of statutory incorporation, the guidelines issued by the chairperson of the Immigration and Refugee Board have recognised gender-related persecution as a valid ground for claiming asylum since 1993 (IRB 1996).

53. It was not clear whether UNHCR considered the withdrawal of these reservations to be important at all, or if, as indicated by one of its reports, it mistakenly maintained that 'the new Refugee Bill 2000 would in fact remove the reservations made by Uganda to the 1951 Refugee Convention and its 1967 Protocol' (UNHCR 2000c).

54. This arrangement for refugee management is at variance with the Disaster Preparedness and Management Bill, 1998.

2

Getting In

Introduction

For asylum-seekers, leaving the place where their lives are threatened is only the first obstacle: getting across a border and into a country of asylum often presents a greater challenge. In Africa, the OAU Convention allows entry into a country of asylum, but the array of policies and practices developed by many potential host countries make reality different (cross-border operations, non-admission policies, preventive protection, safe havens). Furthermore, border police, immigration officials, and police often worsen the plight of refugees. If the rights of asylum-seekers at this stage are to be upheld, it is not only essential that all the actors that play a role in admission have basic knowledge of refugee law; there must also be a proper system in place, rather than ad hoc arrangements, to prevent abuses. One mistake at any point in the process leading to the recognition of refugee status can make a crucial difference to a asylum-seeker's fate.

The influence of donor countries

Over the last two decades, an array of restrictive measures has been developed by many rich countries in an attempt to control migration. The critical notion behind these measures is interception – that is, the idea that it is preferable for the state to 'prevent, interrupt or stop' the movement of people through actions on land or sea before they cross the border (Brouwer and Kumin 2003). Interception practices have included 'carrier liability', 'visa requirements', 'cross-border operations', and 'security zones'. (e.g., Bloch 2000; Crock and Saul 2002; Garry 2002), and state practice in this area is constantly evolving. For example, in the wake of the much-publicised case of refugees rescued from a sinking vessel off the coast of Australia, inter-state cooperation in the South Pacific has resulted in a significant curtailment of the right to seek asylum in Australia and in the 'offshoring' of refugee status determination to poorer countries in the region – the 'Pacific Solution' (Barnes 2004; Goodwin-Gill 2003; Pallis 2002). In the European Union, Britain has sought support for the transfer of refugee status determination to centres 'off-shore', but with little success so far (UK Government 2003). States have also concluded international agreements to crack down on human trafficking – a phenomenon which is to a large extent a consequence of their own restrictionist policies.[1]

Interception practices are part of a shift in refugee policy characterised by 'a preference for containment of refugees in countries of origin over the grant of asylum' (Rutinwa 1999: 8).[2] Restrictionism has not spared those who have succeeded in 'getting in': the asylum-seekers' freedom of movement and their economic and social rights have been severely curtailed, and many of them have been detained in 'reception centres'.[3] Despite the resources that have been poured into efforts to keep refugees out of countries in the 'developed world', many doubt their effectiveness. Interestingly, some state officials in Europe are beginning to realise that the 'closed borders' approach is costly and fails to deliver the expected results.[4]

European countries have often encouraged humanitarian operations – undertaken by NGOs and by the UNHCR or other UN agencies – aimed at providing assistance on site or close to the conflict zone. The benefit for them is that these operations limit the movement of victims of conflicts and persecution, encouraging them to stay in their home countries: if the victims do not leave in the first place, they will never make it into 'Fortress Europe' (Chimni 1994). In East Africa, the cross-border operation at the Kenya/Somalia border in 1992–93 is a case in point.[5] This operation 'aimed at stabilising the Somali communities inside their countries to curtail the refugee influx to Kenya' (Sokoloff 1994; UNHCR 1994b). One of its effects, according to UNHCR, was that it 'spared refugees the debilitating effect of camp life'. At the same time as it was seeking to prevent Somalis from leaving, UNHCR's assessment of the security situation and of the prospects for the work of international organisations in Somalia was bleak. It recognised that the 'prevailing instability will not allow UNHCR to continue fielding quick impact projects in the southern region' and that 'the prospect that conditions would improve to allow international agencies to work effectively in the region is dim' (UNHCR 1994b). UNHCR and the other international and foreign organisations operating in Somalia, unlike ordinary Somali civilians, could rely on armed escorts for their protection.

Donor countries influenced the admission practices in Africa also by choosing which training activities to fund. For example, donors funded human rights training courses for the police and prison wardens, but, for whatever reason, did not include either immigration or border police officials. Canadian and British officials did train their Ugandan counterparts in how to recognise forged passports.[6] It is becoming common practice in international airports throughout countries in the 'developing world' to have foreign officials checking passports of passengers just before they board planes for Europe and North America.[7]

The OAU Convention and group recognition

In Africa, 'closed borders' and 'fortresses' would not only be unfeasible and impractical, but would also be largely illegal, in that the OAU Convention widens the scope of the principle of *non-refoulement* by spelling out that rejection at the frontier is tantamount to *refoulement* (art. 2(3)) (e.g., Marx 1995; Goodwin-Gill 1998a: 121ff).[8] Under the OAU Convention, the grounds for claiming refugee status are the objective situation in the country of origin (art. 1(2)) and individual persecution (art. 1(1)), the latter defined in an identical manner to the 1951 Convention. The OAU Convention is meant to encourage the prima facie recognition of groups of refugees, especially since it is far more economical than an individualised status-determination procedure, not a negligible advantage for poor countries in the 'developing world'.[9] Whether a person's status has been determined individually or under group determination on prima facie grounds, it should not affect the rights that accrue to refugee status.

In some countries, prima facie recognition has been done through official government statements declaring that all persons of a particular nationality are to be automatically granted refugee status by virtue of the conditions in their country of origin.[10] But, in most situations, prima facie recognition of refugees usually amounts to little more than registration upon arrival.[11] This may be carried out by border police or immigration officials, although NGOs are often delegated this task. The involvement of humanitarian organisations in the registration of refugees is related more to the provision of humanitarian assistance than to the proper recognition of their refugee status with their attendant rights. It is rare that such refugees receive any document indicating their status. The only means of identification for the vast majority of refugees in Africa is a ration card that merely indicates the quantity of 'food and non-food items' that the 'international community' provides, commonly viewed as an act of charity rather than as a means of upholding their rights (Harrell-Bond 1999a; Miller and Simmons 1999; Miller 1999: 14).

Admission: standards and procedures

Asylum-seekers are most vulnerable upon arrival in a country of asylum because of their yet undetermined legal status and because of the lack of support networks. The process of admitting them involves numerous actors, ranging from border police, local officials, and the nationals first encountered upon arrival, to an array of UNHCR officials and NGO workers.[12] At this critical stage, those seeking asylum need to be distinguished from other immigrants in order to ensure that they are protected from the risk of *refoulment*. They also need to be given guidance on how to apply for asylum.

It is not known how many asylum-seekers are denied entry to Kenya and Uganda. In Uganda we found more than one case where immigration officials *refouled* asylum-seekers by rejecting them at the frontier (Lomo 1999c; *see also*: UNHCR 1999a; Lomo 1999d). One Ethiopian asylum-seeker had been denied entrance at both Busia and Malaba at the Kenya/Uganda border (case no. 182/ETH/U/1998). He had to leave his luggage with other Ethiopians on the Kenyan side of the border and make his way through the bush into Uganda, where he then reported to UNHCR.[13]

In Kenya, statutory provisions could be relied upon to reject refugees at the frontier. In fact, under the Aliens Registration Act 1973, the minister responsible for matters relating to internal security can prohibit aliens 'from landing in or otherwise entering Kenya either generally or at certain places' (sec. 3(a)). This provision does not make an exception for persons seeking asylum, although, as mentioned, under the OAU Convention Kenya cannot deny them entry. It is a clear example of a provision that needs to be repealed or at least interpreted consistently with the OAU Convention. For the most part the problem with the legislation in force was precisely that it failed to take full cognisance of the 'refugee exception' in all immigration matters.

While the decision to admit refugees is taken by states, UNHCR should play an important role in monitoring their conduct and formulating guidelines. Indeed, UNHCR's statute includes the duty to promote 'the admission of refugees, not excluding those in the most destitute categories' (art. 8(d)). Given the lacunae in the law, training border officials and other relevant actors in international refugee law could be particularly beneficial.[14] In one of its earlier conclusions, the Executive Committee of UNCHR (EXCOM) emphasised:

> The competent official (e.g. immigration officer or border police officer) to whom the applicant addresses himself at the border in the territory of a Contracting State, should have clear instructions for dealing with cases which might come within the purview of the relevant international instruments. He should be required to act in accordance with the principle of *non-refoulement* and to refer such cases to a higher authority (EXCOM conclusion 8(e)(i)(ii)).

The same conclusion also stipulates that at the point of entry 'The applicant should receive the necessary guidance as to the procedure to be followed.'

Regrettably, UNHCR did not offer training for immigration and border police personnel in Kenya or Uganda – unlike South Africa, where the senior protection officer personally visited all entry points to ascertain the situation in the mid-1990s, and arranged courses in refugee and human rights law for immigration officials.[15] However, sometimes UNHCR intervened on behalf of individuals to facilitate their admission to Kenya and Uganda, for example in the case of a group of Ugandans who fled to Kenya claiming persecution at the hands of Museveni's army. Upon arrival the group was detained and sentenced to a year's imprisonment without their asylum claims being considered. UNHCR managed to secure their release and transfer to camps after eight months of detention (case no. 001/UGA/K/1997).

Legal hurdles to admission

Only a small minority of people in Africa possess passports. For individuals who have fallen out with their governments, it is generally more difficult to obtain them than for others. When the Rwandan government introduced new passports in 1995–96, for example, Rwandans seeking asylum suffered serious consequences. Only a few countries were prepared to admit those travelling with the old passports. Kenya stopped recognising them in July 1997 in the wake of a political rapprochement between the two countries. By 1998, with the exception of a few West African countries (for example Togo), all other countries in Africa had ceased to recognise the old Rwandan passport. This situation fuelled the market for forged passports, which the unavailability of Convention Travel Documents (CTDs) only contributed to strengthen.

Some refugees were able to obtain forged immigration documents, including passports (case no. 154/DRC/U/1999). In one case, a Congolese woman who had asylum in Belgium 'borrowed' passports to rescue her children from Uganda (case no. 092/DRC/U/2000). One Burundian, who had been a refugee in Zaire since childhood, managed to escape to Kenya using a passport obtained under false pretences. He had returned to Burundi in 1993, but then had to flee again in 1995. He went back to Bukavu, Zaire. When the war broke out there in 1996, he fled to Uganda. He described what happened next:

> I decided that I could not stay in Uganda mainly because I am Burundian and apparently the Ugandans are not good to people of our ethnie [*sic*], so I did not want to risk [staying]. I presented myself as a Zairean because I

knew the language a bit, and I even arrived here with a Zairean passport. But I had to change the name. The name on the passport is not my real name.

Q: *How did you obtain this passport?*

I went to the Zairean immigration [the embassy in Uganda]. I convinced them that I was Zairean and they eventually gave me the passport. This was during the war and it was very easy to find a passport anywhere in Zaire (case no. 049/BUR/K/1997).

Recognising the difficulties and dangers associated with escaping from a country where one is persecuted and one's life is at risk, the 1951 Convention prohibits states from applying sanctions against refugees 'on account of their illegal entry or presence' (art. 31(1)). Prospective refugees are under an obligation, however, to present themselves to authorities and 'show good cause for their illegal entry or presence' (ibid.). Thus no refugee who has a reason for using forged documents, or has gained entry into a country avoiding border controls, should be punished.

In practice, however, we found cases in Uganda and Kenya where refugees who had used forged documents were prosecuted and even deported. For instance, five Iraqis, including a woman and a small child, were held in Entebbe because they had used forged documents to flee Iraq. They had travelled from Iraq to Jordan, then from Jordan to Yemen, from where they had flown to Nairobi and from there to Entebbe. At Entebbe, they presented their documents to immigration officials and declared that they were seeking asylum, but this did not prevent their arrest and eventual deportation to Kenya.[16] In the aftermath of this case, which had been brought to our attention when it was too late, we interviewed the principal immigration officer in Uganda. When we asked her what instructions were given to immigration officials in the case of a refugee with forged documents, she replied, 'A forged document is a forged document. There is no bargaining with the law.' She added that in her view most of the cases that her department handled were 'crooks rather than refugees'.[17]

Police stationed at entry points like Entebbe airport and Busia[18] were generally ignorant of refugee law, maintaining that asylum-seekers using false documents, or no documents at all, would face prosecution and even deportation. One police officer stated that he would charge an asylum-seeker caught with false documents with 'uttering false documents' [*sic*] even if he knew that the asylum-seeker was using the documents as a means of escaping persecution. He explained: 'The law is for everybody. It does not favour anybody. Forgery is an offence and if the asylum-seeker uses forged travel documents, then he is a criminal and he will be charged and prosecuted just like any other person.'[19]

A member of the special branch at Busia told us that immigration officers 'would know' which people asking for asylum they should or should not allow in. Those whom they should not admit, according to this officer, *'are persons they know are not refugees and will be a burden to the taxpayer'* [emphasis added]. [Anyway] 'we do not have troubles with Kenya, so any Kenyan could not be a refugee.'[20]

The cases that ended up in court included that of a 16-year-old Congolese, who was charged with unlawful presence in the country (*Uganda v. Muhamed Abdul*). In another case, two Congolese students, aged 15 and 27, were accused of illegal entry since they did not possess a valid passport (*Uganda v. Katanga and Kasaleka*). The argument submitted by one of the accused that, despite several attempts, he had failed to meet anyone from UNHCR, was dismissed:

> *Prosecutor*: [One of the men] came to Uganda on 9.10.96 through Ishasha border post. When he came to Kampala, he first stayed with a trailer driver in Nakawa. He moved to stay with a friend on Dewinton road. The time between when the accused entered the country and the time of his arrest in January 1996 [*sic*, = 1997] was enough time to have gone to UN agency for refugees. The fact that he never went to the UN agency for refugees means that his allegation that his passport was taken at the border and [that he is] therefore a refugee cannot hold in this incidence [*sic*, = instance].
>
> In the criminal cases, the accused should face the law for having stayed in Uganda without a passport contrary to the Immigration Act.
>
> *Accused*: It is not true. It is only one thing which is not true. I came on 9 of October 1996. After two days I went to UN office. I was given four days then I go back to UN office. I found very many people in the office. I was to go back again. In that process, 1996 ended. The secretary for UN told me that if I am arrested, they would inform UN who would help me. That is the only part I wanted to put right.
>
> *Court*: Accused 1 is convicted on your own plea of guilt.
>
> *Prosecutor*: No record.
>
> *Accused*: I pray that court finds out from UN office whether I've not been going there for assistance. It is UN office that delayed me.
>
> *Court*: Adjourned to 28.1.97 for sentence.

From the court record it is not clear what happened afterwards. After several adjournments, the magistrate appears to have decided that 'Basing on the accused's prayer, Court will be lenient [*sic*] since there is war in the accused's country, they are to be handed over the UNHCR'. Later, however, the court order of 14 February 1997 reads 'Immigration department to deport the accused' after one week.

In the other recorded cases that we reviewed, the Ugandan Immigration Department was successful in its prosecution, although the accused persons were clearly asylum-seekers. For example, one case (*Uganda v. Katanga Mwendeluwa and four others*) heard in the Nakawa Magistrates' Court, involved five Zaireans who were charged with 'unlawful presence' in the country. They had arrived in Uganda around October 1996. Some came with 'visitor permits', others with proper visas on their travel documents. As the war in the then Zaire intensified, they were unable to go back and were arrested when their visas expired. Although they did not couch them in the appropriate legal terminology, the reasons they gave for having overstayed the permitted time made it clear that they were *sur place* refugees:[21] 'I had no idea of going back because of the war'; 'I left my country because they were looking for me to be killed'; 'I was also a visitor and I had run because of the war'; 'I had intenty [*sic* = intended] of going back to my country but there was no way through to go back to Zaire.' The five were convicted on their guilty plea and deportation orders were issued by the court as requested by the prosecution on behalf of the Immigration Department.

In Kenya it was not at first easy to obtain information on the prosecutions brought by the Department of Immigration against refugees for 'unlawful presence in the country'. In addition to displaying an authoritarian attitude, some officials in the department, including senior ones, appeared to ignore basic facts about refugee and immigration law, and about the Kenyan legal system. A senior official told us that there was a refugee act in force in Kenya, and, when asked for a copy, he declared it was confidential.[22] He informed a member of our team that the prosecutions and court decisions on refugee cases could not be shared with researchers – they were 'secret'. Although it was immediately pointed out to him that there was no law in Kenya making court records secret, it took several attempts before a still more senior official summoned the person who was conducting these prosecutions and told him that there was nothing secret or confidential about these cases, and that he and others working for the department should cooperate with our research. Despite his intervention, we still managed to gain only limited access to files and only succeeded in viewing the files that concerned certain prosecutions in 1997. The Department of Immigration maintained that they never charged 'protected persons' but only asylum-seekers who broke the law, and that they notified UNHCR whenever an asylum-seeker was arrested. However, we found cases that contradicted these statements.

In *Republic v. Christine Niyitegeka*, a 16-year-old Burundian refugee travelling via Kenya to reach her sister in Belgium was arrested and charged with unlawful presence in the country because her Kenyan visa was forged. The court ordered her to pay a fine of KSh 10,000 or spend three months in prison – after which she should be taken to Belgium.

In another case, *Republic v. Maurice Nsabimana*, a Rwandan refugee was arrested at Jomo Kenyatta airport and accused of forging a Belgian passport, of unlawful presence in Kenya and of failure to register as an alien. The accused pleaded guilty. His lawyer, himself displaying little knowledge about the law, said that his client was remorseful, that she was an orphan who had lost both parents in 1994 and was trying to reach Brussels to see a relative (he did not mention, however, as he should have, that his client was a refugee). A sentence of KSh 20,000 was imposed.

In *Republic v. Bonaventure Ntamakemana*, the court was even less lenient. A Rwandan national who lived in Kenya was found to have used a stolen Zimbabwean passport to travel to Europe. He was given a KSh 15,000 fine and served with an order of repatriation to Rwanda, which he was granted leave to appeal within fourteen days. He said in court that he had sent the passport back by DHL to the owner who worked for the UN and who had helped him on humanitarian grounds. An order of repatriation was also served to a Somali refugee accused of having a false UK certificate of identification (*Republic v. Abdi Musa Said*). These cases violated the principle of *non-refoulement*, which, as mentioned, under the OAU Convention allows for no exceptions – prohibiting not only rejection at the frontier but also expulsions for serious crimes or reasons of national security.[23]

Judicial attitudes were not uniform. For example, in Makadera court in Nairobi the foreigners who were arrested and prosecuted in 1997–99 were normally served with repatriation orders only if the magistrate found no evidence of refugee status. It was not only those with UNHCR protection letters who were acquitted and released, but also those who did not have such letters and who claimed to be refugees.[24]

Ordeals of arrival

Whether they arrived by air, land, or sea, asylum-seekers faced uncertainty and perils. In some cases, they were denied entry, contrary to the provisions of the OAU Convention. In others, they were kept in limbo, incarcerated at airports and other entry posts. Some managed to gain entry into the country and to remain inconspicuous finding sanctuary amongst the local population in border villages and towns.

Airports as dumping grounds

It was not possible to get reliable data on the number of asylum-seekers who were either admitted or *refouled* each year at the international airports in Kenya and Uganda (Jomo Kenyatta and Entebbe).[25] It would probably be at least as difficult to get such sensitive information in any other country: immigration controls normally take place in limited-access areas within airports. However, we managed to collect evidence on the practice of rejecting asylum-seekers on arrival at Kenyatta and Entebbe airports by interviewing them and, occasionally, by direct observations during our own travelling. For example, on one occasion in 1996, on arrival at Kenyatta airport and before reaching the immigration desk, we discussed some of these practices with a security officer, a relative of the Kenyan academic with whom we were travelling.[26] The officer said, among other things, that he had been ordered to apprehend Sri Lankans or Pakistanis *before* they reached the immigration desk so that they could be put on the next plane back without applying for asylum.

African airports are routinely used as convenient dumping grounds by countries in the 'developed world'. A Kurdish family from Iraq with two children, aged 4 and 1, spent five months in Entebbe airport (case no. 231/IRAQ/U/1999). They had spent approximately six weeks in Sweden before being separately deported to Entebbe via Brussels. Their treatment by the Swedish authorities and the immigration police at Brussels airport was brutal. Although declared medically unfit to travel by both a Swedish doctor and a doctor at the airport hospital in Brussels, the woman, whose youngest baby was still breastfeeding, was manacled throughout the flights. Their case received extensive press coverage (Mwesige 1995; Nabeta 1995), but, when we met them, they said they had never been visited at the airport by anyone from UNHCR. The family was finally rescued from the airport by the intervention of President Museveni himself. Knowing the president was visiting the airport, an immigration officer advised the Iraqi woman to 'fall at the president's feet'. The president demanded to know why this family was being held and ordered that they be housed at government expense. Their ordeal was not yet over, however: when the case finally reached the Refugee Eligibility Committee (REC), it stated that 'Swedish police observed G.'s movement for a period of one month before being deported. This is a sign that he is not a good man' (GoU-REC 1996). They were eventually given 'mandate' status by UNHCR, and in 2000 the family was resettled in Canada.[27]

Another case in which refugees were dumped at the airport in Entebbe was that of two Burundian women, both of 'mixed Hutu/Tutsi parentage', who in May and June 1999 were forcibly deported from Brussels to Uganda on Sabena Airways – sometimes referred to as 'Air *Refoulement*' by refugees (case 224/BUR/U/1999; 237/BUR/U/1999). One had both her hands and feet tied during the flight and was sedated. She was unconscious on arrival and taken to the nearby Entebbe hospital, where she remained for three days. The second, a 19-year-old woman, was also given injections presumably of sedatives meant to prevent her from screaming at the airport in Brussels. Both women were detained for a number of days at the airport where they were not visited by UNHCR staff (Mugagga 1999). An immigration official explained that the reason they were admitted to Uganda was that Sabena officials had contended they were obliged under the 'first country' rule, which is not part of general international law.[28]

These deportations from Belgium generated an interesting initiative of transnational advocacy. The first woman was in contact with the *Collectif contre les expulsions*, an NGO in Brussels. We established contact with them and were warned in advance of the imminent deportation of the second woman. We could then pass the information on to the Immigration Department, the DoR, and the press, advising them that Uganda had no responsibility to admit her. Nevertheless, she was admitted and detained at Entebbe for several days. However, the story was carried in the national press (Mugagga 1999) and picked up by the press in Belgium, where the *Collectif contre les expulsions* had been gathering support against expulsions. The actions it took included getting passengers from flights on which expelled refugees were expected to travel, to demonstrate against the airlines and even to refuse to board the plane. The professional association of pilots in Belgium declared that they would henceforth refuse to fly planes carrying persons being forcibly deported. A member of the cabin crew, who was dismissed because she had objected to the practice, regained her position. Vincent Decroly, a Belgian MP, offered to travel to Uganda to collect first-hand evidence if such an incident occurred again.[29] All this created enough pressure in Belgium to halt the planned deportation of a third Burundian woman.[30]

Demonstrating just how essential it is to maintain constant pressure on recalcitrant states, another instance of deportation to Entebbe on a Sabena flight occurred on 26 November 1999. After five unsuccessful attempts, a Congolese man was finally forced to board a plane. He had a valid passport and a visa to enter Germany, but in August 1999 he had been stopped in transit in Brussels, where, when detained and prevented from proceeding to Germany, he had applied for asylum (case no. 155/DRC/U/1999).[31]

Although in Kenya we did not come across cases of deportation from countries in the 'developed world', as reported by UNHCR itself, they did happen (UNHCR 1997a). UNHCR also complained that 'The government has also tightened its policy on allowing asylum-seekers and refugees to return to Kenya as their first country of asylum. On several occasions UNHCR has been involved in negotiations to allow asylum-seekers entry at Jomo Kenyatta International Airport after having been returned from countries in Western Europe' (UNHCR 1997a: 2). Did UNHCR exercise a similar measure of pressure on those 'countries in Western Europe' from which the refugees had been expelled?

The Tingi Tingi refugees

A striking example of the hostility often faced by new arrivals is the case of the Tingi Tingi refugees who were stranded at Wilson airport in Nairobi at the end of February 1997. At the time, as war flared up in the then Zaire, many Rwandans, who had sought refuge in the eastern part of that country, found themselves trapped in a war in which one of the sides, Laurent

Kabila's forces, were at that time supported by the Rwandan Patriotic Front (RPF) government, and strongly anti-Hutu. The invidious choice that hundreds of thousands of Rwandans had to make was between going back to Rwanda and staying in eastern Zaire where the pogroms against Rwandan refugees were making many victims – some estimate that as many as 200,000 Rwandan refugees were killed in Zaire in 1996–97 (UN 1997). Those who fled before the onslaught and those who survived it by hiding in the forests ahead of the attackers tried to reach the part of Zaire that had not yet fallen to Kabila (Umutesi 2000). Others managed to leave Zaire, but they too faced gloomy prospects, since neighbouring Tanzania, having *refouled* Rwandan refugees en masse with the support of UNHCR in December 1996, was an improbable safe haven. The same applied to Burundi and Uganda, at the time close allies of Rwanda and entangled in the conflict in eastern Zaire, in which they openly supported Kabila.

Unlike other East African countries, Kenya was viewed by many Rwandan refugees as safe for 'Hutus', because President Moi had been lukewarm towards the RPF. Most of those who reached Kenya during and in the aftermath of the conflict in eastern Zaire did so by travelling through Tanzania or Uganda, but smaller groups of refugees flew directly to Nairobi. The most conspicuous of the groups that arrived at Wilson airport in Nairobi from eastern Zaire came from Tingi Tingi camp.[32] It comprised some 105 Rwandans, including 60 children.[33] For nearly four weeks this group was denied entry into Kenya and repeatedly threatened with *refoulement*,[34] even though the gravity of the situation in Zaire was widely reported.[35] Owing to their direct experiences of the failures of the 'international community' in eastern Zaire, and in Tingi Tingi in particular, the refugees themselves were determined to come under the direct protection of the Kenyan government rather than UNHCR.[36]

The reception of this group of Rwandans at Wilson airport reveals the extent to which the relationship between refugees – Rwandans in particular – and their international 'protector' had deteriorated. The refugees' insistence on dealing with the Kenyan government did not endear them to UNHCR, which early on declared that there were 'no persons of concern to UNHCR' in the group. The group was first accused of refusing to cooperate, but eventually UNHCR interviewed the adults in the group, reportedly for less than one hour each.

One refugee described the situation at the airport where, as she put it, on arrival they were 'sort of jailed':

> Immigration officials asked the pilot to take us all back to Zaire. He refused. We remained in Wilson airport for two days and then were transferred to the international airport where they tried to force us to go back to Rwanda. I remember there were only ten men and the rest of us were women and children. We refused to be taken back to Rwanda. After that we were once again transferred back to Wilson airport, escorted by armed

policeman. No shower for all these days. We spent the first three days without food.

When we were back in Wilson airport, some UNHCR workers came. Among them was a tall lady, a white lady, the senior protection officer, and a Belgian, 'Thomas'. At that very moment, they brought a very bad interpreter and he told them that we refused to talk with UNHCR. When UNHCR first came, I was so sick that I was not there. I was lying on the cement [in another part of the airport]. The second time they came, they brought this interpreter, a Rwandese, who still works at JRS [Jesuit Refugee Service].

Q: Who is he?

I could not tell because I was so sick. When I woke up, people told me that they did not want to see UNHCR because of that bad interpreter. Because I know a bit of English, when Thomas came back, I was asked to go translate for the group. I told UNHCR that the group *wanted* interviews with UNHCR. In all, we spent three weeks there. We stayed from the 28th of February and reached Kakuma camp on 24th March.[37]

The refugees feared that UNHCR's interpreter was associated with the RPF government. The forced intimacy, especially in camps, with persons who had been strangers to each other before often aroused such fears. In fact, one of the interpreters used by UNHCR at Wood Avenue, the office where UNHCR asylum-determination interviews were conducted, was a former captain in the RPF. Before it was acknowledged that he was likely to have been misinterpreting refugee accounts, many refugees had been found 'not to be of concern to UNHCR' (e.g., case no. 020/RWA/K/1998).[38]

UNHCR's unwelcoming attitude towards this group of refugees in Nairobi was not a peculiarity of the Nairobi office; on the contrary, the hostility appeared to emanate from the top of the organisation. For example, as detailed by Amnesty International, UNHCR issued a statement expressing its concern about reports that Tingi Tingi camp was under the control of Hutu extremists and about 'the prospect that refugees will not be allowed to freely decide if they wish to return to Rwanda' (Amnesty International 1997c). UNHCR had not addressed the presence of *genocidaires* in the camps in eastern Zaire for nearly three years and its belated recognition of the problem appears to have been prompted by the need to present the mass return of Rwandans as voluntary and to attribute the behaviour of those who resisted return to the pressure of extremists.

It was only after considerable dithering and after Amnesty International had issued an urgent action on their situation (Amnesty International 1997), that the Rwandan refugees at Wilson were eventually admitted to Kenya and transferred to Kakuma at the request of the Kenyan government. More than a year later, they were given access to asylum 'screening', a controversial procedure organised specifically for Rwandans with a view to identifying and excluding *génocidaires*.

Arriving en masse

Kenya's recent experience with refugees arriving en masse began in 1991 with the 'walking boys', the Sudanese children for whom Kakuma camp was created (UNICEF 1994). Shortly thereafter, the arrival of hundreds of thousands of Somalis in the early 1990s was dramatised by the fact that many fled on overloaded fragile boats to Mombasa (Farah 2000), with unknown numbers perishing when their boats sank in the shark-infested waters off the coast of Somalia. The first refugees who were allowed to disembark in Mombasa were housed in the fenced agricultural trade fair premises. Some were able to find shelter in stands but most slept outside, on the bare ground. The World Food Programme (WFP) provided the rations, while Kenyan police and civilians took responsibility for its distribution and for guarding the enclosure.

In April 1991, during a visit by one of us before the time of our research, a ship full of these Somali refugees was anchored in Mombasa harbour (Harrell-Bond 1991). Stranded on the decks in the scorching sun, the refugees were decimated by sickness. The only water or food available to them was provided by Mombasa residents who were paddling out to the ships in dugout canoes. One desperate Somali, standing on the embankment, was threatening to throw himself into the sea in an attempt to reach his family so that 'they would die together'. We found a member of the UNHCR staff in his flat and asked whether he had been negotiating with the Kenyan authorities for the Somalis to be admitted. He shouted, 'I am not a protection officer!' When reminded of Mr Hocké's – the then high commissioner's – admonition that *all UNHCR staff persons are responsible for protection*, and asked if he had alerted the UNHCR branch office in Nairobi of the seriousness of the situation, he shrugged his shoulders and waved his hand towards the beach, reminding us that this was Easter holiday and 'all of them were sunning themselves down there (ibid.).'[39]

The 'right' place to arrive

The point at which asylum-seekers entered the host country had a bearing on what happened to them. For example, by 1996, UNHCR had determined that Sudanese entering Kenya would only be 'processed' at Lokichokio, a town on the Kenyan side of the border with Sudan where it had established a reception centre. Sudanese arriving in Nairobi were not to be 'received' unless, as noted in the protection report for that year, 'they are able to present a ticket and/or passport with an entry visa showing that Nairobi was their port of entry' (UNHCR 1996a: 9). This restriction helped UNHCR achieve its objective of controlling and concentrating a group of asylum-seekers in a defined area, and – owing to the proximity of Lokichokio to Kakuma – it made it easier to 'catch recyclers' (the term applied to those who attempt to register in more than one place, or more than one time in the same place, in order to maximise their access to food). The protection report went on to explain:

> The purpose of the interview is mainly to try to establish whether the asylum-seeker is a recycler. At present, the Somalis normally come through Harehare and walk to the refugee camps in Dadaab where the same type of screening takes place. Exceptions are the Burundians who are also interviewed in Nairobi as there is no camp at their point of entry (ibid.).

Such practice breached the OAU Convention and the 1951 Convention in at least two respects. Firstly, it made the recognition of refugee status for certain nationalities contingent on their point of arrival in the country. Secondly, contrary to article 2(6) of the OAU Convention, it supported the practice of settling refugees near the border with their country of origin. Those Sudanese who happen to present themselves at the UNHCR offices in Nairobi would be asked to undertake a long (and perilous) journey to Lokichokio.[40] There, according to one UNHCR staff member, '... our response is immediate, well-co-ordinated and humane. The sick and injured are normally hospitalised at ICRC [International Committee of the Red Cross] Lopiding and others at the camp hospital after being screened at the reception centre/police station near the camp awaiting further screening and procedural registration.' However he insisted that, as far as UNHCR was concerned, all of this 'is for the purposes of determining the genuine asylum-seekers as opposed to Recyclers [*sic*] posing as new arrivals' (Masumbuko 1997: 1).

To have designated Lokichokio, where personnel from the Sudan People's Liberation Army (SPLA) were visibly present, and to have given the South Sudan Relief Agency (SSRA) responsibility for managing the reception centre, was tantamount to giving the SPLA power to determine who 'gets out and who gets in'.[41] When we visited this reception centre in April 1998 with the Kakuma UNHCR protection officer, the policy was that food rations were not to be distributed to new arrivals. We found people who were kept waiting inordinate amounts of time for transport to Kakuma – another means of deterring recyclers. The people we saw were from Torit. They had been ordered by the SPLA to evacuate because of a planned attack on the Sudanese army. With the exception of a Dinka woman who, with her children, was well stocked with food, and was assumed by the UNHCR protection officer to be the wife of an SPLA officer, the others were in dreadful physical condition.

In Uganda, convoluted procedures were in place to identify 'recyclers'. For example, the settlement commandant in Adjumani explained to us that all asylum applicants arriving in Adjumani and Moyo districts had to go through his office.[42] 'We are the people who receive and give asylum and not UNHCR.' However, asylum-seekers who came to his office could not claim asylum without any documents. There are places at the border posts, he said, 'where refugees must collect letters. We do not allow people who have no documents to claim that they are refugees.' The 'document' required was a letter from the Local Council (LC) chairman at the point of entry. Since there were no signs on the border giving such instructions to people entering Uganda, asylum-seekers were apparently expected to walk all the way back to the border to obtain such a letter. Perhaps it is not surprising that the settlement commandant in Adjumani asserted, 'We know genuine refugees because they look tired and sick.'[43]

New arrivals and local people

Refugees who settle amongst their hosts without receiving official assistance or formal recognition are variously described by humanitarian organisations as 'self-settled', 'spontaneously settled', and 'free livers'.[44] No one knows how many there were but they have been estimated to be the vast majority (Clark and Stein 1984; Kibreab 1987a). They settle in local villages, towns, and cities. Such an unorganised response to human suffering occurs long before the central authorities and/or UNHCR arrive to intervene, providing relief and opening up camps. This pattern, which finds the majority of refugees in most African countries (if not throughout the world) living amongst their hosts and outside the umbrella of aid (Chambers 1979; Hansen 1982; Harrell-Bond 1986; Kibreab 1983, 1989), also characterised Kenya and Uganda.

The laissez faire policy towards refugees in Kenya before 1991 allowed them to live throughout the country. In Uganda, as early as 1986, Sudanese were seeking refuge, most of them settling among the Ugandan returnees.[45] But when another group of southern Sudanese arrived with cattle, they were advised to settle across the Nile in Moyo district since cattle could not be kept in Ogujebe. The only assistance this group ever received came from International Aid Sweden, an NGO that concentrated mainly on expanding existing national services so that they could accommodate the self-settled refugees.

Uganda's border with Sudan was porous. An immigration officer was stationed only at the border post in Oraba, but there were immigration officers in towns close to the border like Koboko and Arua. Most refugees entering from Sudan simply walked across the border. There were more posts on the border with Congo, but it was still easy for people to cross the border unchecked. Reasons for the generally positive reception of refugees include the fact that familial relationships extend across borders and – as is so frequently the case – people on both sides of a border have alternated the role of refugees with that of hosts (Shack et al. 1979). In fact, there are places in Uganda and Kenya where kinship ties between refugees and hosts are so strong that no one would dream of identifying a new arrival from across the border as 'a refugee' (Munson and Obomba 1999).[46] In northern Kenya, ties between the Oromo from Ethiopia and the Borana have facilitated refugee self-settlement. The existence of cross-border kinship ties has also facilitated the reception and settlement of Rwandans in southern Uganda. However, the role played by kinship ties has been transformed and self-settlement in rural areas is perhaps tolerated more for the commercial value of an expanding population. In Uganda, for example, self-settled refugees pay local taxes and, if they are in business, market taxes. In fact, a tax receipt has been found to provide more protection than a ration card.

There were refugees who had local connections – for example, businessmen – who settled in towns and cities throughout Kenya and Uganda. In both capital cities there were districts where particular nationalities concentrated and where they had, in many cases, been resident for many years. It was in such places that new refugees were also absorbed. For example, in Nairobi, many refugees, especially from Burundi, Rwanda, and the DRC, settled in poor areas like Kawangware and Kangemi among Kenyans and some of their fellow nationals who had been long-term residents. These refugees included those waiting for their asylum-determination interview, and those recognised as refugees who had been 'instructed' to go to camps and had refused to do so, as well as those whose application for asylum had been rejected.

In Kenya, a sizable population of Somalis was historically settled predominantly in Eastleigh.[47] The vast majority of these Somalis never approached UNHCR. Others had escaped from camps. Some of those interviewed 'asked why they would not return to camps ... agreed that they loathe life in refugee camps because it gives them a sense of imprisonment and confinement' (Shiekh 1997). One of our assistants, who did a study in Eastleigh, describes what he found:

> Eastleigh in general has undergone a tremendous transformation since the influx of the refugees. New buildings have come up while old ones have been razed and in their place new ones established. Residential houses have been turned into lodges, business premises have been opened, new opportunities have emerged and the whole area is different from what it was in 1990 ...

> The host community have contrasting views on the refugees' presence ... Many are of the opinion that the refugees have brought a lot of suffering and destruction to Kenya, hence cursing them. However, there are those who hold milder views: that the refugees are in fact a source of blessing to Kenyans. While the former advance increasing cost of living, high inflation, exorbitant prices of goods, high house rents, prostitution, increased crime rates, forgery and competitive business as their woes, the latter argue that the refugees have brought employment, cheap materials and

goods, new business opportunities and have developed Eastleigh struc-
turally and economically (Shiekh 1997).

Conclusion

In their attempts to gain admission, asylum-seekers were faced with the
failures and inadequacies of virtually all actors involved in the process –
from the border police to the immigration department, from the local
authorities to the police, from UNHCR to NGOs. For those who managed
to get in and were not rejected at the frontier or deported shortly after
their arrival, the next challenge was to have their refugee status recognised and to survive while awaiting the outcome of that legal process.

Asylum-seekers, while not automatically entitled to the standard of
protection that under refugee law accrues to the conferral of refugee status, are entitled to protection as potential refugees; for example, they cannot be *refouled*. Furthermore, asylum-seekers, like all other human beings,
are entitled to protection under human rights law. The need for the protection of the rights of asylum-seekers becomes acute in situations of mass
influx, when, mainly because of unwillingness to grant group recognition,
their status can remain undetermined for a long period of time. EXCOM
conclusion 22 identifies, in addition to other fundamental human rights,
respect for family unity, assistance with tracing relatives, and the provision of material assistance covering basic necessities as important minimum standards in the treatment of asylum-seekers in situations of mass
influx.[48] State practice has occasionally granted a more generous treatment than that recommended in the EXCOM conclusion. For example,
asylum-seekers have at times been allowed to seek employment, which
can transform them into net contributors to the hosts' economy and min-
imize their dependence on material assistance.[49]

In both Kenya and Uganda, asylum-seekers were often denied their
basic human rights, and were not given favourable treatment, relative to
other aliens, in view of their potential refugee status. Most of them were
not assisted by either UNHCR or the government. The JRS dispensed
some assistance in both Uganda and Kenya. In Uganda, the small programme for asylum-seekers came under intense pressure from both
UNHCR and from JRS's own country director, who believed that it was at
odds with JRS's much larger programme in countries in the 'developed
world', where, as a UNHCR 'implementing partner', JRS was responsible
for refugee education. With very limited resources, the process of deciding who would receive assistance was erratic. In Nairobi, at Wood
Avenue, Fr Birrer inspected the asylum-seekers who were waiting to be
interviewed and in a fraction of a second decided whether he would give
individuals some pocket money or some used clothes. Amongst the

asylum-seekers, rumours quickly spread about what triggered Fr Birrer's 'charity'. Many believed that he was only inclined to help single mothers and was hostile towards young men. Most asylum-seekers in Nairobi and Kampala had to fend for themselves, relying mainly on their own resourcefulness, and also on local churches and mosques, and on relatives, friends, and neighbours.

Notes

1. See, in particular, the two Protocols to the UN Convention against Transnational Organised Crime (on Trafficking in Persons and Smuggling of Migrants), which were adopted in 2000.
2. Temporary protection is another aspect of restrictionism. A pervasive critical analysis of this practice, and of UNHCR's ill-advised support for it, is conducted by Roxström and Gibney (2003).
3. These practices have been severely criticised by civil liberties groups and have also come under judicial scrutiny. For example, in the UK, the detention of asylum-seekers was challenged under the Human Rights Act: after the High Court ruled in favour of the asylum-seekers, the Court of Appeal and then the House of Lords found against them (*Secretary of State for the Home Department ex Parte Saadi and Others*).
4. For example, officials responsible for refugees in the Ministry of Internal Affairs in Italy expressed their frustration at having to implement the 'Fortress Europe' policy in a country with a long coastline and contiguous to such refugee-generating regions as the Middle East and Africa. They would have preferred an approach that was at the same time pragmatic and humanitarian, and favoured abandoning the visa requirement, since 'Italy will have to deal with a migratory flow from Albania' and 'illegal migration is much more difficult to manage than a legal, controlled flow' (Interview with Mr Compagnucci, head of the refugee section at the Ministry of Home Affairs, Rome, May 1998).
5. Operation Lifeline Sudan (OLS) is another example: OLS is one of the longest running relief programmes operating inside a country at war. Its aims are to attenuate the consequences of the conflict and, by giving civilians access to relief in the conflict zone, to provide a disincentive for people to leave. It also aims to prevent the commission of war crimes by training combatants in international humanitarian law. *See* de Waal 1997: 148–50; Karim et al. 1996.
6. Personal communication with immigration official at Entebbe airport in 1998.
7. This development is linked to the growth of interdiction practices in the 'developed world' (Aiken 2003). In some cases, as a result of the absence of controls on immigration officers at airports, refugees have been *refouled* (ibid.).
8. 'No person shall be subjected by a member state to measures such as rejection at the frontier, return or expulsion which would compel him to return or remain in a territory where his life, physical integrity or liberty would be threatened for the reasons set out in Article I, paragraphs 1 and 2 [the refugee definition].' However, as highlighted by Goodwin-Gill, state practice since the adoption of the 1951 Convention suggests that even in states that are not party to the OAU Convention the view that '*non-refoulement* applies to the moment at which asylum-seekers present themselves for entry has affirmed itself' (Goodwin-Gill 1998a: 123–4).

9. The amounts spent on status-determination procedures in 'developed' countries are astronomical, especially when compared with the humanitarian assistance that actually reaches the refugees (Loescher 1993: 93 ff; Harrell-Bond 1996b: 184).

10. In countries like Tanzania, where such official statements have been issued in the past, this was normally done by 'gazetting' refugees – that is, by publication in the official gazette. Combined with the obligation not to reject potential refugees at the frontier, such 'gazetted' statements would oblige border police to grant access to certain categories of persons and would significantly reduce some of the difficulties faced by refugees when they flee.

11. Information recorded includes the name and gender of the family head, the names of dependants, and the part of their country they came from. Sometimes they may be asked why they left, but there is no space on the form UNHCR currently uses to record such information.

12. Local voluntary organisations, for example, the national Red Cross, could also play a role in facilitating the admission of asylum-seekers, if they are properly trained in human rights and refugee law. In some cases, individuals played such a role.

13. This luggage, he was told, would only be returned on payment of a large sum. It contained, among other things, evidence of the ownership of his house in Ethiopia. Later, he learnt that his wife and children were evicted from the house because she could not prove ownership. He wanted to risk the trip to the border to try at least to obtain this document, but he was dissuaded because of the dangers that this would involve.

14. In Uganda, a member of the police who had attended a training session we organised at Makerere University called us to seek advice on cases, wanting to be sure that his and his colleagues' practice was consistent with what they had been taught.

15. Interview with Mrs Pia Prütz Phiri, senior protection officer, Nairobi, April 1998.

16. In fact, they were simply dropped in the 'no man's land' between immigration posts. We contacted the National Refugee Secretariat (NRS) in Kenya, UNHCR, and the press, but never heard what became of this unfortunate group.

17. Interview with Ms Violet Kaliisa, principal immigration officer in charge of investigations and prosecutions, 7 August 1998.

18. One of the two border posts between Kenya and Uganda.

19. Interview with Detective Constable [name withheld], special branch, Entebbe international airport police station, 11 January 1999.

20. Interview with Detective Superintendent of Police, special branch, Busia police station, February 1999.

21. This means that, as a result of political or other developments in their country of origin subsequent and unrelated to their initial departure, they were no longer able to go back in safety and had thus become refugees while they were outside their country.

22. Similarly in Uganda, the camp commandant of Adjumani refugee settlement told us in an interview in his office in February 1998 that the Control of Alien Refuees Act was a confidential document.

23. In these cases, Ugandan courts should have also considered that the principle of *non-refoulement* is part of customary international law. The lack of incorporation of the OAU Convention in a statute did not prevent the application of this prin-

ciple, since in common law customary international law can be applied by the courts.

24. Report of Praxidice Wekesa Saisi, magistrate, Makadera court, Nairobi, 1998.
25. In Kenya another international airport – Moi international airport in Eldoret – was just opening at the time research in Kenya was completed. We did not collect any data on arrivals at Mombasa airport.
26. Making structured observations at the airports was not possible for a number of reasons. First, immigration authorities would have denied us access, as the Department of Immigration told us clearly when we sounded out one of their officials about this. Second, the behaviour of an official is likely to change if he or she is monitored by researchers, and only after repeated and prolonged observations can one expect the official gradually to resume his or her own 'ordinary' way of working. Nevertheless, this consideration alone probably not have stopped us from making these direct observations since, although research was our primary aim, we also intended to have an impact on practice: we would of course have treated data thus acquired with a pinch of salt, but would probably have seized the opportunity to have an impact, albeit limited, on practice.
27. Not, however, without a considerable amount of personal intervention and even 'bullying' the Canadian authorities ourselves. UNHCR's resettlement officer seemed to have forgotten them. This was, however, during the period when allegations of corruption within the resettlement programme in Uganda were rampant and before they were fully exposed in Kenya (e.g. Blomfield 2002).
28. In Europe, state parties to the Dublin Convention, which entered into force in 1997, have created a mechanism for establishing the country responsible for determining an asylum application (Convention Determining the State Responsible for Examining Applications for Asylum Lodged on One of the Members States of the European Communities).
29. Emails from Liebmann, 13, 15, 28 July 1999, 7 August 1999.
30. Email from Decroly, 6 December 1999.
31. Methods used in the Brussels airport include beating, and, as described by the Belgium MP, attaching 'a self-tightening (*auto-serrant*) plastic wire (*fine languette de plastique*) generally used by electricians to attach several other wires together' (Email from Decroly 6 December, 1999). The marks left by this wire were still visible on the legs of the first Burundian woman two weeks after she had been released from Entebbe. The Belgian police caused serious injuries to the left hand and fingers of the Congolese man, whose arms and legs had been tied 'with plastic handcuffs' during the deportation (case no. 155/DRC/U/1999). To confirm these practices, the MP took a Belgian doctor to see other asylum-seekers who had been subjected to similar treatment in Belgium, and then presented at a press conference the doctor's 'complete medical report' (Decroly, 6 December 1999). Such treatment as described and confirmed by various sources amounts at least to a form of 'cruel, inhuman or degrading treatment'.
32. Wilson is Nairobi's second airport, mainly used by light aircraft and local air charter companies.
33. Their number is known to have been over 100, but, according to the urgent action that Amnesty International issued about them, the total number was 101 and not 105, and the number of children in the group was 59 (Amnesty International 1997b).

34. Our data on what happened at Wilson airport come from interviews with refugees who were part of the group and UNHCR protection officers.
35. Amnesty International, for example, had released a number of reports and 'urgent actions' on the situation. UNHCR was itself aware of the dramatic situation in Tingi Tingi as Amnesty's February 1997 report on eastern Zaire reveals: '... tens of thousands of Rwandan and Burundian refugees (the International Committee of the Red Cross (ICRC) estimates 270,000, the UNHCR 330,000) remain in eastern Zaire, in and around Shabunda, Tingi Tingi and Amisi, where they are receiving very little humanitarian assistance. ... Many are sick and wounded. UNHCR has stated that up to 15 refugees are dying daily at Tingi Tingi camp, where food shortages have led to conflict between refugees and the local population. According to UNICEF there has been an alarming increase in child mortality in the camp, with twelve deaths of children under the age of five in one day alone.'
36. One Rwandan refugee who survived Tingi Tingi wrote about her experience after reaching France: 'When my neighbour informed me of the imminent visit of the Commissioner [the UN high commissioner for refugees] – information which he had heard on international radio stations – I replied to him jokingly that it was time for us to pack our bags because this visit would soon be followed by that of Kabila and his rebels (Umutesi 2000: 183).' On the other hand, they recognised the efforts of the then EU commissioner for humanitarian affairs, Emma Bonino, in favour of Rwandan refugees (ibid.: 182).
37. Interview, Nairobi, 9 May 1998. This interview was conducted after the woman, a nurse who had worked with Médecins sans Frontières (MSF) in Tingi Tingi, had escaped with her two children from Kakuma where she had also been employed in the hospital run by IRC. She fled Kakuma because of UNHCR's plan to relocate the entire Tingi Tingi group to Dadaab. The last time we heard from this refugee, she was in a southern African country.
38. *See* Chapter 3 **Interpreters**.
39. The crisis caught UNHCR completely unprepared. The Kenya office had been understaffed for some time and some key senior officials had not been replaced by the time the crisis began to unfold (UNHCR 1992c: para. 34).
40. Most staff flew to Kakuma. There were frequent armed attacks on the road between Eldoret and Kakuma. Ekuru Aukot, a member of our team, narrowly survived one of these ambushes in which others were wounded and died. The insecurity of this road increased during our research.
41. The SPLA played a similar role in Adjumani, according to one camp commandant interviewed in August in Kampala, a practice he intended to oppose.
42. Interview, Pakele, 7 February 1998.
43. This contrasts sharply with the views of how you can recognise a real refugee expressed by the head of the NRS in Nairobi. He said, 'I can tell you who are the genuine refugees: affluent people who give up more in their home countries in order to come Kenya' (Interview with Nimrod Waweru, Nairobi, 10 July 1997).
44. There are two examples in Africa where governments received refugees without accepting international assistance: Sierra Leone and Guinea in the 1960s. Refugees were allowed to move freely throughout the country and integrate themselves amongst the local population (Harrell-Bond 1990).
45. In 1986 a reception centre was established at Mirieyi; its inhabitants were mainly young Dinka men fleeing forced conscription into the SPLA.
46. The presence of Kenyan nomads in Uganda, uprooted by the 'ethnic clashes', has already been noted.

47. The government of Kenya estimated that the number of Somali refugees residing outside the camps was around 100,000. UNHCR's estimate was lower at some 50,000 (UNHCR 1999f).

48. The Executive Committee (EXCOM) meets once a year to review UNHCR's budget and to advise the high commissioner on protection issues. Its composition has changed over the years; in 2004 it comprised representatives of sixty-four states. In 1977 EXCOM adopted its first Conclusion on international protection, to be followed by over ninety more since then. Although not legally binding, EXCOM conclusions are generally considered authoritative.

49. On socio-economic rights, *see* Chapter 5.

3

Status-Determination Procedures: '... and when you go to UNHCR, pray'

Introduction

When the 1951 Convention was adopted, it was taken for granted that states would assume full responsibility for determining whom they would recognise as a refugee. Under its 1950 statute, UNHCR's role was clearly defined as being primarily to promote the adoption of the refugee law instruments and respect for the rights of refugees they enshrined. Its involvement in refugee status determination was initially very limited: in some countries it sat as an observer on national status-determination bodies, and it was generally responsible for asylum-seekers who had been wrongly denied asylum, helping them find another host country. The fact that fifty years on UNHCR is in charge of determining refugee status in at least sixty-four states (Crisp 2002; *see also* UNHCR 1999b) would have astonished the drafters of the convention.[1]

In countries that are not party to the 1951 Convention, and where UNHCR has offices, there is a justification for its taking a proactive role in identifying and protecting refugees under its mandate (Alexander 1999). However, out of the fifty-five states where, in 1998, UNHCR was taking sole responsibility for determining who was a refugee, thirty were actually parties to the 1951 Convention and, of these, nine had also ratified or acceded to the 1969 OAU Convention. The tenth, Libya, was a party only to the 1969 OAU Convention (which, however, incorporates the refugee definition in the 1951 Convention). It is true that the attitude of some governments, like that of Egypt, which became a party to the conventions but refused to take over individual status determination, may have put pressure on UNHCR to step in. Nonetheless, UNHCR's decision to assume responsibility for status determination also resulted from perceived advantages: it could control the numbers of people it assisted and demonstrate to its donors in countries in the 'developed world' that it was responsive to their interests in restricting refugee movements.

Based on the scant data available, the recognition rate in UNHCR-led status-determination procedures seemed to vary a great deal from country to country; in 1999 it was on average 36 percent (UNHCR 1999b). Where governments maintained responsibility for the refugee status-determination process, they were sometimes criticised by UNHCR branch offices for recognition rates that were considered too high – for example, the Tanzanian authorities were reprimanded for accepting 'too many' refugees (their recognition rate was 96 percent).[2]

Another major problem with UNHCR-led status determination was that in Africa it did not always apply the OAU Convention, thus contravening its own mandate as laid down by the General Assembly. On various occasions we were told by UNHCR officials that the OAU Convention was not part of the mandate of UNHCR.[3] This position is wrong: UNHCR is a subsidiary organ established by the General Assembly which, as its parent organ, is legally empowered to amend its statute (Verdirame 2001b: chap. 2), as it did on a number of occasions. In 1979, for example, the General Assembly 'fully' endorsed the recommendations of the 1979 Arusha Conference on the Situation of Refugees in Africa, and instructed UNHCR to apply the OAU Convention (GA res. 34/61). The view that UNHCR is bound to apply the OAU Convention for its operations in Africa is shared by commentators (Jackson 1999: 194) and, ironically, UNHCR itself recognised it as correct in a report:

> Through the recommendations of the 1979 Arusha Conference on the Situation of Refugees in Africa, endorsed by the OAU Assembly of Heads of State and Government and by the General Assembly in its resolution 34/61 of 29 November 1979, the OAU Refugee Convention *has been clearly identified* as a basis for the Office's protection work in Africa. This is of special importance as in so far as it confirms the Office's protection role with regard to persons falling within the wider 'refugee' definition which figures in the OAU Refugee Convention [emphasis added] (UN Doc. A/36/12 para. 11).

Procedural standards in status determination

The 1951 Convention and the OAU Convention lay down broad standards for refugee status determination with which states should comply, but do not make provision for specific implementation procedures. Given the variety of legal systems in the world, it would have been difficult to come up with universally acceptable procedures. Procedural fairness in the assessment of asylum applications is nevertheless a requirement deriving from general human rights law as well as constitutional provisions such as the right to a fair trial.[4] It also finds a basis in the principle of good faith, which governs the performance of any international legal obligation (Bliss 2000: 95–96).

Despite being absent from the text of the refugee conventions, some specific aspects of procedural fairness have been spelt out in other refugee instruments. The conclusions of the Executive Committee of the UNHCR (EXCOM) – in particular conclusion 8 (XXVIII), 1977 – and the *Handbook on Procedures and Criteria for Determining Refugee Status* (UNHCR 1992a), lay out basic procedural requirements. The General Assembly has repeatedly referred to the need to establish 'fair and efficient procedures' in the asylum process (e.g., GA res. 51/75 and GA res. 50/152). State practice has also over the years fleshed out standards of procedural fairness that apply to refugee status determination, both through case-law and through statutes or administrative regulations.

In assessing UNHCR practice in southeast Asia, Alexander identified a number of specific core standards, which ought to apply to all refugee status determination. These include: the provision of information to asylum-seekers; availability and access to independent legal advice; assistance and representation during the interview; access to information on a person's file and to any other information used in decision making; accuracy and availability of transcripts of interviews; reasons for rejection; and the right of appeal (Alexander 1999: 266–82).[5] EXCOM conclusion 8 also lists 'the services of a competent interpreter' as one of the basic requirements.

Our research in Kenya and Uganda revealed some important additional requirements which are not normally emphasised – probably because they are taken for granted. The first is the need for refugees to read and sign as true the statements that are attributed to them by interviewers (Mumby 2002). The second is the protection of the confidentiality of the information provided by the asylum-seeker. When, as was frequently the case in both countries, information leaked, the consequences could be very serious, putting individuals at personal risk and undermining confidence in the asylum process.

Who is in charge?

Kenya

Until 1991 the Kenyan government conducted refugee status-determination interviews. Refugee status was determined by an Eligibility Committee that included representatives of the Ministry of Home Affairs, Office of the Vice-President, and the Immigration Department. UNHCR's role was as an observer/adviser. A panel of senior officers from the same ministries heard appeals against negative decisions. Although decisions did not normally state reasons – unlike other administrative acts – in principle they could have been judicially reviewed, although we did not see any case of judicial review. Rejected applicants received a letter informing them of the decision and requiring them to 'find another country' within three weeks or regularise their stay as a 'normal alien'. Even before the decision on their case, applicants were given documents, normally a visitor's pass. There was a reception centre at Thika, outside Nairobi, where 'needy' asylum-seekers could reside while their cases were being considered. Once recognised, 'the refugee is automatically issued with a refugee identity card, aliens card, and class M Entry Permit, which allows him to seek employment' (UNHCR 1987a: para. 2.1.6).

Final clearance by the special branch, an arm of Kenya's security apparatus, was required. Those who were recognised by the panel but did not receive such clearance were accorded 'mandate' status by UNHCR, which then took responsibility for finding another country for them. Notwithstanding the role of the special branch, in 1987 UNHCR described the government's policy as 'liberal' since these people were allowed 'to remain in the country for an indefinite period until they are resettled' (ibid.: para. 2.2.1).

As long as the government was in charge of refugee status determination, UNHCR's ability to discharge its protection function and to supervise compliance with refugee law was not seriously compromised.[6] In 1987, UNHCR was negotiating the right to participate as an observer in the special branch interviews. It offered to organise a seminar on refugee law and interviewing methods for 'frontier officers'. It attempted to persuade the government to introduce the right to appeal against the decisions of frontier officers. It also reported 'that the [government] officials conducting interviews have co-operated in applying in some situations the broad criteria for granting refugee status' under the OAU Convention (UNHCR 1987a: para. 2.1.5), although the OAU Convention was not ratified by Kenya until June 1992.[7] In the same period, UNHCR was expressing serious concerns for the protection of Ugandans and did not encourage repatriation. Within a few years, after UNHCR had assumed responsibility for determining status, the situation changed. By then it was UNHCR which denied a proper appeal to asylum-seekers and which flouted the OAU Convention. UNHCR also became intensely preoccupied with repatriation – forecasting in 1992, at the height of arrivals of Somalis and Sudanese into Kenya, that 1993 would be a year of repatriation, not reception (UNHCR 1992b: para 1.3.1).

It is not entirely clear if the assumption of responsibilities for status determination on the part of UNHCR was of its own making or whether UNHCR reluctantly accepted this role. The protection reports of 1992 and 1993 mentioned that UNHCR was trying to persuade the Kenyan government to resume status determination, thus lending support to the latter interpretation. However, it remains a mystery why in 1992 UNHCR believed that it was in a better position to undertake such a resource-intensive task than the government. In that year, UNHCR had only one protection officer in Kenya, while there were at least a handful of Kenyan government officials with some experience in determining refugee status. As discussed in Chapter 1 *Phase Two: The balance of power shifts*, it is more likely that the breakdown in relations between UNHCR and the government that occurred at this time (and this was *not* mentioned in UNHCR's protection reports) was one of the main causes for the transfer of responsibilities. Whatever the reason, this abdication of responsibility by the Kenyan government was not excusable, and constituted a serious mistake.

By 1991, UNHCR, in full control of the procedures of status determination, operated out of its office in Wood Avenue, Nairobi, in a joint partnership with the Jesuit Refugee Service (JRS).[8] The JRS facility was originally designed to provide health and limited welfare services to refugees.[9] With JRS assuming responsibility for the first screening of asylum-seekers, the atmosphere deteriorated.

It must be emphasised, however, that the Kenyan government had never officially accepted that UNHCR's status-determination procedure would be given full recognition in Kenya.[10] The 'status determination' which UNHCR provided inevitably resulted in an unclear status and the protection letter issued was merely an invitation by UNHCR to the Kenyan government to consider the holder *as if* he or she were an officially recognised refugee. The procedures were thus summarised by UNHCR:

> Pre-screening and eligibility interviews are carried out at the premises of the Jesuit Refugee Services [*sic*], UNHCR's implementing partner. Pre-screening is carried out by social counsellors, eligibility interviews are carried out by a legal counsellor and UNHCR protection officers.

> During the reporting period there has been no systematic access to appeal for rejected asylum-seekers. Irregular movers have systematically been requested to return to their first country of asylum (UNHCR 1997c: chap. 2).

In 1998 a crisis occurred between UNHCR and the government. On 20 August, in the aftermath of the bombing of the US embassy, Shariff Nassir, the minister of home affairs, took the drastic decision to refuse to recognise the protection letters that UNHCR had been issuing to refugees. The government announced that UNHCR had no authority to grant refugee status in Kenya and demanded that refugees hand over these papers to the Immigration Department (Warigi 1998: 28). When refugees did so, they were issued with a 'Notice to Prohibited Immigrant' on the basis of the Immigration Act. This notice required them to leave Kenya within fourteen days, and, if enforced, would have amounted to *refoulement*. In practice, those who received this notice generally ignored it. However, it still had the effect of making many refugees in Kenya insecure and vulnerable to arbitrary arrest.

In September 1998, the government also decided to revive its own refugee status-determination procedures and a National Eligibility Committee (NEC) was established with UNHCR's assistance. However, it only met sporadically in the period between November 1998 and December 1999, when it 'adjudicated some 200 asylum claims', mainly from Rwandan asylum-seekers (UNHCR 1999e). UNHCR's role was to give 'recommendations on particular cases and the committee is supposed to decide on the basis of those recommendations. For all intent [*sic*] and purposes UNHCR did the status determination (75 percent of all asylum application are rejected)' (Email from RCK, 13 July 2000). UNHCR reverted to its previous mistake, stating that 'In the absence of a full fledged and fully operational Government status determination procedure, UNHCR established its own eligibility procedure on 1 January 1999, independent of the Jesuit Refugee Services who administered the procedure for UNHCR from 1991 up to the end of 1998' (UNHCR 1999e). The situation thus began to resemble that in Uganda described below: the government and UNHCR simultaneously conducting status-determination interviews, with an unclear division of responsibilities between the two but with UNHCR clearly taking on the lead role.

Uganda

The procedure for status determination in Uganda appeared at first sight to comprise two parallel systems, one put in place by UNHCR and the other by the government. In practice, the balance of power was heavily on UNHCR's side. The bulk of the cases were determined by UNHCR and its implementing partner InterAid, with only a small number being referred to the government. UNHCR, purportedly only an 'adviser/observer', actually played a key role, presenting the facts and making recommendations for many cases. With a few notable exceptions, the government followed UNHCR's recommendations.[11]

The Refugee Eligibility Committee (REC) was established in 1988, when large numbers of refugees were arriving in Uganda from the Sudan. Its membership, which has remained essentially unchanged, included the permanent secretary/director of refugees from the Ministry of Local Government,[12] one member each from the Ministries of Internal Affairs and Justice, an official of the Ministry of Foreign Affairs, a representative from the special branch (the security arm of the police), and a UNHCR official in observer capacity. The REC never developed formal rules of procedure, one reason being that, for several years between 1988 and

1996, the REC ceased to function.[13] Lack of formal procedural rules contributed to the state of uncertainty about the role of different actors.

In 1998, only 464 cases were referred to the REC, and 98.4 percent of them were accepted.[14] There was no appeal against negative decisions, a problem that UNHCR had been raising with the government since 1988. The practice of disbursing 'sitting allowances' to the members of the REC (UNHCR 2000c) enhanced UNHCR's influence over it. Another factor that gave UNHCR leverage was that it presented itself as the infallible 'expert' on refugees (*see* UNHCR 1999g).

Throughout our research in Uganda, the asylum-determination process in Kampala was marked by competition over who had the authority to grant refugee status. Was it the government, through the Directorate of Refugees (DoR) and the REC, or was it UNHCR? The government normally insisted that it was in control. For instance, the deputy director of the DoR asserted that the 'offer of asylum is a prerogative of government. UNHCR has no right to offer asylum on Uganda['s] soil' (Twesigomwe 1995). However, as a result of the influence that UNHCR exercised over it and because of the relatively small numbers that it dealt with, status determination by the REC could be described as secondary to the process controlled directly by UNHCR – the latter being the principal way for refugees to be recognised in Uganda. This is confirmed by the conspicuous absence of the role of the REC in this summary of status-determination procedures in Uganda prepared by UNHCR:

> Asylum-seekers who arrived at Kampala and reported to the UNHCR claiming asylum will follow the following procedures [*sic*]: (1) they will be asked to report to the police that they are in the country and wish to apply for asylum. The police will record their personal data and conduct a brief interview and determine that they are no security concern to the Uganda [*sic*]; (2) they are then directed to report at the InterAid/Urban Refugee Project (URP) whose couselors [*sic*] will interview them and have them fill a standard questionnaire; (3) UNHCR officers will then interview them (UNHCR 1997d: chap. 2).

UNHCR's protection report of 1999, however, did mention the REC, along with the UNHCR process. It presented a picture of two complementary and parallel systems for status determination. It maintained that the competence of each body depended on the country of origin of the applicant, and summarised the situation thus:

> Cases from Sudan, especially Khartoum, have been the competence of REC, while cases from the rebel held areas have been dealt with by the Secretariat [of the Directorate] unless the Directorate decided that they be dealt with by the REC.

> Cases from Rwanda, Burundi, and Ethiopia and other countries have been the competency [*sic*] of the REC.

Cases from other countries have been dealt with by the REC and in many cases redirected to UNHCR (UNHCR 1999d).

Refugees were not provided with any information on the responsibilities of the government or UNHCR in determining status. At times it seemed that the system in Uganda left room for 'forum shopping', giving asylum-seekers the possibility of choosing where to apply for asylum, but in practice UNHCR viewed refugees who approached the government first with disapproval. One refugee, who had obtained his status directly through the government's procedure without passing through InterAid, was refused a form to apply for resettlement by UNHCR. As one UNHCR protection officer explained to him, 'There are two restaurants. One has spicy food, at the other the food is bland.' In short, UNHCR was punishing him for going through the government procedure by denying him access to resettlement, over which it had full control.

In another case, an Ethiopian asylum-seeker who had been rejected by UNHCR applied and was granted refugee status by the DoR (case no. 182/Eth/U/1998). It was not clear if this discrepancy of outcomes was the result of the application of different criteria, or just happenstance. On one occasion, the deputy director of the DoR suggested that 'clear cases' were sometimes decided by his office, as in the case of 'a peasant of no circumstance', whereas cases that were not clear were forwarded by him to the REC.[15] UNHCR's policy on submissions to the REC was at least as inscrutable as that of the DoR: it sent certain cases to the REC, while it decided others, particularly 'security cases'.[16]

Despite the uncertainty and the competition, there were moments of cooperation between the government and UNHCR. For instance, a Congolese medical doctor who had sought asylum with the government was sent to the UNHCR senior protection officer with a note asking for advice on whether this individual was a prima facie case or not.[17] At times, the cooperation was premised on shared prejudices. For example, in a note sent from the government a UNHCR staff member was told: 'Make a test case to refer IC to Kyangwali and see if he is accepting. Some of these guys may be aliens manipulating the current situation in Eastern Congo.'[18] Did this mean that going to the camp was a test of whether the person was a 'real' refugee?

On another occasion, in February 2001, the Office of the Prime Minister and UNHCR announced a joint policy to prohibit Sudanese asylum-seekers from registering for refugee status in Kampala. The reason, according to UNHCR, 'was to stop recognized refugees from seeking placement in other refugee settlements'. A crisis had developed as the numbers of Sudanese in Kampala with no place to reside and no means of subsistence grew. After a meeting with the Refugee Law Project (RLP), UNHCR finally agreed to give transport for asylum-seekers to the northern settlement of their choice. RLP was asked to compile a list of people who found this an acceptable compromise: 'However, many Sudanese, notably young men, refused outright stating that staying in Kampala without identification papers and means of support would be preferable to daring the violence and possibility of abduction endemic in the North' (RLP 2001a: 1–2,8, 2001b.).

The existence of two separate systems could, in some rare circumstances, work to the benefit of refugees. In particular, the vetting by security organs of REC applicants posed a problem for refugees fleeing conflicts, like those in the Democratic Republic of Congo (DRC) and Sudan, in which Uganda was involved. The availability of a separate procedure controlled by UNHCR arguably offered these refugees a safer route for obtaining asylum, as illustrated by the case of the Rwandan students who sought asylum in Uganda in December 1999. Around sixty students from Rwanda arrived in Uganda and claimed asylum (Mugabi 2000). After their arrival had attracted the attention of the press, UNHCR responded by saying that there were no refugees among the students, explaining in the newspaper that they had 'contacted Kigali' (UNHCR 1999g). As a result, the students were not to receive humanitarian assistance from UNHCR (UNHCR 1999f; *see also* OCHA 1999: 2). We emailed the deputy director at the DoR, reminding him that 'You could accept *en masse,* but you could not reject them *en masse'*, and that each person had to be interviewed. On the following day, the offices of InterAid were closed to all other refugees except the Rwandans, but UNHCR protection staff interviewed only about eight students and rejected them all (*see* Harrell-Bond 2000b: 13). In the meantime, the DoR attempted to distance itself from UNHCR. A letter by Carlos Twesigomwe appeared in *New Vision* (1 January 2000), saying that the students were being interviewed by the special branch 'which then compiles details which the committee [REC] uses in its final decisions' (for response, *see* Harrell-Bond 2000b). On 4 January 2000, UNHCR again became involved, reiterating that its office in Kigali had carried out the investigations leading to its negative decision, and that it had not exchanged information with the 'government' of Rwanda, but with local UNHCR offices (Saidy 2000; *see also* Kakande 2000, 2000b, 2000c.). In the meantime, the refugees were hidden (to avoid *refoulement*), and were protected and fed by officials from the Office of the President (Harrell-Bond 1999b, 2000b: 13).[19]

Eventually, UNHCR headquarters in Geneva took action as a result of the intervention of the military adviser to President Museveni, who happened to be the brother of the deputy director of the Division of International Protection in Geneva. He ordered that all the students be interviewed to have their status determined by different officials from those who had been involved in the interviews with the first group of eight. The regional protection officer was sent to Kampala to interview the students along with the senior protection officer, who had been on holiday during this period and was thus considered not to be prejudiced by the earlier actions of UNHCR branch office. All were eventually declared refugees and were subsequently resettled, most in Norway, the others in the US.

These exceptions notwithstanding, for the most part the fact that there were two systems with an uncertain division of responsibilities was problematic. It disoriented refugees,[20] and it hindered the development of a clear and coherent status-determination process in Uganda. By July 2002, the situation had not improved (RLP 2002).

The role of NGOs

A feature common to both Kenya and Uganda was the presence of NGOs as UNHCR's sub-contractors in the status-determination process. The involvement of NGOs aggravated the anomaly: not only was UNHCR exercising functions that should normally be exercised by governments; it also delegated some of them to private humanitarian organisations, the Jesuit Refugee Service (JRS) in Kenya and InterAid in Uganda.

In Kenya, JRS staff were even allowed to determine status at the end of a cursory interview and to issue their decisions on UNHCR letterheads (Gitari et al. 1998: 10), until Pia Phiri was appointed senior protection officer in August 1997. One refugee, Alfred Buregeya, now a lecturer in linguistics at Nairobi University, wrote a graphic twenty-page account of his experiences at the JRS office in Wood Avenue during the two years he waited for an interview.[21] As he put it, UNHCR could not:

> ... condescend so low as to deal directly with the refugee when they first come to seek protection and assistance. Such a dirty job has been delegated to a kind of 'subsidiary' called Jesuit Refugee Service ... It is here your problems start, and it is here they usually end, solved or not. It is here you have to go to 'open your file' – so they call it. It is here you must go prepared to pocket frustrations, humiliations, anguish, despair ... you name it' (1998: 1).

The first problem for refugees was literally to get past the gates and into these JRS/UNHCR offices. By controlling access, the JRS guards were given an inordinate power over refugees. They were also known to take money from individual refugees before allowing them inside (Gitari et al. 1998: 11). The scene outside the Wood Avenue office was described in these terms:

> An asylum-seeker arrives at JRS Wood Avenue sometimes having first been referred there by the UNHCR Branch Office at Westlands. The distance between these two offices is about 1½ hour walk. She waits at the gate which is always closed and is guarded by two uniformed guards armed with batons and one civilian guard. Numbers of hopeful asylum-seekers approaching the Wood Avenue office for protection or assistance

vary but in 1998 numbered as many as 150 or 200 waiting on one day, before UNHCR established its Ngong Road Screening Centre in June 1998 for Rwandan and Burundian refugees ... Now the figures are more in the vicinity of 60–80. Mondays are busier than other days because of needs that have arisen ... over the weekend. They start arriving at about 6: 30 or 7:00 a.m. Some have spent precious shillings to get there. Others have walked long distances. Occasionally people sleep outside the gate over night. If it is raining, they will crowd at the gate under a narrow yellow plastic shelter. They wait, ever hopeful of being let in.

On the days observed by the Evaluation Co-ordinator, of the estimated 50 or 60 asylum-seekers waiting at the gate, between 4 and 6 were allowed to enter. For example, a total of 9 protection interviews were scheduled for 10 August 1998. About five had pre-arranged interviews. The balance was selected from the crowd outside. The names of those not selected for inter-view are not recorded; priorities are not set. These people will return on another day in the hope that they may be selected for interview. Some at the gate had been waiting for 3, 4 and sometimes 7 or 8 days to be admit-ted through the gates. Would-be beneficiaries become extremely frustrated and some are visibly distressed (Gitari et al.1998: 11).

The priest who directed the JRS programme in Kenya was loathed by many refugees, although others, who had received assistance from him, had a different view. The main reason why he aroused such contrasting feelings was that he had the invidious job of gatekeeper. For many refugees, he embodied their frustration with the capricious way in which assistance was dispensed and access to protection was given:

I observed that this gate serves as a first barrier where the receptionist, who is always none other than the Director [the JRS priest] or his second, beckons the needy visitors for brief interview while standing, and then passes them on to the next reception, or pushes them out. It is at this point that many refugees begin to feel extreme bitterness and hopelessness in their lives at the hands of UNHCR.

At this first interview Fr. Eugene Birr [*sic*] is habitually flanked by an aide who, at times, does the translation. Within a couple of metres stand green uniformed security guards who push failures out. Most of those turned away are the ones who resort to sitting sadly at the gate awaiting a chance to address their problems to any UNHCR officer entering. Aware of this, some officers close the windows of their car. Hence, the affected refugees keep trying, noting that maybe the opportunity will come (Otim 1998: 9).

In addition, those who were able to gain access often did so because they presented themselves in ways that fitted with 'acceptable' categories – single mothers and widows often being given preference. As one refugee put it, 'You know there is some little assistance that they give when you get there [to the JRS office at Wood Avenue] the first time. But, if the wife says that she is married, they do not give the assistance. They expect the husband to be capable of supporting the family and the chil-dren' (case no. 048/BUR/K/1997). This practice is also extended to the protection letter: 'women without husbands were often allowed residence in the city, but [those] with husbands were sent to a camp' (Otim 1998: 10). Not surprisingly, many families decided to 'cheat': the man would be left at home, while the woman went alone or with her children, saying that her husband had been killed or was missing.

Upon their arrival at JRS and InterAid in Uganda, refugees had to assimilate a set of unwritten rules regulating their interaction with staff – about the places in the compound where they were allowed to sit, how and when they could ask questions, and so on. 'Teaching the client role' and 'dispensing psychological benefits and sanctions' are functions typical of any street-level bureaucracy (Lipsky 1980: 61), but the arbitrary way in which these functions were exercised at Wood Avenue and InterAid engendered humiliation and chagrin in the refugees. Those who could get past the gatekeepers were kept waiting for hours without explanation, and often sent home without having had their interview. Staff members were bad-tempered and their behaviour could be vexatious and unpredictable. Refugees' requests for explanations were met with reprimands, indifference, and, in some cases, with petty vindictiveness or outright cruelty.

Neither JRS nor InterAid had a professional and humane approach to refugees' dissent, dissatisfaction, or frustration; nor did JRS or InterAid appear to realise that they were working as part of a legal process. They did little to ensure such fundamental attributes of proper status determination as fairness and impartiality, probably not appreciating their importance; nor did they pay due attention to security and respect for confidentiality. In fact, refugees had to wait outside in full visibility of anyone passing by.

As JRS and InterAid began to come under pressure from both refugees and UNHCR for different reasons, humanitarian benevolence began to wither away, 'fatigue' increased, and refugees became a 'problem' with which they had to deal and for which they believed they received no reward – either from UNHCR or from the refugees themselves. Negative stereotyping of refugees as 'liars' or ungrateful 'free-riders' trying to take advantage of humanitarian assistance proliferated among InterAid and JRS staff. At Wood Avenue, the atmosphere became 'intimidating, hostile and dehumanising' (Gitari et al. 1998: 20), a description that is fitting for InterAid too. Such limited benevolence as remained was usually reserved for small numbers of individuals.

Refugees who were particularly 'disobedient' or 'obstinate' were beaten up with batons. Excessive force was used on various occasions. In Uganda, in August 1996, a serious incident occurred at InterAid, when a woman walked out of the office in tears and told other refugees that the InterAid social worker had pulled a knife and had attacked her (case no. 231/SUD/U/1997). The InterAid official maintained that the woman had hit her hand on the desk and had cut herself. Refugees at the scene demanded that she be taken to hospital.[22] When InterAid refused, a riot erupted and the police were called in. InterAid reported that property was damaged – a fan, some chairs, a wall clock, and a car. A UNHCR official was reportedly standing at the front door of InterAid, directing the police to the refugees who were the 'ringleaders' and deserved to be found and beaten. At the end of the riot, five people were arrested: the Sudanese refugee woman, another woman (her friend and interpreter), and three Sudanese men. One of the Sudanese men had been beaten so severely that he was coughing up blood: 'I was even crying because I thought he was near death.' The five were held at Central police station for two weeks. The refugee women were released on bail, while the three Sudanese men were detained on remand in Luzira prison. The case came up several times for hearing but was adjourned until all the accused were released. One of them, Moses Wani, was released at the end of March 1997. He was suffering from severe internal injuries attributed to the beating. Although UNHCR's senior protection officer wrote to InterAid asking for urgent medical assistance, it was never granted, and Mr Wani eventually underwent surgery on his colon, paid for by a Ugandan friend.[23] He was eventually resettled in Australia.

The outcome of the riot was not an improvement in the procedures. On the contrary, from then on it became mandatory for every asylum-seeker to go through the police before opening a file at InterAid. Before long, InterAid moved its offices close to Kampala old police station, and had employed armed guards.

In Kenya, when the senior protection officer who took office at the end of 1997 introduced changes in the system in order to improve the quality of status-determination interviews, tension with the JRS staff on the 'front line' grew. For JRS, an improved process meant longer interviews, and more paper work, which appeared to conflict with the imperative of identifying the beneficiaries of the humanitarian assistance as expeditiously as possible. Partly as a result of this tension, JRS decided to review its project at Wood Avenue. The evaluation team recommended the immediate withdrawal of JRS from a project that had created a conflict with 'JRS's mandate as expressed in its mission statement: to accompany, serve and advocate for refugees' (Gitari et al. 1998). This withdrawal was implemented in 1999. However belated, JRS's decision was important, but it could only be taken because JRS's relative financial independence allowed it to pull out while keeping its entire staff in employment. InterAid, on the other hand, was totally dependent on UNHCR's funding and continued to act as UNHCR's implementing partner.

Confidentiality

Minimum safeguards of confidentiality were not in place in either Uganda or Kenya. Names of asylum-seekers were regularly posted outside the JRS and InterAid offices, either to call them for an interview or to give them the results of their asylum claim. In order to find out the whereabouts of opponents, all that governments in the region needed to do – and we found out that they often did – was to have someone check these lists. Such breaches of confidentiality caused many a refugee to stay away from the InterAid office.

Notes on the testimonies given by refugees during the interviews were not treated with the necessary respect for the confidentiality of the information and for the security of the refugees. It was often reported that files had gone missing from InterAid in Uganda, or that an important document had disappeared. Many refugees believed that this was systemic.[24] An Ethiopian refugee once found another Ethiopian reading his file (case no. 168/ETH/U/1998). Security personnel from both Uganda's internal and external security services were constantly present at InterAid and had access to the offices. Files were also reported missing from the offices that gave 'security clearance' to refugees before their interviews with the REC.

Although the fact that information was leaking from 'all pores' at InterAid was well known, for a long time UNHCR did little to address the situation. It did however display sudden concern about confidentiality when it was unwarranted. For example, the representative in Uganda refused us permission to observe interviews *with the consent of* the refugee, because:

> Although I fully subscribe to the need for in-depth research on refugee protection. [*sic*] I have to balance this need against the asylum-seekers' right to privacy and confidentiality of the information they give to this Office which information is in most cases sensitive. I regret that after a lot of reflection, I have come to the conclusion that the protection of the refugees and the smooth functioning of the refugee status procedure are of higher importance.[25]

After the problems with confidentiality were pointed out to him, the senior protection officer who arrived in Kampala in 1998 decided that files would be kept on UNHCR's premises, and that every morning the files of the people who were going to be interviewed would be hand-delivered to InterAid. Even then one refugee in Kampala was horrified to see that his file was being read by a receptionist at InterAid, in full view of other refugees and staff members. The senior protection officer confirmed that on that day he had taken out this refugee's file and had been absent from his office for only a few minutes (case no. 062/DRC/U/1999). We subsequently learned from InterAid staff who interviewed refugees (on referral from the Kampala old police station) that they always made a copy, and that these continued to be kept at InterAid in an unlocked filing cabinet.[26]

In Kenya, reports of disappearances of files and leaks of information were not so widespread. On one occasion, however, the office where the 'screening' of Rwandans was taking place was broken into at night and computers containing extremely confidential information were stolen. After a police investigation, which did not result in the apprehension of any of the culprits, UNHCR attributed this to ordinary criminals. In a country that had broken diplomatic ties with Rwanda only a couple of years before because of the activities of 'hit squads' sent from Kigali, many refugees were understandably suspicious of this explanation.[27]

Decisions on individual cases were normally taken locally, but some cases, deemed to give rise to special considerations, were referred to Geneva. Decisions to exclude, in particular, were taken by headquarters. Consultations with other branch offices in the region were also frequent. Many refugees feared that in the process of consulting with other branch offices confidentiality could be breached. Such fears, particularly rife among Rwandans and Burundians, were to some extent justified. A UN official interviewed after a mission in Burundi said that UN offices in that country were 'infiltrated', and that local staff were often related to somebody in the government. This official observed that 'we cannot trust our own staff in these conditions. Nothing is kept confidential.'[28] The same is likely to have been the case in Rwanda.

Interpreters

Interpretation is one of the most delicate aspects of a status-determination interview, in terms both of the security of refugees and of the credibility of their testimonies. It would normally be preferable to have interpreters who, while fluent in the language of the applicant, do not come from the same country. UNHCR's training modules warn against the risk that, when refugee interpreters are used, applicants may be deterred from giving certain information (UNHCR 1995a). This would be especially important when the interviews take place in countries that are geographically contiguous to the country of origin, and where, as a result, fears about infiltrators from the country of origin are rife and often justified. In Kenya and Uganda, UNHCR and its sub-contractors almost exclusively used refugees, and it appears that neither their professional qualifications nor their political affiliations were adequately taken into account. For example, in Kenya, a former officer in the Rwanda Patriotic Front (RPF) was employed by JRS. After many complaints from refugees over a long period (e.g., Rwandan/Burundian Fellowship 1995), he was finally removed.

However the negative decisions in cases where he had served as interpreter were not reviewed.

In Uganda, there were at least two separate interviews that required interpreters, at the police station and at InterAid. Fluent speakers of French and Swahili, the main languages of Congolese refugees, were not available and they either had to respond in English, of which only a few had slight knowledge, or to rely on other refugees who were at the office. Many, however, did not want a stranger to sit through their interview, and preferred to plough through it in poor English (e.g., case nos. 033/DRC/U/1999; Odhiambo-Abuya 2004). Some would bring an interpreter they trusted, but the interviewer often rejected that person in favour of another refugee.

Advocacy

As noted in the Introduction, we had set out to use our research as an opportunity to promote changes in policy and as a way of advocating on behalf of refugees and asylum-seekers. The attitude towards legal assistance and representation for asylum applicants was generally hostile. Alexander, who observed a similar attitude in southeast Asia, notes the 'breathtaking' fact that UNHCR's own training modules differentiate between status determination conducted by UNHCR and status determination conducted by the government (1999: 272): for the former presence of counsel is unnecessary, while for the latter it is considered helpful – a reflection of the bureaucratic assumption within UNHCR that its staff are beyond reproach.

Upon our arrival in Kenya, we sought advice from a former UNHCR protection officer, who had since gone on to set up his own law firm in Nairobi.[29] He said that the wisest way to proceed, in the best interests of the asylum-seekers, was to help them draft a letter stating the facts correctly. Including references to the *Handbook* (UNHCR 1992a) or to case law was not, in his view, a good idea and could even be counterproductive: 'people who come across as too smart do not always go down well'.[30] Since his departure from UNHCR, he had helped some asylum applicants on this basis. He had to be particularly circumspect, since he had left UNHCR on bad terms with the senior protection officer. He believed that if it were known that he had been advising a certain applicant, the case would be 'spitefully' rejected. When we interviewed another UNHCR protection officer, who had left the organisation in mid-1997,[31] she confirmed that the method suggested by her former colleague was the one that could serve asylum-seekers best.

In June 1997, before procedural changes were introduced into the status-determination system, we advised a group of asylum-seekers to use the purely factual letters that we had jointly drafted but to sign them in their own name. This group consisted of people who were appealing against first decisions: they believed that the first decision had been based on a cursory interview and wanted to be interviewed again. It was not possible to do the kind of follow-up on this group that we had envisaged, since, in the aftermath of the police swoops in July 1997, which prompted many to seek asylum in other countries, we lost contact with some of them. A significant number of those arrested were forcibly transferred to camps on UNHCR buses. Of those with whom we kept contact, only a handful were recognised as refugees on appeal; a few had their applications rejected and most had not received a response after a year.

In August 1997, with the appointment of a new UNHCR senior protection officer, the situation began to change. The senior protection officer encouraged us to assist refugees with their cases and gave us a framework within which we could operate. We then made numerous written submissions on behalf of applicants. For a few months in 1998, Ekuru Aukot, earlier our research assistant, worked on refugee cases from the Kenya section of the International Commission of Jurists (ICJ), mainly in relation to refugee status-determination procedures. Since then, the Refugee Consortium of Kenya (RCK) has been established and employs lawyers to advise refugees.

In Uganda, for most of the research period we operated under an arrangement similar to that of Kenya: the senior protection officer received our written submissions and used them for his decisions. We frequently made such submissions, but, as mentioned, the UNHCR representative there decided against our presence in an interview to represent an asylum-seeker (obviously with his or her consent) in the interest of 'privacy and confidentiality'. Members of the research team were occasionally allowed to act as interpreters.

Standards of evidence

Asylum-seekers, as noted, were not normally told at the beginning of the interview what the refugee definition was, and what standard of proof they had to meet, even though providing this information is broadly recognised as a fundamental requirement of procedural fairness (*see* Alexander 1999: 266; Bliss 2000: 100). The final item in the UNHCR application form used in Uganda, which had to be filled before the interview, was: 'Do you have any other details which you think will assist in determining whether you are entitled to refugee status?' How could anyone answer this question without knowing what the legal definition of a refugee is?

UNHCR staff commonly justified their silence on the grounds that if applicants knew exactly what the definition and the burden of proof was, they would change their testimony accordingly. These beliefs were shared by senior UNHCR staff in Geneva, as observed by a member of the research team during a meeting organised by the Lawyers Committee for Human Rights (LCHR) in March 1998.

Not informing refugees about the applicable standard of proof vitiated the whole process, since in asylum applications this burden falls on the asylum-seeker. In both Kenya and Uganda, the OAU refugee definition was applicable and, consequently, an asylum-seeker had to prove either that his or her country of origin was beset by 'foreign external aggression, occupation, foreign domination or events seriously disturbing public order in part or in the whole of the country' (art. 1(2)), or that he or she had a well-founded fear of persecution (art. 1(1)). Many asylum-seekers were considered 'economic migrants' and as such were found not to fall under the refugee definition. In many of these cases, however, it was a combination of political and economic factors that had caused the person to flee. Not knowing what the process was really about and since they viewed UNHCR principally as a provider of assistance, these applicants thought that it was in their interests to stress their economic hardships. UNHCR failed to understand the simple fact that, even if no information was provided to them, applicants still developed a mental image of the interview and decision-making process, often fuelled by rumours about what the interviewers were after. For most, lack of information meant that the image was a distortion of the real process. During the interviews they would frame their answers accordingly, often omitting information, the importance of which they did not appreciate.

Withholding information on the refugee definition and on the standard of proof required from applicants helped to shroud the status-determination decision in mystery, thus shielding UNHCR from the accusation that it was applying a much higher standard of proof than the correct one. An indication that it was probably doing so was that, for most groups, its recognition rates were lower than those found in other countries. Some 20 percent of Rwandans were recognised as refugees in Kenya,[32] whereas recognition rates in Belgium, France, Germany, Canada, and the UK for this group are significantly above 50 percent.[33] The 'real chance' (Australia) or a 'reasonable chance' (UK) (Goodwin-Gill 1998a: 39) of persecution suffices in other jurisdictions, but this would hardly have been enough for applicants in Kenya or Uganda. As for article 1(2) of the OAU Convention, many refugees unwittingly discharged their burden of proof under it by discussing the conflict that had compelled them to leave their countries of origin. However, their accounts were often cut short in the interview, since, as has been mentioned, with the exception of Somalis and Sudanese, the policy was not to apply this article, even when, as was the case in Zaire, Burundi, and Rwanda, reports on the conflict abounded in the press as well as in sources of information available to UNHCR staff.[34]

Decisions

Based most commonly on cursory interviews, decision making on asylum applications could hardly have been the result of a rational legal process. Interviewers often relied on such non-legal categories as 'impressions' in order to reach a decision. This approach also created a sense of omnipotence and infallibility among those carrying out the interviews, which became the main cause of the proliferation of rejections on the grounds of lack of credibility. A UNHCR resettlement officer in Kenya, who had also conducted status-determination interviews, said: 'I can understand if someone is lying or not in the first minute of the interview.'[35] The fact that interviewers did not give reasons for their negative decisions facilitated this subjective and erratic decision making.

The *Handbook* (UNHCR 1992a) was available to the interviewing staff, but internal guidelines were given greater importance, while some of the most basic points in the conventions – even the refugee definition – were overlooked. The case of a Congolese asylum-seeker in Kenya showed how the rudiments of international refugee law were often ignored in decision making. His rejection letter (8 August 1997) referred selectively to the grounds of asylum, failing to mention the prima facie grounds in article 1(2) of the OAU Convention, although the letter explained that his application had been:

> ... carefully considered ... against the refugee criteria contained in the 1951 Convention relating to the Status of Refugees *and the* 1969 OAU Convention Governing the Specific Aspects of Refugee Problems in Africa ... [emphasis added]

> You were required to show a well-founded fear of persecution based on any one or more of the five grounds contained in the Convention: race, religion, nationality, membership of a particular social group, or political opinion (case no. 047/DRC/K/1997).[36]

In Uganda at one point, the protection office even appears to have been under the impression that prima facie status was reserved for 'rural refugees' (UNHCR 1991: para. 16.1.2).

Such attitudes towards certain groups did not usually derive, as would be expected, from an objective assessment of the situation in the country of origin. For example, group recognition was denied to Burundians and Rwandans in both countries, and to Somalis in Uganda (UNHCR 2000c),[37] although the conflicts in these countries would certainly have warranted such recognition. It was clear that, particularly in the case of Rwandan refugees, local staff were expected to implement an unequivocally restric-tionist policy that originated from Geneva and that had, in the previous months, led to the forced repatriations from Tanzania and Zaire. It was only in 2000 that it was finally acknowledged that: 'Due to the complexi-ties of the politics of the Great Lakes Region, and in particular the ever changing nature of relationship between former allies Uganda and Rwanda, it is increasingly becoming difficult to protect some of the Rwandan Hutu or Congolese Hutu refugees in Uganda' (UNHCR 2000c).

The policy towards the recognition of Sudanese asylum-seekers was also significantly influenced by attitudes towards the southern Sudanese conflict. In Kenya, the government did not give the Sudanese People's Liberation Army (SPLA) open support, as was the case in Uganda (e.g., Tumusiime 1998), but there was still considerable sympathy for it. The Immigration Department at Lokichokio in Kenya issued temporary per-mits to live in Nairobi to those who had a close connection with the Southern Sudan Relief Agency (SSRA) – a relief and logistics arm of the SPLA, which was also known to issue documents and give clearance to people entering SPLA-controlled areas. These permits had to be renewed every three months. SPLA officers were also allowed to spend time in Nairobi. As one southern Sudanese lawyer, who had also served as an officer in the SPLA, put it: 'Sudanese refugees are honestly in a better position than other refugees. Kenya is sympathetic to our cause, and the treatment they reserve for us is not the same [as for other refugees].'[38] He probably had the situation of his fellow SPLA commanders and of the elite in mind because the rank and file of the Sudanese refugees were in fact confined to Kakuma refugee camp, where the leadership of the Sudanese community was appointed by the SPLA and where, as we shall see, conditions were harsh. In Uganda, where Museveni and the SPLA had been close allies since the 1980s, SPLA cards were recognised as valid forms of identification by the authorities. Refugees who did not support the SPLA had to conceal their political opinions. Consequently, the Sudanese refugees in Uganda reporting for protection from UNHCR (or for legal assistance from our team) were fleeing forced recruitment, tor-ture, and other forms of persecution perpetrated by the SPLA itself.

As noted, reasons for negative decisions were not normally stated. In Kenya, in October 1997, UNHCR maintained that it had begun to give reasons for rejections. However, these were still grossly inadequate, and limited only to perfunctory comments such as 'lack of credibility', 'lack of co-operation', or 'transit from another country of asylum'. In Uganda, nei-ther the REC nor UNHCR usually stated reasons in their letters to the refugees. However, partly because of the small number of cases it was handling, the notes from the REC meetings reveal that their discussions about individual cases had in fact been quite detailed.

The failure to state reasons frustrated the exercise of the refugee's right to appeal against a negative decision. Refugees could only surmise what the reasons for the rejection of their applications had been. In most cases, when they wrote their appeal themselves, they would therefore simply restate their claim, and their appeal would almost always be rejected. In addition, the appeal procedure itself was at best severely flawed, at worst non-existent. As mentioned, there was no formal right of appeal against decisions of the REC in Uganda, despite article 42 of the Ugandan Constitution, which demands the establishment of an appeal procedure for administrative decisions. In the course of the research, however, we succeeded in getting one case reviewed by the REC on the grounds of new evidence and had the first decision reversed (case no. 168/ETH/U/1998).

Decisions on appeals in Kenya usually consisted of a 'reexamination' of the case, often by the same officer who had taken the first decision. 'What is considered is the whole file, and the statement of the asylum-seeker to appeal against the decision. Decisions can be taken immediately or the person is called for another interview.'[39] Such a procedure was in blatant contravention of basic procedural guarantees, not to mention UNHCR's own *Handbook* and guidelines. Another problem was that refugees were not informed about progress on their case. In one case in Kenya, a Rwandan refugee, whose first application had been rejected, submitted an appeal on 17 June 1995. Two years later, after having been at Wood Avenue many times and being eventually told not to come again and to wait for a letter to be sent to her by mail, she was still writing to UNHCR asking for information (case no. 028/RWA/K/1997).

The JRS evaluation team summarised the ordeal which the procrastinations, the unpredictable decision making, and the needless red tape produced for the refugees:

> If granted an interview, she will sit in the waiting area from early in the morning probably until late afternoon and even then she may not be interviewed. The JRS lawyers are usually late because they are required to report first for duties at UNHCR Westlands and the UNHCR Protection Officer may or may not turn up. This means the planned number of interviews is unlikely to be completed. She will then be invited to return on another given date. Delays may also be occasioned by the failure to transfer files from the UNHCR Branch Office file registry. If she is interviewed, their interview will probably be interrupted a number of times. She may be issued with a rejection without appeal letter or a rejection with a 14 day appeal right. Otherwise, she will be asked to return on a specified date and issued with a 'pending letter' in the meantime.

> When she returns she will be delivered with her decision. She will be told that her letter is available for collection at the gate of the Wood Avenue compound. She will be handed it by one of the guards stationed at the gate. Reasons for the decision are not given. If it is a rejection she will have to deal with the shock, disappointment and distress alone for she will be told

that there is nothing anyone can do for her. If she is lucky, someone may find her and comfort her at the gate, but she will not be allowed in again.

If she has received a rejection with a 14 day appeal right she can go to the UNHCR Office at Westlands to make her appeal. No one tells her this. And the letter does not tell her either. If she finds out what to do it will be by chance or because she comes back to Wood Avenue on another morning to make her appeal only to be told that she must go to the Westlands Office (Gitari et al. 1998: 12–13).

'First country of asylum'

Most asylum-seekers in Africa end up seeking refuge in a country neighbouring their own. Many, however, leave their 'first' country of asylum and seek asylum elsewhere for various reasons that range from the fact that their rights were violated by their country of first asylum to the existence of family or friendship ties in other countries. In Kenya and Uganda, there were refugees from as far as Iraq, not to mention the large numbers of refugees from African countries with which Kenya and Uganda do not share a border. Almost all of them had not travelled to Kenya or Uganda directly. The reasons they were seeking refuge there were insecurity, the denial of fundamental rights, family reunion, or the threat of *refoulement*. Despite being rejected by UNHCR, many of them remained in Kenya and Uganda.

There is still no place in general international refugee law for the so-called 'first country of asylum' or 'direct flight' rule under which refugee claimants would have to seek asylum only in the first country in which they arrive (Hathaway 1991: 46; Marx 1995: 392). With the exception of the European countries that are parties to the 1990 Dublin Convention,[40] the lack of uniformity in existing state practice (Goodwin-Gill 1998a: 341) and the absence of *opinio juris* would inevitably lead to the conclusion that the 'first country of asylum' rule has not acquired customary status under international law.

At the time of the research, UNHCR's official policy on the first country of asylum 'rule' was ambivalent. Sometimes it affirmed that people who faced persecution and threats to their lives in their country of first asylum should not be returned there (UNHCR 1997b), although we found many instances in which this guideline was disregarded.[41] Occasionally, UNHCR offices in Europe criticised the notion of first country of asylum. Nevertheless, UNHCR usually promoted the application of the first country 'rule' in countries in the 'developing world'[42] because it:

> … has no objection to the idea of safe or first country of asylum which constitutes a useful basis for readmission agreements within states. Such agreements provide for the return of refugees and asylum-seekers to countries where they had or could have sought asylum and where their safety

would not be jeopardized, either within that country or by an act of *refoulement.*

Following the example of the European Union, such agreements could be drawn up within the framework for intergovernmental cooperation and coordination established by various sub-regional organizations throughout the world ... Where such agreements do not yet exist, UNHCR should periodically examine whether and how it may promote their setting up through its active mediation and by assisting the receiving state in responding to its obligations (UNHCR 1997b: 8).

UNHCR's acquiescence in and, later, active encouragement of the restrictive practices of European states regarding admissions probably goes back to the late 1970s, as revealed by a series of EXCOM conclusions. The erosion within UNHCR of the asylum-seekers' right to choose the country in which they can claim asylum began with EXCOM conclusion 15 adopted in 1979. This conclusion stated that the intentions of the asylum-seekers 'should *as far as possible* be taken into account', thus leaving a significant margin of discretion to states. Later, in 1985, EXCOM noted 'with concern the growing phenomenon of refugees and asylum-seekers who, having found protection in one country, move in an irregular manner to another country and expressed the hope that the problem this represents can be mitigated through the adoption of solutions in a spirit of international co-operation and burden-sharing' (EXCOM conclusion 36).

The reference to burden-sharing is particularly incongruous given that it is through such 'irregular movements' that states end up sharing the 'burden'.[43] The total number of refugees whose movement to other countries of asylum is organised through resettlement is insignificant compared with the numbers of those who leave their first country of asylum. Indeed, the strict enforcement of the first country of asylum 'rule' would result in countries adjacent to the conflict having to accommodate all the refugees.

In 1989, EXCOM conclusion 58 clarified the basis for UNHCR cracking down on 'irregular movements'. It referred to the 'destabilising effect which irregular movements ... have on *structured international efforts* to provide appropriate solutions for refugees' [emphasis added], and emphasised that 'refugees and asylum-seekers, who have found protection in a particular country, should normally not move from that country in an irregular manner'. As acknowledged by EXCOM, 'irregular movers' are 'composed of persons who feel impelled to leave, due to the absence of education and employment possibilities and the non-availability of long-term durable solutions by way of voluntary repatriation, local integration and resettlement'.[44] It goes on to condemn the 'use, by a growing number of refugees and asylum-seekers, of fraudulent documentation and their practice of wilfully destroying or disposing of travel and/or other documents in order to mislead the authorities of their country of arrival'.

While the adoption of these regressive conclusions might have been the result of pressure from donor states, which controlled over twenty out of the fifty-three seats in EXCOM in 2000,[45] UNHCR's application of this 'rule' in Kenya and Uganda dramatically exposed its failure to stand up for the convention – the main international instrument for the protection of refugees, the application of which UNHCR is mandated to supervise (sec. 8(a) statute 1950).

The term 'irregular mover' was with time expanded to include movements of refugees even *within* countries of first asylum, where refugees are expected to remain in camps and settlements. This is explicit in UNHCR's 1996 Comprehensive Urban Policy (UNHCR 1996c).[46] The presence of refugees in towns and cities, like those who move between countries, is seen as a threat to the present structure of international assistance as conceived by UNHCR. In fact, in another document, UNHCR complained that:

> ... urban refugees ... demand a disproportionate amount (estimated at 10–15%) of the organisation's human and financial resources. This has become an issue of concern if one observes that donors have become increasingly selective in terms of the programmes they support. They typically prefer activities focusing on local integration or voluntary repatriation and show little enthusiasm for long-term care and maintenance of urban cases, including upper secondary and tertiary education (UNHCR 1997b: 5).

Donors deserve part of the blame for the omnipresent fear of recyclers and irregular movers among UNHCR field officers, the headcounts routinely conducted in camps and settlements, and the efforts to impede free movement out of them. Such practices confirm that UNHCR's most salient concern is with maintaining its 'structured efforts' for the provision of humanitarian assistance – to which refugees are expected to adapt, rather than vice versa – and this takes precedence over the refugees' right to choose their country of asylum.

The shifts in policy emanating from Geneva were reflected in UNHCR practice in Kenya and Uganda. As early as 1988, the UNHCR protection report gave the 'first country of asylum rule' as a reason for denying refugee status to anyone who 'has immediately before coming to Uganda sojourned for two weeks in a city abroad where there is a UNHCR office' (UNHCR 1988: para. 2.1.2). In the case of a Congolese woman, whose application was rejected in Kenya, UNHCR wrote that it was 'of the opinion that you could have sought asylum in your first Country of Asylum in accordance with the standards laid down in International Conventions' (case no. 051/DRC/U/1998).[47] Was this misstatement of the law deliberate or due to incompetence?

In Kenya, Rwandans, Congolese, and Burundians were particularly affected by the blanket application of the first country of asylum 'rule'.

Although it was clear by late 1996 and early 1997 that neither Congo/Zaire, Tanzania nor Uganda were 'safe' countries of asylum for many refugees from the Great Lakes region, their cases were still systematically rejected. They ended up remaining in Kenya, but with no legal protection, sometimes for many years. A Rwandan refugee who was first interviewed in 1995 and was rejected was told by the protection office, 'Don't you know you have to go back to Zaire which is your first country of asylum?' He did not receive any reply to his appeal and, when he protested, his denial of status was reaffirmed. When, in 1998, Rwandan files were reopened, his was included 'pending word from Geneva' (case no. 032/RWA/K/ 1997).

The case of a Rwandan refugee who received an almost identical rejection letter was harrowing (case no. 01/RWA/K/1997). A 20-year-old man, G., was taking care of his 14-year-old brother. In December 1996, shortly after their mother had died in exile in Tanzania, they were forcibly repatriated to Rwanda. Within a few months, G. and his brother returned to Tanzania where they registered as Burundians for fear of being *refouled* again. They had to abandon the camps once other refugees threatened to reveal their real nationality to UNHCR.[48] G. decided to flee to Kenya where his application was denied. Submitting the case to UNHCR on appeal, we observed that it was wrong to state, as UNHCR had done once again, that the principle of first country of asylum is 'in accordance with the standards laid down in international Conventions'. We added:

> Your decision is also in contravention of Conclusion No. 15 of UNHCR's Executive Committee – 'Refugees without an Asylum Country' – which states that 'regard should be had to the concept that asylum should not be refused solely on the ground that it could be sought from another state'.

> In the light of these remarks, we believe that the best case that can be made for the first country of asylum rule is that it is not unambiguously illegal. However, we trust that you share our view that UNHCR should offer an example to states and, whenever it has an opportunity, it should apply the *best* practice, as well as that which reflects the highest possible standard of protection and which is in more definite conformity with established legal principles of refugee law as enshrined in the 1951 Convention (case no. 33/RWA/K/1999).

The senior protection officer in charge at the time had expressed her intention to stop applying this 'rule' when she had first taken office. During the so-called screening of the Rwandan and Burundian 'caseload' in 1998–99, the decisions on individuals who had been rejected on the basis of the 'first country of asylum' were also reviewed, and this time it was maintained that a 'blind' application of this rule was not going to be followed.[49] Yet G.'s case was decided in February 1999 and UNHCR itself admitted in its protection report that 'Branch Office has further applied the country of first asylum concept to irregular movers from neighbouring countries. However, all new asylum-seekers have had access to the asylum procedure (UNHCR 1999f).' Perhaps the only step forward was that at least in this document, the 'first country of asylum' was referred to as a 'concept' rather than a 'rule'.

In Uganda, there were only a few occasions when UNHCR did not promote a strict application of the first country of asylum 'rule'. As explained by UNHCR's protection officer in Kampala: 'UNHCR is not happy with this principle and is criticising its use in Europe, but we uphold it here in Africa to avoid pull factors.'[50] The application of the first country of asylum 'rule' had led to denial of refugee status to some 3,000 Rwandan Hutus who were staying in Oruchinga settlement in Mbarara district and who had 'explicitly made it clear that they don't want to repatriate' despite UNHCR's 'mass information campaign about the situation in Rwanda.'[51] On this occasion, UNHCR defended the Rwandan refugees' right to be 'screened'.[52] It argued that 'although the exercise would be enormous ... there may be refugees with compelling reasons not to return to Rwanda ... [and] these refugees are not criminals unless proved so.'[53] UNHCR's stance on this group of Rwandans was the exception. Many individual applications for recognition were rejected on grounds of 'first country of asylum'.[54] When the government rejected 700 Somalis on these grounds, UNHCR did not object.

Further evidence that the application of the first country of asylum 'rule' emanated directly from Geneva and was not simply the result of isolated bad practices is contained in a 1995 report. During a mission to Uganda, UNHCR's senior legal adviser for Africa discussed the case of the '3,500 Somalis who were to be transferred from Kampala to Nakivale camp' (UNHCR 1995e), only fifty of whom had accepted the move. UNHCR decided that 'those remaining in Kampala are no more receiving from UNHCR any material assistance except a group of 120 vulnerable cases. So far, there is no major problem as far as this caseload is concerned (ibid.).' This senior UNHCR official then suggested that 'as most of these Somalis came from first countries of asylum, mainly Kenya, the BO [branch office] may wish to apply more vigorously the principle of first country of asylum whenever possible (ibid.).'

There have been some important decisions by courts on the first country of asylum 'rule' that stand in marked contrast with the regressive and restrictionist practice of UNHCR. Interestingly, some of these decisions come from the UK, which, as a party to the Dublin Convention, is to an extent bound by this rule, unlike Kenya and Uganda. The House of Lords affirmed a decision of the Court of Appeal which had prevented the Secretary of State from deporting refugees to their 'first country of asylum' – Germany and France in this case – on the grounds that they would in all likelihood have been sent back to their countries of origin, since courts in

Germany and France do not recognise non-state persecution as coming under the refugee definition in the 1951 Convention.[55]

Credibility

In part owing to difficulties in obtaining evidence in refugee cases, 'lack of credibility' has become one of the main grounds for denying refugee status in many countries (Goodwin-Gill 1998a: 39ff).[56] National and UNHCR guidelines on the assessment of credibility (UNHCR 1989; IRB 1999) were not followed by UNHCR in Kenya and Uganda.[57] Rejections on grounds of lack of credibility were numerous, especially in the context of the 'screening' of Rwandans conducted in Nairobi in 1998–99, since it was difficult to find evidence that could justify exclusion: 'You do need to go into exclusion, if you can catch them on credibility.'[58] Lack of credibility could easily be abused as a reason for rejection because specific details for rejections were not given. UNHCR interviewers were not therefore encouraged to structure their analysis of a testimony and their decisions in rational terms. Had they been required to spell out which aspect of a particular testimony revealed 'lack of credibility', many bad decisions could have been avoided.

In both countries, interviews seldom lasted more than thirty to forty minutes, and some were much shorter.[59] Although friendly formalities sometimes preceded interviews, applicants were told nothing about their rights, the refugee definition, and the burden of proof that they were expected to satisfy.[60] The style of interviewing was inquisitorial. As Buregeya put it, 'It is not the number of questions as such that was overwhelming; it is the cynical, arrogant, and intimidating tone in which they were asked. Cold cynicism, hot arrogance and subduing intimidation. She [the interviewer] displayed a good combination of all three' (1998). Another refugee, a lawyer, reported that some of the people that he had been assisting were 'body searched' by JRS staff in order to verify if they were hiding documents, since it was believed that Rwandans often misrepresented themselves as Burundians (Bucyana 1997: 18).

It was often the credibility of the applicant as a person that was assessed rather than the credibility of the facts adduced in the application for asylum. Inconsistencies that were immaterial to the basis of the claim were considered decisive, as one interviewing officer in Kenya explained: 'Since he [the applicant] has not been consistent before, I cannot know if the story about his persecution is credible.'[61] In Kenya, great importance was given to 'consistency in the chronology of events.'[62] In Uganda, a subjective assessment of credibility took clear precedence over the analysis of the facts. For example, when an Ethiopian asylum-seeker told the UNHCR associate protection officer who was conducting the interview that he had used a pseudonym to escape from Sudan, the response was:

'Oh, so you tell lies.' The interview was abruptly concluded, and his asylum application rejected (case no. 168/ETH/U/1998).

With few exceptions, the climate of the interviews was dominated by disbelief and suspicion, and at times it was overtly hostile and aggressive. Most of the applicants were presumed to be 'liars' and the interviewer saw it as his or her job to 'catch' them. In Kenya, during a status-determination interview in May 1997, questions like 'Why should I believe you?' were asked in a confrontational tone. In another case, a Rwandan refugee, who, having being granted status, was referred to Kakuma refugee camp, explained that, as a Tutsi, he would not feel safe in Kakuma camp, where the Rwandan community was comprised almost exclusively of Hutus. His request to remain in Nairobi was supported by UNHCR's social services section but, when he met the person in charge of 'screening' at Ngong Road, he was told dismissively that nothing else could be done about his case, and that he and his family had no option but to go to the camp. Frustrated at this response, the man asked the UNHCR official if that meant he thought that everything he and his wife had said were lies. 'Yes, they are lies', replied the official, as he walked away shrugging his shoulders. This particular refugee had worked as an interpreter for the Human Rights Field Operation in Rwanda and had been forced to flee because of his refusal to pass confidential information to the Rwandan authorities. He had managed to withstand the pressure while the field operation was still in the country but, after its abrupt termination, like a number of his colleagues, he found himself in a vulnerable position (case no. 34/RWA/K/1999).

The assessment of credibility frequently depended on what the interviewer was capable of believing. If the testimony did not come within the interviewer's *Weltanschauung*, the application was likely to be rejected as 'non-credible'.[63] Although interviewers cannot be expected to be infallible, they should be prepared to question their assumptions and broaden their knowledge. When they do not do so, they can make serious mistakes.[64] Instead of asking themselves, 'Why do people omit or change information, and, what can I do to minimise the chances of this happening?', interviewers engaged the applicant in what for them was tantamount to a battle of wits. 'They think they can cheat us, but we can understand when they are lying,' said another UNHCR protection officer. Believing someone who lied was a sign of naiveté; unmasking or catching the 'liar' a sign of competence and shrewdness. Interviewers attached excessive importance to the assessment of demeanour – a manifestly problematic exercise especially in cross-cultural encounters – looking out for signs that betrayed the applicant and interpreting demeanour on the basis of an over-simplified hermeneutics of human communication: failure to show emotions = callousness and a coldly planned 'story', not looking at the interviewer in the eyes = lack of honesty, and so on.

The impact of this subjective bias can be reduced by up-to-date and comprehensive information on the country of origin, an in-depth knowledge of the cultures of the applicants, and, most importantly, by approaching each individual case with an open mind. In Kenya, consultants hired to interview Rwandan asylum-seekers in 1998–99 were actually offered a more exhaustive training than had been the case in the past. However, wrong decisions based on the lack understanding of the socio-cultural and political context of Rwandan refugees were still frequent. For example, one of these consultants argued that 'a person who says that somebody in Arusha [an accused person at the International Criminal Tribunal for Rwanda (ICTR)] has not killed is clearly not credible and we will reject him for lack of credibility' – a position premised on the assumption that 'wrong' beliefs (in someone else's innocence or in any other fact reported by others) are necessarily held in bad faith.[65] As it happened, a couple of years later, the ICTR did acquit an accused person.[66]

UNHCR sometimes attempted to verify the credibility of a testimony by soliciting information from other refugees or NGO officials who worked closely with refugees. For example, one applicant was asked to provide information about other Congolese refugees (case no. 026/DRC/U/1999). Reception centres such as the hostel run by the Salvation Army in Kampala were usually hotbeds of gossip. The captain of the Salvation Army was asked by UNHCR to write down information that he heard in the centre.[67] Refugees were aware of such tactics and this resulted in great distrust of UNHCR. In one case we interviewed in Kenya, D. said he felt insecure because he was discriminated against by other refugees, who frequently accused him of spying for UNHCR (case no. 003/SUD/K/1998).

In some cases, refugees realised that it was unwise to tell the truth. In Kenya, owing to the strict application of the first country of asylum 'rule', many refugees omitted details about their journey because they feared that, if they said they had spent some time in another country, their applications would be rejected. In the words of one such refugee:

> They often force us to tell lies in order to receive their protection. If you don't lie, it is really difficult to obtain a protection letter at the JRS [Wood Avenue]. When you tell the truth, they will tell you outright to go back to your first country of transit, or they just look for some other way of denying you the protection letter (case no. 030/BUR/K/1997).

Status-determination interviewers should realise that questions about travel and documents are those to which many refugees are hesitant to give truthful or complete answers, because they 'are often suspicious, or reluctant to identify those who helped them, when asked to reveal the details of how they left their country' (Monnier 1995: 314). Although 'these questions rarely have relevance except as another test of credibility' (ibid.), interviewers liked to dwell on them as they saw that this was one area in which they could 'catch' applicants.

Exclusion

Article 1(F) of the 1951 Convention refers to the 'exclusion' clauses, which allow states to exclude from refugee status certain categories of asylum-seekers – such as those who have committed war crimes, crimes against humanity, or serious non-political crimes. These clauses were not the object of much attention until after the Rwandan crisis. The UN responded to the calls for prosecuting those responsible for the genocide by establishing the ICTR in November 1994, which, four years later, delivered its first judgment.[68] In the meantime, reports by human rights organisations (African Rights 1995a) and the media claimed that 'UNHCR was feeding the *génocidaires*' and that the 'real' refugees in the camps for Rwandans in eastern Zaire and Tanzania were under the iron fist of the extremists, some even questioning whether there were any 'real' refugees at all in those camps. At the same time, UNHCR was criticised by many Rwandan refugees for discriminatory practices. For example, the Rally for the Return of Refugees and Democracy in Rwanda (RDR) hired a lawyer who wrote to UNHCR in December 1995 to complain about its handling of the Rwanda problem and its perceived siding with the Kigali government.[69] One accusation was that UNHCR was using lists of *génocidaires* that originated from Kigali. The RDR represented a small minority of Rwandans in Nairobi who could at least afford to hire a lawyer to voice their concerns; the others, who did not subscribe to the RDR's extremist political agenda, could not.

As a result of a shift in foreign policy in the mid-1990s that brought the US close to the Kigali government, the treatment accorded to Rwandan refugees in the region deteriorated. UNHCR, which was administering the camps in eastern Zaire and Tanzania where hundreds of thousands of Rwandans lived, came under pressure to identify *génocidaires*. Some of UNHCR's main sponsors also wanted a 'quick' solution to this problem by repatriating Rwandans as soon as was possible. A summit of the heads of state of Burundi, Rwanda, Tanzania, Uganda, and Zaire, organised by the Carter Center in Cairo in November 1995, called on UNHCR to take steps to identify the 'intimidators' in the camps who were allegedly preventing people from going back voluntarily. In practice, an 'intimidator' became anyone – not only Rwandan refugees but also NGO workers – who dissented from the 'party line' on repatriation and the situation in Rwanda under the RPF.[70]

UNHCR then instituted a comprehensive 'screening' process for Rwandans in various African countries.[71] In Kenya, this took place in

1998–99 and affected all Rwandans and Burundians, including those who had been granted status before. UNHCR maintained that this 'screening' did not have to be viewed as an exclusion process or as a typical asylum-determination procedure, but rather as a *sui generis* exercise, at least in part justified by the suspected presence of excludable elements. But the establishment of an ad hoc process without a precise legal standard was, to say the least, problematic.

Firstly, it does not seem that *génocidaires* were actually identified and captured as a result of this revival of the exclusion clauses. As an NGO worker who had worked with Rwandans for years put it: 'the real killers just would not go to the UNHCR screening'.[72] Indeed, the vast majority of those who had committed crimes in Rwanda during the genocide and who were in Nairobi in 1997, never sought UNHCR's protection. For example, in July 1997, Kenya transferred at least ten Rwandans (and a Belgian citizen) to the ICTR, but it is almost certain that none of them had a UNHCR protection letter.[73]

Secondly, there were some legal problems with the 'screening' (O'Neill et al. 1999). The *Handbook* does contain guidelines on the application of the exclusion clauses, but these are very general and had hardly ever been applied. UNHCR produced revised guidelines to deal with the screening of Rwandans (UNHCR 1997j), which stated that the evidentiary test for exclusion should be 'more likely than not', similar to the balance of probabilities standard which normally applies to civil cases. The expression 'serious reasons for considering' in article 1(F), however, suggests that a *higher standard of proof* ought to have been applied, as recommended by the Lawyers Committee for Human Rights (LCHR) (Bliss 2000).

Thirdly, decisions were normally taken only after 'verification' with the UNHCR office in Kigali through UNHCR's Great Lakes unit based in Nairobi, and the prosecutor's office of the ICTR. Another channel for verification was through the UNHCR headquarters in Geneva. Although neither the complete files nor the photograph of the applicant were sent to Kigali or to Geneva, the fact that names of Rwandans seeking asylum in Kenya were circulated in this manner is in itself problematic.

Finally, a presumption of guilt pervaded the process: 'during the interviews, we cannot assume that the person in front of us has *not* killed in the genocide', said one of the UNHCR lawyers conducting the 'screening'.[74] The interviews began with questions on events after 6 April 1994, and often gave no chance to the asylum-seeker to explain why he or she feared return to Rwanda. Rwandans were therefore subjected to an unusually severe test in having to prove not only a strictly individualised fear of persecution but also their lack of involvement in the genocide. Not surprisingly, the recognition rate was only 20 percent. This screening produced significant 'collateral damage', feeding into the negative stereotyping of Rwandans and resulting in a huge number of rejections mainly on grounds of 'lack of credibility'.[75]

In Uganda, there was no large-scale screening process as had happened in Kenya, but exclusion was invoked by UNHCR in the case of a Sudanese refugee who, having been forcibly recruited by the SPLA, had decided to defect and escape to Uganda (case no. 232/SUD/U/1999). This refugee had lived in Keyo III, a settlement in Adjumani district, for nine years where he had been an upstanding family man participating in community and NGO activities. He escaped to Kampala when the SPLA launched a recruitment drive. We brought the case to the attention of the protection officer, since this refugee believed that he and his family would be more secure if transferred to Kyangwali ('If I could go to Kyangwali where I would be a bit safer and join my uncle, I would say thanks to the Lord'). Our submission, however, elicited a totally unexpected result. The senior protection officer raised the applicability of the exclusion clauses to this case, arguing that '… generally speaking rebels are not refugees …. they are armed combatants … and the difficulty for UNHCR has been to isolate refugees from combatants' (Email: 16 September 1999). The application of the exclusion clauses should not normally be appropriate in the case of defectors, unless there is evidence that they have committed excludable crimes. It would be adding insult to injury if defectors or victims of forced recruitment were excluded from international protection. Moreover, if this refugee had lived in an official settlement for so long, why did UNHCR not raise the exclusion clauses earlier?

We also found two cases that had been brought to the REC in which exclusion was considered in all but name. They were Burundian soldiers suspected of involvement in the coup against President Ndadaye on 21 October 1993.[76] One of them was accused of being the driver for the man who was supposed to become president after the coup (GoU-REC 1997a); the other, who was stationed in Bujumbura the night of the coup, claimed that he had refused to drive a tank to the presidential palace and had not participated in the coup. The REC decided not to grant refugee status to either of them on account of their 'alleged participation in the military coup' (GoU-REC 1997c). In one case, the REC stated that the person had to be exonerated by 'a competent court or International tribunal' before it could grant status (ibid.). From the records of the REC meetings, it appears that the facts, as known to the REC, suggested that these two men's participation in the events of October 1993 in Burundi had been marginal. There was no indication that they had committed acts which could have been considered as war crimes or crimes against humanity (art. 1(F)(a)), or serious non-political crimes. This decision of the REC was taken under pressure from UNHCR. Senior UNHCR officials had conducted a mission to Uganda the year before and had examined the case of these Burundians. Until that point, the REC had seemed inclined to grant them status, a decision which UNHCR 'did not endorse' (UNHCR 1996i). It was therefore 'recommended that efforts should be made to obtain more information from Burundi and, also to inform the International Commission of Inquiry' (ibid.). The fact that the Ugandan government had decided to proceed with caution and to give the applicants the benefit of the doubt should have prompted UNHCR to do the same, in the absence of other clear and convincing evidence that pointed to their excludability.

The identification of combatants in refugee camps is related to the question of exclusion. EXCOM conclusion 94 refers to both the application of the exclusion clauses and the screening of refugee population in order to identify 'armed elements' as tools for preserving the civilian and humanitarian character of asylum. If exclusion as a legal process is fraught with difficulties, the screening and internment of combatants is even more problematic. The standards that should apply are not clear; nor is it clear how such a complex process could be put in place in the midst of an emergency.

Cessation

The cessation clauses (art. 1(C)(2)(5) of the 1951 Convention), covering the withdrawal of previously granted refugee status, have also been applied inappropriately on various occasions. This was sometimes done in respect of individual cases, but on other occasions – and even more problematically – the cessation clauses were applied to entire groups. An example of the application of the cessation clauses to individuals was UNHCR's decision to cease the status of a Congolese refugee in Uganda (case no. 052/DRC/U/2000). UNHCR wrote to him:

> On or about 25-11-99 after what we may consider a coincidental encounter with one of our staff members you then showed up at our offices in Kololo. We then inquired with Salvation Army and they confirmed that you had left the hostel in a diplomatic vehicle belonging to the Congolese Embassy.

> UNHCR believes that by your actions you have clearly demonstrated that you are no longer at the same level of danger in this country as previously assessed by our office. UNHCR also considered your actions and your relations with the embassy of your own country as amounting to availing yourself of the protection of your country of origin.

Having referred to the cessation clauses in the 1951 Convention, the UNHCR letter then concluded that 'UNHCR would henceforth stop any action related to your assistance and protection'.

This action was simply punitive. UNHCR had been protecting this refugee at the Salvation Army as a high-profile security case. They had agreed to have his case transferred to Kenya where he would be further away from RCD intelligence. When UNHCR discovered he had not used the transport money to go to Kenya, but was still waiting for his wife (who was crippled), they evicted him from the Salvation Army hostel. As it happened, this refugee had been persecuted by the Rassemblement Congolais pour la Démocratie (RCD), not the Congolese government, a fact that he explained in a letter addressed to the high commissioner, Mrs Ogata (9 December 1999). Furthermore, the chargé d'affaires of the embassy in Uganda was a personal friend of his. When he was thrown out of the Salvation Army, he had no place to go and accepted the offer of his friend.

We wrote to the UNHCR senior regional protection officer in Addis Ababa, arguing that UNHCR had improperly applied the cessation clauses. In fact, legal precedents and writers' opinions indicate that reavailment of the protection of the country of origin on an occasional basis should not automatically warrant cessation of status (Goodwin-Gill 1998a: 81–84; Hathaway 1991: 192–6).

Cessation of refugee status en masse is also problematic, as acknowledged by UNHCR itself (2003a).[77] In Uganda, a controversial issue was the status of a group of Rwandan refugees who had lived there since 1959–60 and who, unlike most other Rwandan refugees in Uganda, had decided for various reasons not to go back to Rwanda in 1994. In one case the REC commented: 'On the issue of clarification of the status of the 1959–65 Rwandese caseload following the end of humanitarian assistance by UNHCR in view of article 1(5) of the 1951 UN convention, the Chairman informed the committee that the cabinet is to discuss the issue and come out with a clear policy in regard to this caseload' (GoU-REC 1996). In one case, despite the absence of a clear policy, the REC records reveal that 'The Chairman informed the committee that a letter to the above effect [cessation of refugee status] was signed and served to him. Immigration department informed the committee that following the cessation of his status, it has given him a 30 days notice to leave the country' (ibid.).

The policy was later revised and a memorandum was prepared by the Ministry of Local Government (MoLG) – a noteworthy example of good practice. It noted that most of the Rwandans from this early period had repatriated, and that UNHCR had ceased giving humanitarian assistance to them. It outlined the three durable solutions that were available to the Rwandans who were left in Uganda: voluntary repatriation; naturalisation which was now available to them under the 1995 Constitution; and application for continued recognition as refugees (GoU-MoLG 1997).

Another instance of cessation of status en masse was in respect of pre-1991 Ethiopian refugees – that is, those who had fled the Mengistu regime. UNHCR took this step in 1999 for all Ethiopian refugees from this period in the Horn of Africa and East Africa regions, despite the still repressive human rights situation in Ethiopia: 'Wide-scale human rights violations ... in the context of the government's suppression of armed insurgency and political dissent' (HRW 1999b); the arrest by militias of the Ethiopian People's Revolutionary Democratic Front (EPRDF) of 'thousands for months without charge or trial' targeting in particular 'opposition activists, editors of the private press, and leaders of labor organisations' (ibid.). Only a handful of opposition parties could maintain a 'precarious presence' in Addis Ababa, but not in the rural areas (ibid.). Amnesty International stated that '10,000 political prisoners arrested in earlier years remained in detention, most without charge or trial' and that '"disappearances" and extrajudicial executions' were reported (Amnesty International 1999).

To justify its actions, UNHCR presented an almost rosy picture of the situation in Ethiopia in a inter-office protection memorandum:

> With the collapse in 1991 of the military regime of Mengistu which had banned all opposition activities in Ethiopia (1974–91) and had led to the exodus of thousands of Ethiopians in search of protection outside their country, a fundamental and durable change took place in that country so as to generally remove the reasons for fearing persecution of those Ethiopian refugees who had sought protection outside their country before 1991. A coalition government was formed from many political organisations and regional and local government elections were held. A new constitution was ratified in 1994 by an elected constituent assembly and a federal system of government was established. In 1995, democratic elections were held. The government of Ethiopia has, in addition, taken a number of measures to create conditions conducive to the return home of its nationals who had sought asylum outside. These include, *inter alia*, the proclamation of the right and freedom of every Ethiopian national to return to Ethiopia without fear of prosecution on account of having been a refugee. The government also announced its commitment to facilitate the return to Ethiopia of any Ethiopian refugee who wished to do so. It signed various tripartite voluntary repatriation agreements with UNHCR and countries of asylum in 1991, 1993 and 1994 … (UNHCR 1999i)

Refugees were given a deadline of 1 March 2000 'to come forward with any request for continued protection' (ibid.). UNHCR also stressed that 'acquired rights which individuals concerned may possess' ought to be protected. 'Particularly compelling reasons' which could justify failure to return were 'strong family, social or economic links' and the case of 'former refugees' whose children could be de jure or de facto stateless (ibid.). However, UNHCR simply 'recommended that the authorities' in the countries of asylum should allow continued presence in these circumstances. The memorandum concluded that 'governments are expected to consult with UNHCR in order to meet the requirements of Conclusion No. 69' (ibid.). The memorandum also contained the outrageous proposition that 'international law also recognises and, indeed, requires that exile should not go on or be perpetuated forever particularly without a good cause' (ibid.). *Even if* this were a case of supererogation on the part of host states, why did the 'refugees' protector' consider it necessary to call on states to do *less*? In reality, there is no evidence, in treaty or customary international law, of a principle that exile should not go on 'without a good cause', and this was yet another unsettling example of the way in which an institution created to supervise and promote compliance with refugee law was prepared to distort that law in order to promote its own bureaucratic priorities.

Conclusion

The widespread unfairness in UNHCR-led procedures in Kenya and Uganda deterred many potential refugees from even applying for refugee status.[78] They also knew that, even if they were accepted, they would only receive a 'protection letter', which meant little or nothing, and that they would in all likelihood be requested to go to one of the camps or settlements. UNHCR chose to disregard those who did not approach its offices; estimates of their numbers, or a statement acknowledging their existence, seldom featured in its reports. When UNHCR was criticised for its procedures, its reply was often couched in the careful language of diplomatic niceties. For example, in response to an enquiry by People for Peace in Africa, a religious organisation which was approached by many refugees from the Great Lakes region, the UNHCR senior protection officer, Annika Linden, wrote: 'Please be assured that UNHCR has an efficient and effective process of conducting interviews for the status determination of refugees. Both initial and appeal interviews are modelled on international UNHCR guidelines, which are uniform throughout our offices worldwide. Applicants who follow the proper procedures have their claims fully addressed under the mandate of UNHCR' (UNHCR 1996h).

The main problem was that, for the most part, refugee-status determination was not seen as proper legal process by those involved. Asylum-seekers were seen simply as 'persons in need of assistance' – rather than as rights holders entitled to an impartial and fair determination of their status. Resource constraints were used to justify the disregard for procedural guarantees. Frequent changes in protection staff meant that there was little incentive to challenge the underlying problems in the system.

Governments, on their part, seemed ambivalent about the role of UNHCR in status determination: they resented what they perceived, at some level, to be a usurpation of power, but were also relieved not to have to deal with the 'problem'. Neither governments nor UNHCR itself realised that UNHCR could not – and should not – replace them, and that by assuming responsibility for status determination UNHCR weakened its ability to promote respect for refugee law. Indeed, when, in the late 1990s, the adoption of new refugee legislation was discussed, UNHCR was noticeable for its encouragement of *restrictive* provisions (UNHCR 1998i).[79] After all, how could it credibly and effectively press national governments and parliaments to introduce the very guarantees of fairness in the status-determination procedures that it was flouting?

Notes

1. UNHCR placed seventeen countries in the 'both/unknown' column, meaning either that it was unknown – to UNHCR in Geneva – just who was in charge of status determination, or that UNHCR and the host government were doing it jointly (UNHCR 1999b). This document covers only 142 countries; it does not include, for example, Israel, one of the countries in which UNHCR determines refugee status. It also puts Uganda in the 'both/unknown' category, although UNHCR's role there, as we shall see, was predominant.
2. Interview with Henry Domzalsky, senior protection officer, UNHCR branch office, Dar Es Salaam, 1 August 2000. The interview was conducted during a fact-finding mission for the organisation Article 19 (Carver and Verdirame 2001).
3. Confusion also arises because of the laws and policies of resettlement countries. They require an individualised status-determination process and the US insists that a refugee meet the criteria of the 1951 Convention since under US legislation the refugee definition coincides with the Convention definition.
4. Art. 77 (9), Constitution of Kenya. The Constitution of Uganda contains two relevant provisions: article 28(1) protects the right to a fair hearing, and article 42 the right to just and fair treatment in administrative decisions.
5. The Lawyers' Committee for Human Rights (LCHR) has produced a similar listing of standards of fairness that ought to apply in status determination, including during the exclusion procedure (Bliss 2000: 99–100). The only difference is that the right to an oral hearing or interview features more prominently in the LCHR list than it does in Alexander's list.
6. Their protection function may however have been limited by the lack of information about country of origin. For example, in 1991, according to the permanent secretary of Home Affairs, a UNHCR protection officer had advised the Eligibility Committee that no one but 'elites' from Ethiopia would have a reason for seeking asylum. The same protection officer had accused one Ethiopian woman whose child had died during the flight to be 'just a prostitute'.
7. However, the instrument of ratification was not deposited by Kenya until February 1993. On 25 February, OAU member states were officially informed. The UNHCR branch office did not find out about these events until June 1993 (UNHCR 1993a: para 1.1.1).
8. It was also responsible for the entire programme organised for refugees in camps.
9. At the time, UNHCR's office was completely chaotic. Fr Eugene Birrer who set up the Wood Avenue facility found boxes of letters addressed to refugees, many containing remittances that had not been delivered for several years. He put up a list of recipients so that such letters could be collected. By 1997, however, with the pressure of the asylum work this office had assumed, this service and many others had declined or disappeared.

10. Although the government had removed itself from asylum-determination procedures, it continued sporadically to assist individuals who came to its offices and to grant asylum on at least some occasions.

11. In one Kenyan case we interviewed, UNHCR referred O. to MoLG for security clearance before considering his asylum status claim. MoLG referred him to the Uganda People's Defence Forces (UPDF) who questioned O. for two weeks before informing him that he would not be granted status in Uganda because of 'a revival in the East African Community.' This decision was apparently not questioned by UNHCR and O. was subsequently deported to the DRC to seek asylum there (case no. 219/KY/U/2000).

12. In 1999, the refugee office came under the newly created Ministry of Disaster Preparedness and Refugees in the Office of the Prime Minister.

13. Interview with Mr Benon Mujuni, Department of Immigration, 9 December 1997.

14. The number of refugees received by InterAid in the same period dwarfs those who went through the government process. In 1998, InterAid saw 8,327 refugees.

15. Interview with Mr Carlos Twesigomwe, DoR, 2 December 1997.

16. This could have been in the interest of these refugees were UNHCR to have taken action to protect them from the major threats such as militia groups from the DRC and southern Sudan.

17. Note from Douglas Asiimwe, 18 November 1999.

18. Note from Douglas Asiimwe, 21 January 2000.

19. In the meantime, protecting them from *refoulement* by the Rwandan government was no small feat, as the testimony of a member of the group, J., shows: 'The RPF government mounted pressure to either swipe, or snipe one of us but failed. We remained indoors for a period of six months, no body could go out even if you could get sick. And also Uganda increased the number of soldiers up to six to guard us' (4 May 2002); '… in an attempt RPF to take any of us [sic], they made three attacks. One involved even exchange of fire with our guards … we are shedding off psychological torture we experienced in that period, through looking forward to over come the challenges of the new land' (6 May 2002).

20. For instance, a Congolese professional couple, who had been escorted by a resident district commissioner to the Directorate of Refugees, were immediately granted refugee status on prima facie grounds. They then heard that to obtain the 'protection' of UNHCR, it was necessary to 'start all over' and they registered with the police station. When we interviewed them, they were attempting to get an appointment with InterAid without reference to the fact that they had already been granted status by the Ugandan government (case no. 183/DRC/U/2000).

21. He sent his manuscript to Mrs Ogata who, as is the usual practice, sent it back to the Nairobi branch office 'for comment'. He learned that his file had been moved as a result, perhaps accounting for the fact that even after waiting for two years, he was never interviewed by UNHCR. Excerpts were also published in the *Financial Times* (Mortimer 1998).

22. Interview with Ms Sicolastica Nasinyama, InterAid, 16 September 1997. Interview with Naome Yar, 22 October 1997.

23. Interview with Moses Wani, 15 October 1997. We have on file a copy of the medical bill and a letter from Dr Moro, Mulago hospital, confirming that the surgery took place. See also InterAid screening interview with Mr Wani, 26 September 1997.

24. The distribution of the post reflected a similar disregard for privacy and confidentiality. A member of staff from InterAid called out the names of those who had received post and handed the letters to whoever responded. No identification was required to ensure that letters were not being given to someone impersonating the real recipient.

25. Letter from Hans Thoolen, UNHCR representative, to Zachary Lomo, 22 October 1998.

26. Since the departure of this senior protection officer in December 2001, careless attitudes towards confidentiality appear to have reemerged.

27. A similar break-in at the offices of InterAid occurred during the research, but it was never reported in the press.

28. Interview with UN official [name withheld], Dar es Salaam, 13 August 2000.

29. Interview with Mr Wilfred Nderitu, Nairobi, 24 April 1997.

30. Ibid.

31. Interview with Ms Njoki Ndung'u, 18 June 1997.

32. Interview with the senior protection officer, UNHCR, 1 April 1999.

33. See UNHCR Statistics on RefWorld, www.unhcr.ch

34. A UN report had talked about 'acts of genocide' already being committed in eastern Zaire in 1997 (UN 1997). Human rights organizations continued to report on the conflict in Congo (e.g., HRW 1997b, 2000a). On Rwanda, Amnesty International reported that 'between December 1997 and May 1998 [at the time of the research] hundreds, and possibly thousands of people "disappeared". Thousands of others were killed by members of the Rwandan security forces and by armed opposition groups' (Amnesty International 1998a). The US Department of State confirmed that 'the RPA committed hundreds of extra-judicial killings … in the course of fighting the insurgency in the northwest … Victims of RPA operations included elderly persons, women, and children, as well as insurgents and suspected collaborators' (US Department of State 1998). A similarly gruesome picture of the situation in Rwanda in 1997–98 was depicted in Writenet (Prunier 1998), a source of country-of-origin information available to all UNHCR staff.

35. Interview with Monique Bama, UNHCR resettlement officer, Kakuma refugee camp, July 1997. In Cairo, a UNHCR interviewer was overheard saying, 'I can tell if they are going to be honest from the moment they walk into my office.'

36. It is hardly necessary to remind readers that 'events seriously disturbing the public order' were taking place in Zaire (then DRC) from at least 1996. This particular refugee was so traumatised by the events that led to his flight that he was suffering from psychotic symptoms. Perhaps it was only the help of friends with whom he lived that prevented his death from his repeated self-destructive actions.

37. The government denied them status en masse, and treated all of them as 'asylum-seekers'; it allocated 'one settlement (Nakivale in Mbarara District) where the Somalis are allowed to settle' (UNHCR 2000c).

38. Interview with T., Nairobi, 18 September 1997.

39. Interview with Peter Alingo, UNHCR, Nairobi, 25 April 1997. Peter Alingo, together with two other UNHCR employees, was later charged with threatening to kill the US ambassador in Kenya and with fraudulently inducing nine refugees to pay almost US$ 30,000 for being resettled (Kimemia and Nduta 2001). The trial was continuing at the time of writing.

40. The Dublin Convention (Convention Determining the State Responsible for Examining Applications for Asylums Lodged on One of the Members States

of the European Communities) did include the 'first country of asylum' rule as one of the rules to be followed.

41. *See* below.

42. In 1993, according to Priscilla Shabangu, then the head of her government's refugee office, UNHCR was trying to convince Swaziland to include the 'first country of asylum 'rule' in its legislation. This report was made during the Refugee Studies Programme's international summer school in 1993 which she attended.

43. The numbers of those refugees who can benefit from resettlement out of the 'developing world' are so few as to not constitute significant 'burden sharing'.

44. Is it not ironic that these are the very criteria, identified by UNHCR, for determining 'resettlement' as the appropriate solution? (UNHCR 1998a: IV).

45. The composition of EXCOM varies over time. Its total membership reached sixty-four in 2004.

46. The document referenced in this section was provided by UNHCR Geneva. We have learnt that it produced such an uproar within UNHCR that its circulation became restricted.

47. This woman did go to Uganda, where we interviewed her. There she was recognised.

48. In spite of his young age and what he has been through, G. was an entrepreneurial young man with a real instinct for business. His relative success attracted the envy of competitors who threatened to denounce him.

49. Interview with Ms Prütz Phiri, senior protection officer, Nairobi, 1 September 1998. Interview with Mr Ngumba, UNHCR consultant for the 'screening' of Rwandans, 3 September 1998. Both these interviews were conducted with Dr Bonaventure Rutinwa, Centre for the Study of Forced Migration, University of Dar es Salaam, during a fact-finding mission on behalf of the LCHR.

50. Interview with Michele De Maio, UNHCR protection officer, 23 January 1998.

51. Minutes of the 4th Meeting of the REC, 1997, 25 July 1997: 2, 3.

52. Interview with Mr Carlos Twesigomwe, MoLG, 2 December 1997.

53. Minutes of the 4th meeting of REC, 25 July 1997.

54. Carlos Twesigomwe, in an interview in December 1997, expressed strong feelings on the issue of first country of asylum 'rule'. He pointed out that if they did not apply this rule, Uganda would be burdened with many more refugees. Two examples of individual cases from our research are case no. 168/ETH/U/1998 and case no. 103/SOM/U/1999 (in both cases, the individual refugees had to flee the first country of asylum due to a lack of respect for their liberty and security; one of them was targeted because of his ethnicity and the other experienced insecurity while staying at Kakuma refugee camp).

55. *See R. v. Secretary of State for the Home Department, ex parte Adan* et al. (Court of Appeal and House of Lords). Under the 'accountability theory', to which countries like Germany and France adhere, the persecutor has to be the state or an entity affiliated with the state. Under the 'protection theory', followed by the UK, the US, Canada, and the majority of other states, refugees who fear persecution from nonstate agents can be recognised as refugees (Moore 2001). On the *Adan* case, *see* Endicott 2001.

56. The Swiss government has taken unusual steps to verify the nationality of asylum-seekers. They have employed 'linguistic experts' to listen to tapes of interviews to ascertain if a person is of the national origin claimed. In the context of the migratory movements that have characterised the history of Africa, the idea that one could 'verify' national origin in this manner is not watertight.

57. The Canadian guidelines are amongst the most useful and detailed. In particular, they assert: a presumption of truthfulness of the claimant's testimony (IRB 1999: 30); the need to substantiate a finding of implausibility with reasons (ibid.: 32); the importance of giving claimants an opportunity to address apparent contradictions and inconsistencies (ibid.: 40); and the precept that status-determination officers ought not to display 'excessive zeal in an attempt to find contradictions in the claimant's testimony' (ibid.: 45).

58. Interview with Mr Ngumba, UNHCR lawyer working in the 'screening' of the Rwandan and Burundian 'caseload', Nairobi, 1 September 1998.

59. This assessment is based on our observations and on interviews with refugees and with former and incumbent protection officers. In Uganda, some refugees reported that their interviews for status took only fifteen minutes. The two interviews which we could observe directly were much longer, but perhaps that was a function of the presence of our team member.

60. In one case, a Rwandan lawyer insisted on being shown the 1951 Convention before being interviewed; his request was denied.

61. Interview with a UNHCR lawyer working on the 'screening' of the Rwandan and Burundian 'caseload' (Njeri Migambi), Nairobi, 3 September 1998.

62. Interview with Peter Alingo, UNHCR, Nairobi, 25 April 1997.

63. Akram has analysed North American decisions in which the orientalist bias of the interviewer led to the rejection of applications (2000).

64. This was vividly illustrated in a documentary, *Well-Founded Fear*, shown on CNN and other networks. At one point, a Romanian asylum-seeker claimed that as a member of the Anglican Church she was persecuted in Romania. The interviewer from the US Immigration and Naturalisation Service asked her who was the head of the Anglican Church, and she replied that it was the archbishop of Gibraltar. The interviewer concluded that this woman was not 'credible' as he believed that anyone who is a practising member of the Anglican Church would know that the head of the Anglican Church is the archbishop of Canterbury. However, as it later turned out, the woman was not wrong: the archbishop of Gibraltar is indeed the head of Anglicans in continental Europe.

65. Interview with Mr Ngumba, *supra* note 58.

66. *Prosecutor v. Bagileshema* (ICTR-95-1A-T).

67. Gossip played a key part in the case of a Congolese family from Kinshasa (case no. 183/DRC/U/2000). Because of their 'Tutsi' physical appearance and their past wealth, this family was singled out by other Congolese. When, after our 'interference', the UNHCR protection office finally met the man, most of the questions were based on the gossip that had been circulating about the man's wealth and his identity. The man was given refugee status, but the protection officer remained sceptical of him and asked to be kept informed about his travels.

68. *Prosecutor v. Akayesu* (ICTR-96-4-T).

69. Letter to UNHCR from Ken N. Ogetto, Ogetto and Company, 7 December 1995.

70. *See* Carver and Verdirame 2001.

71. The UNHCR practice has been examined in detail by LCHR (LCHR 2002). On exclusion in general *see* Gilbert 2001. UNHCR developed new guidelines on exclusion in 2003.

72. Interview, Nairobi, 2 September 1999.

73. One unconfirmed exception may have been that of Chalome Ntahobali. It is undeniable that the presence of 'Hutu Power' extremists in Nairobi had been

a cause of distress for many Rwandan refugees. For example, M., who came from a 'mixed' Hutu/Tutsi family that had suffered many deaths during the genocide, had left Rwanda in the aftermath of the RPF victory. In Nairobi, he soon discovered that some Hutu extremists had settled there. He even met the person who had tried to kill him and who, he believed, was responsible for his father's death. This man, who was later arrested and transferred to the ICTR, harassed him verbally, on one occasion even threatening 'to finish the job [of killing Tutsis] one day'. It took several weeks of interviews and rapport-building with M. before he agreed to talk about these episodes. When asked why so many Rwandans in Nairobi, including those who, like himself, had been targeted in the genocide, still met extremists and, at times, socialised with them, M. explained that this was a 'survival strategy'. Owing to the lack of security and protection in Kenya, they could not afford to 'have enemies' (case no. 010/RWA/K/1998). Before meeting M., we shared the common view that there was at least some measure of collusion among Rwandan refugees with 'Hutu' extremists. In reality, reticence was often a consequence of fear.

74. Interview, *supra* note 58.
75. The zealous way in which some UNHCR offices directly applied the clauses in Africa, or promoted their application, had repercussions in other parts of the world. For example, the senior protection officer for the Middle East stated that '25 percent [of the 69 percent rejected applicants for asylum in Cairo] are *proved* to be war criminals, militia members involved in slavery and torture, or common criminals' (Interview with Vincent Cochetel, senior protection officer, UNHCR, 5 June 2000: 28) [emphasis added]. The total number of applications for asylum in 1998 in Egypt, where UNHCR was in charge of refugee status determination, was nearly 6,000, of which, according to UNHCR, 1,000 came from 'criminals'.
76. The murder of President Melehior Ndadaye was one of the murkiest events in the region and one about which, despite repeated attempts, the facts are still unknown.
77. New guidelines on cessation were developed in 2003. General cessation declarations in situations of mass influx are viewed unfavourably, and it is emphasised that they should never serve as an automatic bar to an application for refugee status.
78. The problems with UNHCR practice in status determination encountered in Kenya and Uganda exist in other countries, too: in Egypt, as we observed after 2000, in southeast Asia (Alexander 1999), and Turkey (Iranian Refugees' Alliance, Inc. 1995).
79. It later funded the drafting process in Uganda, but in 1996, Ulf Kristoffersson, the representative, was already complaining to Geneva that the law Uganda was producing was too liberal. *See* UNHCR 1996j.

4

Civil and Political Rights

Introduction

Refugee law and human rights law accord refugees fundamental civil and political rights, but in neither Kenya nor Uganda were these rights generally respected. Perpetrators of these violations were primarily the host governments, but UNHCR, NGOs, and refugee communities played a surprisingly prominent role in many violations, and at times were the main perpetrators. Even in the instances in which they were not directly involved in a violation, governments retained legal responsibility for failing to ensure compliance with human rights standards. Occasionally, host governments, UNHCR, and NGOs admitted that the rights of refugees were being infringed, relying on implausible arguments to justify their conduct; more often, the occurrence of such violations was denied.

Each right is examined below and illustrations of violations are given. As discussed in the preface, *one* violation is enough to say that the state was in breach of its obligations. The illustrations we have included are not exhaustive. We have selected those that were representative of the ways in which rights were violated.

A conceptual difficulty in this chapter – and in the one that follows on economic, social, and cultural rights – was deciding under which right a particular practice should be subsumed. In fact, practices such as sexual violence, forced recruitment of minors, and collective punishments, result in the violation of more than one human right. While realising that rigidly categorising a complex reality inevitably impoverishes its representation, we have adopted the catalogue of fundamental rights as the basis for the structure of this chapter, attempting, as far as possible, to organise the data under the violated right as seemed most pertinent.

Non-discrimination

A cornerstone principle of human rights law is non-discrimination. The 1951 Convention obliges states to apply its provisions 'without discrimination as to race, religion, or country of origin' (art. 3). Under general human rights law, the principle of non-discrimination covers a broader range of grounds than the 1951 Convention. Article 2 of the International Covenant on Civil and Political Rights (ICCPR) prohibits discrimination on grounds of race, colour, sex, language, religion, political or other opinion, national or social origin, property, birth or other status.

Both Kenya and Uganda are parties to the Convention on the Elimination of All Forms of Discrimination against Women (CEDAW), which entered into force in 1981. The preamble asserts that the principle of non-discrimination is the foundation for 'equality of rights and respect for human dignity'. Article 1 defines discrimination as 'any distinction, exclusion or restriction made ... which has the effect or purpose of impairing or nullifying the recognition ... of human rights and fundamental freedoms in the political, economic, social, cultural, civil or any other field'. Article 5 is particularly important, as it obliges states to 'take all appropriate measures to modify the social and cultural patterns of conduct of men and women' in order to eliminate prejudices and practices that result in discrimination. Other human rights treaties and declarations have confirmed that fundamental rights are to be enjoyed without discrimination.[1]

The constitutions of both countries contain a general prohibition on discrimination. However, Kenya's Constitution still has a gender-discriminatory provision, by allowing for the naturalisation through marriage only of the wife – not the husband – of a Kenyan citizen.[2] Uganda's Constitution of 1995 is far more progressive: not only does it allow for naturalisation of spouses regardless of gender; it also introduces the women's 'right to affirmative action for the purpose of redressing the imbalances created by history, tradition or custom' (art. 33(5)).

Gender discrimination: the role of culture and custom

Gender discrimination is cultural: it results from socially and culturally accepted practices, which governments refuse to challenge despite having a clear legal obligation to do so. For refugee women in Kenya and Uganda, the customary settlement of disputes in refugee camps was a major source of such 'culturally-based' discrimination.[3] The power of the community leaders (in Kenya, all men) was strengthened by the fact that in many cases parties to a dispute had no relatives present to act as mediators. Community leaders were paid by UNHCR to perform their dispute settlement function, and, in the case of the Sudanese community, they were usually associated with the Sudan People's Liberation Army (SPLA). Their facilities included three large cells for the detention of wrongdoers.[4]

Community leaders heard cases which, under Kenyan law, could only be heard by state courts. They also imposed penalties for conduct that was lawful under Kenyan law, for example for adultery: 'The man has to pay 600 shillings to the husband and he will not be detained, but the woman goes to jail. Most people put in the Sudanese prisons in Kakuma are there for adultery.'[5] In March 1997, we found a woman and her infant child in a cell in Kakuma, where they had been detained for seven days because of her alleged adultery. During other trips to Kakuma, we saw more 'adulteresses' detained with their children. The treatment of the man with whom a woman had committed adultery could also be severe. In some cases, he was chased by the husband and his relatives, who could even murder him. Reuer (1998: 7) recounts the case of a Sudanese man who was attacked by twenty men and beaten up. Although the community elders later found that he was not guilty, this refugee's life remained under threat and he had to sleep in a different house every night.

Another case that shows how community leaders were able to discriminate against women was that of S.A., a Sudanese refugee woman in Kakuma (case no. 005/SUD/K/1997). She successfully opposed the forced recruitment of her child by the SPLA, alerting some UNHCR and NGO officials. As a result of the attention that S.A. had managed to attract, the local community leaders apparently ruled out doing what they would normally do in such cases: abducting the child regardless of the mother's wishes. They decided instead to condemn her to 'social ostracism'. Her friends and other Sudanese in the camp did not dare speak to her, help to alleviate her daily hardships in any way, or give her any form of social recognition and acceptance.[6] During food distribution, she was often pushed to the end of the queue, having to stand in line in the scorching sun, while being verbally abused. She spent a few days camping outside the UNHCR compound, but by this time she was regarded as the 'problem'. Eventually she decided to risk the journey to Nairobi. When we discussed this case with the UNHCR protection officer in Kakuma, he responded that it was not in UNHCR's power to force anyone to be 'nice' to a particular refugee, ignoring the fact that the cumulative effect of gender discrimination, social ostracism, and her social powerlessness caused immense suffering and personal risk to her.

UNHCR in Kenya usually reproached critics of the application of customary law in camps with the response that 'it is their culture'.[7] UNHCR's annual protection report for Kenya in 1998 was almost unique in acknowledging the existence of 'a situation of prevalent harmful traditional practices and customs leading to rights violation' (UNHCR 1998b, chap. VI). 'Wife inheritance, sexual violence, domestic violence, forced marriages, and FGM [female genital mutilation]' were identified as the main problems. Despite this admission, UNHCR continued to fund the Sudanese 'courts' in Kakuma refugee camp. Yet, there were isolated instances in which traditional cultural attitudes were successfully challenged. For instance, a Somali refugee woman of 18 in Uganda was reluctant to enter a marriage with a Somali businessman twice her age, as she wanted to continue studying. The Uganda chapter of the International Federation of Women Lawyers (FIDA) took on the case. A lawyer called on the widowed mother and the uncles, telling them that in Uganda the law prevented forced marriages, explaining what sanctions they could face if they pursued the matter. The family gave in and the girl was allowed to pursue her education.[8]

Since gender discrimination was considered a 'cultural' issue, its victims were seldom treated by government and UNHCR officials with anything other than indifference or hostility. For instance, S., an 11-year-old Somali girl who had not been circumcised, had fled with her unmarried mother from Nakivale to Kampala, where her mother had died (case no. 105/SOM/U/1999) (Mwilinga 1999e). The Somali family with whom they had been staying were about to be resettled.[9] UNHCR thought that, once her foster family had left, S., whose only known relative lived in Holland, should 'return to Nakivale', where no specialised agency dealt with children and where, because of her condition, she would have faced even greater risks than those normally faced by unaccompanied girls (*see* UNHCR 1994c). Through the Uganda Association of Women Lawyers, a branch of FIDA, a magistrate appointed a Somali woman, who lived in the same household and was the recipient of remittances from abroad, as her legal guardian, while efforts to unite her with her uncle could proceed.[10]

The stereotyping of gender

The popularity in humanitarian circles of the axiom 'The majority of refugees are women and children' is surprising when one considers that the majority of people within *any* human settlement, community, or society are women and children.[11] By contrast, some refugee situations are characterised by a reverse gender imbalance: in camps like Dadaab and Kakuma, there were more men than women, probably a consequence of the fact that it is often easier for men to flee than for women.

These clichés are far from unusual in the humanitarian discourse on gender. The image of the refugee woman that emerged from the various gender policy documents that UNHCR prepared throughout the 1990s, and especially after the 1995 Beijing Women's Conference, was, ironically, akin to the representation of women in 1950s cinematography – feeble, vulnerable, gentle, kind, and peace-loving. Complementary to this construction of the refugee woman was the representation of refugee men as strong, resistant, heartless, and callous. These two ideas were synthesised in the 'women-first' approach, which pervaded the provision of humanitarian assistance and was usually flaunted by humanitarian organisations as evidence of their 'gender-sensitivity'.

Being assigned to the bureaucratic category of 'vulnerable' individuals, might have created some entitlement for women on the surface, but it was also a disempowering and, in some ways, debasing practice. Some refugees learned 'to simulate vulnerability in order to qualify for certain benefits' (Horst 2003: 75). For example, women who requested assistance from the Jesuit Refugee Service (JRS) in Nairobi sometimes lied about the whereabouts of their husbands, knowing that, if they had said that their husbands were in Nairobi with them, they would have been considered less 'vulnerable' and therefore not in need of assistance. The policy on 'vulnerability' therefore worsened the situation for some of them as they were left to deal with depressed or embittered husbands who had been turned by force of circumstance into liabilities.

UNHCR and NGO staff tended to implement only those measures that paid token respect to gender, required minimum effort, and were often ineffective.[12] In general, the way in which legal principles on gender discrimination were institutionalised and transformed into policy and conduct, resulted in contradictions and duplicity. Gender-awareness workshops were organised, while at the same time the almost entirely male 'community' leadership was given funds to impose its interpretation of customary law on other refugees, regardless of the limits set in international human rights law and even in the law of the host state. As we have seen, such 'traditional' interpretations that UNHCR promoted and supported, or at least acquiesced in, violated the rights of refugee women in numerous ways – from the imposition of penalties on 'adulterous' women, to the lenient sentences meted out to rapists (when sentences were imposed at all), to discrimination in all other matters including child custody, divorce, and dowry.

Ideas that were progressive in origin, like gender mainstreaming, were used as a justification for sidelining the gender-based problems that they were meant to address.[13] In Dadaab, the protection posts that had been created to deal with specific gender issues were abolished under the pretence of ' mainstreaming'. In Kakuma, owing to lack of substantive attention to gender, the wives of male applicants were often given little attention and presumed to have 'no case' for asylum. On one occasion, the claim of a woman who had suffered horrific torture in Uganda was ignored. This woman had been assaulted and burned with boiling oil, while her husband was arbitrarily detained by the security forces. When the family's case was finally submitted for resettlement, her torture did not feature in the referral (case no. 004/UGA/K/1997).

The 'gender movement' in the social sciences also started from the premise that, by looking at gender as one of the key relational and organisational elements in society, one can greatly improve the understanding of society (e.g., Indra 1999). Such ideas are echoed in some UNHCR policy documents.[14] In the institutional practice of humanitarian organisations, the interdependence of the two genders was usually forgotten, despite the incontrovertible fact that many of the problems of refugee women derived from the failure to address the problems of their husbands or their sons. For example, refugees often imputed the high incidence of domestic violence in the camps and settlements to the deleterious psychosocial effects that camp life had on men, in particular the increase in alcohol consumption. Other refugees, such as one Sudanese leader in Ifo camp, Dadaab, pointed to the gender imbalance within the community – *too few* women rather than too many – as a major source of problems for the refugee women.[15] In Kakuma, men outnumbered women by two to one. In Kiryandongo settlement in Uganda, where there was a high (and officially unreported) incidence of sexual and domestic violence, the three main causes identified by refugee women were alcohol consumption, the inactivity of men, and the fact that, because of the lack of sufficient accommodation, co-wives could not be separated (Mulumba 1998: 40).[16] Problems that affected male refugees, such as forced recruitment, were disregarded. To make matters worse, the age and gender of young refugee men were often seen as predisposing them to criminality, especially the commission of war crimes.[17]

The failure to understand the psychosocial needs of refugee men derived in part from misunderstandings of the impact that exile had on gender roles. Contrary to the most commonly held beliefs among humanitarian workers, refugee men were often psychologically more vulnerable than refugee women. The reason for this was that in societies in which men dominate the public sphere, the loss of social status as a result of exile is bound to affect them more than women, often leading to depression (e.g., Mulumba 1998).[18] On the other hand, the role of refugee women can in some respects be enhanced by the experience of exile: as the needs of their families grow, their responsibilities increase – in a sense they cannot afford to get depressed.[19] This does not mean that the psychosocial status of refugee women in Kenya and Uganda was overall better, but simply that their needs were different from the needs of a stereotyped 'vulnerable' woman whom exile had made even more vulnerable.[20]

One of the consequences of creating camps that can never become 'communities' (Hyndman 1996) is to engender a situation that promotes the sexual exploitation of women and girls. In Kakuma town, the emergence of commercial sex predated the establishment of the camp. Kakuma is a truck stop on the way to Lokichokio and the humanitarian operation in Sudan. The famine that hit the Turkana region in the late 1980s 'caused an influx of thousands of Turkana nomads to Kakuma which resembled an international refugee camp', even before the arrival of refugees (Stanley 1998: 14). During this time, the Turkana lost 90 percent of their cattle, 40 percent of their camels, and 80 percent of their small stock (ibid.). In their destitution, women and girls turned to prostitution (e.g., case no. 035/DRC/K/1994). The arrival of a predominantly male refugee population only exacerbated the situation. Very young girls were preferred because it was believed that they did not carry sexually transmitted diseases (STDs). Some Turkana were said to sell their daughters for US$ 0.35 (ibid.). 'Kambi Inama', the 'designated area' for commercial sex workers, consisted of about 150 houses situated just behind the chief's office and was set up by the local administration in Kakuma town, even though prostitution is illegal under Kenyan law. The women and girls working there included refugees (Stanley 1998: 24; *see also* Das Neves Silva 2002). Somali refugee prostitutes operated in secret for fear of reprisals from the religious leaders. The fee for a prostitute was between US$ 1.50 and US$ 4.00 but some could earn up to US$ 50, because Sudanese men were said to prefer Somali women. Turkana women, on the other hand, charged US$ 0.30 for sex (ibid.: 26; *see also* Das Neves Silva 2002).

Racial, ethnic, and other forms of discrimination

Rwandans, whether Hutus or Tutsis, were a group of refugees whose treatment was often discriminatory owing to the domestic and foreign policy interests of Kenya and Uganda. In Kenya, many of the Rwandan refugees who had fled in 1959–60 had been naturalised, while all of them were given permanent residence and work permits; in Uganda, the much larger number of Tutsi refugees from these years were never naturalised en masse, despite their prominent role in helping Museveni's National Resistance Movement (NRM) during the civil war. After most Tutsi refugees in Uganda had returned to Rwanda in 1990–94, the cessation clauses were invoked for the remaining caseload, exceptions being made only for individuals who could rely on 'compelling reasons arising out of previous persecution'.[21] The Hutu refugees who escaped forced repatriation from Tanzania by fleeing to Uganda in December 1996 were singled out because of their social origin. Their lack of protection and security in Uganda was in part the result of discrimination.[22]

In Kenya, Hutu refugees from Rwanda were relatively tolerated until July 1997 (e.g., case no. 001/RWA/K/1998). The Kenyan government, however, closed its eyes to the presence of various individuals linked with the interim government responsible for the 1994 genocide. Following a visit to Nairobi by Rwanda's Vice-President Kagame in July 1997, the Kenyan policy towards Hutu exiles took a U-turn and some were transferred to the custody of the International Criminal Tribunal for Rwanda (ICTR). Although Kenya's collaboration with the tribunal was a welcome change, the wave of arbitrary arrests of ordinary refugees that occurred concomitantly had no justification. Hutu refugees were the primary target of police roundups. They were detained without charge in police stations, in some cases with their children (e.g., case no. 009/DRC/K/1998). A handicapped minor was among those arrested: she was detained together with her mother, sister, aunt, and uncle, and was not released for two weeks (case no. 031/RWA/K/1997). Her father managed to escape arrest on different occasions, once by asking his neighbours to lock the entrance door to the house with a padlock from the outside. Two students in a well-known educational institution in Nairobi, which also catered for refugees, were kept in a cell for three weeks in spite of the interventions of their sponsors. These refugees not only held valid protection letters, but also had special 'authorisation' to reside in Nairobi and complied with the requirement of being able to support themselves. Arrested refugees were also concerned about what would happen to their belongings: 'The house and everything in it is just abandoned. The refugees would like to have a warning in order to have a chance to take the precious documents such as diplomas, or in order to take measure to safeguard their possessions' (ibid.).

Another group that faced discrimination in Kenya were Christian Somalis, who, especially in the camps, were often forced to conceal their religious affiliation for fear of reprisals from some of their fellow nationals. They were often accused of proselytising among other Somalis. Those who had converted to Christianity from Islam were often threatened with death – the punishment for apostates, according to certain interpretations of Sharia. A Somali refugee in Ifo, Dadaab, who had become Christian after being taught the Bible by members of the Canadian Baptist Church of Kenya, was moved to the Sudanese section, but he was still assaulted by a group of Somalis (case no. 027/SOM/K/1997). A Catholic priest told us that it was unsafe for him to visit the camps, because his very presence could jeopardise the safety of these 'closet Christians'.[23] In Kakuma, one Christian Somali was killed; his wife was later found hiding in Lodwar, afraid to go back to the camp. Another Christian family, living in constant fear, had to be kept in the 'special protection area'.

Muslim refugees, who lived as a minority in the predominantly Christian camps or settlements, also complained of discrimination. For example, in Mongola settlement in Uganda, there were sixty-five Muslim Sudanese families. One of them told us:

> ... they are saying we Muslims have our names registered in the SPLA offices and we are considered as collaborators of the Islamic North [the government of Sudan], the Christians consider themselves as the 'genuine' ones collaborating with the SPLA. It is a wound that cannot get cured. It is

already in their hearts and they hate us as Muslims ... There was a man who came from Kampala and cautioned us that our names [those of their leaders] are in SPLA offices and just yesterday, a neighbour was saying we can be picked at any time because we are Arabs and are considered to be part of the 'developed world'.[24]

He also complained that, when Ogujebe was destroyed, the mosque was burnt down, while 'the Christians' were allowed to dismantle their own places of worship slowly.[25]

Another group often discriminated against were Bantu-speaking Somalis, descendant in part from slaves and in part from indigenous minority groups. Some of them, especially in Ifo camp, were Christian. There were various reports in Kakuma and in the camps around the coast of verbal abuse and even assault against 'Somali Bantus'. The leader of their community in Kakuma complained that 'relations between Somali Bantus and non-Bantu Somalis are very poor weak [sic]; Somali Bantu are despised because they are not considered as true Somalis. Somali Bantus have no relatives abroad who sponsor.'[26]

Despite the political military alliance between the Ugandan government and the SPLA, Dinka refugees in Uganda, on account of their association with the SPLA and the war in Sudan, did not escape discrimination by both Ugandans and other Sudanese from Equatoria (e.g., case no. 137/SUD/U/1999).[27] Only a few refugees from this group were placed in the settlements, mainly in Kali I, blocks 6–8.[28] A special 'transit' centre, Mirieyi, was established for the majority. Its residents, which included a few Madi and Kuku wives, were provided with full rations since 'There were not enough women to farm'.[29] Mirieyi had gained a reputation as a place of 'rest and recreation' for members of the SPLA: armed men could often be seen marching from Mirieyi to the border.[30]

A very large proportion of the Dinka youth had been in camps in Ethiopia, and many of them had been abducted by the SPLA as small boys and taken for military training 'under the title of Red Army'.[31] Their handwritten stories of escape through Torit to Uganda are as horrific as those of the 'walking boys' who made it to Kakuma camp. In Kakuma some special programmes were introduced for these minors, but their special needs were completely ignored in Mirieyi.[32] A young man recounted his experience of discrimination under the heading 'The most hated tribe in Uganda is the Dinka':

People say, 'Why did the Dinka tribe follow us to take refuge, yet they were the causers of the war in Sudan' ... I myself when I came, I first stayed at the Catholic Centre of Torit Diocese at Kocha near Pakelle. After one to three months, I was told that we are taking you to the camp where you will be given food ... In the morning when I awoke, I saw a vehicle waiting for me. I rushed inside the tent and pick my little bag and climbed on the vehicle. We were with Catholic brother who was a driver. On the way I asked him, 'Brother, are these people to whom you are taking [us] not going to fight?' No, he said, there you are going to be protected by the chairman of the transit.

When we reached the first camp called Pachara, he stopped and to me he said that this is your place. I saw many people come to me with sticks, some with stones to stone the car ... they were using Acholi language and they were saying God has brought us Dinka. The Brother had seen what has taken place. He proceeded to the next camp and the same happened, until we can back to Kocha to live (ibid.).

As a result, the boy was enrolled in Biyaya Primary School and along with others, remained under the care of the priest until 'This man left [for] England in 1995 due to tribal problems which our tribe is facing in this country [where] everybody came to hate Dinka, including the citizens of Uganda.'[33]

Another boy described what happened in Ogujebe transit centre where he was first placed:

In transit I met some of my fellow Dinkas who came before I could come, therefore, I had to stay with them. The following day we were granted foodstuff and some few days later, we were fought by our fellow Sudanese who are not our tribe. These were most[ly] Acholi and Madi whereby they killed one of us. They fought us on no ground[s], the only reason they gave when they were questioned by the police officer was that we Dinkas are trouble causes in Sudan ... As the situation was arrested by the policeman, three days later we were brought back to Pakelle by UNHCR officers for safe custody. Meanwhile they were glancing for piece of land to accommodate us. As such they found Mirieyi.[34]

Others complained that the 'label of Dinka' had come to mean 'trouble':

... people are identifying us as fighters and impatient people ... The problem is that Dinka are Nilotic people and we are the ones who fight and cause problems. This thing [the stereotyping of Dinkas] they put it in policy. For instance, if I go to the settlement commandant with a request, they will accept someone before me and answer his need first because they see us Dinka as bad and quarrelsome. Most of the [Dinka] students here are self-sponsored in secondary school; they are having to sponsor themselves while others around are getting JRS and UNHCR scholarships. Also, when we go to work – no one will accept us for work here; Dinka teachers are also refused because their certificates are in Sudan. In Adjumani hospital, we have to wait for many hours because we are Dinka. There are now two people injured who passed [died] due to a lack of treatment in the hospital. In October 1996, we had a small boy who went to town in the evening and went to the video and was shot on his way back here. He was taken to hospital but no one cared for him. The RWC [Refugee Welfare Committee] chairman went to the settlement commandant to ask why no one in the hospital would care for him and he was told it's because he is a criminal.

When new people come here – 'new arrivals' – the CC [camp comman-dant] refuses us registration because he accuses us of just coming to collect ration cards and go back to Sudan. Some here have stayed for two years without cards. Those brought by the RWC are even refused. Even those coming from Kenya are refused. The RWC chairman stated that when there is a new arrival, I will write a letter and look at the new documents and take the person to the CC; he says, 'we don't want your people – you are just moving from place to place'; it is just for us Dinka because they say we move from place to place … (ibid.).

Right to life

The death penalty is still legal in both countries. Although capital punish-ment per se has not been prohibited under general international law, it should be imposed at the end of a fair trial and be limited to the most seri-ous offences.[35] In Kenya, it has been argued that these basic conditions are not satisfied (African Rights 1996: 193–8). In Uganda, we knew of many cases of refugees who were awaiting trial for treason, a capital offence, despite the obvious fact that treason is an offence that logically can be com-mitted only by nationals. They included Sudanese who had been arrested by Ugandan military intelligence in Koboko as suspected members of the two 'rebel' groups, the West Nile Bank Front (WNBF) and the Uganda National Rescue Front Two (UNRF II), suspected members of the former eventually being released by a decision of the government in 2000. The death penalty was also imposed for raping a minor ('defilement') (Bouman and Harrell-Bond 1999).

The main violations of the refugees' right to life that we identified resulted from extra-judicial killings, from rebel or bandit incursions into the camps and settlements, and from the deprivation of basic means of livelihood so extreme as to result in loss of life.[36]

In Kenya, the murder of Seth Sendashonga was the most 'high-profile' example of the extra-judicial killing of a political exile.[37] A Rwandan Hutu politician, Sendashonga had served as a minister in the Rwandan Patriotic Front (RPF) government after July 1994, but had subsequently defected to Kenya and publicly denounced the RPF authorities for their treatment of Hutus. A first attempt to kill Sendashonga had failed in 1996. The assailant was arrested and identified as an employee of the Rwandan embassy in Nairobi, but he was not prosecuted. Nevertheless, Kenya broke diplomatic ties with Rwanda, accusing the Rwandan government of having organised the killing. It was not long after the rapprochement between Kenya and Rwanda in July 1997 that the second, successful attempt was carried out. Because of the changes in the regional political situation, the Kenyan government's reaction this time was subdued. Within a few months, diplomatic relations were re-established with

Rwanda, and in 2000 the presidents of Kenya and Rwanda paid official state visits to each other. Sendashonga's wife and children were belatedly resettled, but other members of his close family remained in Nairobi (case no. 003/RWA/K/1998).

Extra-judicial killings like the one carried out against Seth Sendashonga are directly imputable to the country of origin that allegedly sent the hit squads. In such cases, the host countries' obligation to *ensure* the right to life means that they have to investigate the murders and prosecute those who are responsible.

Other evidence of the risks faced by many refugees comes from the testimony of M., a Rwandan refugee, who was subsequently resettled with his family in a European country (case no. 002/RWA/K/1998).[38] A survivor of the 1994 genocide in which many members of his 'mixed' family perished, M. fled Rwanda after members of the RPF arbitrarily took over his family's property and threatened to kill him when he attempted to seek justice. In Kenya, M. won a scholarship to attend a course in nursing at the University of Eastern Africa, Baraton, in Eldoret. He had to interrupt his studies when, in June 1997, he discovered that two Rwandan students who had been threatening him possessed guns. The police, who had arbitrarily arrested his wife in July 1997 and detained her for nearly two months, continued to extort bribes from him. In the previous months M. had been the victim of a whispering campaign that associated him with the *interahamwe* (the 'Hutu Power' militias) and the *abacengezi* (the 'infiltrators' – that is, the rebels that were operating in northwestern Rwanda). On various other occasions, M. and his family received threats to his life and, when we interviewed him in April 1998, he was sleeping every night in a different place for fear of being killed.

Attempts at extrajudicial execution were also made against V., a Ugandan refugee in Kakuma camp (case no. 004/UGA/K/1997). The second of these attempts took place while we were in Kakuma in March 1997. A Ugandan, registered as a refugee but in actual fact a member of the Ugandan external security service, was found in possession of bullets, and of a list of names of those he had been sent to eliminate. V.'s name was on top of that list.[39] He had been accused of being a collaborator of the Lord's Resistance Army (LRA); his name, together with three other officials working for the Northern Uganda Reconstruction Programme, appeared in a letter, found in the suspect's possession, from the director of the Internal Security Organisation (ISO), which instructed the army to apprehend them and 'to inform me about their arrest immediately'.[40] The reason why the Ugandan security suspected V. appears to be that he was an educated Acholi and had been captured twice by the LRA, managing to escape on both occasions. V.'s family included five children and his wife, who, while in prison in Uganda, had been subjected to horrific torture in an attempt to force her to disclose the whereabouts of her husband.

On one occasion in the 1990s, the Kenyan government was directly responsible for a series of extra-judicial killings of refugees in the Dadaab area. During a major security operation in August 1992, following the killing of four Kenyan policemen south of Dadaab, a pogrom against refugees took place. For days after the army left, bodies of Somali refugees were found around Dadaab (FIDA Kenya 1994e). The number of victims was said to be in the hundreds. A public inquest was finally started in 1994 and hearings began in Garissa and Dadaab. The matter was with the attorney general in 1996 (ibid.), but so far no prosecution seems to have been brought against any of the members of the security forces responsible for the killings.

Uganda was probably even worse than Kenya, when it came to ensuring the right to life of refugees against rebel groups such as the SPLA and the Rassemblement Congolais pour la Démocratie (RCD). Indeed, both these groups were supported politically and militarily by the Ugandan government, and the ISO was accused by the Uganda Human Rights Commission (UHRC) of involvement in the disappearances of Rwandan and Congolese refugees (Weddi 1998; Mutumba 1998a).

The *Monitor* in Uganda accused the Museveni regime of complicity with several disappearances of Rwandan Hutus. One of the first cases happened on or around 23 August 1996. K., who had formerly worked for the United Nations Assistance Mission in Rwanda (UNAMIR), was trying to flee to Mali via Entebbe in search of a safe country of asylum.[41] Prior to fleeing to Uganda, K. had been arrested and interrogated by the RPF on three occasions; after he escaped to Uganda with his wife and two children, all of his possessions were reportedly confiscated by the RPF (case no. 007/RW/U/1999). With the support of a columnist at the *Monitor*, he purchased a ticket to Mali. The journalist left him at the airport; a few days later he called the friend in Mali and was informed that K. had never arrived. This information was later corroborated by Ethiopian Airlines who confirmed that K.'s plane ticket had not been used. In February 1997, another *Monitor* columnist wrote an article about the abduction. He said that he was subsequently contacted by the RPF in Rwanda and received death threats. After K.'s abduction, his wife and children hid in Kampala while seeking resettlement through UNHCR with the assistance of her friend at the *Monitor*. At the time of our interview in October 1997, over one year after her husband's disappearance, her papers had still not been processed properly by UNHCR despite her urgent requests. Furthermore, she was not included in the interviews of the Joint Voluntary Agency (JVA) resettlement officers who came from Nairobi for resettlement applications to the US (*see* Amnesty International 1998b).

Reports of deaths in prison were also frequent. For example, in July 2000, a refugee, Mr Ndayizeye, was allegedly beaten to death while in police custody in Nakivale. The refugee had apparently been arrested after a drunken brawl. The policeman was arrested, but the investigation against him was conducted through the same Mbarara police. The surgeon who conducted the post mortem concluded that the man had died as a result of alcohol poisoning.[42]

Insecurity in the camps and settlements deriving from the activities of bandits and rebels often resulted in significant loss of life, as discussed below.[43]

Freedom from torture and from cruel, inhuman, or degrading treatment or punishment

Both Kenya and Uganda are party to the 1984 Convention against Torture and Other Cruel, Inhuman or Degrading Treatment or Punishment (hereinafter, the Torture Convention), as well as being party to other general human rights instruments that prohibit torture.[44] The prohibition of torture is also enshrined in both the Kenyan and Ugandan Constitutions, respectively in articles 73 and 24.

An essential element of torture as defined in the Torture Convention is that the act must be 'inflicted by or at the instigation of or with the consent or acquiescence of a public official or other persons acting in an official capacity' (art. 1). The term 'public official' must not be interpreted restrictively, and includes persons or groups exercising 'certain prerogatives that are comparable to those normally exercised by legitimate governments' (*Elmi v. Australia*). In our cases, the infliction of torture – or of a treatment or punishment of lesser severity than torture but still cruel, inhuman, or degrading in nature – was not always imputable to officials of the state. However, such acts were tolerated and at times instigated by state officials. In some instances, acts constituting torture or cruel, inhuman, or degrading treatment were committed by private security personnel employed by UNHCR, by UNHCR and NGO officials during headcounts, and by refugees themselves, in the exercise of the administrative powers that they had been granted in camps and settlements.[45]

Ideally, host governments, UNHCR, and NGOs should establish programmes to target the psychosocial needs of torture victims, of whom there were many among the refugees in Kenya and Uganda. Through interviews with Congolese refugees in Uganda, we gained a detailed and shocking picture of the situation in 1998–99 in the eastern Democratic Republic of Congo (DRC), where political opponents and members of certain ethnic groups were systematically tortured by the various factions, especially the RCD and the Congolese army.[46] With the exception of one or two voluntary initiatives, there was no support for these torture victims. In one case, in which the SPLA admitted in writing that an individual had been subject to torture in Sudan 'by some unknown SPLA people and killing of his brother', UNHCR still wanted to settle him in a camp in Adjumani or Arua district where the presence of the SPLA was well known and where even the nominal services for assisting torture victims that existed in Kampala were not in place.[47] Before the SPLA, this man had been tortured by members of the Sudanese army who forcibly circumcised him (case no. 131/SUD/U/1999).[48] The report compiled by the African Centre for Treatment and Rehabilitation of Torture Victims (ACTV) stated: 'The patient feels sad, fearful and tearful. He sleeps poorly and eats poorly and has lost weight. He has multiple aches and pains all over including stomach-aches and vomiting blood … He has multiple scars on his arms indicating severe past tying of his limbs.'

Acts by the state

The Kenyan Penal Code (a residue of the colonial period) still allows corporal punishment as part of sentencing, a practice that was inflicted on refugees and nationals alike. Although there was no evidence of harsher sentences being imposed on refugees than on nationals, the fact remains that refugees were subjected to sentences that were clearly in breach of Kenya's obligations under international human rights law. For example, in one unreported case, *Republic v. Mohammed Hassan*, a Somali refugee charged with breaking into a shop (Penal Code sec. 306), was sentenced to ten strokes of the light cane.[49]

In both Kenya and Uganda, conditions in detention often amounted to cruel, inhuman, or degrading treatment. In Uganda, we found refugees in each of the detention centres we visited in the north. The officers in charge of the prisons discussed the problems frankly. The officer-in-charge of Murchison Bay prison, for example, admitted that the prison, built to house 480 inmates, contained 1,642 men, of whom 70 percent were detained on remand. Of those who were serving sentences, a significant proportion had been transferred to Murchison Bay from other prisons because of its hospital.[50]

As for the treatment of refugees compared with nationals, only a few complained about being treated less favourably and about verbal abuses from Ugandan inmates; most of them, however, either did not raise the question or said that there was no difference in the treatment. Although our visits to prisons in Uganda focused on the treatment of refugee inmates, we used them as a way of campaigning for improving prison conditions for all (Harrell-Bond 1999c).

In Kenya, we interviewed refugees held in police cells in the aftermath of a major police roundup in Nairobi in July 1997, when the police rounded up entire families, detaining even young children. We also met refugees held in Lodwar prison. Conditions in the Kenyan prisons have been described as a 'tale of horror' (African Rights 1996: 180–98). The living conditions in the police cells were also appalling and the cells over-crowded, as E., a Burundian refugee held in Kilimani police station, recounted:

> The cell was a bit smaller than this room [the room in which he was inter-viewed measured approximately 5 m by 4 m] and contained forty people, both men and women. There were also four Kenyan children who had been there for some time and they did not even know why. They were not older than 13 or 14. As soon as we arrived at the cell, we were asked for '*kitu kidogo*' [something small]: the food was particularly bad and insuffi-cient and we had to pay bribes in order to receive more food. We had to pay bribes to take a stroll in the courtyard, to see our visitors, and to go to the toilet. Those who did not pay were told to wait for the use of the toilet, but they were never taken there. Many people had therefore to urinate and defecate in the cell. The smell was unbearable. We were all asked if we were Hutus, but in the cells there were also many Somalis, Ethiopians, Congolese, and Ugandans. I think the police were asking this because they were hoping to get more money from Hutus who, they said, had to be screened for the genocide (case no. 041/BUR/K/1997).

The police often demanded larger bribes from refugees than from nationals because refugees were believed to be 'rich', especially the Somalis. Refugee prisoners lacked adequate food, medical care, and cloth-ing, as well as moral support, since only a few had relatives in Nairobi who could visit or bring food or money. Friends and neighbours were sometimes prepared to visit them and provide support. In particular, a group of Burundian and Congolese young men in Nairobi was noticeable for the sense of mutual social responsibility that they had developed. During roundups, however, refugees normally felt too insecure to visit police stations where their friends were detained.

In the camps and settlements, the use of excessive force by police and camp commandants to maintain public order was frequently reported. In many cases, arbitrary beatings occurred. In Uganda, cases of beatings by camp commandants and the police stationed in the camps that were reported to us came mainly from Nakivale:

> More than one refugee reported having been either threatened or beaten – or both – by the Camp Commandant. Refugees fear the commandant, he is said to be seldom at his post, often intoxicated, verbally and physically abusive and takes bribes. Given the frequency and consistency of these complaints from all over the camp, it would appear that there is a duty to investigate the performance of this particular officer. Moreover, the exchange of correspondence between the Mbarara office of the OPM [Office of the Prime Minister] and this camp commandant confirms the problem is long-standing. Persecution experienced by refugees in the set-tlement have included a sadistic mock execution of a young refugee (Elder 1999b; and case no. 225/BUR/U/1999).

Although the actions of this camp commandant certainly did not reflect government policy, the fact that, in spite of many complaints, he was not dismissed shows that the state was unwilling to take action (case no. 053/DRC/U/1999).

Staff at InterAid had no compunction about directing police to use excessive force against refugees. After the review of his case by Dr Swai, UNHCR's medical officer, K., a Congolese, was allowed to remain in Kampala for three months during which he should have received financial assistance and medication. However, in that period, '... every time I was going to InterAid for medicine, I was chased away and [told] that my sickness is chronic and that I should not expect any medical assistance from them anymore. During this three months I did not receive any medical assistance.' At the end of the three months, in October 1999:

> I went to InterAid in order to enquire about my case. I met Mr Frances who immediately, without even listening to me, gave me a letter, asking me to leave Kampala and go to the camp. After reading the letter, I said that I cannot leave for the camp because of my health and that I have not paid the rent for the hostel at Mulago hospital where I have been staying ... I asked him to give me my allowance ... Frances told me to come the next day for it.

> The next day I came, but to my surprise, Frances told me that I would not receive money any more. I could not understand. Then he told me to see Sicola [the social worker] about it. I went to see her. She told me to go back to Frances. I got annoyed and went to Frances and told that they should not play with my mind like this. Frances shouted at me and asked me to stop disturbing him like that and told me to get out of his office.

> He then went out and told the two police guarding the office and told them to get me out of the building by force, which they did. I tried to protect myself by covering my stomach where my incision is [from the recent operation]. Instead of asking me to leave they started beating me inside the building. I implored them to stop beating me, but they refused to hear me. After some minutes, the doctor from InterAid came to rescue me, ask them to stop beating me. They stopped.

> ... Since that day I stopped going to InterAid (case no. 097/DRC/U/1999).

In this case, the policeman had received instructions from InterAid, but, because of his official capacity, his acts were still imputable to the state. In another case, a refugee, H.A., said that he had been walking on the side of the road, 'minding his own business', when a policeman demanded money from him (case no. 106/SOM/U/1999). After H.A. had handed over his money, the policeman took the butt of his gun and hit him on the right side of his face, leaving a permanent scar. He fell to the ground, bleeding, and later went to the InterAid clinic for treatment. He never reported the incident to UNHCR (*also* case no. 008/RWA/U/1999).

Apart from these examples, reports of arbitrary mistreatment by the police in Uganda were rare.

Although there were cases of police brutality against refugees in Kenya, the situation had improved since 1992–94 when, as described above, following the murder of four of their colleagues around Dadaab, the Kenyan security forces killed, tortured, raped, and wounded hundreds of refugees. However, there were still cases of individual refugees who complained of ill-treatment by the police. One such case in Kakuma was that of H.A. (case no. 002/SOM/K/1998), a Somali refugee who worked as a security guard for the Lutheran World Federation (LWF). He had gone to the police to report 'Somali refugees in the camp [who] intended to register false family sizes during the imminent headcount exercise', but ended up being beaten for no reason. As H.A. reported:

> Unfortunately, as soon as I reached the police station and entered the appropriate office, a policeman called me and told me that the police officer-in-charge is going to see me in his office. When I entered his office, he ordered me to sit down for the first time; and few minutes later he told me to lie down on the floor. Surprisingly, that officer seized a whip and started hitting me seriously on the back with at least 10 lashes and at the same time he kicked me on the chest several times. Later on, that cruel man ordered his policeman to take me out of the station with inhuman action.[51]

A medical report confirmed that he had 'trauma, haematoma and bruises on the left shoulder' and 'difficulty in breathing' (Kakuma refugee camp, IRC-UNHCR Hospital, doctor's order sheet, 1 October 1997). In another case, a Somali asylum-seeker, M., was examined and treated by Kamiti prison hospital for a fractured rib, septic wound on his elbow, laceration on his right ear, and torn left ear after being assaulted by police while in custody (case no. 011/SOM/K/1996).

Acts by UNHCR and NGOs

The data collected in Uganda include numerous examples of inhuman treatment of refugees trying to access the services of UNHCR's sub-contractor, InterAid. In particular, the inhuman treatment accorded to refugees waiting for their asylum cases to be heard or to receive services at the offices of UNHCR or their implementing partners has been so widely reported that it can be described as normative (*see* e.g., Buregeya 1998 and Otim 1998).[52] Mark Walkup describes an incident he observed in a refugee camp in Kenya where the UNHCR field officer was trying to get a large group of women to sit down while they were waiting for the distribution of plastic sheeting for house construction:

> When they did not comply with directives to sit, he seized a small tree branch and began beating the women. His beating continued throughout

his time there, which he told me was for 'monitoring purposes' ... He approached a small group of refugees gathered between the refugee women and the distribution centre and grabbed a teenage boy by the neck and roughly slung him to the ground with an audible thud. His threats with the stick persuaded them to disperse. When he approached me later with stick in hand, he said matter-of-factly, 'Beating refugees with sticks is not in UNHCR policy, but sometimes we have to do it'. On the beating, his colleague attested, 'Somali women need this because they don't understand like men' (Walkup 1997a: 83–84).

It must be unusual for a researcher to 'catch' a UNHCR official in the act of beating a refugee, but it is not unusual for humanitarians to be found observing such abuses being carried out by others in their employment, and often on their orders.

Such acts of violence chiefly occur in refugee camps out of sight of the media or independent observers, but attempts by refugees to access necessary services in more public places may also be met with the threat of, or actual, violence. However, such incidents are rarely reported or even observed by those whose testimony is sufficiently credible to interfere effectively. An exception was an incident that occurred in Nairobi on 10 July 1997. On that occasion, we alerted a Human Rights Watch (HRW) lawyer who happened to be in town. She summarised the event in an email she sent to UNHCR:

> ... There are about 80 Somali refugees (1 Sudanese family) who have been there two weeks. They came from Swaleh Nguru camp at the Coast (the camp was burnt down some time back after an attack by the local population) ... this group made their way up to Nairobi and came to the UNHCR office ... to ask to be transported to Kakuma camp in NE [North Eastern] province. They were told that the Nairobi office does not process them and to go back to Mombasa. They have no money and have set up a makeshift camp right between the highway and the UNHCR office. This morning (July 7), they came into the UNHCR compound to ask again for help. It was raining and they crowded under the building awning. According to the refugees a white man ordered the security to get them out. The UNHCR security beat a number of them and got them out of the compound ... One man was injured and his finger appears to be broken. He is lying under a blanket on the side of the road. Another woman I interviewed had a bloody eye from being beaten. I have urged the refugees to file police reports. They had been getting water from the latrine in the UNHCR compound, but have now been denied access to it so they have no water. All they are asking for is transport to be taken to Kakuma camp ... There is no need for excessive use of force by UNHCR security and surely something can be done to help this group? ... (Email from Binaifer Nowrojwe to UNHCR, Geneva, July 1997).

One of the constraints facing InterAid's Ugandan staff employed by UNHCR was the severe restrictions on the budget allocated to provide services to refugees living in urban areas. One Ugandan social worker employed by InterAid asked the rhetorical question: 'How does it feel to be a helper faced with inordinate suffering and be unable to authorise treatment?'(Harrell-Bond 2002: 66; *see also* Reynell 2000; Oliver 2000).

Headcounts are periodically conducted by UNHCR in refugee camps. They are also known as 'revalidation exercises', since new ration cards are issued in this process. The rationale underlying the practice of headcounts is that 'maintaining reliable and accurate population figures and demographic data is to assure continuation of donors' funding for the programme'.[53] Headcounts are almost universally perceived as debasing and humiliating by refugees, who have often protested, at times violently, against them (Harrell-Bond et al. 1991; Verdirame 1999b: 64–66).[54] We know of such protests taking place in both Kakuma and Dadaab camps, and in Nakivale (Byrne 1999; Luganda 1999: 6).

UNHCR does not normally allow visits of outsiders to the camps when headcounts are taking place (Hyndman 1996). We did research in Dadaab camps in the weeks that preceded a headcount in April–May 1998 and we were told that under no circumstances could we prolong our stay into the week when the headcount was scheduled to take place. UNHCR was particularly nervous about this exercise, because a riot had erupted in the course of a previous headcount in Dadaab. However, one of us sat in on preparatory meetings and wrote down these observations in his notebook:

> Two UNHCR training films were shown, the first one on the partially successful headcount in Dadaab in 1994, and the second one about a successful headcount operation in Tanzania. In Dadaab, the staff had to be evacuated at the end of the operation for reasons of security ... At the end of the count, refugees were allowed out of the enclosures and they started running after the UNHCR vehicles. In Hagadera, the operation had to be suspended because gun shots were heard ... UNHCR intimated that the food distribution would not be resumed until the population allowed UNHCR to count them. This did not happen until 'several weeks later', and for all that time no food was distributed.

> ... observing humanitarian staff watch these videos was quite revealing. The inhuman aspect [of the headcounting process] was missed by the viewers, no empathy was shown for the refugees. The staff were busy commenting on practicalities, and giggling when they identified known faces among staff members who appeared in the video.

> ... The UNHCR training video also said that 'the fact that much of the food that was distributed was sold in the local market' demonstrates that some refugees were receiving too much, and that there were people with fake ration cards. Hence, the need for a headcount and revalidation exercise.

> ... At the end of the video, Mr Malik [UNHCR's senior registration officer in charge of headcounts] begins his training and explains the counting process ... he sets off saying, 'All we need for this exercise is ink, wristbands, torches, and scissors.' He pauses after naming each object, picks it out of a bag, and shows it to the audience as a smug grin appears under

his moustache. Then he displays his panoply of simple headcounting devices on the table and declares, 'Nothing else but these four instruments to count thousands and thousands of people.' He pronounces the last words with particular solemnity, slowly turning his head to gaze at his entire audience. The contrast between the simplicity of the tools and the difficulty of the task obviously thrills him ...

UNHCR maintains that refugees protest against headcounts because they are trying to ensure that those carrying two or more ration cards will not be discovered. It is hardly conceivable that a mass protest would take place to protect the privileged few who have managed to obtain more than one ration card. If anything, unfairness in rationing is likely to engender resentment or even revolt among the unprivileged ones.[55]

But why did refugees decide to rebel against headcounts? And why was there hardly any organised protest against the reductions in food distribution, despite the alarming levels of malnutrition? The answer might be found in the sociology of obedience and revolt. It has been argued that, regardless of the social context, revolts occur when there is a clear perception that a certain punishment or treatment is essentially inhuman, and that 'the punishments that are rejected vary in accord with varying conceptions of humanity' (Moore 1978: 29). In the case of headcounts, an important fact is the strong cultural resistance among different groups to censuses (Evans-Pritchard 1940: 20; Harrell-Bond et al. 1991).[56] Moreover, the way in which headcounts in refugee camps are conducted is particularly debasing: refugees are forced in enclosures, sometimes referred to as 'corrals', like cattle, often having to wait in the scorching sun for many hours; the whole process is managed in a cold, impersonal, and bureaucratic manner, engendering a sense of humiliation. Finally, body markings, albeit not indelible, are seen as debasing. For individuals who have already suffered a loss of social status and whom aid has made 'powerless', an imprinted symbol of humiliation can seem like a stigma:

> In 1997, in Nakivale Refugee Settlement, a group of Congolese refugees of Banyamulenge origin initiated a protest against the UNHCR's methods of counting refugee populations. The refugees expressed a fear that the UNHCR's practice of 'marking' each person's elbow with ink, to show that he or she had been counted, had an ulterior motive: to inscribe on their bodies the number '666' and to set them apart for destruction in the impending biblical apocalypse. The end of the world had been prefigured for them, they said, in the renewed war in the Democratic Republic of Congo, in their flight from home, and in their exile in Uganda. Their discourse around the protest clearly linked the 'white men' who controlled the counting procedures to the devil (Byrne 1999).

It is certainly no coincidence that the Geneva Convention (IV) Relative to the Protection of Civilian Persons in Time of War (1949) explicitly prohibits 'identification by tattooing or imprinting signs or markings on the body' (art. 100). The practice of headcounts constitutes 'a conduct of a certain level of severity which lowers the victim in rank, position, reputation or character in his own eyes or in the eyes of his people' (*East African Asians v. UK*), and one in which an individual is 'treated as an object in the power of the authorities' (*Tyrer v. UK*). Yet, headcounting is so ingrained in humanitarian practices that its inhuman and degrading nature is not perceived. As Elder explains, the fact that refugees are construed as liars explains this blindness to the consequences of this practice:

> I asked the Red Cross zone managers why the refugees were not asked to count themselves. My question was greeted with disbelief and, in a condescending tone, I was told that 'it was not wise to let cheats count themselves'. Interestingly enough, I was later informed by a Somali refugee precisely how many Somalis remained in the camp. The number he gave was nearly one quarter of the registered figure – the figure on which funding is determined and relief assistance calculated (Elder 1999b: 8).

Acts by other refugees

Refugees themselves were responsible for inflicting practices on each other that amounted to torture, or cruel and inhuman treatment. Refugees hired as security guards in the camps and settlements often received inadequate training, and some of them were known to beat up other refugees with impunity. In Kakuma, however, we noted that the refugee responsible for security, who was hired by LWF, was aware of his duties, and even of human rights law, in performing the functions that had been assigned to him. Community leaders sometimes also employed refugees as guards. For example, the Dinka community leaders in Kakuma, who – as mentioned – were SPLA officers, posted one or two refugees to guard the prisons where refugees served the sentences imposed on them by the leaders. In Dadaab, security and justice committees existed at block level and were also entrusted with the administration of justice as far as dispute settlement and even certain offences were concerned.[57]

In both the Kenyan camps and the Ugandan settlements, community leaders could impose a sentence of corporal punishment. As will be discussed in the section on fair trial, there were many summary convictions of refugees accused of conduct that at times would not even have constituted a crime under Kenyan or Ugandan law, and the sentence often included lashes. For example, the Refugee Welfare Committee (RWC) for Ibakwe village in Palorinya settlement adopted a set of 'bylaws', which *inter alia* prescribed that someone who shouted at night should be punished by sixty lashes of the cane, 'but because of the trouble that [he] has given 10 more lashes to make 70'. Beer could only be drunk at fixed times, and beer sellers who sold beer outside these hours could be punished with fifty lashes.[58]

Some community leaders also exploited traditional beliefs to assert their power and to harass refugees, the harassment sometimes amounting to a form of cruel, inhuman, or degrading treatment. These acts were often justified (or disguised) as ridding the society of particular threats – such as sorcerers, people who are believed capable of poisoning or bringing about illnesses through magic. Alice Lakwena, the defeated leader of the LRA, who was in Ifo camp, Dadaab, maintained the loyalty of her followers through such methods and tormented those who dared break away. She instilled fear among other Ugandan refugees through explicit threats and through 'witchcraft', especially against members of the other Ugandan community in the camp, which consisted mostly of former members of her group. The leader of the breakaway Ugandan community reported that he found objects associated with witchcraft (a chicken head, hair) on his doorstep (case no. 001/UGA/K/1997).[59] Another refugee, who was still a member of her group, feared that 'due to his close involvement with the movement his life will be endangered if he breaks away', and wanted to be resettled in a third country 'away from the clutches of Mme. Alice Lakwena' (*see* UNHCR protection note in case no. 002/UGA/K/1998).

Sexual violence

Sexual violence is here discussed as a violation of the prohibition on torture, and on other cruel, inhuman, or degrading treatment and punishment, but it also involves a violation of various other rules of international human rights law, and, in certain circumstances, of international humanitarian law and international criminal law.[60] The orthodox legal categorisation of acts of sexual violence against women would have entailed a distinction based on the perpetrator. In fact, one can correctly talk of 'torture' under the current legal definition only in the case of violence inflicted by a public official.[61] In this section, however, we discuss sexual violence against women regardless of the public or private status of the perpetrator. Similarities in the experiences of victims, in particular in their psychological and physical suffering, override – in our view – the need to adhere to legal notions that appear to do little justice to reality: we are committing a misdemeanour in terms of legal categorisation to avoid what would have been an anthropological misrepresentation. After all, various authors, not least the special rapporteur on violence against women, have pointed out the limits of the orthodox legal distinction, making the case 'for defining severe forms of domestic violence as torture' (Charlesworth and Chinkin 2000: 234).[62] UNHCR policy on sexual violence is also inspired by a similar purposive approach (UNHCR 1995 h; EXCOM conclusion no. 73).

The most significant failure to protect refugee women in Kenya was the incidence of sexual violence in Dadaab. Years after it had become a cause célèbre in the international human rights arena following the reports in 1993 by HRW and African Rights, the situation had not improved. In Kakuma, as well as in Kiryandongo and in most of the Ugandan settlements in the north, the situation was scarcely any different: women lived in constant fear of being raped or of being abducted as sexual slaves there also. UNHCR's apparent concern about 'root causes' never translated itself into an examination of the root causes of sexual violence. The solutions that it developed were grossly inadequate: a 'mobile court' initiative did not have a sustained impact; the distribution of firewood was followed by a decrease in the number of rapes outside the perimeter of the camps – where women went to collect firewood – but an increase in rapes inside the camp (UNHCR 1998b);[63] and the creation of a 'safe haven' for women victims of violence in Kakuma was an ill-conceived remedy, based on what amounted to the incarceration of the victims in a secluded space, which worsened their plight by stigmatising them as 'loose women'.[64] In both countries, it often proved difficult to act against policemen or soldiers accused of committing such violence.

Measures that would have been more effective included respect for the refugee woman's right to move away from a place that she found dangerous, and challenging – rather than buttressing – traditional male authority in camps. It was, after all, UNHCR's own 'Geneva' policy that acknowledged a correlation between closed camps and sexual violence (UNHCR 1995h: 12). Nevertheless, as usual, measures that involved a reassessment of the fundamental premise of the encampment of refugees were seldom taken into serious consideration at the field level. UNHCR protection officers were aware of the harm done to the rights of women by their 'tolerance … for such traditional settlements', but chose to acquiesce in them because 'the purpose was to maintain peace and order in camps' (Okoro 1995).

The Kenyan and Ugandan governments were also at fault for failing to ensure proper protection for women and, in particular, to reduce the incidence of sexual violence in the camps and settlements. There were numerous reports of sexual violence perpetrated by members of the security forces who were meant to protect refugees. In Kenya, the situation in the late 1990s had slightly improved compared with 1993–94 – when security forces had attacked Somali refugees in Dadaab, killing or wounding dozens of them and raping many women – but the police and the army still represented a threat to the physical security of refugee women. In Uganda, where many refugee settlements had been located in conflict areas, there were reports of rapes of both refugees and Ugandans committed by members of the armed forces.[65] Neither government investigated reports of rape: the Public Commission of Inquiry into the events of

1993–94 in Dadaab never completed its work, and the Ugandan government did not take action against soldiers or officers accused of rape. As it could not rely on the active cooperation of the authorities of the host countries and in particular of the security machinery, implementing an effective policy against rape was an almost impossibly difficult challenge for UNHCR.[66] The victims were generally women, but it was often overlooked that men, boys in particular, were also victims of rape.[67]

In Dadaab, Goretty Omala, a FIDA lawyer employed by the Women Victims of Violence (WVV) project in 1994–95, dealt with a number of cases in which Somali refugee women reported that policemen had raped them. UNHCR had involved FIDA after HRW and African Rights had denounced the sexual violence and abuses of the Kenyan security forces in the Dadaab camps (HRW/Africa Watch 1993; African Rights 1993). African Rights commented on the fact that UNHCR had never initiated a court case against the Kenyan government or security forces on behalf of a refugee, nor provided any legal representation for a refugee victim. The FIDA lawyer struggled to bring to court at least one of the cases in which the identity of the suspected policeman was known. Another case concerned the abduction by a policeman of a 16-year-old girl. In this case however, the FIDA lawyer was at least 'reliably informed that the arresting officer has been relieved of his duties as a police officer' (FIDA Kenya 1994a).

The case of the rape of two young Sudanese refugee girls in Adjumani exemplifies both the impunity on which the army soldiers and officials could normally rely when they perpetrated these crimes, and the inadequacy of traditional dispute settlement procedures to protect the victims (case no. 129/SUD/U/1998). In July 1998, both of P.'s daughters, H. and B., aged 14 and 16 years – were kidnapped and raped by two different army officers. P.'s relatives arranged to meet the officer who had raped H. in order to settle the dispute. This officer, who admitted the rape, agreed to pay a sum of USh 650,000 (US$ 500), and, the next day, sent a soldier with USh 150,000 as part of the payment. P.'s relatives accepted this settlement, while P., as is customary, had to let his relatives handle the matter and had to remain silent throughout the meeting.

When, after only a week, P.'s elder daughter, B., was kidnapped and raped by another officer, P. stood his ground and demanded that the case be taken to court, but the deputy camp commandant and the commander conspired to keep the case out of the hands of the police. Under Ugandan law, defilement (the rape of a minor) is a very serious offence for which the death penalty can be imposed, although courts normally mete out less severe penalties. The officer in question at first denied that he had raped B. However, at least four witnesses, including a junior officer stationed in the same barracks, came forward and confirmed that he had indeed kidnapped B. and had kept her in his house against her will for some days.

The commanding officer of the barracks and the deputy camp commandant decided that the officer should pay a fine of USh 550,000 to P. for
abducting his daughter. P., not knowing about Ugandan law, could only
insist that the officer be brought to trial but did not know how to go about
it. Some three weeks after the rape, the officer, who refused to pay, went
to see P. and his wife and menacingly told them that they should be 'careful with your daughter because I can shoot her at any time'.[68] When we
met them in Adjumani, they wanted to be resettled in Kyangwali refugee
settlement. They confessed that they were so frightened that they were no
longer prepared to press the case in court. The family first moved to
Kampala and finally were transferred to Kyangwali, but no case was ever
brought against the soldiers.[69]

In another tragic case (case no. 107/SOM/U/1998), A., a Somali widow
with two little children, was pressured to marry a Somali Muslim. When
she refused, she was accused by the Somali refugees in Nakivale of having an affair with a Ugandan Christian with whom she was doing business in the market. One Somali man came to her house, pulled a knife,
and said, 'I am going to show you that Somali men have penises.' A.
escaped, but her 6-year-old daughter was raped.[70] A. went to the police to
report the assault and the rape of her daughter, but the members of her
community asked the police to allow them to settle the matter. On returning home, she found the man who had raped her daughter standing with
members of his family brandishing pangas. She only escaped being killed
because of the intervention of a female neighbour.

A. fled to Kampala, where she was refused help at InterAid and was
referred to the Red Cross – the NGO implementing partner in charge of
Nakivale – and from there she was sent back to InterAid. When she
returned, she was told there was nothing that they could do without official police documents.[71] Eventually, the fact that A. was at great personal
risk was acknowledged and she was given permission by UNHCR to
remain in Kampala. However, it was not long before some Somali men
traced her and she was attacked again, this time by three masked men
who severely beat her. The man who had raped her daughter also came to
her home in Kampala. After the publication of a newspaper article about
her situation, the visits and harassment ceased for a few months (Taylor
1999b).[72] Under the guidelines of UNHCR and receiving governments,
women victims of sexual violence should be given priority for resettlement. Why she was not put on a priority list is incomprehensible.

In Dadaab, the FIDA lawyer also found that traditional dispute settlements often precluded enforcement of the law on sexual violence. In her
report, she observed:

> It was generally felt by most refugees that to report cases of rape, attempt-
> ed rape, defilement of minors, forced early marriages and abduction was

to call for stiff reprisals from the clan elders, otherwise known also as 'gudumiyas'. These 'gudumiyas' wielded immense powers and had hitherto been the ones who adjudicated on the disputes and other matters of concern to the different clans in the refugee camps. There was a very hostile reception to project staff as we were seen as interfering and usurping the powers of the 'gudumiyas' (FIDA Kenya 1995a).

On another occasion, in the case of a woman who had been assaulted by a man during food distribution, the elders went to see her with a proposal to settle the matter:

> ... out of curiosity I wanted to know from them what the out-of-court settlement would entail. They advised me that normally a fine of 100 KSh is paid for such kind of a wrong and that once the leaders are convinced that an offence did take place, then the perpetrator would be charged with KSh 4,000. I told the clan elders to please raise that amount of money and give it to me so that I could then tell the trial Magistrate that the parties had opted for an out-of-court settlement.

> The danger with this is that this money is shared among the clan leaders and the victim ends up getting nothing at all. To guard against this, I attached one condition to the request as put before me, that all the money be given wholly to the victim. The clan leaders never came back to me (FIDA Kenya 1994b).

Goretty Omala's awareness of the inadequacies of traditional dispute settlement and her ability to confront the elders were exceptional. In fact, as we have seen, it was UNHCR's practice to accord significant powers to the community leaders, to pay their salaries, and even to build prisons where, outside any due process of law, those found guilty of 'customary' offences were detained. In Dadaab, the Anti-Rape Committee, which included five women and five men, was put in charge of the initial investigations of rape cases and of reporting them to the police. Although victims were not prevented from approaching the police directly, this was not encouraged. That rape was still underreported was probably a function of a system in which women feared exposure, most particularly to members of their own community, afraid of ostracism or other forms of punishment.

The lack of security in the camps and the involvement of the Kenyan police often meant that victims had no way of averting a rape when they had received clear threats. For example, an Ethiopian refugee woman in Ifo camp, Dadaab, successfully resisted a man who was trying to break into her house at night. She did not know who this man was, but she told her neighbours what had happened. The following day, on her way to work, she met a man who told her that he was the one who had tried to break into her house the previous night, that he was a police officer, and that, if she did not comply with his requests, 'twenty men would rape her and her brother would not be able to help her' (FIDA Kenya 1995b). The woman told her brother about this meeting, but, since the man who was threatening her was a policeman, she could not seek the protection of the police. That same night, two men came to see her, one of them the man that she had met. While he remained outside, the other man came in and raped her 'in the same bed where her children lay' (ibid.). The woman finally managed to hit him and scream for help. The man ran away, and she decided to go into hiding – scared because she had struck a policeman. However, she 'noticed that the man had left without his trousers ... She carried these away with her when she ran away and went into hiding the next day' (ibid.).

Cases like this one, however, could not be followed up by the FIDA lawyer since the 'legal assistance project died a premature death' (Omala 1996). There were some tensions with UNHCR and the FIDA lawyer: she often complained about lack of logistical support – for example, the contentious rule 'that the FIDA lawyer should not use UNHCR vehicles while in Mombasa' (FIDA Kenya 1994d). Logistical support and effective work by the various UNHCR field workers were essential for the success of the project, since the FIDA lawyer had to cover an extensive area that had no public transport and was ridden with insecurity. On one occasion, she complained that she had not received 'all the necessary documents pertaining to a particular case ... in good time so that I can make the necessary arrangements for court attendance' (FIDA Kenya 1994a). The UNHCR field office had not warned the witnesses, and on the same day the case was due for a court hearing, 'we had to drive all the way to Marafa not only to pick the witnesses [*sic*] but to trace them and bring them to court ... this kind of logistical support has to come from UNHCR particularly given the fact that I am based in Dadaab' (FIDA Kenya 1994d).

Later, the collaboration between UNHCR and FIDA resumed. The director of litigation of FIDA 'was hired to assist UNHCR Branch Office in Nairobi in designing appropriate legal training material on Women's rights under Kenyan law' (UNHCR 1999f: 6.5.3). In Kakuma, where sexual violence was prevalent, a 'safe haven' was constructed to receive women victims of violence (ibid.). During a fact-finding mission in Kakuma, the Sudan Human Rights Association (SHRA) was told that there were four or five cases of rape every week and that these were 'rarely reported because of the customary dictates of some of these tribes. Most of the victims, after a rape incident, leave the camp to avoid humiliation and excommunication from the clan' (*Sudan Monitor* March 2001: 4). Sexual violence in Kakuma was notoriously underreported, but horrific assaults did happen; on one occasion, the victim of the rape was an 8-year-old girl (case no. 005/DRC/K/1996).

In 1998, in Ifo camp, Dadaab, we learnt about the case of a 60-year-old man who had married a young woman believed to be only 16. The man was accused by the girl, who had been infibulated, of using a sharp wooden implement on her genitalia causing her to bleed profusely. Although in this case it was not possible for us to interview the girl, we were given UNHCR's reasons for not pursuing this case further: that they were not going to press for a prosecution against this man 'because of insufficient evidence, and of *wanting to avoid a clash with the Somali community*' [emphasis added].[73] It was also pointed out that the Somali elders had intervened and had managed to persuade the husband to divorce his wife, who had sought refuge with her relatives. Finally, the woman's credibility was questioned by UNHCR, because she had apparently talked 'too openly' about what had happened when she had reported the case at the hospital. Furthermore, it was believed that the girl might have been persuaded by her father to concoct this claim as part of a stratagem to be resettled. This, however, was unlikely, given the stigmatisation of rape victims within Somali society, and given that it was not possible to foresee how the man would have reacted to a false accusation. Undoubtedly, both the girl and her father must have been at least aware of the fact that falsely accusing a prominent elder was a very risky, even life-threatening, business. As for the Somali man accused of this act, he was employed by the UNHCR consultant as a facilitator for peace education.

Dadaab also illustrated the failure of protection strategies, which, for the most part, were ill-conceived from the start. In fact, despite the panoply of gender-awareness activities – gender-sensitisation workshops, anti-rape committees, gender 'mainstreaming', offering belated 'protection' to the victim often in the form of lay counselling, and medical examinations (often made by unregistered foreign doctors whose reports could not be used as evidence in court) – there continued to be widespread sexual violence against women. The attitude of the agencies towards sexual violence too often 'paid only lip service to' the right of women to physical safety. In practice, it may even have exacerbated the situation, not only by not attending to the consequences of encampment, but also by establishing ineffective structures and reinforcing the position of the elders.

As noted, the levels of sexual violence had made Dadaab camps a cause célèbre (African Rights 1993). The majority of reported rapes happened while women were collecting firewood, but 'in Somali culture ... the women have the sole responsibility for collecting firewood for subsistence consumption' (UNHCR 1998e: 19). Apparently, although the rapes had been going on since the establishment of the camps, the idea that men should collect the firewood was only mooted in a workshop in 1998. However: 'Some refugee male participants in the workshop felt that rape is a more bearable crime than the death men face in procuring wood. Donkey cart owners (mainly men) face illegal tax for firewood, have their carts burnt, are beaten up and even face death ... Hence, the majority of the women are sent because they will come back alive (albeit assaulted). The women felt this was a slow death' (ibid.).

By the beginning of 1998, the number of *reported* rapes in the Dadaab camps was at least as high as it had been at the height of the crisis that had attracted the attention of human rights organisations in 1993 (African Rights 1993). Jessica Munson, a Sadako volunteer in the Dadaab camps,[74] documented the number of reported cases over a period of three months in 1998 (January–March). She found that there were still significant problems with the reporting system that involved three agencies – CARE, MSF (Médecins sans Frontières), and NCCK (National Council of Churches of Kenya) – and the police, and that the police were 'not aware' of cases that the victim believed had been reported to them through CARE.[75] UNHCR data for 1997 put the total number of reported rapes that year at 155, but it is not clear whether these data refer to the cases reported to the police, to one of the agencies, or to the total number reported to any agency (UNHCR 1998e). However, in the period when Munson was in Dadaab, she went through the reports of each agency involved in the system, and found that in January 1998 there had been a total of thirty-one rapes reported to at least one of the three agencies or the police. In February, the figure in only two of the camps (Hagadera and Ifo) was seventeen, and in March, seventeen cases were reported from all the three Dadaab camps. The victims included at least five children aged between 10 and 15, and two of the victims had been raped more than once.[76]

A much-neglected reason for this high incidence of rape is that camps, like prisons, are institutions that generate certain types of violence. Within an artificial community, characterised by unemployment, lack of future prospects, total dependence on insufficient food rations, and at times, by a preponderance of single and often young men, it is hardly surprising that rape becomes endemic. As the leader of the Sudanese in Ifo camp, Dadaab, observed:

> They are trying to sensitise the community, but there is a problem of gender imbalance: women are not enough. In my community, 80 percent of the population are single men. We have to solve the problems of men in order to solve the problems of women. The first thing they [the agencies] could do is family reunion. Because of the social set-up of the camp, we have no interaction with the Somalis. There have been cases of Sudanese men converting to Islam in order to have social access and to meet Somali women.[77]

WVV was a project aimed at improving the physical security in and around camps, providing specialised medical treatment and counselling, and offering material assistance to the victims, but FIDA's main emphasis was to end the impunity of the perpetrators through the courts. The FIDA component of the WVV project was relatively small, representing only 6 or percent of the budget.[78] In its evaluation of the rest of the WVV project, the Canadian International Development Agency (CIDA) 'identified management problems, endemic to UNHCR, as one of the major obstacles to the project's success from a donor perspective'. Furthermore, while it was able to continue to support FIDA's successful project, the CIDA evaluators found that: '... most of the expenditures made by the time of the mission [the CIDA evaluation, 1994] had gone to fill gaps in the general programme' (FIDA Kenya 1994a; UNHCR 1996e).

After incidents of rape had soared in Ifo camp, Dadaab, in 1997, the project of the 'mobile court', which had initially been proposed by FIDA but left dormant for three years, was revived and implemented in 1998, owing to pressure from Pia Phiri, the senior protection officer. The idea was to offer transport to the magistrate in Garissa for him to hear cases in Dadaab. Despite its important symbolic significance, its impact on the incidence of sexual violence in the camps was probably negligible: in 2000, 'only three perpetrators of sexual violence were punished' (RCK 2001a). Moreover, when the perpetrator of the violence was known, many victims chose – often under family pressure – traditional dispute settlement mechanisms, under which women received compensation (which was often pocketed by the closest male relative) but the perpetrator did not go to prison. The traditional solution was tantamount to another punishment for the victim: she was forced to marry her rapist in order to save the 'honour' of the family.

After a visit of US congressional staff during which meetings were arranged with rape victims, UNHCR received US$ 1.5 million, through the Ted Turner Fund, which was to be used to distribute firewood to women:

> A first blanket distribution was executed in July 1998. The second distribution took place in August 1998. Following both firewood distributions, reported rapes fell considerably and UNHCR, the anti-rape committees and the refugee women themselves concludes [*sic*] that the firewood distribution has had a positive impact in reducing the incidents and exposure to the risk of sexual violence in the outlying bush while fetching cooking fuel. However, despite the downward trend in rape and sexual violence reports in the outlying areas there has been an increase in overall rape and sexual violence reports committed inside the camps in comparison with previous years (UNHCR 1998b: chap. VI).

In the settlements in Uganda, much of the sexual violence that was reported was attributed to the Ugandan army and to the rebels. Two refugee leaders in Mongola settlement described the situation:

> The problem with the mobile forces (Ugandan army) here is that they want to take all of our ladies. They may stay only for one week, one month and then they go and pass through Gulu through here. These mobile teams often come with an appetite for women and they behave in a strange way and they spoil them with money and play sex. This causes a problem with

HIV/AIDS. The ones here based as stationary in Udu also do not stay here for long and also play with our ladies.[79]

Of the girls and boys who were abducted by the LRA, unknown numbers were used as sex slaves; others escaped abduction but were raped during a raid.

Freedom from slavery and forced labour, and the violation of other labour standards

It was UNHCR's policy that refugees who worked in the settlements and camps should only be paid 'incentives' (*see* Chapter 5) – rather than salaries equivalent to what national staff were paid for the same work. This practice constituted a serious violation of the right to equal remuneration for equal work (ICESCR art. 7). Under the International Covenant on Civil and Political Rights (ICCPR), an exception to the general prohibition on forced or compulsory labour can be made only for 'any service exacted in cases of emergency or calamity threatening the life or well being of the community' (art. 8(3)(c)). It would be acceptable only for a very limited period of time to expect people to work without pay, and this would apply only to such serious situations as, for example, the El Nino floods in Dadaab camps in 1997–98 or the cholera epidemic in the immediate aftermath of the exodus of 1 million Rwandans to Zaire in 1994.

Despite these legal provisions, in some cases the UNHCR and NGOs required people to work without any remuneration whatsoever. In Dadaab, a system of 'community self-management' (CSM) was introduced by UNHCR's 'implementing partner', CARE, in 1995 (Hyndman 1996). CSM was based on the realisation that 'refugees were managed, controlled and taken care of without having a say in the whole process of decisions concerning them' (ibid.). Seven committees, one for each vital activity in the camp, were established, but they did not participate in meetings dealing with financial issues, or have any say in the allocation of resources.

In 1997–98, CARE reviewed the CSM system for two reasons. Firstly, some financial cuts were necessary. Secondly, according to CARE, there was some confusion regarding the powers that refugees would have: 'Committee members want to assume power and keep information to themselves. The committee members misconceived the whole thing. They thought they would take over from CARE'.[80] But such a democratic transfer of power was not what CARE had in mind.

The committees that represented a challenge to CARE's authority were dismantled and block leaders were appointed. 'Now if there is a problem, for example, with water, the block leader needs to report it to us. We think that in doing so, refugees will identify their own problem and it will *look* as if it is a partnership, (ibid.). At this point, CARE was using CSM simply as a way of replacing the loss of employed staff, or refugees on incentives, with free labour from the camps.

As a result of the financial crisis, many important activities had to be suspended in the camps and refugee workers were laid off. In Ifo camp, 50 percent of casual workers in social services were dismissed, while the agricultural programme was completely suspended. Adult literacy programmes were also phased out and income-generating activities were trimmed down. In April 1998, CARE envisaged that within a few months, sanitary, logistics, and community development work would have to be done without pay. The block leaders, also unpaid, were to identify people within their block to carry out these duties. However, refugee teachers, nurses, doctors, and guards would continue to receive 'incentives'. At the time, CARE was considering the possibility of using sanctions to force reluctant conscripts to work, but it maintained that it preferred 'persuasion'. The introduction of this practice was presented as an exercise in capacity building aimed 'to prepare refugees for repatriation so that they can go back without a dependency syndrome'.[81]

Liberty and security of the person

Human rights law guarantees the right to liberty and security of the person. Article 9 of the ICCPR and article 6 of the African Charter contain a detailed regulation of the rights of arrested and detained persons, to protect individuals from arbitrary forms of deprivation of their liberty. Refugee law has also addressed some of the specific physical security problems facing the refugees. For example, the OAU Convention provides that 'for reasons of security, countries of asylum shall, as far as possible, settle refugees at a reasonable distance from the frontier of their country of origin' (art. 2(6)). When the OAU Convention was adopted, it was believed that it was both in the interests of refugees and of host states to remove them as far as possible from the threat of 'hot pursuit.' The EXCOM conclusion 48, which condemns such attacks, calls on states and UNHCR to preserve the essential civilian and humanitarian nature of camps.

Physical safety in camps and settlements

Security arrangements varied from one camp to another. In Kenya, there were police posts just outside each camp. Some 120 kilometres of live fences were planted around Dadaab camps to protect the refugees from banditry. In Dadaab, most of the staff lived in a secure compound near the town, and left the camps at dusk. A police escort was necessary to move between camps. Staff in Kakuma lived in a compound behind a fenced enclosure adjacent to the camp, where refugees did not generally have access. Inside the camps, there was a night patrol made up of Kenyan guards and refugees.

The Dadaab camps were located in a part of the country that was fraught with armed banditry: as a result, sexual violence, robberies, theft, and murders were regular occurrences in the camps. Armed bandits, normally referred to as *shifta* by the government, had operated in North-Eastern Province uninterruptedly since the 1960s, when a large part of the ethnically Somali population was believed to favour the irridentist plan to include the province as part of a 'Greater Somalia'. The phenomenon had a clear political connotation, although the government always depicted it as a criminal one. The authorities often chose brutal repression as a response, while the machinery for promoting the rule of law, especially the courts, was either confined to a marginal role or produced what was in practice a travesty of justice (African Rights 1996). As described above, on one occasion in 1994, many refugees died during a 'security operation' by the Kenyan army; other instances of widespread violence by the army and security forces against refugees were documented by human rights organisations (African Rights 1993; Human Rights Watch/Africa Watch 1993). By 1997, the security forces were no longer a main cause of the refugees' fear, at least not to the extent that they had been during the early years of the existence of the camps, but armed attacks by bandits, as well as sexual violence, murders, and theft, continued to pervade life in the camps.

Kakuma was also a far from secure environment for refugees. The security reports compiled by LWF for 1995–96 depict a harsh situation, with suicides, widespread theft, armed robberies, riots, murders, and the discovery of unidentified corpses.[82] Investigations were seldom carried out and they hardly ever resulted in prosecutions. The lack of security affected the life and the livelihood of the entire camp population. One of the main sources of insecurity was clashes between members of different ethnic groups within the camps, mainly southern Sudanese in reaction to the war in Sudan. At the end of 1997 an intern who was working for the Windle Trust, teaching English to the Sudanese 'minors', described the situation:

> We have major trouble here. People are trying to kill each other big time. Dinka vs. Didinga mainly. Ironically we had a peace committee meeting this morning ... My room is in a compound in the camp and I am cut off from it for now. We tried to drive there earlier but had to turn around when boys with spears and shields (where do they get them? Do they make them?) began attacking people in the rear of the vehicle. The police were called in and over 100 rounds were fired into the air but it seems as soon as they control the fighting in one area it breaks out elsewhere. At the

moment, they are having to transport patients up to Loki because there are so many serious cases. The fighting seems to be extending to the Ethiopian community or the Nuer. I can hear noises from here. To top it all, the Bantu Somalis in Kakuma 2 are getting increasingly fed up and rebelling against the state of affairs – dismal, no shelter and it is pouring with rain, no rations, or late or they have to pay for them.[83]

The situation worsened after that period,[84] with UNHCR reporting that, in one instance in 1999, 'inter-ethnic conflict between the Dinka and the Didinga tribal groups resulted in six deaths and seventy-seven refugees seriously injured. 456 shelters were burnt down while 6,500 were displaced within the Kakuma camps' (UNHCR 1999f: sec. 3(2)(2); *see* also case nos. 003/SOM/K/1997; 003/SUD/K/1998). On that occasion, thousands of women and children living in the camp took temporary refuge in or near the UNHCR compound.[85] Tensions also soared between Ethiopian and Eritrean refugees as the two countries went to war, prompting at least one Ethiopian to leave Kakuma in search of safety (case no. 181/ETH/U/1999). Ethnic tension pervaded the small Rwandan community too: Tutsi refugees were recurrently accused of being spies and subject to racist abuse. One of them, who had been in Kenya since 1982 and had moved to Kakuma in 1994 following the government order that all refugees should go to camps, said:

> ... I have been residing mainly with Rwandese refugee who just fled out of Rwanda in 1994. This was before my house's destruction which was set on fire on 25th February 1999 at 2:00 a.m. Day after day I am insulted and abused by Hutus because of my tribal affiliation being a Tutsi ... 'You Tutsis why are you still in exile yet you made us flee our country. You must be working for Rwandese regime. You Tutsis, you have continued to follow us even in exile ... Tutsis must vacate this community'. This is the song of everyday by the Hutu here in the camp. After my house was gutted down completely and having save totally nothing except my life, I was helped by my workmates who contribution 2395 Kenya Shillings to enable me to buy clothes, since I had none left with to put on as I escaped from the burning house with only underwear on my body (case no. 005/RWA/K/1999).

In another case, A., a Tutsi from Rwanda, married a Hutu woman in Kakuma. Not long after the marriage a threatening note was left on the door of their *tukul*. A few days later the *tukul* was set on fire. After reporting these incidents to UNHCR and requesting a travel document to leave the camp, they were told to be 'patient' while their case was investigated. Meanwhile, A. was beaten up by a group of Rwandan refugees. After his request for a travel document was refused, A. was advised by the district officer to apply for a travel document for reasons other than insecurity – for example, to go to Nairobi to meet family members. A. changed his request and managed to obtain a travel document, but he was told not to go to the UNHCR branch office in Nairobi as 'they will not be able to change your situation and you will have to return to Kakuma' (case no. 021/RWA/K/1998).

Kakuma had a 'protection area' for individuals whom UNHCR recognised as facing persecution and harassment in the camp and who could not be protected through the refugee communities system. However, the area was only surrounded by a fragile fence, leaving people vulnerable to attacks at night, and those inside became easily identifiable targets. For many individuals, being admitted to this 'protection area' was a lengthy and uncertain process because of the multi-layered system that was put in place to identify those in danger: cases first had to be assessed by the LWF's social services department and then referred to a UNHCR field office before being passed on to a protection officer (when there was one). The case of a Sudanese woman illustrates these shortcomings: she was the victim of a serious assault by a man who claimed to be her missing husband's brother and wanted to marry her under the custom of 'wife-inheritance'. Although the Sudanese leaders had found in her favour, recognising that she was not obliged to marry him, he continued to threaten her and even tried to kill her. An intern working for LWF recalls:

> The night she decided to flee from her home, he came with a knife trying to kill her. After that she camped outside the compound gates seeking the safety that is guaranteed by UNHCR. Upon hearing this story, I quickly wrote it up and submitted to UNHCR the same afternoon, hoping that a ruling would be made and that she could move into the protection area. No action was taken that afternoon, or the next day, or the next, despite my attempts to convince the officials of UNHCR that this was in fact an urgent case. My internship was done and I left the camp not knowing if this case was ever resolved (Reur 1998).[86]

Another problem was that refugees living in the 'protection area' were seen by others as privileged, because 'security cases' had a better opportunity of being resettled in a third country. UNHCR itself was often incredulous of security complaints by refugees, claiming that many were concocted by refugees seeking a fast route to resettlement.

The security situation in Kakuma can be further illustrated with the case of Ifrah and Oba, two refugee girls from Somalia. Ifra, 14, and her sister, Oba, 21, ended up in Kakuma, after a long saga of years of separation, failed foster families, the attempted abduction of Ifrah by Kenyan Somalis from Dadaab, and her escape to Eastleigh, a part of Nairobi inhabited by large numbers of Somalis.[87] In Kakuma, UNHCR kept the girls in the reception centre with no adequate shelter or protection. A Liberian refugee, who was also staying in the 'reception area' for his family's protection, tried to help them. Notwithstanding his efforts, their ration cards were stolen. A few days after we first met Ifrah, she heard someone call her name outside the 'protection area': it was one of the people who had tried to abduct her from Dadaab. She ran back to Oba who advised her to leave Kakuma. We then found Ifrah sleeping on the street outside UNHCR in Nairobi, at least two dangerous days of travel away from Kakuma.

In Dadaab we also found cases of individuals who faced threats to their personal security and whose plight was not properly addressed. For example, a Dinka refugee from Rumbek was unfortunate enough to be the nephew of someone who had been an SPLA prison guard in Pagera when some prisoners, including Kerubino Kwanyin Bol, a prominent rebel leader, had escaped to Uganda. His uncle was one of those believed to have shot at the prisoners. In Kakuma one night, this refugee and his brother were locked inside a house and the house was set on fire. They managed to break the door and escape, but, as they ran away, one of them was caught by the assailants and killed with spears and pangas. The surviving brother left for Nairobi, but was then persuaded by UNHCR to go to Dadaab, and since 1995 he had lived in Ifo, where we met him. There he was again recognised and threatened by other Sudanese refugees. The UNHCR field officer had to intervene three times and warn the community. On one occasion, an arrow was shot into this refugee's house at night, but luckily it only cut the mosquito net. He then moved to a different section of the Sudanese community and, when we interviewed him, he had just reported to the field office that he had found needles in his drinking water.

The situation in most of the settlements in northern Uganda was even worse owing to the war. When refugees first came to Uganda from the Sudan in 1986–87, most of them were accommodated in the Ogujebe transit centre and in the Palorinya settlements. In the following period, the settlements to which refugees were sent in Adjumani were situated in the buffer zone between Gulu and Kitgum districts. In Moyo district, refugee camps were subject to attacks by rebels of both the WNBF and the UNRF II. When more settlements were established in Adjumani and Moyo districts, people were reluctant to move there because the area was prone to attacks from rebels. The LRA was active across northern Uganda, but particularly in Gulu and Kitgum, while the SPLA operated mainly in Adjumani owing to the proximity of the Sudanese border (RLP 2001b: 3; UNHCR 2000c; Gersony 1997; see also case nos. 1009/SUD/U/1998; 110/SUD/U/1999; 115/SUD/U/1999; 118/SUD/U/1999; 123 SUD/U/ 1999). The head of sub-office in Pakelle observed that nationals were also victims of the insecurity, but 'perhaps refugees suffer the brunt because after food distribution the rebels target them because of the concentration of resources. The rebels can come into the area where the tukuls are all together and easily round up resources. In this sense, refugees can be seen as more vulnerable. We do not think that they are being attacked for politics but for resources.'[88]

Testimonies of rebel attacks against settlements were numerous, often resulting, as mentioned above under the right to life, in loss of life. On 3 November 1997, rebels occupied Waka for twenty-four hours:

> Six people died immediately – three were children, cut and floating in the river and the other three died of bullet wounds ... No one knows exactly why they are attacking the refugees. Waka is now vacant and some have decided to cross back into Sudan through Lafori. There have been abductions before and the exact number of those who died or were abducted no one knows up to now.[89]

A refugee from Palorinya settlement fell victim to three rebel attacks between 1991 and 1997 (case no. 132/SUD/U/1999). In the first attack, the rebels destroyed all his property, and he was beaten and stabbed. In another attack, he was whipped and hung upside down from a tree. Finally he was attacked one more time by the rebels who burnt his body with hot jerrycans. During the same incident, his wife was beaten and lost her left eye. She was pregnant at the time and subsequently gave birth to a paralysed baby. His mother who was also present died as a result of the wounds inflicted by the attackers. On this occasion seventeen refugees from Waka in Palorinya were killed.

Throughout 1997, the United Nations Development Programme (UNDP) considered that the Palorinya settlements were at 'Phase IV' in terms of danger.[90] During August 1998, an attack took place just three kilometres from where we were staying in Adjumani. Twelve people were abducted. Seven boys and men were told to lie on the ground and were beheaded with pangas. The babies on the women's backs were checked to see if they were boys. The women later reported that the rebels had explained: 'We are coming to kill all the men because the men of Adjumani refuse to support us.'[91]

No effort was made to ensure that any of the refugee settlements were 'at a reasonable distance' from the border with the country of origin (art. 2(6)). For example, Kali was only eight kilometres from Sudan and experienced rebel attacks in 1995, 1996, and 1997. Even though detachments were stationed near settlements, the army was largely ineffective at guaranteeing the security of refugees. Many refugees were abducted, raped, or killed. Refugees from Kali settlement repeatedly asked the Ugandan authorities to be relocated to safer places, but these requests were summarily dismissed. There was one settlement, Kyangwali, in Hoima district, designated for 'special security cases' (case nos. 206/SUD/U/1999; 138/SUD/U/1999). However, it was not enough to provide for the protection of the hundreds of thousands of Sudanese in danger in northern Uganda. Moreover, Kyangwali itself was not spared ethnic tensions and feuds between clans (case no. 169/ETH/U/98), and it was far from safe even from the SPLA (case no. 208/SUD/U/1999).

In Moyo district, the staff and a detachment of soldiers were stationed in the centre of Palorinya, and some refugees observed that they themselves were protecting the soldiers rather than the other way around. There were also detachments in Adjumani district, but they too were largely ineffectual mainly because of poor communication and transport facilities. As some refugees in Kali stated:

> ... although some security personnel has been brought, you find that something may happen just near and they do not respond – there is no proper response here. The detachment here in Kali was brought in January 1997. When the attack was about to happen in Waka, a message was brought to the detachment before; at 3 p.m. they were informed and by the second day there had been no action. Some were killed and some brought to the health centre, it wasn't until 11 a.m. the next day when they came. Our means of protection is only to take a report to the military personnel as we have no weapons ourselves to take up against the rebels. But the military pay little attention to it. They only come later.[92]

In some cases, not only did the soldiers fail to protect refugees from rebel attacks, they were themselves responsible for looting and for raping women (e.g., case no. 129/SUD/U/1998):

> Whenever an incident takes place at night, the military does not come until morning and during the day they come late. They do not patrol and they tell us we are their 'eye' and it is our responsibility to watch. Sometimes, the army come and loot and even kill some of the refugees, but if we complain, they will come and blame us that we are the ones.[93]

Obviously, UNHCR did not have the means to ensure security in the settlements. Such security could only be provided by effective security forces, or, more to the point, by allowing refugees to settle elsewhere. Refugees found UNHCR's response to their regular reports of incidents callous:

> Regarding the UNHCR protection officer, we met him last year four times to discuss insecurity. From July up to this time we have not met or seen the new officer. During the time of insecurity here it was very bad and the protection officer came here when the situation was very bad. He discussed about the security problems only. He told us to watch out and to report at any time to the military personnel a strange person; there is however, no proper response – things are always late. We can write to the protection officer only through the settlement commandant. The problem with the settlement commandant is that he is available but his response is always negative. When we wrote a memorandum to them about being taken away from this area, at least fifty miles from this place, the protection officer was at this meeting and was having the same words as the settlement commandant; he said that security is entirely up to the government and they can do this best with the soldiers, and as the UNHCR, they cannot do anything as they are under the government just as we are (ibid.).

In one of the worst attacks, in October 1996, over 100 Sudanese refugees were killed in Achol-Pii and Agago settlements in Kitgum; 48 of them were children (Lomo 1999a: 167; *see also* UNHCR 1997d). Yet President Museveni was quoted as having stated that 'it is common sense that when someone is in danger, he runs away to places of safety. This is common sense ... only an enemy can tell you to remain in a dangerous place (as quoted by Lomo 1999b).' Some decided to flee and to move to Kiryandongo, in Masindi district, but they were not registered for rations, causing enormous hardships for those who had to share their own rations and increasing the overall malnutrition in the settlement (Kaiser 2000).

The attacks were frequent and appeared to follow a pattern:

> ... rebels enter the settlement around 10:00PM to 11:00PM, refugees are captured and bound, the houses and fields are looted of food, pots, clothes and other household items, and refugees are stripped and forced to carry the loot as they are marched to Zoka Forest. Most are then released to find their own way back to the settlements ... They are forced to walk often as far as 20 kilometres barefooted and are beaten up on the way to the forest. Young persons are at particular risk during these incursions: boys are forcibly recruited to become LRA fighters, and girls are forced to become 'wives' to one of the rebels and to follow him (RLP 2001: 6–7).

Children were often a target during these rebel attacks in northern Uganda. P., a refugee in Mongola settlement working for LWF, told us about the his and his son's experience:

> ... from July to August 1997, many boys and girls were abducted. The first village to be attacked was Adidi, where about eleven were abducted and fifteen escaped. The second attack was on Opi village where the dispensary was attacked and twenty-six children were abducted. Mongola and Aliwara were also raided, but they failed to abduct anyone there. The third attack occurred in Esia village where there was looting in the market. Stores and the base were looted, and some people were abducted. During one of the attacks, thirty-eight rebels came and used my compound as a base. They stayed from 10 p.m. to 4 a.m. using children as labour for logistical stuff. It was raining heavy and I ran to the bush to hide. When I returned, everything was in a mess and my child was missing ... the rebels have no base. When they rest, they go deep into the forest and communicate with handsets. They are divided by sections. For two days, the abducted children were given no food or water. When the children got weak, they were given cassava.

> When they reached the forest, religious rituals were performed. They put a cross of oil on their faces after prayers, and said that they are only fighting the government and nothing else, and that they will not fail. They try and convince the children that they are the right persons for the government of Uganda so that each child will have his/her rights. My son was taken through a village only of walls and no roofs – I think it was in Acholi or Gulu area. There are women participating as soldiers according to him. The abductees are put in the middle of the camp and are surrounded by

the rebels to prevent escape. The bush life was hard, without appropriate clothes; the rebels took the ones the children were wearing and gave them dirty underwear or shorts. My son cannot tell why or where exactly they were released. They were given a letter copied to UNHCR that they [the rebels] would be coming.[94]

Among those abducted by the LRA, many were boys and girls. At the school in Mongola they kept a list of primary students abducted or missing: on 18 March 1998 the list had eleven students, one of whom was believed to have been killed while six managed to escape after some time in captivity. One of the teachers reported, during a focus group held in Mongola I, that:

> ... on 17 November 1997, the rebels came and first attacked our families looting all of our properties. My brother and neighbours were abducted. My brother escaped from Pajele County in Kitgum. He reported to the Local Council who took him to the army where he was imprisoned for two weeks in Gulu. He returned to us and his mind is still not settled. He had finished P6 but has not yet returned to school.[95]

In Moyo, settlements were attacked by the WNBF. The sight of a settlement in the immediate aftermath of an attack was harrowing:

> Along our way to Kali we passed the Waka area and there was *tukul* after *tukul* abandoned and some kicked over with the roofs burnt. It was eerie, like a ghost town ... Why is it that the agencies around keep resorting to comparing the refugees to the nationals and state that the refugees are no better off than the locals and that the locals are suffering from the same insecurity. Why is it then that only settlements are targeted?[96]

UNHCR offices and staff were not spared. In 1996, a Khartoum government Antonov plane dropped a bomb near the UNHCR compound in Pakelle, leaving a large crater. In October 1996, UNHCR's sub-office in Pakelle was attacked by rebel forces. During the attack, fourteen motor vehicles were burnt, but miraculously no member of staff was injured (UNHCR 1997d). A family of expatriate staff members had a near escape, as the door to their house was just being demolished when help arrived. After 1997 the situation became progressively worse. Humanitarian newsletters from the region include many reports of rebel attacks against refugees, and yet probably only a minority of attacks were reported (e.g., IRIN 2001; OCHA 2000a, 2000b, 2000c, 2001; *Sudan Monitor* 2000).

A Sudanese refugee, C., whom we first interviewed in Kampala at the beginning of April 1999, was perhaps too cynical about the role of UNHCR in protecting the refugees' security, but his bitterness was far from uncommon amongst refugees (case no. 125/SUD/U/1999). A defector from the SPLA, he had been assigned by UNHCR to Rhino camp despite the well-known SPLA presence in Arua district, where the camp is located near the Congo/Uganda border. It was not long before C. was recognised by an SPLA soldier in the camp who had come to visit his family on 'R and R'. C. decided to leave the camp and return to Kampala. He said:

> In my opinion, the UN of today has no power because there are instances here where our eyes, noses, and ears are cut off and nothing is reported – no action taken. They are here as I see it to get money – get rich and for economic reasons – not to protect or push for the human rights of refugees. Often when the rebels come, we are driven away and then the UN forced us to come back to those places. In Waka across the Nile, people ran and then the UN forced them back saying if you don't go back you won't get food – it's there. They are using our blood for food. All of the instances taking place here have not been reported to the world; they are kept quiet and the sooner there are independent observers to report to the world, the better.[97]

The destruction of Ogujebe transit camp

The final closing and destruction of the Ogujebe transit camp in Adjumani illustrates the disregard of the government and UNHCR for the safety of refugees. Despite being referred to as a transit centre, the area had been inhabited by refugees since at least 1986 (Harrell-Bond and Kanyeihamba 1986). With the help of rations from the World Food Programme (WFP), many refugees had established themselves economically, and most were either self-employed or were in paid employment. They had established new social networks, and also enjoyed more physical security than that in the settlements, which were prone to rebel attack from across the Sudan border via Aringa county and from across the Kitgum/Gulu border. The market in Ogujebe was reported to be the largest in northern Uganda.

When land became available for placing these people in agricultural settlements, efforts were made to persuade all of them to move. Some responded and moved willingly, mainly to the settlements across the Nile in Palorinya. Others were moved to settlements along the Kitgum/Gulu border. But many chose to stay in Ogujebe. Others, who had first agreed to move, returned to Ogujebe after they had suffered rebel attacks in the settlements, where looting, rapes, murders, and abductions had taken place.

In one week, as noted earlier, 24,000 refugees were forcibly uprooted from Ogujebe, where, because of its location near Adjumani town, they had lived in relative safety and to which many refugees from neighbouring settlements had fled when their settlements were under attack. The uprooted refugees were forcibly relocated in Palorinya where, as we discussed above, many refugees had already been killed during attacks. The closure of Ogujebe was to be marked with an official ceremony to hand back the land to the owner 'with people from government and Geneva'.[98]

For the refugees, however, there was little to celebrate. A member of our team wrote in her field notebook:

> When I passed through on 14 February on a trip with AEF [African Education Fund] to go to Palorinya … I was appalled at the level of chaos and devastation. On that day, thousands of people lined the market road with piles of their belongings and all of the shops were taking out their merchandise in order to evacuate. They had been threatened by the settlement commandant that the army would be brought in after Sunday, 15 February, to raze the place to the ground and to force out anyone who stayed behind. The level of anger, frustration and frantic movement was unbelievable. LWF brought in truck after truck to pile up people with all of their possessions and to get them out as quickly as possible because the Geneva delegation was coming and the place had to be completely empty for their arrival. The inhumanity of it all made me determined to spend all of Sunday talking to people, taking photos, and watching the procedure. I was shocked at their [the refugees'] initial anger towards me as they I thought I was with UNHCR. After explaining that I was trying to document their suffering, they calmed down and groups of fifty plus gathered around to voice their anger and opinions on what was happening to them …

> I met up with the local owner of the land who informed us that they had first been told about the transfer in a meeting with ACORD [Agency for Cooperation and Research Development] sometime in mid-January. He and the local elders immediately began lobbying and pressuring the RDC [resident district commissioner] to please not move these people off his land … When we talked with the owner today, he had not even been invited to the closing ceremonies of Ogujebe. Who then are the locals that they are handing this land over to?[99]

According to William Sakataka, head of UNHCR's sub-office in Pakelle:

> In 1994, there was an agreement with the local government to make Ogujebe a local settlement programme where eventually we cut down care and maintenance each year. Each year, however, we have fallen short of the target. I came last August and one quarter of the refugee population was still in Ogujebe and so we set another target to move them out because it was clear that by 1998 there would have been no more funds for Care and Maintenance, and we would have had to spend money that we did not have for these people in Ogujebe. The donors have been persisting in giving funds to make them self-sufficient. It is primarily an issue of shortage of funds. Our financial year begins on 1 February and so we give ourselves two weeks to achieve the closing of Ogujebe … In Ogujebe, demolition is not really demolition. People move out; we have teams pulling down abandoned shacks to prevent recycling and we want to begin environmental rehabilitation. Officials are coming to hand over the site to the local population.[100]

As an official working for Uganda's Transcultural Psycho-social Organisation (TPO), which provided counselling in the camps, explained,

'In my view, the land they give and the food service of Action against Hunger (Action contre la Faim – ACF) in Mongola and Maaji is very adequate; the refugees, I think, appreciate their work. They don't refuse the place because it is a settlement or because it is far; they refuse it because of security.'[101] He added that 'in Mongola, where the refugees were moved from Ogujebe, the suicide cases were almost monthly. It is too early to see the results of the current transitions from Ogujebe. One of the complaints raised by the refugees is that NGOs will say "the situation is normal" on their handsets when they are not on the ground and in the settlements where the situation may actually not be normal.'[102]

The destruction of the transit camp of Ogujebe was part of a policy in Uganda which is explained in one of UNHCR's country operations plans: 'As the government could only consider allocation of additional land once the present settlement capacity is saturated and there are remaining refugees in the transit camps, the local settlement programme for Sudanese refugees will be pursued concentrating on transfer of refugees from transit camps to settlements even if these settlements are equip [*sic*] with only basic life-sustaining services and infrastructures (UNHCR 1996g: 9).' UNHCR's representative, Hans Thoolen, confirmed that the destruction of Ogujebe was 'necessary', because 'The refugees had no rights to their houses because they did not own the land, and it was actually the locals and especially the traders who were trying to obstruct the eviction.' When we pointed out that the landlords were willing to let the refugees stay, Mr Thoolen replied that 'at the end of it all, they would still come to demand for money/payment from UNHCR. You need to distinguish between a job not properly done and real violation of refugee rights.'[103]

In planning the evictions and destruction of Ogujebe, UNHCR and its partners also acted in disregard of the rights of the nationals. Indeed, the nationals had benefited to an extraordinary degree from the presence of the refugees, especially from the infrastructure that had been erected during their residence. Even a Sudanese theological school had been built adjacent to the transit centre. Landlords protested at the closing of Ogujebe.[104] In accordance with UNHCR's determination to ensure that refugees could not return, all developments constructed on the land – including houses, shops, and a 100-bed hospital – were flattened by a bulldozer. Yet, under Ugandan land law, all physical improvements that are fixtures on land are part of the land and revert to the landlord(s). Chattels – that is, things that can be removed without affecting the land – are not part of the land and cannot be retained by those who hold the land. The permanent buildings in Ogujebe were fixtures and the landlords had the right to sue for damages.

When we asked the LWF field coordinator to justify LWF's involvement, he explained:

We are judged by our output and not by methodology. We were constrained by a number of factors, like time. The deadline for the closure of Ogujebe was 15 February 1998. At first refugees accepted to move but later they rejected the idea, arguing that it was not safe for them to move to some of the settlements which were at the periphery. Whereas it was important that we had to move refugees, the context in which we worked must be clearly read ... The business community was one of the interest groups. There were cattle keepers and church leaders. The cattle keepers said they wanted to graze their cattle there. There were also religious leaders who rallied the people behind them [to resist the movement]. They did not address the question of self-sufficiency. They were sure that the nationals would give them land.

Q: If they were going to get land, then why not help them where they feel that they can feel safer and have no problem with land? If the nationals were giving them land, why was this idea rejected?

It would be against the policy of the MoLG [to let refugees live on the land given to them by Ugandan landowners], which is that refugees should stay in settlements. We received the grievances of traders, but how would we reconcile them with other interest groups? If we favoured one group, we would have to consider the others as well. This would affect the policy.[105]

He concluded by observing that LWF's hands were tied and that it had to carry out UNHCR's orders: 'Well, he who pays the piper calls the tune. Unless NGOs have their own resources, they cannot change much.'

From Mombasa to Dadaab: the journey to insecurity in Kenya

In Kenya, there were also examples of the forced relocation en masse of refugee populations to unsafe areas. In October 1997, some 20,000 refugees still had to be relocated from the camps around Mombasa. The hardships of the relocation and the trauma of the decisions being forced upon many of the refugees were witnessed during visits to Jomvu camp just before its final closure and the bulldozing of the structures. In this camp, out of a total population of about 5,200 registered refugees, around 3,000 had opted for repatriation to Somalia instead of relocation to Kakuma. Those who were going to be repatriated would receive US$ 30 each and would be accompanied to the border. For many, awareness of the insecurity in both Dadaab and Kakuma was a key factor in their decision to opt for repatriation. In fact: 'The coastal camps have been blessed with better security due to their proximity to urban areas as compared with the hazardous location on the Dadaab camps which are nearer the Somali border, and often targeted by armed bandits. This factor has attracted many refugees to the coast who would rather be *unregistered and unassisted in urban areas than go to the other camps in Kenya* (Okoro 1995 [emphasis added]).

Others emphasised that the complete lack of prospects and the malnutrition in the camps were 'push factors': 'At least in Somalia we can still try to do something with our lives, although it is not easy because of the fighting. But I prefer Somalia to Kakuma, where there is nothing one can do. If something goes wrong in Somalia, I will die in my country. If I have to choose my death, I prefer to be shot dead in Somalia than to starve to death in Kakuma'.[106]

Security in Kampala

In Uganda, refugees from the Great Lakes region were at particular risk even in Kampala, mainly because of Uganda's military involvement in the war in eastern DRC. In the aftermath of Laurent Kabila's victory, many Congolese who had exposed human rights violations by Kabila's forces and the RCD or who were suspected to be in any way opposed to Kabila fled to Uganda, but did not find the sanctuary they had hoped for. Many of the refugees we interviewed in that period reported harassment, arbitrary arrests, interrogations, abductions, and even disappearances. These are some examples: a Congolese priest was abducted by three armed men (case no. 029/DRC/U/2000); in the case of another Congolese refugee, a student, the abduction did not succeed (case no. 036/DRC/U/1999); a human rights activist who knew of RCD agents in Kampala 'disappeared' for a few weeks (case no. 037/DRC/U/1999); a former national security agent had to leave Kyangwali camp, but was then attacked in his home in Kampala (case no. 042/DRC/U/1999); another Congolese refugee who had worked for a human rights NGO saw members of the RCD intelligence agency at InterAid posing as refugees (case no. 062/DRC/U/1999), a sighting confirmed by a refugee woman who had worked in the governor's office in the DRC (case nos. 059/DRC/U/1999; *see* also 101/DRC/U/1999, 187/DRC/U/ 2000). One refugee, who was better off than most others, thought that the situation in Kampala was so unsafe owing to the presence of RCD agents that he decided to hire guards for his house, after several attempted intrusions. Unsurprisingly, some thought Uganda too insecure, and moved to Kenya (case no. 029/DRC/K/1998).

As discussed above, abductions of Rwandan Hutus in Uganda with the complicity of Museveni's regime had been reported by the media as early as August 1996. One month later, John Mwesigwa, a Rwandan businessman, was reported to have been abducted from Luwum Street in Kampala.[107] There were cases of Rwandan Hutus being abducted from their homes and places of business, and subjected to threats, beatings, interrogation, and deportation (e.g., case no. 007/RW/U/1999). Evidence exists that some were initially arrested on minor charges such as theft, and then turned over to the Rwandan authorities. Reported abductees included a schoolteacher, a former Rwandan judge, a human rights lawyer, a university lecturer, a driver, and a trader. According to some, most of the disappearances were carried out by Ugandan internal security or Interpol (Weddi 1998; Mutumba 1998b). Some refugees evaded abduction only to face intimidation by members of the RCD who did not hesitate to stop, interrogate, and harass their political opponents in the streets of Kampala (e.g., case no. 068/DRC/U/1999).

On 19 May 1998, during a visit by the US ambassador, Nancy Powell, the chairperson of the UHRC, Margaret Sekaggya, confirmed that there was an escalation in abductions of Rwandan and Congolese in Uganda.[108] She estimated that there had been at least ten new abductions in 1998, in addition to at least four documented by the commission in 1997.[109] Two months earlier, the commission publicly alleged that the majority of the abductions and violations were being committed by the Internal Security Organisation (ISO) and the External Security Organisation (ESO) in Uganda, both based in the Office of the President.[110] This finding prompted the director of social affairs, Lt Kasule, to visit the UHRC a few days later, to deny the allegations publicly and to assure the UHRC that ISO would cooperate in identifying any of its members involved in such activities. Around the same time, Amnesty International issued an 'Urgent Action', calling attention to these same cases of abduction and deportation, arbitrary arrest, and extra-judicial execution of Rwandan nationals within Uganda.[111]

In Kampala, the hostel run by the Salvation Army was meant to provide safe accommodation for security cases and to protect refugees from extra-judicial executions or abduction. E., an educated and articulate middle-class woman from the DRC, was one of the residents of this 'safe hostel' (case no. 033/DRC/U/1999). She was placed there after she had been abducted at night from the streets of Kampala and had managed to escape from her assailants on the highway leading back to DRC.[112] For some time after this, she and her children lived outside in the UNHCR compound. Back in the hostel, she openly criticised the way it was run and she was ejected in retaliation. After that, she lived with her two young children in an open hostel with no special security, sleeping on the bare floor, and, at one point, was forced to share her room with nine Sudanese men.[113]

Refugees from other ethnic groups also feared possible abduction by security forces from their country of origin. H. from Burundi reported to us that he had left Oruchinga refugee camp in Uganda after four other Burundians were abducted from there within the space of two weeks. The camp commandant gave him permission to leave the camp and seek resettlement in Kampala through UNHCR. He applied for resettlement, but, at the time of our interview, his application had been delayed because it was purportedly 'lost'. Meanwhile, H.'s fears of abduction were further fuelled by reports that three other Burundians seeking resettlement had recently been abducted (case no. 222/BUR/U/1998). K. from Kenya also reported that he had been seeking resettlement through UNHCR as his family had been confronted twice by 'strange men' enquiring after him and he feared abduction by Kenyan security forces in Uganda. In Kenya, he worked as a campaigner for the Kenya Civil Servants Union and had had four attempts on his life. In Uganda, his own son mysteriously disappeared and later reappeared with signs of mental illness. After contacting the local Amnesty International branch, K. was able to put appropriate pressure on UNHCR to give priority to his claim (case no. 218/KY/U/1999). Many Sudanese refugees in Kampala feared reporting threats from the SPLA to the police or attempted forced recruitment, because of the close alliance between the SPLA and the Ugandan government (case nos. 123/SUD/U/1999; /206/SUD/U/1999).

In a few cases, foreign government officials attempted to use the asylum system to enter a country in order to target or gather information on refugees. A senior officer of the special branch in Uganda reported his success on two occasions in stopping Kenyan government officials who were attempting to use this route as a means of entering the country to eliminate other Kenyans regarded as 'enemies of the state'.[114] In one case, the would-be asylum-seeker was detained and the Kenyan government intervened to have him released and returned to Kenya. That others have been successful is demonstrated by the kidnapping of Koigi wa Wamwere who 'was detained in Kenya in 1990 after he had been abducted from Uganda'.[115] An RCD intelligence officer was granted refugee status in 1999 and was often seen at InterAid, as well as the Amnesty offices in Kampala.[116]

Arbitrary arrest and detention

In Kenya, only a few lawsuits were ever brought against the police for unlawful arrest (Mutunga 1990: 10–12) – none, to our knowledge, by refugees. Arbitrary arrests were common in camps. For example, L., having been arbitrarily arrested and detained in Kakuma, decided to leave the camp and go first to Nairobi, and then on to Kampala, where we interviewed him (case no. 175/ETH/U/1998). His home in Kakuma had been broken into at night by the Kenyan police and looted. He reported this incident to the UNHCR protection staff in the sub-office but no investigation was carried out and he was told to return home. L. refused and demanded protection from UNHCR. The protection staff reportedly called the police who beat him up and then took him to Lodwar prison where he was detained for three days. L. was finally brought before the court on the charge of 'underestimating the ability of the government to provide security', an offence which does not feature in Kenyan criminal law. The UNHCR protection officer (Mr Abuya) appeared in court as a complainant. The magistrate dismissed the case. This is an example of a criminal prosecution against refugees instigated by UNHCR which failed in court.[117]

Lack of identification documents made refugees vulnerable to arbitrary arrest. In Uganda, according to the camp commandant in Palorinya, Moyo district, ID cards were given only to 'adult' refugees; we also found refugees in Nakivale with ID cards issued by the Directorate of Refugees (DoR). Nevertheless, aside from students, it was only a few refugees who possessed proper identification documents. By 2003 the situation had begun to change, with UNHCR and the government agreeing on the need to abandon the old 'protection letters' and to provide refugees with ID cards.

In Kenya, protection letters, normally A4-size sheets of paper with a passport-size photograph of the refugee, simply stated that the bearer was a refugee in Kenya recognised by the office of UNHCR. It normally instructed the refugee to report to one of the camps by a certain date. Only a small minority of refugees had letters that indicated that they could reside in Nairobi on medical or educational grounds, although possession of this letter did not guarantee protection from arbitrary arrest (case no. 020/BUR/K/1996). As in Uganda, the only form of identification possessed by the vast majority of refugees who had registered directly in the camps was their own ration cards. Many refugees tried to get regular visas on their passports as, in practice, visas were a better form of protection than 'protection letters'. Possessing a valid passport was at times viewed as proof of country-of-origin protection by UNHCR, and as a result refugees often denied having them when interviewed by UNHCR.

The many who fell foul of the police had to pay bribes to avoid imprisonment or to gain release from arbitrary arrest, the amount depending on a number of factors. Somalis, often viewed as wealthy and as a good source of illicit earnings for the police, normally had to pay thousands of shillings. In Pangani police station, in 1997, KSh 15,000 (about US$ 100) was apparently extorted for releasing six Somalis.

The amount of the bribe depended as much on the mood of a policeman as on his assessment of the resources of his victim. A Congolese refugee living in Kangemi, a suburb of Nairobi, received a 'visit' in his home by two police officers. An argument ensued over the amount he had to pay to avoid arrest. The police finally realised that M.F. had no money to offer and, as he related, a compromise was struck: 'I had a protection letter that was in order, but they wanted to arrest me anyway. As I did not have the money, they took my shoes and promised that they would come back, but I have not seen them since. I think insecurity and injustice have really reached the peak here in Kenya.' Other circumstances contributed to determining the cost of the bribe: 'The price changed if you were paying when the police came to pick you up or if you were paying to be released after being arrested and taken to a police station. When they just come to your place, 500 or 600 shillings can be enough, but your relatives or friends will need more than that to get you out of the cells!'(case no. 037/DRC/K/1997).

T., a Sudanese lawyer working for the SPLA, was disenchanted with the role of the courts: 'At the end of the day, we know that there is practically no court remedy against arbitrary arrests of refugees here in Kenya. It is something which may not be officially condoned, but indirectly it is approved of. In order to get our people out we try to use other channels, mainly political contacts. We know that through the courts we would not get anywhere.'

To the courts' credit, however, when cases reached them, some of them were known to order the release of the refugees. In Makadera court, in July/August 1997, twenty-five non-Kenyans appeared on charges of unlawful presence in the country. The eight who presented UNHCR protection letters were immediately discharged. The others were either served with a repatriation order, or, if they claimed to be refugees, they were given time to legalise their status.[118]

Immigration officials in fact often complained that courts were 'too lenient'. They also criticised courts, like Kabera court, for failing to penalise refugees for not residing in camps; some magistrates rebutted that there was no statute that mandated residence in camps. According to one official, the Immigration Department preferred to conduct the prosecutions directly rather than ask the police to do it, because they 'do not know how to prosecute. An alien unlawfully in the country would only be charged on three counts by the police who will eventually reduce these to only one count. Instead, such an alien is fit to be charged with at least 7 counts: unlawful presence in the country; forged passport; failure to report entry into the country; failure to register after 90 days of presence in the country; failure to report entry, forged entries onto genuine passport; misleading [sic].'[119]

In addition to UNHCR, which used to visit the police stations during roundups, other groups attempted to obtain the release of refugees. For example, the Sudan Women's Association in Nairobi (SWAN) had at least two lawyers who would intervene on behalf of women who had been arrested. On at least one occasion, 'rights education' proved to be quite effective: having received the training, one member of SWAN whose husband had been arrested, successfully claimed her right to visit him in spite of the attempts of the police to extract a bribe. During the July/August roundups, Amnesty International wrote to President Moi expressing concern about 'the wave of apparently arbitrary arrests of hundreds of foreign nationals in Kenya' (Amnesty International 1997d). In its letter, which had been preceded by numerous appeals sent by individual

Amnesty members around the world, a list of some 140 persons, mainly Rwandan and Burundian, was included and information about their whereabouts was requested.

In Uganda, UNHCR's response to the roundups and imprisonment of refugees was erratic, seemingly depending on who was the protection officer in charge. For example, in Adjumani, the officer in charge of the prison farm, who had been in that position since 1995, said that when the protection officer was one 'Mr Bright', the issue of bail was 'alleviated'. He would write to UNHCR and they would respond in a positive way, paying bail 'in very many cases'.[120] On some occasions, UNHCR hired lawyers to assist and represent refugees. In February 1998, a lawyer, paid by UNHCR, prepared a writ of habeas corpus on behalf of the wife of a Rwandan who had been abducted and detained by a combined force of Ugandan and Rwandan security operatives.[121] In another case, five Somali refugees were arrested, together with the desk officer from the DoR, and charged with 'malicious damage of property' in Mbarara. They were sentenced by a lower Magistrates' Court to six months in prison. On appeal to the Chief Magistrates' Court, they were represented by Ojiambo Wejuli-Wabwire & Co. Advocates, a private firm in Kampala, at the expense of UNHCR. In another case, involving the detention of an Ethiopian on charges of criminal trespass, the combined efforts of the Legal Aid Project (LAP) and Doreen Lwanga, a member of the Human Rights and Peace Centre (HURIPEC) Alumni Club Prisons Project, persuaded UNHCR to stand surety for his bail.

It is not entirely clear on what basis UNHCR decided to provide legal assistance, although, as the director of the division of international protection reminded field offices, UNHCR had funds for legal aid to be spent in conjunction with NGOs.[122] Whenever the charges involve a violation of the 1951 Convention, UNHCR should be expected to intervene in court – and, where necessary, it ought to provide legal assistance to refugees directly or through an NGO. For example, in the case of refugees charged with unlawful presence in the country, it is indisputable that their conviction would constitute a significant breach of the Convention and could result in *refoulement*. UNHCR should also assist those refugees who, in the country of asylum, face criminal charges that are related to the very persecution from which they fled. The many Congolese and Sudanese refugees arrested in Uganda charged with treason are a case in point.

The Constitution of Uganda also prescribes a limit of forty-eight hours of detention before charges are formulated (art. 23(4)(b)). We found in the case of J., a Burundian refugee, that he had been arbitrarily detained and questioned without charge by the Ugandan ISO for a total of five days on his way to Nakivale camp from Kampala. He was also subjected to eighteen days labour in a local prison. After his release, he was told to report to the ISO every Friday for two months (case no. 226/BUR/U/1999). In prisons we visited in Uganda, we found refugees being held on remand for periods far exceeding the constitutional limit of 360 days for capital offences and 120 days for non-capital offences (art. 23(6)). For example, in *Uganda v. Solomon Khemis*, the accused was kept in remand in Moyo for nearly three years, although the charge was petty theft (of a bicycle) committed in Sudan. Overall, however, it should be noted that we found no evidence that the treatment of refugees by the criminal justice system was any more unjust than for Ugandans (Harrell-Bond 1999c: 23).

The majority of the refugees we interviewed during our visits to Ugandan prisons had been arrested by the army. The situation was particularly bad in the north of Uganda.[123] Military personnel arrested the majority of the seventy refugees that we interviewed in prisons in Moyo, Adjumani, and Kampala, although the National Resistance Army (NRA) statute no. 3, 1992 lays down penalties for military personnel who unlawfully detain or confine any other person.[124] The extent to which these rules were breached was alarming.

In Adjumani, the magistrate, Joseph Emodo Nyanga, confirmed that unnecessarily long detentions on remand were a serious problem, affecting refugees and nationals alike. He said that this was 'due to a lack of speedy investigation/prosecution' and added that 'There was one case of a boy who stole something worth only 4,000 shillings [less than US$ 3] and was in remand for seven to eight months before the case ever reached me. I was so bitter.'[125] He also observed that, when a person is taken into police custody, the Constitution obliges the police immediately to inform the next of kin, the lawyer, or the personal doctor, and to grant access to the accused. However, this provision was seldom applied to nationals, and 'it is worse for refugees where it is very difficult to trace the next of kin; for those in the camps, we advise the police to inform the settlement commandant and the protection officer, but I highly doubt whether this is being done'.[126] Another problem, affecting refugees more than nationals, was the failure by the police to communicate in a language that the accused person could understand, as prescribed by the Constitution.

In Luzira remand prison, we found a group of twenty-four Sudanese and Congolese refugees who had spent over two years in prison (*see also* Abbey 1999).[127] The army had arrested them and brought them to Luzira. No charge against them had been formulated, probably because there was no offence that they could have been charged with. They had been refugees in Yei, Sudan, when it fell to the combined forces of the SPLA, the Uganda People's Defence Forces (UPDF), and Kabila's forces, the Alliance of Democratic Forces for the Liberation of Congo (ADFL). In November they were arrested, accused of supporting the Khartoum government, and handed over to the UPDF to be returned to their home country. In February 1998, these men were brought to Uganda and eventually locked up in Luzira; their families were left behind in Yei.

In Luzira, we interviewed M.J., who had been a self-settled refugee in Koboko county. Soldiers had arrested him in October 1993 when he was visiting a market at Keri. He reported being beaten and tortured by his captors who wanted him to confess that he was a member of the WNBF. He was subsequently detained by them in several places, including the military barracks at Gilgil in Arua and Makindye in Kampala. Eventually in 1997, a group of Sudanese refugees, including M.J., all of whom had been arrested individually, were charged *collectively* in court with treason, a crime punishable by death. None had been visited by a lawyer.[128]

Another Sudanese refugee, R.A., interviewed at Luzira, was suspected of being a rebel, and was arrested by soldiers and taken to Monudu barracks, where he was interrogated and given twenty-three strokes of the cane. The soldiers informed him that they had been tipped off that he was a rebel. When he denied that this was true, he was beaten again and told that if he confessed, they would set him free. If he did not, they would kill him. He told them he would rather die since he knew nothing about rebels. He was then transferred to Koboko barracks where he was kept until 27 May 1996, and then to Makindye barracks in Kampala. It was only on 17 March 1997 that he, together with twenty-five others, refugees and Ugandans, was finally taken to Buganda Road court and charged with 'trying to overthrow the Government of Uganda' – that is treason. They pleaded not guilty and the court remanded them for 360 days, ignoring the fact that R.A. had already spent almost two years detained by the army.

R.A.'s nightmare seemed to have come to an end when, on 3 March 1998, he and other Sudanese were released on court bond and told to go back to Arua. They were given release forms. Around 6 pm on the same day, the police told them that since 'it was late' and security in Kampala is 'tight', it was not safe for them to go, and they were invited to spend the night at the Kampala central police station. Then they were locked up and their release forms were collected by police officers. The following morning, a police officer informed them that there 'were impending murder charges against them'. The group was charged with the murder of a local councillor in Koboko who had allegedly been killed in July 1996. M.J. wondered how he could have been accused of having killed someone on this date when he had been in prison since 1995. He was remanded back to Luzira. On 5 March 1998 they were all given new 'prison numbers' indicating they were there on fresh charges of murder.

Visits were made to Onigo and Silili (Moyo) and Openjinji prison farm (Adjumani), and, in Kampala district, the four units of Luzira prison. Both prison officials and refugee prisoners were interviewed and these data demonstrate the seriousness of the problems faced by refugees in gaining access to justice. In Moyo and Adjumani, we found prisoners, including refugees, who had been arrested on charges that can only be tried by the

High Court. However, the High Court had not sat in that region since 1994. Data on conditions in prisons and the problems of refugees who had been detained were also drawn from interviews with individuals. We found, for example, that refugees who were released were often unaware of their right to collect their release paper from the court.

Although we did not dwell on sentencing practice, and we neither sought nor found any evidence that refugees were handed harsher sentences than nationals, exemplary punishment was common; the standard formula in Moyo, for example, was 'to discourage other refugees and for the accused to learn a lesson in the future' (*Uganda v. Lemi and Yopkwe*, criminal case no. 32/96).

As mentioned, some refugees were charged with treason. This was anomalous, given that treason is a crime normally believed to presuppose that particular link of loyalty between the person and the state that is conferred by citizenship – whether through birth or through naturalisation. In Luzira prison alone in August 1999, thirty-one refugees were being held on charges of treason. When we wrote to the UHRC about these cases, the commissioner sitting on the police and prisons committee replied:

> I have several times personally been to Kampala Remand Prison and have met and talked with all prisoners from West Nile region charged with 'Treason'. They were 553 in number. Although they repeatedly told they were arrested from various places in West Nile region and in Southern Sudan none did inform me that some had been arrested from a refugee camp in Arua.

> However, between 11th and 14th October 1999, 147 of them, who had been transferred back to Arua prison on 10th October 1999, were acquitted in Arua Chief Magistrate's Court. The Director of Public Prosecutions has assured us that the rest will also be taken to court in due course.[129]

The security forces suspected these refugees of being associated with the WBNF. Their lack of identification prompted their arrest and detention under the charge commonly used against many Ugandan rebels, and against all those accused of conspiring to overthrow the Ugandan government with violent means. By 2000 most of them had been released, along with the many Ugandans, as the WBNF was declared 'defunct' and the insurgency in the West Nile over.

Forced recruitment

The legal standards for the protection of children in armed conflict have been crystallised with the adoption of the Convention on the Rights of the Child (CRC), to which 192 states are parties. Articles 38 and 39, while arguably not introducing an altogether new rule, have the benefit of synthesising the protection deriving from the two relevant but distinct bodies of international law, international humanitarian law and human rights law. Article 38 obliges states to ensure that children under the age of 15 are not recruited to the army and take no part in hostilities, and it also recalls the obligations towards civilians under the laws of warfare; article 39 concerns the social reintegration of children affected by war. An optional protocol, which raises the minimum age to 18, has been added to the Convention, and Kenya and Uganda have become parties to it.[130]

Despite this progress on the legal side, the recruitment of minors by both official and irregular armed forces remains a dismal feature of contemporary armed conflicts (Cohn and Goodwin-Gill 1994). One of the most publicised UN reports of the 1990s – the 'Machel report' on the impact of armed conflict on children – detailed the ways in which children are recruited and used by armed groups, as well as the challenges posed by their reintegration in society at the end of hostilities (UNICEF 1996: paras. 36–57). By virtue of its being 'often the first to respond to emergencies' (id.: para. 293), UNHCR has a particularly important role to play, according to the report, both in preventing recruitment of minors from refugee populations and in ensuring the reintegration of child soldiers in the host society in the event of return.

By general admission, child soldiers were prominent in the armed groups involved in the conflicts which refugees in Kenya and Uganda had fled, Somalia and Sudan having become particularly notorious for this practice. The proximity of the Kenyan and Ugandan refugee camps to the borders constituted a risk factor in the forced recruitment of minors. In fact, the reality in Kakuma was dramatic: of the 12,000 Sudanese minors who had first arrived in Kakuma, only 3800 were left in 2000–01, when they were resettled in the US (RCK 2001b); the others were not accounted for, and most were believed to have been recruited and sent to the front line in Sudan.[131] According to an intern who worked for UNHCR and LWF:

> Last year, over 5,000 [Sudanese] were taken from Kakuma refugee camp to the war front, where most of them died. The type of clothing found on their dead bodies enable them to be traced to this camp. Because Kakuma is located so close to the Sudanese Border, commanders ... often enter the camp. They meet with Community leaders here, who are required to produce a certain number of youths ... The boys have no choice other than to obey their elders, if they don't wish to be outcast from the society (Reuer 1998).

She concludes, 'I become painfully aware of all of my misconceptions about refugee camps. They were not safe havens; they were not safe places'. Yet, in its protection report for the same period UNHCR stated that:

In general military recruitment out of the Kakuma camp has reduced ... However, this does not exclude the fact that a number of persons are recruited in the camp and community pressure on the individual might lead to a voluntary decision to become a soldier. Also, idleness and boredom resulting in frustration can and has led to choosing recruitment as a way out, although enhanced activities for children have been implemented (UNHCR 1998b: chap. V).

For many children who had escaped the war in Sudan, Kenya turned out to be an unsafe refuge. In 1996 an SPLA mobilisation team was dispatched to Kakuma and over 500 refugees were enlisted, including minors. Some of these boys had been in the SPLA 'Red Army', minors who had been trained in Ethiopia and who had escaped (case no. 210/SUD/U/1999).

The SPLA threatened, harassed, and abducted refugees, including minors, even in Nairobi, as this testimony written by Sudanese children in Nairobi reveals:

> In the last 2 years notorious SPLA ... have been finding their ways to Sr. Louise's compound. In very friendly terms they would request to meet the boys and brief them on the development of the war. Of course Sr. Louise would never take them to our compound but it still makes us fear for our lives even here in Kenya. At one time in 1993 it did happen that SPLA persons were sent at 2.00 a.m. in the night and Chief Gervasio Amotum, his wife, who was still recuperating from a stomach operation, and his daughter were abducted and transported back to Chukudum where he is forced to supply the rebel army with young men from his tribe (case no. 11/SUD/K/1997; *see* also case no. 10/SUD/K/1997).

In Uganda, the situation was even worse. Settlements usually had an SPLA recruiting officer in residence, and recruitment drives were recurrent. The SPLA even wrote to individual refugees in settlements to remind them of their military duties (case no. 128/SUD/U/1999). Individuals who were defecting or escaping from forced recruitment were accorded very little protection by UNHCR. At times, they were considered 'persons not of concern to UNHCR' because they had been combatants. The Ugandan government, a close ally of the SPLA, actively supported their recruitment activities, and this was probably one of the reasons why it so zealously advocated the concentration of Sudanese refugees in settlements in northern Uganda. Referring to the leader of the SPLA, John Garang, a magistrate we interviewed in the north, aptly commented, 'He is just free here in Uganda.' This magistrate also told us that Garang had visited the area three nights before our visit and that he had been escorted by Ugandan soldiers.[132] Abductions by the SPLA were also reported by the camp commandant for Moyo and Adjumani districts. On one occasion he reported that thirty-two refugees, for the most part believed to be former SPLA soldiers, were taken to Kiangoro by SPLA forces. However, he added that 'even though SPLA soldiers have been allowed into the camps with the camp commandant office's permission, upon suspicion or report that they cause violence while there, the police are notified for immediate arrest'.[133]

From June to September 1999, the SPLA was engaged in mass mobilisation. In Kampala, this took the form of house-to-house raids in areas where Sudanese were known to live. Earlier in the year, three refugees, hiding in Kampala while waiting for resettlement because of earlier attempts to recruit them, came to our office to report that four people who had been members of the Sudanese Christian Fellowship had been recruited as 'mobilisers'. All this was:

> ... happening with the notice of the host countries. So all refugees will face problems with the SPLA/M especially those in the North ... For those who are the target, like myself, I would say only 'God will be at my side to protect me from the SPLA/M'. Because most of cadets were my friend before they joined the SPLA/M, but now I am their first and worst enemy because I refused to be with SPLA/M. This means Kampala and Uganda in general is not safe for me at the moment.

> In February 99 A. Ochaya the officer-in-charge of asylum-seekers at Special Branch office told me that I have to get a letter from the SPLA/M office in Kampala. I told him I am not with the SPLA/M nor NIF Government [the National Islamic Front, i.e. the government of Sudan]. He insisted that I have to be with one party at least. I refused to go to the SPLA/M. And that had made A. Ochaya delay my process [for refugee status] (case no. 212/SUD/U/1999).[134]

In July 1999, John Garang addressed the people of Kiryandongo, a settlement where many thought they would be safe from the SPLA because of their distance from the border. In August, the town of Adjumani was raided by the SPLA, with the assistance of the UPDF. A woman working for TPO provided the following eyewitness account:[135]

> I live in Adjumani town, close to the centre, and on 7 August 1999, we got up in the morning as usual. While preparing breakfast with my children, I noticed a neighbour at her door bare-chested talking to a soldier. I thought she had had a fight with her husband, and the soldier came to intervene. I went out of the house about 7 a.m., but before I could go far, I saw armed men going about in uniform. I asked my immediate neighbour what was going on. She didn't know. I saw more soldiers coming. Then I could hear them shouting 'Where are your men? Where are your men?' I said I didn't have any. They said I couldn't have such a house without a man, and said I should bring him out. I invited them in to look.

> After they passed, I got up and went for work on my motorbike ... We have a Freedom Square in Adjumani. It was filled with men and soldiers. I was told they wanted able men to go and work in the Sudan, and that they were looking for SPLA deserters. The soldiers were screening everyone to determine who had identity documents.

I noticed that both the government soldiers and the SPLA soldiers were there. They screened people in the square there with the help of the LCs [Local Councils] and the police, and even the heads of some NGOs were there. The heads of NGOs went there to have their staff freed, because the soldiers said they have no problem with working people …

I eventually learnt that this operation in the town was just a cover … All the men assembled in Freedom Square were eventually released after they could prove they were working … The main operation was in the Miryei and Olua camps. After the screening, they eventually took about fifty youths from Mireyi, mostly Dinka and Nuer … All in all … they took between seventy and a hundred people.[136]

Even though the Pakelle office was only eight kilometres away, UNHCR was totally absent on this day, although NGOs at least went to Adjumani to free their staff. When one woman went to rescue the driver from her NGO, she saw Brigadier Moses Ali, then the second deputy prime minister of Uganda, arriving: 'He was moving around the district all day.'[137] This 1999 recruitment drive was confirmed later in other accounts (RLP 2001b: 11). It became clear that in this period 'the SPLA, with the assistance of the UPDF, rounded up males from Keyo, Olua, Mirieyi, and Adjumani town who did not have any refugee document' (ibid.).

Even when no mass recruitment was taking place, individuals were still harassed by the SPLA and many of them were hand-picked to go and fight in southern Sudan (ibid.: 12–13; *see also* Mugeere 2001). As one refugee put it: 'The situation is very bad and we are always living in uncertainty. Three of my sons and two of my grandsons have been forcibly recruited by the SPLA … We are always being terrorised to give our young children to be trained in the army by the SPLA. I have taken the courage to speak to you this because I know that I am already old and hopeless.'[138]

Members of the SPLA who defected and sought asylum in Kenya and Uganda encountered obstacles, although many of them had been forcibly recruited as children between the ages of 7 and 11 (e.g., case nos. 195/SUD/U/1999; 159/SUD/U/1999; 125/SUD/U/1999; 127/SUD/U/1999). The proximity to the SPLA of various humanitarian NGOs in southern Sudan meant that it would have been difficult to find support from the NGOs during flight.[139] Once in Kenya or Uganda, former SPLA members would have been at risk of revenge attacks by the SPLA. Their cases were considered with great suspicion and many of them were denied asylum. Prospective defectors, including those who had been forcibly recruited when they were still young children, had to weigh the hazard of uncertain asylum against the perils of combat and the possibility of becoming war criminals.

UNHCR's arguments that these people did not qualify for refugee status are not persuasive, given that they were fleeing from civil war, a situation covered by article 1(2) of the OAU Convention. A case could also be made for according them refugee status on the basis of individualised fear of persecution: the fact that both sides in the war in southern Sudan were known to have committed violations of the laws of war and that those who defected were harshly punished meant that defectors *were* subject to persecution, which could be viewed as resulting from their political opinions or their membership of a particular social group.[140] When interviewed, defectors did not always mention their refusal to participate in the commission of war crimes. Nevertheless, these refugees should not have been expected to articulate their fears with well-informed references to international humanitarian law. Expressions like 'I didn't want to kill my brothers' or 'I could not stand this killing any more' should have been taken as clear evidence of dissent from war, not just because of a general conscientious objection but because of the way in which the war was being fought. Why was it not realised that these were individuals eminently in need of protection and that, by protecting them as well as defectors from the Khartoum army, UNHCR would be doing some real 'conflict resolution' work?

An example of a defector whose application for refugee status was rejected was that of R. (case no. 127/SUD/U/1999), who had been abducted by the SPLA from his junior school when he was eleven years old, was interviewed by UNHCR, Uganda, and found to be a person 'out of UNHCR mandate'.[141] The senior protection officer reached this conclusion because R. was allegedly holding back information: '... on his actual involvement in human rights violations (such as throwing grenades at colleagues), but also [because of] his previous activities as a mobiliser of SPLA/SPLM ... his very recent card of membership of SPLM, issued only a few days ago, his officers rank (a lieutenant), and his actual residence in the capital in SPLA quarters all combined with the fact that we cannot really prove defection leaves us with such serious doubts'.[142]

When we interviewed R., he was terrified. A Sudanese student had directed him to the JRS and from there 'Jimmy [of JRS] brought me to InterAid'. He did not go in because he had identified 'two SPLA soldiers who actually act as spies. These were ...'[143] Like most defectors, he had not publicised his intentions and was avoiding raising suspicions. He came to us and we wrote up his case. We also escorted him to InterAid where UNHCR did *not* give him 'the benefit of the doubt'.[144] Despite the UN's proclaimed commitment to end the plight of boy soldiers, this young man, who was no longer a minor but who had been deprived of his adolescence having been forced to fight since the age of 11, was mercilessly excluded from refugee protection and left alone to face the danger of execution.[145] The hypocrisy that underlies this decision is clear in the context of the policy of UN agencies towards the SPLA. As we have mentioned, UNHCR failed to denounce or oppose in any other way the systematic forced recruitment of adults and minors in the settlements in Uganda, although it knew about them (UNHCR 1999e).[146] The UNICEF-led Operation Lifeline Sudan (OLS) also followed policy of *not* denouncing abuses.

Freedom of movement

The 1951 Convention obliges states 'to accord to refugees … the right to choose their place of residence and to move within its territory' (art. 26). The obligation to issue identity papers to refugees (art. 27) is related to the actual enjoyment of freedom of movement, since in many countries people are required to carry identification at all times. Freedom of movement is also recognised in general human rights law, in particular under the African Charter on Human and Peoples' Rights and the ICCPR (both at art. 12).

As noted earlier, freedom of movement is instrumental to the enjoyment of other human rights (Beyani 2000; RLP 2002c).[147] In order to seek employment or education, to secure means of livelihood, and sometimes in order to protect their own personal security, refugees, like all human beings, need to be free to move within the country as well as to be able to choose their place of residence (case nos. 007/DRC/K/1997; 004/DRC/K/1998; 002/DRC/K/1994; 017/DRC/K/1998; 025/DRC/K/1994; 014/SOM/K/1998; 006/BUR/K/1997; 013/BUR/K/1997; 098/DRC/U/1999). Freedom of movement is probably even more important for refugees than for the rest of the population, who can normally rely on the existence of a support network of relatives, friends, and acquaintances in a part of the country. The failure to uphold this right was perhaps the single most important obstacle to refugees recovering from the consequences of being forcibly uprooted (Lomo 1999b).

In Uganda the law criminalises a breach of the order to stay in the prescribed place. Under section 11 (a), Control of Alien Refugees Act 1960, a refugee found illegally in Uganda other than in a refugee settlement, without a permit issued under section 6 of the act commits an offence and is liable to imprisonment for a period not exceeding three months. Section 6 states that a refugee is allowed to remain in Uganda only under the terms of a permit issued by an officer authorised by the regional police commander. From an advocacy point of view, the question of freedom of movement proved especially controversial and almost intractable, not least because many nationals feared that the refugees could vote in elections if they were allowed to choose their own place of residence. When the advocacy group for the refugee bill convened to provide the Drafting

Committee with recommendations, it was difficult to reach a consensus on freedom of movement. In the report of that meeting, it was noted that 'surprisingly much reservation was expressed on the part of certain members in recommending full freedom of movement for refugees due to issues such as voting, insecurity, and political involvement' (Garry 1998c: 5).

In Kenya and Uganda, respect for the freedom of movement of refugees was the exception rather than the rule: refugees were generally expected to live where assigned and only move with a special permit. In Uganda, in order to leave a settlement 'legally', refugees first had to obtain a letter from the chairman of the RWC in order to have access to the camp commandant from whom they would then get another letter permitting them to travel to a specific destination for a limited period of time. The offices of the camp commandants were not always nearby, nor were these officials always available. Moreover, permission was not always forthcoming – both 'gatekeepers' had wide discretion: 'I went at the time as well to MoLG [the Ministry of Local Government] for a permit to stay in Kampala: they refused and said I must go to the camp. I was not willing to go to the camp in Adjumani because I really feared for my security … I don't know why UNHCR is forcing people to the camps when you are in real danger for your lives' (case no. 231/SUD/U/1997).

In Kenya, permits to leave the camps, known as 'safe travel letters', were equally hard to obtain and were issued by UNHCR and validated by the district officer. The latter did not normally require to see in person the refugee to whom he issued a permit; he 'countersigns a UNHCR "Safe Travel Letter" and stamps it with an official Government stamp' (UNHCR 1999f: 34). Nevertheless, obtaining these permits was very difficult: refugees were often unable to gain access to a protection officer and, even when they did, they were often denied the permit.

In practice, in both countries most refugees could not get the permits and took great risks to leave the camps and travel without them.[148] In Uganda, there were fewer complaints about the police, but the main danger for a refugee man travelling without a permit was arrest or detention by the military, sometimes on suspicion of being a 'rebel'. In Kenya, travelling without work permits basically meant that in budgeting for their travel, refugees had to include casual payments to policemen at the various roadblocks. In fact, the protection officer stationed in Kakuma complained that the movement of refugees out of the camps had become a business for the police 'who never arrest a single refugee'.[149] He said that UNHCR had lodged a complaint with the district officer about police accepting bribes in lieu of a travel permit, a practice that did not allow UNHCR to control movement out of the camp as effectively as they would have wished.[150]

In Kenya, Convention Travel Documents (CTDs)[151] were available only to the category of 'convention refugees', a term that, as we have seen, was given an entirely new meaning in the Kenyan context and essentially referred to refugees whom the government had recognised before 1991 (UNHCR 1999f). In Uganda, CTDs were issued by the Ministry of Internal Affairs, but in practice 'it is a nightmare to obtain a CTD ... because civil servants are not paid enough and require incentives'. In order to receive a CTD, a refugee first had to obtain a letter from UNHCR to the MoLG in which his or her application for a CTD was supported by UNHCR.[152] The MoLG would then write to the Ministry of Internal Affairs. As explained by the director of the Hugh Pilkington Trust, whose organisation funded the studies abroad of many refugees and often had to go through the process of obtaining CTDs for them:

> I personally know people in the MoLG who I can just ring, but for the individual on his own – it's a nightmare. I can also ring UNHCR to see an individual refugee: otherwise, they have difficulty getting into the compounds. For example, I had a Somali who applied on his own when I was in Northern Uganda. He paid so much – nearly USh 450,000! The actual total amount is US$ 50. This applies both to Ugandans and to refugees. However, there is an idea that those who can travel who are refugees are 'rich' or will be rich wherever they are going. I can also assist refugees with obtaining ID documents from the MoLG. The MoLG doesn't recognise the OAU IDs given in mass determination status at the local level – thus refugees must in effect seek refugee status twice when they need to obtain a CTD and travel.[153]

The vast majority of officials from the government, UNHCR, and NGOs working for refugees ignored the fact that their policies violated freedom of movement. They attempted to rationalise such violations with the most improbable excuses. For example, the camp commandants in Adjumani and Moyo admitted that strict conditions existed for issuing 'movement permits to refugees who wanted to travel outside the district because we have to control their movements and, after all, this is for the good of refugees. Moreover, whenever refugees go to Kampala, they go to disturb the people in the UNHCR offices and those in the Directorate of Refugees.'[154]

UNHCR maintained that the policy of keeping refugees in camps and settlements, and the attendant restrictions on their freedom of movement, were imposed by the host governments. However, as we explained in Chapter 1, UNHCR encouraged the adoption of this policy as it perceived it to be in its own interest. For example, a protection report from Kenya states that:

> ... be that as it may, mandate refugees are restricted to the designated camp in the country of asylum with the exception of those authorised to travel for medical, education or resettlement purposes. It is therefore in our inter-

est that freedom of movement is restricted to those people who have a genuine reason to travel. If the refugees see that the only punishment for illegal movement is a return ticket to the camp, the travel letter loses its significance and we lose control over the movement (UNHCR 1997g).

UNHCR's senior protection officer in Uganda confirmed this approach when he argued that '... the group so declared [prima facie refugees] may be subjected to reasonable restrictions as to the location of residence and movement, a situation which will be strongly criticised by human rights activists who favour a "complete freedom of movement for refugees" which, in our view, it not tenable even in the most civilised society' (UNHCR 1998i).[155]

Access to courts and right to fair trial

Article 16, which enshrines the refugees' right of access to courts, is one of the few provisions in the 1951 Convention that cannot be the object of a reservation by state parties.[156] Human rights law does not use the terminology of 'access to court', but talks instead of the right to fair trial, which it defines by identifying minimum procedural guarantees. Under article 14 of the ICCPR, 'in the determination of any criminal charge against him, or of his rights and obligations in a suit at law, everyone shall be entitled to a fair and public hearing by a competent, independent and impartial tribunal established by law.' (*see also* African Charter art. 7).

Fair trial and access to courts are complementary concepts, and the paucity of references in human rights law to the principle of access to courts, which is a sine qua non of fair trial, is probably a reflection of the fact that the enforcement of human rights law in countries in the 'developing world' was not given due consideration when human rights treaties were drafted. In fact, in developing countries access to courts is hindered by various factors: courts are remote, costly, and intimidating; individuals are often denied any sort of trial, let alone a fair one. Refugees in Kenya and Uganda were also thwarted in their attempts to access national courts by the policies of humanitarian organisations which chose to allow a parallel 'justice' system in the camps and settlements that conformed neither to the national legal system nor to international human rights standards.

Distance, restrictions on travel, and costs were all factors that undermined the refugees' access to courts. In Kenya, the nearest courts to the refugee camps in Kakuma and Dadaab were the resident Magistrates' Courts in Lodwar and Garissa, respectively around fifty and sixty kilometres away. The journeys to Lodwar and Garissa were perilous owing to the insecurity in the region. Refugees needed a special permit from

UNHCR and the district officer to travel but such permits were usually granted to attend court hearings.

In Kenya it cost KSh 300 to file a petition in a subordinate court, while 'a *habeas corpus* or an application for an appeal costs KSh 1,500; costs for filing, depositing documents and calling witnesses reach thousands of shillings' (African Rights 1996: 37). Given that the highest incentive that was paid to refugees was KSh 1,800 a month, these costs, which did not include the cost of hiring a lawyer, were already prohibitive. Since there was no lawyer based in the whole of Turkana and the North-Eastern Province in Kenya, or in Adjumani and Moyo in Uganda, it would have been necessary to pay for transport and accommodation in addition to the legal fee.

One way of remedying the problem of access to courts was by establishing a mobile court as discussed above. It is hard to assess its impact on crime in the camps since it only heard a handful of cases. However the few decisions that were reached appeared to be well-reasoned and fair.[157]

The idea of 'bringing justice' to camps and settlements with mobile courts has some positive aspects: in refugee-affected areas, mobile courts can strengthen the rule of law to the advantage of refugees and hosts alike. However, the problem of lack of access to courts cannot be separated from the denial of freedom of movement: had refugees been free to choose their residence, they might have included public order considerations, including the existence of courts, as one of the criteria for preferring one place over another. Instead, they were forced to reside in places where they had no access to courts, a situation for which the mobile court was only a sporadic and inadequate solution.

Overview of national judicial systems

When it came to refugees, the main problem with national courts was that they were not used as much as they should have been. Only a few cases did go through national courts, as is discussed below. Courts were organised differently in the two countries: Kenya had essentially maintained the pre-independence structure, whereas Uganda had adopted some important reforms.

In Uganda, Local Council Courts (LCCs) were introduced in 1987 by the Resistance Committees (Judicial Powers) Statute, which came into force on 22 January 1988 and defined their jurisdiction and procedures. These courts operate at the parish, sub-county, and county levels within the jurisdiction of formal Magistrates' Courts, and have an internal system of appeals, from LCC1 to LCCII and LCCIII, and a special appellate procedure to the chief Magistrates' Courts.

The LCCs may hear civil disputes involving debts, contracts, assault and/or battery, conversion of and/or damage to property, and civil trespass. The LCCs also have jurisdiction over civil disputes governed by customary law including land disputes relating to customary tenure, disputes concerning the marital status of women, paternity, identity of customary heirs, impregnating a girl under 18, or eloping with her, inheritance rights, and 'customary' land issues. There are no monetary limitations on the LCCs when they hear cases allowed under customary law. In cases involving matters of customary law, a magistrate explained to us that courts normally invited the local elders:

> ... who testify before the court on the existence and tenets of the law. I have not personally had such cases. When these elders are invited, they are subject to cross-examination by the parties and by the court, and the court normally invites three or even four if not just to test their consistency and to prevent elders using the law to their own ends. Their testimony is treated as expert evidence of a doctor or lawyer subject to cross-examination.[158]

If damages are awarded in excess of USh 5,000 in *any suit*, such cases must be referred to the chief magistrate of the area, who may find the judgement excessive and reduce it (sec. 4(3)). LCCs have no powers of detention. All prisons are under the supervision of the commissioner for prisons. Even when the LCCs were allowed to impose 'civil custody', the chief magistrate of the area had to make the order. In fact, in all but the most minor cases, these courts are to be directly supervised by the chief magistrate of the area.

Museveni's government saw the LCCs as an alternative to the formal court system. However, the danger that these courts would discriminate against women, was already a matter of concern in the 1987 debates in parliament. A 1998 evaluation of these courts suggests that these and many other problems in the dispensation of justice by LCC remain to be addressed (Mukassa 1998). Some were also known to have exceeded their jurisdiction by trying criminal cases.

In Kenya, the lowest level of courts is represented by the Magistrates' Court. The jurisdiction of the resident Magistrates' Courts is countrywide, whereas the jurisdiction of the lower District Magistrate's court is limited to the geographical area in which they operate. Residents magistrates can hear cases of a value not exceeding KSh 120,000, while the limit for the district magistrates is KSh 75,000; these limits do not apply to customary law cases. Criminal jurisdiction depends on the sentence that can be imposed for the offence. For example, District Magistrates' Courts can only deal with offences for which the sentence is not more than seven years imprisonment, corporal punishment of twenty-four strokes, or a fine of KSh 20,000. With the consent of the parties, *Khadis* courts have jurisdiction over family law disputes between followers of the Muslim faith. They operate under the supervision of the High Court and they have to follow two guiding principles on the assessment of evidence.

Firstly, they have to admit evidence without discriminating on grounds of religion, sex, or otherwise. Secondly, they cannot assess evidence simply on the basis of the number of witnesses (Khadis Court Act sec. 6). Their procedures must be in accordance with the Civil Procedures Act. Neither *Khadis* courts nor customary ones have criminal jurisdiction. Finally, Juvenile Courts have been established under the Children and Young Persons Act in order to deal with the anti-social behaviour of children and taking into account their special needs (Kuloba 1997: 36–44).

Refugee cases tried in courts

Identifying refugee cases in national courts was a challenge.[159] Adjumani and Moyo districts were an exception because most of the charge sheets indicated when a person was a refugee and gave the address.[160] Interviews and searches of case files were conducted in four Magistrates' Courts in Kampala – Buganda Road, Nakawa, Mengo, and Makindye. We also interviewed the registrar of the High Court and the Supreme Court.

Bail, as noted, was a problem and affected both refugees in settlements and those outside. As one magistrate put it:

> Because my personal experience here is that once they are granted bail, they almost in all cases abscond and go back to Sudan, we normally require surety, to ensure their payment, but they find it difficult to get credible sureties. For those in refugee camps charged with serious offences, we normally write to the UNHCR protection officer and camp commandant to send a representative who can stand as surety and this has happened in many cases. They usually come when notified. For less serious offences we may not bother; in these cases, citizens are at an advantage to find surety and to be bailed (*see also* case no. 071/DRC/U/1999).[161]

In none of the cases we examined from the court records in Adjumani or Moyo were the refugees represented by a lawyer; lack of legal representation equally affected Ugandans since there were no practising advocates in either district. Under the Constitution, all those charged with offences that carry a term of imprisonment of fourteen years or more (art. 28(3)(e)) are entitled to legal representation paid for by the state, but this was rarely provided (case no. 133/SUD/U/1999). As pointed out by a magistrate:

> The problem is that these refugees do not have the means to seek legal representation. I have never had a refugee before me with an advocate; none has been represented … It may have happened in the 1994 High Court session in which they must have legal representation at the expense of the state. It is only the well-to-do who can afford lawyers. The nearest law firm is in Arua and you have to pay for transport, food, fees. I have a few cases in Moyo where advocates come from Kampala, but never here in Adjumani.[162]

The same magistrate observed that it was often difficult to guarantee the accused person's right to an interpreter, although this is enshrined in the Ugandan Constitution: 'although we have a lady here who lived in Sudan for fifteen years and knows many of the languages, there are still cases that cannot be tried. Interpreters need to be paid for the work and we cannot afford to do that.'[163] Apart from these problems, it was our general conclusion, from the cases we examined, that once refugees were 'in the judicial system', the courts did not discriminate against them.

The majority of court cases involving refugees were related to criminal charges ranging from simple theft to aggravated robbery and 'defilement' – that is, the rape of a minor. Refugees did not usually use courts to file civil lawsuits to protect their property or their contractual or other rights. Those living in the settlements and in the camps were expected to use the dispute settlement process through the community leaders, while 'self-settled' refugees in Kampala were understandably reluctant to use courts, given that the vast majority of them were either waiting for recognition of their refugee status or had already been rejected. In rural areas, however, the situation was generally different. We found two cases brought by self-settled refugees in the Magistrates' Court in Arua – one for the recovery of property (*Nimaya Lodu v. Aminia Amandua and Anor*, civil suit no. MM 19/97) and the other brought by a woman against her husband seeking compensation in tort in a case of domestic violence (*Josphine Wude v. Machael Sabe*, civil suit no. MM 15/97).

As has been noted above, in both Kenya and Uganda a significant proportion of the cases that ended up in national courts concerned 'unlawful' presence in the country.[164] In both countries, magistrates played an important role in mitigating spurious actions initiated by the police or by the Immigration Department against refugees.

'Justice' in the refugee settlements – Uganda

The settlements were organised into clusters and blocks with elected leaders. The highest authority were the community leaders – the RWCs – who were empowered to hear and decide cases. The justification normally given for assigning these functions to leaders was that it allowed refugees to settle disputes according to their own cultural norms and traditions. In addition, cases were heard in their own language, and costs were lower than in national courts.

Unlike in Kenya, the establishment of the RWC courts has some basis in the law. The Control of Alien Refugees Act (cap. 64) gives settlement (or camp) commandants power to '... give such orders or directions either orally or in writing, to any refugee as may be necessary or expedient ... to ensure that the settlement is administered in an orderly and efficient manner' (sec. 13(2)(a)), and 'to preserve orderly conduct and discipline in the settlements' (sec. 13(2)(d). Settlement commandants may detain those refugees who commit a 'disciplinary offence' for up to thirty days in a settlement 'lock-up' (cap. 64, sec. 21(2)(a)(b)). A disciplinary offence is defined as any refugee leaving or even *attempting* to leave the settlement without permission, or disobeying any order or direction made by the DoR or settlement commandant, or who is guilty of conduct that is 'prejudicial to good order and discipline' (sec. 21(3)(a–c)). The only appeal is to the DoR, whose decision 'shall be final' (sec. 21(4)). Section 23 gives the settlement commandant the powers to use force, 'including the use of firearms, as may be necessary to compel any refugees to comply with any order or direction, whether oral or in writing'. In practice, so far as observed, settlement commandants in Uganda did not carry weapons.

The fact that settlement commandants reported directly to the central government rather than to local authorities was one of the 'imperfections' in Uganda's decentralisation, which made them essentially independent of any effective local control. Settlement commandants were given an important role in dispute settlement; in practice, they tended to delegate their dispute settlement functions to the RWCs. Tensions between settlement commandants and the RWCs were not uncommon. One commandant, for example, complained that 'once refugees have power they do not want to relinquish one bit of it, and that the refugee leaders benefit from exploiting their power' (Munson 1999b: 26).[165] In Rhino camp, the commandant requested that monthly reports be submitted by the RWC, but they refused to cooperate (ibid.: 28).

The way in which settlement commandants exercised their supervisory function varied a great deal from one settlement to the other. In some cases, it was the settlement commandants who resisted the involvement of the police even for crimes for which the jurisdiction of the RWC courts was expressly excluded. For instance, when two soldiers raped two minor girls in Adjumani, the camp commandant attempted to settle the case according to 'customary law' rather than by reporting it to the police.[166]

The de facto criminal jurisdiction exercised by the RWCs, as well as logistical problems (such as lack of resources, no means of transport, and distance from the settlements), limited police investigation of criminal affairs. Providing transport for the police took time and the collection of evidence was affected by these delays. Rhino camp was sixty kilometres from the nearest station; in one case, the body of a man who had apparently committed suicide in Rhino camp had to be left hanged for twenty hours while waiting for the police (Munson 1999b: 10).

RWC-appointed *askaris*[167] played a role in the maintenance of public order in settlements. They could arrest suspects on orders from RWCs or settlement commandants. Munson reported: 'One Secretary for Security specifically told me that when they arrest a suspect they bring him in peace without torturing him. However, we saw several *askaris* armed with a variety of locally made weapons, from thin, stout clubs to forked rubber whips with wooden handles. If a person is given a punishment involving community work, it is also the *askaris'* responsibility to supervise the work' (Munson 1999b).

On other occasions, settlement commandants decided to involve the police if a particular refugee was 'stubborn' – the word usually being applied to a person who refused to conform to the often arbitrary rules imposed on refugees, or whose behaviour offended one or other person in authority. For example, the police were called to detain an adolescent Burundian refugee who had 'irritated' the settlement commandant in Nakivale. His punishments included beating and detention and, allegedly, being threatened by the police with execution.[168] Although the facts were not all clear, the situation was serious enough for the senior settlement commandant to take the unusual step of admonishing his junior in writing.[169]

In Adjumani, the limits on the exercise of jurisdiction by the RWC courts were spelt out by the settlement commandant after he had received complaints. In a letter, he informed them that 'what you used to refer to as "judiciary committee" were to be abolished'.[170] The letter instructed the RWCs to appoint 'five elders of reputation, who have not served on the defunct "Judiciary Committee" to assist the RWC Chairman'. Enclosed with the letter was a list entitled 'Roles of Refugee Welfare Committee (Dispute Settlement)'. Specific cases that could be heard included: recovering a debt; contracts or matters concerning agreements; minor assault and battery provided that 'no wounding or cut was sustained as a result of the assault'; wrongly taking ownership or using another person's property; damage to property; and trespass – that is, 'entering people's land without permission (if the value of the thee [*sic*] claim does no [*sic*] go beyond Shs 5000'. Concerning 'matters of customary law', the RWCs were allowed to hear disputes about customary land, whether a woman is married or not, who the parent of a child is, who a customary heir is, customary bails, and eloping with a girl under 18 years. The letter concluded with the warning that the RWCs should 'remember' that they have 'no power to impose a fine of more than 5,000 Shs for any disputes' that they settle and that:

> ALL OTHER DISPUTES AND CRIMES MUST BE REPORTED TO THE POLICE AND THE CAMP COMMANDANT ON THE SAME DAY IF POSSIBLE! IF THIS IS NOT DONE A FULL EXPLANATION WILL BE REQUIRED.
>
> … IF YOU DETAIN A PERSON YOU WILL BE COMMITTING A CRIME. (ibid. [emphasis in original])

Our data revealed that the powers the RWCs exercised were wider than those of the LCCs, although in principle the jurisdiction of the RWCs ought not to have exceeded that of the LCCs. In Mongola settlement,[171] we found seven cases of assault, four of theft, two of debt, two of 'adultery' cases, one of dowry, a 'witchcraft' case, and a case in which a refugee was found guilty of threatening to shoot another refugee. With the exception of simple debt and customary marriage, all the other cases ought to have been heard in a higher court of law. Furthermore, although LCCs were not allowed to impose monetary penalties or to award damages above USh 5,000 without the approval of the chief magistrate of the area, the RWC courts in Mongola imposed fines as high as USh 150,000, with fines below USh 5,000 being imposed only in a few cases. The issue of monetary limits also raises the question of where the money charged went.

In Rhino camp, the RWCs were cluster-level committees, with zone committees above them, and with a Refugee Welfare Council at the top of the hierarchy. Elections for cluster-level committee members took place every two years, but there was no secret ballot: every refugee would line up behind the candidate of their choice or raise their hands. The cluster-level committee members then chose the members of zone-level committees, who in turn elected the members of the overall council (Munson 1999b: 11). Members of the committee could be dismissed if they 'misbehaved', but this happened only once in Rhino camp, when the refugee in charge of security was replaced after it had been found that he had 'tied, beaten and tortured' people (ibid.). It was generally believed that the greater than usual powers vested in the RWCs in the administration of justice were to be credited with the reduction in the high crime rates that had beset the settlement in 1996–97 (Munson 1999b: 10).

As noted, the jurisdiction of the RWCs in Rhino camp, as in Mongola, stretched far beyond the statutory limits that would apply to LCCs. If cases were beyond the RWC's jurisdiction, the council was supposed to take a statement and, after discussing the case with the camp commandant, refer it to the police and to the court in Arua. However, 'In practice I saw and heard of the Council judging these cases' [for example, rape, adultery] (Munson 1999b: 12). Parties had to pay a court fee of USh 500 each (USh 1,000 at the zone level, and USh 2,500 at council level). In Rhino camp, the RWC was authorised to hear cases involving damages up to USh 30,000, at zone level the limit was USh 60,000, and USh 100,000 at council level (Munson 1999b: 11).

Among the offences that were dealt with by the RWCs in Rhino camp, were some alcohol-related ones, especially fights in the drinking places or after drinking. For theft, there was a fine of USh 10,000, as well as the restitution of the stolen property. Five strokes of the cane were inflicted on a man who had stolen a goat and could not pay the fine in a case reported by Munson (1999c: 17). There were problems between Sudanese and Ugandans, particularly when Ugandan-owned cows ate Sudanese-owned crops. 'Some Sudanese react by "arresting" and tying the cow, but many are afraid that the owner will perform witchcraft in retaliation' (Munson 1999b: 18). RWCs and LCs sat together when disputes involving refugees and Ugandans arose. Refugees complained that in such cases fines imposed on Ugandans were seldom enforced.

The administration of justice in Rhino camp had one good aspect, in comparison with other settlements: the infliction of corporal punishment appeared to be in steady decline and most punishments, although excessive, consisted of monetary fines. In other settlements, corporal punishment, either as the main penalty or in default of payment, remained the norm. For example, during a focus group meeting with the members of the RWC in Mongola, one remarked, 'If fines cannot be paid and someone is stubborn not to do it, then we cane: 500 shillings equals one stroke.'[172] In Ibakwe village, a handwritten note containing the RWC bylaws indicated the measure of corporal punishment to be inflicted for the following 'offences':

> ... if you shout at night, the Chairman shouldn't judge the case. The person(s) should be cane[d] 60 lashes. But because of the trouble that has given [caused] 10 more lashes to make 70.
>
> BEER SELLING
>
> There should be time limited for drinking beer. If the seller doesn't take care the person shall be caned 50 lashes.
>
> Concerning borehole use and 'stubbornness', not to respect the people made responsible ... 20 lashes any stubborn persons.
>
> Concerning nightwalkers [who] knocking (wizards) at the people's door. It is the work of the landlord of Ibakwe responsible to act upon such people the best way he knows.

In Rhino camp, imprisonment was used,[173] but the RWCs were reluctant to publicise their practice in this respect because they knew that in principle they were not authorised to detain. The RWC eventually admitted that there was a cell for keeping 'suspects' for up to forty-eight hours while statements were taken; arrested persons could be bailed for USh 1,000 (Munson 1999b: 13). Rhino was not exceptional in this respect. In Adjumani, the senior settlement commandant maintained that none of the settlements in his area had lockups. However, the testimony of refugees visited in the prisons in these two districts suggests *all* of the settlements did have some facility for detention, perhaps just outside the settlement.[174] Moreover, Uganda's draconian Control of Alien Refugees Act gave the camp commandant the power to detain, and the fact that RWCs in practice detained refugees illustrates the problematic growth of their powers.

Despite their high incidence, cases of domestic violence were only seldom dealt with by the RWCs. When domestic violence arose as an incidental matter in another case (for example, adultery or divorce), the RWCs would barely take notice of it. While domestic violence was neglected, adultery cases frequently ended up in the RWC courts, another indication of the RWC system's inability to protect the rights of refugee women. The 'adulterous' woman and the man with whom she committed adultery had to pay a fine of USh 5,000 to the committee, and USh 35,000 in 'damages' to the woman's husband. If the man and the woman denied the charges, but were found guilty, the fines increased – USh 12,000 to the committee, and a goat and food to the woman's husband in addition to the USh 35,000 to the husband (Munson 1999b: 16–17).[175]

'*Justice' in the refugee camps – Kenya*

We have already noted that the Sudanese 'court' in Kakuma tried, amongst others, cases of adultery, imprisoning the woman and fining the man. It was also well known that these 'courts' dealt with criminal cases, mainly theft, although under Kenyan law there is no place for customary law in criminal cases. The leader of the Sudanese in Kakuma summarised this arrangement:

> The Sudanese court decides on smaller cases, like family, adultery, and petty theft. The cells in the Sudanese area are used primarily for these cases. For adultery, the traditional punishment for the man was six or ten bulls. Here we had to change it into a sum of money because people do not normally own cattle. So, we fine him KSh 1,000, which is much smaller than the price for ten bulls, but we consider the economic hardships in the camps. Sometimes, we can also accept a promise to pay the bulls upon return to Sudan. For more serious cases, like murder, the Kenyan police is called in. But in some cases, the culprit decides to confess to the elders in our community and he is put in the prison cells in our area. At times it is the culprit himself who prefers to be put in our cells.[176]

As the Sudanese leader hinted, a number of cases that involved offences more serious than theft were still tried by the Sudanese court. LWF, in charge of security, normally did refer most cases to the police for further investigation, but it admitted that 'there were many other cases, which were not reported to us owing to complainants reporting direct to police or social services, *or solved in communities, by their community leaders*' [emphasis added] (LWF Kakuma 1997a). Furthermore, LWF also decided not to refer certain cases to the police, particularly if they had an inter- or intra-communal dimension. For example, on one occasion, LWF security was dispatched to hand over through the elders a Somali woman to her mother, because the woman was having a relationship with an Ethiopian refugee. Neither the Somali woman nor the Ethiopian man were minors. The woman was first taken to the camp hospital 'for treatment of some parts of her swollen head and left eye which had been beaten by her mother on that night after her mother had realised about her love affair'. The woman had voluntarily moved to the Ethiopian man's house, but 'LWF security, Ethiopian security and Somali group 61B security and their leaders arranged' to pick her up and hand her over first to her mother, and then to her uncle 'where they thought it was ... far from her boyfriend to interfere with her' (LWF Kakuma 1996).

Another case in which LWF omitted to refer a serious matter to the police was that of 'a young Sudanese of Dinka tribesmen' who 'materialized at the compound gate on 19/02/97 claiming that he was abducted by the members of the SPLA, while coming back from Kakuma town, and transported up to a place called KIBES PASS [an SPLA base] accusing him of killing people at their places of origin before soughting [*sic*] refugee status, but he managed to escape'. LWF 'notified' the protection officer, but did not report this case to the police (LWF Kakuma 1997c).

The UNHCR senior protection officer who took office at the end of 1997 expressed her unease about customary dispute settlement in Kakuma. She decided to establish a monitoring system. The 1998 protection report thus envisaged the launch of 'a pilot project with SWAN/SSLS [South Sudan Law Society] to assess the current judicial system applied by the Sudanese community in order to ensure compliance with international legal standards and to curb abuses' (UNHCR 1998b). A project of this kind was long overdue, but whether the SSLS, which is the legal branch of the SPLA, was really capable of challenging an SPLA-dominated customary 'court' was debatable.

In Dadaab, under the community self-management (CSM) system, Security and Justice Committees were established in each camp. Some of these committees included among the members refugees who had practised law in their country of origin. In Hagadera, the Security and Justice Committee 'hears cases and has had a great impact on the case-load that has to be dealt with by the offices [of CARE and UNHCR] ... They [the members of the Committee] apply Somali culture and only if there is a major problem they refer it to the CARE office. If their decisions conflict with our general policies, we may intervene.'[177]

Neither the Sudanese 'court' nor the Justice and Security Committees in Dadaab (nor the RWCs in Uganda) constituted a 'competent, independent and impartial tribunal established by law' (ICCPR art. 14). While the settlement of *some* disputes through the application of custom can be considered on a par with any other form of alternative dispute resolution, the exercise of jurisdiction by these bodies has to be subjected to clear limitations, as indeed prescribed under Kenyan or Ugandan law.

Collective punishment in Kakuma

Collective punishment was imposed on the whole refugee population of Kakuma camp on two separate occasions – a measure that affected the refugees' access to court and right to fair trial, as well as their right to food, liberty, security, health, and freedom of expression.[178]

In April 1994, a number of refugees demolished the enclosures that had been built for food distribution and for headcounts. In retaliation, UNHCR decided to suspend food distribution for twenty-one days. After the demolition of the enclosures, refugee leaders were asked to attend a meeting with agency representatives and the district commissioner in Lodwar. To their surprise, the leaders found that the meeting had been an excuse to entice them to Lodwar where they were arrested and charged with incitement, destruction of property, and theft of building materials.

The protection report for 1994 simply stated that '7 refugees were detained and charged with destroying UNHCR property, inciting refugees to rioting and stealing property, following the destruction in April of enclosures which had been set up for the census. The magistrate acquitted all of them for lack of evidence ... in all the cases the sub-office was contacted by the authority and granted access to them (UNHCR 1994a).' It said nothing about the deprivation of food for twenty-four days, and that it had been UNHCR itself that had called in the police.

After the seven refugees had spent two months in prison in Lodwar and Nairobi, court hearings began, some taking place in Kakuma. In the end, all the leaders were acquitted, but the legal fees were paid with contributions from the refugee community. Afterwards, the leaders met to discuss the possibility of suing UNHCR and the government for compensation. Although UNHCR had softened its tone once it became clear that the prosecution's case was very weak, the refugees maintained that UNHCR had been behind their arrest and prosecution. They were reminded by the lawyers of not only the costs involved, but also the immunity enjoyed by UNHCR.

The second incident in April 1996 was recalled by Mr Dau, leader of the Sudanese community:

> The agencies wanted to show a video on food distribution to some women and children [the unaccompanied minors] in the camp. The video was about the distribution in some other camp and the agencies hoped to convince their audience that that was the best way of distributing food. They intended to introduce that new system in Kakuma, too, but until then the reception had not been very good. At the end of the video, everyone started asking questions and the children especially were quite upset. The agencies [UNHCR, WFP and LWF] started getting nervous and dismissed the protest saying that whether they liked it or not, that new system would be introduced. At that point the situation got out of control. The minors

rioted on the spot and destroyed the same premises which had already been destroyed once in 1994 and had been rebuilt thereafter.[179]

The distribution of food was again suspended, this time for fourteen days. With the exception of refugees working in health, water logistics, and security, incentives were punitively withdrawn. In a memorandum to the refugee community leaders, copied to the agencies, the district officer, and the district commissioner, the conditions for resuming food distribution were spelt out by the officer-in-charge, UNHCR sub-office, Kakuma:

> Following the visit of Kenya Government officials, UNHCR Representative and Deputy Representative, WFP Country Director, to the camp on 2 April 1996, and a meeting with the heads of UNHCR Sub Office and implementing partners and WFP in Kakuma, it was decided that the March 1996 incentives for all refugee workers will be forfeited.
>
> Please note that this decision was made jointly by the Government of Kenya, UNHCR, WFP, LWF [Lutheran World Federation], IRC [International Rescue Committee] and Radda Barnen.
>
> April 1996 incentives will be paid only to those workers employed in the essential sectors, i.e. health care, water, logistics and security.
>
> Payment of incentives for other refugee workers for the month of April 1996 will depend on the co-operation on the part of refugees during the reconstruction of the destroyed facilities, recovering all the looted properties and providing the names of the culprits responsible for the damages, etc. This will be evaluated by my office and our implementing partners shortly after this reconstruction starts.
>
> Your co-operation and performance will be closely monitored by respective supervisors. Anyone whose performance proves to be unsatisfactory will be dismissed without prior warning. Thank you for your co-operation (UNHCR 1996f).

This suspension of food[180] and the withdrawal of incentives had a tragic affect on the entire population in Kakuma. The refugees were left with no choice but to accept these conditions. The leader of one of the communities explained what was behind this episode: 'It is the colonial idea that some individuals are always children and that you have to punish them, however hardly and indiscriminately, because you need to educate them. After the incident was over and the refugees had rebuilt the food distribution centre, the people in the UN compound were saying "The refugees have learnt the lesson, although it was a hard punishment."'[181]

Collective punishments are paradigmatic examples of the violation of the right to a fair trial. Indeed, it is generally considered so abhorrent a practice that it is prohibited even in time of war (Geneva Convention (IV) art. 33). Moreover, in this case, other rights, such as the right to food, and the dignity of refugees, were violated. There can be no legal justification for the imposition of collective punishment on some 40,000 persons, half of whom were probably minors, by a UN agency *and* in time of peace.[182]

Privacy and family life

Respect for privacy, family, home, correspondence, honour and reputation, already featured prominently in the Universal Declaration of Human Rights (UDHR) (art. 12). The ICCPR strengthened the protection of the family by recognising the right to marry and found a family, in which spouses have equal rights and responsibilities (art. 23).

Separation during flight is an experience common to many refugee families. Once in exile, tracing their lost family members and bringing them together again is for many of them a priority. Family reunion is however a complicated and resource-intensive process, which may involve UNHCR, the United Nations Children's Fund (UNICEF), and the International Committee of the Red Cross (ICRC), and often requires the cooperation of governments. When one of these governments is that of the country of origin, it may be impossible to effect family reunion. At times families are separated when they are in the same country or even in the same camp. For example, when people were forcibly moved from Koboko town to Ikafe settlement, members of a family sometimes travelled on different lorries and found themselves separated in a camp that spread over many kilometres (Harrell-Bond 1994). It took months before their situation could be sorted out (ibid.: para. 16.5). Members of a family often left their country of origin at different times and might have no idea how to locate relatives who might themselves be dispersed among settlements.

A large number of refugee families became separated in flight and found themselves in different countries. Although ICRC has a tracing programme to find lost relatives, most refugees are unaware of the services available. The majority of refugees did not have passports which would have allowed them to travel across borders even if they had the wherewithal. Even when it was known that close family members were on the other side of the border, there was resistance to facilitating their reunion, probably because of lack of resources. One member of our team hand-carried dozens of letters from the settlements in Adjumani and Moyo districts to family members in Kakuma camp in Kenya. On one occasion, it required the serious intervention of a human rights organisation to convince the authorities to issue CTDs to two individuals who needed to travel to Kenya to try to find their relatives (case no. 108/SUD/U/1997). When informed of their right to a travel document, members of a focus group discussion in Mongola settlement said: 'The CTD has not even reached the whole of us in the North of Uganda. Some of us have parents in Kenya and since separation we have not seen each other. We may not see each other before reaching the grave.'[183]

The case of B. illustrates the risks that some refugees were prepared to take to reunite their families (case no. 092/DRC/U/2000). B.'s husband was a medical doctor, a health inspector in eastern DRC. When the rebellion broke out, he had escaped arrest and probably death only because he was absent from home when members of the RCD came for him. He flew from Bukavu to Nairobi and then on to Belgium. His wife, who was travelling abroad at the time, returned home to their six children. Some army personnel became threatening when they heard that her husband had reached Belgium. B. fled to Kampala with the children. She did not report to UNHCR in Kampala because she 'feared that, since Uganda was involved in the conflict in her country, it was unsafe'.

In Uganda, not having enough money, she purchased tickets to Belgium for herself and three of the children, leaving the others with her cousin, M.[184] In Belgium she was granted refugee status. She applied for a CTD, purportedly to go on a pilgrimage to Lourdes, but in reality in order to travel to Kampala to collect the children who had been left behind and who, she had been informed, had fallen ill. She 'borrowed' documents for these children from another Congolese family in Belgium, attaching her children's photos. On 6 November 1999, she left Uganda with the children, but the false papers were recognised in Nairobi. B. and her children were sent back to Kampala where they were detained at Jinja Road police station.

Her cousin in Kampala managed to obtain their release, having left his own passport as surety that the children would leave the country at his expense. B.'s brother arrived from the DRC to collect the children, accompanied by the children's grandmother. To ensure that they left Uganda, a policeman accompanied them to the Rwanda border.[185] On 15 November, all alone, B. headed for Belgium, but in Nairobi the Kenyan immigration authorities said that her CTD was forged and cut it with scissors. B. was returned to Entebbe,[186] where she was put in a cell, after the immigration officer had confiscated her now damaged CTD and her tickets. Her cousin once again rescued her. In the meantime, the Belgian consulate declared that her CTD was genuine, and B. finally managed to fly back to Belgium. The three children remained in the DRC, still separated from their family.[187]

The case of Fabien (case no. 014/BUR/K/1997), a 29-year-old man, illustrates how easily the protection of children can be compromised by both state authorities and UNHCR (UNHCR 1994c). Escaping what he believed to have been the total massacre of his family in Burundi, Fabien arrived in Kenya in 1994. Four months later, when he was standing outside the JRS, a car carrying a Burundian family drove up and his 4-year-old brother, Fiston, stepped out.[188] Fabien immediately tried to get Fiston included in his protection letter, but someone at UNHCR asked, 'How do we know that he is your brother?' We wrote to UNHCR, drawing attention to the fact that apparently no one at UNHCR considered the implications of Fiston being an unaccompanied minor in wrong hands, if he was not allowed to stay with Fabien. As a result of our letter, Fiston was eventually added to his brother's protection letter – more than three years after his arrival in Kenya. In December 1997, Fabien learnt that his small sister, Tekla, who was not yet 4 years old, had been found with relatives in one of the camps near Kigoma, Tanzania. He went there by lorry and brought her back (across an international border) to Nairobi. In 1998, this child was added to the protection letter and it was understood that Fabien and the children would be resettled. Fabien got enrolled in a JRS training course.

In September 1999, after the Kenyan government announced it would no longer recognise UNHCR's protection letters,[189] Fabien was detained in a police station and given a prohibited immigrant notice. A month or so later, little Fiston was also detained for a week. Fabien used the money we had sent him for the school fees to bribe the police. Just after these events, Fabien was run over by a truck and killed. The children moved back in with a Congolese pastor but their situation is not being supervised by any authority responsible for children, either of the Kenyan government or UNHCR.

Sometimes families got separated simply out of the sheer vindictiveness on the part of humanitarian workers (*see* Harrell-Bond 2002). O. had fled from Goma alone (case no. 042/DRC/U/1999) but as soon as he reached Kampala, where he was granted asylum, he contacted his wife through the Red Cross. O. had just been informed that he had to leave the Salvation Army hostel where he had been staying and go to a camp, when his wife arrived, ill, eight months pregnant, with two small children, one of whom was also ill. InterAid said that she must stay in Kampala to have her claim for refugee status examined and they refused to give her a room unless her husband immediately left for the camp. O. refused to leave his wife and children alone and a FIDA lawyer was asked to intervene. After several trips between UNHCR and InterAid, it was finally agreed to include their names on O.'s protection letter. The whole family was to travel to the camp together the next day. As InterAid had refused to attend to O.'s wife's medical condition, the lawyer took her to her own private doctor for an examination which found O.'s wife anaemic, suffering from a urinary tract infection, and apparently about to deliver. Armed with a letter advising against travel, she was seen by the InterAid nurse who was sympathetic and agreed she should not travel. She was asked to bring the husband to the InterAid office. When the social worker saw that the husband was O., she shouted, 'I won't help you. You are the one who reported *us* to FIDA.' The FIDA lawyer was again summoned. After going back and forth between InterAid and UNHCR, the lawyer finally gave up and arranged public transport to take O. and his wife to the camp. At least, the lawyer consoled herself, the family was together.

Freedom of expression, thought, conscience, and religion, and freedom of assembly and association

All human beings, not only citizens, are entitled to the 'right to hold opinions without interference' and 'to seek, receive and impart information and ideas of all kinds' (ICCPR art. 19). Under international law, freedom of expression is subject to restrictions more pervasive than under the constitutional law of many countries. In particular, states have an obligation to prohibit by law 'any advocacy of national, racial or religious hatred that constitutes incitement to discrimination, hostility or violence' (ICCPR art. 20) – a provision which is especially relevant in the context of ethnic divisions and conflict.

One of the few provisions in the OAU Convention that can be described as retrogressive deals with freedom of expression. Article 3 prohibits what it broadly defines as 'subversive activities', which include 'attacking' any OAU member state 'through the press, or by radio'. As observed in a report by the London-based organisation Article 19:

> ... this unfortunate provision provides an underpinning for an attitude that most governments probably instinctively share: refugees are in their country by sufferance and should not rock the boat by expressing unwelcome opinions. Yet such an attitude is in direct conflict with the freedom of expression provisions of the international human rights treaties and the African Charter, with which the refugee instruments are supposed to be in harmony (Carver and Verdirame 2001).

Whether political activities by refugees are tolerated normally depends on the relationship between the host country and the country of origin. Moreover, as a general rule, rights limitation clauses, such as article 3, have to be interpreted narrowly. This seemed to be ignored by UNHCR, when, in its Uganda protection report for 2000, it stated that, 'as a signatory to the 1969 OAU Convention', Uganda imposed limits on 'refugees' political rights', including 'refugees' right to freedom of association and carrying out political activities either through print or other media' (UNHCR 2000c). Such a blanket prohibition, however, does not feature even in the OAU Convention's restrictive provision on political activities, which only prohibits 'subversive' activities that are likely to engender interstate tensions.

For refugees, access to information becomes particularly important when repatriation is considered, since information and discussion on conditions in the country of origin are essential for deciding whether it is safe to repatriate or not (*see* Carver and Verdirame 2001). Freedom of conscience, thought, and religion, and freedom of peaceful assembly and association constitute discrete rights, protected under articles 18 and 21–22 of the ICCPR. Under the 1951 Convention, two provisions, articles

4 and 15, deal with religion and freedom of association. However, article 15 only applies to 'non-political and non-profit making associations and trade unions'.

Like freedom of movement, freedom of expression is also a right on the exercise of which the enjoyment of many other fundamental rights is contingent. Many of the cases examined above involved a violation of freedom of expression: from the discrimination cases to the suppression of the right to protest and the forcible relocation of the human rights activist to Dadaab. In camps and settlements, it was difficult for cultural, political, and religious dissidents to escape social condemnation, persecution, and – as we have seen above under right to security – even assaults. Violations of economic and social rights were also often accompanied by infringements upon free expression – for example, in the case of a doctor who revealed the extent of malnutrition in Kakuma.[190]

Fearing bad publicity, UNHCR controlled access to camps, and often tried to limit researchers' and journalists' access to refugees.[191] On our first visit to Kakuma, we were told by UNHCR that we were not 'allowed' to go to the camp to interview refugees after dark because of 'security concerns'. Over and over again, we were told that we needed 'UNHCR clearance' to visit a camp or a settlement, or to conduct interviews there. The fact that many camps are located in remote areas and that UNHCR controlled transport facilities made it a very effective gatekeeper.

If external researchers found obstacles, refugees trying to have their voices heard outside camps found it an arduous enterprise. One group of refugees, for example, told us about their experiences when they tried to send information on the security situation in the settlements in northern Uganda:

> Last year, in Ogujebe, 7 refugees were killed by government security persons. I [a teacher] was in charge of security for the Emergency Committee and we wanted the world to know about what had happened. We sat down and wrote letters and posted up to Geneva. We got personal replies and people from Geneva even came to talk to us. Afterwards, the government realised we used our own means, our committee was threatened and stopped. We are not allowed to give our own opinion in the media. For example, Eritreans in Khartoum publicised their own news magazine to sensitise the world to human rights abuse – why cannot the voices of we southern Sudanese also be heard?

> The Protection Officer has not come to verify reports or facts on the ground: there is a misrepresentation of numbers – for example, in Waka, where 13 were killed and not all were reported. With our exiled community, we had a delegation come from Kampala of MOLG and they threatened us that we are doing political activities and must stop or action would be taken; information must not be leaked out of the refugee settlements ... (Focus group, Kali Women's Committee, 11 March 1998)

At times UNHCR officials interfered with freedom of speech in a direct way. For example, one Ethiopian refugee was subjected to punitive relocation in Dadaab camp. Ironically for an organisation that is meant to promote respect for human rights, UNHCR identified this person as a 'trouble-maker' because he had organised a series of human rights seminars. UNHCR's senior protection officer at the time wrote to him:

> You will recall that you were transferred from Kakuma Refugee Camp due to security problems following a series of human rights lectures given by you. It is the view of UNHCR that the lectures were a direct cause for the wave of tension and the disruption of public order in the camp.
>
> As you are aware, UNHCR has already taken the decision to transfer you to the Dadaab area. UNHCR has noted your unwillingness to be transferred to Dadaab but regrets to inform you that there are no viable options available at the moment. Once in Dadaab, you will be expected to refrain from any conduct likely to disrupt public order in the camp. This includes the organisations of such lectures as you conducted in Kakuma Refugee Camp. Your attention is drawn to Article III of the 1969 OAU Convention and to the Geneva Convention both of which provide:
>
> 'Every refugee has duties to the country in which he finds himself which require in particularly that he conforms with its laws and regulations as well as with measures taken for the maintenance of public order.'
>
> Accordingly, you are required to report at our Office as soon as possible so that appropriate arrangements for your transport to Dadaab may be made.[192]

Refugee associations

There are many examples of refugee self-help associations.[193] Impediments placed before refugees in officially registering cultural or 'development' associations inhibited their ability to help themselves.

Despite the prohibition on 'subversive activities', in both Kenya and Uganda, as we have seen, the SPLA was tolerated – not only its political activities, but also its military recruitment. Other groups found it much harder to organise associations for either cultural or development purposes. Throughout the research in Nairobi, we observed the plight of many intellectuals, some of whom had been academics in their countries of origin, who tried to continue their work (teaching and research) by organising themselves in associations. There often appeared to be a 'gentlemen's agreement' with the authorities, whereby refugee organisations were tolerated so long as they kept a low profile. This in turn meant that only a few of them received funding from external sources. In Kenya, some Rwandan and Burundian groups used existing Kenyan religious organisations as an institutional cover to obviate the lack of official recognition and to get around the registration requirements under the NGO Act. SWAN was almost exceptional in that its registration under the act was said to be imminent in April 1998.

In Nairobi, we also found two associations of refugee lawyers. The SSLS was in the process of registering as an NGO. It was very close to the SPLA and was mainly preoccupied with drawing up a constitution for an independent southern Sudan. The SSLS did not concern itself with the immediate problems facing refugees. The Inter-African Organisation of Jurists consisted mainly of lawyers from Rwanda and Burundi. Some of the members were also involved in teaching at the Hope International School. They published a report on the massacres of Rwandans in the DRC.

In Uganda there was generally greater respect for freedom of expression than in Kenya. The Sudan Human Rights Association (SHRA), located in Kampala, made regular visits to camps including Kakuma in Kenya (as finances allowed) and published a newsletter, the *Sudan Monitor*. Their reports were impartial and they did not omit to discuss the abuses committed by the SPLA as well the treatment of refugees in camps by the host government and UNHCR. They also held training sessions on refugee rights and organised various conferences. Southern Sudanese Students of Makerere University was another association which had among its objectives addressing the problem of women's education and fighting illiteracy. Another refugee association in Uganda was the Congolese Refugees Development Association (COREDA), which we helped to register as an NGO.

Conclusion

The violations of human rights of which refugees were victims in Kenya and Uganda were imputable to different actors. Governments bore the main responsibility for the violations that were perpetrated outside the camps, while UNHCR and humanitarian NGOs were at fault for many of the violations committed in refugee camps and settlements, where they exercised governmental powers of administration. A minimalistic approach to refugee rights was adopted by both government and humanitarian officials who believed that refugees were entitled to little more than physical survival. The political 'earthquake' that occurred in December 2002 in Kenya appears to have shaken some of these approaches too, as the new minister of home affairs announced the intention to adopt a refugee policy that is respectful of the rights of refugees.

Fundamental to the long catalogue of rights abuses that we have detailed was the violation of the refugees' sense of dignity. When they were compelled to queue for food in the camps in the scorching sun, when they were superciliously guarded and sometimes lashed by *askaris*, when they were chased away from offices and called 'liars' and 'parasites', when they were forced to pay a bribe in order not to be arbitrarily arrested, when they saw that their social status – for example, as elderly people, or as women – was given no recognition by the humanitarian bureaucracy or government officials, when they were discriminated against owing to their gender or race, and were subjected to various forms of sexual violence and exploitation, refugees felt a deep sense of degradation. For many, the most difficult struggle was against the negative stereotype created by the host government's authorities and the humanitarian bureaucracies, '... someone who has no shelter ... nothing to eat; cannot afford medical care; dresses poorly; is a beggar; and lives in fear ... someone who has no freedom and [who] *other* people think is not self-reliant or self dependent' (Lammers 1998: 43).

Notes

1. *See also* the International Convention on the Elimination of All Forms of Racial Discrimination (1969), the Declaration on the Elimination of All Forms of Intolerance and of Discrimination Based on Religion or Belief (1981), and the Convention on the Rights of the Child (1990).
2. Such discriminatory laws on naturalisation are not limited to Kenya. In Tanzania, a similar provision exists and, when refugees were forcibly rounded up and put in the camps, many Tanzanian wives found themselves with no alternative but to live there also (Whitaker 1998; HRW 1999a). In Botswana, this law was successfully challenged and the decision on that case – *Unity Dow v. Botswana* – became a landmark precedent. In Egypt, the children of Egyptian women and Sierra Leoneans found themselves in limbo: they were denied Egyptian citizenship, they could not go back to Sierra Leone because of the war, and they were not recognised as refugees.
3. *See also* the section on fair trial below.
4. When we first visited Kakuma in 1997, these small cells were guarded by a young man with a whip, one holding three minors and one a mentally disturbed woman.
5. Interview with Deng Dau Deng, leader of the Sudanese community, 17 July 1997.
6. Ostracism is a common social sanction against 'dissidents' in a society. *See* Martha Nussbaum's example from Bangladesh (Nassbaum 2000: 82). On the use of psychological sanctions in traditional dispute settlement, *see* e.g. Köbben (1969: 130).
7. Interview with Njoki Ndung'u, 18 June 1997.
8. Interview with Goretty Omala, 1997.
9. They too had been the victims of discrimination – the parents were of mixed parentage and they refused to have their daughters circumcised.
10. It took some persuading to get UNHCR to pay the school fees of the young girl and to maintain her as an urban refugee. It also took more than a year to persuade the senior protection officer to work seriously on this case when his second idea, of sending her to an orphanage in the US, was not considered by

us as in the best interests of the child since she had a relative in Holland. By August 2003, four years later, she had not yet been re-united.

11. This statement is sometimes followed or preceded by similar cliché statements about men. For example the inter-agency guidelines on gender mainstreaming contain this truism about men: '... b) in complex emergencies, men account for the largest numbers of combatants while women and children comprise the largest section of civilians affected by conflict' (Inter-Agency Standing Committee 1999).

12. Another common gender policy was to have female members of staff interview refugee women. A recommendation to this effect featured in the Guidelines on Reviewing National Refugee Legislation, prepared by UNHCR (IOM/UNHCR draft 2000). The assumption was that gender is the only determinant of a person's level of comfort with his or her interviewer and interpreter, while psychological, cultural, or other factors were underplayed (*see* Harrell-Bond 1986: 283 on the over-socialised concept of man). However, while it is reasonable to assume that, in most cases, a victim of sexual and gender-based violence will feel more comfortable talking to another woman, there might also be gender reasons for which a woman, or a man, might feel comfortable with a person of the opposite gender. For instance, it is usually women who perform genital mutilation on other women – in Sierra Leone and Liberia, as part of rituals of the women's secret societies (the *Bundu* societies). A woman *might* feel more comfortable recounting these experiences to a man from a completely different cultural background than to a woman from her own background, whom she might assume to favour these practices.

13. A parallel can be drawn between gender mainstreaming in institutions and gender blindness in the law. Both are purportedly corollaries of the principle of equality, as they are apparently based on non-discrimination between men and women. Both, however, can mask 'the fact the they do not always take into account women's particular needs and rights' (Garling 2003: 35). Garling also expresses concerns about gender mainstreaming (ibid.: 38).

14. For example, the UNHCR policy on sexual violence recognises that combating male refugees' 'immense frustration, boredom and feeling of dependency generated by camp life' is instrumental to the prevention or reduction of sexual violence (UNHCR 1995h: 14).

15. Interview with Maler Mathiang Malek, Ifo camp, Dadaab, 30 April 1998.

16. Since the debate on domestic violence is dominated by western sociocultural models, it often fails to acknowledge the peculiarities of the problem in societies where polygamy is practised. Some women associated the idea of 'violence in the home' with fights among co-wives, but, in spite of this, only 6.3 percent of the women interviewed were in favour of abolishing polygamy as a way of eliminating domestic and sexual violence (Mulumba 1998), revealing a certain resilience of traditional cultural norms. The incidence of domestic violence among co-wives should not mislead one into believing that other more 'predictable' forms of domestic violence – that is, the husband using violence against his wife or against sons and daughters – did not occur.

17. For example, when we conducted research in Liberia on behalf of the Lawyers' Committee for Human Rights (LCHR), we were frequently told by UNHCR and NGO officials that in the camps for Sierra Leonean refugees in Vahun and Kolahun there were many 'war criminals'. When asked what evidence there was to support this statement, the answer was usually, 'There are quite a number of young and fit men.'

18. But there is conflicting evidence on the gender incidence of post-traumatic stress disorder (Karunakara et al. 2004).
19. *See also* Nurrudin Farah's narrative account of the life of Somali refugees in *Yesterday, Tomorrow*, especially the section on Somalis in Italy: Somali women managed to find employment as domestic workers, while men generally remained unemployed. By becoming 'bread-winners' women increased their power and, as Farah notes, they could 'afford' to deal with men in ways that were almost unthinkable in Somalia – for example, by asking them to do housework, denying them money, and so on (Farah 2000).
20. *See*, e.g., UNHCR 2000c where it is argued that displacement is a more dis-empowering experience for women than for men.
21. *See* Chapter 3 **Cessation.**
22. Hutu refugees were clearly disadvantaged in terms of access to status-determination procedures. *See* Chapter 3 **Decisions.**
23. Interview: anon.
24. Interview with Mr I. and Mr J., Mongola settlement, Adjumani district, 17 March 1998.
25. Ibid.
26. Letter from the Somali Bantu Committee, Kakuma refugee camp, to Guglielmo Verdirame, 9 December 1997.
27. Another cause of this discrimination was the identification of the Dinka with the SPLA, which in 1986–88 had attacked the camps of Ugandan refugees in southern Sudan. The Equatorians had been adamant in 1983, when the war erupted, that they would not join the struggle. They had even sided with the Nimeiry government in the 'decentralisation' policy, which demanded that every person return to their place of birth. 'The Dinka sold us out in the 1972 agreement. If the Dinka want a war, let them fight it', was the almost univer-sal sentiment expressed in Equatoria at the time.
28. Kali I was described as the 'stubborn village'. It was said that as soon as food was distributed. Kali I residents crossed the border to Sudan. They were also accused of selling rations, affecting the market prices. The Dinka were also said to sell their hoes the moment they received them. 'They can't stay with a hoe.' On 27 November 1997, an SPLA mission was reported to have brought women and children in five lorries from Ogujebe. In the morning a hand grenade was found at the Lutheran World Federation (LWF) warehouse.
29. In Ikafe settlement, a few Dinka had initially arrived with cattle and they were segregated from the main camp in an area which could offer limited grazing. Many Dinka youths without cattle were initially given plots in the settlement but found it more 'comfortable' to join the others in the area set aside for cattle. There was an argument on whether these young men should be allowed to receive rations since they were not conforming to camp rules.
30. UNHCR never openly objected to this militarisation. It continued the practice of assigning all Dinka and Nuer to Mirieyi, including defecting soldiers. It must have been an extremely dangerous place for those who did not have sympathy for the SPLA and for the minors who were especially vulnerable to forced recruitment.
31. Field notes: Personal narratives 1998.
32. Field notes: Personal narratives – Mirye Transit, Adjumani.
33. Ibid.
34. Field notes: Handwritten account 1998.
35. *See*, e.g., ICCOPR art. 6.

36. The deprivation of livelihood and the violations of the right to food will be discussed in Chapter 5. Suffice it to say that the fact that refugees are confined against their will in camps, where they cannot become even self-reliant in food production, means that those responsible for their confinement and for the provision of the essentials of life – host states, UNHCR, the World Food Programme (WFP), or NGOs – are obliged to provide the refugees with necessities such as shelter, water, food, and health care. Keeping refugees on inadequate rations is a breach of the right to food, but when loss of life occurs as a result of these deprivations, it is a breach of the right to life.

37. We do not know if Mr Sendashonga had a UNHCR protection letter. It would not be surprising if he did not, since prominent political exiles at times manage to obtain papers through normal immigration or asylum channels. However, members of his family, whom we interviewed after he had been killed, possessed UNHCR 'protection letters'.

38. *See also* the case of the Rwandan family killed in Nairobi in a 'secure residence' run by UNHCR (HRW 2002b).

39. After the Uganda carrying the hit list was identified, the head of security in the Ugandan sector in Kakuma wrote to UNHCR requesting that some action be taken. Members of our team and the Windle Trust, which had sponsored V.'s masters studies in the UK, intervened on his behalf too. In spite of this, no secure accommodation outside the camp was arranged for him for two years, by which time his resettlement to Canada had almost been completed.

40. Letter from Col. Kahinda Otafiire, 18 February 1996.

41. Interview with Ms Laurence Harerimana, Kampala, 27 October 1997. We also interviewed David Balikowa, the sub-editor of The *Monitor*, who was a friend of Ms Harerimana's husband and accompanied him to the airport.

42. Information about this incident came to us from Mary Byrne and Martin Zak. The camp commandant was simply transferred to another camp.

43. The distinction between bandits and rebels is not, of course, a clear-cut one. Both groups are armed, but the rebel groups of northern Uganda appear to have a set of political claims, while the phenomenon of 'banditry' in the North-Eastern Province (NEP) of Kenya seems more akin to organised crime exacerbated by the political and administrative neglect of that province.

44. Most important is art. 5 of the African Charter on Human and Peoples' Rights, and art. 7 of the ICCPR.

45. The attribution of an act to the state has been one of the main areas codified by the International Law Commission under its state responsibility project (*see* arts. 4–11, Responsibility of States for Internationally Wrongful Acts, Annex to the UNGA res. 56/83). The rules on attribution are not discussed in this book, but they have been taken into account in attributing acts to different entities.

46. In particular case nos. 024/DRC/U/1998; 073/DRC/U/1999; 079/DRC/U/1999; 090/DRC/U/1999; 096/DRC/U/1999; 140/DRC/U/1999; 151/DRC/U/1999; 189/DRC/U/1998.

47. The research team persuaded UNHCR to change the order and send him to Kyangwali.

48. *See* case nos. 127/SUD/U/1999; 131/SUD/U/1999; 203/SUD/U/1999; 210/SUD/U/1999.

49. This was a relatively mild sentence, considering that the draconian Kenyan Penal Code would have allowed imprisonment for up to seven years, together with corporal punishment for this felony.

50. Visited on 18 September 1999.

51. Letter from H.A. to the senior protection officer, 22 February 1998.
52. An observation in Tanzania is also telling: '... a pregnant mother ... carrying a baby and with a toddler following her was pushed out of the queue. The *sungu sungu* [uniformed refugees employed and armed with sticks by UNHCR to police other refugees] then began hitting her on the legs with their sticks. The woman was pleading and crying, the toddler screaming. This scene was observed by UNHCR and other agency staff, *but none of them interfered* ' (Harrell-Bond 2002: 63).
53. Presentation of Mr Malik, UNHCR's senior regional registration officer, in preparation for the headcount, Dadaab, 29 April 1998.
54. One of us was also told of analogous incidents in the refugee camps in Vahun and Kolahun, Liberia, hosting Sierra Leonean refugees, when a fact-finding mission was conducted on behalf of the LCHR in July–August 1998.
55. Even inmates in Nazi concentration camps reported to the guards individuals who received larger rations. Such episodes are recounted both by Primo Levi (1979a) and by Bruno Bettelheim (1988). On social revolt originating from concepts of distributive justice, *see* Moore 1978: 37.
56. Censuses are also prohibited under the Jewish Torah (*Exodus*, 30, 11–13) and have a bad press in the New Testament too.
57. In the camps for Burundian refugees in Kibondo, Tanzania, we found that refugee guards, the *sungu sungu*, were given far too much power. 'It was a general view among those refugees with whom we spoke that the introduction of police into the refugee camps and the payment of some refugees to serve as *sungu sungu* has increased insecurity rather than reduced it. They say that salaried *sungu sungu* no longer feel responsible to the block chairpersons but to the police, not even to UNHCR who pays them. They accuse some *sungu sungu* of co-operating with police to extort money from refugees who infringe rules, for example, being caught outside the four kilometre camp limit or using the land near Kanembwa that was declared inside the conservation area and excluded from such use. They are even accused of being responsible for some of the cases of rape that take place. The block chairpersons of some blocks have now organised another layer of security, asking men, including *sungu sungu* they had appointed, to station themselves outside particularly vulnerable households at night' (Harrell-Bond et al. 2000: 17).
58. Meeting of the RWC of Ibakwe, 16 February 1998. 'Shouting at night' would not probably fall under 'common nuisance' under section 156 of the Penal Code Act, for which the maximum sentence is one-year imprisonment. (cap. 106 of the Laws of Uganda).
59. The US embassy was also the target of Ms Lakwena's delirium. She wrote a letter to the US ambassador, berating her for having arrested 'the Prophetess Madame Lakwena and all her followers ... We had time and time and again wanted to know who is trying to confine us with the Refugee Camp but have now confirmed it is you. Do you want to prove whether the Holy Spirit has now landed on Earth?'
60. In a landmark decision, the ICTR held that acts of rape can constitute genocide (Verdirame 2000b). On sexual violence against women, *see also* Declaration on the Elimination of Violence against Women (GA res. 48/104, 20 December 1993), and the reports of the Special Rapporteur on Violence Against Women, appointed for the first time in 1994 (available at www.unhchr.ch). The literature on gender and human rights, and on sexual violence, is vast. A thorough analysis can be found in Charlesworth and

Chinkin 2000: 201–49. On sexual violence as a ground for claiming asylum, *see*, e.g., Haines 2001.

61. Convention against Torture, art. 1(1).

62. The work of Rebecca Cook in this area is particularly relevant. By proposing ways in which states should be made accountable for acts of non-state actors, she has tried to break through the public/private dichotomy and create a more purposive set of rules (Cook 1993).

63. 'This analysis of rape demonstrates a decrease of 45% in firewood collection rapes during periods of full firewood coverage. However, these periods also see an increase in rapes in other locations and contexts by between 78% and 113%. It is therefore difficult for the evaluators to conclude that firewood provision is a wholly successful rape prevention strategy. Our findings suggest that firewood collection provides a convenient context or location for rape, but should not be viewed as its "cause"' (UNHCR 2001b: 4).

64. The expression is used by Chimni in respect of the 'safe havens' established by the international community in the former Yugoslavia and in northern Iraq (1994).

65. *See* case no. 004/UGA/K/1997.

66. Because of their fear of the police, women victims of rape were usually reluctant to report it to the police, afraid of 'repercussions, despite our assurances that additional measures will be taken to safeguard their security' (Okoro 1995). 'Improper handling of medical evidence by clinical staff of the implementing partner' was adduced as another obstacle towards the prosecution of the perpetrators of the sexual violence.

67. In Kenya and Uganda, male rape does not exist in the law. The rapist can only be charged with sodomy (if this was part of the rape), which is punished whether consensual or not under the Kenyan Penal Code.

68. Case no. 129/SUD/U/1998.

69. Ibid.

70. The girl was injured during the rape and was incontinent after that.

71. Later she found out that the man who raped her daughter also raped a Rwandan woman. He was imprisoned but released two weeks later.

72. The research team was fortunate in having two experienced journalists working as interns for a few months during 1998–99, who wrote up this story in the local press.

73. Concerns about maintaining good relations with the Somali community did not prevent UNHCR from seeking the intervention of the police when one of their staff members was the victim of a much less serious offence: 'On 30th of November, our Field Officer for Ifo was assaulted by a Dadaab resident. Awaiting the departure of the regular escort, some locals forced their way into the UNHCR vehicle in order to secure a lift to the camp. The driver got out and urged them to leave the car. They alighted reluctantly and one of the locals approached the Field Officer at the passenger's seat. He started talking to her in agitated manner and at this point struck her in the face twice. A police officer was nearby, but did not intervene, not even after a specific request from our Field Officer. The matter was reported to the District Officer and a police report was drawn up' (UNHCR 1997j).

74. This was a volunteer scheme organized by the former high commissioner to encourage students and young graduates to go to refugee camps and write reports about their experiences.

75. Munson's field notes, 1998.

76. Ibid.

77. Interview with Maler Mathiang Malek, Ifo camp, Dadaab, 30 April 1998.
78. The FIDA consultant was initially employed for a period of three months, after a struggle, she managed to have the project extended for another year.
79. Interview, Mongola settlement, Adjumani district, 17 March 1998.
80. Interview with CARE camp manager, Mr Weru, Ifo camp, Dadaab, 28 April 1998.
81. Interview with Mr Hussein, CSM focal point for the camps in Dadaab, 29 April 1998.
82. One of these was a Sudanese man whose 'head was completely damaged' (Weekly Security Report, 30 January 1996), and a decomposed Turkana girl (Weekly Security Report, 22 October 1996).
83. Email from Lucy Weir to Barbara Harrell-Bond, 6 December 1997
84. When we were in Kakuma and Dadaab, there were continuous reports of attacks on cars and *matatus*. As noted earlier, a research assistant nearly lost his life on the road from Lodwar to Eldoret.
85. Email from Mauro De Lorenzo, 2 February 1999; *see also Sudan Monitor* 2001.
86. She added: 'The most difficult part ... was not the not knowing for myself, but it was the not knowing for Susan. Whenever I left the compound, she would come running up to me, hoping that I would have an answer. At that point, I would have to assure her that indeed, the UNHCR was working as fast as they could and that people inside the compound did care about her well-being. I served as a sort of buffer between the reality of the refugee, and the seemingly bureaucratic world inside the compound. A frustrating position, as I had so little power, but so many responsibilities to both the refugee and the UNHCR' (ibid.).
87. In this period the Italian press was reporting on the sex traffic of Somali girls and women. Sister Louise, who maintained a home for refugees outside Nairobi, reported that on several occasions she had been approached by supposed philanthropists who claimed that they were interested in providing education abroad for Somali girls.
88. Interview with William Sakataka, head of sub-office, Pakelle, 11 February 1998.
89. Interview with Augustino Henry, assistant field coordinator, TPO, Palorinya, 17 February 1998. *See also* letter from Augustino Henry to the field coordinator, TPO, Adjumani, 'Report on the tortured refugees who sustained injuries', 12 November 1997.
90. Phase IV is the stage at which expatriate staff of UN agencies are evacuated. The UNHCR representative had requested UNDP, which was responsible for coordinating security for UN agencies in Uganda, to assign this level of danger to the settlements in Palorinya (Letter from Ulf Kristoffersen to the high commissioner, 21 October 1996).
91. Reports of such attacks were still continuing in August 2002: 'Sudanese refugees in Uganda have come under rebel attack again, this time at Achol-Pii camp, after July's raid on refugees in the Adjumani area. Eight refugees were reportedly killed and four local aid workers kidnapped. "Twenty-four thousand refugees are in flight" said UNHCR spokeswoman Bushra Malik ... The refugee camp manager, who managed to flee on foot 15 km to the town of Rachkoko together with a group of some 10,000 refugees, spoke by radio to UNHCR staff in the northern Ugandan town of Kitgum' (UNHCR News Stories 2002).
92. Interview with the RWC, Kali I, Village 2, 18 February, 1998.
93. Interview with RWC at Belameling School, Palorinya, 22 February 1998.

94. Interview with P., Mongola settlement, 18 March 1998.
95. Focus group with teachers at Mongola Primary and Secondary School, Mongola I settlement, 18 March 1998. This series of attacks were also described in detail by other refugees in Mongola settlement, including in a focus group with the RWC and court members of Mongola I. Interview with Patrick Manson, registration clerk, LWF/Adjumani, refugee in Mongola settlement, 18 March 1998.
96. Hannah Gary's field notes, 18 February 1998.
97. Interview, 17 March 1998, Mongola settlement, Adjumani district.
98. Interview with William Sakataka, head of UNHCR sub-office Pakelle, 11 February 1998.
99. Hannah Garry's field notes, 17 February 1998.
100. Interview with Mr William Sakataka, head of sub-office UNHCR Pakelle, 11 February 1998.
101. Interview with Augustino Henry, assistant field coordinator, TPO, Palorinya, 17 February 1998.
102. Ibid.
103. Notes on meeting with Mr Hans Thoolen, UNHCR representative, Kampala, 16 July 1998.
104. Letter from the landlords to the RDC, 17 January 1998.
105. Interview with LWF project manager, 21 February 1998.
106. Interview with Somali refugee, Jomvu camp, 15 October 1997.
107. *See* the *Monitor*. 1996.
108. *See* Mutumba, 1998a, b.
109. Ibid. *See also* Omara 1998. Named abductees in 1997 included Safari Marembo, Lusakweno Mawakana Dodo (Congolese), and Paul Bagalabo (Ugandan Rwandan). Named abductees in 1998 included Emmanuel Ngomiraronka, Nathanael Nsengiyumva, and Venest Ruvumwabo.
110. *See* Weddi 1998; Mutumba 1998a,b.
111. *See* Amnesty International 1998b.
112. Police stopped the car and ordered her abductors to get out. She managed to slip out of the door near the ditch and roll away from the car. After the car drove off, she stood up and identified herself to the police.
113. Although clearly a woman at risk who should have been a candidate for resettlement, she was still writing from Uganda in August 2002, hoping soon to have an interview soon.
114. Communication with member of special branch, 7 August 1999, after the course on refugee/human rights law, in which he participated.
115. '... and released in 1992. He was saved by his popularity, otherwise he could have been killed. Between the years 1986 and 1989 someone by the name of Abongo masqueraded as a refugee and was assisted by senior clergy ... in Uganda, who convinced the UNHCR to resettle him ... in Norway ... Today that same man is the Commissioner of the entire police force in Kenya. In 1994, 150 people who had escaped ethnic violence to Uganda disappeared mysteriously when they were convinced to go back to Kenya. It is therefore very true that Kenya's security detail has been crossing to Uganda from time to time to trap escapees' (Email from Issac Newton Kinity, 27 August 2002).
116. Name withheld.
117. Another example is the case of refugees charged with the destruction of facilities which led to the imposition of collective punishment, discussed below.
118. Report, Praxidice Wekesa Saisi, magistrate, Makadera court, Kenya 1998.
119. Interview with Mr Kyambo, senior immigration officer, 29 October 1997.

120. Interview with officer-in-charge, Mr Andrew Ongai, 6 February 1998.
121. This information was obtained from the files of the JRS, Kampala. The case was handled by M/S Kiyingi and Co. Advocates, Kampala.
122. Inter-Office Memorandum No. 28/98, Director of the Division of International Protection, Dennis McNamara, to All Representatives, Chiefs of Mission and Correspondents, All Directors of Bureaux and Divisions, All Protection staff, 20 March 1998.
123. This was confirmed by Father Waliggo of the UHRC, who said that 'in his prison visits in the North, he has found many refugees in remand for various reasons' (Garry1998c: 6).
124. Under section 43, 'A person subject to military law who unlawfully detains any other person in arrest or confinement, or unnecessarily detains any other person without bringing him to trial, or fails to bring that other person's case before the proper authority for investigation, commits an offence and shall, on conviction, be liable to a term of imprisonment not exceeding ten years'.
125. Interview with magistrate grade I, Moyo and Adjumani districts, 19 March 1998.
126. Ibid.
127. The Luzira prison is made up of the women's prison, remand prison, Murchison Bay, for men, and the maximum or upper prison, where capital offenders are held.
128. We sent a summary of this case to LAP with a request that they take up their cases.
129. Letter from Commissioner Karusoke, UHRC to Doreen Nakasaga Lwanga, 28 October 1999.
130. On the international legal regulation of children in armed conflict, *see* Kuper 1997.
131. Some might have been abducted to be sold as slaves (*see* Fitzgerald 2002).
132. Interview, 19 March 1998.
133. Interview with Mr Charles Opio, desk officer, MoLG, Pakelle, 6 February 1998.
134. *See also* SHRA 1999: 4. Reporting on the same events, it says 'The abducts [*sic*] have been taken to Ajulu and Patiko Prisons in Kitgum and Gulu respectively for training. The old and the starving have been forcibly been made to give contribution on failure to submit to conditions ...'
135. That this roundup was going to happen was a well-known secret. The Hugh Pilkington Charitable Trust, an educational NGO, had warned all the scholarship holders to come to Kampala in advance.
136. Interview, 11 September 1999.
137. Interview with an eye witness, 7 August 1999.
138. Interview by SHRA's field officer (SHRA 1999).
139. A humanitarian worker, for example, recounting his harrowing experience in southern Sudan in the aftermath of a fierce battle that had left many wounded, wrote:
    I found [SPLA] Commander G ... and explained my mission in detail to him. He then explained to me the politics of the medical evacuation process that led to there being no wounded ready to be evacuated. Part of the issue is that anyone that is evacuated to the ICRC [International Committee of the Red Cross] facility in Loki is lost to him forever. When they recover from their wounds the ICRC makes it impossible for them ever to return to their units. Plus there is a security aspect of using the ICRC, which is well known for being biased towards the Khartoum regime. If we could agree that the

wounded will be evacuated only to hospitals within New Sudan then he will make it his highest priority to support it. I assured him that we would only evacuate wounded to Loki when there was no other option. We agreed and shook hands (Norbury 2002).

140. The political opinion is that which prevents the refugee 'from taking part in a type of military action that is contrary to the most basic international rules of conduct' (*Zacarias Osorio Cruz* cited in Hathaway 1991: 182); the social group is that of individuals within the regular armed forces or within the insurgents' forces who intend to uphold respect for humanitarian law.

141. Email: 16 July 1999.

142. Ibid.

143. Names withheld.

144. Yet UNHCR certainly knew that forced recruitment was one of the main causes of the influx of refugees from Sudan (e.g., UNHCR 1996k, 1996l).

145. One of those defecting told us of an incident that occurred in Kigali. Garrang, Museveni, and Kagame – he claimed – were all present when a group of defectors who had been captured were shot by a firing squad made up of young SPLA recruits (case no. 159/SUD/U/99).

146. Some local UNHCR officers confirmed the occurrence of forced recruitment. For example, one of them said that the 'persecutors and the persecuted often live side by side in refugee camps and we [UNHCR] can never provide full protection as the SPLA are free to move around' (Interview with Sofi Elg, UNHCR protection officer, Pakelle-Adjumani and Moyo, 19 March 1998).

147. Chambers and Kibreab also noted the harmful effect of the denial of freedom of movement on self-reliance (Kibreab 1987b: 277; Chambers 1979).

148. In both Kenya and Uganda, we sometimes wrote our own 'protection' letters for those without a means of identifying themselves as refugees. Addressed 'to whom it may concern', it stated that the person was a refugee who was seeking asylum or travelling from a to b. We explained that we were doing research on refugee rights and gave our government research clearance number. These letters were apparently respected.

149. Interview with Sten Hansen, Kakuma, 10 March 1998.

150. Ibid.

151. CTDs are travel documents to which refugees have a right under article 28 of the 1951 Convention (*see* Schedule in the 1951 Convention which gives details about provisions and rules that member states must abide by). CTDs are issued by the host government. As explained by Goodwin-Gill, '... the words of this provision [art. 28 of the Convention] may well place the refugee in a better position with regard to the issue of travel documentation than the citizen of the State in which he or she resides' (1998a: 302). The predecessor of the CTD was the Nansen Passport (Skran 1988; 1992; 1996).

152. We helped one refugee obtain a CTD in order to travel to Tanzania. The Ugandan, Kenyan, and Tanzanian immigration officials he met en route would not recognise it and he had to bribe his way across two borders (case no. 088/DRC/U/1997).

153. Interview with Yossah Wawa, director, Hugh Pilkington Trust, 8 May 1997.

154. Interview with Mr Opio and Mr Choko, 21 August 1998.

155. In a footnote he added that the complete freedom of movement for refugees was 'A situation most favoured by Ms. Barbara Harold-Bond [*sic*], now visiting professor at Makerere University of Kampala and her research team'.

156. On the Ugandan reservations, *see* Chapter 1 **The legal framework in Uganda**.

157. An example was the acquittal of a Somali woman charged with assaulting a policeman. The provincial authorities had been trying to ban *khat* (or *miraa*) in North-Eastern Province (NEP) but the legality of this ban was in question. She had been selling *khat* in the market when a policeman approached her. A confrontation occurred and she was accused of physically assaulting the policeman. She claimed she was acting in self-defence. The magistrate discarded the evidence of the policeman and his colleague. He also held that there was 'no administrative order or legal notice, lawfully gazetted in the Official Kenya Gazette' that contained the ban on selling *khat*. The magistrate concluded that 'if the accused did slap the complainant as alleged by the prosecution, it was out of provocation' (*Republic v. Lul Ali Hassan*). *See also* UNHCR Dadaab, 'Note for the File: The Mobile (Visiting) Court Session in Dadaab (8th to the 10th of April 1998)', Note of 22 April 1988.
158. Interview with magistrate grade I, Joseph Emodo Nyanga, Moyo and Adjumani districts, 19 March 1998.
159. It must be noted, however, that, even in Uganda where we collected refugee cases from national courts more systematically than in Kenya, the data are not exhaustive and point to areas for further research.
160. Moreover, in Adjumani, the court clerk helped in identifying cases involving refugees and we were able to copy twenty-two cases from the 1997–98 records. Notes on sixteen additional cases were made in August 1998 in the same court: one of these was from 1994, all the rest were from 1997.
161. Interview with magistrate grade I, Joseph Emodo Nyanga, Moyo and Adjumani districts, 19 March 1998.
162. Ibid.
163. Ibid.
164. Another string of cases that ended up in courts in Uganda had to do with work permits and will be examined in Chapter 5.
165. Munson, a member of our team, conducted a study of dispute settlement in Rhino camp (Munson 1999b); interviews were made and documentary evidence on the administration of justice was collected from other settlements.
166. Resort to the 'customary' track rather than the proper judicial one in this case protected the soldiers, who could have faced a long prison sentence or even the death penalty if convicted in court of 'defilement'.
167. Kiswahili for guards.
168. There are no police stationed in the settlements in Adjumani and Moyo districts, but there are police posts in settlements in other parts of the country.
169. According to a letter, dated 2 January 1999, from the regional refugee desk officer (RDO) to the camp commandant in Nakivale, two young men (including the Burundian who alleged this threat) had complained to him of '1. Torture 2. Harrassment 3. Threats 4. General Fear'. The RDO requested the camp commandant to respond to these four allegations 'so as to assist me in making a decision'. He went on: 'In the meantime let the two stay without any further harassment. If you think they are a security risk I hope there [are] better ways of handling the matter than torture.' Signed Baraki Charles RDO.
170. Letter of 22 September 1995 from C.B. Opio, settlement commandant, Adjumani refugee settlement to all RWC chairmen.
171. The only settlement where we could find written records, albeit incomplete.
172. 17 March 1998, Mongola settlement, Adjumani district.
173. For example, Munson found out that one woman had been in prison for a week on suspicion of 'bewitching'.

174. Further confirmation of lockups in settlements comes from an interview with Mr Nabongo Fred, the former head of the Mbarara police station, now deputy commandant, Kibuli Police Training School, Kampala, 23 July 1999.
175. Most sexual offences in the customary law of the different peoples in Uganda carry a penalty of payment of compensation, either monetary or in kind – for example, 5 goats or 2 cows. Imprisonment is always a last resort when the culprit fails to cooperate (Email from Zachary Lomo, 22 August 2002).
176. Interview with Deng Daw, leader of the Sudanese community, Kakuma, 23 July 1997.
177. Interview with camp manager, Hagadera, Dadaab, 3 November 1997.
178. The imposition of collective punishments in refugee camps is not exceptional. On at least two occasions it was imposed on refugees in Dadaab as well.
179. Interview with Deng Dau Deng, leader of the Sudanese community, Kakuma, 17 July 1997.
180. This memorandum mentioned only the 'incentives', but, through interviews with refugees and NGO workers, we could confirm that the suspension of food was part of the punitive measures.
181. Interview with Luwi Buchike, leader of the Rwandan community, Kakuma, 15 July 1997.
182. In addition, these cases illustrate how the law on immunity of international organisations, which shields them from the jurisdiction of national courts even when they exercise de facto powers, can conflict with the right to a fair trial (Verdirame 2001b).
183. Interview, 17 March 1998.
184. She had been assisted by the Bishop of Bukavu to leave the DRC and he had also arranged her visa for Belgium.
185. Only then was M. able to reclaim his passport. The deported children were a boy, 18; a girl, 13; and another girl, 11.
186. By coincidence one of us was on the same plane from Uganda to Nairobi and we talked. We had no inkling, however, of the problem, that B. would face when she attempted to board the plane for Belgium.
187. Emails from J.P. Muongo, 11 and 13 January 2001. When this case was recorded, we referred them to the ICRC and the National Red Cross.
188. The two of them moved in with a Congolese pastor who had been in Nairobi for many years.We interviewed him for the first time in April 1997. Our main concern at the time was to get Fiston, then 7, into a school.
189. *See* Chapter 1 *Phase Two: The balance of power shifts*.
190. *See* Chapter 5 *Malnutrition and the conspiracy of silence*.
191. Chapter 6 *Image management: reporting the field*.
192. Letter from the UNHCR's protection officer, Roberto Quintero, 19 July 1997.
193. The Lutaya School, built and run by refugees in southern Sudan, is only one example (Wilson et al. 1985).

5

Economic, Social, and Cultural Rights

Introduction

Economic and social rights are often assumed to be 'new' rights compared with civil and political rights. Whereas this might be true as far as national constitutions are concerned, it is not true for international law (Grant 1998: 76). Historically, freedom from slavery and labour-related rights were the first human rights to be recognised under international law.[1] The 1948 Universal Declaration of Human Rights (UDHR) already contained provisions on economic, social, and cultural rights (arts. 22–29). The International Covenant on Economic, Social and Cultural Rights (ICESCR), adopted in 1966, is the fundamental international instrument in this area.

An importance difference between the International Covenant on Civil and Political Rights (ICCPR) and the ICESCR is in the nature and scope of state obligations (Alston and Quinn 1987). Article 2(1) of ICESCR 1 obliges a state party 'to take steps, individually and through international assistance and co-operation, especially economic and technical, to the maximum of its available resources, with a view to achieving progressively the full realisation of the rights recognised in the present Covenant by all appropriate means, including particularly the adoption of legislative measures'.[2] This provision has been contrasted with its counterpart in the ICCPR, which uses more compelling language, imposing on state parties an obligation 'to respect and to ensure' the rights under the Covenant. As a result, endless and rather otiose debates on the legal character of socio-economic and cultural rights have for a long time dominated their analyses. Of far greater relevance, and much more neglected, is the question of the enforcement of these rights: which measures can states adopt to promote them, in respect of their nationals and of refugees alike? What is the role, and what are the duties, of international organisations and non-governmental organisations (NGOs)?

Both Kenya and Uganda are parties to the ICESCR,[3] and as a result of the combined effect of the obligations deriving from it and other relevant instruments – most notably the African Charter on Human and Peoples' Rights, the 1951 Refugee Convention, the 1969 OAU Convention, and the Convention on the Rights of the Child (CRC) – both countries have committed themselves to protecting the economic and social rights of all human beings in their territory, including refugees.

The 1951 Convention refers to specific economic and social rights to which refugees are entitled, including the right to gainful employment and education. Interestingly, the Convention also provides that refugees are to be accorded the same treatment as nationals with respect to rationing systems and public relief and assistance (arts. 20, 23). The fear of the drafters of the 1951 Convention was that states would exclude refugees from humanitarian assistance during national emergencies. They had not contemplated the current situation, in which refugees throughout countries in the 'developing world' are made dependent on a parallel system of humanitarian assistance.

Employment

The right to work is defined in the ICESCR as the right 'of everyone to the opportunity to gain his living by work which he freely chooses or accepts' (art. 6). To achieve the full realisation of this right, states are also required to provide 'technical and vocational guidance and training programmes' and to adopt 'policies and techniques to achieve economic, social, and cultural development and full and productive employment under conditions safeguarding fundamental political and economic freedoms of the individual' (art. 6(2)). The right to work does not mean that individuals have an automatic right to paid employment, but that, at the very least, they should not be denied the opportunity to seek it.

The provision in the ICESCR has to be read in conjunction with articles 17–19 in the 1951 Convention, which regulate the refugee's right to engage in wage-earning employment, or in self-employment, or to join the liberal professions. As regards the right to engage in wage-earning employment, the 1951 Convention adopts the 'most favoured alien' standard of treatment, and even provides that restrictive measures imposed on aliens or on the employment of aliens for the protection of the national labour market do not apply to refugees who have completed three years of residence in the country. As far as self-employment (art. 18) and employment in the liberal professions (art. 19) are concerned, states have to treat refugees as favourably as possible, and in any event not less favourably than they treat aliens in the same circumstances.

Work permits

Until 1991, before the Kenyan government suspended its status-determination process, refugees received a class M permit, which allowed them to work. This class of work permits featured in the special schedule of the Immigration Act (amended in 1972) (cap. 172), which established that work permits would be given to a refugee 'and any wife or child over the age of 13 years of such a refugee'. The definition of refugee referred to in the schedule was the one contained in the 1951 Convention – making the Immigration Act the only piece of legislation in force in Kenya to make any mention of the refugee definition, or rather of part of the refugee definition given that the additional grounds for claiming asylum contained in the OAU Convention are not mentioned.[4] Although the Immigration Act indirectly recognised the status of refugees by making them the beneficiaries of a specific class of work permits, it did not go as far as unequivocally stating that they had a justiciable right to obtain the permits. However, in practice there were no significant obstacles to obtaining work permits, as proved by the fact that UNHCR's main concern at the time was that its training for refugees be tailored to meet the demands of the Kenyan labour market and that land should be made available for those refugees who would prefer to make their living in agriculture (UNHCR 1987b).

After 1991, with the mass influx of refugees from Somalia, the Kenyan government abandoned its previous laissez-faire policy. All newly arrived refugees were considered to be under UNHCR's mandate and the government controversially decided that it would not accord them 'full' 1951 Convention rights including employment rights. Those who had come before 1991, however, were still able to renew their work permits. The existence of two 'classes' of refugees was reflected in the way NGOs operated. On one hand, for example, the African Refugee Education Programme (AREP), a refugee-based organisation,[5] continued to provide vocational training and job-seeking skills to pre-1991 refugees who were in possession of work permits. But for the vast of majority of refugees who arrived after 1991, the vocational training offered by agencies merely scratched the surface of the need, as those who were trained could not put their skills to use in gainful employment. For example, the Jesuit Refugee Service (JRS) in Nairobi trained a few refugees to make crafts that they sold in a little shop next to the office: the meagre proceeds from the sales were not normally sufficient to sustain even the very few refugees who managed to obtain a place on the programme.

One of the ironies of the situation was that it was easier for the post-1991 refugees to obtain a work permit if they concealed their status and applied as regular aliens. Of course, it was only the few who had a valid passport on which to stamp the work permit who could avail themselves of this possibility. For example, a small number of academics, including a Rwandan writer, managed to obtain class A work permits to work in a university.[6] However, obtaining these permits was difficult, especially because of the 'Kenyans first' policy that put severe constraints on employers seeking to hire foreign workers. In addition, even when refugees were successful in obtaining a work permit in this way, they could not renew it once their passport expired.

In Uganda, there were no special class work permits for refugees, either under the old Immigration Act 1969 or under the Immigration Act 1999. The Control of Alien Refugees Act (sec. 15, cap. 64) did, in theory, allow refugees to enter paid employment at the rates prevailing for similar work done by nationals. However, this right was curtailed by a proviso in the legislation which stated that 'it shall not be *obligatory* to pay a refugee for any employment in connection with the administration, internal arrangement or maintenance of refugee settlements' (sec. 15(a)). As refugees were expected to live in settlements, it could be expected that the majority of them would have come under this exception. We found that refugees, working with NGOs in Adjumani were paid less than their Ugandan counterparts, even though they had the same qualifications. The Bill for the Refugee Act 1998 maintains a restrictive approach to matters of employment.

Under the Immigration Act (sec. 13(a)), 'engaging in gainful employment without an entry permit' constitutes an offence. The conferral of refugee status should, normally, be equivalent to an entry permit, but, as a result of the uncertainties in the legislation and in the refugee status-determination process, this is not the case. In *Uganda v. Teshome Nood*[7] and *Uganda v. Tamenez Bezabeh*,[8] two refugees, who had been granted refugee status in November 1996, were charged with the offence under section 13. Their case was tried at the chief Magistrates' Court of Mengo at Nakawa, and, unlike most refugees, they had lawyers representing them. Although the prosecution knew about their refugee status, it was decided to proceed with the case. Both refugees pleaded guilty, and the court imposed a relatively lenient sentence – a fine of USh 80,000 and imprisonment for four months in default of payment. However, court records show that they were eventually pardoned: '... being a refugee ... each was cautioned and set at liberty' (ibid.). In this case, the lawyers acting for the accused did not invoke article 17 of the 1951 Convention, although the lack of legislation incorporating this provision in Ugandan law would almost certainly have constituted an insurmountable obstacle.[9]

Delays in the refugee status-determination process had repercussions on the enjoyment of the right to work. For instance, C., a refugee from the Democratic Republic of Congo (DRC) (case no. 198/DRC/U/2000), had applied for asylum as a refugee *sur place* in 1997. When in January 2000 he received an offer of employment from the Uganda Polytechnic Kyambogo to teach in their French language department, he applied to the Immigration Department for a work permit. Immigration contacted the Directorate of Refugees (DoR) and they reported that he had not yet been granted refugee status. Apparently his file had been lying untouched for nearly three years. Pamela Reynell, then director of the Refugee Law Project (RLP), wrote to the directorate explaining that in order to help C. and to partly make up for the inordinate delay, all that was needed was 'a letter to assure his prospective employer that it is OK for him to be legally employed in Uganda. Would it be possible for your office to assist him with such a letter? I can't envisage any obstacles but your advice would be welcome.' This request did not receive a response (*see also* case no. 121/SUD/U/1999).

To complicate matters, UNHCR decided in 1999 to 'rationalise' the urban caseload by demanding that refugees who wanted to remain in Kampala appear before the deputy director of refugees with proof that they could support themselves. We do not know of any refugee who complied with this stipulation since most refugees worked in the informal sector, without work permits or contracts of employment, to give as evidence (e.g., case no. 173/ETH/U/1999). One likely consequence, however, was that refugees without work permits in Kampala had one more reason to stay away from UNHCR and from the office of the DoR.

Incentives

The labour practices of all humanitarian organisations fell short of basic standards.[10] Refugees working for UNHCR and NGOs were not paid salaries but 'incentives', lower than the salaries paid to nationals for the same work. Meanwhile, their Ugandan and Kenyan counterparts, who worked side by side with them, not only earned proper salaries, they collected additional 'hardship' allowances because life in a settlement was regarded as more difficult and dangerous than in other parts of the country. 'Incentive' workers were not normally given contracts. In Uganda, this was clearly inconsistent with the Employment Decree of 1975 which applies to any 'person' in Uganda regardless of status, and stipulates the written form for employment contracts for periods longer than six months (sec. 10); failure to comply with this requirement is an offence.

Refugees were also subject to arbitrary dismissal without notice. Dismissal was even at times used as a punitive measure against refugees as in the two instances of collective punishment in Kakuma described in Chapter 4 (UNHCR 1996f).

The UNHCR head of sub-office, Pakelle, Adjumani, attempted to justify the UNHCR policy that refugees should be paid less than their Ugandan colleagues:

First, refugees already get assistance in terms of food, building materials, etc. This puts refugees at an advantage compared with nationals. Second, refugees are helping their own people. Third, they are being given an opportunity to practice the skills they have acquired; otherwise they would in the long run lose them. Anyway, refugees are always free to leave their jobs if they feel they are not well paid. There is no conscription here.[11]

Later in the interview, this UNHCR official admitted that lack of resources was another important factor behind the 'incentives' policy. He added that it was UNHCR's policy not to give contracts to refugee employees, especially in sectors like education and, when we pointed out that we knew of one NGO that had contracts with refugee teachers (which we regarded as an example of 'good practice'), he observed that this was 'illegal'.[12] Another argument was that UNHCR and NGOs had no choice but to employ refugees under less generous conditions than those applying to nationals because refugees did not have work permits. Nevertheless, UNHCR and NGOs did not lobby for work permits for refugees in general, or for their refugee staff. Moreover, there is no good reason why the incentives paid by the humanitarian organisations should not have been at the same level as salaries. As for the argument that the refugees worked for their own communities, it could apply to national teachers, academics, doctors, and nurses the world over. And even counting the additional 'benefits' that refugees received, the disparity of treatment remained striking.

Except for the fact that it gave written contracts, the African Education Fund (AEF) followed UNHCR's guidelines on the employment of refugee labour. The conditions of employment indicated in the contracts were draconian. A standard clause provided: 'Employment is at the sole discretion of AEF. The conditions of service listed are subject to revision and amendments as may be deemed necessary by the Team leaders. All amendments shall be binding upon distribution.' It was also at the complete discretion of AEF to grant time off to the refugee and to compensate for work done on holidays, including Ugandan public holidays. AEF was allowed to terminate a refugee's employment without notice and without giving reasons, only paying for fourteen days in lieu of notice. Pressure from UNHCR to standardise the treatment of refugee employees by its implementing partners according to its discriminatory policies was such that the Deutscher Entwicklungsdienst (DED) in Rhino camp found that they had to 'apologise [to UNHCR] for not having followed' the rules on the employment of refugee teachers, 'since we have been paying teachers whether refugees or not according to their qualifications and Ugandan scales'.[13]

Not all NGOs discriminated against refugee employees. In Kyangwali and Achol-Pii, the Associazione Volontari per il Servizio Internazionale (AVSI) attempted to follow a transparent policy and formulate precise criteria to calculate the differential treatment between Ugandan and refugee staff. It based its payments to refugees on the official salary of a Uganda labourer and then subtracted the value they estimated for free medical care, drugs, food, non-food items, and social services (AVSI n/d), and determined that refugee employees would receive 70 percent of a Ugandan labourer's wage, which was better than what refugee workers would receive in most other camps and settlements.[14] Yet these calculations failed to take into account the fact that nationals working in the settlements and camps normally received a hardship allowance over and above their normal salary, and, in practice, had free access *at least* to health services.

The Agency for Cooperation and Research Development (ACORD) was the only NGO with an entirely non-discriminatory employment policy: it had written contracts with all employees, refugees and nationals, at the same conditions, including remuneration. As explained by their coordinator in Palorinya:

> For our employment policy here, refugees and nationals have the same salaries; they pay taxes; have the same contracts written and the same interviews: we've got a set system. We try to avoid local politics by hiring the position of coordinator, assistant coordinator, and administrator in London. Normally these posts are for people working for some time in ACORD. For heads of sectors and finance officers, these positions are announced as open all over Uganda and one must apply to Kampala. Refugees here can apply through this office and we direct the application to Kampala where they sit and decide ... In Moyo, 20 percent of our staff are refugees and mostly are field staff. For termination of employment, we do not decide on our own but must do so according to the labour laws of Uganda. If we mess around with the rules we can be brought into a lawsuit which is what is happening with some of our programmes in West Africa.[15]

The ACORD coordinator also complained about pressure from UNHCR: '[They] used to talk to us about using their incentive system but we've got our own policy which complies with the Uganda labour laws according to our legal adviser.'[16]

In Kenya, CARE's treatment of refugee employees in the Dadaab camps was a clear example of unfair labour practices.[17] By 1998 CARE was in the process of implementing a programme of 'voluntary work' whereby, with the exception of refugee teachers and guards, the payment of 'incentives' to refugee employees would be phased out. CARE argued that this programme would relieve refugees of their 'dependency syndrome' and enhance their sense of responsibility towards their communities. Progressive as they might sound, these methods of encouraging responsibility for others were unlikely to be successful in refugee camps. Most people living in the camps are not there by choice. They are populations rather than 'communities' (Hyndman 1996, 2000). Indeed, one of the salient features of the refugee experience is the loss of social and economic support networks (Harrell-Bond 1986; Lammers 1998). As a result, expecting refugees to work without pay, which is premised on a communitarian spirit that would be hard to find even in affluent and well-established neighbourhoods, was not only against human rights law but also ill-advised.

Refugee teachers in Uganda

The case of refugee teachers in Adjumani and Moyo refugee settlements in Uganda illustrates the unfair working conditions imposed on refugee workers. Refugee teachers, who formed a union demanding contracts of employment, were met with a harsh response from aid agencies. A UNHCR official explained that shortage of funds was one of the main reasons why the organisation could not afford to give refugees contracts: 'Unfortunately, UNHCR does not have guaranteed funds each year so it would be impossible to enter into long term agreements, involving pensions etc. The teachers and communities have been informed that it is the community's responsibility to give contracts to teachers ...'[18] Yet, although their dependence on voluntary contributions from states is a constraint for UNHCR programmes the world over, it does not prevent UNHCR from employing permanent staff at much higher international salaries. In reality, the type of financial commitment that would be required to offer proper contracts to refugee teachers would not be significant.

In Adjumani and Moyo, JRS, which was the implementing partner for education, rigorously adhered to the UNHCR policy. It denied refugees written contracts, justifying this policy with the argument that it was not JRS that employed the refugee teachers, but, as explained by UNHCR's education coordinator, 'their own community recruits them ... Each settlement raises [sic] the teacher. Then we train and uplift them ... The contract is with the parents, the school belongs to the parents. We just come to push them up. The parents are the employers because they opened the schools.' The coordinator added that, as a Christian organisation, JRS was concentrating on education and pastoral work, and its ultimate aim was to 'prepare refugees to go home'. He asserted that it was important to 'give them [the refugee teachers] motivation', and noted that, 'Training is a very big motivation – a big gift.'[19]

Policies like this one were supposed to evoke a genteel spirit of communitarianism, but since refugee 'communities' did not have any legal status as such, either as companies or as NGOs, the 'contracts' that the teachers were supposedly concluding with their communities were legally worthless. Furthermore, given that refugee communities were not in a position to raise and administer their own funds, how could they be financially more stable than UNHCR itself or than JRS?[20] Treating refugees as employees hired by their own community was a creative solution for shielding UNHCR and JRS from their duties vis-à-vis their employees, while in practice they exercised powers wider than those that employers possessed under Ugandan law. For instance, the JRS coordinator explained: 'In cases of misconduct [of the teachers], the parents come to complain. We may take action.' JRS also retained the power to dismiss teachers, and, according to many refugee teachers we interviewed, it often dismissed 'those who argue'. JRS paid the 'incentives' and, after pressure from the district officer, began to deduct pay-as-you-earn taxes.

In Adjumani and Moyo, as noted, refugee teachers decided to protest against their treatment. As early as 1993, the refugee teachers, supported by their Ugandan colleagues, organised a teachers union. The parents were supportive of the teachers' grievances, which were over low pay, lack of teaching materials, poor accommodation, and general welfare.[21] They also complained of being constantly transferred from school to school. As one of the teachers said, 'Before you can even settle and put your life in order, he [the JRS education coordinator] may decide that you are taken to another school in another settlement.' In the staff meetings, which were held on the fifth of every month, 'There is no discussion of issues. JRS just dictates.'

In 1997, supported by their Ugandan colleagues, the refugee teachers went on strike. The strike started around October and lasted more than a month. Exams had to be postponed, and the term ended late. Students sympathised with the teachers' protest and at a coordination meeting in 1998 they concluded that although education is a fundamental right of refugees, it had not been a priority for humanitarian organisations. They also agreed that teachers' salaries were inadequate, and that written contracts should be given. The children of nationals were also affected and Ugandan teachers joined the strike. In a focus group with teachers, the refugees talked about some of their complaints:

> The group had heard that in the settlements in Palorinya across the river, teachers were paid more – up to [USh] 68,000 per month by AEF. They stated that they bring this up not to complain that they want to be just like them; however they want a uniform grading system which provides at least a balance between the [USh] 30,000 vs. 68,000 disparity. The teachers expressed adamantly that they would like a grading system which pays according to training, capability and experience; however, they were informed that UNHCR does not want a grading but a flat rate. Anyway, the teachers agreed to go back to work after this meeting being given the verbal promise that their demand for a contract be looked into. The group was not sure if their salaries would be increased at all. They expect some results this month.

> When asked their plan of action if their request is not looked into, they stated that our plan of action is to write a letter to request that Mr Charles Atim, the JRS education coordinator be removed. We see the problem is

with him because he wrote a letter to all teachers and headmasters in a circular teacher's news bulletin criticising us. 'Apparently, the parents were behind the teachers on this issue of a contract and higher incentives and felt that the teachers were being mistreated.'[22]

The teachers also complained about the 'poll tax', arguing that 'even though we are not employed under this system and are getting incentives only, they deduct USh 52,000 per year from our salaries as a poll tax.' They claimed that before JRS took over, the government had been paying their salaries and a food-for-work system was in place; they got groundnuts, oil, sugar, salt, and soap. The government paid them the national average salary and payments were usually received on time. Under the UNHCR/JRS system, they said that they had no benefits, including medical care. Their contracts could be terminated without notice (and without any pay in lieu of notice). The only benefit they received from JRS was an annual bonus of an extra month's salary, but, even with this payment, their annual salaries were still significantly inferior to those of their national colleagues. Moreover, if, upon termination of the contract, the bonus had been delayed, the person would never receive it. The teachers said that they had written to UNHCR 'many times' but they did not know what happened to their letters along the way and suspected that they were never delivered because UNHCR's education coordinator, Tim Brown, had told them during a visit to Adjumani that he did not know about the letters.

The teachers' strike caught UNHCR and JRS by surprise. JRS could not accept the existence of a teachers' union, and summarily dismissed some of the 'ring leaders'. The dispute escalated. The teachers accused the JRS education coordinator of having written 'very bad things about the teachers' and having, in a newsletter, referred to them as 'terrorists' and 'gangsters'.[23] The acting district education officer, together with other members of the District Council, acted as mediators in the dispute, but, according to the teachers interviewed, since the education officer was partly reliant on funding from JRS, he could hardly be considered a disinterested party. The UNHCR head of sub-office in Pakelle told the strikers that 'they were striking against their own children, against themselves' and reaffirmed that the NGOs 'are just a conduit for delivering support and therefore cannot conclude contracts with refugee teachers'.[24]

The teachers said that if they had had contracts, they would have gone to the labour office and to the courts. The JRS coordinator told them that the labour office was only for those permanently employed. He and the 'education consultants' advised them that, if they went ahead, they would be digging their own grave.[25] In fact, the teachers could have used the courts since, as we have mentioned, JRS was obliged under Ugandan law to give them a written employment contract. The fact that taxes were being deducted from their incentives was clear evidence of the fact that, despite the nomenclature 'incentive', they were actually JRS employees receiving a 'salary'. In the end, the refugees could claim little success: the JRS education coordinator was removed, but their conditions of employment were left unchanged. This is not so surprising, given that an employer will be ready to compromise only when the strike is seen as causing political or economic damage. In the case of the strike of a group of disenfranchised refugees employed under exploitative terms, neither UNHCR nor JRS had to bear any cost for their intransigence.

'... people capable of work'[26]

The refugees we interviewed came from many different backgrounds and brought a variety of skills to their host countries.[27] Despite the constraints, many refugees continued to struggle to earn their own living, preferring insecure or unfair employment to receiving handouts in camps and settlements – like Mr R. and his wife who left Agago refugee settlement without 'permission', preferring to eke out an existence in Kampala repairing shoes and weaving baskets – to life in the camp (case no. 066/DRC/U/1997).

In Nairobi, many of the Rwandan and Burundian refugees were secondary school and university students, as well as academics such as Dr Alfred Buregeya, a writer and linguist trained at Reading University in the UK, and Dr Augustin Nsanze, a Burundian historian who had studied at the Sorbonne in Paris and who in 1999 succeeded in leaving Kenya, obtaining an academic post at the University of Leiden, Netherlands. Dr Nsanze's asylum application had been rejected in Kenya on the basis of the first country of asylum 'rule'.[28] During his stay in Nairobi he worked to complete and publish his two-volume history of modern Burundi. He had to pay to use the library and a computer. He was unable to find employment in a Kenyan university and eventually left for Europe – one more African intellectual who was left with no choice but to join the 'brain drain'.[29] Other Rwandan academics 'stranded' in Nairobi included the former dean of the law faculty of the National University of Rwanda, two lecturers at the same university, and a social scientist who had studied in Russia and who was using his time in Nairobi to conduct a survey of the educational needs of Rwandan refugees in the hope that this could be used to raise funds.

Finding a job was often purely fortuitous. As one refugee told us:

> After loitering around in Kampala, I found a certain boy in the Taxi Park. I told him I was looking for some place to stay and for a job. I just approached him and he understood English. I discussed with him some of my predicaments. He was selling second-hand clothes. He told me that if I had capital, I would join him ... I tried every day and finally I got a job as a night and day watchman ... I was entitled to a salary of USh 15,000,

lunch, breakfast, and supper, but I was not supposed to move away without my boss's permission at any time, day or night. I was given a bow and arrows [to guard the premises] ... I had no liberty. I could not move away, in fact, not even during daytime. The day I decided to go away and look for other job opportunities is when my boss got to know about it. He sacked me ... He refused to give me my salary for that month ... I had to continue looking around ... I met a Sudanese Dinka who was working as a shoe shiner on [*sic*] IPS building ... He allowed me to join him. I started shining shoes. I would get some little money for eating and to contribute to rent (case no. 209/SUD/U/1999).

Some refugees worked, usually for a pittance, for voluntary organisations, like the Sudan Women's Association (SWAN) and Hope International School in Nairobi, which normally received no support from UNHCR or other donors.[30] These examples of voluntary work succeeded because 'voluntariness' was not imposed from above, as CARE tried to do in Dadaab.[31]

Some refugees in urban centres set up businesses and, in some cases, created employment opportunities for others, including nationals. This was particularly the case with Somalis and Ethiopians who arrived in Kenya and Uganda in the 1970s and 1980s. As mentioned above, it was material to their success that the government in those days did not hinder their entrepreneurship and accorded them the basic legal protection they needed. For refugees who arrived in Kenya after that period, self-employment opportunities were mainly in the informal sector – as street-vendors, guards, drivers, and so on (Lukoba and Cheluget 1992), not to mention prostitution (Stanley 1998).[32]

Another constraint on refugees was the lack of a Convention Travel Document (CTD).[33] This limited both their access to economic opportunities outside the country of asylum and their ability to set up trade and businesses across the border, the latter being an almost 'natural' form of self-employment for refugees. The experiences of self-settled refugees who owned businesses in Moyo town demonstrate this. Many wished to be able to engage in import-export businesses. They complained of their inability to travel to and from Dubai where most national traders went to buy commodities for resale in Uganda.

An adequate standard of living

Under the right to an adequate standard of living, the ICESCR protects the right to adequate food, clothing, and housing, and to the continuous improvement of living conditions (art. 11). This right featured originally in the UDHR (art. 25), which is considered part of customary international law (Sieghart 1983: 53). The qualifier 'adequate' does not mean simply what is necessary for physical survival; it also includes the idea of what is needed to lead a dignified way of life.[34] While the idea of human dignity undoubtedly has a core universal component, to an extent it has to take into account cultural perceptions. For example, nomads might perceive aspects of sedentary life as 'undignified', whereas for a sedentary population the notion of an adequate home assumes a permanent dwelling. This is not, of course, tantamount to adopting a cultural relativist approach.

It is often argued that poor countries like Kenya and Uganda cannot absorb large numbers of refugees and provide them with an 'adequate standard living' when large sections of their own populations do not enjoy such a standard. As discussed above, states' obligations in the field of social and economic rights start with the negative duty '*not* to interfere' and move up to the positive duty 'to ensure' a certain right by providing the necessary means. States also have to take appropriate measures, usually commensurate with the level of their resources, towards the realisation of social and economic rights.

In order to gauge the standard of living of refugees, UNHCR has normally used as a yardstick the 'economic level' of the local population, which, since all societies are economically differentiated, has in practice meant equating refugees with the poorest segment of the host population (Harrell-Bond 1986).[35] For refugees in Kenya and Uganda, this situation – combined with the encampment policy and restrictions on their freedom to seek paid work or self-employment – meant that they were unable to achieve anything like an adequate standard of living.

The Ugandan settlements differed from the Kenyan camps because refugees were given some land, although the plots varied widely in quality from settlement to settlement and within settlements. Furthermore, there were significant differences between households in terms of their ability to take advantage of the opportunities for supplying their own food – for example, the ratio of people who could do productive work to the number of dependents within one household differed significantly (Lester 1998). In Kenya, conditions in the camps were such that the physical survival of the refugees depended almost entirely on food aid. In Kakuma refugees were not even allowed to keep animals or poultry, whereas in Dadaab they could keep poultry, but in neither camp did they receive any land for cultivation.[36] In the impoverished economy of refugee camps, the meagre 'incentives', which in any case only a small percentage of the population was receiving (around 3 percent in Kakuma in 1996), nonetheless 'played a pivotal role' in ameliorating living conditions for many refugees (Boudreau et al. 1996: ii). Other ways of supplementing humanitarian assistance included engaging in petty trade in the market and, for those who had relatives abroad, remittances.

Food

The Committee on Economic, Social, and Cultural Rights, established under the ICESCR, distinguished three different levels of state obligations vis-à-vis the right to food: the obligations *to respect*, *to protect*, and *to fulfil* – the latter comprising both an obligation *to facilitate* and an obligation *to provide* (ICESCR Committee 1999).

States can comply with the obligation to *respect* – the minimum component of a state's obligation vis-à-vis the right to food – regardless of their resources. The obligation to *respect* imposes a negative duty, requiring states simply '*not* to take any measures that result in preventing' access to food (ICESCR Committee 1999: paras. 14–15). The obligation to *protect* means that states have 'to ensure that enterprises or individuals do not deprive individuals of their access to adequate food' (ibid.). Finally, the obligation to *fulfil* includes both the obligation to 'proactively engage in activities intended to strengthen people's access to a utilisation of resources and means to ensure their livelihood' (*facilitate*), and the obligation to *provide* food directly to individuals or groups who are 'unable, for reasons beyond their control, to enjoy the right to adequate food by the means at their disposal' – for example, 'victims of natural or other disasters' (ibid.). The Committee on Economic, Social and Cultural Rights has also emphasised that the right to food should 'not be interpreted in a narrow or restrictive sense which equates it with a minimum package of calories, proteins and other specific nutrients' (ibid.: para. 6). These comments are aimed primarily at governments, but, as we have argued throughout, the exercise of de facto governmental functions by UNHCR and NGOs, particularly in refugee camps and settlements, means that they bear legal obligations analogous to those of states.

The approach of the World Food Programme (WFP), UNHCR, and NGOs to the right to food was premised on the very 'narrow and restrictive' interpretations criticised by the committee.[37] For the most part, they only referred to the minimum package of calories, ignoring other specific nutrients that any human being should receive.[38] Malnutrition in the camps as a result of poor rations and of the periodic cuts was treated as an inevitable 'fact of life', not as a shocking violation of the right to food and, in the worst situations, of the right to life of refugees.[39] Nor did WFP, UNHCR, and NGO officials see themselves as the perpetrators of this violation, or as accomplices to it.

Food rations were often used by UNHCR and governments as a way of enforcing the unpopular settlement policy on refugees or as a push factor for repatriation.[40] Although this was officially denied and 'problems with the pipeline' were routinely blamed for reductions and interruptions in food distribution, the fact that reduction in rations was used to deter new arrivals (if not encourage repatriation) was crudely confirmed in the minutes of an inter-agency monthly meeting of UNHCR, the International Federation of Red Cross and Red Crescent Societies (IFRC), the Uganda Red Cross Society (URC), and the Ministry of Local Government (MoLG) in Mbarara on 19 December 1997: 'Conflicting instructions on the amount of food rations to the various groups were expressed by URC [Uganda Red Cross]/IFRC. It was explained that the GoU [government of Uganda] strongly feels that the Rwandese refugees formerly in Tanzania should receive life sustaining quantities of food below the normal rations as a deterrent against attracting more refugees.'

Another common practice was to withhold food rations from newly arrived refugees in order to determine if they were 'true' new arrivals or 'recyclers'. The idea behind it was that a 'true' refugee would withstand the hardship, whereas a 'recycler' would give up. In Lokichokio, refugees waited days or weeks without rations for a lorry to drive them to Kakuma. In Dadaab, Médecins sans Frontières (MSF)-Belgium reported in February 1998 that, out of an estimated population of 1,300 new arrivals in Hagadera, 80 of the 280 children under 5 were severely malnourished (UNHCR 1998c). In Arua district in Uganda, in 2000, refugees arriving from Sudan who chose to go to a settlement had to first report to the transit camp in Koboko for 'screening'. During this time, they were provided with neither food nor health services. Processing time in the centres took between a few days and a couple of weeks. In Adjumani district, a group of newly arrived Acholi refugees from Sudan had been encamped on a rocky hill site and were not receiving any food. We observed that they were cooking wild grasses and roots in their pots.[41]

Dr Greg Elder, a physician, found a similar situation in Nakivale:

> One of the issues raised at the earlier interagency evaluation was the length of time it was taking to register/verify new arrivals so that they could receive rations and other non-food items. The excuse given was that care has to be taken to identify recyclers, i.e. people who were already registered and attempting to cheat the system. As a consequence, new arrivals may have to wait for up to three months before receiving assistance. As new arrivals do not receive any assistance until they are verified, they are forced to share the meagre rations of their compassionate hosts, family or friends already residing in the settlement ... The impact of these delays has contributed to the deterioration of the nutritional status of the population as a whole. More serious, when the Rwandans from Tanzania started to arrive, a decision was taken at district level to suspend registration for a month to discourage others from following. This attempt at deterrence had not decreased the numbers arriving from across the border (Elder 1996).

A nutritional survey in Oruchinga, where most of the new arrivals were settling at the time of the evaluation, showed a global malnutrition rate of 5.5 percent in June 1996. What was alarming was the fact that the rate had doubled in six months. While there were many reasons for this trend, one of the factors was the sharing of rations with newly arrived refugees. In one case, a family of nine was hosting a related family of eight: this meant that seventeen people in one dwelling were sharing one family's ration. This was happening at a time when many of the refugees in Oruchinga were receiving only 50 percent rations and the drought was seriously affecting the harvests.

No one has a complete picture of the nutrition situation of refugees in camps and settlements, since nutritional surveys normally only measured malnutrition in a segment of the population – that is, children from 0 to 5. The rest of the population is unlikely to be better off than this group, since they do not benefit from special feeding programmes; nor do they receive the particular attention that is given to small children. However, there was much evidence that suggested that malnutrition was not confined to the 'new arrivals'. In Uganda, a survey of all the refugee settlements was undertaken by Action contre la Faim (ACF-USA) on behalf of UNHCR in 1998 (ACF-USA 1998). It found that the rates of malnutrition among children aged 6 to 29 months in 'all settlements is high' (page 4). Where rations were still being distributed, they fell 'short of the "ideal food ration"' (ibid.: 16). Unsurprisingly, children in households receiving 50 percent rations were 'more malnourished than children in the other groups' (ibid.: 17). This report made a clear connection between lack of freedom of movement and standards of living and nutrition, explaining that it was necessary to 'allow/encourage movement to continue as a *legitimate* activity because it would appear ... [that] the inability to move [is what] ... makes households more vulnerable' (ACF-USA 1998: 61 [emphasis in the original]). The report also noted that: 'Women are generally more restricted in their capacity to move than men to generate income ... An increase in income-generating opportunities in and around the settlement would make women less dependent upon their own cultivation (and food ration) as the primary source of household food (ibid.).'

Some nutritional reports were questionable. For example, in March/April 1997, Save the Children Fund (SCF) conducted nutritional surveys in Kenya and Uganda on behalf of UNHCR. The assessment of the household food economy in Moyo and Arua in April 1997 – which reached different conclusions and made different recommendations from a mirror study in Kakuma (Boudreau et al. 1996) – concluded, debatably, that 'the majority of refugee families have, even on half the official ration, been able to cover their minimum energy needs and do not currently face a problem of acute hunger' (Lawrence et al. 1997: iii). It then recommended that rations should be targeted – that is, reduced for certain groups and increased for others – and that, in particular, the very poor sector of the population in the settlements (typically woman-headed households with three to four young children) should receive increased rations because of their low income. The Ugandan study did not contain any data on the level of malnutrition in the settlements. Furthermore, as recognised by the assessment team (ibid.: vii), uncertainties over levels of crop production made it impossible to assess food security. The study was thus based on the land available in the different settlements rather than on the harvest per household without taking into account the quality of the land.

From the outset of our research in the Kenyan camps in March 1997, we found a deplorable nutritional situation. In Kakuma, one of the most affected groups was that of the teenage boys from Sudan, many of whom suffered from severe anaemia (Boudreau et al. 1996). Two years, and a few reports later, the Centre for Disease Control (Atlanta) still found a prevalence of 47 percent anaemia among adolescents in Kakuma camp. The study added that there was a correlation between the length of stay in the camp and the level of anaemia: 'Those who stayed longer had higher rates of anaemia (Woodruff et al. 1998 as quoted by Estephanos 1999: 21).' The report also noted that anaemia was one of the three main health problems in the antenatal clinics (ibid.: 21).

Other micronutrient deficiencies that were reported both in Kakuma and in Dadaab included deficiencies in iron, vitamin C, and vitamin B12. In 2000, it was believed that cases of scurvy were in decline (INTRAC 1999: 22), but the fact that scurvy was still affecting a population under the protection of the 'international community' in the twenty-first century is shocking. Moreover, the improvements in the incidence of scurvy that were periodically announced seldom lasted. For example, following epidemics in 1994 and 1995, a decline in cases of scurvy in Dadaab had been reported in 1997, but surveillance data before the year ended showed an increase in the number of cases (UNHCR 1997a: 16). During one of the worst epidemics, some 700 cases of scurvy per month were reported (MSF-B 006/11/96; UN ACC/SCN December 1996).

The ineffectiveness of agencies' response to malnutrition was highlighted by the fact that the rate of moderate and severe malnutrition continued to increase in Kenya and Uganda: the September 1997 survey reported a global malnutrition level of 14 percent, but in October 1998 this went up to 15.6 percent and, in May 1999, it shot up to 18.3 percent with some variations inbetween (INTRAC 1999: 22; Estephanos 1999: 22). This was despite the fact that the amount of kilocalories per person per day distributed in Kakuma had apparently been increased to 2100 in 1998 (compared with 1900 in 1997).[42]

In both countries, responsibilities for providing food were divided between UNHCR and WFP, although the secrecy that often surrounded the agreements between UNHCR and WFP meant that they often blamed each other when things went wrong. For example, when we first visited Kakuma refugee camp in March 1997, UNHCR officials implied that it was WFP that was responsible for the scarcity of food there. However, when we eventually got hold of the memoranda of understanding between WFP and UNHCR – both the general one between the two agencies and the one signed by the respective branch offices of these organisations in Kenya – it became clear that UNHCR had actually assumed responsibility for distributing certain food items. In fact, this was how responsibilities were allocated under the memoranda of 1997:

> 4.1 WFP is responsible for mobilizing the following commodities, whether for general or selective feeding programmes: cereals; edible oils and fats; pulses and other sources of protein; blended foods; salt; sugar; and high-energy biscuits. Where beneficiaries are totally dependent on food aid, WFP will ensure the provision of blended foods or other fortified commodities in order to prevent or correct micronutrient deficiencies. UNHCR is responsible for mobilizing complementary commodities. These include: local fresh foods; spices; tea; and dried and therapeutic milk ... (*see also* UNHCR 1998k: chap. 4)

> 4.5 In particular cases where micronutrient requirements cannot be met through the ration, UNHCR will assume responsibility for the provision of the necessary micronutrients until the ration can be adjusted or fortified to meet these needs. (UNHCR-WFP 1997).[43]

The actual provision of food in the camps by UNHCR and WFP revealed that both organisations failed to meet the standards they had set themselves in their memoranda. During nearly all food distributions, WFP, avowedly because of 'problems in the pipeline', only distributed the main staple, with at least one of the other items missing. As for UNHCR, its commitment to supply 'local fresh foods, spices, tea, and dried and therapeutic milk' was seldom carried out (Bennett et al. 1999: 6).

In addition to shortages in micronutrients, it was established through food basket monitoring that refugees were not receiving the minimum amount of calories they were supposed to get. In the refugee camps in Dadaab, from August 1996 to July 1997, refugees never received the recommended minimum of 2,100 Kcal; the closest they ever got to it was in May 1997 when 2,063 Kcal were distributed. In April of the same year, they received as little as 1,463 Kcal, and the average over the whole period was 1,870 Kcal. In Kakuma, during the same period, refugees received on average only 1,800 Kcal per person per day.

A standard food distribution in Dadaab was described as including a daily ration of '458 gm of cereals, 50 gm of lentils, 25 gm of oil, and 5 gm of salt', although, as mentioned, at least one of these items was often missing.[44] In Kakuma, in August 1997:

> The general ration ... is composed of: 9 oz whole grain (maize or sorghum); 7 oz milled grain (wheat flour); 1.5 tablespoons vegetable oil; 1 tablespoon salt; 3 tablespoons pulses (beans or lentils) – per person per day. Shortages mean that refugees often do not get even this deficient diet, or they get maize without oil or salt, or salt without flour. In February 1997, refugees had not received any beans or lentils for eight weeks – their only source of

protein. In fact oil, salt, wheat flour were the only commodities given during that distribution (Reznick 1997: 10).

Despite routine commitments to improve matters, increases in food rations were always short-lived. In Dadaab, where alarm bells about the nutritional situation had frequently been ringing for the eight years, the situation in 2001 was described in these terms:

> Of the 2100 daily calories, only 1400 have been distributed in April, May, and June: a 30 percent reduction. Wheat has disappeared, oil is finishing, maize is running out. The result has been that malnutrition cases have soared. The three hospitals in the camp, run by Médecins sans Frontières, have been filled with worn-out, emaciated children on the brink of death. The alarm has been raised, but the appeal has not yielded any results. The only government that firmly continues to send food aid is that of the US. The European Union and Japan are absent. Not to mention Italy (Veronese 2001) [our translation].

It must be pointed out that in all these cases the real situation was even worse than that suggested by the Kcal per person per day indicator: this presumed a completely equitable distribution – which rarely happened (MSF-B 1997: Annex 1) – and did not take account of the balance of staples, proteins, and vitamins that an adequate diet should contain.

Supplementary feeding, aimed at pregnant and lactating women, and debilitated patients such as those suffering from tuberculosis or from HIV/AIDS, was irregular and unsystematic. In Kakuma, despite the much publicised introduction of therapeutic feeding centres in 1998 – following the news about the rates of malnutrition in 1997 – the situation in 1999 remained serious: these centres were catering for relatively small numbers of people and, even then, providing an inadequate service, as reported by the UNHCR/WFP evaluation mission (Bennett et al. 1999: 5). Although the UNHCR-WFP memoranda of understanding had incorporated the recommendation of the Committee on Economic, Social and Cultural Rights that 'products included in international food trade or aid programmes must be safe and culturally acceptable to the recipient population' (ICESCR Committee 1999: para. 39), in practice it was concluded that 'in these camps harbouring refugees from over 13 countries with many clans and sub-clans having diverse cultural differences, it would be impossible to satisfy anyone's food preference. So, the option for the refugees is to sell what they do not like and buy what they prefer' (Estephanos 1999: 24). In fact, refugees traded or bartered food rations not only because they were culturally inappropriate but also in order to buy other essential food and non-food items, such as milk for children, sugar, clothing, footwear, and fuel – items that were distributed in grossly insufficient quantities, if at all. Pupils often sold some of their food rations to buy pens and notebooks.

Trade and barter in food rations was usually frowned upon by UNHCR. In some cases, the food was even confiscated. For example, in Dadaab, police were instructed to confiscate the food because 'the sale of food in large quantities is not allowed, but we tolerate it in the market within the camp. We do understand that the food is an exchangeable commodity, but donors do not like this.'[45] An Ethiopian refugee confirmed this: 'Selling food in the market is allowed and tolerated by the authorities, but too much food exchange is not.'[46] These policies, which effectively restricted access to a balanced diet, represented a violation of the obligation to *respect* the refugees' right to food.

Moreover, the sale or barter of food items was not an offence under Kenyan criminal law. The situation was similar in Uganda, as was pointed out by a police officer, when his junior officers arrested a refugee who was selling his ration. He asked them to find out with what offence the refugee would be charged. After some research, the junior officers went back to the officer and admitted that they could not find any offence in the penal code.

By the late 1990s, WFP appeared finally, if somewhat reluctantly, to have accepted that trade and barter of food rations was one of the strategies used by refugees to secure their livelihood. But this belated acceptance had one negative effect: WFP decided that the variety of the food basket was no longer important, provided that the KCal content reached the recommended level. Single-item distributions became more frequent throughout the region. The consequent excess of supply in certain items meant that the market value of the ration fell dramatically, and refugees still could not ensure adequate food for themselves.

Factors such as conflict, which had a significant impact on food security, were not taken into account when food was phased out, and NGOs sometimes complained that their reports regarding land assessments were ignored. For example, the ACORD coordinator for Palorinya, pointed out to us:

> To me at the moment, even with the older settlements, this is not the time for food reductions because of insecurity. In June 1994 Palorinya opened; by 1995 we must prepare to phase out agricultural inputs; in 1996 UNHCR had reduced some of the funds. It happened that the food assessment done by WFP was during a time of good harvest. Then in September 1996, people were all displaced after the attack; but women used to sneak and harvest for survival. This year, everything was looted and some have lost agricultural inputs and there has been a poor harvest. Afterwards, we agreed with UNHCR to supply these people again with seeds; for the food being reduced, if people are displaced tomorrow they will have nothing.

> All our soil figures are given to the UNHCR agricultural assistant and he analyses and sends them to UNHCR [Kampala] without giving back to us for our independent opinion or cross-checking of accuracy of the numbers. Policies made then in Kampala are based upon Ernest's report made off of

[*sic*] our statistics. We just give the raw data and are not allowed to comment. Some of the final reports produced and acted upon do not reflect the findings on the ground. The community in turn blames us for the crop analysis because they believe it comes straight from us without filtering through UNHCR. We have our own independent reports on the soil analysis and on the ability of refugees to be self-sufficient. It is not our role with UNHCR to recommend; we give data and they analyse and make the decisions ...

This [UNHCR] agricultural consultant does not always go to the settlements. He sits in Pakelle and in Kampala. There is also one based in Arua who only comes once during the time for producing quarterly reports. This consultant had an eight month contract and arrived three months late and never comes to this area and the field. We feel we should at least sit and discuss the figures with the UNHCR consultant to get some independent opinion and to verify figures; we are merely a conduit for collection of raw data ...

Under UNHCR we used to have the funding for a post of technical adviser which we were responsible for hiring. Our last was an Asian who was in the field constantly and advised us; we worked together on the reports. But, in 1996, this was abolished and UNHCR unilaterally imposed an external consultant using our allocation in the budget. He is supposed to be with us under our budget and yet he never goes to the field. We have to give over our data to him. We've never protested against this action by UNHCR – what can we do?[47]

Malnutrition and the conspiracy of silence

UNHCR and humanitarian organisations were usually loath to report accurately on the nutritional situation in camps and settlements, and on mortality and morbidity rates. As Sen points out (Sen 1981), free expression and availability of information on famines could be the cause of such public uproar as to force governments and international agencies to take immediate action. In refugee camps, information was normally controlled and the under-reporting of mortality rates became standard practice. In Goma, DRC, Waldman found an enormous gap between the number of deaths reported at the official health facilities and the number of actual deaths as evidenced by the bodies that were collected by the road.[48] He noted that in a period of three weeks between 77 percent and 94 percent of deaths went unreported, but the relatively low number of deaths reported by the health stations allowed WFP to claim that no increase in mortality had resulted from its reductions in the food rations. Similarly, in Kakuma, there was a cholera epidemic in May–June 1997, but while the International Rescue Committee (IRC), which was UNHCR's implementing partner for health services, reported that only nine people had died of cholera, fifty-one deaths were recorded by the leader of the Sudanese community alone,[49] and some women working for the JRS whispered to us that deaths from cholera in the whole camp had 'been in the hundreds'.[50]

In reporting on emergencies, humanitarian organisations attempt to strike a difficult balance between different interests.[51] On the one hand, they want to persuade donors that the situation warrants more funds; on the other hand, they are keen to portray themselves as being effective in tackling the problems. As a result, in the first phase of an emergency, they often exaggerate the seriousness of the situation in order to attract more funds (de Waal 1997). Later, however, they become more inclined to *understate* the gravity of the situation to show that their work has improved it.

In both Kenya and Uganda, our research took place during the post-emergency phase – the 'understatement phase' – when rations were being harshly cut or phased out altogether and malnutrition rates were steadily increasing. UNHCR's protection reports for Kenya 1994–98, and Uganda 1996–97 did not even refer to any violation of the right to food of refugees in camps. And yet its protection mandate would have required an accurate presentation of the situation, which could have been used as a way of raising funds. While donors could be criticised for their propensity to become easily 'fatigued' by unsolved humanitarian crises, the fact that UNHCR opted for what it presumably believed to be 'face-saving' reporting clearly contributed to making the crisis even more insoluble.

The lengths to which UNHCR and NGOs were prepared to go in order to avoid taking the blame for the malnutrition in the refugee camps and settlements were shown by the treatment meted out to a doctor who worked in Kakuma for IRC.[52] His account of his time in Kakuma is telling:

> When I arrived in August, I found that refugees were expected to survive on 1,800 Kcal per day, theoretically made up of a combination of cereals, pulses, oil, salt and sugar ... After my protests, WFP promised to increase the ration to 1,900 Kcal, which is still grossly inadequate. WFP has an agreement with UNHCR and its Memorandum of Agreement indicates that UNHCR is responsible for supplementing the diet with vegetables, meat/fish and fruits. With the exception of a one-off hand-out of 1 kg of fish per household, distributed the last week in March, 1997,[53] during my stay, these vital foodstuffs never arrived.

> Even if the full ration in terms of Kcal had always been made available, it would have been insufficient for the most vulnerable which included pregnant women, lactating mothers, children and the large numbers of single adolescents which are present in this camp.

> The problems in Kakuma were aggravated by the fact that WFP often had to substitute foods to make up the required number of Kcal. For example, oil instead of cereal. For one period of three months, no pulses, hence no protein source, were available. No sugar was supplied during the entire period of my employment. For many of the nationalities living in Kakuma, the food supplied by WFP was culturally inappropriate and was always traded at exchange rates which were disadvantageous to the refugees. Moreover, because only an armful of wood is distributed to each house-

hold, all refugees had to exchange food for fuel, not to mention access to other non-food items (such as even matches) which are required for survival. UNHCR never provided the food supplements for which it was responsible during the time I was there.

I had patients whose haemoglobin rate ranged from 4 to 1 gram per cent. The overall population was so anaemic that it was almost impossible to find blood donors [for transfusions]. The group most affected was predominantly young Sudanese males. Unlike the Somalians and Ethiopians in the camp who had access to the resources of petty trading to augment WFP's rations, the Sudanese were totally dependent on these rations.

... there was great controversy over my reporting of the health consequences of the under-nutritional state of the population and the alarming number of refugees who suffered anaemia which was nutritionally related. My reporting included frank discussions with other medical staff and with journalists from Dutch television who visited the camp.

The problem for medical personnel working in such a situation is to *prove* to the agencies which are responsible for supplying food that the anaemia was the consequence of their failures to provide adequate rations. I arranged for all those who had been diagnosed as anaemic to be tested for other causes of blood loss such as malaria, blood-sucking intestinal parasites and other causes of low haemoglobin. The majority of the most extremely anaemic were not suffering either malaria or intestinal parasites.[54] I also compared the haemoglobin results of the refugees with that of the local population which had been seen at the local mission hospital located next door to the camp and also with that of the District General hospital in Lodwar, 45 kilometres from the camp. It was found that anaemia among the local population was very low; as noted above, the Turkana have access to both milk and meat.

Even when you prove that refugees are suffering from severe under-nutrition, the problem may not be resolved. In November, 1996 a team including the staff of WFP and UNHCR from Rome and Geneva arrived in Kakuma to assess the food situation and to find ways to reduce costs. I took members to the hospital to see the anaemic patients. I pointed out the differential food requirements by age and sex and believed that I had managed to persuade them to increase the rations, particularly for the most vulnerable. A second meeting was held in Nairobi where my recommendations were again seemingly accepted. The new ration would be increased to 2,134 Kcal (Guluma 1997b).[55]

In addition to the issues addressed in this letter, during his posting in Kakuma this doctor repeatedly informed UNHCR that the water situation was critical. On several occasions, he analysed samples of water and found chloroform bacteria in it, notwithstanding the fact that water was 'officially' safe. He trained refugees to clean the tanks adequately, and also asked UNHCR to supply new buckets to carry the water. He spoke frankly about the health situation in Kakuma to various teams of researchers and journalists. In March 1997, he heard that his position had been advertised. He had a meeting with the UNHCR medical coordinator,

Dr Babu Swai,[56] and an IRC official. He was told that his 'name had come up too many times in relation to malnutrition in Kakuma'. The following day he received a letter that terminated his employment and asked him to leave Kakuma within two days.[57]

After Dr Guluma was dismissed by IRC, veiled allegations about his medical competence and insinuations about the reasons for his dismissal circulated. In particular, it was held against him that he had made a great fuss about a suspected case of haemorrhagic fever that turned out to have been misdiagnosed. However, as the US specialist who was flown in on this occasion confirmed: 'When we arrived at the camp, we were greeted by Dr W.V. Guluma. We discussed the case with him and the hospital staff before visiting the patient. Dr Guluma believed that viral haemorrhagic fever was very low on the diagnostic differential list of possible aetiologies, but had provided adequate isolation procedures until it could be ruled out. I felt the patient had received proper care given the local situation.'[58]

With this IRC doctor disposed of, it was easier to conceal the real situation. In Kakuma, according to the 'official statistics' compiled by the IRC (1997: 8), malnutrition accounted for eleven deaths, 5 percent of the total 235 deaths (ibid.). The IRC report for 1997 omitted to mention the existence of a direct causal link between malnutrition and the severe anaemia found in the camps, which SCF had postulated in 1996 (Lawrence et al. 1997: 12) and the IRC doctor had conclusively demonstrated.[59]

Upon returning from our first trip to Kakuma, we discussed the malnutrition with the political counsellor at the US embassy in Kenya, Dr Lucien Vandenbroucke, who replied to us:

Regarding your points about anaemia, I regret to say that information reaching us from other sources tends to confirm the details relayed to you by Dr Guluma. The matter of anaemia as a consequence of under-nutrition first came to our attention earlier this year. We immediately informed Washington of these issues, which raised US government concerns with UNHCR headquarters in Geneva.

One result of Washington's raising this issue was the decision by the UN Agencies in the camp to begin a school feeding program. Unfortunately, the program was plagued with a number of start-up problems. Nevertheless, the move to begin such a program did suggest a desire on the part of the UN agencies in Kakuma to correct shortcomings in their care and maintenance operations.[60]

At the same time, Dr Onyango, director of the African Network for the Prevention and Protection against Child Abuse and Neglect (ANPPCAN), whom we had briefed about the situation in Kakuma, wrote a letter to UNHCR acting representative asking for comment and enclosing an email we had sent.[61] At the time, UNHCR was receiving many letters from abroad because of an article about malnutrition in Kakuma that had appeared in a Scottish religious newsletter (*see* Scottish Churches Sudan

Group 1997). Receiving this email at this time, they assumed that the campaign originated from the members of the research team and blamed Dr Guluma for briefing us.[62] Our access to senior UNHCR officials in Kenya in the first months of the research was compromised by this incident, but the situation improved later in the year.

Adequate clothing and housing

Refugees received only one distribution of clothing and were expected to manage on their own after that: in Kakuma the group of Sudanese boys stood out from the rest of the population owing to their tattered clothing. Minors, particularly girls, sometimes decided not to go to school because they found their bedraggled appearance too shameful and undignified (*see* Lester 1998).

The right to adequate housing was described by the ICESCR Committee as the 'right to live somewhere in security, peace and dignity' (ICESCR 1991: para. 7). Clearly, 'Durable shelter, provided to satisfactory physical standards, using appropriate materials and related to prevailing cultural parameters, constitutes one of the basic needs for refugees' (Zetter 1995).

Given that our research was conducted in the post-emergency phase, it was not surprising that some of the refugees had managed to improve their dwellings.[63] Nevertheless, the poorest continued to live in huts (*tukuls*) that did not provide adequate shelter from the elements. In Kakuma, for example, many refugees continued to depend on the plastic sheeting provided during the emergency as their only shelter, and which was recognised to be of poor quality (UNHCR 1992c). Some places of worship stood out for their elaborate construction, an indication of the priorities of refugees themselves, or of the power of the religious leaders to mobilise labour and resources.

The Lutheran World Federation (LWF), which was sub-contracted by UNHCR to provide social services in Kakuma, dealt with many complaints about inadequate shelter and submitted reports to UNHCR, but the response was far from prompt in most cases. Its reports tell a story of neglect and inefficiency. Again, new arrivals suffered serious hardship, partly because of a deliberate policy aimed at deterring 'recyclers'. In Kakuma, a special area was reserved for them, next to the 'special protection' area. Yet, the provision of shelter was so inadequate that their security was threatened. For example, the LWF report had this to say about a Somali woman who had been transferred to Kakuma with the children of her sister-in-law (who had died after being raped): 'M.'s situation in Kakuma is quite difficult because she is caring for so many children. She has no one to protect her and feels insecure. Bandits target her because she has so much food when she is first given her ration. She has also had problems because she hasn't been given any shelter materials. Karanja [a

member of LWF's staff] has written three letters on M.'s behalf, requesting shelter, but at present no action has been taken' (case no.
024/SOM/K/1998). In another case concerning a Burundian refugee who
had fled to Kenya after being detained and tortured in Burundian prisons,
LWF wrote to UNHCR asking for some action: 'A. has been living in
Kakuma for over five months and still hasn't received any shelter materials or non-food items. He and his family have been living with a friend,
but fear being asked to leave. His family is sick and he has been getting
regular nosebleeds from the heat' (case no. 047/BUR/K/1998).

One of UNHCR's protection reports for Kenya was unusually candid
about the lack of adequate shelter for refugees, especially 'new arrivals'.
It admitted that 'many refugees have had to wait for unacceptable periods for shelter materials', and added that the problem 'has been
addressed in Kakuma with the implementing partner', thus implying that
the blame lay with the NGO. The report then notes that 'Culturally insen-
sitive outlays [i.e. layouts] of the camps and calculation of needs have
exposed refugee girls and young adolescents to unnecessary security
problems as they often are relegated to sleep under the open sky'
(UNHCR 1999f: 3.5).

The effect of forced evictions

Forced evictions constitute a prima facie breach of the right to adequate
housing protected under article 11 of the ICESCR. Indeed, possessing 'a
degree of security of tenure that guarantees legal protection against
forced eviction and other threats' is an essential component of this right
(ICESCR Committee 1997: para. 1). The ICESCR Committee also called
upon international agencies to 'scrupulously avoid involvement in projects which ... involve large scale evictions or displacement of persons
without the provision of all appropriate protection and compensation'
(ibid.: para. 6).

Forced evictions occurred in both countries, as part of a UNHCR/gov-
ernment plan to resettle refugees in different areas. Not only did they
amount to a violation of the refugees' right to adequate housing and the
right to property; they were also a traumatising form of cruel, inhuman,
and degrading treatment to impose on individuals who had already been
uprooted from their homes.[64] The most glaring example of forced eviction
en masse in Uganda was the demolition of Ogujebe transit centre in
Adjumani in February 1998.[65] When we visited the site in February 1998,
we observed the rapid pace at which the destruction of the centre was
proceeding so as to comply with the deadline that UNHCR had set. The
main 'implementing partner' for this programme was LWF.

The bulldozing of the Ogujebe transit centre resulted in the destruction
of the standard of living the refugees had achieved. They lost much of

their property; those supporting themselves through trading or other businesses were deprived of their means of livelihood. They lost their homes and were given only plastic tarpaulins for shelter. Expected to rebuild their homes and grow their own food in the settlements to which they had been moved, they were supplied with sickles, axes, and pangas: these tools were of such a poor quality that many broke on the first day of use. The refugees were given beans, and dry maize with no means to grind it. Some families got salt, others did not.

Somali refugees in Kenya were also forcibly evicted. Arriving in 1991 by sea, many were settled into camps, not far from the urban area, and a large number were able to self-settle, mainly in the town of Mombasa. Some Somali refugees were able to establish businesses along the coast, and they were highly visible in the main market in Mombasa. At the same time, the camps became centres of economic activity in the area because business carried out within the confines of the camps was not subject to taxation. This had the effect of skewing the local Kenyan economy in favour of the camp locations, much to the resentment of the local business community, who were losing customers to the unfair competition.[66] It is not surprising that powerful segments of the Mombasa business community put pressure on the government to order the closure of the camps.

UNHCR's response to this largely iatrogenic state of affairs was to give refugees the choice of repatriating or being relocated in either Dadaab or Kakuma camps as the camps on the coast would be destroyed. As in Ogujebe, the whole camp infrastructure was razed to the ground: at the end of the exercise, only one clinic was left standing. UNHCR maintained that it had no choice as the government had decided that these camps should be closed. The refugees who chose repatriation received US$ 30 and were taken to the border (*see* Waldron and Hasci 1995).[67] The others were taken by bus or truck to the camp of their choice.[68] Between 1995 and 1997, some 35,000 people were transported from the coastal area to the camps in the deserts of the northeast and northwest. In October 1997, around 20,000 still needed to be moved from the coast. The hardships of the relocation and the trauma of the decisions being forced upon many of the refugees were witnessed during visits to Jomvu camp in October 1997. The Somalis living in Jomvu camp came from Kismayo and belonged to the Bajuni clan, who are, for the most part, fishermen and, as such, must have found life in an arid region even more alienating. Out of a total population of about 5,200 registered refugees, around 3,000 opted for repatriation to Somalia instead of relocation to Kakuma.

The highest attainable standard of physical and mental health

Article 12 of the ICESCR protects the right to the *highest attainable standard* of physical and mental health.[69] As is the case with other economic and social rights, there are three levels of states' obligation 'to respect, protect and fulfil' (ICESCR 1990, 2000). The obligation to fulfil in turn entails obligations to facilitate, provide, and promote (ICESCR 1999). The full implementation of the right to the highest attainable standard of health raises the question of scarcity of resources perhaps more dramatically than any other economic and social right. The provision of curative health care, in particular, can be very expensive, and there are enormous and ever-widening disparities between scientific and technical advances in countries in the 'developed world' and what 'developing countries' can afford for their own people. The attendant right 'to enjoy the benefits of scientific progress and its applications' (ICESCR art. 15) is limited to the few who can afford it, or who live in those countries in the 'developed world' where extensive public or private social welfare systems exist.

A common feature across countries in the 'developing world' was that private NGOs and international organisations provided a significant portion of the health services. For instance, in Kenya, in 1998, 71.9 percent of the health care available in the whole country was provided by the private sector while in Uganda the figure was 61.8 percent (WHO 2001: Annex, Table 5, 160–66).[70] Of the US$ 11 per capita spent annually by Uganda on health, US$ 4 was spent by the government (including external aid) and US$ 7 was private expenditure (ibid.), whereas US$ 12 per capita is often assumed to be the minimum acceptable expenditure (Mulumba 1999). In the same year, in Kenya, US$ 30 per capita was spent on health – US$ 8 in the public sector and US$ 22 in the private (WHO 2001). However, these statistics might be misleading since the private component of the expenditure might in part reflect high spending by the better off, rather than spending on the poorest. Moreover, the bulk of government health expenditure was devoted to curative treatment of preventable problems, leaving preventive measures substantially under-funded. Last but not least, currency devaluations affected the provision of health care, as they made drugs, medical equipment, and supplies more expensive.

Establishing a parallel system

For an international organisation like UNHCR, operating both in the 'developed' and in the 'developing' world, the provision of health services to refugees in different countries raises a difficult legal and ethical dilemma. Whenever UNHCR provides health care, directly or through a partner NGO, should the standard of care for refugees be the same the world over?

The idea that UNHCR should make some types of costly curative health care available to the refugees it assists in countries in the 'developed world', but not to those in countries in the 'developing world', clashes with a principle of distributive justice – that is, that the same institution should ensure equal treatment for all its beneficiaries. UNHCR's solution to this problem is: 'Ultimately, refugees are entitled to the best possible health care: that is, to the same level of care that the local community has access to, and/or to the same level of services as previously available in their home country' (UNHCR 1998f). While this approach could, on the face of it, be accused of being discriminatory, the alternative – equal standard of health care to all refugees in the world – would be open to a similar criticism, with those discriminated against being 'the hosts'.

Nevertheless, a problem with the 'national standard of care' approach avowedly followed by UNHCR was that the standard of care actually available to the host population in countries like Kenya and Uganda varied considerably from place to place, and was also contingent upon social class. When UNHCR talked about 'the same level of care that the local community has access to', which local community was it referring to – the local Turkana or, for example, the professional classes in Nairobi? The reference to the 'level of services available in the home country' as an additional criterion for determining the level of health care to be made available to refugees was even more problematic. Did it mean that African refugees in Europe should be offered a standard of health care similar to the one they would have received in Africa? In practice, it was probably only seldom that UNHCR used the level of health care that had been available to the refugees in the home country as a yardstick for determining what it would provide. One example when it did so was the case of a small group of refugees from the former Yugoslavia in Kenya. UNHCR covered the costs of their accommodation in hotel rooms in Nairobi and of their medical care at Nairobi hospital, one of the country's leading private hospitals.

A more fundamental flaw in the approach of UNHCR and NGOs to health care in camps and settlements was that the health services for refugees were separate from those that catered for nationals. Strengthening existing local institutions to enable them to provide for both nationals and refugees would have been a better solution, and economically less costly. It would have also helped defuse xenophobic attitudes towards refugees.

In Kenya and Uganda, the parallel system approach presented a number of problems. Firstly, the establishment of parallel systems was difficult to reconcile with the standard of care that UNHCR had set as its goal – 'the same level of care that the local community has access to' – since NGOs which took responsibility for health as implementing partners were not normally prepared to adopt this standard. Secondly, the establishment of these parallel services was expensive and difficult to sustain over the long term (e.g., case no. 056/DRC/U/1999). Thirdly, parallel services undermined local health institutions by attracting staff away from them.[71] As mentioned, resentment among the local host population grew as they were excluded from these services. For instance, in Kakuma, one of the motives for the recurrent tension between the agencies working in the camps and the local Turkana population was their exclusion from the refugee health services. As a way of reducing tensions between hosts and refugees, in the 1990s UNHCR sometimes made the services established for refugees available to nationals living in the area of the settlement or camp. Fourthly, while it was commonly believed[72] that refugees had access to a higher standard of health care, including preventive, primary, and curative, than the host population, these parallel health structures could in fact be precarious (Lomo 1999b). Such services were entirely dependent on one, or at the most, two sources of external funding. When UNHCR faced a funding crisis for a certain programme, the standards dropped dramatically. Given that 'there is strong presumption that retrogressive measures taken in respect of the right to health are not permissible' (ICESCR Committee 2000: para 33), the right to health of refugees was often violated in the downsizing or 'phase out' stage. Since UNHCR knows in advance of any emergency that donor funding is insecure, it should be expected to spend its resources prudently in local institutions so as to make the provision of health services at their proposed standard sustainable.

Finally, parallel health systems did not necessarily deliver 'better' health and they ignored the consequences of encampment on refugee health and welfare. In fact: 'Camp conditions affect physical, mental and social well-being … Because of increased transmission through overcrowding, epidemics of measles, cholera, dysentery and meningitis become major killers in camps, more than in any other situation. The bigger the camps are, the more pronounced these effects become' (van Damme 1998: 195).[73] Studying the provision of health care to self-settled refugees in Guinea, van Damme observed that the limited impact of epidemics there was due to 'the dispersion and the general situation of the refugees … more than the effectiveness of epidemic control measures'. Since health care was provided through local institutions, the cost of the medical programme was limited to some US$ 4 per refugee per year, against a reported cost of medical assistance in camps of up to US$ 20 per refugee per year. Some of the benefits of providing health care through local institutions have been highlighted since the early 1980s – for example, by Simmonds (Simmonds et al. 1983) and Harrell-Bond (1986).

UNHCR often prided itself on its health programmes, maintaining that refugees usually got a better deal than nationals.[74] However, a closer look at the official statistics offers a different picture.[75] In Uganda, according to

UNHCR's official figures, the numbers of doctors in the settlements were as follows: 0.29/10,000 (Adjumani), 0.5/10,000 (Moyo), 0.45/10,000 (Rhino), 0.31/10,000 (Imvepi), 0.30/10,000 (Orukinga), 0.0/10,000 (Nakivale), 0.33/10,000 (Achol-Pii), 0.46/10,000 (Kyangwali), 0.0/10,000 (Kiryandongo) (UNHCR 1999g). Because of a computation mistake, the UNHCR table for 1999 said that there was an average of 2.73 doctors per 10,000 people in the settlements in Uganda. The actual figure is 0.33/10,000, which was below the Ugandan figures of 0.40/10,000 in the period 1992–95 (UNDP 2000: 193). As for the various categories of nurses and midwives (registered nurse, registered midwife, enrolled nurse, enrolled midwife), there were in total sixty-seven nurses and midwives serving an official population of 329,056 refugees and nationals in the settlements. This means that there were roughly two nurses for every 10,000 people – again below the Ugandan figures, as reported by the United Nations Development Programme (UNDP) for the period 1992–95 (2.8/10,000). Two of the settlements (Kiryandongo and Nakivale) did not have a doctor; in Nakivale, there was only one nurse, one midwife, and one medical assistant, whereas in Kiryandongo there was a marginally larger presence of such personnel.

Individual violations of the right to health

A significant number of the refugees we interviewed had suffered a violation of their right to health. Most of them complained about receiving inadequate or no attention for their condition as a result of lack of staff or resources, of bureaucratic complications, or simply of indifference on the part of humanitarian workers.

NGOs often responded defensively to criticism about inadequacies in the health services in camps and settlements. One illustration is the case of a Congolese refugee who left Achol-Pii in Kitgum because he was suffering from a serious health problem for which he was not getting treatment. Once in Kampala, this refugee contacted AVSI, an organisation he knew since it was responsible for health care in Achol-Pii. We wrote a letter in support of his case, but AVSI responded:

> According to his [the refugee's] explanation, he was directed to AVSI by your office, since he is coming from Achol-Pii Settlement area. Unfortunately I could not be of any help to him, since by mutual agreement we are not responsible for Refugee care in Kampala, as InterAid has availed its services [sic] in this field ... Additionally, to my knowledge, there was no problem in Achol-Pii concerning drug supply and Staffing at the time mentioned in the documents here attached, therefore he should have got either treatment or a referral document if needed without problem from there at that time.[76]

In another letter we explained why this refugee had not obtained a referral letter from the camp: 'One of the findings of our research on refugee rights is that it is often impossible for refugees to secure appointments with camp officials. Sometimes, the chairmen of welfare committees are the "gate keepers" and if a particular refugee is not in good standing, for whatever reason, with this individual s/he will not be given the first letters that open the door to the camp commandant.'[77] Acknowledging that the refugee was in need of assistance would have implied recognition of the fact that something had gone wrong with the services that AVSI provided in the settlement.[78]

A 35-year-old Rwandan refugee, who, following the protocol, went to Kampala only after referral from the settlement, died before he could make it past the receptionist at InterAid. Unusually, news of the circumstances of his death reached the local press and created uproar in Kampala.[79] A journalist wrote an article describing what had happened:

> Assisted by his uncle, he had arrived directly to InterAid on 11 January 2000. Told they were too busy to attend to him that day, InterAid staff directed them to the Salvation Army hostel where other refugees in Kampala were residing.[80] The Salvation Army Captain, according to his own testimony, had been told to starve them out.

> Although in terrible pain, Mr Kaijuka returned with his uncle to InterAid again the next day. Without money for transport, this involved a long journey on foot. Again, At InterAid, Mr. Kaijuka sat waiting in the sun for several hours outside the main offices. The staff eventually told Mr. Kaijuka they could not take him to the hospital because ... they were again too busy.

> Mr Kaijuka staggered into an empty room and laid on a small grass mat. Sometime during the night, he curled up into a ball and pulled his threadbare blanket up close to his neck. He tucked his hands under his chin, perhaps for warmth. Then Mr Kaijuka's humble struggle for survival, his flight from Rwanda, his years in the camp; all slipped away late in the night of January 12 2000, on the floor of the Salvation Army compound ... Mr Kaijuka died alone (Oliver 2000).

Scarcity of resources and the particular institutional ethos sometimes led to absurd procedures. For example, requests to spend money on serious medical cases had to be forwarded to Geneva for approval by a special committee.[81] One Ugandan social worker explained a case with which she had been confronted and how her appropriate reaction almost cost her her job:

> Three refugees lived together. One was paralysed from the waist down. He was not only dying, he smelled so badly it was impossible to live in the same room. His roommates locked him in the room and abandoned him, but one reported to this social worker. She immediately investigated, called an ambulance and transferred him to a hospice. However, as the cost

was significantly above what UNHCR would tolerate, she was warned if she ever did such a thing again, she would be sacked (Kalyango 2000).[82]

The 'parallel system' approach was followed for the urban programmes too, although there were parts of the city – like Eastleigh or Kangemi in Nairobi, and Kisenyi or Makerere West in Kampala – where many refugees were known to live and where the funds that were available could have been channelled through existing health services in order to permit them to cope with a larger number of beneficiaries. In particular, primary health care projects in the suburbs were normally left to manage with scarce resources.[83] A small health programme existed for refugees living in Nairobi and Kampala. In both cities, however, owing to the presence of large numbers of refugees who were not recognised by UNHCR or who had been referred to a camp and had refused to go, most refugees had to seek health services from national clinics.

The assistance provided to those exceptional cases with official permission to live in Kampala, who received money from InterAid, was far from sufficient to sustain good health.[84] Health services provided by UNHCR even for those on the approved urban caseload list in Kampala were limited to primary health care. It was rumoured that staff in Kampala were forbidden to give any assistance, including medical, to anyone over 70 years of age. Although InterAid staff denied this, our experiences with elderly refugees would appear to confirm the rumour.[85]

Violations of the right to health often occurred in conjunction with, or as a result of, violations of other fundamental human rights. Restrictions on the freedom of movement and on the right to choose one's place of residence generated violations of the right to health. For instance, a Sudanese refugee had to postpone his operation in Kampala because permission to leave Kyangwali camp was delayed (case no. 157/SUD/U/1999).

Moreover, when refugees were uprooted – as in Ogujebe or from Mombasa – there was a total disregard not only of the psychosocial impact, but also of the health problems of some individuals. For instance, a Somali refugee interviewed in Hatimy camp suffered from bi-ventricular failure, a condition that had been diagnosed by two doctors. Medical resettlement for his case had been discussed since 1995, but UNHCR argued that they had no more places for medical resettlement and that the only treatment he could receive was what was available in Kenya. As was explained in a letter which was copied to him: 'It has been made clear to him that there is no medical resettlement so he will be treated by medication till death' (case no. 029/SOM/K/1997).

The medicines he was taking could only alleviate the pain. In order to solve the medical problem, he needed heart surgery. Dr Aseso, a cardiologist at Kenyatta national hospital, wrote to UNHCR on 6 February 1997, advising that 'since he needs to see us monthly and for some time, it may be more reasonable and economical to settle him in Nairobi'. In spite of this medical recommendation, and even the intervention of a Kenyan member of parliament, UNHCR was still determined that Abdi Abdullahi would be relocated to Kakuma refugee camp where his medical condition 'can be monitored through the medical referral system'.[86]

In prisons in Kenya and Uganda, there was inadequate health care for both refugees and nationals. What made the situation of refugees worse was the fact that they could not rely on a support network of relatives and friends to bring them food and medicines. An illustration of the health conditions in prison was the case of I.J., who was only 17. He had been arrested in 1996 with his brother, and charged as an accomplice with 'illegal possession of firearms'. When arrested, both were badly beaten and imprisoned, initially in Silili prison in Moyo. In December 1996, I.J.'s brother escaped from prison, and in January 1997, I.J. was transferred to Openjinji prison. I.J. suffered from leprosy but never received treatment. The court was prepared to allow him bail if a surety could be found and USh 100,000. The officer-in-charge of the prison tried to help him by contacting UNHCR, but received no response.

The mental health dimension of the right to health was usually neglected, despite the high percentage of refugees who had been traumatised by direct acts of torture or by being witness to atrocities (Karukanara et al. 2004). In Nairobi, although JRS employed far more counsellors than protection officers, they were not working as such and most of them had not been trained as mental health counsellors.[87] Refugees appearing for status determination often required emergency mental health services, but their symptoms of distress were often ignored and, on at least one occasion, UNHCR even called the police (case no. 103/SOM/U/1999). The psychological and physical humiliation to which refugees were subject certainly took its toll on their mental health.

Mental health issues affecting refugee children should have been a priority. One study revealed that 'most of these children [the Sudanese in Kakuma] suffer from anxiety and depression, sometimes even considering suicide' (Refugees International 2000). Out of 174 children, 168 stated that they did not feel safe and mentioned fears of being killed or attacked. A Sudanese refugee child in Nairobi listed his problems:

1. I am bored of being lonely since I do not have any body who can exchange with me ideas. But I had one of my best friends M. who has just gone to Canada recently.

2. I do not have any job which can make me busy all the time but reading Novels and go to bed.

3. I used to dream for my parent night after another since I miss them for about ten years since I left them in Chukuduni.

4. I miss my elder brother, E.L. who had been struggle for so many years to be a priest but now I heard that he was succeeded a priest now.

5. My sister who is in Kakuma camp is suffering together with my youngest brother, they are really stuff [*sic*] because of hunger and I have nothing to help them.

6. It is so difficult for me to get something which I like to get for myself, such things like money to send to my sister and brother in camp.

7. The education that I want it is not yet enough to me for my future because I want to get well educated so that in future I can use my talent to help my children in future to have a better life that they might achieve.

8. I used to wake up very early in the morning reading some novel or newspapers to improve my language.

9. I used to cook for myself and for my group, washing my clothes, lifting water from a deep hole about 10 cm from the ground level, but it is too dirty some time it cause coughing also typhoid.

10. I don't have anywhere to go since I have a problem of the financial, even I don't have my relative in Kenya to visit, even I don't have any here who scholarly [*sic*] for example my brother (case no. 12/SUD/K/1997).

For most of the children, flight had been a deeply traumatic experience, having to leave behind not only their homes but also friends, relatives, and in some cases their parents and siblings. Their accounts were harrowing (case nos. 007/SUD/K/1997; 008/SUD/K/1997; 009/ SUD/K/1997).

A pattern that has already been seen in the context of the right to food and that also characterised the health sector was the tendency to blame the beneficiaries rather than confront the inadequacy of the service being provided. A recurrent accusation was that refugees over-consume health services, a subtle way of suggesting that the provision of health care would be adequate in itself were it not for the fault of refugees. This accusation was levelled in Uganda.[88] In Dadaab a similar line was taken when in 1997–98 the funding cuts imposed a 'rationalisation' of the services. An MSF doctor was asked to conduct an evaluation of the health programme and, in particular, of the question of 'over-utilisation', but her findings refuted the argument that 'over consumption' was really taking place. Instead, she found that the apparent over-distribution of certain medicines (in particular chloroquine for malaria) was a function of the shortcomings in first-line health care, which was provided by the health posts: these were staffed by Somali refugees who had secondary education but had only received limited training in nursing at the beginning of the emergency in the early 1990s. Patients were given a standard packet of medicines, and there was a risk that 'a lot of cases who are really in need of higher level care' were being turned down (Boelaert 1996: 21). First-line health care thus became a 'rather expensive and probably inefficient triage system, to block the road to the hospital' (ibid.). But, most importantly, the main reason for the apparent over-utilisation of the health service was the level of malnutrition, since 'refugees are over-consulting because they are not getting what they are looking for: health care and adequate diet ... They ask in fact not to be fed like animals' (ibid.). In other words, the refugees' 'fault' in Dadaab was that they got sick because they were malnourished, and their demand for health services was greater than the supply.

In particular, the report explained:

> ... the current utilisation rate of 2.3–2.9 NC/p/yr is indeed high compared to utilisation rates in a stable situation ... although mortality rates have been brought under control since June 1993, life in the refugee camp is not really 'healthy'. The recurrent problem of the scurvy outbreaks is in striking contrast with all international commitment to 'ending hidden hunger'. When one listens to the refugees, they see the food issue as the main health problem. The budgetary restrictions urging WFP since 1995 to restrict the quantity and the quality of the food rations have a clear impact on rising malnutrition rates in the camps. The question might be raised whether there is a deliberate strategy behind the policy. Is it a policy 'to starve refugee back into Somalia?' The experiences from Sudan and more recently from Zaire, show that it is mostly factors external to camp policy which influence on [sic] decision ... Everybody seemed to be aware that the emergency situation was over in Hagadera, but putting it a little bluntly, the adaptation made was rather in terms of cutting down on budgets: doing the same with less (less money, less people), then in terms of rethinking the response ... It is up to NGOs as MSF to decide to what extent they will take up the voice of the refugees and give it the audience it deserves (ibid.).

Scarcity of resources undeniably posed ethical dilemmas for governments, UNHCR, and NGOs providing health care. In Dadaab, a Sierra Leonean doctor explained some of the difficult choices he had to make to a journalist from the Italian newspaper *La Repubblica*: 'He recounts that the serious cases from the three hospitals in the refugee camps have to be evacuated to Nairobi and Garissa. But the number is limited; there is a monthly quota that cannot be exceeded and so every time that he decides to evacuate someone he asks himself whether he is not sentencing to death a patient who will arrive later in the month and will end up outside the quota' (Veronese 2001 [our translation]).

Triaging was inevitable, but, as observed by Lipsky in respect of street-level bureaucracies in countries in the 'developed world', '... the problem with triaging in public service is not primarily that it is sometimes destructive. It is that discretionary judgments are subject to *routine abuse*' (Lipsky 1980: 106 [emphasis in original]). The implementation of the refugees' right to health could have been improved to a significant extent

– within the available resources – had their other human rights (in particular freedom of movement, the right to work and the right to food) been respected, had resources been channelled through existing health structures, and had the humanitarian organisations developed a more caring attitude towards the needs of refugees.

Reproductive health

The ICESCR does not use such expressions as 'reproductive rights' or 'reproductive health', but the right to highest attainable standard of physical and mental health, protected under article 12, is generally interpreted to encompass these notions (ICESCR General Comment 14). Moreover, the Covenant recognises that mothers are entitled to special protection 'for a reasonable period during and after childbirth' (art. 10). More generally, maternal health and disability have been found to affect four groups of rights: rights relating to life, survival, and security of the person; rights relating to maternity and health; rights to non-discrimination and due respect for difference; and rights relating to information and education (Cook, Dickens and Wilson 2001).

Reproductive issues have featured prominently in the final acts of international conferences, most notably the Cairo Conference on Population and Development (1994) and the Fourth World Conference on Women held in Beijing (1995).[89] An inter-agency manual on reproductive health has been developed by the UN and it constitutes the basis for their operational programmes (UNHCR 1999j). Some authors have praised UNHCR for its standard-setting work and for its guidelines on reproductive issues (Gilbert 1995). Nevertheless, despite the existence of a 'clear mandate for governments, UNHCR and NGOs to meet the reproductive rights of refugees' (Girard and Waldman 2000), a gap existed between the high-level policy of the organisation – emanating from Geneva – and the middle-level to field-level policies. The reasons for this gap between standards and practice are manifold. Scarcity of resources was undoubtedly a factor. In addition, as we have seen in other instances, the role played by legal standards tended to gradually diminish as one moved from the upper echelons in policy-formulation to the level of field implementation. Difficulties in devising effective public health policies in a context that was complex and fluid presented another challenge, particularly since relevant data were not always collected and analysed in an accurate and prompt manner. For example, in Uganda, while mortality statistics were not disaggregated according to gender, morbidity ones were.[90]

Education was an important component of the reproductive health programmes, but the impact of educational initiatives was often undermined by the refugees' lack of trust in the humanitarian organisations. In Kenya, the National Council of Churches of Kenya (NCCK), was 'mandated by UNHCR and the Ministry of Health to carry out the awareness programmes for the reproductive health services in the camps in Mombasa, Kakuma and Dadaab' (NCCK 1997: 2). A Christian organisation, NCCK was not at first accepted by many Somalis. NCCK also complained that 'The NGOs concerned with health made it impossible for NCCK to get into the camps (ibid. 5).' According to NCCK, this was because 'the refugees had threatened them so much that there was a fear of introducing anything new just in case it antagonises what co-operation they had already achieved' (ibid.). Over time, and working with the elders, including the imams and sheiks, NCCK managed to make some progress and was still in charge of reproductive health and family planning in Dadaab and Kakuma in 1997–99.

In Uganda, in 1997, an appraisal was carried out in five refugee camps/settlements to '… establish which reproductive health services were on the ground, what the quality of services is and where the biggest gaps are' (UNFPA 1997). The report concluded by saying that the:

> … quality of reproductive health services, i.e. services in the health system of the settlement/camp addressing safe motherhood family planning, sexual and gender violence and RH [reproductive health] harmful practices, HIV/AIDS and STDs and emergency obstetrics, are generally rated as mediocre and health staff are not competent in reproductive health … it is worth mentioning here that one camp/settlement has no trained TBA's [traditional birth attendants] at all and two camps/settlements have no doctor.

> … A range of factors prevent the women from using the services [that are there]. Some women are not aware that the services are there, others are intimidated by rude and/or incompetent staff, while others feel they are prevented by their husbands' attitude and the culture and religion of the community.

> … Family planning services are provided in all camps/settlements, but the quality of services is generally rated poor. Again lack of trained staff is mentioned as a major weakness … Only one camp/settlement has services for removal of IUDs and implants and for provision of post-coital contraception (UNFPA 1997).

Regarding sexual and gender-based violence and harmful practices, the report stated:

> This is definitely the most neglected area of RH services in refugee camps/settlements. Only one camp/settlement provides the services and here the quality is rated as poor. Lack of knowledge about the magnitude of the problem and lack of openness of sexual and gender violence from the women are cited as the major weaknesses. Still there are reports of rape, defilement, sexual coercion or other types of sexual and gender violence in all but one of the camps/settlement (ibid.).

Among refugee populations, programmes to address the scourge of HIV/AIDS have been noticeable by their absence, although in 1999 an inter-agency field manual *Reproductive Health in Refugee Situations* was produced. It reminded readers that STDs and HIV/AIDS:

> ... spread fastest where there is poverty, powerlessness and social instability. The disintegration of community and family life in situations leads to the break-up of stable relationships and the disruption of social norms governing sexual behaviour. Women and children are frequently coerced into having sex to obtain basic needs, such as shelter, security, food and money ... refugee situations are like large urban settings and may create conditions that increase the risk of HIV transmission (UNHCR 1999j: chap. 5: 2).

In Kakuma, Stanley (1998) conducted research on prostitution and the spread of sexually transmitted diseases, including HIV/AIDS, and the impact of these practices on both refugees and the host population where the extreme poverty of Turkana women and girls also forced many into prostitution. In Kakuma, 27 percent of the blood donors tested between January 1997 and February 1998 were HIV positive (ibid.: 27; *see also* Das Neves Silva 2002).[91]

Determinants of sexual attitudes included the ratio of men to women within the refugee population. In Kakuma, men outnumbered women by two to one and most men were bachelors, 'not least because many of them are "grown up" unaccompanied minors' (Stanley 1996). Alcohol abuse, frustration, ennui, and low morale were other factors, and, according to Stanley, so was the pornography available in the camp. She also found general ignorance of the physical signs and symptoms of STDs. In Kakuma, there was little attempt to prevent STDs other than distribution points for condoms. At the time Stanley conducted her research, supplies had run out at all the condom dispensers in bars in Kakuma town (ibid: 32).

As was the case with many other human rights issues, reproductive health matters were negatively affected by the fact that other rights were not adequately protected. Some refugee women in Kali (Uganda) commented on the link between their destitute condition and lack of autonomy, and their access to reproductive health services:

> Women are overburdened with child care. Anyway, if there was some kind of assistance for mobilising us to form groups for income generation, we could manage to take care of ourselves ... As for sanitary pads, the material is not good and the pads do not last for a long time. They used a petticoat at least and smelling soap to protect ... AAH [Aktion Afrika Hilfe] assisted us, but it was limited – only being distributed in Zone A and partly Zone B without safety pins; UNHCR has been trying to encourage the mobilisation ... There was a lady concerned with income generation who promised they'd be channelled through the community leaders; up to now, there has been no action and we leaders have been accused of eating the money.[92]

UNHCR's general policy towards reproductive health was called into question when some NGOs criticised the content of a new manual for reproductive health. OXFAM and SCF decided to remove their names from the manual because the practices that were recommended – such as the insertion of ultra-uterine contraceptive devices, long-term contraceptive implants, and surgical abortion – cannot, they maintained, be performed safely in refugee camps, given the unhygienic conditions and the high risk of infection. OXFAM pointed out that 'there were hardly any properly equipped medical centres in the camps. Local hospitals needed to be supported, and the very few were too far away for emergency use' (Phillips 1998). However, the UNHCR reproductive health officer pointed out that the manual advised aid workers to use these procedures only when safe to do so and that it was not true that most refugee camps were unhygienic and medically dangerous. 'I've been to some of the most incredible health facilities in refugee camps' she said (ibid.).

The impact of exile on fertility has been studied by Karunakara (2004), who has collected data on Sudanese refugees in northern Uganda, Sudanese stayees, and Ugandan hosts. He found that Sudanese refugees had the lowest fertility rates of the three groups. As he points out, it is not the experience of forced migration per se that has an impact on fertility, but:

> ... family separation, experience of child death and reduced access to food, health and education services, exacerbated by conflict, affect fertility through the proximate determinants. Loss and death of a sexual partner affects the proportion of women in sexual unions thereby inhibiting fertility. The experience of child death affects postpartum infecundability through lactation effects, increasing chances of subsequent pregnancies. Experiences of child mortality can also result in intentional, socially reinforced pro-natalist behaviour. Reduced food intake resulting in malnutrition affects a woman's ability to conceive thereby reducing fertility (id.: 156).

Education

As set out by ICESCR and CRC, states are obliged to make primary education compulsory and free to all, including nationals and non-nationals. Secondary education should be made 'generally available and accessible to all by every appropriate means, and in particular by the progressive introduction of free education' (ICESCR art. 13). The CRC places emphasis on 'measures to encourage regular attendance at school and the reduction of the drop out rates' (art. 28). Higher education should be 'equally accessible to all on the basis of capacity'. Before these treaties, the 1951 Convention had already established that states 'shall accord to refugees the same treatment as is accorded to nationals with respect to elementary education', and as favourable a treatment as possible with respect to other levels of education (art. 22).

In addition, the Ugandan Constitution provides that 'All persons have a right to education' (art. 30), and that 'a child is entitled to basic education which shall be the responsibility of the state and the parents of the child' (art. 34(2)). During the presidential elections in 1996, Museveni announced that, when elected, he would introduce universal primary education (UPE), which would begin by providing free primary education to four children per family.[93]

While for humanitarian organisations, education is the last priority in an emergency, for refugees it is among the first. The variety of educational initiatives that were developed by refugees outside the aid umbrella shows this. In Uganda, lessons were conducted 'under trees and in temporary erected structures. The majority of the teachers were the boys and girls whose education has been disrupted by the war in Sudan' (Ucanda 1993). Alere Secondary School, 'set up by the parents in the settlements' (Sesnan 1992), began as a copy of Lutaya, a self-help senior secondary school built by Ugandans when they were refugees in southern Sudan. 'Some very minor help with books, stationery etc has been given by EPSR [Education Programme for Sudanese Refugees]' (Sesnan 1992).[94] In Nairobi, despite having arrived only a few years before, Rwandans and Burundians were among the most active in establishing educational programmes. The Hope International School was established mainly by Burundian and Rwandan refugees who had taught in universities before fleeing their home country. It offered primary, secondary, and tertiary education in French. Another school, Kabiria, was established by a committee of Rwandan parents concerned about the education of their children, with the support of a priest of the Padri Monfortani Order and of a small Belgian Catholic grant-making body – Fondation Catholique des bourses d'études pour Africains (FONCABA) – and provided affordable education in French mainly to Burundian and Rwandan children. The Methodists also had a small primary education programme for Rwandan children based on the Rwandan curriculum.

Despite these initiatives undertaken by the refugees themselves, lack of educational opportunities, including primary education, was one of the main problems for refugees in Kenya and Uganda. JRS in Kenya had a small scholarship programme, which was run by Sister Louise Radlmeier. She lived outside Nairobi and housed many refugee children with extreme security problems. There were tensions within the JRS office as to the future of this programme, and complaints that the management intended to downsize it. With its meagre funds, the programme could not satisfy the educational needs of all refugees. Despite their numbers in Nairobi, Somalis hardly ever benefited from these scholarships, but the reason was probably also that many of them chose not to approach a Christian organisation or did not want to be educated in parish schools.

When Otim (1998) interviewed refugees at the JRS Mikono centre in Nairobi, he found that other nationalities often complained that the scholarship programme unfairly favoured Sudanese, whilst some Sudanese said that it was only Dinka who were favourably treated. Selecting refugee students in those circumstances posed real problems: carrying out meritocratic selection is difficult when the demand is so high, the backgrounds so different, and the funds so scarce.

A survey carried out between April 1995 and April 1996 of 2,342 Rwandan refugees, for the most part living in Nairobi but also including some in other cities like Mombasa, Eldoret, Thika, and Machakos, revealed that there were 510 children requiring primary education and 380 requiring secondary education.[95] Since educated Hutus were particularly targeted in Rwanda, a relatively large number of these refugees had completed a first degree at university (136) and wanted to pursue their studies at postgraduate level, including 65 people who held a *maitrise* and were hoping to undertake a doctoral degree. 205 refugees had completed their secondary education and wanted to study for a degree at university (Karara 1997: 31). One problem with offering scholarships for qualified refugees to attend Kenyan universities was that 'the funds required for each student in private university in Kenya are very large' (Karara 1997: 29).[96]

In the camps in Kenya, primary education was for the most part available, but secondary education had been phased out in Dadaab by 1996. Plans to reintroduce it were considered in 2000, and in 2001 a small secondary school was opened. In both Kakuma and Dadaab the general conditions in the camp affected the refugees' ability to go to school and to study. Lucy Weir taught English in Kakuma in 1997–98 and described some of the difficulties in teaching children who had to struggle for survival:

> Observation of these students revealed that they had to struggle extremely hard to meet the basic requirements for survival, and the additional strain of trying to meet their 'tertiary' needs, if that label can be applied to further education, often meant that they suffered to attend class. Many of the students skipped meals and others missed the only opportunity they had to collect water during the evening in order to be able to attend evening meetings or class committee meetings (which the students themselves organised). Attendance was interrupted frequently by illness, particularly malaria, brucellosis and typhoid, with those students whose personal histories were most traumatic experiencing the worst bouts.
>
> Initially, students expressed, both directly and indirectly (in debates and discussion) anger and frustration at a system which seemed designed to keep them on the very verge of survival. Certainly their essays and any creative work they were given to do reflected their need to express the degree of their suffering, in terms of lack of adequate nutrition, lack of shelter materials, lack of water and lack of security. Any discussion activities we had initially quickly dissolved into tirades of accusation of a lack of under-

standing on the part of workers in the camp of the harsh daily realities they had to face (Weir 1998).[97]

In Uganda, educational services for refugees, like all other services, were provided in the settlements. Primary education was provided by UNHCR in all the settlements, whereas secondary schools were present only in some and most of them had been started as self-help initiatives by the parents. Access to tertiary education was extremely limited, although Makerere University took a commendable decision in August 1998 to charge refugees the same tuition fees as nationals. The Hugh Pilkington Charitable Trust supported quite a few students in Makerere and other private universities like Ndejje Christian University. Another funding programme for tertiary education of refugees in Uganda – Deutsch-Afrikanische Frauen Initiative (DAFI) – was run by UNHCR, but in 1998 'DAFI had expressed regret to freeze this year's new sponsorship. It is therefore, clearly seen that, students who will pass to the university – 1998/99 will not be supported' (GoU-UNHCR 1998b).

In Uganda, between 1997 and 2000, there was a programme for providing secondary school scholarships to refugees. The programme, funded by UNHCR, was operated through the DoR at the MoLG. It worked with varying degrees of success, but camp commandants who selected the students were often accused of favouritism and embezzlement. Another problem was that resentment emerged in the local community not only because refugees were receiving scholarships but also because Ugandan students believed it unfair that refugee students were kept in school even when payment for their fees was delayed, while Ugandans were immediately expelled if their parents failed to pay punctually. The UNHCR/MoLG programme was abruptly stopped in 1999 after some Ugandan students had gone on strike against the perceived injustice of the system; at this point, UNHCR took over secondary education. It recommended that students be prepared for the inevitable costs that would be associated with any opportunities for post-primary education. UNHCR explained that:

> The present system with sponsorships given to students to study at boarding schools all over Uganda has become extremely expensive and benefits only a few refugee students. Due to shrinking funds the sponsorship scheme is being reduced and eventually eliminated.
>
> UNHCR is therefore making an effort to assist the district secondary schools to enable them to accommode [sic] additional refugee students and to encourage the students to enrol in local day schools which will be less costly and thus MoLG/UNHCR will be able to assist more students.[98]

At a meeting between UNHCR and secondary school authorities, it was announced that a plan to invest in the district secondary schools in order to build enough capacity to absorb additional refugees would be drawn and agreed upon with each secondary school in the district.

> This is the first meeting to inform the schools and initiate the process. The chairman suggested that agreements should be made with the local secondary schools such that UNHCR assist the respective schools to improve or add facilities that are required for the additional students and also to provide appropriate secondary education for the existing students.

> In exchange for the assistance the secondary schools enter into an agreement with MoLG/UNHCR to enrol a specific number of refugees for a number of successive years.[99]

UNHCR sub-office Pakelle concluded such an agreement with Moyo Town Day Secondary School.[100] Under a two-year agreement, the school would admit ninety refugee students at a reduced fee, USh 10,000 per term instead of USh 25,000, while UNHCR would pay the difference 'in the form of assistance with identified infrastructure development'.[101] Although this was supposedly a step towards the integration of services, the question was what would happen at the end of the two years? Would the school demand more infrastructural development before allowing the ninety refugee students to continue? By linking the improvements to the schools to individual students, UNHCR put the refugee students in a vulnerable position – giving school authorities a justification for dismissing them the following year if more infrastructural improvements were not provided.

Unsurprisingly, refugee students were not supportive of this scheme. They said: 'We are opposed, however, to the policy of conning NGOs to develop national schools that are *hostile* to refugee students. Past experience from the brutal expulsion of students from Metu S.S. [Secondary School] and Moyo S.S. ... [and] the issue of the alleged 18m shillings MoLG owes Metu S.S. tells us that national school administrators are not predictable.'[102]

Yet UNHCR had earlier ostensibly embraced a policy of integrating the educational services for refugees with those existing in the host communities,[103] and one of the key recommendations was: 'Admission quotas for refugees are undesirable (UNHCR 1995c: 31).' The same report proposed 'that the area around the camps and settlements be considered a "refugee-affected area" and that everyone working in these areas should make some provision for *Ugandans,* if their main focus is refugees, and for *refugees,* if their man [*sic*] focus is Ugandans' (UNHCR 1995c [emphasis in original]). Other recommendations on education included:

Recommendation Three
That all concerned should recognise that for Sudanese refugees in Uganda there is no reasonable alternative to education using the Ugandan system. However, Arabic and acceptable Sudanese History and Geography options should be available.

Recommendation Thirteen
Capital investment must be matched by an allocation of recurrent funds for a reasonable number of years.

Recommendation Fifteen
That neither refugees nor nationals should be excluded from education in any institution in the refugee-affected area simply because of nationality (ibid.: 21, 15, 27).

However, JRS opposed the implementation of this policy and for some time the idea of integrating educational services was shelved.

Although UNHCR appeared to be working hard to promote the education of refugees, its overriding concern with the possible 'pull factors' undermined these efforts:

Education is an important ingredient for a refugee child's development and survival but it could also be a pull factor attracting an excessively large number of refugees into a country … How do we distinguish between refugees who are really genuine from migrations who are just drifting between countries looking for possibilities of free (higher) education? … Possibilities for continuing studies after secondary school are extremely limited, but implications of a substantial increase will have to be carefully studied to avoid the 'official' establishment of a boarding school centre in exile for Southern Sudan (Brown 1999).

Thus, one of the fears with offering 'real' secondary education was that it could attract more students from Sudan. Such fears were not entirely unfounded, since in Juba alone there were fifteen secondary schools that were adopting Arabic as a language of instruction under a new policy of the government (Sesnan 1992). Moreover, in meetings we held with elders, students, and Refugee Welfare Committees (RWCs) in settlements in Palorinya, many of the refugees said that they had left Sudan because there were no educational opportunities owing to the war and – and although this was not explicitly stated – the fact that many would have been conscripted into the rebel sudan People's Liberation Army (SPLA).

In Kenya, in the period where no secondary education was available in Dadaab, the only form of post-primary education was 'peace education'.[104] While 'peace education' provided some educational activity in the camps at a time when only primary education was available, it could be argued that those resources should have been used to fund refugee students to attend Kenyan secondary schools. Donor policies, however, certainly played a role in decisions on how to allocate the scarce resources available, and, by the late 1990s, peace education and conflict resolution had become a fad. The peace education programme in Kenya in 1997–98, for example, was financed with earmarked funds. Peace education was defined as:

... the process of promoting a non-violent and co-operative way of living through teaching ideas about peace, and the skills to put these ideas into practice. The ideas can include the philosophy of peace, the theory of peacemaking, and the fact behind particular conflict situations. The skills, which are learned through experience can include co-operation, listening, empathy, communication and conflict resolution.

Peace education is about empowering people with the skills, attitudes, and knowledge:

- To build, maintain, and restore relationships at all levels of human interaction.

- To develop positive approaches towards dealing with conflicts – from the personal to the international.

- To create safe environments, both physically and emotionally, that nurture each individual.

- To create a safe world based on justice and human rights.

- To build a sustainable environment and protect it from exploitation and war.

Peace education is based on a philosophy that teaches non-violence, love, compassion, trust, fairness, cooperation and reverence for the human family and all life on our planet (Refugees and Educations Resources 1999).

Leaving aside the old Socratic question as to whether virtue can be taught, it is hard not to be sceptical about peace education programmes, which seem to be based on an oversimplified assumption about conflict: the idea that wars happen because people have not been taught that war is bad, and the corollary that hiring consultants to 'teach' peace amounts to 'conflict prevention'. This is simply 'nonsense upon stilts'. In Kenya and Uganda, the peace education programmes contained very little 'hard law', and human rights were normally presented in an insipid sermonising manner by people who often had little idea about the *legal* dimension of such rights. Moreover, the pedagogic effects of such programmes on refugee children who, unlike many of their peace educators, had direct experience of war, were not likely to be significant.

In setting up these peace education programmes while phasing out secondary education, UNHCR paid little attention to the law. As far as legal obligations are concerned, as mentioned, it is clear that there is an obligation to provide free primary education, and to make secondary education 'available and accessible to all by all appropriate means'. Peace education, however worthy an activity according to its proponents, is not the object of a specific right. Furthermore, as was the case for health care, retrogressive measures can amount to a prima facie violation of the right to education. The social cost of dismantling the secondary schools, of depriving many refugees of the possibility to pursue their studies, and of interrupting the studies of many others, was enormous. In this respect, the United Nations Relief and Works Agency (UNRWA) for Palestinian refugees offers an example of good practice. Early in the course of its existence it decided to focus on education, and this has continued to be its single largest area of activity, accounting for half its budget and two-thirds of it staff.[105]

In neither Kenya nor Uganda was UNHCR's policy of 'education for repatriation' being implemented. This was fortunate given that 'education for repatriation' means that refugees are taught in the curricula of their countries of origin and, at the end of their studies, their qualifications risk not being recognised in either the country of origin or the country of asylum. However, UNHCR often sees this approach as a corollary to the idea that repatriation is the best durable solution. As the UNHCR education coordinator in Kampala put it: 'Education/skills training for country of asylum may help refugees become self-reliant in the short term but may detract from the preferred durable solution of voluntary repatriation of country of origin' (Brown 1999).[106]

In Kenya, the Burundian and Rwandan self-help schools in Nairobi were following the curricula of the countries of origin. However, they were doing so somewhat reluctantly. In 1996 they tried to switch to the Kenyan syllabus but there were two problems. First, their teaching staff often did not speak English and did not feel competent to teach the Kenyan curriculum. Second, it was difficult for them to obtain recognition from the Kenyan Ministry of Education.

Another questionable aspect of the educational policy in Kenya and Uganda was that it was premised on the idea that the fairest way of using scarce resources was to offer a mediocre education to 'more' rather than a better education to 'fewer'. Thus, with the exception of the scholarship programme for Makerere, the tendency in both Kenya and Uganda was to place refugees in 'second-league' universities in those countries – that is, private religious universities. Even students of outstanding ability had thus little opportunity to go to the more reputable academic institutions in the host countries. Obviously, many nationals faced similar hardships. However, Kenyan and Ugandan students from underprivileged backgrounds had at least the possibility, albeit limited, of raising funds through work, from relatives, or from their communities, or, as is customary in Kenya, through *harambees*.[107]

Cultural rights

Article 15(1)(a) of the ICESCR provides that 'The States Parties to the present Covenant recognise the right of everyone to take part in cultural life' and incorporates article 27(2) of the UDHR which states that 'Everyone has the right to freely participate in the cultural life of the community.'

Article 246 of the Constitution of Uganda is a model provision since it spells out that 'any custom, practice, usage or tradition relating to a traditional leader or cultural leader which detracts from the rights of any person as guaranteed by this Constitution, shall be taken to be prohibited under that article' (art. 246 (4)).

In refugee camps and settlements, the idea of culture was subject to the interpretations of UNHCR and NGOs. The establishment of customary courts, the organisation of refugees in communities,[108] and the concession of wide and arbitrary powers to camp leaders were part of the system of indirect rule. Far from being neutral and respectful of cultural identities and processes, UNHCR in this way legitimised one particular interpretation of a given culture and gave support and funding to one party (normally the strongest one), thus contributing to the suppression and marginalisation of other voices and interpretations. As a result of these policies, 'cultural dissidents' were a group at particular risk. In Kakuma, the only remedy for refugees who were not prepared to accept the imposition of cultural norms as interpreted by their community leaders was their incarceration in the 'special protection area'.

In this respect, the example of the Sudanese Dinka refugees in Kakuma is telling. As has been discussed, officers of the SPLA were the self-appointed leaders of this 'community'. In the camp, they were tacitly allowed both to forcibly recruit minors and young men in the SPLA, and to divert some food aid to the rebels in southern Sudan. They were treated as the sole legitimate voice of the Dinka 'community', whereas dissident individuals and groups were not given any recognition. Indeed, when tension arose between the leaders and sections of the Sudanese population, UNHCR usually espoused the cause of the leaders, at times actively, more often by omitting to intervene even when it was required under its mandate. A frequent source of inter-community tension in Kakuma was the presence of thousands of Sudanese boys – for the most part Dinka – who, in exile, had developed their own set rules. For instance, these boys often refused to undergo military training and they rejected much Dinka custom on marriage and sexual relations.[109] UNHCR's policy on the Sudanese boys in Kakuma (usually still referred to as the 'unaccompanied minors' although most of them were no longer children) was to deny the acceptability, let alone the legality, of the practices that did not conform to Dinka traditional custom as interpreted by the SPLA-controlled leadership in Kakuma, and to encourage their forced assimilation into their 'community' of origin. The (sub-)culture developed by these boys was thus considered unworthy of protection, because it differed from Dinka 'custom'. The SPLA-dominated group of Sudanese refugees in Kakuma, like their counterparts in Nairobi, had relatively easy access to the staff of UNHCR and other UN agencies. A consequence of the policy of identifying 'authentic' representatives of certain communities was that UNHCR could at all times claim to be 'in contact with the Sudanese community', or to be 'aware of the claims' of the Sudanese refugees simply by having relations with one group of these refugees while neglecting the claims of others ('unaccompanied minors', women, draft-dodgers, mixed couples, political or cultural dissidents).

The problem, however, was not simply one of implementation. Some of the policies themselves were flawed. For example, UNHCR guidelines on children pay tribute to the cornerstone principle of child protection – the best interests of the child[110] – but specific policies often failed to achieve this. These guidelines referred to 'the conservation of culture' as a human right, explaining that: 'The social upheaval caused by the involuntary movement of individuals, families and communities, can dramatically affect the coherence of their culture. Normal social rules, values and controls begin to break down when the social group which provides the framework for their application disintegrates' (UNHCR 1994c: chap. III, 1). The guidelines then talk about 'restoring cultural normalcy' (ibid.: chap. III, 3) as one of the objectives of assistance and protection activities for children. The preservation of the status quo, and the promotion of traditional leadership, are seen as values in themselves. If there is no traditional leadership, then the aid worker can help identify the new leaders:

> A refugee population may already include part, if not all, of its traditional leadership. The aid worker can help to strengthen and reinforce traditional leaders by consulting and working through them. Preservation of the refugees' traditional form of social organization enhances not only their well-being but also the effectiveness of assistance efforts.

> New leaders: where a fragmented refugee population lacks traditional leaders, it may be necessary to assist the community in identifying new ones. In this situation it is of critical importance to ensure that the non-traditional leaders given support and credibility by the aid worker have the best interests of their community at heart rather than their own self interest (ibid.: chap. III, 3).

The UNHCR policy towards the Sudanese 'unaccompanied minors' in Kakuma was therefore probably viewed as part of the restoration of 'cultural normalcy'.

A misrepresentation of cultural rights and the corresponding obligations of states underlay these UNHCR policies and attitudes. At the field level, UNHCR officers often saw themselves as the defenders of endangered cultures and this led to a situation in which they were, in effect, supporting, encouraging, and funding practices in breach of human rights.[111] Moreover, such practices also constituted a violation of the very cultural rights they purported to protect as they interfered in a cultural process by giving legitimacy, as well as powers and funding, to the strongest voices. Human rights law does not recognise the right of groups to exact compliance with cultural practices (or certain interpretations of these) from individuals; instead, it enshrines the right of the individual to opt out of his or her own culture, or to embrace its norms and customs selectively. Finally, the use of mandatory customary practices in refugee camps also relied on the ill-conceived and pre-Freudian belief that individuals are always happy to adhere to the cultural norms of their groups.[112]

Cultures are open to challenges from within as well as from the outside. They normally accommodate a variety of often conflicting interpretations and voices, and they constantly undergo processes of social transformation and adaptation even to the extent of abandoning a particular custom. In some cases, such transformation is a legal requirement. For example, the Convention on the Elimination of All Forms of Discrimination against Women (CEDAW) requires states 'to take all appropriate measures to modify the social and cultural patterns of conduct of men and women' in order to eliminate 'prejudices and customary and all other practices', based on the stereotyping of gender roles or on ideas of gender inferiority or superiority (art. 5(a)). Those who are in power naturally perceive this potential for change as a threat. As observed by Pascal, who also saw this as a risk rather than a value, any custom may be overcome from within once its arbitrary nature is unmasked.[113] By promoting the forced membership of individuals in rigidly defined groups and their subjection to the 'cultural' norms of these groups, NGOs and UNHCR thus suppressed this intrinsic potential for change and reform, and promulgated the immutable authenticity of certain interpretations of a culture.[114]

Conclusion

In the refugee context, the UNHCR and NGOs, as the main providers of services such as education and health that are essential to the enjoyment of socio-economic rights, must be viewed as co-holders of the human rights obligations incumbent upon states, under treaty law or under customary international law (Verdirame 2001b). Delegating functions to international organisations and NGOs does not relieve host governments of their obligations under international law; in principle, they still bear responsibility at the international level for any wrongful acts committed by these organisations. At the very least, host states have a legal duty to monitor the extent to which UNHCR and NGOs are furthering socio-economic and cultural rights.

In both countries, violations of these fundamental rights were widespread, resulting from direct actions as well as from policies the consequences of which had been wilfully or negligently ignored. In some cases, governments, UNHCR, and NGOs failed to comply with their basic obligation – the obligation *to respect* that simply requires states *not* to take actions that can interfere with socio-economic and cultural rights. In other cases, they failed to take active steps to protect these rights, or to promote and facilitate their implementation. Encampment is as irreconcilable with economic, social, and cultural rights as it is with civil and political rights.

Notes

1. The Slavery Convention was adopted in 1926. The International Labour Organisation was established in 1919 and promoted labour standards through treaties from its very first year of existence, when it adopted conventions on hours of work and night work in the industry, and on maternity protection. The Forced Labour Convention (ILO Convention no. 29 of 1930) became one of the most important treaty instruments in the area of labour protection.
2. *See also* General Comment 3 adopted by the ICESCR Committee.
3. They have not entered reservations except for Kenya's one reservation to art. 10(2) – special protection of mothers before and after childbirth.
4. The last amendment to the Immigration Act was in 1972. It did not refer to the broader refugee definition under the OAU Convention. Kenya signed the OAU Convention in 1969 but only ratified it in 1992.
5. For some time, in the 1980s at least, it received funding from the World University Service, London.
6. Class A work permits are reserved for 'A person who is offered specific employment by a specific employer, who is qualified to undertake that employment, and whose engagement in that employment will be of benefit to Kenya'.
7. Criminal case no. IMM/MN/33/97.
8. Criminal case no. IMM/MN/35/97.
9. On the Ugandan reservations, see Chapter 1 **The legal framework in Uganda**.
10. *See*, e.g., UDHR art. 23 and ICESCR art. 7. Art. 24 of the 1951 Convention obliges states to treat refugees like nationals for various matters such as 'remuneration, including family allowances where these form part of remuneration, hours of work, overtime arrangements, holidays with pay, restrictions on home work, minimum age of employment, apprenticeship and training, women's work and the work of young persons, and the enjoyment of the benefits of collective bargaining'.
11. Interview with William Sakataka, Pakelle, 22 August 1998.
12. Ibid.
13. Letter from G.A. Adrabo, head of section – education, to the programme coordinator, DED, Rhino camp, 30 December 1997.
14. UNHCR later terminated its implementing partnership with AVSI, which had been the main implementing NGO for Kyangwali and Achol-Pii.
15. Interview with Stephen Wani, coordinator for Palorinya, 23 February 1998.
16. Ibid.
17. *See also* Chapter 4 **Freedom from slavery and forced labour and the violation of other labour standards**.
18. Email from Tim Brown, UNHCR, 18 August 1999.

19. This and subsequent data comes from Hannah Garry's field notes and interview, Adjumani district, February 1998.
20. Projects are often funded for only one year, but there is no reason why refugees could not be given one-year contracts.
21. They were earning USh. 31,000 with JRS, 42,000 with AEF. At the same time, a driver in Kampala working for a primary school was earning USh. 100,000 (case no. 040/DRC/U/1998).
22. Focus group with teachers, Adjumani, 12 February 1998 (Hannah Gary's field notes).
23. Focus group, Adjumani, 18 February 1998.
24. Interview, 13 March 1998.
25. Focus group, Adjumani, 18 February 1998.
26. Throughout, we were reminded of Kapuscinski's words: 'What could this man have been yesterday? A sower in the spring, a harvester in the fall ... And today? A refugee, with a bowl in his hand, queuing for soup. What a waste of human energy, I think, an abasement of dignity ... a billion people capable of work with nothing or almost nothing to do for the duration of their lives ... If they could be given worthwhile occupations, humanity could make dizzying progress. The world's wealth would be doubled. Pyramids of Merchandise would rise in even the poorest countries. Granaries would overflow. Water would flood the deserts' (Kapuscinski 1991).
27. These ranged from factory packers (case no. 155/SUD/U/1999) to mechanics (case no. 026/DRC/U/1999), medical doctors (case no. 214/DRC/U/1999) laboratory assistants (case no. 031/DRC/U/1999), businessmen (case no. 183/DRC/U/2000), artists (case no. 184/DRC/U/1999), priests (case no. 029/DRC/U/2000), hairdressers (case no. 195/SUD/U/1999), engineers (case no. 155/DRC/U/1999), and musicians (case no. 037/DRC/K/1997).
28. *See* Chapter 3 *'First country of asylum'*.
29. Dr Buregeya found a position at the University of Nairobi.
30. *See* Chapter 4 **Freedom of expression, thought, conscience and religion, and freedom of assembly and association**.
31. *See* above *Incentives*.
32. *See* Chapter 4 *The stereotyping of gender*.
33. *See* Chapter 4 **Freedom of movement**.
34. This is the position of the Committee on Economic, Social and Cultural Rights: 'In the Committee's view, the right to housing should not be interpreted in a narrow or restrictive sense which equates it with, for example, the shelter provided by merely having a roof over one's head or views shelter exclusively as a commodity. Rather it should be seen as the right to live somewhere in security, peace and dignity ... As both the Commission on Human Settlements and the Global Strategy for Shelter to the Year 2000 have stated: "Adequate shelter means ... adequate privacy, adequate space, adequate security, adequate lighting and ventilation, adequate basic infrastructure and adequate location with regard to work and basic facilities – all at a reasonable cost"' (ICESCR 1991: para. 7).
35. This was, albeit not officially stated in these terms, the practice in some countries in the 'developed world'. Combined with the restrictions on the right to seek paid employment, the erosion of social security has resulted in the relegation of refugees to a sort of *Lumpenproletariat*, even more marginalised socially than nationals in similar conditions of deprivation.
36. In Kakuma an agricultural programme was started by the International Rescue Committee (IRC), but the plots each measured one square metre.

37. *See* footnote 34.
38. The standard provided for by the Geneva Convention (III) Relating to the Treatment ofPrisoners of War is higher than the policy and practice of UNHCR/WFP for refugees. Art. 26 of this Convention states: 'The basic daily food rations shall be sufficient in quantity, quality and variety to keep prisoners of war in good health and to prevent loss of weight or the development of nutritional deficiencies. Account shall also be taken of the habitual diet of the prisoners.' This provision obliges states to measure performance in terms of results, something which neither UNHCR nor WFP normally do.
39. Malnutrition is not a cause of death per se, but death can result from a disease which either has been contracted because of malnutrition or has become fatal because of it (Rangasami 1989; de Waal 1997).
40. The UNHCR representative, Hans Thoolen, defended the policy of pegging food assistance to the encampment at a workshop organised by UNHCR/OPM on 'Who does what and how?', 17 February 1999.
41. Observations by Mauro De Lorenzo in Adjumani, August 2000. We also observed similar conditions among new arrivals in the camps for Burundi refugees in Kibondo, Tanzania (Harrell-Bond et al. 2000).
42. In Tanzania, Porter (2001) found that in health status, refugees do not do as well as locals, with morbidity levels much higher in the new camps and still considerably higher in the old camps than in the nearby villages. He found that the supplementary feeding programme resulted in a stunting in the growth of children and that the stunting was 'dose-related' – that is, the more food they got the less they grew (2001: 194–99 and email 21 March 2002).
43. The 1994 Memorandum of Understanding was equally comprehensive (UNHCR/WFP 1994).
44. Interview with WFP, Dagahaley, 2 November 1997.
45. Interview with Mathijs La Rutte, protection officer, Dadaab, 26 April 1998.
46. Interview with M.R., Ifo camp, 28 April 1998.
47. Interview with Stephen Wani, coordinator for Palorinya, ACORD, 13 February 1998.
48. It was possible for Waldman to collect these data because the volcanic soil in Goma made burials impossible, and people had to lay their dead on the side of the road to be collected for mass burial elsewhere (Toole and Waldman 1997).
49. Interview with Daniel Deng Dau, Kakuma camp, 23 July, 1997.
50. Interview, 15 July 1997.
51. Chapter 6 *Image management: reporting the field.*
52. Before coming to Kenya, he was medical director of Lofa County, Liberia, for five years and subsequently served in refugee and displaced camps in and around Monrovia as a volunteer. He was trained at the Hadassah Medical School, Jerusalem, and completed postgraduate training in surgery in the UK in 1981.
53. [Footnote in the passage quoted] 'I was told that this distribution would be repeated every three months. I protested that this distribution would have no nutritional impact. I was informed, however, that this distribution had been determined to be sufficient by the senior medical co-ordinator of UNHCR, Nairobi.'
54. [Footnote in the passage quoted] 'Subsequently, it has been brought to my attention that in April 1996, preceding my arrival in Kakuma, that food had been withdrawn from the entire population for 14 days, part of the collective punishment imposed for an incident in which the food distribution centre had been destroyed by a few individuals and it was suggested that this might have been the cause of the high rates of anaemia I diagnosed on my arrival. In fact, the rate of anaemia remained more or less constantly high throughout

my tenure. I found that the food distributed every two weeks was normally consumed in three to four days.'

55. For another reference to the low haemoglobin count of 1.8 of a Sudanese minor, *see* Stanley 1998: 4 fn 1.

56. We came across Dr Babu Swai later in our research when he was transferred to Uganda. Months after the Red Cross had recommended one seriously ill refugee for follow-up medical care after surgery in Kampala, he was referred by the new senior protection officer to Dr Swai. According to this refugee, 'The next morning I went there and the doctor told me that he would not do anything and that I should return to the camp ... I was shocked to hear such a thing from this doctor as he did not apparently like to talk with a patient who is almost dying' (case no. 097/DRC/U/1999). Unlike in the case of Dr Guluma, we did not come across other evidence to verify this testimony.

57. Interview with Dr Guluma, Nairobi, 28 June 1997.

58. Letter from Lt. Col. Bonnie L. Smoak, MD, US army medical research unit-Kenya, US embassy, 14 October 1997.

59. This 1997 IRC report also includes a report of a project, Household Food Security, which describes vegetable growing in the camps. It includes a table indicating that a total of 3,422 people were farming a total 10,591 plots. The table does not remind the reader that there are at least 40,000 people in Kakuma. Nor does it elaborate on the *size* of the plots, which were dependent on 'household waste-water, or on free land near the public water tap-stands ...' All it says is that 'plots vary between 1 square meter to over 100 square meters accumulatively ...' (IRC 1997: 35).

60. Letter, 5 November 1997.

61. Letter from Dr Philista Onyango, director of ANPPCAN, to Mr Ebrima Camara, acting representative, UNHCR, 1 April 1997; Email from Marguerite Garling to Philista Onyango, ANPPCAN, 27 March 1997.

62. When discussing the case of Dr Guluma, a WFP employee commented on how unwise he had been to speak out, and added that one had to make compromises to keep one's job.

63. A few community leaders, like Alice Lakwena in Dadaab, having access to the free labour of her 'boys', as she called them, had a relatively spacious and solidly built dwelling.

64. Art. 17 of the ICCPR also guarantees that 'No one shall be subjected to arbitrary or unlawful interference with his privacy, family [or] home'.

65. *See* Chapter 4 *Physical safety in camps and settlements.*

66. This is a common problem because humanitarian organisations are often unaware of the unfair competition and the consequent resentment against refugees felt by the local population that a 'tax free status' introduces in such situations. For instance, in both Dadaab and Kakuma camps, the same situation was instituted and similar tensions were experienced.

67. Many of the Somali refugees who were 'repatriated' actually returned to Kenya within a few weeks after realising that the situation in Somalia was not yet safe.

68. A decision based upon what they knew of security for their clan in either place.

69. *See also* African Charter on Human and Peoples' Rights (1981), art. 16. The specific human rights instruments, like the CEDAW (1979, art. 12) and the CRC (1989, art. 24), also enshrined the right to health.

70. In 1990, over 40 percent of health expenditure in sub-Saharan Africa was private, and about 10 percent of public expenditure was financed through foreign aid (van Damme 1998: 31, figure 11).
71. There are some exceptions. For example, the government attempted to avoid the parallel system in Malawi in the early 1990s and received support from the UNHCR representative at the time. In Guinea a similar policy was followed at least in the health sector (van Damme 1998).
72. This is normally the view of UNHCR, host governments ,and the local population, but is not, however, shared by refugees. For example, in her study Mulumba reported that, 'All persons interviewed expressed the view that refugees were receiving better quality health services than their hosts. The Director of District Health Services in Arua summarized it thus "refugee services are better, access is better, staffing is higher and morale is better"' (1999). It is impossible, however, to judge whether UNHCR and NGOs are meeting the health needs of particular age or gender groups since health data is not disaggregated.
73. Nancy Godfrey has added other factors specific to refugees: there are marked demographic changes, with higher or lower than average proportions of women, children, and elderly; illness and death may be more frequent, more severe; mental stress is an overriding problem; health and nutritional conditions may change rapidly; and there are usually increased injuries, trauma, and disability from armed conflict (1991).
74. Asylum-seekers did not receive health care in either country, except for the sporadic and limited assistance offered in Nairobi and Kampala by the JRS.
75. It must be emphasised that these statistics normally need to be taken with a pinch of salt. The data are not generally disaggregated and, as a result, it is not possible to know whether the health needs of a particular age group or of one gender are met.
76. Letter from Mr Stefano Pizzi, AVSI, to Zachary Lomo, 5 January 1999; case no. 78/DRC/U/1998.
77. Letter from Zachary Lomo to Stefano Pizzi, AVSI of 15 January 1999.
78. *See also* case no. 097/DRC/U/1999, in Chapter 4 *Acts by the state.*
79. Word also reached UNHCR Geneva as the articles were scanned and transmitted by email. *See* Reynell 2000; Mohammed 2000; Editorial 2000; Oliver 2000; and Oroma 2000.
80. These were refugees who had been placed there because they were at risk of abduction by agents from their countries of origin and could not be protected from such a risk even in refugee settlements. Ironically, several weeks earlier these refugees had been given notice to quit the place and find their own housing. They did not leave, and their food was cut off (31 December 1999).
81. Information from Ronald Kalyango (2000).
82. This threat would not be taken lightly, because people employed by UNHCR are in a privileged position as regards salaries and unemployment among university graduates is very high in Uganda.
83. This was the case, for example, with Eroni Nakagwa's Kabiro clinic, a primary health care project in Kawangware, Nairobi. Ms Nakagwa, a Ugandan refugee, set up this programme in the 1980s to provide for both the local and the refugee population. The latter at the time comprised primarily Ugandans. In 1997, the project with its limited funds still helped Ugandan refugees from the 1980s, as well as nationals and other refugees, for the most part from the Great Lakes.

84. In 2001, a refugee eligible for assistance received USh 57,000 per month or roughly US$ 33 to cater for rent, water, electricity, food, clothing, and all other basic needs. The cheapest one-room accommodation without proper sanitary facilities, water, or electricity costs USh 20,000. How much would a refugee have available to pay for health services after paying for food, clothing, and other basic needs?

85. One of them was Mr Gaspard Rutama, mentioned by Harrell-Bond (1999d), an elderly Rwandan who had spent most of his life in Uganda. His medical report by Dr Lydia AZ Mpanga MRCP (UK), compiled in April 1997, contained a long list of health problems arising from chronic malaria and malnutrition, but he complained that, because of his age, he received no attention.

86. At the time of our visit to the Hatimy camp in September 1997, it seemed inevitable that his relocation to Kakuma, threatened since 1993, would take place as planned before December 1997. Mr Abdullahi feared that he was not even going to survive the long journey from the coast to Kakuma.

87. They were doing 'first screening' interviews, filling in a form with personal data for the applicant and taking decisions on status determination, for which they were not qualified.

88. Interview with Dr Deppner by Deborah Mulumba, 9 March 1998.

89. The Vienna Declaration and Programme of Action, adopted at the end of the World Conference on Human Rights, should also be mentioned, although the reference to reproductive issues in it is short.

90. Interview with Dr Deppner by Deborah Mulumba, 9 March 1998.

91. In Adjumani there was a sign announcing an HIV/AIDS NGO but if it was active at all, it did not work among the refugees.

92. Focus group with Kali Women's Committee, 11 March 1998.

93. While the Kenyan Constitution does not protect the right to education, or any other social and economic right, following the December 2002 elections, the government announced as its first action that free primary education was being introduced. The primary schools were immediately overwhelmed as children (and their parents) asserted their right to education.

94. But later UNHCR stepped in and funded the school.

95. This study was done in the hope that it would be useful for fundraising. It was conducted by a Rwandan refugee. He travelled to all of these places and distributed the questionnaire to a non-random sample. He had no funding except some contributions for his expenses.

96. These data confirm that the educational profile of the Rwandan refugee population in Nairobi was very high in comparison with national statistics for Kenya and Uganda: the secondary school enrolment rate was 9 percent in Uganda in 1998 (UNDP 2002) while no data were available for Kenya; the tertiary education enrolment rate was 1.46 percent in Kenya and 2.05 percent in Uganda in the last year when data were available (available from the statistics section at www.unesco.org).

97. In Kakuma, one easily remediable factor that prevented many Somali boys from attending school was that it was 'compulsory' for them to wear shorts rather than trousers (Weir 1998). As for the girls, non-attendance during menstruation was common, since girls were not given sanitary pads and there were no separate toilet facilities in the schools. Boys' taunts were probably another factor negatively affecting girls' attendance.

98. Minutes of the Consultative Meeting between UNHCR and Secondary School Authorities on Refugee Students' Education, sub-office Pakelle, 5 February 1998.

99. Ibid.

100. Agreement between UNHCR sub-office Pakelle and Moyo Town Day Secondary School, 22 July 1998. UNHCR reference SOP.L.030H-98.
101. Ibid.
102. Interview with refugee secondary students, Moyo town, 27 February 1998.
103. A similar pattern characterises UNHCR's approach to social services all over Africa. For example, in Ivory Coast, which opposed the settlement of refugees in camps and allowed them to settle freely among the local population, parallel health structures and separate schools for refugees were imposed by UNHCR until it ran out of money in 1997. At that point, it started to speak the language of integration of services (Kuhlman 2001).
104. 'Peace education' programmes have indeed blossomed throughout refugee camps in the whole East African region, as we could confirm during research trips in camps for the Burundians in Kibondo, Tanzania, where, again, with the exception of Kanembwa camp, there were no secondary schools in the camps.
105. *See* 'Programme Management', www.un.org/unrwa/progs/edu/pro.html.
106. In Tanzania, UNHCR was following this policy and the refugees in Kibondo were educated in the Burundian syllabus. In 1999, UNHCR negotiated an agreement with the Buyoya government – from which those refugees had fled – for the Burundian Ministry of Education to participate in the marking of the final year exams and to issue 'proper' Burundian diplomas. It surprised only a few that in the end the Burundian government did not honour its commitment and the students literally sat in their classrooms waiting for examination papers that never arrived.
107. A practice whereby the community raises funds for worthy causes.
108. As noted by Hyndman, in spite of so much rhetoric to the contrary, 'a refugee camp is not a community ... (it) is an institution organized as a temporary solution to displacement', and in which refugees 'are the subjects of a tacit and unsatisfactory policy of containment by which camps are enforced 'colonies', not communities defined by voluntary association ... In exchange for temporary asylum and the provision of basic needs, refugees forfeit a number of entitlements' (Hyndman 1996).
109. Particularly unacceptable to the Dinka leaders is the fact that a number of Sudanese boys 'take other boys as their wives' (Interviews with Deng Dau, leader of the Sudanese Dinka community, July 1997).
110. *See* Convention on the Rights of the Child.
111. On the institutional ethos of humanitarian workers, *see* Walkup 1997a. On the imagery of self-appointed defenders of endangered natives, *see* Sontag 1991: 86.
112. In *Civilisation and Its Discontents* Freud argued that subjection to social and cultural norms is often a source of discontent and neurosis (1984).
113. *See* Pascal (1961: 152–3): 'The art of opposition, of revolt against States is to undermine established customs, reaching to their foundations in order to unveil their lack of authority and justice ... and they [the people] should not realise the fact of appropriation; the law, introduced once without reason, has become reasonable; it must continue to be regarded as authentic, eternal, and its origin must be concealed, unless we want it to come to an end.'
114. *See*, for example, case no. 107/SOM/U/1998, discussed in Chapter 4 *Sexual violence*.

6

Refugee Protection:
What Is Going Wrong?

Introduction

As we have shown in the preceding chapters, the human rights of refugees in Kenya and Uganda were violated in a variety of ways. Encampment was the worst aspect of refugee policy in both countries; a radical change in this respect might not have been a panacea for all the problems faced by refugees, but would have certainly gone a long way at improving respect for their human rights. Among the plethora of negative consequences of refugee camps that have been documented are the link between encampment and epidemics (e.g., van Damme 1996, 1998), environmental degradation (e.g., Black 1998), the radicalisation of ethnic identity (e.g., Malkki 1995), and the breakdown of 'community' (e.g., Harrell-Bond 1986; Hyndman 1996). Camps (and settlements) are wrongly perceived as an efficient way of depoliticising refugees by controlling their movements (Karadawi 1983; Malkki 1995), and as expedient for the provision of humanitarian assistance (Harrell-Bond 1986). Encampment also violates the fundamental right to the freedom of movement that is essential to the enjoyment of all other rights. It also constitutes a unique setting for the arbitrary exercise of power.

As a long-term strategy, camps are not good for host states because the presence of refugees cannot be used as a catalyst for economic development (e.g., Kuhlman 1990, 2001; Mollett 1991; Zetter 1992), and because they undermine local institutions (e.g., Goyen et al. 1996). Camps can also become enclaves of political ferment and even bases for military activity. They are not good for donor states either, because they cost more (with less return) than investments geared towards integration and development (Harrell-Bond 1996a).

If encampment is bad for everyone, why does it remain the preferred solution to long-term refugee crises in Africa? The short answer is that the 'camp pathology' has become entrenched in UNHCR's modus operandi in Africa and elsewhere, since it satisfies the *short-term* needs of donors and host states. The empirically (and historically) false assumption that refugees are temporary has buttressed this approach: once exile is seen as temporary, it is easy to justify the hardship as a short-term purgatory before the 'inevitable' journey home. More original solutions leading to the socio-economic integration of refugees through developmental assistance are for the most part ignored. Early on, the 'integrated rural development land settlement schemes' developed by the World Bank and other donors in the 1960s in order 'to *modernise* Africa and other backward parts of the world' (Daley 1989; Harrell-Bond and Voutira 1997: 14) have also contributed to UNHCR's adherence to the policy of encampment. The idea that people had to be uprooted and resettled in an organised and efficient manner in order to promote development found support both in centrally-planned socialist economies and in free-market capitalist countries.

UNHCR's promotion of repatriation as the best 'durable solution' to the refugee problem has consolidated the policy of encampment, on the grounds that refugees are temporary. The other two potential 'durable solutions' – integration and resettlement – have been sidelined: integration because UNHCR does not consider it feasible or appropriate, and resettlement because it can be available to only a small percentage of the refugee population in countries in the 'developing world'. Having embraced the 'camp solution' and exercising administrative control in refugee camps and settlements in Kenya and Uganda, UNHCR and NGOs were less able to act as advocates for refugee rights. For their part, host governments left policy making and the day-to-day running of refugee affairs to UNHCR and international NGOs, only becoming involved when security or foreign policy interests were perceived to be at stake (*see* Karadawi 1977, 1983, 1999).

In this synergy of dysfunctions, misperceptions, and ossified modi operandi, each actor involved with refugees – host countries, donors, UNCHR, NGOs – played a different role.

Host countries

In Kenya and Uganda, government officials responsible for refugee matters often asserted that refugees were 'the responsibility of UNHCR'. In Kenya, the government maintained that Kenya was a country of transit. However, the fact that UNHCR had upstaged host governments in the management of refugee policy cannot absolve states of their international legal commitments (Verdirame 2001b: 113–28). Government officials did not seem to be aware of this, and, in a vicious circle, UNHCR, the organisation that was supposed to remind governments of their international legal obligations, was loath to do so.

As explained in Chapter 1, it is not entirely clear whether the 'power shift' from the governments to UNHCR happened as a result of pressure from UNHCR, or whether governments requested a reluctant UNHCR to take over. The most likely explanation is that this handover of refugee matters to UNHCR was seen by both the governments and UNHCR as in their mutual interests, and, from UNHCR's point of view, it was also seen as in the refugees' interests. UNHCR was thereby in a position to seek more funds from donor countries, while governments believed that they were ridding themselves of a 'burden'.

Accusations of endemic corruption in the host states give UNHCR and NGOs another reason to justify their control over refugee matters, even after UNHCR's own problems with financial accountability came to light. Despite a series of articles published in the *Financial Times* (*FT*) in 1998, and the resettlement scandal in the Nairobi office in 2000,[1] donor countries continued to prefer to support UNHCR rather than host governments in Africa.

Uganda enjoyed a good reputation with donor countries in the 1990s, but it failed to exploit it to solicit funds for refugee programmes.[2] On the other hand, Kenya's relations with donor states in the 1990s were troubled. A series of financial scandals had brought corruption in Kenya under the international spotlight. International financial institutions put pressure on the government to adopt new legislation to fight corruption and in 1997 an International Monetary Fund (IMF) loan for over US$ 200 million was suspended. In 1997–99 no disbursements were made from the IMF to Kenya, worsening the economic crisis. The government reacted by setting up the Kenya Anti-Corruption Authority, which was later declared unconstitutional by the High Court, forcing the ruling party to repackage the authority and present it to parliament as a constitutional amendment. One positive consequence of the fact that funds for refugee programmes were entirely channelled through UNHCR and NGOs was that this crisis in the relationship between Kenya and donor institutions did not affect funding for refugees directly.[3]

Ubiquitous corruption had a direct effect on the life and security of refugees: there was a clear nexus between corruption in the police and the arbitrary arrest and detention to which refugees were routinely subjected. As discussed in Chapter 4, periodic police swoops became a fund-raising exercise for the police, with most refugees having to pay bribes to 'buy' freedom from detention or avoid arrest in the first place.[4] In Nairobi, many refugees we interviewed cited police abuse and corruption as one of the main sources of insecurity. The practice of extorting bribes from refugees had not permeated the police in Uganda to the same extent as in

Kenya, and our work with the police revealed that there was room for improving the situation through training. However, with police salaries being very low in Uganda, the risk of such a pattern developing was considerable.

Owing to the lack of diplomatic protection from their country of origin and the uncertainty concerning their status, refugees – more than any other group – were vulnerable to failures in the rule of law. The 'face' of the host state that they saw was usually repressive: police roundups, detention, forced recruitment, and, in the worst cases as in parts of northern Uganda and in Dadaab in the early 1990s, torture, sexual violence, and assassinations by the security forces. Nor did the refugees' segregation in camps run by UNHCR and NGOs shield them from abuses by authorities in Kenya and Uganda.

Legal reform, and in particular the adoption of the Ugandan Constitution of 1995, meant that there was, arguably, more potential in Uganda than in Kenya for using the law to advance refugee protection. The Ugandan Constitution not only formally enumerated human rights but also provided an enforcement machinery. The Uganda Human Rights Commission (UHRC), a quasi-judicial body set up under the new Constitution and entrusted with the promotion of human rights, took an active interest in refugee matters.[5] The UHRC also began to investigate a case involving a refugee's claim against UNHCR, but concluded that it had no jurisdiction because of the provision that prevents it from investigating 'a matter involving the relations or dealings between the Government and any doctrine of the State or international organisation' (art. 53(4)). In Kenya, on the other hand, by 1997 the Bill of Rights had been dead letter for nearly a decade.[6] The Kenyan government's Standing Committee on Human Rights was neither a quasi-judicial body nor an independent one, and its ability to promote respect for human rights was limited. The chairman himself displayed a rather nonchalant attitude to human rights, asserting during a public presentation that 'freedom of expression has to be put in context and interpreted against the background of what is right and what is wrong to say'.[7] The committee played no role and took no active interest in refugee matters.

Weaknesses in the rule of law were compounded by the failure to adopt adequate legislation on refugees. Xenophobia and slowness in the law-making process cannot fully account for this failure. The political class – majority and opposition alike – seldom engaged with refugee issues at all. Most politicians, as well as civil servants in departments that were not directly concerned with refugees, were simply oblivious to refugee issues. UNHCR might be criticised for failing to play its part in raising awareness of refugees amongst politicians, but this does not justify, for example, the compliant silence of the Kenyan opposition when President Moi made the inflammatory statements against refugees and foreigners that normally preceded police swoops. Civil society was left at the margins of the law-making process: in Kenya, officials at the Ministry of Home Affairs and at the Office of the Attorney General were generally reluctant to consult with local activists on law making about refugees and, when approached directly by activists, they were hesitant to cooperate.

Both Kenya and Uganda had laws to regulate NGOs (*see* Adiin-Yaansah 1995). Yet provisions in the legislation aimed at making NGOs accountable were seldom invoked and never thoroughly applied. International NGOs working with refugees, except for submitting annual reports, were basically exempt from regulation. In Kenya, many had failed to register as required by the Non-governmental Organisations Coordination Act. In both countries, foreign doctors employed by NGOs to work in refugee camps did not normally seek permission to practice from the Ministries of Health. This meant, for example, that their reports in cases of rape could not be used as evidence in court. Government attitudes towards NGOs were ambivalent. It was exclusively foreign NGOs that could benefit from this laissez-faire attitude on the part of the authorities. National NGOs, especially human rights ones, were at times obstructed in their work and exposed to harassment – or they protected themselves by self-censorship (Lomo 1999a).

Foreign policy played a role in decisions to grant asylum, and in the treatment and freedoms accorded to refugees. An example of the impact of foreign-policy considerations on refugees in Kenya was the reaction to the shift in the balance of power in the Great Lakes. By 1996, the US had begun to actively support the Rwanda Patriotic Front (RPF) government in Rwanda. In April/May 1997, the Rwandan–Ugandan alliance managed to oust Mobutu from Kinshasa. Before these events, Kenya had broken diplomatic ties with the RPF government following the attempted assassination of Seth Sendashonga, a minister in the first RPF government in 1994, who had defected to become a prominent dissident and refugee in Kenya.[8] Its attitude to the International Criminal Tribunal for Rwanda (ICTR) had been defiant, with the president stating that Kenya would never surrender any Rwandan on its territory.

In the run-up to the December 1997 elections, the political climate was inflamed. The electoral registration process was denounced as deeply flawed and opposition leaders complained of harassment by the government. Anti-government rallies took place in June–July 1997, '*Moibutu*' being sometimes chanted by the demonstrators. On 7 July ('Saba Saba') about fourteen demonstrators were killed, mainly in Nairobi. Between August and October 1997, ethnic strife on the Coast Province caused the death of dozens and led to the displacement of thousands. The elections also took place at a time of great regional unrest, which saw the fall Mobutu in Zaire and the isolation of Kenya on a regional scene dominated by the Rwanda–Uganda alliance. Given the support of the US government for Rwanda and the 'wait-and-see' position adopted by the British, the Kenyan establishment had some reason to feel under siege internationally as well as domestically. Several civil servants we interviewed feared the fall of the regime, and conspiracy theories were rampant. The comments of one civil servant reflect this mood of apprehension:

> Many countries in this region have been destabilised by influxes of refugees. Museveni, Kagame, Kabila, all gained power through the gun. Uganda and Rwanda have now admitted their direct involvement in the Zairean war. Kenya has to be very cautious because dangerous elements could come to the country as refugees and try to start something similar to what happened in neighbouring countries. What if Museveni decides to sponsor a guerrilla movement in Kenya through refugees who are not real refugees?[10]

In the end, the divisions in the opposition proved providential to the Moi regime and were probably one of the main factors that delayed its fall by five years.

The attitude of the Kenyan authorities towards refugees, and towards Rwandans in particular, hardened after July 1997, following a visit by members of the Rwandan government in Nairobi – the first encounter between representatives of the two countries since diplomatic relations had been severed after the Sendashonga incident. In some respects, this was a positive change. Kenya finally decided to cooperate with the ICTR over ten Rwandan suspects. However, the change in policy also meant that 'Hutu' refugees in general, from both Rwanda and Burundi, suddenly became a target for arbitrary arrest and detention. The precarious 'protection' from abuse that these refugees had enjoyed until then was over, and dozens, if not hundreds, were rounded up in July 1997. Thereafter police swoops continued with regular frequency.

Kenya's attitude towards Sudanese refugees was also deeply influenced by its foreign policy. The Kenyan government had traditionally taken a benign attitude towards the Sudan People's Liberation Army (SPLA), even allowing it to have an office in Nairobi in the 1990s. Moreover, as noted, the SPLA controlled the leadership of the Sudanese refugee community in Kakuma (UNHCR 1995b: 2; Crisp 2000a). This government support for the SPLA meant that large numbers of Sudanese refugees, who had escaped *from* the SPLA, did not find security and protection in Kenya.[11] However, after the assassination of Kerubino Kuanyan Bol in September 1999, allegedly by members of the SPLA, Kenya's hospitality cooled.

In Uganda, the alliance between the SPLA and Museveni's government was even closer, dating back to the 1980s when the National Resistance Army (NRA) had counted on the help of the SPLA to force refugees in settlements in Southern Sudan back to Uganda. By 1986, the SPLA had attacked settlements in the East Bank of the Nile, and was guilty of sexual violence, torture, and looting. In 1987–88, the settlements in the West Bank of the Nile became the target of these SPLA attacks aimed at pushing Ugandan refugees back. As a result of this alliance that went back a long way, leaders of the SPLA, including John Garang, had free rein in Uganda, as the widespread forced recruitment and military training showed. Refugees from the Democratic Republic of Congo (DRC) and Rwanda paid a heavy toll in terms of insecurity in Uganda because of the Uganda People's Defence Forces (UPDF) involvement in the conflict in the DRC and its close links with the RPF government (at least until late 1999–2000).

Uganda differed from Kenya because the politicisation of refugees had been an important feature of its political life at least since the 1970s. For example, during Amin's rule, Sudanese refugees were not only recruited into the Uganda army, sometimes as officers, but they were also believed to have been the main executioners in Amin's infamous 'State Research Bureau'. Museveni's NRA drew decisive support from Rwandan refugees. Its intelligence section was headed by Major (later Major General) Paul Kagame, who became the head of the Rwandan Patriotic Army (RPA) after the death of Major-General Fred Rwigyema in the first days of the 1990 attack on Rwanda.[12] He then became vice-president in 1994, and president in 2000. The officers in charge of northern Uganda in 1986 were almost exclusively Rwandans.[13]

Short-sighted political and economic calculations, foreign policy, and disregard for the rule of law were the key factors that hindered a positive engagement by national governments with refugees. The fact that refugees were politically disenfranchised meant that they could not seek to benefit from the softening of authoritarian rule that took place in both countries in the 1990s. With the collapse of the Moi regime in Kenya in December 2002, a new window of opportunity for a significant shift in refugee policy has opened up. A process of policy reassessment is on the way, and various comments by the new minister of home affairs, Moody Awori MP, indicate that the government is considering an integration-based approach to refugees in Kenya.

Donor countries

Donors have had a significant impact on refugee assistance policy in Kenya and Uganda – for the simple reason that their funding accounts for the vast majority of services that exist for refugees. Kenya and Uganda were not spared the contradictory message that donor countries usually send to refugee-hosting countries in the 'developing world': on the one hand, they emphasise respect for human rights and the strengthening of democratic institutions; on the other hand, they impel developing countries to adopt restrictive policies in order to protect the boundaries of 'Fortress Europe' (or 'Fortress Australia').

Ironically, the likelihood is that, if the rights of refugees in host countries in the 'developing world' were respected, if refugees were given an opportunity to integrate into their host societies, and if they could find safe asylum in countries of the 'developing world', for many of them the need to leave in search of another country of asylum would cease to exist. Restrictionism, as currently practised, thus becomes a contributing factor to the 'problem' that it aims to solve – namely the apparently high number of people seeking asylum in the countries of the 'developed world'. Yet donors still choose to promote the inhumane and unworkable logic of control and containment of refugees in countries in the 'developing world'. They have found states in the 'developing world' to be for the most part responsive to it, and they have 'domesticated' UNHCR and NGOs to ensure that they, too, follow the same approach.

In some cases, donors' urge to contain refugees manifests itself in even more negative ways. For example, the Swedish International Development Agency (SIDA) admitted that it was 'prioritising activities inside the Sudan to make the refugee to return [*sic*] or for the habitants of the Sudan to stay back'.[14] To the extent that these activities had the effect of making flight more difficult for the people, donors and NGOs were interfering with the very right to seek asylum. They did not realise that creating safe conditions for people to remain in their country of origin is, in nearly all situations, an objective that is beyond the reach of a government development agency or of an NGO. In conflicts like the one in Sudan, there were no activities that SIDA, or any other donor agency, could realistically have put in place to make a particular area secure. Security depended on the settlement of the political dispute and on the end of the fighting. Moreover, NGOs operating in southern Sudan had to rely on the consent of the host government and of the SPLA, the main perpetrators of the abuses that prompted people to leave. NGOs could do little more than alleviate the consequences of the fighting by offering basic assistance to the wounded combatants and to civilian victims of the conflict, but they could not realistically put an end to the conflict or direct its future course.[15]

To some extent, however, lack of imagination and institutional inertia can also account for donors' continued support for encampment rather than the integration of refugees. In both Kenya and Uganda, when we met the staff at the embassies in charge of development aid, we normally found ourselves in front of competent individuals, whom it would be hard to associate with restrictionist policies. For the most part, they had joined the development agencies of their governments out of an idealist commitment to a cause. Furthermore, they were often aware of UNHCR's and NGOs' limits, and about problems with their operations. In Nairobi, for example, the US embassy's political officer knew about the malnutrition in Kakuma and sent the embassy's refugee officer on a mission to find out more. The official who worked for SIDA in Nairobi had had her own negative experiences with UNHCR in Angola and Zaire. Yet the widespread negative opinions about UNHCR were not translated into pressure on UNHCR to change its policies or any attempt to monitor UNHCR's activities. Many in the donor community probably saw the encampment of refugees as 'inevitable', and UNHCR's autonomy as a fact of life.

The other factor that influenced the response – or rather the lack thereof – of the local donor communities in Kenya and Uganda to UNHCR was the distinction between development aid and relief aid. Refugees are traditionally placed in the 'relief' category as they are viewed as a temporary emergency and as separate from the long-term developments needs of the host country (Harrell-Bond 1996a). The officials working in Nairobi or Kampala for Britain's Department for International Development (DFID), for Sweden's SIDA, or for the other government development agencies, were not responsible for relief and emergency budgets, and refugees did not therefore come within their purview or budget. For its part, UNHCR raised funds through annual appeals, and did not liaise with development institutions (Värynen 2000). As a result, assistance to refugees was planned and delivered in a vacuum, with little, if any, attention to the socio-economic context and with no attempt to use the presence of refugees as a catalyst for development.

An attempt to redefine relations with UNHCR was made by Britain's DFID after 1998. In Uganda, DFID decided to stop the direct funding of NGOs in the refugee sector, and instead to channel a higher level of funding through UNHCR to be allocated to NGO projects. DFID and UNHCR signed a memorandum in April 1998 which committed DFID to disbursing an initial £3 million. DFID's rational for this change was that:

> DFID managers increasingly felt that there might be more effective ways of ensuring that this funding was used to achieve key objectives such as the promotion of self-reliance among refugee groups and the provision of assistance which benefited refugees and host populations alike. The logical choice of partner seemed to be UNHCR.

> … This arrangement is intended to replace CHAD's [Conflict and Humanitarian Affairs Department, part of DFID] own direct support for NGO refugee projects, and to complement any funding of refugee projects by DFID's Regional Departments (UNHCR/DFID1998).

Other limits of the previous scheme were detailed in the same document:

> Under the previous arrangements whereby DFID funded NGOs bilaterally, projects were selected for support in an *ad hoc*, responsive manner, with little regard to how they fitted in with other NGO activities or with any Governmental or other strategy for handling the refugee caseloads.

Appraisal of the projects was constrained by lack of on-the-ground presence and knowledge, and monitoring was minimal ...

Under the new scheme, projects selected for support are part of a clear and comprehensive strategy agreed between the Government and UNHCR, which fits well with DFID's preferred approach. Channelling funds through UNHCR is assisting them in their efforts to reduce duplication and improve co-ordination between the NGOs operating in refugee areas, thus encouraging a more effective response. Appraisal, selection and monitoring of projects appears to be more thorough than under previous arrangements (ibid.).

However, UNHCR's experience in providing assistance to refugees and hosts alike was limited, as later acknowledged by DFID (2000). This new arrangement weakened the position of the NGOs that were recipient of DFID funding vis-à-vis UNHCR since it increased UNHCR's control over the allocation of resources. If, previously, they had had to account for their field performance primarily to DFID, now, under the new arrangement they had to respond to UNHCR (DFID 2000).

Reading between the lines, it also seems that some strain might have emerged between UNHCR and DFID on how to allocate this funding, since:

... it was only after the DFID/UNHCR meeting in London in April 1998 that it became clear to UNHCR that DFID was expecting it to give special consideration to the projects which had previously been bilaterally funded. UNHCR Geneva then contacted its Field Offices, including Kampala, to ask them to look into possibilities for funding such projects, where possible using funding already allocated to them for their country programmes. At the same time UNHCR Geneva indicated it might be able to find supplementary funding for particularly deserving projects (from the small portion of the £3 million grant which then remained unallocated) (UNHCR/DFID 1998).

Of the NGOs that DFID had been funding directly before the new policy, only one, the Equatorian Civic Fund,[16] received funding from UNHCR under the new arrangement. The UNHCR/DFID report said that 'once informed of the need to give special consideration to former DFID-funded projects, UNHCR Kampala appear to have looked seriously into the possibilities of providing support. They have yet to provide funding of any [of these projects]' (ibid.).

One of the supposed benefits of the new arrangement was that it would remedy DFID's own lack of field monitoring. Under the new arrangements, DFID would continue periodically to send evaluation teams to Uganda, but these teams would rely on UNHCR for information about their field-monitoring activities. Moreover, owing to the short-term nature of their missions, DFID hardly had a chance to verify the effectiveness of this monitoring system, which was described as follows:

Both at country and field level, UNHCR appears to have a close and constructive relationship with its NGO implementing partners, combining policy dialogue with thorough monitoring and appraisal. Partners are consulted in the formulation of strategy objectives, and proposals are appraised against their contribution to that strategy. Quarterly financial and six-monthly narrative reports from partners are supplemented by frequent monitoring visits, and periodic audits and evaluations, both internal and external. Monthly meetings are held at national and local levels between UNHCR and implementing partners: one of the aims is to improve co-ordination between partners. These are supplemented by periodic workshops on aspects of project management and sector-specific meetings.

Relations with the Ugandan Government, at both national and local levels, appeared excellent. The Head of the UNHCR sub-office in Pakelle and his staff have built good relationships with the local Resident District Commissioners and the local Council leader (UNHCR/DFID 1998).

In practice, the UNHCR/DFID mission lasted only a week and included field visits. Notwithstanding their competence, it would not have been possible for the team members to review all the aspects of this new relationship in such a short time.

Exclusive reliance on UNHCR's own reports is ill-advised, since it is precisely the work of UNHCR and NGOs that donor countries ought to monitor. Clearly, setting up an effective monitoring mechanism capable of gathering up-to-date information from the various sites in which UNHCR and NGOs are assisting refugees would be costly. But even if longer-term field missions are not possible, a more accurate picture of what is happening in those camps and settlements that donors have paid to create could be gained by lateral thinking and with a flexible approach. In Kenya and Uganda, donors relied too little on the journalists, activists, and academic researchers who were visiting the camps – let alone the refugees themselves. Moreover, the follow-up was usually construed narrowly as a way of monitoring the financial side of the operation. Follow-ups based on a 'rights assessment' – that is, on the extent to which a particular project was improving the enjoyment of the refugees' rights – were virtually non-existent.

Donors were also to blame for some unrealistic conditions that they placed on UNHCR and NGOs. For instance, 'revalidation exercises', which were taxing for UNHCR staff and caused great anger and at times riots among refugees, were imposed by the World Food Programme (WFP) to please donors.[17] Thus, donors expected 'credible' figures of the refugee population before disbursing the necessary funds, despite the fact that in 1992 Kenya was in the midst of a humanitarian crisis with the refugee population suffering one of the highest child mortality and malnutrition rates in East Africa (UNHCR 1992c: para. 51) and with thousands of refugees arriving every month from Somalia. UNHCR explained to its staff that 'budgeting is dependent on accurate statistics' (ibid.: para. 29), landing an overstretched and understaffed office with the burdensome and invidious task of organising a headcount.

Another example of this unrealistic approach was resettlement. One of the main problems in the process was that, in compliance with their national policies, resettlement countries – all of which were also donor countries – only considered cases submitted by UNHCR.[18] Strict adherence to this procedure defied common sense. In Nairobi, Australia, Canada, and the US had the largest resettlement programmes, with full-time staff based at the high commissions and the embassy; the US also subcontracted an NGO, the Joint Voluntary Agency (JVA) to help in the process. During the year, staff from the national headquarters of the immigration departments flew in to interview refugees – partly for procedural reasons and partly because the local offices alone could not cope with the numbers.[19] Embassy staff dealing with refugees were surely aware of how resource-intensive this process was. Yet they expected UNHCR's resettlement unit – which, in Nairobi, only had one international member of staff and one assistant – to submit cases to fill the quotas of all the resettlement countries, a process that, at the embassies' end, required the full-time work of many people. Unsurprisingly, UNHCR did not submit enough cases to fill the available places (*see also* Nowrojee 2000).

Embassy staff were often unwilling to accept UNHCR's limits and, for the most part, their commitment to the system was unwavering. Occasionally they would admit some problems, while always emphasising that they were working to improve them. This is illustrated by a letter sent by the official responsible for resettlement at the Canadian high commission:

> Canada relies on the UNHCR as one of its main partners in identifying and referring refugees for third country resettlement. Canada Immigration has been engaged in dialogue with UNHCR in Geneva and in the field over the past twelve months to better streamline the refugee referral system, and more work will be done with the regional offices to improve referral systems locally. I understand that you have concerns about the UNHCR and clearly some of the individuals you have met did not have faith in the system or the people working here. I agree that there is more work to be done to improve the existing system. Nonetheless, Canada Immigration recognizes that progress has already been made, and I can reassure you that dialogue with the UNHCR offices in this region of Africa will continue …

> We would therefore ask that the individuals whom you would like us to consider go through normal UNHCR channels. You may wish to make representations to the UNHCR directly about their situation. Referring cases to this office directly can only lead to false expectations on the part of the refugees.[20]

1998 was a difficult year for UNHCR, and its operation in Kenya was suffering from significant budget cuts. How could it be expected to improve its system at this time? Moreover, was this official not aware of the fact that it was UNHCR that administered the camps and that refugees had great difficulty accessing UNHCR personnel even when they were in imminent danger?[21]

Resettlement

The resettlement process suffered from the legal and institutional failures of the various actors involvement – referral agencies, UNHCR, and resettlement countries. Resettlement is one of the three 'durable solutions' for refugees, the others being integration and repatriation. It is a solution that is in practice available only to a minute number of refugees. Only a few countries, the most significant still being the US, Canada, and Australia, have resettlement quotas and, despite the increase in the 1990s in the quota for Africans, the total number is still in the order of tens of thousands out of millions – little more than a drop in the ocean. UNHCR was right in reminding refugees over and over again that there is no right to be resettled. Nevertheless, for many refugees who face imminent security risks in their countries of asylum, resettlement can be the route to survival. Moreover, for the vast majority of refugees in Kenya and Uganda the other two solutions were not available, and resettlement represented the only possibility to obtain a 'durable solution'. In these circumstances, the need for the resettlement process to be fair, transparent, and efficient is paramount, but none of these attributes could be ascribed to the procedures in place for resettling refugees from Kenya and Uganda.

A serious problem was the role that refugee leaders played in identifying cases for resettlement. An illustration of this is the case of Hassan A. (case no. 002/SOM/K/1998). This refugee had problems with the Somali community because of his membership of a very small clan and because, as a Lutheran World Federation (LWF) security officer, he had denounced some refugees' attempt to obtain extra ration cards. His letter to the senior protection officer detailing these problems, as well as a problem he had with the Kenyan police was stamped – 'Chairman, Somali Community Kakuma R. Camp' – and below it there was a short statement by the chairman: 'I the above named of the Somali Community Chairman [*sic*] do hereby testify that the above explained problem is absolutely true as stated above. So that any assistance accorded to him will be helpfully appreciated' (ibid.). In this case, the system somehow worked, because the chairman had agreed to support the submission of this refugee, despite the criticism it contained of other Somali refugees. The protection officer in Dadaab admitted that this practice was problematic:

Resettlement is a 'lottery ticket'. Disproportionate number of those work-ing for the agencies seem to receive it. This is because they have greater access to UNHCR. 'Accessibility' is the key factor in resettlement. The other problem is that we rely too much on the elders who, in some cases, are part of the system, or they are the problem! We do not have a rigid referral system, but we still rely too much on certain 'referors'.[22]

The UNHCR practice of identifying 'priority groups' also gave rise to problems, although behind this practice there were often the resettlement countries, which demanded that certain categories of refugees be referred to them for resettlement. In Uganda, where resettlement was overall more difficult to obtain, UNHCR identified Rwandan and Congolese Hutu refugees as groups in need of resettlement because 'it is becoming increas-ingly difficult to protect' them (UNHCR 2000c). In Kenya, the Sudanese minors in Kakuma and the Rwandan refugees of mixed parentage (Hutu/Tutsi) were indeed all identified as 'priorities' at first by the US, which has the largest resettlement programme, and UNHCR went along with this decision.

'Somali Bantus' were also resettled from Kenya to the US at the end of a long saga. Before the US agreed to resettle them, UNHCR had approached Mozambique and Tanzania. Although there is no reason why African countries should not become resettlement countries (and in fact there are many good reasons for them do so), Tanzania and Mozambique had been considered as suitable countries of resettlement for this group of refugees for reasons that were, to say the least, anthropologically unsound. It was believed that, since 'Somali Bantus' were the descendants of slaves who had been taken to Somalia from central and eastern Africa, it would be culturally appropriate to resettle them in countries like Tanzania and Mozambique. However, a putative cultural affinity dating back many generations is a relatively weak ground on which to build a successful resettlement.[23] Other factors, such as the particular socio-eco-nomic conditions in the host countries, were far more important and yet neglected. In fact, the project foundered in the end, at least the Mozambican plan, because the national authorities were not persuaded that enough funds would be made available, at a time when they were already struggling with their 'own' returnees.

As for the Sudanese 'walking boys' in Kakuma, the decision to make them a priority for resettlement was generally welcomed, as this was one of the largest groups of 'unaccompanied minors' in a refugee camp (by the time they were resettled most of them had become adults), and credit should be given to UNHCR's protection staff in Nairobi in 1998–99 for finding a 'durable solution' for them (UNHCR 1999f: 5.4.2 and 5.4.3). There was, however, a concern that some of them might be left behind. Around 1,500 cases were reported to be proceeding 'too slowly', and a child welfare specialist was 'attempting to determine which of the minors would benefit from resettlement' (Refugees International 2000).

Priority groups were often criticised by the rest of the refugee population, which accused UNHCR of favouritism. Rumours circulated about how these groups had managed to obtain this 'durable solution', yearned for by all. In the period that preceded their resettlement, members of these groups often found themselves in greater danger than before as other refugees' resentment intensified. They were often the target of armed robbery in the camps. At a tense meeting of the Anti-Rape Committee in Dadaab, a refugee member of the committee argued that 'UNHCR created tension by considering resettlement of mixed marriages. This meant that Somali girls were tempted to marry Sudanese or Ethiopian men to obtain resettlement. These girls were referred to as prostitutes (by the mere fact that they have relationship with non-Muslims).' The UNHCR assistance protection officer replied that:

> ... the Committees should not forget the essence of their role: to create awareness of the community to social and cultural bias against members of the same community. Rape victims were resettled much less because of the rape, than because of the reaction that they were subjected to by the community. The same applies to mixed marriages. If people do not get harassed or persecuted, there is less need for resettlement (UNHCR 1997j).

Given the scarcity of resettlement places, resettlement could easily 'provide a market opportunity' (Elder 1999b). In both Kenya and Uganda, refugees told us about 'companies' that preyed upon them – promising global job searches, visas to the US, tickets, green cards, and so on. In Uganda, one company claimed that all of this could be available after payment of an initial deposit of some US$ 45. One refugee was swindled by a company based in Alabama, which claimed to be able to get him a job and a work permit, and arrange a flight. He wrote to us:

> If I had the means I would sue that company. The way they have changed my brain, all the false hopes that company have given me is having devastating effects on me. We had such high hopes. I do not know if I am going to be able to tell my wife. Maybe I should not tell her. I really thought that God had heard our prayers and that we had an alternative. Now is there any way that you can advise me about the effects that this will have on me and my family?

> ... When a blind man is offered something, he cannot distinguish. He cannot say, 'No I don't want that, I want this.' He cannot make choices, he cannot see if something is a good thing or a bad thing. A blind man cannot make choices.[24]

Being lured by bogus companies was, to some extent, a consequence of the despair experienced by refugees deprived of prospects. Among Somalis in Dadaab, such despair took a particular form, which has been analysed by Cindy Horst and named *buufis* (Horst 2003). As one of her interviewees put it:

> The word *buufis* stems from the Somali language and involves a person who has sent his or her application letter to outside countries. When the first rejection letter arrives, stating that he has to go back to the motherland and find peace there, the person may nearly go mad. He starts running to the UNHCR offices every day, looking for a chance to go ... In fact, *buufis* is a kind of disease that is spread through verbal expressions. It can have an advantage, because when someone goes to the UNHCR every day consecutively, he may be given resettlement. But it can also be life threatening, because if the person recognises that he cannot go overseas, he may kill himself, starve himself or simply run mad (Horst 2003: 124).

For those who had relatives abroad, *buufis* often amounted to the almost obsessive hope that these relatives would one day be able to help them out of the camp into a safer country, preferably a western one. And some relatives do try to help, by sponsoring them or even sending money – as much as 6,000 dollars – to allow them to buy their way abroad (Horst 2003: 145).

The 'market opportunity' offered by resettlement was also exploited by UNHCR members of staff, some of whom were put on trial in Kenya (Blomfield 2002). Many refugees believed that the payment of a bribe was essential for resettlement, and newspaper reports confirmed some accounts of improprieties in the resettlement process. For example, the *Monitor* reported on the 'resettlement' to Sweden of ten Ugandan youths posing as refugees (Onyang 1999).

The main problem was, of course, those who were denied access to the resettlement process. For instance, the Congolese students who had survived the Lumumbashi massacre ten years before satisfied all the criteria for resettlement and had also been in camps for a long term, but were still not identified as a priority group. In addition, many refugees who had security problems and who were at most urgent need of resettlement were excluded from the process, because they did not live in camps. 'There is only resettlement in the camps and in the settlements,' refugees in Nairobi and Kampala were frequently told.

In a sense, some of these problems were a function of the way the resettlement process had been arranged: the lack of transparency, the powerlessness of the refugees, and the almost absolute powers of the officials. If one adds the weakness of internal mechanisms of accountability within UNHCR, it becomes clear that within such a system refugees could easily become the victims of blackmail, malice (e.g., case no. 139/SUD/U/1999), or requests for bribes (case no. 128/SUD/U/1999). It was, in other words, a fertile ground for corruption. It was also an environment in which suspicions and sometimes even paranoia among refugees could thrive. In addition to accusations of favouritism for certain groups, rumours circulated about UNHCR officials (Elder 1999b), in particular those from the protection and resettlement units, accused of being corrupt: as a result, many refugees were even more guarded in their interviews. The rumours often contained some truth. For example, Abel Mbilinyi told us that, upon his arrival as UNHCR senior protection officer, he had been approached by a 'committee' of Somalis and Ugandans saying that they would like to 'cooperate' with him, but he refused. He also admitted that a UNHCR staff person was known to have been taking bribes for resettlement for the past five years, but they could 'never get hard evidence'. During his term of office, he managed to have this member of staff removed from the resettlement unit. Refugees believed that, because of his integrity, this official was encountering serious resistance (ibid.).

The most disconcerting case of corruption to be unveiled in the east African refugee programme concerned resettlement. Some UNHCR officials were arrested in 2000–01 and put on trial (Kimemia and Nduta 2001), while others were transferred. At least one Kenyan national was believed to have benefited from the sale of resettlement papers. The damage done to thousands of refugees has been enormous and the remedial action taken by UNHCR and by resettlement countries has been inadequate. In particular, UNHCR does not seem keen to give up its monopoly on referrals for resettlement, and resettlement countries still expect UNHCR to devote an unreasonable amount of resources to making these referrals.

UNHCR

UNHCR and encampment

UNHCR's attitudes towards encampment were two-faced. On the one hand, senior UNHCR officials stated that refugee camps were not 'good places' for refugees. The former high commissioner Sadako Ogata wrote on one occasion that 'Refugee camps are not a fitting place for person, anywhere' and that therefore 'The goal is to make refugee camps unnecessary' (Ogata 1994), a comment subsequently echoed by high commissioner Lubbers.[25] UNHCR officials in the field normally blamed host governments for imposing the encampment of refugees on UNHCR, claiming that governments were responsible for refugee policy and that all UNHCR could do was to assist refugees as well as it could in difficult circumstances. On the other hand, these officials, both at the field level and in Geneva, normally shared a belief in the inevitability of camps, maintaining that 'alternatives to camps *in toto* were "simply not working" or "politically not feasible" despite the fact that little information on such issues was actually available to most staff' (Schmidt 1998). Even those protection officers who took a rights-based approach to their work – as was the case during the latter phase of our research in both Kenya and Uganda – did not challenge the policy of encampment.

There was also another reason for UNHCR's failure to press for the refugees' freedom of movement and to promote the end of encampment. It was clear that, at least as far as Kenya was concerned, far from reluctantly acquiescing to the host government's policy of putting refugees in camps, UNHCR had played a pivotal role in key phases of the policy-making process that led to the adoption of camps as the principal way of assisting and hosting refugees.[26] By the late 1990s, the claim that UNHCR grudgingly went along with the encampment policy was clearly at variance with documents that were emanating from its headquarters in Geneva. UNHCR's urban policy, in particular, was openly premised on the 'containment' of refugees in confined spaces, and viewed movement to urban centres and 'irregular movements' in general as an undesirable phenomenon (UNHCR 1997b). Encampment thus became part of UNHCR's general policy, as confirmed by the experience in other countries (e.g., Karadawi 1999; van Damme 1996, 1998), and by research conducted in Geneva (Schmidt 1998).

The reasons for UNHCR's acceptance and promotion of camps, despite their manifestly negative impact on the protection of refugees, are numerous. Firstly, the greater 'visibility' of encamped refugees makes it easier for the organisation to raise funds from donors (Harrell-Bond et al. 1991). Secondly, refugees can be more easily controlled in camps. Such control serves the institutional purpose of simplifying the provision of humanitarian assistance, and, as noted, it also has an immediate appeal both to host governments in the 'developing world' and to donor countries in the 'developed world'– the former short-sightedly regarding the control and concentration of refugee populations as being in their interest, and the latter viewing this as a way of containing refugees in the 'developing world' and reducing the numbers of those who could make it to 'Fortress Europe'. Thirdly, UNHCR's modus operandi has by now been crystallised over decades. To some extent, institutional inertia is responsible for the perpetuation of the camp policy, and experience or knowledge of other ways of assisting refugees is almost entirely lacking.[27] Fourthly, encampment is bolstered by UNHCR's approach to 'durable solutions': with repatriation being viewed as the 'best' solution, asylum is regarded as temporary and camps become 'acceptable' as intermediate holding grounds until repatriation is effected.

Finally, UNHCR's isolated attempts in the past to develop approaches to refugee assistance that were based on using funds for integration through developmental assistance were met with resistance. A senior UNHCR official in Geneva recalled that, when UNHCR proposed a joint developmental scheme for assisting Ghanaian refugees in Togo in the early 1960s, donor countries scrapped it because of concerns over costs.[28]

The 1984 Second International Conference on Assistance to Refugees in Africa (ICARA II) was an attempt to revive this approach, but it was not followed up (*see* Gorman 1987, 1993; Weighill 1996; Harrell-Bond 1996a). The existence of separate categories of budgets (emergency and relief as opposed to development) and the donors' insistence that refugees constitute an emergency have consolidated UNHCR's approach and the refugees' relegation to the relief budget.

The 'demise of protection'

The mid-1980s are often described as a critical time when restructuring led to the 'downgrading of protection and of UNHCR's legal culture' (Loescher 2001: 249); until then the division of international protection had 'dominated a rigid hierarchy' within the organisation (Goodwin-Gill 1999: 235). In the early 1990s, the relegation of protection to the back seat culminated in a comprehensive management review known as 'Project Delphi' (UNHCR 1996m) and the rise in prominence of the 'care and maintenance' sector, comprising logistics workers, project managers, and field officers – all involved with the provision of material assistance (Loescher 2003: 13). This institutional transformation reflected a pattern that was already visible in the aid world at large – the emergence of the 'aid worker' as a professional figure.[29] Recent years have witnessed a reawakening of the debate on protection issues, of which the initiative on global consultations on international protection is the main illustration.[30] Whether this debate will lead to concrete policy changes remains to be seen.

In Africa and throughout countries in the 'developing world', however, unlike Europe and North America, UNHCR's work was never protection-driven. The institutional changes in the 1980s meant that the prospect for improving the protection side of UNHCR work in Africa diminished substantially. The approach that UNHCR traditionally followed was premised on the assumption that in Africa UNHCR could not 'depend on asylum governments to provide relief and NGOs were more scarce' (UNHCR 1997f). This assumption was not always true. In the 1960s Sierra Leone and Guinea refused to allow UNHCR to set up an office and implement a relief programme that would have included the encampment of refugees from, respectively, Guinea and Guinea-Bissau. (Harrell-Bond 1990).[31]

In addition, the 'full-belly' theory – the idea that rights and legal protection were pointless for 'starving' refugees – provided an ideological guise to this approach. As a result, UNHCR in Africa did not really monitor compliance with refugee law, nor did it facilitate bringing cases about the treatment of refugees to courts, as it did at times in Europe. Nor did it establish a link between refugee assistance and development programmes and seek the sustainable integration of refugees in the host country. Underlying these attitudes amongst staff were probably deep-seated cultural relativist beliefs: the fact that for African refugees a different, and lower, standard was applied was not perceived as shocking because the different socio-cultural context was believed to warrant different standards.

This combination of disregard for protection and a flawed assistance policy characterised UNHCR's work in Kenya and Uganda and resulted in a vicious circle of economic and legal marginalisation of refugees from their hosts (Harrell-Bond 1990). UNHCR programmes in Kenya and Uganda clearly suffered the consequences of the weakened status of protection work within UNHCR headquarters. In the 1990s, at a time when in both countries a local human rights community was growing, UNHCR's institutional weakness meant that it often missed the opportunity to exploit such an important social development to the benefit of refugees. Thus, for example, when the Kenya chapter of the International Commission of Jurists (ICJ) developed a programme of legal aid for refugees and went knocking at UNHCR's door for collaboration, not only was that door shut abruptly but UNHCR even attempted to undermine ICJ's work, as discussed below.[32] Protection posts remained unfilled for many months in some places, including Kakuma and Adjumani: field officers with no legal training were asked to do protection work, for which they could not find any guidance in UNHCR's Manual – probably the main operational handbook used by field staff – as the 1998 edition did not contain a chapter on international protection.[33] In Nairobi, the senior protection officer, who arrived in September 1997, found that a large part of her already limited budget for personnel was earmarked for social counsellors rather than lawyers, despite the huge backlog of cases in status determination. Despite some considerable resistance, she eventually managed to hire more lawyers. The fact that status determination and resettlement absorbed the time and resources of the protection staff in both Kenya and Uganda only aggravated the shortcomings in protection.

Probably the most harmful consequence of the diminution of protection in its institutional ethos and its procedures was that UNHCR staff and programmes had became almost impervious to arguments based on the law. As explained by Goodwin-Gill, 'that portion of UNHCR protection work that was rooted in international law, standards and principles, has been eclipsed by so-called pragmatic approaches to refugee problems, in which everything seems to be negotiable' (Goodwin-Gill 1999: 235). The belief that 'in extreme cases, principles and standards can seem almost academic in deciding action' (Morris 1997: 494) pervaded the work of the organisation.

The relegation of protection to the periphery of UNHCR's work was worsened by the 'evolution of solutions' (Harrell-Bond 1996b), which culminated in UNHCR's declaration that the 1990s was going to be the decade of repatriation. Resettlement was available to only a small percentage of refugees, and integration was dismissed as unfeasible or undesirable. The sidelining of other solutions, and in particular of integration, closed the circle: UNHCR saw itself as a relief-provider with the duty to keep refugees alive until the time when they could return home. The refugee experience was reconceptualised as a triptych: flight occupied the first panel, UNHCR-administered camps the central one, and repatriation the last panel.[34]

UNHCR as a welfare agency

With the strengthening of the 'care and maintenance' sector and the consolidation of its institutional identity as a provider of humanitarian aid, UNHCR developed many of the problems – or 'pathologies'[35] – that are common to national welfare institutions: the negative stereotyping and disempowerment of the beneficiaries (Lipsky 1980); the role of gatekeepers (ibid.); bureaucratic rigidities; the gradual dehumanisation of helping (Harrell-Bond 2002); blaming the refugees for institutional failures; imperviousness to the law (Halliday 2000); the ossification of a certain modus operandi; and the weakening of the idealist commitment to the cause – refugee protection in UNHCR's case – in the ethos of the institution and its replacement with bureaucratic loyalty. These problems were exacerbated by the fact that UNHCR was subject neither to judicial control nor to the complex forms of administrative control that act as checks and balances on national welfare bureaucracies (*see* Walkup 1997a, 1997b).[36] Finally, as a transnational welfare institution, UNHCR was also faced with peculiar moral dilemmas, as illustrated by the decision of the standard of health care it had to provide in its different operations.[37]

Like most bureaucracies, UNHCR produced a plethora of documents (handbooks, guidelines, and so on) for the use of its field staff. There was no evidence that UNHCR's practice improved in areas on which this paper production thrived. Gender and children are cases in point: despite the long list of reports and handbooks, UNHCR's protection record on 'vulnerable' refugees was abysmal. Part of the problem was that there were flaws in the conceptualisation of some of these policies and guidelines. For example, UNHCR's policy on 'vulnerable' refugees was premised on the existence of immutable 'vulnerabilities' – such as woman-headed households, unaccompanied minors, women victims of violence, and, more seldom, the elderly. But other potentially vulnerable groups were ignored – for example, adolescents,[38] defectors, cultural dissidents, and young men of 'fighting age', many of whom were at risk of forced recruitment. The bureaucratic categories of 'vulnerable' refugees were assumed to be exhaustive; those refugees who did not fit into these categories were sometimes seen as having no special protection needs. Moreover, even the measures that were taken to protect refugees who were recognised as 'vulnerable' were, for the most part, wholly inadequate.

Another problem was that, as pointed out in a UNHCR evaluation:

> ... the many guidelines on the protection and care of refugee children were criticized by the evaluation team as being overlapping. Furthermore, their combined volume is overwhelming. As a consequence, existing materials only serve as references documents occasionally consulted by specialised staff. Much needed is a single set of programme development guidelines that integrated the most essential lessons of the various existing materials along with a concise operationally oriented checklist, encapsulating key policies and the action required (UNHCR 1997k).

These reports did serve an important bureaucratic function: UNHCR could be seen to be active in areas that donors, or public opinion in general, considered important. Since only a few observers actually investigated the situation on the ground, many were left with the impression that UNHCR was really addressing the problems of refugee women or refugee children.

'Blaming the refugees' is by no means a new phenomenon (Harrell-Bond 1986; Waldron 1987; Walkup 1997a). UNHCR, like national welfare institutions, resorted to it whenever funding cuts made a reduction in services necessary – rather than admitting that resources were scarce and its policies in need of rethinking. As noted previously, in Kenya and Uganda, refugees were blamed for the inadequacies of health services and food rations. In Hagadera camp, Dadaab, humanitarian workers believed that refugees were to blame for the 'over-utilisation rate' of the health services, with psychosomatic problems and fraud cited as the most important causes (Boelaert 1996: 4). The consultant hired by Médicins sans Frontières (MSF) to investigate the causes and possible remedies for this phenomenon found that 'They [the refugees] are overconsulting because they are not getting what they are looking for: health care and adequate diet' (ibid.).

Another example of 'blaming the refugees' was CARE's decision to phase out its small agricultural programme in Dadaab at the beginning of 1998. The justification that was offered was that the programme had not been productive because refugees had not been able to take advantage of it.[39] Yet, in its report to the Overseas Development Administration (ODA) in 1996, CARE – UNHCR's main implementing partner in Dadaab – had claimed that the food harvested in the agricultural sites had far exceeded their objectives and that: 'Impacts of agriculture activities are very evident in all the Dadaab camps, and in the town, spinach is now available throughout the year. Agencies operating in Dadaab are meeting 30 percent of their vegetable needs from the local/camp market. The refugee community now has these nutritional supplements in their diet, even if not regularly' (CARE 1996: 6). Which of these two versions is to be believed – the positive 'face' shown to the donors or the bitter one shown only two years later when funding cuts imposed a reduction in the programme?

Rather than appreciate that food represents the only tradable commodity entering the camps and that it is often necessary for refugees to sell it to provide other basic necessities for themselves (such as matches to light fires), at times humanitarian organisations even blamed malnutrition on the refugees' lack of certain skills. For example, a UNHCR report suggested that if, despite receiving close to 2,100 Kcal daily, the Sudanese unaccompanied minors in Kakuma still developed nutritional deficiencies, training in the form of 'home science education' should be offered to them. The report observed: 'A housewife would probably not serve an enormous meal on distribution day and let her family go without food until next time, but the boys have not learned how to divide and stretch food to make it last' (UNHCR 1995b). 'Training', 'sensitisation', and 'raising awareness' became catchphrases in the humanitarian community, welcomed with profuse nodding at meetings and recurring in reports and workshops as a solution to all problems. Adequate food, rather than training in 'home science education', was what these malnourished children needed.

In addition to blaming them, humanitarian staff often tended to 'dehumanise' refugees. To some extent, switching off one's empathy is a way of deflecting the sense of powerlessness and the pain that one might experience in certain situations: feeling overwhelmed by the sheer size of the suffering that surrounded them, many humanitarian workers reacted with indifference. 'Helplessness generates cynicism', as psychologists have shown (Dörner 1996: 18). The response of a UNHCR official to a case on which we solicited her intervention is illustrative. We were telling her about the experience of a refugee woman from Burundi who had fled the camps in eastern DRC where she had lost all her family members and where she had been gang-raped at gun point. This woman was pregnant from the rape, when we met her in April 1997 in Nairobi, and her neighbours were seriously worried that she might take her own life. The UNHCR official cut our account short and, sighing, said, 'You know ... There are just so many of them! Anyway' – she continued, changing her tone – 'How are you?'. In another case, in Uganda, a Congolese refugee, who suffered from a medical condition which required major specialised surgery, was met with growing irritation by InterAid staff and told to go back to the camp, which he could not do because of his poor health. Finally, the Inter-Aid workers unleashed their frustration by verbally abusing Mr K., threatening to withdraw his assistance. They even allowed the security police to beat him and it was only through the intervention of the InterAid doctor that he was saved (case no. 097/DRC/U/1999).

As is the case with street-level welfare bureaucracies, UNHCR staff 'can impose costs of personal abuse, neglectful treatment, or inconvenience without necessarily paying the normal penalty of having the other party retaliate' (Lipsky 1980: 56). The UNHCR–refugee relationship was characterised by an even greater power imbalance than the one between national welfare institutions and their beneficiaries. Petty abuse, systematic humiliations and, not infrequently, beatings were inflicted on refugees by guards who were following the instructions of UNHCR and NGO staff (Harrell-Bond 2002). Such abuses did not occur simply because of individual wickedness; they were a symptom of power relations between refugees and their 'helpers' that were so imbalanced as to give rise to this 'socio-pathology'. Indeed, 'The structure of humanitarian assistance programmes is organised in such a way as to make it almost inevitable that some people will act crassly and sometimes cruelly' (ibid.: 68). In a sense, the surprising thing is not so much that such abuses took place, but that UNHCR was prepared to accept their occurrence and failed to put in place an effective system to prevent them or punish those responsible for them. Instead, it chose to adopt an image-saving attitude of obstinate and defensive denial.[40]

Abuse and humiliations were among the key factors that caused the breakdown in the relationship of trust between refugees and their international 'protector', UNHCR. Refugees' views of UNHCR were disenchanted at best, but more often cynical. One embittered refugee explained why he preferred having to deal with government officials than with UNHCR:

> I've been to the Ministry of Local Government [MoLG] two times and to UNHCR at InterAid hundreds of times – the famous InterAid. We saw him [the protection officer] once only; if you see him, he tells you to come back – he postpones appointments. They always say 'come back' and the transport there costs so much. Ahhhh these people! First, they (InterAid) say 'go to the camp' or second, they say, 'come next week' … Sometimes you get tired and don't go to InterAid and give up.

> The Ministry of Local Government is better than those men from the UNHCR; at least they can understand you. The man [the UNHCR assistant protection officer], he is interesting because of his famous responses and special attitudes towards refugees. He says the same response to everyone though you are in a big difficulty the response is the same: 'go to the camps' or 'come back next week.' If we claim we need health care, he'll tell us that we should go to the camp because there are 'so many doctors' there. Or if we want resettlement, to go there and apply and wait. Sometimes when you go to UNHCR, they tell you to go to MoLG and that once I get my documents, then they are obliged to help me. For me, once I get my document, I will NOT go to UNHCR (case no. 232/DRC/U/1997).

From UNHCR's point of view, the problem lay in the refugees' unrealistic expectations or in their lack of gratitude – yet another illustration of 'blaming the refugees'. In other situations, UNHCR reacted to its inability to cope with a crisis, by making refugees 'invisible', a pattern also referred to as 'eliminating the organisational problem' (Walkup 1997a, 1997b).[41] This is exemplified in an evaluation report prepared by UNHCR in the midst of the crisis in 1992, when thousands of Somalis were arriving in Kenya. The report described the frustration of staff 'sieged' [*sic*] by refugees in a 'particularly inadequate space' with 'toilet facilities which have to be shared with the hundreds of refugees waiting to be attended, and a comparatively large caseload to manage under a tense atmosphere of insecurity emanating from desperate and frustrated asylum-seekers and refugees' (UNHCR 1992c: 26). The response to this was:

CONFINEMENT OF REFUGEES TO ESTABLISHED CAMPS AS A SOLUTION
In view of the present over-crowding of refugees in Nairobi, it would be realistic for the asylum-seekers to return to their camps. UNHCR appealed to asylum-seekers through the press to return to the camps. Resettlement countries were also requested to visit the camps from time to time to interview resettlement cases (UNHCR 1992c: 28).

The overcrowding that had to be alleviated was not in the city of Nairobi, as stated in the report, but in the UNHCR office. Eliminating the refugees' presence was a bureaucratic way of getting rid of the 'problem'.

Like most bureaucracies, UNHCR guarded what it perceived to be its territory – programmes for refugees – from 'intrusions', even when it was clear that such intrusions could be to the advantage of refugees. Resettlement was a case in point. As mentioned, the embassies of resettlement countries expected UNHCR to submit the cases for their consideration, but UNHCR lacked the resources to meet these demands. If UNHCR cannot be blamed for not having enough funds to employ at least a dozen or so people for its resettlement activities, it can be accused of institutional hubris. It was blind to its own limits in identifying resettlement cases, in particular the high-priority 'security cases' (e.g., case nos. 231/IRAQ/U/1999; 004/UGA/K/1997; 018/SOM/K/1997). These limits resulted from a number of different factors: the fact that UNHCR was the de facto authority in camps; the limited contact that its staff could have with tens of thousands of refugees; the existence of various 'filters' or 'gatekeepers' that refugees had to go through before having access to a UNHCR official in the camps; and understaffing in the protection teams, which in Nairobi and Kampala focused almost exclusively on status determination. The submission of cases to the embassies suffered from the same problems that beset the UNHCR-led status determination, such as perfunctory interviewing, superficial assessment and, deciding on the basis of first impressions.

A solution to some of these problems would have been to increase the number of actors allowed to make submissions for resettlement. Resettlement countries feared being overwhelmed with requests if individual refugee applications were given parity with those coming from UNHCR. Nevertheless, the problem at the time for nearly all resettlement countries was that they received *too few* rather than too many submissions. They could at least have allowed NGOs to make such submissions. Moreover, UNHCR could have found more imaginative ways of making up for its understaffing and increasing the number of submissions for resettlement: it could, for example, have hired interns from a local law school to help its staff prepare these submissions,[42] or it could have asked an NGO to prepare them under its supervision. The main reason for maintaining the status quo was UNHCR's reluctance to relinquish power, as well as its fear that, should a solution be found, it could no longer use understaffing as a ground for seeking funds from donors.

Dirigisme

The welfare-institution mentality that UNHCR has developed over the years may account for the otherwise astonishing fact that, in an era dominated by economic liberalism and free-market reform, UNHCR and the relief world in general appear to be trapped in a time warp, obstinately continuing to pursue centralised planning. This is apparent particularly in UNHCR's approach to issues such as integration, self-reliance, and 'urban' refugees. We have already seen how the policy of self-sufficiency (or self-reliance) for Ugandan settlements retained the separation of refugees from their hosts, and how it was used to justify the phasing out of funds and the withdrawal of UNHCR assistance. Self-sufficiency was construed as meaning that refugees in settlements had to produce enough food for themselves, and had to be capable of providing for their medical or educational needs without depending on outside assistance.[43] Like agricultural communes of a bygone era, refugee settlements had to be controlled; and like agricultural communes, they had to forgo any aspiration to embark on productive activities in the manufacturing or tertiary sectors, nor could they rely on trade. A laissez-faire approach to self-reliance was distant from the socio-economic philosophy that underpinned UNHCR's humanitarian programme and that was inspired instead by a dis-empowering and controlling paternalism.

Agriculture in the settlements was seen as 'subsistence farming'. Despite the potentially higher market values of certain products, 'there is an active discouragement of growing perennial crops (tea, coffee, matooke) on the basis of the idea that, should refugees return to their countries, they could claim compensation' (UNHCR-OPM 1998: 5). In the same document, UNHCR recognised that this policy had to be revised, but again it could not resist the temptation of central planning and decided that the diversification of production had to be 'determined through market surveys which will analyse demand on the market and make recommendations on areas of production' (UNHCR-OPM 1999: 27). Furthermore, the denial of freedom of movement was not seen by UNHCR as a key factor impeding the pursuit of an economically meaningful policy of self-reliance, although the fact that any businessperson needs to move around would seem self-evident. As in the various failed experiments of socialism and collectivisation, like the Soviet *kolkhoz* or the Tanzanian *ujama* policy, market forces were not taken into account and individual initiative was discouraged – when not openly obstructed or impeded. The notion that refugees could, for example, decide for themselves which crops to produce was in contrast with the *dirigisme* of humanitarian bureaucrats.

The most oppressive consequence of this settlement/camp approach was the uprooting of refugees from places where they had found relative security and had managed to improve their economic conditions. Examples of this cruel 'uprooting of the uprooted' were the destruction of Ogujebe transit centre and the transfer of tens of thousands of Somalis from the camps around Mombasa to Dadaab and Kakuma refugee camps, or back to Somalia.[44] In these cases, UNHCR showed its Janus-face again: it silenced those who criticised it, saying that these were government policies that it was implementing reluctantly and that its involvement was at least a guarantee that damage would be minimised. In reality, UNHCR had been behind these decisions from the beginning. It had even decided to mark the occasion of the completion of the demolition in Ogujebe with a special ceremony, in which a senior UNHCR official from Geneva symbolically planted a tree. In the context of the immense suffering and destruction that the destruction of Ogujebe involved, UNHCR's public 'face' was grotesque. One of us observed in her notebook:

> As we waited for the arrival of the honoured guests, I just wandered around the plot which was arranged with small trees ready for planting. Besides each tree was a signpost for all the VIPs – one for Alain Peters/UNHCR, one for the minister of state for local government, Ssali, MOLG, and one for Hans Thoolen/UNHCR, and then for the various NGOs. The Alerere Secondary School [a refugee school] choir came and practised in the hot sun and I wandered around amidst the rubble of what used to be Ogujebe, a booming place of 24,000 people. The *tukuls* were all completely knocked down and a few of the refugees were left picking through the remains. I walked and stood in the shells of the *tukuls* amazed that just one week earlier thousands of people were rushing about as their houses were knocked down, scrambling to get their properties and load the trucks to the settlements. It was very sad. I talked to two of the Alerere students and they said that some of those having to act as entertainment in the choir were from Ogujebe and had just been displaced from their homes.[45]

Urban policy

The policy of concentrating refugees in designated 'self-sufficient' settlements was complemented by UNHCR's urban policy. Based on the notion that African refugees are essentially 'rural' peasants, this policy regarded 'urban refugees' as an exception, a problem deriving from the refugees' 'irregular movements'. Only a small number of refugees were 'allowed' to reside in the cities – as few as 500 at one point in Kampala – provided that they fell into one of the special categories (medical cases, students on scholarships); the others 'belonged' to the rural camps or settlements.

UNHCR defined an 'urban refugee/asylum-seeker' as: 'A person of urban background in the country of origin and who is neither an irregular mover, nor part of a *prima facie* case load, and, if of rural background, for whom in the country of asylum the option of rural settlement which offers an opportunity for self-sufficiency does not exist' (UNHCR 1997b: 11).

Thus, in its own economic interests, UNHCR decided that no person whose status was determined on a prima facie basis, who 'moved independently to an urban area in the same country', or who was an irregular mover from another country of asylum, could be 'considered for assistance in urban areas' (ibid.). The only 'possible exception' that could be made, and only for irregular movers from another country, was 'life-saving medical care' (ibid.: 29). It would appear that, later, UNHCR Geneva allowed branch offices to assist single women with children 'because otherwise, it is likely they will resort to prostitution for their survival'.[46]

UNHCR's urban policy was based on a complete denial of the demographic and economic trends in Africa that had begun more than 200 years ago (e.g., Harrell-Bond et al. 1977). The policy paid respect to and aimed to perpetuate the class structure that was in place in the country of origin, and did not take into account the possibility of upward social mobility and the process of urbanisation. UNHCR's urban policy explains:

> Perhaps the most commonly used definition of an urban refugee is that of an individual of urban origin, usually a student, former politician or civil servant, a professional, a trader or a skilled, non-agricultural labourer. Other definitions add people with rural backgrounds seeking work or education, one-parent (female) families, sick and disabled people who have been referred from camps and rural settlements for treatment or rehabilitation, or refugees who have left the country of first asylum. Many individual cases among these groups may indeed have special needs, over and above those of a *prima facie* rural caseload. However, by itself, life in urban areas does not constitute an answer to their problem and may well be significantly *more* difficult than in a rural settlement, where appropriate community support can be generated. In the case of medical referrals, these should normally be temporary, lasting only for the duration of treatment. The Working Group concluded that self-selecting irregular movers who had already had access to protection and assistance elsewhere, but have chosen to move on in search of something 'better' should be excluded from UNHCR's assistance.

> For individuals sent from rural settlements to an urban area for medical assistance, every effort should be made to promote their return to the rural centres as soon as essential medical treatment has been completed.

Similarly, for students sent from rural settlements to an urban area for the purpose of study, every effort should be made to promote their return to their communities once their studies are complete ... Those moving temporarily to an urban area should be required to sign an undertaking to return to the rural area before travelling to the city for the stated purpose (UNHCR 1997b: 11).

Refugees who were not deemed to be 'truly' urban and had to spend some time in a city for educational or medical reasons were to be sent back to the rural settlements as soon as possible. For the 'stubborn' refugees who insisted on living in the urban areas, the sanction was deprivation of educational or material assistance (UNHCR 1997b: 11). In Nairobi and in Kampala, we were frequently given the 'party line' by UNHCR officials, according to which these harsh measures were imposed by the host governments. Again, this policy, emanating directly from UNHCR's headquarters, reveals UNHCR's true 'face' and its zealous endorsement of the logic of control and containment of the refugee population in segregated rural areas.

Image management: reporting the field

In one of the most important passages in *Discipline and Punish*, Foucault argued that the social organisation of the 'plague-stricken town' in the sixteenth century in Europe constituted the blueprint of the 'disciplinary power' that lies behind such institutions as prisons and mental hospitals (1977: 195–200). Hyndman has used Foucaultian concepts, such as disciplinary power and governmentality,[47] to analyse power in refugee camps and UNHCR's report-writing practice (1996; 2000),[48] and has observed that 'UNHCR meticulously orders the field through exercises of counting, calculating, and coding refugees', and often represents refugees 'as statistical and moral deviations' in its official reports (Hyndman 1996: 85).[49] Foucault also observed that, in the representation of its administrators, 'the plague-stricken town, traversed throughout with hierarchy, surveillance, observation, writing ...' became 'the utopia of the perfectly governed city' (Foucault 1977: 198). As in Foucault's plague-stricken city, the humanitarian administrators of refugee camps also sought to transform a dystopia into a utopia. In blatant contrast to the painful reality of refugee camps, representations of the refugee camp as the perfectly administered city featured in much official literature. And, in nearly all cases, the life of refugees and events in camps 'are reduced to a compilation of statistics'[50] in order to convey the efficiency of the administration. In some cases, life in camps was represented as idyllic.[51] In others, for example UNHCR's 1999 protection report for Kenya (1999f), after a truthful, albeit selective, account of the human rights violations suffered by minors in Kakuma camp, the impulse to insert a utopian description prevailed. In addition to peace education, the long list of activities that, it was submitted, the refugee camp offered to its resident children included: field visits outside Kakuma for children and adolescents to promote gender issues and to exchange experiences; six educational trips; environmental education with activities such as planting trees, watering plants, utilisation of used water, cleaning their schools and compounds, small-scale agricultural activities, and participation in the Global Learning Observation to Benefit the Environment (GLOBE); economic skills training such as weaving, blacksmithing, carpentry, poultry, brick-making, embroidery, crocheting, knitting, pottery, shoe-making, bakery, spaghetti-making, wood-work, metalwork, restaurants, hairdressing. The sports programme included football, volleyball, netball, and basketball. A youth programme offered drama, debate, poetry, painting, drawing, sculpture, art and craft, creative writing and music, training in leadership, decision making and career development, and cultural activities focusing on cultural dances, music, and aesthetics. There was also language training and special activities for children with special needs and a day care centre for traumatised children offering counselling, reflexology, massage, drawing and painting, doll making, and other therapy activities such as play therapy and recreation (ibid.: para. 5.8).[52]

All this sounds more like a brochure for a summer camp, than a *protection* report about refugee children who included one of the most deprived, traumatised, and malnourished groups of adolescents in the world – the Sudanese 'walking boys' in Kakuma camp. The key problems that affected the walking boys – forced recruitment and malnutrition – were glossed over.

Refugee camps were represented as particularly joyful places on occasions like International Refugee Day and official visits (*see* Harrell-Bond 1999a; Thoolen 1999). For instance, refugees in a Ugandan settlement were said to have gratefully cheered the high commissioner: 'After one and a half hour drive, Mrs Ogata saw school boys and girls clapping and singing to welcome her convoy alongside with leaders of Oruchinga settlement' (UNHCR 1998h: 2). On another occasion, refugees were said to 'display cultural pride in their national costumes and dances, encouraged by UNHCR and partner agencies' (UNHCR 1997a: 16).

Visitors to the camps were also regularly treated to these utopian representations.[53] As part of induction and briefing upon arrival, they were usually driven around in an air-conditioned, four-wheel-drive vehicle with a UNHCR staff member, who pointed to the well-ordered components of the camp mosaic, outlining its perfectly tessellated social structure: 'This is where the Somalis stay ... This is one of the places where they get their water ... The number of bore-holes in this section is ... This is their community centre ... This is the health post ...' UNHCR or NGO personnel would normally be prepared to acknowledge that there were some cracks in the mosaic, but the underlying assumption of encampment was never called into question.

But there were other problems that marred UNHCR reporting. The authors of the reports – the senior protection staff, the representative, the head of sub-office, or the protection officer in a camp – were submitting these reports to their superiors, often at UNHCR's headquarters in Geneva, who usually had a say in their promotions or reassignments. All people have a strong instinct for self-preservation and self-promotion, and it would be naive to expect bureaucrats to report candidly on their failures. Unsurprisingly, field reports became an opportunity for showing 'all the good work' that was being done, while glossing over problems and even misrepresenting facts.[54] Furthermore, all officials were aware of UNHCR's dependence on voluntary contributions, and of the need to keep donors satisfied. Even if the reports they were preparing were meant for an in-house readership, they knew that, by reporting problems or institutional failures, they were putting their superiors in the invidious position of having to decide whether to suppress these problems to risk spoiling the institutional image.

The concern about image management is illustrated by UNHCR's Uganda Country Operation Plan for 1997. Setting out the priorities for the following year, the plan identified 'public information/private sector fund raising activities' (UNHCR 1996g). At a time when budget cuts were affecting food distribution for refugees, UNHCR still found it necessary to make provision for public-information activities that included various pieces of computer and publishing equipment, a travel budget to allow the public information officer to travel in the region to receive training and attend workshops, a separate budget for 'frequent travel and extra monies ... to take journalists to various parts of Uganda to report on UNHCR's activities', and the organisation and advertisement of Africa Refugee Day (ibid.). There was no reference to the situation of refugees: public information was not aimed at raising awareness about the predicament of refugees living in insecure settlements with little land and surviving on meagre and ever-decreasing food rations; it was meant to disseminate information about UNHCR's 'good work'.[55]

Since in both Kenya and Uganda UNHCR exercised significant powers over refugees, especially in the camps and in the settlements, a truthful protection report would have had to account for the exercise of such powers, and for any violation of the refugees' human rights that resulted from it. But the annual protection reports for Kenya and Uganda had hardly anything to say about this. The imposition of collective punishment on Kakuma[56] – one of the most serious violations of the human rights of refugees in Kenya – was not mentioned, nor were the violations of procedural fairness in UNHCR's refugee status determination in both countries. When the camps around Mombasa were demolished, the infrastructure destroyed, and refugees forcibly uprooted, UNHCR's reports omitted any discussion of the sufferings of refugees who were the victims of these events, preferring instead to sing the praises of the organisation for the success of the operation. One report even commented: 'By 1998 the presence of large refugee populations in the Coast of Kenya will belong to the history of the province' (UNHCR 1997a: 15). Similarly, the destruction of Ogujebe was treated as an institutional success, not as the forcible uprooting of thousands and the destruction of their livelihoods.

An exception to this disingenuous way of reporting was UNHCR's protection report on Uganda for 1996. This contained a detailed description of abductions and *refoulement* by the SPLA – the occurrence of which in camps and settlements was normally denied by UNHCR since the fact that this happened in 'their' camps did not fit the image of everything being satisfactory (UNHCR 1996d). The same report also described various incidents in which the physical safety of refugees had been threatened, other fundamental rights had been violated, and minors had been forcibly recruited by the SPLA. It did so without the usual concern for image management, and even contained frank admissions of failure: 'It was not possible to reduce the level of SPLA activity in the camp, and in fact this has increased'; 'Branch Office's resettlement policy has been a fairly conservative one'; 'for those rare cases when children are truly unaccompanied no special arrangement exists'. This type of candid and truthful reporting was rare.[57]

We noted some general improvement in the quality of annual protection reports from Kenya and Uganda, with those from the late 1990s being more accurate and detailed than the previous ones. Such an improvement was both a consequence of changes in the protection staff in the late 1990s and of the development by UNHCR Geneva of a comprehensive standardised format for these reports.

Field reports are one of the key instruments through which UNHCR's headquarters in Geneva are informed about the situation of refugees in various countries, and about the activities of UNHCR's country offices. Policy making is said to depend on this constant flow of information from the field, and the monitoring of country and field offices cannot be carried out adequately without it. However, writing reports took up the time and resources of field staff. If the outcome was, as in most cases, simply an exercise in self-promotion, this use of staff resources appeared pointless.[58] Some UNHCR staff expressed resentment about reporting obligations, complaining about having 'to write report after report to Geneva' and hearing nothing in return.[59]

With operations the world over, UNHCR headquarters could not rely on sending its senior staff on missions to the each field location in order to obtain more accurate information. However, for such reports to be truthful and accurate – especially regarding any problem with a field operation – it is necessary to overcome both the bureaucratic interest in image management and individual self-promotion. One way of doing this would be to have reports written by independent and impartial officials – to create, in other words, the type of administrative control normally found in national bureaucracies. This was the idea behind the 'protection audits' proposed by Guy Goodwin-Gill in the 1990s (2001).

An example of good practice in this area comes from UNHCR's evaluation and policy analysis unit. Since the late 1990s it has published and made available on the Web reports on refugee situations in various parts of the world. A significant number of these reports were written by academics or independent specialists and were based on research conducted for academic or other purposes, and some of them contained severe criticism of UNHCR operations. This is an efficient way of creating a flow of information from the field to headquarters which is not marred by the problems discussed above, while avoiding setting up a costly system of evaluation through hiring external consultants.

Image management: dealing with bad publicity

The same bureaucratic instinct for self-promotion and image management that was behind UNHCR field reports was set in motion when UNHCR became the object of criticism in the press.[60] Its dependence on contributions from governments ('soft funding') compounded the pathology of institutional defensiveness.[61] For instance, during the police roundups in Kenya in July and August 1997, UNHCR hired buses to transport refugees to the camps with a police escort. It was keen to do this out of the public eye, presumably aware of the fact that its image as the 'international protector' of refugees would be blemished by the sight of refugees put on buses against their will and escorted by police. Katie Jenkins, a BBC World Service journalist in Nairobi, was alerted, and when she arrived at the scene she began interviewing refugees on the buses. Within a few minutes, the UNHCR public information officer appeared, asking her to leave the bus and to see him in his office: 'I now have to go and get the party line' she commented.[62]

One of the most serious instances of 'negative publicity' for UNHCR was the series of articles that London's *FT* published in July 1998 on mismanagement and lack of financial accountability (*FT* 1998a, 1998d; Burns and Williams 1998e). It was reported that UNHCR was beleaguered with 'incompetent management, dubious accounting practices and alleged fraud' as well as breaches of their own guidelines on protection (Burns and Williams 1998a). UNHCR was criticised for scrapping the post of 'mediator' – a neutral ombudsman for staff complaints – whose holder, Anne-Marie Demmer, had produced various critical reports, which had been distributed to all staff members and obtained by the *FT*. Some of the articles also dealt with UNHCR's failures to implement its protection mandate on behalf of women and children, with its participation in the forced repatriation of Rwandans from Tanzania, and with its silence on arms movements (Burns and Edgecliffe-Johns 1998).

The response from UNHCR was written by Søren Jessen-Petersen, assistant high commissioner for refugees, who criticised the article as 'deeply flawed' and expressed disappointment with the fact that only one UNHCR staff member, himself, had been contacted by the *FT* journalists (Jessen-Petersen 1998).[63] He also claimed that his comments had been mis-interpreted. He maintained that UNHCR's 'board of auditors gave an unqualified bill of clean health to UNHCR after last year's inspection', and forewarned that 'a detailed, point-by-point response' was being prepared (ibid.). A few days after, a nine-page rebuttal was distributed to the media and sent to all UNHCR offices.

This UNHCR document maintained that the 'FT's articles contain gross errors and misrepresentations, half-truths, and distorted facts which seri-ously undermine the credibility of its reports' (UNHCR 1998g). However, it focused almost exclusively on the accusations of mismanagement and improper accounting, and 'did not tackle allegations that it [UNHCR] had not adequately monitored its compliance with UN policy guidelines on the protection of women, children and the environment' (Edgecliffe-Johnson 1998a). UNHCR was no doubt concerned that, following these articles, donors could threaten to withdraw funding and that UN bodies entrusted with financial accountability could intervene. Britain's contri-butions to UNHCR were indeed affected by these reports (Burns and Williams 1998c; DFID 2000), and there were also some repercussions with-in the UN, with, for example, 'Annan call[ing] for full details on UNHCR books' (*FT* 1998e) and 'UNHCR call[ing a] meeting of donors' (*FT* 1998b).

In the case of financial irregularities, there is at least a system for mon-itoring and imposing sanctions. One individual who did comment on the broader questions of UNHCR's accountability for violations of its man-date was Goodwin-Gill, who, in a letter to the *FT* published alongside Mr Jessen-Petersen's, said that UNHCR had 'disabled itself from fulfilling its primary duty of protection' and that:

> This is most notable in the failure to integrate the basic principles of pro-tection (human rights and refugee-specific rights) into policy-making and programme design, in its emasculation of the one research activity that can provide the basis for coherent operations (country of origin information collection and competent analysis – also much valued by governments and NGOs), and in the loss of institutional integrity that comes with the repeat-ed pursuit of billion-dollar budgets.
>
> To these woes remarkably poor management can indeed be added. As the few competent managers in UNHCR can confirm, the general sense of

non-accountable unsinkability prevails, towards donors and towards staff (Goodwin-Gill 1998b).

Others found the *FT*'s criticism inappropriate. For instance, Kathleen Newland wrote that 'a blast like this can do real damage to the work of the organisation, to say nothing of a High commissioner who is almost universally admired for her education, intelligence and rectitude' (Newland 1998; *see also* Taft and Skogmo 1998; Lambsdorff 1998). Like most press exposés, this one ran out of steam within a few weeks. That there was hardly any follow-up, on the part of states or NGOs, is a function of the inadequacy of existing mechanisms for ensuring UNHCR's accountability.[64]

UNHCR and compliance with refugee law

In principle, refugees should be able to rely on one of the largest UN agencies for monitoring and promoting compliance with refugee law; in practice, however, with the redefinition of UNHCR's functions from protection to assistance and because of the inadequate dispute settlement mechanism under the 1951 Convention, control over compliance with refugee law was lacking. Moreover, UNHCR's involvement with refugee status determination and its assumption of wide administrative functions in camps and settlements meant that, as we have seen, in some situations, UNHCR itself was a perpetrator of violations of refugees' human rights.

One structural weakness has to do with the 1951 Convention itself. Article 38 of the Convention is a 'classic' treaty provision on the settlement of disputes. It allows state parties to the Convention to bring any dispute 'relating to its interpretation or application' to the International Court of Justice. However, states are unlikely to bring lawsuits against other states unless their national interests are involved. Unsurprisingly, article 38 has never been used to bring a case against a non-compliant state to the International Court of Justice. The system of mutual monitoring of compliance, which might work for other types of international law obligations, has therefore proved ineffective for refugees.[65] In human rights treaties of the later generation – from the International Covenant on Civil and Political Rights (ICCPR) and the International Covenant on Economic, Social and Cultural Rights (ICESCR) to the Convention on the Rights of the Child (CRC) – mechanisms for monitoring and enforcing compliance have been devised. These normally consist of a body which receives periodic reports from state parties and which makes observations; in some circumstances, these bodies have been entrusted with judicial powers and can receive complaints from individuals. This type of mechanism would have been appropriate for the 1951 Convention, but one of the problems with being among the first international law instruments to create a comprehensive legal regime for a category of individuals is that lessons learnt afterwards are difficult to incorporate; amending a treaty is a complicated process.

The ancillary use of human rights bodies such as the European Court of Human Rights, the Inter-American Commission on Human Rights and Court of Human Rights, and the Human Rights Committee (HRC), has already played an important role in advancing standards, most notably on the scope of the principle of *non-refoulement* and on the standards of treatment of refugees.[66] In Africa, the main regional organ entrusted with the protection of human rights is the African Commission on Human and Peoples' Rights, established under the African Charter on Human and Peoples' Rights. Both Kenya and Uganda are parties to the Charter, while Uganda has also ratified the protocol to the Charter for establishing an African Court, which is not yet in force. The African Commission has so far considered a limited number of cases on refugee issues (Odinkalu and Zard 2002: 263–7), but the African Charter has perhaps more potential for refugee protection than any other human rights instrument. In particular, article 12 enshrines 'the right to seek and obtain asylum', which entails the obligations on states 'to establish institutions and fair procedures for status determination' (ibid.: 266), an obligation which both Kenya and Uganda manifestly breached.

Gil Loescher has proposed the creation of an 'independent monitoring mechanism or ombudsman ... to provide oversight of state activities in refugee protection' as a way of addressing some of these problems (Loescher 2003: 17). Clearly, there is a need for an international body to 'aggressively promote and monitor the obligations states have taken on through international refugee and human rights instruments' (id.: 16), and, for the reasons we have seen, UNHCR is not at present capable of performing this function. Despite the actual and potential role of human rights bodies, the promotion of compliance with refugee law will depend primarily on the much-needed transformation of UNHCR and on its 'rediscovery' of protection. Many of the cases discussed in the previous chapters reflect the inadequacy of existing mechanisms to monitor UNHCR and improve its performance: the problem was not limited to the injustice and abuses that refugees were exposed to; it also had to do with their powerlessness to challenge decisions and to obtain a remedy. The only channel for complaint (not a legal redress) against violations of rights committed by the staff of UNHCR was by writing to 'Geneva'. This channel was only available to refugees who had enough education (or funds to pay someone else to write for them) and the wherewithal to post a letter. When refugees did take such action the procedure followed by 'Geneva' could be very dangerous for the complainant. UNHCR Geneva routinely referred such letters back to the local office and to the specific official who stood accused, asking 'for comment'. This practice was based on the notion that 'colleagues' could do no wrong and, even if they did make a mistake, it would be inappropriate and discourteous to use it against them. In some cases, refugees who wrote to Geneva were punished.[67]

Because of the jurisdictional immunity it enjoys, UNHCR cannot be sued in national courts (Verdirame 2001b). A rare case of review of UNHCR actions by a national quasi-judicial body in an individual case was *Ahmed and Ahmed v. UNHCR*. Two Somali refugees brought a complaint against UNHCR to the UHRC (which can sit as a court ordering people out of detention and awarding compensation), submitting that they had been 'tossed about by the UNHCR and the Uganda Red Cross on the issue of who should have the responsibility to pay for their school fees.'[68] The Commission concluded that if the men had been accepted as refugees by UNHCR, 'then the UNHCR should take up the matter seriously thus protecting and promoting the rights of refugees, among which is the right to education' (ibid.). In another case, the UHRC dealt with a complaint by a Sierra Leonean asylum-seeker who had been denied refugee status because West Africans were not apparently accepted in East Africa (*Kromah v. UNHCR*). The Commission wrote to UNHCR: 'Given the fact that Sierra Leone is embroiled in a civil war, it is pertinent that you be pleased to grant the said Complainant refugee status.' The chairperson of the UHRC reported that there were more refugee complaints registered at the Commission, ranging from arbitrary arrest to alleged violations of economic and social rights to 'lack of access to the officers of the UNHCR so as to explain their problems' (ibid.). The chairperson also pointed out that although the Commission had competence over refugee rights 'as stipulated in all the relevant international instruments', it did not 'have the legal mandate to enforce such rights [refugee rights] against UNHCR' (Sekaggya 1999).

Individuals

An individual's incompetence produces the most harmful consequences when combined with an institutional dysfunction. For example, the report compiled by a senior UNHCR official on a mission to Kenya and Uganda in 1995 illustrates what can happen when professional incompetence is combined with the 'demise of protection' (UNHCR 1995e). This mission reviewed some protection issues in the two countries, one of which concerned a Kenyan who had sought asylum in Uganda in May 1992. UNHCR had rejected his application for refugee status 'on the grounds that he was still involved in subversive activities' (ibid.). The UNHCR decision was flawed: 'subversive activities' might have been a reference to article 3 of the OAU Convention, but even this provision, which prohibits 'subversive activities', does not suggest that the commission of a 'subversive act' should lead to the loss of refugee status. While waiting for UNHCR's decision, this refugee had been arrested and detained by the Ugandan authorities for several months without appearing before a judge. The case had attracted considerable media attention in Kenya and Uganda, and had strained relations between the two countries. The Ugandan government did not want to *refoul* him, but was eager to find a third country where he could be resettled so as to alleviate the political tension with Kenya. Ghana responded positively to the request and agreed to admit this refugee, as well as another Kenyan in a similar situation. The Ugandan Ministry of Foreign Affairs later announced that 'the decision to resettle was jointly taken by the Government of Uganda and UNHCR Kampala' (ibid.). However, 'The Government of Kenya, which had in the meantime requested Mr Odongo's extradition, protested with UNHCR's representative in Kenya and accused UNHCR of recognising "criminals" as refugees in Uganda' (ibid.).

The review revealed a lack of knowledge of the basic principles of refugee law: 'after thorough review of IC's [individual case's] file including the reading of the interview report and different press reports, we came to the conclusion that IC could not qualify for refugee status, in view of his activities since he came to Uganda. His activities were confirmed by the President of Uganda in person in an interview to the daily "New Vision"' (UNHCR 1995e). It was apparently the opinion of the senior official and the other UNHCR lawyers involved in this review – as well as of those involved in the initial rejection of this refugee's application – that an asylum-seeker's application could be rejected on account of his or her presumed activities in the country of asylum. However, the conduct of an asylum-seeker in the country of asylum has nothing to do with recognition of refugee status, whether the claim arises out of individualised persecution or out of the objective situation that obtained in the country of origin. Under the 1951 Convention, the refugee's conduct in the host country can lead to expulsion when the person is found guilty of certain crimes. In this case, the man had not even been convicted of a crime by a court of law. At any rate, the OAU Convention broadens the protection against *non-refoulement* and eliminates the exception on expulsion that features at article 32 of the 1951 Convention.

This case also illustrates how, once the centrality of the protection function under the UNHCR statute is given up, political factors can be decisive in difficult decisions (Goodwin-Gill 1999). In the case of Mr Odongo, the anomaly was also that the roles were reversed: Uganda, the state that UNHCR was meant to be monitoring, was trying to find a solution for this refugee despite the political turmoil that his presence had caused; meanwhile UNHCR was trying to thwart the government's attempts for reasons of political expediency. Incompetence, or ignorance of the law, underlay the process. Seldom did UNHCR display such zeal in individual cases, when Kenya or Uganda wrongfully rejected asylum applications. The UNHCR report recommended that all cases of Kenyan refugees and asylum-seekers in Uganda be reviewed and updated, and that interview reports and recommendations should be sent to headquarters. When the reporting official travelled to Kenya, a copy of the Kenyan refugee's file was given to the UNHCR representative and 'it was agreed that it should be left to Headquarters to inform the Kenyan authorities on UNHCR's comments on this issue' (UNHCR 1995e). Surprisingly, in this case, UNHCR was informing the government of the country of origin even though the refugee had been granted status.

This review was not an isolated case of incompetence. Numerous decisions on status determination taken by UNHCR in both Kenya and Uganda were poorly reasoned – when reasoned at all – or wrong in law (discussed in Chapter 3). The lack of experienced staff was also a major problem at a critical time in Kenya, when the exodus of Somalis began in 1992 (UNHCR 1992c: 35–39). In general, UNHCR suffered from flaws in the recruitment system used by the UN. For example, the protection posts at field level were normally filled by junior professional officers. Although these individuals normally had good academic qualifications, they seldom had much experience. Yet they were landed with some of the world's most difficult jobs – such as being put in charge of the protection of tens of thousands of refugees in Kakuma or Adjumani. Moreover, junior professional officers were not always assigned to the UN programme of their choice. As a result, for some of them, personal frustration was added to the difficulties of their work; this was the case, for instance, of a highly qualified UNHCR official in Dadaab who had specialised in international environmental law but had found 'UN work' only at UNHCR.

More worrying was the fact that, in many instances, bad and even legally flawed policies were implemented *notwithstanding* the presence of competent individuals. When certain procedures become entrenched in an institutional culture, individual competence often succumbs to bureaucratic loyalty. The policy of encampment is an example: it was followed scrupulously, *despite* the competence in refugee law of at least some officials who knew that it meant a violation of the rights of refugees.

As argued by Walkup, three options are available to the competent UNHCR official who has to implement a policy that he or she does not agree with, or that is unlawful: 'exit, voice and loyalty' (1997b: 42). The official can decide to quit 'because of the build-up of stress, unresolved conflicts, and perceived hopelessness' (ibid.), or to 'voice' his or her 'frustrations in efforts to expose organisational problems' or bad policies (ibid.: 43). The final option available to the disillusioned official is 'loyalty', often justified with the argument that 'it is better to work within the system than not to work at all' (ibid.: 43).

In UNHCR in Kenya and Uganda, 'loyalty' was, as in most bureaucracies, the commonest reaction. There were a few dissenters, officials who chose to 'voice' their dissent in the hope that this could bring about institutional change. We witnessed a vivid illustration of internal dissent during a closed-doors meeting at UNHCR Nairobi in March 1997, to which we had been invited as observers. This meeting took place three months after the forced repatriation of Rwandans from Tanzania and while the dramatic events in eastern Zaire were still unfolding. A member of staff who had worked in Ngara, Tanzania, during the repatriation, said that UNHCR's direct involvement in the forced repatriation had upset her. She related that the field staff kept being told that they should not resist the repatriation because 'Geneva wanted it'. After describing some of the most dramatic scenes from those days, she asked rhetorically, 'What is the point of our work if we then do something of this kind to refugees?' Her outburst was met with embarrassed silence. She then commented, 'Well, if saying these things will make me lose my job, that's fine. I can go and work for an NGO, or something.'[70]

Dissenters tread on dangerous grounds when they have to make a considered assessment of how far they can go in voicing their dissent. If they go too far, they can be punished with assignments to the most inhospitable locations, or even with dismissal.[71] This is illustrated by the case of Dr Guluma, who was dismissed by UNHCR and an NGO, the International Rescue Committee (IRC), for having 'overstepped the boundaries' by speaking to various visitors and external researchers in Kakuma about the appalling nutritional situation in the camp.[72] The doctor was flabbergasted when he found out that his contract was not going to be renewed, periodic renewal being more or less a routine formality. He said that he would not have acted differently, even if he had considered the possible risks of voicing his dissent, but psychologically he had not prepared himself for the consequences.

The UNHCR staff appraisal system creates a major incentive to demonstrate 'loyalty', and a strong disincentive to voice criticism. In UNHCR, heads of office are responsible for evaluating the performance of junior members of staff. A protection officer or a field officer working for UNHCR in one of the camps or settlements would have had his or her appraisal written by the head of sub-office and countersigned by the head of branch office in Kampala or Nairobi. Without a good appraisal, the prospects of promotion are virtually nil; an excellent appraisal almost always assures it. Junior professional officers, who had fixed-term contracts, were particularly eager to obtain good appraisals, as most of them aspired to continuing to work for UNHCR or another UN agency.

This fear of a negative appraisal undermines the possibility of bottom-to-top changes within UNHCR, and limits the scope for staff challenges to institutional policies. In addition, the main criterion for appraising members of staff is whether they have 'met the objectives', which will have been identified by their superiors. 'Organisational commitment' and 'political and organisational awareness' are other criteria employed to assess the performance of a member of staff. If newly hired protection or field officers find that the objectives they have been assigned conflict with their interpretation of the mandate, the choice will be between a career sacrifice and 'loyalty' (which might mean a sacrifice of the mandate instead).

At first glance, this system might seem similar to that for civil servants in national bureaucracies. There is however a substantial difference: in UNHCR the built-in checks and balances are completely inadequate, leaving staff vulnerable to abuses of power. Members of staff are shown their appraisal forms, and, after reading them, have to choose one of two boxes, depending on whether they agree with the appraisal or not. In the latter case, they can explain the reasons for their disagreement in the space provided in the form, 'continuing on one separate piece of paper if necessary' (UNHCR 1996n: 9.3). Members of staff can also avail themselves of a 'formal rebuttal procedure' by submitting a statement to the performance monitoring unit in Geneva within thirty days. UNHCR's manuals repeatedly state that disagreements with the appraisal should be avoided as far as possible, and differences of opinion should be settled through 'dialogue' between the members of staff and their supervisor (a head of suboffice or a head of unit) and the reviewer (normally the head of branch office). Those few who, having received a negative appraisal, decide to record their disagreement and to follow it up with a formal statement sent to Geneva usually realise that their career prospects in the UN are at that point diminishing. Furthermore, unlike civil servants, UNHCR staff cannot use the law to enforce their rights or take action against abusive colleagues or superiors; the remedies that exist are all internal.

The combined effect of these practices is entrenched conservatism, 'especially in the repetitive rituals of the lower levels of some bureaucracies. Rules and procedures are revered' (Chambers 1997: 65). As one UNHCR member of staff, talking about UNHCR status determination, remarked: 'My responsibility is to follow the procedure 100% and so I should not be concerned if I send 100 back and one or two is killed; we just try to avoid this the next time and cannot be blamed when we've done our duty according to protocol.'[73]

Thus, the 'rules and procedures' that are revered are not the legal principles of refugee law or the UNHCR statute, but 'the protocol' – internal bureaucratic rules, some written down in handbooks and manuals and some unwritten. This employee was able to be casual about the possible consequences that a mistake might have for a refugee because he knew that he would never be called to account for that mistake. Staff behaviour in bureaucratic organisations 'tends to drift towards compatibility with the ways the organization is evaluated' (Lipsky 1980: 51). In the case of this protection officer, a negative appraisal was not going to follow from a poor or wrong decision; it could, however, have resulted from, for example, deciding too few cases, since UNHCR and other bureaucracies 'tend to measure what they can readily quantify without intruding on workers' interactions with clients' (ibid.: 52). In fact, in its handbooks UNHCR includes 'measurability' as an essential feature of a 'good objective' – providing as examples of 'good' objectives 'eligibility interviews of X refugees by (date)' or 'to assess and report on all unaccompanied minors in the camp by (date) so as to ensure that appropriate Protection measures can be taken' (UNHCR 1996n).

Meeting quantifiable objectives serves the bureaucratic purpose of creating the impression of increased institutional efficiency and good staff performance, but these measurements are seldom reliable indicators of real improvements. While the fulfilment of the institutional objective of determining the status of a certain number of asylum applicants by a certain date would have produced the semblance of efficiency, this numbers-led exercise would have concealed the experience of the many whose applications had not been fairly assessed and had been rejected. Lispky gives the example of measurements of police performance based on the number of arrests carried out by each officer: 'Do increases in arrest rates signal improved police performance? Or do they signal deteriorating police performance, indicating an increase in criminal activity and thus in the number of criminals available to catch?' (1980: 51). Such 'agency-generated statistics are likely to tell us little about the phenomena they purport to reflect, but a great deal about the agency behaviour that produced the statistics' (ibid.: 53).

Some competent individuals chose 'loyalty', while trying to improve UNHCR practice. Kenya and Uganda illustrated the limits of what competent and committed individuals could achieve. As mentioned, in both countries, the senior protection officers who took office after 1998 succeeded in introducing some positive changes, in particular by making the status-determination procedures fairer. They were responsive to criticism, and were prepared to follow up on individual cases with greater professionalism. Both of them were critical of the status quo on refugee policy in Kenya and Uganda. However, despite their efforts and some important results, the fundamentals of the situation did not change: encampment remained the policy in both countries, disguised as 'settlements' and 'self-sufficiency' policy in Uganda.

NGOs

'NGO' is an umbrella term that refers to the most disparate organisations. NGOs can be distinguished on the basis of their activities (humanitarian/emergency, development, human rights, environment, and so on) and their geographic spread (from international down to small grassroots initiatives). Our data and analyses, unless otherwise indicated, refer, for the most part, to international and national humanitarian NGOs, and do not apply, as such, to other types of NGOs.

A prominent feature of the UNHCR–NGOs relationship in Kenya and Uganda was that NGOs seldom, if ever, challenged UNHCR policies towards refugees. The docility of humanitarian NGOs vis-à-vis UNHCR in Africa contrasts with the confrontational stance of human rights, development, and environmental NGOs opposed to the policies of international financial institutions like the World Bank (Fox and Brown 1998). It is undoubtedly to the credit of the transnational coalitions of these NGOs and grassroots movements that they succeeded in putting the accountability of the World Bank on the political agenda.[74] It has by now become almost accepted wisdom that international financial institutions can get it wrong, that they do tend to act in an unaccountable manner, and that they can have a negative impact on human rights. Yet such accepted wisdom has yet to appear when it comes to the work of UNHCR with refugees, despite the fact that it is now nearly twenty years since *Imposing Aid* (Harrell-Bond 1986) and *The Quality of Mercy* (Shawcross 1984) first cast a critical light on the world of humanitarianism.

Why is it that NGOs in the refugee and humanitarian sector have not challenged UNHCR? Political pressure to refrain from criticism against UNHCR is unlikely to have been greater than that withstood by NGOs that criticised the World Bank; after all, the economic and political interests that international financial institutions represent are generally viewed as more important than humanitarian causes by countries in the 'developed world'.

An important reason for the NGOs' subordination to UNHCR in Kenya and Uganda was that UNHCR did not hesitate to use its position of power to enforce obedience. For instance, when MSF-Holland announced that it would not be involved in a headcount, the MSF representative was told that 'if his agency were to be UNHCR's implementing partner, he would do as he was instructed or leave. The census was carried out' (Elder 1999b: 8).

Other factors contributed to making NGOs subservient to UNHCR. Firstly, the 'transnational coalitions' of grassroots movements and NGOs against the World Bank were largely possible because grassroots movements could mobilise a constituency of *citizens* around a set of interests and a programme of political action. In both Kenya and Uganda, refugee associations did exist, but they never found a local or international spokesperson capable of furthering their claims. After all, who could this spokesperson have been? The local and national political class was unlikely to take up their complaints, because refugees did not vote; the refugees' international protector, UNHCR, was part of the problem; NGOs working with refugees had a vested interest in defending the status quo. As for international human rights organisations, such as Amnesty International or Human Rights Watch (HRW), they were aware of these refugee groups but they only took up individual refugee claims on an isolated and sporadic basis.[75]

Secondly, in Kenya and Uganda, nearly all NGOs that had an interest in refugees were at some point sub-contracted by UNHCR to provide certain services in refugee camps and settlements, or to help with the status-determination process or with the much smaller programmes for urban refugees. Even those NGOs that were not in a contractual relationship with UNHCR were probably loath to take any action that could compromise their future chances to enter into such a relationship and to have access to funds.

An 'implementing partnership', normally hailed as a positive example of dialogue and engagement between UNHCR and civil society, proved to be a death toll to civil society, since sub-contracting created a synergy of interests between NGOs and UNHCR, and it disabled the former's potential for critical action against the latter.[76] NGOs developed an interest in maintaining good relations with UNHCR, from whose funds the continuation of their refugee programmes and the employment of their staff depended. This type of arrangement transformed them: they became 'service contractors ... NGOs which function as market-oriented non-profit businesses serving public purposes ... They are distinguished from voluntary organisations in that they are driven more by market considerations than by values, and thus have more in common with private businesses ...' (Robinson 1997: 59). Therefore, commitment to the cause (or the value) quickly succumbed to the more compelling needs of remaining in business, preserving jobs, and beating the competition of other NGOs.

Of the organisations that worked on refugees in Uganda and Kenya, only the Refugee Law Project (RLP), established at Makerere University in November 1999, and the Refugee Consortium of Kenya (RCK) have never been sub-contractors of UNHCR.[77] In Kenya, the partnership between UNHCR and the Jesuit Refugee Service (JRS) ended only in 1999. In Uganda, the small assistance project that JRS ran for asylum-seekers in Kampala operated under significant pressure from both UNHCR and its own country director, who took the view that the 'independent' urban programme was at odds with UNHCR/JRS partnership in northern Uganda because it was encouraging refugees to remain in the town. For other NGOs, their dependence on UNHCR was almost total: the LWF, for example, had a budget of US$ 1.5 million for 1997 and US$ 1.6 million for 1998, which 'dwarfs the funds available from other independent sources (US$ 361,000 in 1998), rendering LWF almost completely dependent on UNHCR, with little scope for responding to needs which UNHCR is unprepared to fund' (Seddon et al. 1998).

It was important for NGOs to conceal the effects of the transformation in their role so as to preserve the image of themselves as part of a civil society movement driven by a cause rather than by profit. In countries in the 'developed world', organisations that are sub-contracted by governments and provide certain services normally cease to be regarded as humanitarian organisations, both because they have lost their independence and because their work ceases to be humanitarian in nature: for example, an NGO providing security services for a detention centre for asylum-seekers in Britain would not be viewed as working for a 'cause' and as deserving of the 'civil society' label.[78] Yet in Kenya and Uganda, and across countries in the 'developing world', the moral legitimacy of NGOs was not undermined by the fact that, to all intents and purposes, they acted as business enterprises and got involved in activities that had little to do with the cause or were even harmful to refugees.

The main reason for this was that the trustees, donors, and the media that were conferring moral legitimacy on these NGOs were removed from the operational reality: to these people the NGOs could continue to successfully present themselves as activist and value-driven organisations.

Sub-contracting offered advantages to UNHCR too. In particular, it could claim that it was acting 'in partnership' with civil society and decentralising its activities, although, in practice, this decentralisation was only apparent since UNHCR controlled the funds and therefore determined policy.

Whither civil society?

Although there is a general myth that NGOs are closer to the people, a problem with NGOs administering refugee camps – as illustrated by the situation in Kenya and Uganda – was the distance they maintained between themselves and the refugees. For example, the 'zone managers' employed by the Uganda Red Cross Society (URCS) and with responsibility over some 1,500 people were supposed:

> to provide the interface between the refugee community and the Red Cross ... With so few beneficiaries under their responsibility one would expect that they would be acquainted with them, know precisely where they lived and how many were in each family. It became clear during the census preparation meeting that they knew very little about those in their charge. Why this is the case became clear during the few days that I was in the settlement. Not once did I see any of them leave the base camp' (Elder 1999b: 8).

The cooptation of civil society organisations through contractual agreements and the disenfranchisement of refugees in host states create a 'power bloc' of interests, which has thus far proven impenetrable. Interestingly, the thinker who is credited with developing the concept of civil society,

Antonio Gramsci, never regarded it as an intrinsically progressive force: he considered civil society as part and parcel of power, the other complementary face of 'political society' (Gramsci 1992). In the humanitarian arena, civil society operates precisely as Gramsci had envisaged.

In the late 1990s, humanitarian NGOs belatedly reacted to criticism by engaging in a standard-setting exercise, aiming to get closer to their beneficiaries. They developed codes of good practice and minimum standards for sanitation, shelter, food, and so on, to apply to the provision of humanitarian assistance. The most important of these initiatives is the Sphere Project, joined by more than 200 NGOs, and which resulted in a Humanitarian Charter and Minimum Standards in Disaster Response, to which all members are signatories.[79]

The idea of measuring performance represents a step forward in some respect from the view that NGOs are only doing 'charity' work, but this approach is still a far cry from questioning the encampment policy and using the enjoyment of the rights of the beneficiaries – that is, refugees – as the yardstick for gauging the performance of humanitarian work. Stockton has observed that this 'renewed clarion call for the setting and imposition of standards for humanitarian aid is increasingly offered as a panacea for solving all the ills of emergency interventions' (1996: 8). Indeed, much of the Sphere Project's work duplicates the Geneva Convention (III) Relative to the Treatment of Prisoners of War which contains 'an exhaustive, even obsessive, regulation of the confinement of a human group in a restricted space', making 'meticulous provision for every aspect of the life of prisoners of war in a camp, including registration, hygienic standards, provision of food, clothing, underwear and footwear, frequency of health inspections, types and standards of shelter, religious, intellectual and physical activities, the wearing of badges, correspondence, etc' (Verdirame 2001b: 209). It made sense for the Geneva Convention to contain this detailed regulation, because it dealt with prisoners of war. Refugees *are not* prisoners of war, and the standard of treatment that ought to apply to them is significantly better.[80]

To the extent that these humanitarian codes reinvent the wheel, initiatives like the Sphere Project are superfluous. Unfortunately, they also conceal a dangerous trend: reducing rights to measurements on the assumption that liberty and dignity consist of giving human beings a certain number of items, regardless of the fact that their fundamental rights – movement, work, fair trial, etc. – are violated.

Human rights organisations

Unlike humanitarian NGOs, human rights organisations were not usually sub-contracted by UNHCR, and guard their political and financial independence. Nevertheless, despite a few and generally short-lived exceptions – the Foundation for Human Rights Initiative (FHRI) in Uganda in 1997, ICJ in Kenya until 1997, and the Kenya section of the International Federation of Women Lawyers (FIDA) in 1995–96 – they did not generally include refugees in their work.

The political disenfranchisement of refugees, discussed before, was probably the main factor that could account for the very limited involvement of national and local human rights NGOs in refugee matters. In addition, some human rights organisations, like humanitarian ones, viewed refugees as a 'humanitarian' issue rather than a human rights one. More generally, the human rights abuses of which citizens were victims absorbed the energy and resources of national human rights organisations, probably causing them to adopt a rather inward-looking attitude. The significant risks associated with advocating refugee rights and making enemies with the government played a role too (Lomo 1999a). Finally, money for refugee rights programmes was not as easily available from the main donors as for other activities, and donors were also wary of activism that they perceived as too confrontational (ibid.: 169).

As a result, monitoring of respect for refugee rights by local human rights NGOs was limited, and systematic fact-finding about the refugee situation almost non-existent. When over 100 Sudanese refugees were killed in one attack of the Lord's Resistance Army (LRA) in Achol-Pii and Agago camps in Kitgum in 1996, only the Sudanese Human Rights Association (SHRA) and Amnesty International denounced this. In Kenya, when Ekuru Aukot started working for ICJ as an intern in 1998, he became frustrated as 'None [of the NGOs] was interested in refugee matters. KHRC [Kenyan Human Rights Commission] kept on sending to ICJ refugees with a slip addressed to me stating "Please assist the bearer as his problem is of a refugee nature and we do not have a refugee programme here."'

International human rights organisations compensated for some of the shortcomings of national human rights groups. Amnesty International, HRW, the Lawyers Committee for Human Rights (LCHR) at one point or another produced reports on the situation of refugees in Kenya and Uganda.[81] Nevertheless, the impact of this reporting activity, crucial as it was, was limited by the fact that resources and time constraints only allowed for narrow follow-up activities. Moreover, some human rights violations that had less visibility and that required more long-term advocacy – such as, for example, those resulting from encampment – did not receive the attention they deserved.

Another problem was that, in many cases, international and national human rights NGOs had not found the most effective way of combining efforts and resources to achieve their common goals. The modus operandi of international human rights organisations is based on documenting and publicising human rights violation in an attempt to improve compliance. Methods include campaigns through letter-writing, the adoption of cases by local groups, submissions of 'shadow' reports to treaty-based and charter-based human rights bodies, and missions and meetings with government officials. Since the time when international human rights organisations, like Amnesty International and HRW, began their work, most countries in the 'developing world' – and certainly Kenya and Uganda – have witnessed the development of a thriving national human rights community. This is a significant change, the benefits of which remain to be fully reaped.

International human rights organisations are, of course, aware of the existence of national organisations and use them as sources of information, along with others (journalists, private individuals, lawyers, academics, clergy, etc.). What is sometimes lacking is greater strategic coordination, playing on the strengths of different organisations. For example, international human rights organisations, which are generally better-resourced than their national counterparts, can offer assistance to help bring cases to court; they can develop advocacy programmes for refugees, or facilitate national human rights organisations with raising funds; and they can draw the attention of donors and policy makers in the 'developed world' to the failures of UNHCR. A useful blueprint for the type of strategic coordination that is needed is the experience of NGOs that have worked to promote the accountability of the World Bank (Fox and Brown 1998). Advocacy campaigns on the World Bank have been carried out by 'transnational coalitions' of activists in which each actor played on its expertise and resources, trying to maximise the benefits of the political and geographic context in which it operated. Grassroots organisations gathered data and were pivotal in setting the agenda for the movement. National and international NGOs organised the material from the field, wrote reports, and disseminated them widely. Washington lobbyists used this information to ensure dissemination at the highest policy decision-making levels, while activists organised campaigns in Europe and North America, where the main donor countries of the World Bank can be found.

Human rights organisations, and other NGOs, have learnt to regard the World Bank as a powerful actor to be tackled in the same way as they tackle states. UNHCR, on the contrary, is too often considered by human rights organisations as an 'ally' working for the same cause. Although it might be so in the case of UNHCR's work in Europe, this is not so in all those situations, especially in the 'developing world', where UNHCR has assumed governmental powers, administering refugee camps and conducting refugee status determination. Despite some important examples of reporting critical of UNHCR (e.g., African Rights 1993; LCHR 1995; HRW 1997a), the predominant approach was too often 'soft' on UNHCR. As a result, violations of the human rights of refugees committed by governments – for example, through arbitrary arrest or refoulement – were given significantly greater attention than those committed by UNHCR or humanitarian NGOs.[82] This is part of a more general phenomenon that has seen human rights organisations broaden their mandates from the initial focus on civil and political rights to social and economic rights and to human rights in the private sphere. This shift has caused them 'to reposition themselves in relation to the state', as well as to other actors such as international organisations (Garling 2003: 58).

PARinAC: a case study in cooptation

The implementation of the Partners in Action (PARinAC) process in Kenya is a good example of how such apparently progressive ideas as promoting the 'development of civil society' can be put into operation in such a way as to destroy what they purportedly set out to create or strengthen. At the time of the PARinAC initiative, Kenyan civil society had not only expressed a willingness to take refugee matters on board; it clearly also had the ability to do so effectively. That all of this occurred without any facilitation from UNHCR was perhaps the crux of the matter: UNHCR was not in control. Once the Kenyan NGOs with an interest in refugees attempted to intrude themselves into the PARinAC process, UNHCR was quick to set about destroying a spontaneous and dynamic local initiative.

PARinAC was launched in 1993 in response to the fact that the number of humanitarian NGOs had mushroomed,[83] working relationships between them and UNHCR had been less than ideal, and the participation of national NGOs in refugee matters was minimal. A series of regional meetings was held to discuss the potential for a more 'harmonious' partnership between UNHCR and NGOs. Following the regional meetings, a PARinAC Global Conference took place in Oslo in June 1994 bringing together '182 NGOs from 82 countries' (ECRE 1994). At this conference, a Plan of Action containing 134 recommendations was approved.[84]

Before the PARinAC process started, some momentum had been created within Kenyan civil society to deal with refugee issues. This had been triggered by the Kenya section of the ICJ, which since 1991 had been assisting refugees in Nairobi with advice on their asylum claims and with other problems. In February 1992, the council of ICJ decided 'to establish a Refugee Programme'.[85] ICJ began to develop contacts with other organisations with a view of creating a network of Kenyan NGOs dealing with refugees. The director of ICJ, representatives of other NGOs and the Centre for Refugee Studies, Moi University, interested Kenyans, and refugees formed 'The Joint NGO/Refugee Group'. Their first meeting took place in May 1993. The initial goals of the Joint Group were to: increase public awareness of the plight of refugees in Kenya, challenge adverse press coverage of refugee issues, coordinate the activities of the

various NGOs who offered services to refugees, encourage the government to enact legislation on refugees, and promote research on refugees
in Kenya. The ultimate objective of the Joint Group was to improve the
protection of the rights of refugees in the country.[86]

ICJ remained the leading player in the Joint Group, as its refugee programme made progress. Nevertheless, its attempts to get UNHCR's support for this initiative, as well as for asylum cases, were often frustrated.
In one case, it took ten months for ICJ to get a response from UNHCR. In
another letter, the senior protection officer acknowledged the receipt of
'various letters from your organisation during the last months' and apol-
ogised 'for not having answered on time your inquires regarding asylum-
seekers or refugees who have requested your intervention'.[87] By contrast,
the response of the government of Kenya to ICJ's initiative was positive.[88]

By 1993 the Joint Group had become more than just a network of NGOs
involved in refugee matters. Its activities included visiting refugees in the
Thika reception centre, as well as dealing with individual refugee cases.
The Joint Group was in communication with the LCHR, which was planning a mission to investigate the protection problems of refugees in
Kenya: the Joint Group took responsibility for setting up appointments
for this mission and provided names of individuals whom the LCHR
team could meet in the course of its fact-finding mission. The group
sought to be inclusive, declaring that 'all NGOs who in their operations
are already undertaking work relating to refugees and asylum-seekers, or
are seriously considering taking up such work, qualify to be members of
the Joint NGO/Refugee Group'.[89]

A workshop on the protection and rights of refugees in Kenya was
planned and took place in December 1993. As part of the agenda, the preliminary reports of HRW/Africa Watch (1993) and African Rights (1993)
were considered. The minutes of the workshop reveal that a UNHCR official dismissed the results of the report by African Rights because the
author had:

> ... visited the camps but never contacted UNHCR. It appears that his
> observations were obtained from refugees directly [*sic*]. He said that NGOs
> in the camps were not aware of this person. It appeared that the person
> came with a certain bias in mind ... resulting in a perverted report of
> events in the camp. He said that it was not the policy of UNHCR to hide
> anything. Mr. Quintero said that it was not true that UNHCR had failed to
> protect Somali refugees and offer legal assistance. He said that the report
> drew the serious conclusion that Somali refugees were not safe in Kenya.
> The impression created was that Somali refugees were not receiving prop-
> er protection from the government and UNHCR.[90]

During the workshop, a draft refugee bill was also discussed.
Participants compared it with a model for national refugee legislation prepared by the OAU, and with the OAU Convention. The workshop also

planned to revise the NGO directory to include all NGOs that 'are or might be concerned with issues of refugee protection'.[91] It was also agreed that there would be a visit to the camps in Kenya and Somalia by members of the Joint Group, and plans for a national conference on refugees were debated.

Following the workshop, in a letter to the LCHR, the Joint Group explained that its objectives included:

> (1) the application of the international refugee law and the determination of the juridical status of asylum-seekers and refugees in the country ... (3) dissemination of refugee law; (4) the incorporation of international refugee law into municipal law and the enactment of domestic refugee legislation; (5) provision of legal services to refugees and asylum-seekers in matters related to violation of their rights, and (6) examination into the root causes of refugee movements.[92]

Summarising the purpose and the history of its involvement in refugee matters, ICJ explained, 'Two years ago the International Commission of Jurists (Kenya Section) started a small project whose main objective was *to protect refugee rights against the UNHCR and Government bureaucracy.* This project involved simplifying refugee law and UNHCR policies to the aggrieved refugees so that they may seek redress from the two organs procedurally and without being necessary tied down by 'red tape' [emphasis added].'[93]

Research was also part of the activities of the Joint Group. In January 1994, a research project on the refugee situation in Kenya was discussed and a draft proposal was presented to the government and to UNHCR. The need for such a study derived from the fact that:

> Given the pressure of the needs on the ground, much of response has been assistance-oriented, so that only limited research has been undertaken to assess the refugee situation in the country. Most of the literature is in the form of piecemeal agency reports on specific aspects of their operations. It is thus the intention of this study to undertake a comprehensive assessment of the phenomenon of forced migration in Kenya.[94]

In February, the chair of the Joint Group received another letter from the Office of the President, welcoming his proposal for research into the refugee situation in Kenya.[95] The ICJ and the Joint Group were growing increasingly pro-active. The uneasiness expressed by the UNHCR official about their December 1993 workshop should have rung alarm bells. By February 1994, UNHCR was taking steps to sideline the NGOs involved in the Joint Group. An unexpected help in achieving this goal was offered by the PARinAC initiative.

The regional PARinAC meeting was held in Addis Ababa, on 21–23 March 1994, but none of the NGOs involved in the Joint Group was invited. In fact, as the chair of the Joint Group explained in letters to UNHCR senior staff in Geneva, the group had not even been informed about the PARinAC process by UNHCR, but had found out 'in a circuitous way ...' that 'five names of NGOs involved in relief work' had been chosen for 'the regional meeting to be held in Addis Ababa'.[96]

In the same period, the chair of the Joint Group also wrote to the chief of the NGO liaison section in Geneva expressing similar concerns and requesting that the participation of:

> ... at least one of the seven legal NGOs in the country and which belong to the Joint NGO Refugee Group ... The attendance at the regional conference in Addis Ababa would of course make it easier for a representative of the legal NGOs to attend the global Conference scheduled to be held in Oslo (6–9 June, 1994). Such inclusion would be in accordance with the declared intention (as per PARINAC Information Note and Update No. 1 (which I obtained from Mr Kishindo), that is to say: 'The organisers will ensure the participation from a broad cross section of NGOs from each region.'[97]

Although not invited to attend the Addis Ababa Conference, following the protest, some of the NGOs participating in the Joint Group were invited to the PARinAC Global Conference in Oslo, but not ICJ which had spearheaded the Joint Group. The Kenyan NGOs represented at that meeting decided that ICJ ought to be the national focal point for the implementation of the Oslo Plan of Action. Meanwhile, UNHCR had selected the Islamic African Relief Agency (IARA) as the NGO responsible at the regional level for the coordination of PARinAC activities.[98] Its main task was to organise consultative meetings in conjunction with the national NGOs. IARA held a meeting in Nairobi, only two months after Oslo, in order to elect the NGO that was to be the national focal point. Only four NGOs attended the meeting called by IARA – far fewer than those who would normally attend the meetings organised in the 'non-PARinAC' context of the Joint Group chaired by ICJ. Nonetheless elections were held, and the Crescent of Hope was chosen as the national focal point. ICJ and other NGOs that were part of the Joint Group had not been invited to that meeting.

The chair of the Joint Group wrote once again to the chief of the NGO liaison section in Geneva observing that:

> ... Since Oslo, NGOs have been briefed on the Oslo Plans of Action. However, as we met to discuss the implementation of the Plans of Action, we became aware of several developments which are counter-productive to the philosophy and spirit of the PARinAC process.

> On the 21st of July 1994, as we met to discuss PARinAC, IARA was holding another meeting, purportedly to hold elections for the national focal point. The election was postponed due to lack of quorum. A week later, on the 28th of July, 1994, the elections were held with only 4 NGOs concerned with refugees in attendance, and Crescent of Hope, a local NGO, was elected as the national focal point. (The International Commission of

Jurists (Kenya Section) was not invited to the meeting in which the elections were held.)

This development, which many NGOs in the refugee area never anticipated and which, in the opinion of ICJ was uncalled for, raises fears on the possibility of reinventing the wheel and creating parallel structures. Democracy is a way of doing things and it is imperative, for the PARinAC process to succeed, that there is genuine involvement of all parties involved ...

... There is also something else we wish to point out, as we think it might be lying underneath the attempt to cause a fissure within the already existing Joint NGO Refugee Group, namely, the misconception that the solution to the refugee problem lies in material and humanitarian assistance only, which is of course not the case. Indeed, we believe it might have been partly this misconception which resulted in the omission of legal/human rights NGOs from Kenya from the list of participants to the regional meeting held in Addis Ababa. It was noteworthy that all the five names of the NGOs provided by the Co-ordinator, Mr Andrew Kishindo, of the All African Conference of Churches, were all involved in relief work and none from the NGOs involved in the international protection of refugees, something which was counter to the declared objective of the PARINAC initiative ...[99]

IARA and the Crescent of Hope remained respectively regional and national focal points, and the marginalisation of ICJ and of the Joint Group was completed. When considered in the light of UNHCR's poor performance in the protection of the rights of refugees in Kenya at the time – detailed in other sections of this book – perhaps it should come as no surprise that UNHCR decided to sideline an initiative which aimed at promoting respect for the human rights of refugees and which had not hesitated to criticise the actions of UNHCR and of the government.

PARinAC's lacklustre history in the region continued. At a regional meeting in Addis Ababa in November 1998, various levels of red tape were added as part of the PARinAC structure.[100] It was recommended that UNHCR and the NGO community should establish their national PARinAC focal point; that NGO groups should be set up, or reinforced where they already existed, with UNHCR's assistance; that other coordination mechanisms – NGO/UNHCR, government/UNHCR/NGO, as well as with other intergovernmental organisations – should be established; and that UNHCR should set up a UNHCR/NGO task force that included regional focal points. In addition, UNHCR/NGO country focal points had to produce a PARinAC newsletter; the NGO regional focal point had to produce an annual report; UNHCR should include funding for as many national NGO focal points as possible to enable them to attend pre-EXCOM and EXCOM meetings; and that an annual East and Horn of Africa PARinAC meeting should be held.[101] Clearly the amount of staff time and resources to fulfil these recommendations would require a significant diversion from services to refugees.[102] As a final exercise in futility, the Addis Conference discussed the adoption of a definition of

PARinAC. It eventually produced a circuitous definition, while giving no clue whatsoever as to what exactly the multi-layered PARinAC structure was supposed to do:

> Partnership in Action, PARinAC, is every activity in which UNHCR and NGOs are involved together. It encompasses all NGOs who have interest in refugees. PARinAC, regardless of whether it is referred to as such, is an important part of all protection and operational activities, whether in emergency response, care and maintenance or the pursuit of solutions. Solutions comprising (*sic*) repatriation, local settlements or resettlement in a third country. It is also an important part of *our* [emphasis added] relationship with those NGOs who are primarily concerned with advocacy – either directly on behalf of refugees or as part of a broader human rights focus.[103]

The only substantive recommendation coming out of the conference that was not given adequate prominence was that 'Partners should promote refugee law and improved refugee legislation, as well as raising public awareness on the rights and obligations of refugees'.[104] This was the only recommendation for which no follow-up was established.

Conclusion

Common to all actors dealing with refugees was what Dietrich Dörner, a cognitive psychologist, calls the 'logic of failure' (1996). Dörner designed some imaginative experiments in which participants were asked, via computer, to deal with various situations that involved suffering on a large scale resulting from different causes (poverty, pollution, drought, and so on). Different measures were available to the participants, and, once a particular measure was chosen, its short- to long-term effects were shown. Dörner found that a surprisingly large number of individuals, including highly educated ones, chose measures that, despite some immediate benefits, were overall detrimental. One of the main reasons for this human tendency 'to produce calamity' (Sunstein 2002) is the failure to take into account systemic effects – in other words, to deal with complexity. Most individuals tend mentally to isolate a set of effects – usually the most noticeable ones – and neglect others, generally those that are system-wide or manifest themselves in the longer term. An illustration of this obdurate human tendency in the humanitarian arena was Bob Geldof's defence of Live Aid, the fund-raising initiative in the 1980s to relieve the famine in Ethiopia. When a BBC interviewer asked him about the benefits that the Menghistu regime derived from the aid that was pouring into the country, Geldof was dismissive, saying that even if only one child received aid the whole operation was still worth it.

Although similar research on institutions' tendency to produce calamity through neglecting certain effects has not, as far as we know, been conducted, it can be hypothesised that an institutional setting in which modi operandi and guidebooks dictate action can further blind individuals to the broader consequences of the policies they are implementing. When they are under pressure, individuals tend to apply established measures (Dörner 1996: 33). In the field of refugee policy, a 'power bloc' of bureaucratic and political interests stymies much-needed and long-awaited changes; a combination of institutional dysfunctions and individual misperceptions has thus become 'the foe of refugee rights' in countries in the 'developing world',[105] containment of refugees through humanitarianism being the main policy objective, and encampment the chief means of achieving it.

Notes

1. *See below Image managements dealing with bad publicity.*
2. The administrative structure that was envisaged under the Disaster Preparedness and Management Bill, 1998, however, would provide the basis for integrating refugees and victims of natural disasters in the development plans of the government. Whether this opportunity will be concretely taken up remains to be seen.
3. The fact that UNHCR was hit by a funding crisis around the same time and had to impose cuts on its programmes in East Africa was coincidental.
4. *See* Horst for the way in which the Kenyan police rounded up Somalis in Eastleigh and extorted bribes from them (Horst 2002).
5. *See* Chapter 4, **Right to life** and *Security in Kampala.*
6. But *see* Chapter 1 *The Legal Framework in Kenya* on the development of procedural rules for challenging the constitutionality of laws under the Bill of Rights in 2001.
7. Address by Professor Mutungi (chairman of the Standing Committee on Human Rights), Italian Cultural Institute, Nairobi, 9 June 1997.
8. He was eventually murdered in 1998 just outside the UN compound, but on this occasion the reaction of the Kenyan government was only a mild protest.
9. The role of members of the ruling party in orchestrating this and other instances of ethnic violence throughout the 1990s was finally confirmed by the commission of inquiry chaired by Justice Akiwumi. The report was completed in 1999 but was only made public in October 2002, following a court order.
10. Interview, Nairobi, 10 July 1997.
11. *See* Chapter 4, *Forced Recruitment.*
12. In charge of the RPA was Col. Fred Rwesigye.
13. These soldiers were highly undisciplined. They 'nationalised' and wrecked fourteen new lorries belonging to UNHCR, the last being smashed in Moyo by its drunken Rwandan driver in October 1986. Observations by Barbara Harrell-Bond during EU Mission, October 1986.
14. Email from Linnea Ehrnst, programme officer, 19 December 1997. SIDA was also supporting an altogether different initiative for refugees living outside

settlements in Uganda, International Aid Sweden's work in Moyo district, but it explained that its support for this agency was an 'isolated case'.

15. Elsewhere in the region, other humanitarian operations aimed at reducing the numbers of those who fled abroad were the cross-border operation in Somalia (Kirby et al. 1997) and Operation Lifeline Sudan (OLS). The idea that humanitarian action should address the 'root causes' and attempt to prevent the flight of refugees in the first place has been popular since the 1990s and is behind such disasters as the 'safe havens' policy in the Balkans.

16. A Sudanese NGO registered in the UK, operating an educational programme in Kiryandongo. UNHCR has since stopped funding this NGO.

17. *See* Chapter 4 **Freedom from torture and from cruel, inhuman, or degrading treatment or punishment**.

18. The standard letter sent by the Joint Voluntary Agency (JVA) in Kenya, the NGO contracted by the US government to help in the resettlement process, enumerated the categories of refugees who could be considered for resettlement:

    '(1) UNHCR-referred or Embassy-identified persons in immediate danger of loss of life and former political prisoners or dissidents facing compelllng security concerns in danger or refoulement
    (2) UNHCR-referred vulnerable cases including women-at-risk, victims of violence, torture survivors, and individuals in urgent need of medical treatment not available in the first asylum country.
    (3) UNHCR-referred cases of individuals for whom the other durable solutions are not feasible and whose status in the place of asylum does not present a satisfactory long-term solution' (Letter of 21 May 1996 to Hicayezu Numviyabagabo).

19. Other countries – New Zealand, Norway, Finland, Sweden, and the Netherlands – offered resettlement to smaller groups and on an irregular basis.

20. Letter from Robert J. Orr, Counsellor, Canadian high commission, Nairobi, to Dr Barbara Harrell-Bond, 5 November 1998.

21. Nonetheless, there had been examples of cooperation between embassies and selected individuals and NGOs in the past in order to get more cases for resettlement. For instance, the resettlement team at the Canadian high commission that had been in office until the end of 1997 had established an informal partnership with Sister Louise Radlemeier, from the Jesuit Refugee Service (JRS), for identifying security cases for resettlement.

22. Interview with Mathijs La Rutte, protection officer, Dadaab, 30 April 1998.

23. Anthropologists sent by the Mozambicans did find some ancestral link with the Somali Bantus, evidenced in dances, clan structure, and language (Email from Ken Wilson to the authors, 3 April 2004).

24. Letter from Sungwon Jim, Imvepi settlement, 3 October 1999.

25. 'A refugee camp – no matter how well it is run – is no place to spend a childhood, commented high commissioner Ruud Lubbers, in a statement addressing the allegations of exploitation of refugee children in West Africa, 1 March 2002 (UNHCR 2002a).

26. *See* Chapter 1. In Uganda, as explained, the situation was more complex and the settlement policy dated back to the 1960s; it featured in the 1960 Control of Alien Refugees Act, enacted in the aftermath of the Rwandan refugee crisis of 1959.

27. Individuals taking difficult decisions under pressure show a tendency 'to apply overdoses of established measures' and an 'inability to think in terms of nonlinear networks of causation rather than of chains of causation – an

inability, that is, to properly assess the side effects and repercussions of one's behaviour' (Dörner 1996: 33).

28. Interview with Jacques Cuenod by Anna Schmidt, 5 September 1997. However, in part owing to the determination of the Togolese government to pursue the integration of the Ghanaian refugees in Togolese life, UNHCR used the little resources it could raise for integration programmes which were overall successful (Holborn 1975 II: 1039–42).

29. It was not until the late 1990s that humanitarian organisations began, albeit somewhat hesitantly, to give some attention to the role of the law, of human rights, and of refugee protection in their activities through the 'minimum standards' movement.

30. Documents from the three phases of the consultation are available on UNHCR's web site (www.unhcr.ch). The consultations culminated in the adoption of the Agenda for Protection in October 2002.

31. The experience of Sierra Leone destroys another myth – that governments in Africa cannot maintain peaceful relations with the country of origin of the refugees they host. Sierra Leone and Guinea had a mutual defence pact. Siaka Stevens even relied on Guinean troops to protect his person while also hosting refugees from Guinea in Sierra Leone (Harrell-Bond et al. 1977).

32. *See below PARinAc: A case study in cooptation.*

33. A caption in one of the first pages explained that the need for having such a chapter had been recognised.

34. Representations of refugees in UNHCR's web site are normally based on this triptych *(see,* e.g., http://www.unhcr.ch/images/images.htm; and the online documentary on refugees in Mauritania, *infra* note 51).

35. Barnett and Finnemore (1999) adopt a neo-Weberian approach to the analysis of international organisations to explain their dysfunctional behaviour, to which they refer as 'pathology'.

36. As Barnett and Finnemore argue, international organisations 'can become autonomous sites of authority ... because of power flowing from the legitimacy of the rational-legal authority they embody, and control over technical expertise and information' (1999: 707), and, one would add, control over resources.

37. *See* Chapter 5 *Establishing a parallel system.*

38. These groups, which also include women and children, because of their stage in the life cycle, require special consideration and protection (Voutira et al. 1995: paras. 4.6, 4.7, 4.8, and 4.9).

39. Interview with Mr Weru, Ifo camp manager for CARE, 28 April 1998.

40. *See,* e.g., the letter that Hans Thoolen, UNHCR's representative in Kampala, sent to Zachary Lomo. Having referred to him as an 'unsolicited champion of refugees ... making public statements of a very critical nature regarding refugee policy and practice in Uganda', the letter then attacked Lomo because 'More cumbersome for me is that you are making rather wild allegations against UNHCR, its staff and that of its implementing partners' (Letter, 19 June 1998).

41. See Chapter 1, *Phase Three: Eliminating the organisational problem.*

42. It would not have been difficult to find students at Nairobi or at Makerere Universities willing to take up this opportunity. Throughout our research, we always found an enthusiastic response from university students, a good number of whom became involved in the research. In this way, UNHCR could also 'build capacity' and could create interest and awareness of refugee law in the next generation of Kenyan and Ugandan lawyers.

43. *See* Chapter 1 *Phase Three: Eliminating the organisational problem.*
44. Chapter 4 *The destruction of Ogujebe transit camp.*
45. Field notes, 17 February 1998.
46. Interview with Vincent Cochetel, UNHCR senior protection officer, Cairo, 28 March 2000.
47. Governmentality is the capacity of power to order a disordered reality 'across the boundaries of family and economy, public sector and private sector' (Dumm 1996: 133).
48. Although Foucault never included refugee camps in his analyses of space and power, few institutions lend themselves as well as refugee camps to such an analysis.
49. Hyndman examines UNHCR's Country Operation Plan for Kenya (1995f) as an example of governmentality and technologies of surveillance. In this report, UNHCR announced that it had 'addressed the intractable problem of discrepancies between feeding figures, registered numbers, and total populations, by camp site as well as by overall caseload and nationality, through physical headcounts and registration of refugees in the camps. These discrepancies are due to acts of *refugee sabotage*' [emphasis added].
50. This vivid image of human life being reduced to statistics is used by Nuruddin Farah in his novel *Gift* (1993) and in his account of the life of Somali refugees around the world (2000). A UNHCR official, who wants to remain anonymous, would have agreed: '... it is interesting to me to see that some of the greatest "authoritarians" are our social services types. They love counting (and re-counting) vulnerable groups, targeting assistance, assessing the needs of individual, "gender-disaggregated data", etc. Perhaps the only saving grace is the WFP is getting even sillier than we are' (Email, January 2001, anon.).
51. *See*, e.g., UNHCR's online documentary *Road to Refuge 2: Into the Sahara* about a refugee camp for Tuaregs in Mauritania (http://www.unhcr.ch/witness4/III_Stans/html/toc/toc_set.html); and UNICEF, *Children of War: Wandering Alone in Southern Sudan* (1994), where it is also claimed that since they arrived in Kakuma camp the thousands of Sudanese unaccompanied minors could 'resume normalcy' (at 21–22).
52. *See also* UNHCR's protection report on Uganda that claimed that 'Refugees in Uganda are provided with basic civil rights' (2000c).
53. In particular, the visits of the high commissioner are carefully staged events, which resemble the visits of heads of states: a show is organised with refugee dances and music, and he or she receives little presents from refugees.
54. *See*, e.g., Mugumya 1997, discussed in Chapter 1, footnote 36.
55. *See also* Chapter 5 *Malnutrition and the conspiracy of silence.*
56. Chapter 4 *Collective punishment in Kakuma.*
57. Another example of a remarkably honest protection report came from Iran (UNHCR 2000e).
58. Chambers's observations on the 'survey slavery' of outsiders working on rural development in the 'developing world' are fitting for the reporting of UNHCR and NGO field staff (Chambers 1983: 51–55).
59. Interview with Dr Wandhe, June 1997.
60. This is not a recent phenomenon. An early example is in the archives of the refugee historian, Louise Holborn: a UNHCR staff person, commenting on one of her chapters, suggested certain cuts to avoid embarrassment to UNHCR. Her reaction was to write 'Quatsch' (codswallop) next to this comment (Copeland 1997).

61. In every office, not just Kenya and Uganda, UNHCR employs a public information officer whose main responsibility is not to build awareness of refugee situations, but to make sure that UNHCR's public image is not tarnished.

62. Observations, 30 July 1997.

63. A similar criticism had been directed at African Rights when they published their report on treatment of Somali refugees in Kenya (*see below*: *PARinAC: A case study in cooptation*).

64. This is also a reflection of UNHCR's narrow construction of the notion of 'accountability', which was defined in the Delphi Project as a 'management requirement to be answerable for something to someone ... an individual obligation to perform against an agreed objective. It is evidently not about UNHCR's accountability to mandate' (Goodwin-Gill 1999: 237). The idea that 'Transparency and accountability ... are not only about dollars, but also about consistency and conformity to principles' does not come under this limited approach to accountability (ibid.: 223).

65. Lord Steyn said in the *Adan* case, 'The prospect of a reference to the International Court of Justice is remote' (*R. v. Secretary of State for the Home Department, ex parte Adan, R. v. Secretary of State for the Home Department, ex parte Aitseguer* [2001] 2 Weekly Law Reports 143). *See also* Kalin 2001.

66. For a full discussion of the impact and potential of the human rights machinery, *see* Fitzpatrick 2002.

67. During the course of this research refugees reported many such threats being made against them for having complained to Geneva about the actions of individuals. For example, some refugees wrote to UNHCR expressing their complaints and suspicions about the resettlement process (e.g., Letter to the UNHCR representative from the Nuer Elders, Kyangwali refugee settlement, 10 January 1999). On a different occasion, a group of Congolese refugees in Tanzania had formed an association and had been vocal in their protest against UNHCR. By the senior protection officer's own admission, the decision to deny them status, taken before his arrival in Dar Es Salaam, had been clearly tainted by the desire to castigate them for their perceived insolence (Carver and Verdirame 2001).

68. Letter from the chairperson, Uganda Human Rights Commission, to Tim Brown, education adviser, UNHCR Kampala, 15 April 1997.

69. This was a speech at a workshop organised in 1999. In 1997, when this research was first initiated, the commission noted with regret that all its attempts to communicate with UNHCR on particular cases failed to get a reply.

70. Her reaction stood in sharp contrast to that of other UNHCR officials at that meeting. One of them said 'Why don't NGOs sue us as the ones in Bangladesh are planning to do?'. Another one remarked that, from a logistical point of view, the Tanzanian repatriation had been a success.

71. Dismissal was the 'punishment' for the UNHCR accountant who wrote a damning internal report about accounting irregularities – a case of which the authors have direct knowledge. His findings were later confirmed by the auditors, and by the investigation that the *Financial Times* conducted in 1998 (*see above*: *Image management: dealing with bad publicity*).

72. *See* Chapter 5 *Malnutrition and the conspiracy of silence*.

73. Interview with UNHCR protection officer (JPO), 28 January 1998.

74. This might be changing, as 'operational collaborations' between the Bank and NGOs are on the increase (Covey 1998).

75. *See*, for example, the urgent actions concerning refugees in Uganda and Kenya that Amnesty issued on at least two occasions: Chapter 4 *Security in Kampala* and *Arbitrary arrest and detention*.

76. That 'implementing partnership' or 'operational collaborations' are almost universally regarded as a good thing, despite their negative impact on NGOs, is the result of a rare convergence of opposite political views: for 'neo-liberals', the use of private organisations appears to be in line with the mantra that 'the private sector always does it better'; many on the left consider the allocation of funds to avowedly value-driven organisations in the voluntary sector as a positive phenomenon (Robinson 1997: 61).

77. The RLP is not an NGO, but a programme of the Faculty of Law, University of Makerere. The statement in the text refers to organisations that operated at the time of the research. ICJ-Kenya, which, as discussed at various points, had a refugee programme in the mid-1990s, was not sub-contracted by UNHCR.

78. An NGO sub-contracted by a state tends to behave in a similar manner, as Monnier observed in the context of refugee status determination in Switzerland. The NGO official who is allowed to sit in on interviews with asylum-seekers developed a sort of 'complicity' with the status-determination interviewer (Monnier 1995: 310).

79. Their manual and other training and evaluation materials can be seen on: http://www.sphereproject.org/handbook_index.htm

80. In Plato's *Republic* – the archetype of utopian imagination – Socrates at one point also lists the staples which should be part of the diet of the dwellers of this perfect city. Glaucon's reply is as refreshing and pertinent as ever: this approach and measurements could be used 'if you were founding a city for pigs' (Plato 1997: 1011).

81. *See*, e.g.: African Rights 1993; HRW 1993, 1997a, 2000b; Amnesty International 1997b, 1998b; LCHR 1995.

82. The fact that the latter took place for the most part in isolated refugee camps is another important factor that can explain the underreporting of abuse in camps.

83. For example, in 1994, over 100 NGOs were operating in Rwandan refugee camps in eastern Zaire, 150 NGOs were operating in Mozambique, and 250 in Bosnia-Herzegovenia.

84. It is worth noting here that not one of the recommendations dealt with the integration of refugees, and only two vague recommendations were on accountability/transparency, stating only that 'UNHCR/NGO partnerships must be transparent' (UNHCR-ICVA 1994: recommendation 115), and that 'UNHCR and NGOs, acting as operational partners should undertake regularly joint project evaluations' (ibid.: recommendation 122).

85. 'The Refugee Project. Promoting and Protecting the Human Rights of Refugees Through Education and Legal Aid' (undated document of the Joint NGO/Refugee Group, certainly after April 1993).

86. Minutes of the Steering Committee of NGOs/Institutions Concerned with the Legal Protection of Refugees in Africa, March 1993.

87. Letter from Roberto Quintero Marino, 9 November 1992.

88. Letter from the Office of the President to Chris Mulei, 31 March 1993.

89. Minutes of the Steering Committee of NGOs/Institutions concerned with the Legal Protection of Refugees in Africa, 28 October 1993.

90. Minute 13/93, Minutes of the Joint NGO Refugee Group Workshop, held at Nairobi Safari Club, 8 December, 1993.

91. Ibid.

92. Letter to Arthur Helton, 18 January 1994, ref: ICJ/SM/94.
93. Undated document referred to above (note 85).
94. Project Proposal, Joint NGO/Refugee Group Research Project: The Refugee Situation in Kenya (Document also not dated, but from the context it can be inferred that it is from January 1994).
95. 8 February 1994, ref. no. HA 13/6/27.
96. Letter from the director of the International Crescent of Hope and chair of the forum to Mr Olusyi Bajulaiye, conseiller juridique principal (Afrique), 21 February 1994, ref. ICJ/SM/94.
97. Letter to Mr Santiago Romero-Perez, chief NGO liaison section, UNHCR, Geneva, 24 February 1994.
98. The region included Ethiopia, Somalia, Kenya, Uganda, Tanzania, and Sudan.
99. Letter to Mr Santiago Romero-Perez, chief, NGO liaison section, UNHCR, 19 August 1994.
100. By this time the Crescent of Hope had disappeared from the scene as its money had dried up.
101. There were also economic considerations. Organising these conferences is rather costly and UNHCR did not do it on the cheap: the Addis Ababa meeting, for example, took place at the Hilton Hotel, one of the most expensive hotels in the region.
102. The budget for the NGO local focal point for Uganda in 1999 alone was $56,590. This was only a fraction of the total PARinAC budget which presumably included a budget for UNHCR for each local focal point, a budget for the regional focal points, a budget for regional meetings, and a budget for the various other components of the plan (InterAid-Uganda, NGO Local Focal Point Budget, 1999). This budget included provision for $10,000 for two people for two five-day trips to attend the PARinAC workshop conferences outside the country.
103. Report on the UNHCR/NGO Regional Partnership in Action (PARinAC) workshop for East and Horn of Africa, Addis Ababa, Ethiopia, 9–13 November 1998, prepared by InterAid, Uganda.
104. Ibid.
105. Barnett makes a similar argument (2000).

Conclusions

This book has examined the ways in which the human rights of refugees have been violated by a variety of actors – most importantly, governments, UNHCR, and humanitarian organisations. As mentioned in the Preface, we did not set out to write about the injustices which refugees suffered before their flight. During our interviews we did collect sufficient material to write a broader ethnography of injustice, especially since our interviews with refugees normally began with the events in their countries of origin that had prompted them to leave. Nevertheless, we decided to adhere to our initial research questions and to focus on the treatment they received once they became refugees in Kenya and Uganda. It might thus appear to some that our criticism of humanitarian organisations and UNHCR is excessive, or even unfair, and that there is a risk of throwing the baby out with the bath water. Certainly, the emergence of a 'humanitarian conscience' is a positive moral development. Traditionally, individuals did not make donations for the benefit of strangers, and the recipients of charity were defined by the religious, social or ethnic identify of the donor (Hufton 2004). The fact that humanitarian organisations can raise funds from people prepared to donate to help strangers in distant places is to their credit. The failures and shortcomings of humanitarian organisations should not prompt a retrogressive development and undermine this humanitarian spirit with a sense of fatalistic powerlessness about our ability to make a difference. However, donors – individuals and institutional alike – should use their position of power to ensure that humanitarian organisations are accountable to their beneficiaries and fulfil their mandates; if they do not do this, their humanitarianism could end up being fruitless. Naiveté can undermine the humanitarian action, as Pierre Bezuchov's artless philanthropy in Tolstoy's *War and Peace* shows.[1]

We have analysed the formation and implementation of refugee policy, highlighting the progressive sidelining of national authorities by UNHCR. Failures in the protection of refugees resulted from a complex combination of bad policies, bureaucratic dysfunctions, and ossified modi operandi. All actors – host governments, donor countries, UNHCR, NGOs – bear some responsibility for the situation. But, if the repressive face of the state does not come as a surprise, the duplicity of humanitarian organisations, both UNHCR and NGOs, is astonishing. The face of these organisations that refugees encountered was often callous, sometimes cruel, and – nearly always – ineffectual. Their public face, however, was almost the opposite. They wanted to be seen as organisations consisting of compassionate cosmopolitans driven by ideals and values, and committed to helping refugees.

The public face was the one on display especially in countries in the 'developed world', when soliciting funds from the public or from governments. It also helped in dealings with the host government: NGOs posed as 'civil society', UNHCR as a member of the UN family and representative of the 'international community'. 'Civil society' and 'international community' are loaded terms that come with a significant amount of soft power.[2] Refugees, on the other hand, whether in camps and settlements, or in Nairobi and Kampala, were more accustomed to the other face of humanitarians, and discovered that power exercised under a humanitarian guise was not so different from power in other guises. Against abuses of this power they found little remedy.

Failures in refugee protection started with rejections at the frontier, and continued with the refugee status-determination process in which murky arrangements between UNHCR and its implementing NGOs gave rise to procedures that were arbitrary to an extent that would be considered unacceptable in any legal process. NGOs – InterAid in Uganda and the Jesuit Refugee Service (JRS) in Kenya – were 'screening' asylum-seekers. The conflation of various kinds of assistance with the *legal* process of determining who was a refugee corrupted the status-determination process. By the late 1990s, both governments had refugee status-determination procedures in place, but UNHCR continued to play the pivotal role.

In both countries, assistance to refugees was premised on their segregation in camps and settlements. While integration, resettlement, and repatriation are based on the idea – whether in practice successful or not – that refugees have to become part of the surrounding social, political, and cultural environment, encampment *means* separation from the host community. The full catalogue of human rights – both civil and political, and economic, social, and cultural – were violated. This situation obtained not in the 'camps of the very worst kind' – like those for Rwandans in Tanzania and Zaire, to which some have ascribed the 'revival of interest in the question of refugee camps' (Crisp and Jacobsen 1998: 27) – but in camps that had been established for the better part of a decade (Kenya) and in settlements that were at times even flagged as 'models' of refugee assistance and protection (Uganda).

As we have shown throughout, camps and settlements constituted spaces in which the law of the host country virtually ceases to apply. Compounded by the absence of any form of independent and impartial adjudication, camps are spaces that are virtually *beyond the rule of law* and in which the life of refugees ends up being governed by a highly oppressive blend of rules laid down by the humanitarian agencies and the customary practices of the various refugee communities. In Kenya and Uganda, there were some camps and settlements in which respect for human rights could be described as better than others, and there were also occasional improvements. But respect for human rights cannot ultimately be reconciled with encampment: the violation of freedom of movement, which is the defining feature of encampment, was only the precursor to violations of all other human rights.

The impact of repressive state policies on the refugees' enjoyment of their rights should not be underestimated. As we have discussed, governments, especially the Kenyan one, were responsible for hundreds of cases of arbitrary arrest and detention. Both were to blame for unfair trials, for appalling conditions in detention, for some cases of *refoulement*, not to mention the failure to protect the security of refugees. They also failed to protect refugees from forced recruitment, by being either passive (Kenya) or active (Uganda) accomplices to rebel movements like the Sudan People's Liberaton Army (SPLA). Nevertheless, it would be wrong to surmise that humanitarian agencies were doing a favour to refugees by exempting them from the application of the law of the often authoritarian states which host them. Even in a country like Kenya, with all its chronic institutional and judicial failures at the time of the research, injustice suffered by refugees outside camps at the hands of the Kenyan authorities was more 'remediable' than injustice perpetrated in camps: such indefensible violations of human rights as the imposition of collective punishment on tens of thousands of people were perpetrated against refugees in camps.

Further research is called for. In particular, cost-assessment studies of encampment are much needed. If, as we would hypothesise, camps are more expensive than interventions aimed at local integration and development, then there should be no obstacle to making the pursuit of the latter the primary objective of humanitarian assistance programmes for refugees. Politics is by nature dynamic (MacFarlane 2000: 5), and any political hostility to this solution could be surmounted through a concerted effort involving international and local actors. In Kenya and Uganda, however, UNHCR and humanitarian organisations have seemed more bent on encouraging such hostility than seeking to reduce it.

This book was not about solutions. We did not set out to collect data specifically on repatriation, integration, and resettlement, and it might seem odd that we discuss solutions only in our conclusion. Yet our research can offer important insights into the debate on solutions, since, whichever solution is opted for, respect for the human rights of refugees has to be the essential prerequisite: this is a legal and moral imperative. Kenya and Uganda were paradigmatic, because for the vast majority of refugees none of the three 'durable solutions' – repatriation, integration, and resettlement – was available. They were trapped in the fourth 'durable (non) solution': 'the relief void ... the space of protracted care and maintenance programming', centred upon their encampment (Elder 1999b: 11; *see also* Jamal 2000; Crisp 2000b).

The adoption of the policy of encampment in Kenya and Uganda was not a 'local accident'. The urban policy document prepared by UNHCR headquarters in Geneva confirmed that encampment was UNHCR's policy of choice (UNHCR 1996c; 1997b). Two versions of this document exist, the first one so draconian that it had to be hastily withdrawn after criticism from the protection section. The second version reiterated, albeit in a slightly toned-down form, the overall assumption that assistance should be provided in camps and settlements, and that very little would be done for urban refugees. As was pointed out in a report by UNHCR's own evaluation unit (UNHCR 2001a), refugee protection took the back seat in these policy documents.

There is a close conceptual and practical link between UNHCR's focus on repatriation and its ineffectiveness as a protector of refugee rights. The issue of repatriation came to dominate refugee policy at every level and had an impact on refugee protection. Since the 1980s UNHCR has regarded repatriation as the preferred solution (Harrell-Bond 1989: 45; Loescher 2003: 10), an approach crystallised later with the high commissioner's announcement that the 1990s would be 'the decade of repatriation'. The call for repatriation has permeated UNHCR's work since then, and repatriating large numbers is regarded as an institutional achievement. By viewing countries of asylum as 'waiting rooms' before repatriation, UNHCR has virtually given up on integration, choosing instead to coerce refugees to the margins of host societies and to segregate them in camps. Even those within UNHCR who are aware of the fact that 'camps are not good' for refugees continue to support encampment as an intermediate stage before the 'durable solution' of repatriation can be effected.

Repatriation is premised on the notion that refugees have an eternal and visceral tie with the country of origin – 'home' – the place to which they will always 'belong'.[3] This somewhat reactionary conception of unalterable identities and loyalties is in marked contrast with the idea of fluid and dynamic personal and collective identities that seems to underlie our 'era of globalisation'. To the extent that this focus on repatriation as the best solution creates or reinforces the refugees' resolve to go back rather than encourage their integration in the host country, it could also act as a factor that worsens conflicts.[4] Leaving educated élites stranded in a refugee camp without work opportunities, while continuing to feed them the dream of repatriation, can lead to the creation of the leadership of insurgent groups, since, as has been repeatedly argued (Douglas 1986; Richards 1996), intellectuals excluded from economic and political power often form the basis for radical and ever violent political movements.

Repatriation also appears as an anachronism if viewed in a broader historical context. In fact, 'Throughout history, most refugee movements have tended to result in permanent exile of the refugee population' (Rogge 1994: 21). What prompted UNHCR to sail against the stream of overwhelming historical precedents? Donor countries short-sightedly tend to view repatriation as a less costly and 'simpler' solution (Harrell-Bond 1989), although in most countries in the 'developed world' integration, even if somewhat undermined by the idea of temporary protection, remains the predominant approach to recognised refugees. However, the failure of the repatriation-based approach to refugees is becoming increasingly evident, and some authors are now talking about local integration as the 'forgotten solution' (Crisp and Jacobsen 1998; Jacobsen 2001).[5]

Integration is a complex socio-economic and cultural process that is the result of different variables, but a sine qua non for successful integration is that legal barriers that impede or obstruct it are removed. In neither Kenya nor Uganda were these barriers removed. Before 1991, Kenya's laissez-faire refugee policy meant that, despite the absence of a systematic piece of legislation, in most cases refugees could integrate. However, without a law that clearly spelt out their rights and obligations, the status of refugees was susceptible to sudden changes at the behest of the government, as what happened in the early 1990s showed. From then on, the policy centred on the encampment of refugees in remote areas, making local integration impossible for nearly all refugees. As detailed in Chapter 1, UNHCR was behind this shift in policy. It admitted that the issue of local integration was never 'seriously discussed with the government' in the 1990s (UNHCR 1997a: 20), although it was clear that for most groups of refugees (Sudanese, Somalis, Rwandans, and Burundians) an end to the conflict that had caused them to flee was not in sight. Rather than acting as a catalyst for re-introducing integration, at least after the end of the acute phase of the Somali emergency and once the numbers of refugees had begun to stabilise, UNHCR invested exclusively in the 'fourth solution' – that is, encampment.

It was not until 1998 that UNHCR finally brought up integration in discussions with the Kenyan government – one of the positive outcomes of changes in protection staff. The senior protection officer achieved some important results: the government was persuaded to proceed with the naturalisation of the pre-1991 caseload (UNHCR 1999f: 4.2). The imposition of taxes on the commercial activities undertaken by refugees in camps, which UNHCR had usually resisted, was agreed upon and even regarded as a positive step by the senior protection officer, and business licences were granted to refugee traders in the camps. Significant as these results might be, there was still no concerted effort to put into practice a developmental model for assisting refugees as an alternative to camps. Such an effort would have involved a U-turn from established UNHCR policies and practices in assisting refugees, in fundraising, and in its relations with other UN agencies and with NGOs.

With the elections in 2002 and the change of government, Kenya had the best chance in a generation to radically reform its refugee policy and become a model for countries in the region. The publication in the Kenya Gazette of the Refugees Bill 2003 shows that the government is keen to review legislation and policy. With this renewed political will and as donors are better disposed towards Kenya than in the past, UNHCR and humanitarian organisations should take this opportunity to promote an integration-based approach to refugees.

In Uganda, the situation was different from Kenya because the government and UNHCR maintained that the settlements were part of a policy of refugee self-reliance, or self-sufficiency, and of integration (MoLG 1993). The self-reliance policy, however, far from allowing refugees to integrate in their host societies, kept them isolated and separated in areas that were often highly dangerous. It was based, as we have seen, on an outdated *dirigiste* economic approach and did not take into account the importance of certain rights – freedom of movement, right to work – for socio-economic integration. Self-reliance also gave UNHCR a justification for its programme cuts, arguing that, for refugees to achieve self-sufficiency and to integrate, they had to free themselves from the 'dependency syndrome' (ignoring though that, even if such a syndrome ever existed, it was entirely iatrogenic). UNHCR pulled out of certain settlements expecting the local authorities, which it had neglected and even undermined for years, to now take over its role. Self-reliance thus became a paradox: a concept intended to improve the situation of refugees and the enjoyment of their rights became the basis for a strategy that ended up worsening their plight.

In Uganda, UNHCR did not use the debate on the adoption of a new refugee law to promote local integration as a durable solution for refugees. In some respects, its comments on draft bills were heavy-handed. On the provision in the Ugandan legislation on camps, for example, UNHCR Geneva recommended, 'Perhaps under this section there should be added positive powers to establish or designate specific areas as transit centres, camps or settlements where refugees will be required to stay or settle rather than just including a provision that empowers the Commissioner to specific certain areas out-of-bounds for certain refugees' (UNHCR 1996j). Therefore, not only was it not considered appropriate to raise objections to encampment, it was even suggested that certain areas be designated for refugees by statute, like permanent 'mini-bantustans' for refugees.

Respect for the human rights of refugees can only be improved once encampment is abandoned as the policy of choice and integration is again pursued as the best solution. Integration is after all the solution that historically has been the predominant and probably the most successful one. UNHCR could assist refugees in a way that would benefit hosts and persuade states of the worth of this approach rather than encourage them, as it does at present, to adopt encampment and the establishment of separate health and welfare services for refugees.

The pursuit of integration does, of course, pose serious challenges. Nevertheless, integration remains the best solution, if only by a process of elimination of the others. Only small numbers of refugees can be resettled, and, difficult as they may seem, the challenges of integration almost pale in comparison with those posed by repatriation. The second half of the *Odyssey* is often forgotten: once he arrives home, a new series of violent vicissitudes begins for Ulysses. Similarly, for refugees, reintegration into their countries of origin is likely to be arduous and often more difficult than integration into countries of asylum (Allen 1988; Arhin 1994; Harrell-Bond 1989; Majodina 1995, 1998; Pottier 1999; Rogge 1994; van Hear 1994; Zetter 1988, 1992, 1999).[6] Furthermore, the timing of repatriation has the disadvantage of being beyond the control of UNHCR and humanitarian organisations: no one can claim sufficient prescience as to be able to predict when a conflict will end and when conditions for return will be acceptable. Pacifying countries and preventing conflicts is beyond the statutory and practical limits of UNHCR;[7] persuading host governments to integrate refugees, and using relief resources as a lever, is not.

That, of all people, those who are uprooted should be relegated to camps at the margins of society and be denied their freedom of movement is a tragic irony. Hopefully, in a not-so-distant future, confining refugees in camps will be perceived for what it really is: a breach of the most fundamental human rights, a cruel and dehumanising absurdity which neither economic nor political factors can justify. The dysfunctions and misperceptions that led to the adoption and implementation of this policy by UNHCR and humanitarian organisations will be viewed as a tragic accident of history. Refugee camps will then join the array of total institutions (mental asylums, internment camps, Bantustans) premised on the segregation of human beings that human kind has learnt to regard as aberrant.

Notes

1. Having decided to fund schools and hospitals for the farmers working on his land, he was not prepared to do any serious follow-up. He visited the land for only a very short time, congratulating himself for all his good charity. His vanity blinded him to the reality of deception, diversion, and corruption, and

to the fact that the vast majority of 'his' farmers were no better as a result of his charity.

2. Soft power is a concept developed in the context of international relations to explain the ability to influence behaviour by cooptation rather than coercion (Nye 2002: 8ff.). For the UN and for humanitarian organisations, which lack the military and economic means of the most powerful states, such soft power based on the values they profess is crucial and helps them shape the political agenda.

3. UNHCR chose as one of its slogans one of the very few rather anodyne lines – one could say even a cliché – to be written by Aeschylus: 'There is no place like home'. Laura Hammond has observed the implication of the construction of this ideal home and of the terminology that is normally used to describe repatriation (reintegration, return, reassimilation, readaptation, and so on): 'returnees should seek to move backward in time, to recapture a quality of life that they are assumed to have enjoyed before becoming refugees or that those who remained behind currently enjoy. Because post-repatriation life, or "home" in the discourse of repatriation, is rooted in the country of origin it is considered by outsiders to be necessarily better than life in exile' (Hammond 1999: 230).

4. Malkki has noted that Burundian refugees who lived in the camps in Tanzania had an 'unfaltering belief in the temporariness of exile' (Malkki 1995: 228, 228–31). See also her postscript on 'return to genocide' (ibid.: 259 ff.).

5. On the other hand, the insistence that local integration remains the exception, to be pursued only in 'protracted refugee situations', is ill-advised: how could UNHCR know in advance if a refugee situation will become 'protracted' or not?

6. As Dolan has shown (1999: 106–107), lack of integration can even have the effect of holding refugees back in their countries of asylum, even when they desire to repatriate: disruptions in employment and vulnerability ensuing from lack of status meant that many Mozambicans in South Africa were not able to accumulate the minimum capital that they thought necessary to start again in Mozambique.

7. The cross-border operations in Somalia in the first half of the 1990s (Waldron and Hasci 1995) and the ongoing Operation Lifeline Sudan (OLS) are examples. Studies of the impact that such programmes have on potential refugees by interfering with their right to flee and to seek asylum abroad are needed.

Bibliography

Abdullahi, A.M. 1993. 'Protection of Refugees under International Law and Kenya's Treatment of Somali Refugees: Compliance or Contrary', unpublished manuscript.

————. 1997. 'Ethnic Clashes, Displaced Persons and Potential for Refugee Creation in Kenya: A Forbidding Forecast', *International Journal of Refugee Law* 9: 196–206.

ACF-USA (Action against Hunger). 1998. 'An Overview of Food Security Issues in Adjumani, Palorinya, Rhino Camp, Imvepi, Kiryandongo and Nakivale Refugee Settlement', draft version of a report prepared for UNHCR. August.

Adiin Yaansah, E.A. 1995. *An Analysis of Domestic Legislation to Regulate the Activities of Local and Foreign NGOs*. Oxford: Refugee Studies Programme and Centre for Socio-Legal Studies.

————. 1996. 'Domestic Legislation to Regulate the Activities of Local and Foreign NGOs : A Comparison of the Experience of Zambia & Kenya', report of main findings of research to Nuffield Foundation & Polden-Puckham Trust.

ADFER (Groupe d'action pour la Défense des Droits de la Femme et de l'Enfant). 1997. 'Reaction au Rapport d' African Rights intitulé "Not So Innocent: When Women Become Killers"'. Nairobi.

Africa Watch. 1991. 'Kenya Taking Liberties'. New York.

African Rights. 1993. 'The Nightmare Continues ... Abuses Against Somali Refugees in Kenya'. London.

————. 1995a. *Death, Despair and Defiance*. 2nd edn. London.

————. 1995b. *Not So Innocent: When Women Become Killers*. London.

————. 1996. *Kenya: Shadow Justice*. London and Nairobi.

Ahmed, J.A. ed. 1995. *The Invention of Somalia*. Lawrenceville, NJ.

Aiken, S.J. 2003. 'Of Gods and Monsters: National Security and Canadian Refugee Policy', *Revue québecoise de droit international* 14: 2.

Akram, S.M. 2000. 'Orientalism Revisited in Asylum and Refugee Claims', *International Journal of Refugee Law* 12: 7.

Alexander, M. 1999. 'Refugee Status Determination Conducted by UNHCR', *International Journal of Refugee Law* 11: 251–89.

Allen, T. 1988. 'Coming Home: The International Agencies and the Returnees in West Nile', *Journal of Refugee Studies* 1(2): 166–75.

Allen, T. and Morsink, H. (eds.) 1994. *When Refugees Go Home*. London.

Al-Omari, G. 1995. 'Notes on the Act to Make Provisions for the Proper Control of Alien Refugees, for Regulating their Return to the Country of Residence and for Making Provision for their Residence While in Uganda', unpublished manuscript, Refugee Studies Programme, University of Oxford.

Alston, P. and Quinn, G. 1987. 'The Nature and Scope of State Parties' Obligations under the International Covenant on Economic, Social and Cultural Rights', *Human Rights Quarterly* 9: 156.

Amnesty International. 1997a. 'A 10 Point Program for Women's Human Rights in Kenya', *Nairobi Law Monthly*, August/September.

_____. 1997b. 'Urgent Action: Threat of Refoulement/Fear for Safety. 101 Rwandese Refugees in Kenya', London. 6 March.

_____. 1997c. 'Great Lakes Region: Still in Need of Protection: Repatriation, *Refoulement* and the Safety of Refugees and Internally Displaced', London. February.

_____. 1997d. 'Letter to President Daniel arap Moi from Derek Evans, Deputy Secretary General', London. 30 July.

_____. 1998a. 'The Hidden Violence: "Disappearances" and Killings Continue'. AFR/47/23/98, London.

_____. 1998b. 'Urgent Action: Possible "Disappearance"/Fear of Return to Rwanda/Fear of Extrajudicial Execution: Emmanuel Ngomiraronka, Nathanel Nsengiyumva', AFR/59/01/98, London. 23 April.

_____. 1999. *Annual Report*. London.

An-Na'im, A. 2001. 'The Legal Protection of Human Rights in Africa: How to Do More with Less', in Sarat, A. and Kearns, T.R. (eds.) *Human Rights: Concepts, Constests, Contingencies*. Ann Arbor: 89–115.

Annan, K. 1999. 'Foreword', in *The Universal Declaration of Human Rights: Fifty Years and Beyond*. New York.

Arhin, K. 1994. 'The Reaccommodation of Ghanaian Returnees from Nigeria in 1983 and 1985', in Allen, T. and Morsink, H. (eds.) *When Refugees Go Home*. London: 268–75.

Aukot, E. 1998. 'Is it Better to be a Refugee than a Turkana in Kakuma: Relationships between the Hosts and Refugees', unpublished paper presented at the 6th IRAP Conference, Jerusalem. December.

AVSI (Associazione Volontari per il Servizio Internazionale), 1996. 'Acholpii Refugee Camp, Kitgum, Uganda. Narrative Performance Monitoring Report', Kampala.

_____. 1997a. 'Assistance to Sudanese Refugees in Kitgum District – Acholpii Refugee Settlement Narrative Performance Monitoring Report', Kampala.

_____. 1997b. 'Care and Maintenance for Rwandese Refugees: Kyangwali Refugee Settlement, Hoima District. Narrative Performance Monitoring Report', Kampala.

_____. 1999. 'Who Does What and How', Kampala. 17 February.

_____. no date. 'Salary Scale for the Refugees Settlement in Kyangwali', Kampala.

Baker, J. and Zetter, R. 1995. 'Shelter Provision and Settlement Policies for Refugees: a State of the Art Review', Studies on Emergencies & Disaster Relief, report no. 2, Uppsala: Nordiska Afrikainstitutet.

Barnes, R. 2004. 'Refugee Law at Sea', *International and Comparative Law Quarterly* 53: 47–77.

Barnett, M. 2000. 'Humanitarianism with a Sovereign Face: UNHCR in the Global Undertow', paper presented at the Conference Commemorating UNHCR at 50: Past, Present and Future of Refugee Assistance, New York. 13–15 May 13.

Barnett, M.N. and Finnemore, M. 1999. 'The Politics, Power and Pathologies of International Organisations', *International Organization* 53: 699–732.

Barutciski, M. 1996. 'The Reinforcement of Non-Admission Policies and the Subversion of UNHCR', *International Journal of Refugee Law* 8(1/2): 49–110.

Bascom, J. 1998. *Losing Place: Refugee Populations and Rural Transformations in East Africa.* Oxford.

Bayefsky, A.F. 2000. 'Introduction', in Bayefsky, A.F. and Fitzpatrick, J. (eds.). *Human Rights and Forced Displacement.* The Hague: ix–xii.

Behrend, H. 1999. *Alice Lakwena and the Holy Spirits: War in Northern Uganda, 1986–97.* Oxford.

Bennet et al. 1999. 'Assistance to Somali and Sudanese Refugees in Kenya', final report of the joint WFP-UNHCR evaluation mission.

Besteman, C. 1999. *Unraveling Somalia: Race, Violence, and the Legacy of Slavery.* Philadelphia.

Bettelheim, B. 1988. *The Informed Heart: A Study of the Psychological Consequences of Living under Extreme Fear and Terror.* London.

Betts, T. 1974. *The Southern Sudan: The Ceasefire and After.* London.

Beyani, C. 2000. *Human Rights Standards and the Movement of People Within States.* Oxford.

Black, R. 1998. 'Putting Refugees in Camps', *Forced Migration Review* August (2): 4–7.

Black, R. and Koser, K. 1999. *The End of the Refugee Cycle? Refugee Repatriation and Reconstruction.* Oxford.

Bliss, M. 2000. '"Serious Reasons for Considering": Minimum Standards of Procedural Fairness in the Application of Article 1F Exclusion Clauses', *International Journal of Refugee Law* 12 (Special Supplementary Issue: Exclusion from Protection): 92–132.

Bloch, A. 2000. 'A New Era or More of the Same? Asylum Policy in the UK', *Journal of Refugee Studies* 13: 29–42.

Boelaert, M. 1996. 'Over-consumption or Under-supply? MSF Refugee Health Program in Hagadera', Brussels: MSF. November.

Bookman, M.Z. 2002. *After Involuntary Migration: The Political Economy of Refugee Encampments.* Boulder, CO.

Boudreau, T., Lawrence, M. and King, A. 1996. 'Household Food Economy Assessment of Kakuma Refugee Camp, Turkana District, North West Kenya'. London: SCF.

Brouwer, A. and Kumin, J. 2003. 'Interception and Asylum: When Migration Control and Human Rights Collide', *Refuge* Spring.

Brown, T. 1999. 'Dilemmas in Refugee Education', Kampala: UNHCR.

Brownlie, I. 2003. *Principles of Public International Law.* 6th ed. Oxford.

Bucyana, J. 1997. 'La condition juridique des réfugiés rwandais à la lumière des conventions onusiènnes sur le statut des réfugiés', unpublished manuscript, Nairobi.

Buregeya, A. 1998. '… And When You Go to UNHCR to Seek Protection', unpublished manuscript, Nairobi.

Byrne, M.M. 1999. 'Religion, Protest and Concepts of Dignity in Refugee Camps', unpublished research proposal. Kampala.

——. 2000. 'Understanding Benefactor and Beneficiary: Protest Stories in Nakivale', paper presented at the Conference on Conflict and Peace-Making in the Great Lakes Region, Entebbe. 10–12 July.

CARE International. 1996. 'Final Project Status Report for the Overseas Development Administration, Refugee Unit. Reporting Period: April 1, 1995 to March 31, 1996', Nairobi.

Carver, R. and Verdirame, G. 2001. 'Voices in Exile', London: Article 19.

Cassanelli, L.V. 1982. *The Shaping of Somali Society: Reconstructing the History of a Pastoral People, 1600–1900.* Philadelphia.

_____. 1995. *Victims and Vulnerable Groups in Southern Somalia.* Ottawa: Immigration and Refugee Board of Canada. May.

Chambers, R. 1979. 'Rural Refugees in Africa: What the Eye Does Not See', paper presented to the African Studies Association Symposium on Refugees, London. September.

_____. 1983. *Rural Development: Putting the Last First.* Essex.

_____. 1997. *Whose Reality Counts? Putting the First Last.* London.

Charlesworth, H. and Chinkin, C. 2000. *The Boundaries of International Law: A Feminist Analysis.* Manchester.

Chimni, B.S. 1994. 'The Incarceration of Victims: Safety Zones or Refugee Status for the "Internally" Displaced?', paper presented at the Conference on International Legal Issues Arising under UN Decade of International Law, Doha, Qatar. 22–25 March.

Chrétien, J.-P. 1993. 'Des sédentaires devenus migrants: Les départs des Burundais et des Rwandais vers l'Ouganda (1920–1960)', in Chrétien, J.-P (ed.) *Burundi: L'histoire retrouvée: 25 ans de métier d'historien en Afrique.* Paris: 71–101.

Clark, D.L. and Stein, B. 1984. 'Documentary Note: The Relationship between ICARA II and Refugee Aid and Development', Washington: Refugee Policy Group. 16 November.

Clay, J. 1984. *The Eviction of the Banyarwanda: The Story behind the Refugee Crisis in Southwest Uganda.* Cambridge, MA.

Cochetel, V. 1999. 'Interview', in 'An Asylum Seeker's Guide to Applying for Refugee Status at the UNHCR, Cairo, Egypt', draft document prepared with the cooperation of the UNHCR by members of the refugee community and volunteers. 5 June: 29.

Cohn, I. and Goodwin-Gill, G. 1994. *Child Soldiers: The Role of Children in Armed Conflict.* Oxford.

Cook, R. 1993. 'Accountability in International Law for Violations of Women's Rights by Non-State Actors', in Dallmeyer, D. (ed.) *Reconceiving Reality: Women and International Law.* Washington, American Society of International Law: 93.

Cook, R., Dickens, B.M. and Wilson, A.F. 2001. *Advancing Safe Motherhood Through Human Rights.* Geneva: WHO.

Copeland, E.A. 1997. 'Louise W. Holborn Archives, Schlesinger Library, Radcliffe College', *Journal of Refugee Studies* 10: 503–6.

Core Group on Psycho-Social Support. 1997. 'Proceedings and Recommendations of the Workshop on Psycho-Social Support Programmes in Northern Uganda', Jinja. 24–25 July.

Covey, J.G. 1998. 'Is Critical Cooperation Possible? Influencing the World Bank through Operational Collaboration and Policy Dialogue', in Fox, J.A. and Brown, D.L. (eds.) *The Struggle for Accountability: The World Bank, NGOs, and Grassroots Movements.* Cambridge, MA: 81–119.

Craig, J. 1998. 'Notes on Kenyan Education', unpublished manuscript, Kampala.

Crisp, J. 2000a. 'A State of Insecurity: The Political Economy of Violence in Kenya's Refugee Camps', *African Affairs* 99: 601–32.

_____. 2000b. 'Thinking outside the Box: Evaluation and Humanitarian Action', *Forced Migration Review* 8. Oxford: Refugee Studies Centre.

Crisp, J. and Jacobsen, K. 1998. 'Refugee Camps Reconsidered', *Forced Migration Review* 3. Oxford: Refugee Studies Centre.

Crock, M. and Saul, B. 2002. *Future Seekers: Refugees and the Law in Australia.* Sydney.

Daley, P. 1989. 'Refugees and Under Development in Africa: The Case of Barundi Refugees in Tanzania', unpubl. D.Phil. thesis submitted in the Faculty of Anthropology and Geography, University of Oxford.

———. 1991. 'Gender, Displacement and Social Reproduction: Settling Burundian Refugees in Tanzania', *Journal of Refugee Studies* 4: 248–66.

DANIDA (Danish International Development Agency). 2000. 'Strategy for Danish Support to Civil Society in Developing Countries', Copenhagen: Ministry of Foreign Affairs. October.

Das Neves Silva, M. da. 2002. 'Impact of Kakuma Refugee Camp on Turkana Women and Girls', a study for UNIFEM African Women in Crisis Program, Nairobi.

DED (Deutscher Entwicklungsdienst) Rhino camp. 1997. 'Letter of the Head of Section-Education to the Programme Co-ordinator'. 30 December.

De Lame, D. 1996. *Une colline entre mille ou le calme avant la tempête*. Tervuren: Musée Royal de l'Afrique Centrale.

De Lorenzo, M. 1998. 'Report of Activities, July–September 1998', unpublished report, Kampala & Oxford.

De Waal, A. 1997. *Famine Crimes: Politics and the Disaster Relief Industry in Africa*. Oxford/Bloomington, IN.

Deng, F.M. 1995. *War of Visions: Conflict of Identities in the Sudan*. Washington DC: Brookings Institution.

———. 2000. 'Further Promotion and Encouragement of Human Rights and Fundamental Freedoms, Including the Programme and Methods of Work of the Commission: Human Rights, Mass Exoduses and Displaced Persons', in Bayefsky, A.F. and Fitzpatrick, J. (eds.) *Human Rights and Forced Displacement*. The Hague: 229–35.

Denza, E. 2003. 'The Relationship between International Law and National Law', in Evans, M. (ed.) *International Law*, Oxford: 415–42.

Des Forges, A. 1999. *Leave None to Tell the Story: Genocide in Rwanda*. New York: Human Rights Watch.

DFID (Department for International Development) (UK). 2000. 'United Nations High Commissioner for Refugees', London.

Dolan, C. 1999. 'Repatriation from South Africa to Mozambique: Undermining Durable Solutions?' in Black, R. and Khoser, K. (eds.) *The End of the Refugee Cycle: Refugee Repatriation and Reconstruction*. Oxford: 85–108.

Dörner, D. 1996. *The Logic of Failure: Recognising and Avoiding Error in Complex Situations*. Boulder, CO.

Douglas, M. 1986. 'The Social Preconditions of Radical Scepticism', in Law, J. (ed.) *Power, Action, and Belief: A New Sociology of Knowledge* (as cited by Richards, P. 1996. *Fighting for the Rain Forest: War, Youth and Resources in Sierra Leone*. London).

Doyal, L. and Gough, I. 1991. *A Theory of Human Need*. London.

Dumm, T.L. 1996. *Michel Foucault and the Politics of Freedom*. London.

ECRE (European Council on Refugees and Exiles). 1994. 'PARinAC Final Update', meeting held at the Documentation Centre of the Refugee Studies Programme, University of Oxford.

Elder, G. 1999a. 'OPM/IFRC-URC/UNHCR/WFP Review: Mbarara Refugee Programme', evaluation report. July.

———. 1999b. 'Institutional and Structural Constraints on Supporting Refugees in Nakivale Transit Camp, Mbarara District, Southwest Uganda', unpublished report. August.

Eliah, E. 1999. 'Makerere Aids Refugee Cause', *Times Higher Education Supplement*, 12 February.

Elmadman, K. 2002. *Asile et Réfugiés dans les Pays Afro-Arabes*. Casablanca.

Endicott, T. 2001. '"International Meaning": Comity in Fundamental Rights Adjudication', *International Journal of Refugee Law* 13: 280–92.

Equatoria Community in the UK. 1999. 'Meeting of 10.07.99: Resolutions, Recommendations and Proposals for Action on the Chukudum Crisis', Leeds.

Estephanos T. 1999. 'Review of the Household Food Security, Nutrition and Health Status in Dadaab and Kakuma Refugee Camps in Kenya'. Nairobi: UNHCR & WFP. October.

Evans, M. (ed.) 2003. *International Law*. Oxford.

Evans-Pritchard, E.E. 1940. *The Nuer*. Oxford.

Farah, N. 1993. *Gifts*. London.

_____ . 2000. *Yesterday, Tomorrow: Voices from the Somali Diaspora*. London.

FIDA (International Federation of Women Lawyers) Kenya. 1994a. 'Update on Cases under Legal Assistance Project', memorandum from the FIDA legal liaison officer, Dadaab, to the coordinator, WVV Project, Nairobi. 22 August.

_____ . 1994b. 'Legal Follow up on the Individual Case of … Criminal Case No. 244/94- *Republic v. Aden Abdi Hussein*', file note. Nairobi.

_____ . 1994c. 'Legal Follow up on the Individual Case of … Criminal Case No. 511/264/94- *Republic v. Mohammed Abdi Noor Ahmed*', file note. Nairobi.

_____ . 1994d 'Marafa Rape Case: Complainant … Criminal Case No. 648/94', file note. Nairobi.

_____ . 1994e. 'Public Inquest', file note, Nairobi.

_____ . 1995a. 'The Legal Assistance to Refugees Project', file note, Nairobi.

_____ . 1995b. 'Investigation into the Rape of … on 15th June 1995', file note, Nairobi.

Fitzgerald, M.A. 2002. *Throwing the Stick Forward: The Impact of War on Southern Sudanese Women*. Nairobi.

Fitzpatrick, J.M. (ed.) 2002. *Human Rights Protection for Refugees, Asylum-Seekers, and Internally Displaced Persons: A Guide to International Mechanisms and Procedures*. Ardsley, NY.

Foucault, M. 1977. *Discipline and Punish*. London.

Fox, J.A. and Brown, D.L. 1998. *The Struggle for Accountability: The World Bank, NGOs, and Grassroots Movements*. Cambridge, MA.

Freud, S. 1984. *Civilisation and Its Discontents and Other Essays*. Reissued edn. New York.

Garling, M. 2003. 'Enhancing Access to Human Rights', draft report for consultation, Geneva: International Council on Human Rights.

Garry, H.R. 1997. 'Peace and Human Rights in the Great Lakes Region of Africa: Prospects for the Third Millennium', rapporteur report, HURIPEC, Kampala: Faculty of Law, Makerere University. 11–12 December.

_____ . 1998a. 'The Right to Compensation and Refugee Flows: A "Preventative Mechanism" in International Law', *International Journal of Refugee Law* 10(1): 97–117.

_____ . 1998b. 'Applying the "Plumb Line" of Uganda's Bill of Rights: Human Rights and the Draft Bill on Refugees', *East African Journal of Peace and Human Rights* 5: 1–31.

_____ . 1998c. 'Report on Meetings Held to Discuss Uganda's 1996 Draft Refugee Bill', Kampala: Makerere University.

_____ . 2001. 'When Procedure Becomes a Matter of Life or Death: Interim Measures and the European Court of Human Rights', *European Public Law Journal*, 7(3).

_____ . 2002. 'Harmonisation of Asylum Law and Policy Within the European Union: A Human Rights Perspective,' *Netherlands Human Rights Quarterly* 20(2): 163–84.

Gasarasi, C.P. 1984. *A Tripartite Approach to the Resettlement and Integration of Rural Refugees in Tanzania*. Uppsala: Nordiska Afrikainstitutet.

———. 1990. 'The Mass Naturalisation and Further Integration of Rwandese Refugees in Tanzania', *Journal of Refugee Studies* 3: 88–109.

Gersony, R. 1989. *Why Somalis Flee: A Synthesis of Accounts of Conflict Experience in Northern Somalia by Somali Refugees, Displaced Persons, and Others*. Washington DC: US Department of State.

———. 1997. 'The Anguish of Northern Uganda: Results of a Field-Based Assessment of the Civil Conflicts in Northern Uganda', submitted to US embassy, USAID mission, Kampala. August.

Gilbert, G. 2001. 'Current Issues in the Application of the Exclusion Clauses', paper prepared as part of the UNHCR Global Consultations on International Protection, Geneva.

Gilbert, L. 1995. 'Rights, Refugee Women and Reproductive Health', *American University Law Review* 44: 1213–52.

Gingyera-Pinycwa, A.G.G. (ed.) 1996. *Uganda and the Problem of Refugees*. Kampala.

Girard, F. and Waldman, W. 2000. 'Ensuring the Reproductive Rights of Refugees and Internally Displaced Persons: Legal and Policy Issues', *International Family Planning Perspectives* 26(4): 167–73.

Gitari, A., Lester, E., Munge, J. and Ndungu, N. 1998. 'Report on the Evaluation of the JRS Wood Avenue Project', Nairobi.

Godfrey, N. 1991. 'Refugee Health: An Overview', London School of Hygiene and Tropical Medicine, London. 15 July.

Goffman, E. 1961. *Asylums: Essays on the Social Situation of Mental Patients and Other Inmates*. Garden City, NY.

Goodwin-Gill, G. 1998. *The Refugee in International Law*. 2nd edn. Oxford.

———. 1999. 'Refugee Identity and Protection's Fading Prospect', in Nicholson, F. and Twomey, P. (eds.) *Refugee Rights and Realities*. Cambridge: 220–49.

———. 2000. 'Refugees: Challenges to Protection', paper presented at the Conference Commemorating UNHCR at 50: Past, Present and Future of Refugee Assistance, New York. 15–18 May.

———. 2001. 'Refugees: Challenges to Protection', *International Migration Review* 35: 130–42.

———. 2003. 'Refugees and Responsibility in the Twenty-First Century: More Lessons from the South Pacific', *Pacific Rim Law & Policy Journal* 12: 23.

Gorman, R.F. 1987. *Coping with Africa's Refugee Burden: A Time for Solutions*. Boston, MA.

Gorman, R.F. (ed.) 1993. *Refugees Aid and Devleopment: Theory and Practice*. Westport, CO.

Goyen, P., Porignon, D., Soron'gane, M.E., Tonglet, R., Hennart, P. and Vis, H.L. 1996. 'Humanitarian Aid and Health Services in Eastern Kivu, Zaire: Collaboration or Competition', *Journal of Refugee Studies* 9: 268–80.

Gramsci, A. 1992. *Prison Notebooks*. New York. 1992.

Grant, S. 1998. 'The Social and Economic Human Rights of Non-Citizens', *East African Journal of Peace and Human Rights* 5(1): 75–89.

Guluma, W.V. 1997a. 'Health Sector Report for February 1997 for Kakuma Refugee Camp', Kakuma.

———. 1997b. Unpublished letter to *The Lancet*, London. 4 October.

Haines, R. 2001. 'Gender-Related Persecution', paper prepared as part of UNHCR's Global Consultations on International Protection, Geneva.

Halliday, S. 2000. 'The Influence of Judicial Review on Bureaucratic Decision-Making', *Public Law*: 110–22.

Hammond, L. 1999. 'Examining the Discourse of Repatriation: Towards a More Proactive Theory of Return Migration', in Black, R. and Koser, K. (eds.) *The End of the Refugee Cycle: Refugee Repatriation and Reconstruction*. Oxford: 227–44.

Hansen, A. 1982. 'Self-Settled Rural Refugees in Africa: The Case of Angolans in Zambian Villages', in Hansen, A. and Oliver-Smith, A. (eds.) *Involuntary Migration and Resettlement: The Problem and Responses of Dislocated People*. Boulder, CO.

Hansen, A. and Oliver-Smith, A. (eds.) 1982. *Involuntary Migration and Resettlement: The Problem and Responses of Dislocated People*. Boulder, CO.

Harrell-Bond, B.E. 1986. *Imposing Aid: Emergency Assistance to Refugees*. Oxford.

_____. 1989. 'Repatriation: Under What Conditions Is It the Most Desirable Solution for Refugees? An Agenda for Research', *Africa Studies Review* 32: 41–69.

_____. 1990. 'Breaking the Vicious Circle: Refugees and Other Displaced Persons in Africa', in Adeji, A. (ed.) *The African Social Situation*. London.

_____. 1991. 'Mission Report: Moi University, Eldoret, Kenya', unpublished report, University of Oxford: Refugee Studies Programme. 29 March–12 April.

_____. 1994. 'The Ikafe Refugee Settlement Project in Aringa County', report to OXFAM, Oxford: Refugee Studies Programme. December.

_____. 1996a. 'Refugees and the Reformulation of International Aid Policies: What Donor Governments Can Do', in Schmid, A.P. (ed.) *Whither Refugee?* Leiden: 183–200.

_____. 1996b. 'Refugees and the International System: the Evolution of Solutions after the Second World War' in *Oxford International Review* (Special Issue) 3(2): 2–9.

_____. 1997a. 'Are Refugee Camps Good for Kids?', paper presented at the Continental Conference on Children in Situations of Armed Conflict, ministerial level meeting of the OAU. July.

_____. 1999d. 'Disposable People? Refugees, Migrants and the Church's Mission Today', keynote address to the World Mission Institute, Lutheran School of Theology, Chicago.

_____. 2000a. 'Can Humanitarians Be Humane?', paper presented at the Conference on Recovery and Development After Conflict and Disaster, Norway. 5–6 April.

_____. 2002. 'Can Humanitarian Work with Refugees Be Humane?', *Human Rights Quarterly* 24: 51–85.

Harrell-Bond, B.E., Howard, A. and Skinner, D. 1977. *Community Leadership and the Transformation of Freetown (1801–1976)*. The Hague.

Harrell-Bond, B.E. and Kanyeihamba, G.W. 1986. 'Returned Refugees', report of a mission to Uganda for the EEC.

Harrell-Bond, B.E. and Dunbar-Ortiz, R. 1987. 'Who Protects the Human Rights of Refugees?', *Africa Today* 34(1–2): 105–25.

Harrell-Bond, B.E., Voutira, E. and Leopold, M. 1991. 'Counting the Refugees: Gifts, Givers, Patrons and Clients', *Journal of Refugee Studies* 5: 205.

Harrell-Bond, B.E. and Zetter, R.W. 1992. 'Governments, NGOs and Humanitarian Assistance to the Uprooted in Central and Southern Africa', report, Oxford: Refugee Studies Programme.

Harrell-Bond, B.E. and Voutira, E. 1995. 'In Search of the Locus of Trust: The Social World of a Refugee Camp', in Daniel, V.E. and Knudsen, J.C. (eds.) *Mistrusting Refugees*. Berkeley: 207–24.

_____. 1997. 'Refugees and Oustees: Competing or Complementary Concepts? The Challenges of Resettlement', unpublished manuscript.

Harrell-Bond, B.E., Asiku, E., De Lorenzo, M., Lammers, E. and Lutaakome Kayiira, J. 2000. 'DanChurchAid Evaluation of the Tanganyika Christian Refugee Service (TCRS) Refugee Project in Kibondo District, Tanzania, 5–19 January 2000: Report and Recommendations', Copenhagen and Dar es Salaam. February.

Harris, O. (ed.) 1996. *Inside and Outside the Law*. London/New York.

Hathaway, J.C. 1991. *The Law of Refugee Status*. Toronto.

————. 1997. *Reconceiving International Refugee Law*. The Hague.

Hathaway, J.C. and Dent, J.A. 1995. *Refugee Rights: Report on a Comparative Survey*. Toronto.

Headly, W.M. 1986. 'People on the Move: In Service to Them'. Nairobi: Religious Superiors' Association of Kenya & Catholic Overseas Development Fund.

Helton, A. 2002. 'The Future of Refugee Protection', in Bayefsky, A.F. and Fitzpatrick, J. (eds.) 2000. *Human Rights and Forced Displacement*. The Hague: 213–28.

Hitch, P. 1983. 'The Mental Health of Refugees: A Review of Research', in Baker, R. (ed.) *The Psychological Problems of Refugees*. London.

Holborn, L.W. 1975. *Refugees: A Problem of Our Time: The Work of the United Nations High Commissioner for Refugees, 1951–1972*. Two volumes. Metuchen, NJ.

Holt, P.M. and Daly, M.W. 2000. *A History of the Sudan: From the Coming of Islam to the Present Day*. 5th edn. Harlow.

Hopkins, T. et al. 1990. 'Refugees in Kenya: An Assessment of Needs/Resources, Opportunities, and Institutions for Self-Sufficiency', report to UNHCR and the Ford Foundation, Nairobi.

Horst, C. 1999. 'Somali Refugees in Dadaab, North-Eastern Province of Kenya: Towards a Transformation of Academic Societies', paper presented at the International Conference on Refugees and the Transformation of Societies: Loss and Recovery, Soesterberg, Kontakt der Kontinenten, University of Amsterdam. 21–24 April.

————. 2002. 'Vital Links in Social Security: Somali Refugees in the Dadaab Camps, Kenya', *Refugee Survey Quarterly*, 21(1–2) (special issue 'Displacement in Africa: Refuge, Relief & Return').

————. 2003 *Transnational Nomads: How Somalis Cope with Refugee Life in the Dadaab Camps of Kenya*. Ph.D. thesis, University of Amsterdam.

Hovil, L. 2001. 'Refugees and the Security Situation in Adjumani District', working paper no. 2, Kampala: Refugee Law Project.

HRW (Human Rights Watch) 1997a. 'Uncertain Refuge: International Failures to Protect Refugee', New York.

————. 1997b. 'What Kabila is Hiding: Civilian Killings and Impunity in Congo', New York.

————. 1998. 'Sudan. Global Trade, Local Impact: Arms Transfers to All Sides in the Civil War in Sudan', New York.

————. 1999a. 'In the Name of Security: Forced Round-ups of Refugees'. New York.

————. 1999b. *World Report*. New York.

————. 2000a. 'Eastern Congo Ravaged: Killing Civilians and Silencing Protest', New York.

————. 2000b. 'Rwanda: The Search for Security and Human Rights Abuses', New York.

————. 2001a. 'Congo: Reluctant Recruits: Children and Adults Forcibly Recruited for Military Service in North Kivu', New York.

————. 2001b. 'Uganda in Eastern DRC: Fueling Political and Ethnic Strife', New York.

_____. 2001c. 'Eastern Congo: Rebels' Persecution of Rights Activists', press release, New York. 21 August.

_____. 2002. 'Rwanda: Observing the Rules of War?', New York.

_____. 2002b. 'Hidden in Plain View: Refugees Living without Protection in Nairobi and Kampala', New York.

HRW/Africa Watch. 1993. 'Seeking Refuge, Finding Terror: The Widespread Rape of Somali Women Refugees in North Eastern Kenya', London.

Hufton, O. 2004. *Poverty and the Purse*. Cambridge.

Hulme, D. and Edwards, M. 1997. *NGOs, States and Donors: Too Close for Comfort*. New York.

Hyndman, J. 1996. 'Geographies of Displacement: Gender, Culture and Power in UNHCR Camps', Ph.D. thesis, University of British Columbia.

_____. 2000. *Managing Displacement: Refugees and the Politics of Humanitarianism*. Minneapolis.

Hyndman, J. and Nyklund, V. 1998. 'UNHCR and the Status of Refugees in Kenya', *International Journal of Refugee Law* 10: 21–48.

ICG (International Crisis Group). 2000. 'Uganda and Rwanda: Friends or Enemies?' Nairobi/Brussels.

ICRC (International Committee of the Red Cross). 1994. 'Red Cross and Red Crescent Regional Workshop', Mombasa. 15–17 March.

Indra, D. 1999a. 'Not a "Room of One's Own": Engendering Forced Migration Knowledge and Practice' in Indra, D. (ed.) *Engendering Forced Migration*. Oxford: 1–22.

Indra, D. (ed.) 1999b. *Engendering Forced Migration*. Oxford.

Inter-Agency Standing Committee. 1999. 'Policy Statement for the Integration of a Gender Perspective in Humanitarian Assistance', XXI Meeting, Geneva. 31 May.

INTRAC (International NGO Training and Resource Centre). 1999. 'UNHCR-WFP Evaluation', Oxford. September.

IOM (International Organisation for Migration)/UNHCR. 2000. 'Guidelines on Reviewing National Refugee Legislation', draft document, Geneva.

Iranian Refugees' Alliance, Inc. 1995. 'Evading Scrutiny: Refugee Determination Procedure Measure up to International Standards?', Turkey. May.

IRB (Immigration and Refugee Board). 1995. 'Human Rights Brief: Women in India', Documentation and Research Branch, Ottawa. September, as cited in KIMS CD-ROM, UNHCR, Geneva, January 1999.

_____. 1996. 'Guidelines on Women Refugee Claimants Fearing Gender-Related Persecution', issued by the chairperson pursuant to section 65(3) of the Immigration Act, 1996 update, Ottawa.

_____. 1999. 'Assessment of Credibility in the Context of CRDD Hearings', Ottawa.

IRC (International Rescue Committee). 1994. 'Review of Health Activities in Kenya and Somalia – July 18–23 1994', conducted by Michael Alderman.

_____. 1997. 'Integrated Health Care, Community-Based Rehabilitation, Women's Development, Forestry, Agriculture, Adult Education and Micro-Enterprise Programs. Kakuma Refugee Camp, Kenya, final report, 1 January 1997–31 December 1997'. Nairobi.

IRIN (Integrated Regional Information Network). 2001. 'Uganda: LRA Actions Restrict Relief Work in Northern Districts'. 11 July.

Jackson, I.C. 1999. *The Refugee Concept in Group Situations*. Dordrecht.

Jackson, T. 1992. *The Law of Kenya*. Nairobi: Kenya Literature Bureau.

Jacobsen, K. 2001. 'The Forgotten Solution: Local Integration for Refugees in Developing Countries', New Issues in Refugee Research, working paper no. 45. Geneva: UNHCR.

Jamal, A. 2000. 'Meeting Essential Needs in a Protracted Refugee Situation: A Case Study Review of Kakuma Camp, North-Western Kenya', Geneva: Evaluation and Policy Analysis Unit, UNHCR.

James, W. 1979. Kwanim Pa: The Making of the Uduk People: An Ethnographic Study of Survival in the Sudan-Ethiopian Borderlands. Oxford.

Jennings, R. and Watts, A. 1992. Oppenheim's International Law. London.

Johnson, D.H. 2002. The Root Causes of Sudan's Civil War. Oxford.

Joly, D. 1999. 'A New Asylum Regime in Europe' in Nicholson, F. and Twomey, P. (eds.) Refugee Rights and Realities. Cambridge.

Kaiser, T. 2000. 'Participatory and Beneficiary-based Approaches to the Evaluation of Humanitarian Programmes', Geneva: Evaluation and Policy Analysis Unit, UNHCR.

_____ . 2001. 'UNHCR's Withdrawal from Kiryandongo: Anatomy of a Handover', New Issues in Refugee Research, working paper no. 32, Geneva: UNHCR.

Kalin, W. 2001. 'Supervising the 1951 Convention on the Status of Refugees: Article 35 and Beyond', UNHCR background paper for the 2nd Expert Roundtable as part of Global Consultation on International Protection, Cambridge. 9–10 July.

Kalyango, R. 2000. 'Nongovernmental Organisations and the Provision of Humanitarian Assistance to Urban Refugees in Kampala', unpublished M.A. thesis, Makerere University, Uganda.

Kamau, K. and Vasquez. 1991. 'Judges and Human Rights: The Kenyan Experience', Journal of African Law 35: 142.

Kapuscinski, R. 1992. The Soccer War. New York.

Karadawi, A. 1977. 'Political Refugees: A Case Study from the Sudan, 1964–1972', unpublished M.Phil. thesis, University of Reading.

_____ . 1983. 'Constraints on Assistance to Refugees: Some Observations from the Sudan', World Development 11(6).

_____ . 1991. 'The Smuggling of the Ethiopian Falashas through Sudan to Israel', African Affairs 90: 23–49.

_____ . 1999. Refugee Policy in the Sudan, 1967–1984. Oxford.

Karara, J.-D. 1996. 'Etude sur la situation des réfugiés rwandais vivant au Kenya,' unpublished manuscript, Nairobi. April.

Karim, A., Duffield, M., Jaspars, S., Benini, A., Macrae, J., Bradbury, M., Johnson, D.H. and Larbi, G. 1996. Operation Lifeline Sudan: A Review. Birmingham: School of Public Policy, University of Birmingham. July.

Karunakara, U.K. 2004. 'The Demography of Forced Migration. Displacement and Fertility in the West Nile Region of Northern Uganda and Southern Sudan', Ph.D. thesis, Johns Hopkins University.

Karunakara, U.K. et al. 2004. 'Experience of Traumatic Events and Symptoms of Post-traumatic Stress in Sudanese Forced Migrant and Ugandan Populations of the West Nile', African Health Sciences.

Katalikawe, J. 1999. 'Judicial Review of Administrative Action in Uganda: The Case of Asylum Seekers and Refugees', paper presented at the Judicial Seminar on Asylum and Refugees, Faculty of Law, Makerere University. 15–17 April.

Keen, D. 1992. Rationing the Right to Life: The Crisis in Emergency Relief. London.

_____ . 1994. The Benefits of Famine: A Political Economy of Famine and Relief in Southwestern Sudan 1983–1989. Princeton, NJ.

Kibreab, G. 1983. *Reflections on the African Refugee Problem: A Critical Analysis of Some Basic Assumptions*. Uppsala: Nordiska Afrikainstitutet.

_____. 1987a. 'How Durable are "Durable Solutions" to the Problem of African Refugees?', overview paper for the Refugee Research Workshop, Nairobi. 14–17 December.

_____. 1987b. *Refugees and Development in Africa: The Case of Eritrea*. Lawrenceville NJ.

_____. 1989. 'Local Settlement in Africa: A Misconceived Option?', *Journal of Refugee Studies* 2: 468–90.

_____. 1991. 'Integration of African Refugees in First Countries of Asylum: Past Experiences and Prospects for the 1990s', paper commissioned by the Program on International and U.S. Refugee Policy, Tufts University. Boston.

_____. 1996. 'Eritrean and Ethiopian Refugees in Khartoum: What the Eye Refuses to See', *African Studies Review* 39(3): 131–78.

Kirby, J., Kliest, T., Frerks, G., Flikkema, W. and O'Keefe, P. 1997. 'UNHCR's Cross Border Operation in Somalia: The Value of Quick Impact Projects for Refugee Resettlement', *Journal of Refugee Studies* 10: 181–98.

Köbben, A.J.F. 1969. 'The Cottica Dyuka of Surinam', in Nader, L. (ed.) *Law in Culture and Society*. Berkeley: 117.

Koos, N. and Ros, D. 1996. 'A Participatory Review of the Ikafe Refugee Response', report for OXFAM-UK&I, Oxford. April–June.

Koser, K. 1997. 'Information and Repatriation: The Case of Mozambican Refugees in Malawi', *Journal of Refugee Studies* 10: 1–18.

Kostanjsek, N. 1996. 'Strengthening Institutional Development in the Context of Integrated Refugee Settlement Programmes: A Case Study of Rhino Camp Refugee Settlement', report for DED. May.

Krulfeld, R.M. and Macdonald, J.L. (eds.) 1998. *Power, Ethics and Human Rights: Anthropological Studies of Refugee Research and Action*. Oxford.

Kuhlman, T. 1990. *Burden or Boon? A Study of Eritrean Refugees in the Sudan*. Amsterdam: Anthropological Studies VU no. 13.

_____. 1995. *Asylum or Aid? Economic Integration of Ethiopian and Eritrean Refugees in the Sudan*. Research Series, no. 2. Leiden: African Studies Centre.

_____. 2001. 'Appropriate Responses to Protect Refugee Situations: The Case of Liberian Refugees in Côte d'Ivoire', report of a mission for UNHCR. August–September.

Kuloba, R. 1997. *Courts of Justice in Kenya*. Nairobi.

Kuper, J. 1997. *International Law Concerning Child Civilians in Armed Conflict*. Oxford.

Lammers, E. 1998. 'Refugee Experiences: From Theory to Daily Life in Kampala', Amsterdam: Department of Cultural Anthropology, Free University of Amsterdam.

Landau, L.B. 1997. 'Beyond Dependency: Is Human Development an Appropriate Model for Refugee Assistance?', unpublished manuscript, Berkeley.

Lauterpacht, E. and Bethlehem, D. 2001. 'The Scope and Content of the Principle of Non-Refoulement (Opinion)', paper prepared as part of the UNHCR Global Consultations on International Protection, Cambridge, June.

Lawrence, M., King, A. and Lejeune, S. 1997. 'Household Food Economy Assessment of Sudanese Refugees. Moyo and Arua Districts, Uganda', report on a study undertaken by Save the Children Fund on behalf of WFP Uganda and UNHCR Uganda. April.

LCHR (Lawyers Committee for Human Rights). 1995. *African Exodus*. New York.

_____. 2002. *Refugees, Rebels and the Quest for Justice*. New York.

Lemarchand, R. 1970. *Rwanda and Burundi*. London.

———. 1973. 'Selective Genocide in Burundi'. London: Minority Rights Group.

———. 1995. *Burundi: Ethnic Conflict and Genocide*. Washington, DC/Cambridge, UK.

Leopold, M. 2002. '"Trying to Hold Things Together": International NGOs Caught Up in an Emergency in North-Western Uganda', in Barrow, O. and Jennings, M. (eds.) *The Charitable Impulse: NGOs and Development in East and North East Africa*. Oxford: 65–78.

Lester, T. 1998. 'Addressing the Needs of Vulnerable Individuals/Households in Refugee Settlements in Adjumani District', unpublished manuscript, Kampala.

Levi, P. 1979a. *If This Is a Man*. New York.

Levi, P. 1979b. *The Truce*. New York.

Lewis, I.M. 1961. *A Pastoral Democracy: A Study of Pastoralism and Politics Among the Northern Somali of the Horn of Africa*. London.

———. 1988. *A Modern History of Somalia: Nation and State in the Horn of Africa*. Boulder, CO.

———. 1993. *Understanding Somalia*. London.

———. 1994. *Blood and Bone: The Call of Kinship in Somali Society*. Lawrenceville, NJ.

Lipsky, M. 1980. *Street Level Bureaucracy: Dilemmas of the Individual in Public Services*. New York.

Loescher, G. 1993. *Beyond Charity: International Cooperation and the Global Refugee Crisis*. New York.

———. 2001. *The UNHCR and World Politics*. Oxford.

———. 2003. 'UNHCR at Fifty' in Steiner, N., Gibney, M. and Loescher, G. *Problems of Protection: The UNHCR, Refugees and Human Rights*. New York and London.

Lomo, Z. 1999a. 'The Struggle for the Protection of Human Rights in Uganda: A Critical Analysis of the Work of Human Rights Organizations', *East African Journal of Peace and Human Rights* 5: 161–74.

———. 1999b. 'The Role of Legislation in Promoting "Recovery": A Critical Analysis of Refugee Law and Practice in Uganda', paper presented at the International Conference on Refugees and the Transformation of Society: Loss and Recovery, Amsterdam: InDRA, University of Amsterdam. 21–24 April.

———. 1999d. 'Do I Owe Minister Butime an Apology?', unpublished manuscript, Kampala.

Lukhoba, G. and Cheluget, K. 1992. 'A Bundle of Belonging: Not the Only Thing a Refugee Brings to His New Country', paper presented at the National Seminar on Refugee Law and Rights, Moi University, Kenya. 6–10 September.

Lwanga-Lunyiigo, S. 1996. 'Uganda's Long Connection with the Problem of Refugees: from the Polish Refugees of World War II to the Present', in Gingyera-Pinycwa, A.G.G. (ed.) *Uganda and the Problem of Refugees*. Kampala.

LWF (Lutheran World Federation) Kakuma. 1996. 'Security Section: Weekly Report', 27 February.

———. 1997a. 'Security Section: Annual Report', 17 December.

———. 1997b. 'Security Section: Weekly Report', 14 January.

———. 1997c. 'Security Section: Weekly Report', 24 February.

LWF Uganda. 1998. 'Adjumani (East Moyo) Sudanese Refugees Resettlement Programme 1998', Kampala.

Macchiavello, M. 2001. 'Urban Refugees: An Under-Utilised Asset?', unpublished report, Kampala.

MacFarlane, S.N. 2000. 'Politics and Humanitarian Action', occasional paper no. 41, Providence, RI: Thomas J. Watson Institute for International Studies.

Macklin, A. 1998. 'Truth and Consequences: Credibility Determination in the Refugee Context', paper presented at the International Association of Refugee Law Judges Conference on the Realities of Refugee Determination on the Eve of a New Millennium: the Role of the Judiciary, Ottawa. 12–17 October.

Majodina, Z. 1995. 'Dealing with Difficulties of Return to South Africa: The Role of Social Support and Coping', *Journal of Refugee Studies* 8(2): 210–27.

———. 1998. 'Home at Last: The Re-Entry Adaptation of Returned South-African Exiles', Ph.D. thesis, Department of Psychology, University of Cape Town.

Malkki, L.H. 1995. *Purity and Exile: Violence, Memory, and National Cosmology among Hutu Refugees in Tanzania*. Chicago.

Mamdani, M. 1996. *Citizen and Subject: Contemporary Africa and the Legacy of Late Colonialism*. Princeton, NJ.

———. 2001. *When Victims Become Killers: Colonialism, Nativism, and the Genocide in Rwanda*. Princeton, NJ.

Marx, R. 1995. 'Non-Refoulement, Access to Procedures, and Responsibility for Determining Refugee Claims', *International Journal of Refugee Law* 7: 383–406.

Masumbuko, M. 1997. 'Implementing Protection in Kakuma', unpublished manuscript, Kakuma.

Mathews, J.T. 1997. 'Power Shift', *Foreign Affairs* 76: 50–66.

Merkx, J. 2000. 'Refugee Identities and Relief in an African Borderland: A Study of Northern Uganda and Southern Sudan', working paper no. 19, Geneva: UNHCR.

Meron, T. 1996. *Human Rights and Humanitarian Norms as Customary Law*. Oxford.

Mijere, N.J. (ed.) 1995. *African Refugees and Human Rights in Host Countries*. New York.

Mollett, J.A. 1991. *Migrants in Agricultural Development*. London.

Monnier, M.-A. 1995. 'The Hidden Part of Asylum Seekers: Interviews in Geneva, Switzerland: Some Observations about the Socio-Political Construction of Interviews Between Gatekeepers and the Powerless', *Journal of Refugee Studies* 8(3): 305.

Moore, B. 1978. *Injustice. The Social Bases of Obedience and Revolt*. New York.

Moore, J. 2001. 'Whither the Accountability Theory? Second-Class Status for Third-Party Refugees as a Threat to International Refugee Protection', *International Journal of Refugee Law* 13: 32–50.

Moore, S.F. 1993. 'Changing Perspectives on a Changing Africa', in Bates, R.H. et. al. *Africa and the Disciplines*. Chicago.

Morris, N. 1997. 'Protection Dilemmas and UNHCR's Response: A Personal View from within UNHCR', *International Journal of Refugee Law* 9: 492–99.

Morrs, E. 1984. 'Institutional Destruction Resulting from Donor and Project Proliferation in the Sub-Saharan Countries', *World Development* 12: 465–70.

MSF (Médicins sans Frontières)-Belgium. 1997. 'Nutritional Survey Report for Ifo, Dagahaley and Hagadera Camps', Dadaab. August.

Mtango, E.-E. 1989. 'Military and Armed Attacks on Refugee Camps', in Loescher, G. and Monahan, L. (eds.) *Refugees and International Relations*. Oxford.

Mugumya, G. 1997. 'Final Report of Kiryandongo Phase Out: Evaluation of Work Done by InterAid and Recommendations', Kampala. 2 April.

Mukassa, S. 1998. 'Baseline Survey on the Local Council Courts System in Uganda', report for Nordic Consulting Group, Uganda.

Mulei, C., Laketch D. and Garling, M. 1996. *Legal Status of Refugee and Internally Displaced Women in Africa*. Nairobi.

Mulumba, D. 1984. 'A Study of the Rwandese Refugees' Attitudes towards Repatriation', unpublished B.A. thesis, Makerere University, Kampala.

_____. 1998. 'Refugee Women and the Traumas of Encampment in Uganda', *East African Journal of Peace and Human Rights* 5: 32–44.

_____. 1999. 'Towards the Integration of Health Services in Refugee Affected Areas in Uganda', report to the Ford Foundation, Nairobi.

Mumby, T. 2002. 'Arguments re: UNHCR Administrative Decision-Making Procedures', unpublished paper, Ruskin College, University of Oxford. 1 March.

Munson, J. 1999a. 'The Role of Government for Uganda's Refugee Populations: Observations from the Office of the Prime Minister, Directorate of Refugees', unpublished manuscript, Kampala.

_____. 1999b. 'Conflict Resolution and Justice in Rhino Camp Refugee Settlement', Kampala.

Munson, J. and Obomba, J. 1999. 'Report on the Refugee Situation in Nebbi District, April 21–27 1999', Kampala.

Murungi, T.I. 1999. 'Kampala Urban Refugee Needs Assessment Report', for Jesuit Refugee Service, Kampala.

Musirika, M. 1999. 'Self-Reliance for Sudanese Refugees: Opportunities and Challenges', paper presented at the Monthly Seminar Series on Forced Migration, Makerere Institute of Social Research, Kampala. 28 March.

Mutibwa, P. 1992. *Uganda Since Independence: A Story of Unfulfilled Hopes*. London.

Mutunga, W. 1990. *The Rights of an Arrested and an Accused Person*. Nairobi.

Nabuguzi, P. 1998. 'Refugees and Politics in Uganda', in Gingyera-Pinycwa, A.G.G. (ed.) *Uganda and the Problem of Refugees*. Kampala: 53–78.

Nader, L. 1969. *Law in Culture and Society*. Berkeley.

Nagey, B. 2000. 'Turn Back to Look Ahead? Central European Observations on the Future of Regimes Affecting Refugees', in Bayefsky, A.F. and Fitzpatrick, J. (eds.) *Human Rights and Forced Displacement*. The Hague: 245–61.

NCCK (National Council of Churches of Kenya). 1997. 'Integrating Family Planning into Health Services in Refugee Situations: Kakuma and Dadaab, Kenya', Nairobi: NCCK.

Newbury, C. 1988. *The Cohesion of Oppression: Clientship and Ethnicity in Rwanda, 1860–1960*. New York.

Nobel, P. 1982. 'Refugee Law in the Sudan', research report no. 64. Uppsala: Nordiska Afrikainstitutet.

Norbury, F. 2002. 'Playing God in Hell', field report from Western Upper Nile area, Sudan. 28 February.

Nowrojee, B. 2000. 'In the Name of Security: Forced Round-ups of Refugees in Tanzania, Human Rights Watch, vol. 11, no. 4A, New York.

Nussbaum, M. 2000. *Sex and Social Justice*. Oxford.

Nye, J. 2002. *The Paradox of American Power*. Oxford.

OAU (Organisation of African Unity)/UNHCR Working Group. 1980. 'Guidelines for National Refugee Legislation', adopted by OAU/UNHCR Working Group on Arusha Follow-up, second meeting, Geneva. 4–5 December.

Obi, N. and Crisp, J. 2000. 'Evaluation of UNHCR's Policy on Refugees in Urban Areas: A Case Study Review of New Delhi', Geneva: UNHCR. November.

Odhiambo-Abuya, E. 2004. '"Parlez-vous l'anglais ou le Swahili?" The Role of Interpreters in Refugee Status Determination Interviews in Kenya', *Forced Migration Review* 19, January: 48–50.

Odinkalu, C. and Zard, M. 2002. 'African Regional Mechanisms That Can Be Utilised on Behalf of the Forcibly Displaced', in Fitzpatrick, J.M. 2002. *Human Rights Protection for Refugees, Asylum-Seekers, and Internally Displaced Persons: A Guide to International Mechanisms and Procedures*. Arsdley, NY: 259–314.

Ogata, S. 1994. 'Keynote Address at the Opening Ceremony of the PARinAC Global Conference', Oslo. 6 June.

Okoro, U.R. 1995. 'Protection Problems of Refugee Women: The Case of the Coastal Refugee Camps in Kenya', paper presented at the NGO Workshop on African Refugee Protection Issues, Dakar. 16–18 June.

Oloka-Onyango, J. 1998. 'Forced Displacement and the Situation of Refugee and Internally Displaced Women in Africa', *East African Journal of Peace and Human Rights* 5(1): 1–31.

Omala, G. 1996. Letter to Barbara Harrell-Bond. 30 September.

O'Neill, W., Rutinwa, B. and Verdirame, G. 2000. 'The Application of the Exclusion Clauses in the Great Lakes', *International Journal of Refugee Law* 12 (special supplementary issue): 135–70.

Opondo, E. 1994. 'The Stranger Among the Luo of Kenya – Some Notes on Attitudes Towards Asylum Seekers, Refugees and Other Forced Immigrants in an African Community', Oxford: Refugee Studies Centre.

Otim, J. 1998. 'A Study of Problems Affecting Refugees Accessing Their Rights and Ways of Survival within Nairobi City', report for the EU research team, Nairobi.

Pallis, M. 2002. 'Obligations of States Towards Asylum Seekers at Sea: Interactions and Conflicts Between Legal Regimes', *International Journal of Refugee Law* 14: 329–64.

Pascal, B. 1961. *Pensées*. Paris: (ed.) Garnier Freres.

Payne, L. 1996. *Rebuilding Communities in a Refugee Settlement: A Casebook from Uganda.* OXFAM Development Casebook Series. Oxford.

_____. 1997. 'Impact of Food Delays on Refugees', *Emergency Nutrition Network: Field Exchange.* August.

Pérouse de Montclos, M.-A. and Kagwanja, P.M. 2000. 'Refugee Camps or Cities? The Socio-Economic Dynamics of the Dadaab and Kakuma Camps in Northern Kenya', *Journal of Refugee Studies* 13: 205–22.

Petrasek, D. 2000. 'Through Rose-Coloured Glasses: UNHCR's Role in Monitoring the Safety of the Rohingya Refugees Returning to Burma', in Bayefsky, A.F. and Fitzpatrick, J. (eds.) *Human Rights and Forced Displacement.* The Hague: 114–36.

Pirouet, L. 1988. 'Refugees in and from Uganda in the Post-Colonial Period', in Hansen, H.B. and Twaddle, M. (eds.) *Uganda Now: Between Decay and Development.* London.

Plato. 1997. Cooper, J.M. (ed.) *Complete Works.* Indianapolis.

Porter, K. 2001. 'Growth, Health and Physical Work Capacity of Adolescents in Refugee and Non-Refugee Communities in Tanzania', unpublished D.Phil. thesis, University of Oxford.

Pottier, J. 1999. 'The "Self" in Self-repatriation: Closing Down Mugunga Camp, Eastern Zaire', in Black, R. and Koser, K. (eds.) *The End of the Refugee Cycle? Refugee Repatriation and Reconstruction.* Oxford, New York 142–70.

Prunier, G. 1995. 'Burundi: Descent into Chaos or a Manageable Crisis?', Geneva: UNHCR/WRITENET. March.

_____. 1996. 'Identity Crisis and the Weak State: The Making of the Sudanese Civil War', Geneva: UNHCR/WRITENET. Available at http://www.unhcr.ch.

_____. 1997. *The Rwanda Crisis: History of a Genocide.* Revised edition with a new chapter. London.

_____. 1998. 'Rwanda: Update to End of February 1998', Geneva: UNHCR.

Rangasami, A. 1989. 'The Study of Social Responses to Disasters: The Case of "Scarcity" and "Famine" in India', unpublished Ph.D. thesis, Jawaharial Nehru University, New Delhi.

RCK (Refugee Consortium of Kenya). 1999. 'Project Proposal on the Legal Protection of Refugees and the Establishment of an Advocacy Centre', Nairobi. July.
_____. 2000. 'Report on the One-day Seminar "Reflections of the Past, Visions for the Future"', Nairobi. 6 April.
_____. 2001a. 'Dadaab: The Nightmare That Just Won't End', *Refugee Insights* 1 (April): 3.
_____. 2001b. 'Kakuma Camp – Refugee Camp or Recruitment Ground?', *Refugee Insights* 1(April): 13.
Refugees International. 2000. 'Dying to be Safe: Get the Minors out of Kakuma', *Refugees International Bulletin*. 24 April.
Reilly, R. 2000. 'A New Role for Human Rights Organisations in Refugee Protection?', in Bayefsky, A.F. and Fitzpatrick, J. (eds.) *Human Rights and Forced Displacement*. The Hague: 26–49.
Reuer, K. 1998. 'The Dangers of Living in Kakuma Refugee Camp', paper presented at the IASFM-IRAP Conference, Jerusalem. December.
Reyntjens, F. 1994. *L'Afrique des Grands Lacs en crise: Rwanda, Burundi (1988–1994)*. Paris.
_____. 1995. *Rwanda: Trois jours qui ont fait basculer l'histoire*. Paris.
_____. 1999. *La guerre des Grands Lacs: Alliances mouvantes et conflits extraterritoriaux en Afrique centrale*. Paris.
Reznick, N. 1997. 'Report of Student Intern, EU Health and Welfare Project'. New Hampshire. September.
Richards, A.I., (ed.) 1956. *Economic Development and Tribal Change: A Study of Migrant Labour in Buganda*. Cambridge.
Richards, P. 1996. *Fighting for the Rain Forest: War, Youth and Resources in Sierra Leone*. London.
Rizvi, Z. 1984. 'The Protection of Refugees', paper presented to the International Symposium on Assistance to Refugees: Alternative Viewpoints, Oxford: Refugee Studies Programme. March.
RLP (Refugee Law Project). 2000. 'Report on the Two-Week Intensive Court on Refugee Law and Human Rights', Kibuli Police Training School, Uganda. 14–25 February.
_____. 2001a. 'Sudanese Asylum Seekers Stranded in Kampala', fact sheet no. 1, Kampala. 21 February.
_____. 2001b. 'Refugees and the Security Situation in Adjumani District', working paper no. 2, Kampala.
_____. 2002a. 'War as Normal: The Impact of Violence in the Lives of Displaced Communities in Pader District, Northern Uganda', working paper no. 5.
_____. 2002b. 'Refugees in the City: Status Determination, Resettlement, and the Changing Nature of Forced Migration in Uganda', working paper no. 6, Kampala.
_____. 2002c. 'Refugees in Kyangwali Settlement: Constraints on Economic Freedom', working paper no. 7, Kampala.
Robinson, M. 1997. 'Privatising the Voluntary Sector: NGOs as Public Service Contractors?' in Hulme, D. and Edwards, M. 1997. *NGOs, States and Donors: Too Close for Comfort*. New York: 59–78.
Rogge, J.R. 1994. 'Repatriation of Refugees', in Allen, T. and Morsink, H. (eds.) 1994. *When Refugees Go Home*. London.
Rothman, D.J. 2000. 'The Shame of Medical Research', *New York Review of Books*. 30 November.
Röxstrom, E. and Gibney, M. 2003. 'The Legal and Ethical Obligations of UNHCR: The Case of Temporary Protection in Western Europe', in Steiner, N., Gibney,

M. and Loescher, G. *Problems of Protection: The UNHCR, Refugees and Human Rights*. New York and London.

RRAP (Refugee Rights Advocacy Programme) 2000–2002. *In the News: A Compilation of Newspaper Cuttings on Refugees and Internally Displace Persons from the Ugandan Press, Sudan Human Rights Association*. Kampala.

Rutinwa, B. 1997. 'Forced Displacement and Refugee Rights in the Great Lakes Region', paper presented at the Conference on Peace and Human Rights in the Great Lakes Region of Africa, Makerere University, Kampala. 11–12 December.

_____ . 1999. 'The End of Asylum? The Changing Nature of Refugee Policies in Africa', New Issues in Refugee Research, working paper no. 5, Geneva: UNHCR.

Rwandese/Burundian Prayers Fellowship. 1995. 'Report on the Meeting with JRS Representatives, held on 1st October 1995 at Calvary Worship Centre', Nairobi.

Samatar, S.S. 1991. *Somalia: A Nation in Turmoil*. London: MRG (Minority Rights Group).

Schmid, A.P. (ed.) 1996. *Whither Refugee?* Leiden.

Schmidt, A. 1998. 'How Camps Become Mainstream Policy for Assisting Refugees', paper presented at the 6th IASFM-IRAP Conference, Jerusalem. December.

Schrijvers, J. 1991. 'Dialectics of a Dialogical Ideal: Studying Down, Studying Sideways and Studying Up', in Nencel, L. and Pels, P. (eds.) *Constructing Knowledge: Authority and Critique in Social Science*. London: 162–79.

_____ . 1995. 'Participation and Power: A Transformative Feminist Research Perspective', in Wright, S. and Nelson, N. (eds.) *Power and Participatory Development: Theory and Practice*. London: 19–29.

Scottish Churches Sudan Group. 1997. 'Sudan: the Shame', Edinburgh. February.

Seddon, D., Harrell-Bond, B.E., Wamai, G. and Onweng Angura, T. 1998. 'Evaluation Report: Lutheran World Federation, Uganda Programme', University of East Anglia: Overseas Development Group. December.

Sekaggya, M. 1999. 'Who Does What and How for Asylum Seekers in Uganda: The Role of the Uganda Human Rights Commission', brief at a workshop organised by UNHCR, Kampala. 17 February.

Sen, A. 1981. *Poverty and Famines*. Oxford.

_____ . 1999. *Development as Freedom*. Oxford.

Sesnan, B. 1992. 'Education: Policy and Pencils', paper presented at the Refugee Studies Programme Summer School, Oxford.

Shack, W.A., Skinner, E., Percival, C. and Sullivan, H. 1979. *Strangers in African Societies*. Berkeley.

Shah, P. 2000. *Refugees, Race and the Law in Britain*. London.

Shawcross, W. 1984. *The Quality of Mercy*. London.

_____ . 2000. *Deliver Us from Evil: Peacekeepers, Warlords and a World of Endless Conflict*. New York.

Shiekh, H. 1997. 'Somali Refugees in Eastleigh', unpublished report, Nairobi.

SHRA (Sudan Human Rights Association). 1999. 'Human Rights Field Assessment Report: Refugee Camps in Northern and Central Uganda: 20 July–2 August 1999' Kampala.

Sieghart, P. 1983. *The International Law of Human Rights*. Oxford.

Simmonds, S., Vaughan, P. and Gunn, S.W. 1983. *Refugee Community Health Care*. Oxford.

Skran, C. 1988. 'Profiles of the First Two High Commissioners', *Journal of Refugee Studies* 1(4): 277–96.

_____ . 1992. 'The International Refugee Regime: The Historical and Contemporary Context of International Responses to Asylum Problems', in

Loescher, G. (ed.) *Refugees and the Asylum Dilemma in the West*. University Park, Pennsylvania: 8–35.

———. 1998. *Refugees in Inter-War Europe*. Oxford.

Sokoloff, C. 1994. 'Review of UNHCR's Kenya-Somalia Cross Border Operation', Geneva: UNHCR.

Sontag, S. 1991. *Under the Sign of Saturn* (reprint edn). New York.

Sperl, S. 2001. 'Evaluation of UNHCR's Policy on Refugees in Urban Areas: A Case Study Review of Cairo', Geneva: UNHCR.

Sphere Project. 2000. *Humanitarian Charter and Minimum Standards in Disaster Response*. Oxford.

Stanley, A. 1998. 'An Examination of the Impact of Refugees on Host Populations with Reference to Prostitution and the Spread of Sexually Transmitted Diseases and HIV/AIDS', Independent Study Project conducted in Kakuma Refugee Camp. London.

Steiner, N., Gibney, M. and Loescher, G. 2003. *Problems of Protection: The UNHCR, Refugees and Human Rights*. New York and London.

Stockton, N. 1996. 'Rations or Rights? Humanitarian Standards', Newsletter of the ODI Relief and Rehabilitation Network, no. 6. London. November.

Strange, S. 1996. *The Retreat of the State. The Diffusion of Power in the World Economy*. Cambridge.

Sunstein, C. 2002. *Risk and Reason: Safety, Law and the Environment*. Cambridge.

Toole, M. and Waldman, R. 1997. 'The Public Health Aspects of Complex Human Emergencies and Refugee Situations'. *Annual Review of Public Health* 18: 283–312.

Towle, R. 2000. 'Human Rights Standards: A Paradigm for Refugee Protection?' in Bayefsky, A.F. and Fitzpatrick, J. (eds.) *Human Rights and Forced Displacement*. The Hague: 26–49.

Tuitt, P. 1999. 'Rethinking the Refugee Concept', in Nicholson, F. and Twomey, P. (eds.) *Refugee Rights and Realities: Evolving International Concepts and Regimes*. Cambridge: 106–18.

———. *False Images: The Law's Construction of the Refugee*. London.

Ucanda, J. 1993. 'The Report on the Education of Refugee Girls and Women in the Refugee Camps of East Moyo and Kiryandongo', paper prepared at the 2nd Forum on Education for Southern Sudanese, Alere, Uganda. 8–24 March.

———. 1996. 'Access to Education for Refugee Girls: A Case of East Moyo Sub-District', Kampala: UNHCR. May.

Uganda Refugee Law Group. 1998. 'Recommendations to the Joint Drafting Committee for Developing Uganda's *Draft Refugee Bill*'. Makerere University, Kampala.

Umutesi, M.B. 2000. *Fuir ou mourir au Zaïre: Le vécu d'une réfugiée rwandaise*. Paris.

UNHCR (United Nations High Commissioner for Refugees) 2000. *The State of the World's Refugees 2000: Fifty Years of Humanitarian Action*. Oxford.

USCR (United States Committee for Refugees) 2000. *World Refugee Survey 2000*. Washington, DC.

US Department of State. 1998. 'Country Reports on Human Rights Practices for 1998 – Rwanda'. Washington, DC: US Department of State.

van Damme, W. 1996. 'Do Refugees Belong in Camps? Experiences from Goma and Guinea', *The Lancet* 346: 360–62.

———. 1998. *Medical Assistance to Self-Settled Refugees*. Antwerp.

Van Hear, N. 1994. 'The Socio-economic Impact of the Involuntary Mass Return to Yemen in 1990', *Journal of Refugee Studies* 7(1): 18–38.

Värynen, R. 2000. 'The Dilemma of Voluntary Funding: Political Interests and Institutional Reforms', paper presented at the Conference Commemorating UNHCR at 50, New York. 16–18 May.

Verdirame, G. 1999a. 'Response to Jeff Crisp and Karen Jacobsen', *Forced Migration Review* 4: 36.

_____. 1999b. 'Human Rights and Refugees: The Case of Kenya', *Journal of Refugee Studies* 12(1): 54–77.

_____. 2000. 'Ethnic Conflict and Constitutional Change in Rwanda and Burundi', in M. Andenas (ed.) *The Creation and Amendment of Constitutional Norms*, London, British Institute of International and Comparative Law: 302–18.

_____. 2000b. 'The Genocide Definition in the Jurisprudence of the *Ad Hoc* Tribunals', *International and Comparative Law Quarterly* 49: 578–98.

_____. 2001a. 'Testing the Effectiveness of International Norms: The Provision of Humanitarian Assistance and Sexual Apartheid in Afghanistan', *Human Rights Quarterly* 23(3): 733–68.

_____. 2001b. 'UN Accountability for Violations of Human Rights', unpublished Ph.D. thesis, London School of Economics and Political Science (on contract with Cambridge University Press, 2005).

Vidal, C. 1991. *Sociologie des passions (Côte d'Ivoire, Rwanda)*. Paris.

Voutira, E. et al. 1995. 'Improving Social and Gender Planning in Emergency Operations', Oxford: Refugee Studies Programme. July.

Voutira, E. and Whishaw Brown, S.A. 1995. 'Conflict Resolution: A Review of Some Non-governmental Practices. A Cautionary Tale', Studies on Emergencies and Disaster Relief, report no. 4, Uppsala: Nordiska Afrikainstitutet.

Waldron, S. 1987. 'Blaming the Refugees', *Refugee Issues: British Refugee Council and Queen Elizabeth House Working Papers on Refugees* 3: 1.

Waldron, S. and Hasci, N.A. 1995. *Somali Refugees in the Horn of Africa*. Oxford/Uppsala: Refugee Studies Programme and Nordiska Afrikainstitutet.

Walkup, M. 1997a. 'Policy and Behaviour in Humanitarian Organizations: The Institutional Origins of Operational Dysfunction', Ph.D. thesis, University of Florida.

_____. 1997b. 'Policy Dysfunction in Humanitarian Organizations', *Journal of Refugee Studies* 10: 37–60.

Weighill, L. 1996. 'ICARA II – Refugee Aid and Development', unpublished manuscript, Oxford: Refugee Studies Programme.

Weiner, M. 1998. 'The Clash of Norms: Dilemmas in Refugee Policies', paper presented at the Conference on the Growth of Forced Migration, University of Oxford. 25–27 March.

Weir, L. 1998. 'Research into the Health and Welfare of Refugees in and out of Camps in Kenya and Uganda', report for the EU research project, June.

Weiss, P. 1995. *The Refugee Convention, 1951: The Travaux Préparatoires Analysed with a Commentary*. Cambridge.

Whitaker, B.E. 1998. 'Hosting Neighbours: The Impact of Refugees on Tanzanian Communities in Ngara, Kibondo, and Kasulu Districts', unpublished summary of Ph.D. thesis, University of North Carolina, Chapel Hill.

Wilde, R. 1998. 'Quis Custodlet Ipsos Custodes? Why and How UNHCR Governance of "Development" Refugee Camps Should Be Subject to International Human Rights Law', *Yale Human Rights and Development Law Journal* 1(5).

Wilson, K. 1992. 'Thinking About the Ethics of Fieldwork', in Devereux, S. and Hoddinott, J. (eds.) *Fieldwork in Developing Countries*. Boulder, CO.

———. (n/d) 'Thinking about the Ethics of Fieldwork', unpublished manuscript, held at the library of the Refugee Studies Centre, Oxford.

Wilson, K., McGregor, J., Wright, J., Myers, M., de Waal, A., Pankhurst, A. and Ayling, R. 1985. 'The Lutaya Expedition: A Report on Research in Yei River District', occasional paper no. 1, Oxford: Refugee Studies Programme.

Wilson, R. 1997. *Human Rights, Culture and Context: An Introduction*. London.

World University Service (Uganda). 1992. 'Education Programme for Sudanese Refugees', Kampala.

Zetter, R. 1988. 'Refugees, Repatriation and Root Causes', *Journal of Refugee Studies* 1(2): 99–106.

———. 1992. 'Refugees and Forced Migrants as Development Resources: The Greek Cypriot Refugees from 1974', *Cyprus Review* 4(1): 7–38.

———. 1995. 'Shelter Provision and Settlement Policies for Refugees: A State of the Art Review', Studies on Emergencies & Disaster Relief, report no. 2, Uppsala: Nordiska Afrikainstitutet.

———. 1999. 'Reconceputalizing the Myth of Return: Continuity and Transition amongst the Greed-Cypriot Refugees of 1974', *Journal of Refugee Studies* 12(1): 1–22.

Newspaper/Newsletter articles

Abbey, Y. 1999. '24 Sudanese, Congo Refugees Languish in Luzira Prisons', *New Vision*, 15 September.

Aliro, O.K. 1997. '*Hutucide:* Museveni's Moment of Shame', *Monitor*, 14 September.

Black, I. and Watt, N. 2002. 'Britain Drops Plans to Link Asylum to Overseas Aid', 21 June.

Blomfield, A. 2002. 'UN Shaken by Refugees' Extortion Allegations', *Guardian*, 21 December.

Bouman, M. and Harrell-Bond, B.E. 1999. 'Men: The Victims of Defilement', *New Vision*, 2 December: 24.

Brooker, E. 1997. 'A Long Decade's Journey into the Night', *Independent on Sunday*, 26 January: 4–5.

Burns, J. and Edgecliffe-Johnson, A. 1998. 'UNHCR "May Have Paid for Ammunition Flights"', *Financial Times*, 7 August: 1.

Burns, J. and Williams, F. 1998a. 'Refugees' Agency Lost in Wilderness of Bungling and Waste', *Financial Times*, 29 July: 7.

———. 1998b. 'Ideals Fall Prey to Political Pressure', *Financial Times*, 29 July.

———. 1998c. 'UK Attack on UNHCR Emerges', *Financial Times*, 1–2 August.

———. 1998d. 'Warning to UN on Refugee Aid', *Financial Times*, 29 July: 1.

———. 1998e. 'US Calls for Urgent Review of UNHCR', *Financial Times*, 31 July.

Edgecliffe-Johnson, A. 1998a. 'UNHCR Denies Allegations of Dubious Accounting Practices', *Financial Times*, 10 August: 1.

———. 1998b. 'UN Refugee Agency Scraps Mediator Post', *Financial Times*, 12 August.

Financial Times. 1998a. 'Annan Calls for Full Details on UNHCR Books', 30 July.

———. 1998b. 'UNHCR Calls Meeting of Donors', 31 July.

———. 1998c. 'UN Seeks Report on UNHCR's Books', 30 July: 1.

———. 1998d. 'Editorial: Refugees and UN Reform', 30 July.

Goodwin-Gill, G. 1998b. 'Board of Auditors Has Awarded UNHCR Clean Bill of Health Following Last Year's Inspection', letter to the editor, *Financial Times*, 30 July.

Harrell-Bond, B.E. 1997b. 'Must Africa Keep its Refugees in Camps?' *Monitor*, 26 September: 12.

_____. 1999a. 'Should We Forget Our Bitter History?', Letter to the Editor, *New Vision*, 21 June.

_____. 1999b. 'What's the Fate of the Rwandan Students?', *New Vision*, 31 December: 23.

_____. 1999c. 'What's Wrong with Our Justice System?', *New Vision*, 29 September: 23.

_____. 2000b. 'More Awkward Questions Yet for UNHCR', *New Vision*, 5 January: 13.

Jessen-Petersen, S. 1998. 'Board of Auditors Has Awarded UNHCR Clean Bill of Health Following Last Year's Inspection', letter to the editor, *Financial Times*, 30 July.

Juuko, S. 1998. 'Refugee Kids Stunted', *Monitor*, 4 August: 7.

Kakande, J. 2000a. 'RPF Forced Us to Flee Home', *Sunday Vision*, 30 January: 29.

_____. 2000b. 'Stranded Students Rap Rwandese Leaders on Persecution', *New Vision*, 31 January: 3.

_____. 2000c. 'Rwandese Students Are Spoilt Kids, Says Official', *New Vision*, 1 February: 5.

Karpf, A. 2002. 'We've Been Here Before', *Guardian Weekend*, 8 June: 21–31.

Kimemia and Nduta. 2001 'Man Weeps at Judgment', *Daily Nation*, 17 May.

Kizito. 1997. 'Why God Has a Soft Spot for Refugees', *Sunday Nation*, 21 September.

Lambsdorff, O. 1998. 'UN Member States Have Heaped Pressure on UNHCR', *Financial Times*, 3 August.

Leak, O. 2001. 'UNHCR is Playing Politics', *Monitor*, 29 August, from *In the News: a Compilation of Newspaper Cuttings on Refugees and Internally Displaced Persons from the Ugandan Press'*, Refugee Rights Advocacy Programme (RRAP), Sudan Human Rights Association: 37.

Lomo, Z. 1999c. 'Butime Wrong to Send Away Nigerian Rebel', letter to the editor, *Monitor*, 5 April: 15.

Luganda, A. 1999. 'Refugees Refuse to Be Counted', *Monitor*, 27 February: 6.

Malaba, T. 1998. 'Gunmen Abduct Rwandese Refugee', *Monitor*, 2 February.

McKinney, C. 2000. 'Clinton Is Assisting Uganda, Rwanda to Wreck Havoc', *East African*, 7–13 August.

Miller, C. 1999. 'Chicken for Kosovo Refugees, No Water for Africans', *Monitor*, 26 May: 14.

Miller, C. and Simmons, A. 1999. 'Relief Camps for Africans, Kosovars Worlds Apart', *Los Angeles Times*, 21 May.

Mohammed, K.G. 2000. 'One Dead After Govt, UNHCR Dump Refugees in Ntinda', *Monitor*, 14 January.

Monitor 1996. 'Police Roughs up *Monitor* Staffer', 4 September.

_____. 1999. 'Cruel Shave in Gulu Can't Be UPDF – Brig. Mugume', 8 June: 22.

_____. 2000. 'How Many Refugees Must First Die Off?', 14 January: 8.

Mortimer, J. 1998. 'The Daily Menu of Hard Choices', *Financial Times*, 20–21 June.

Mugabi, J. 2000. 'Exile: More Students Leave for Uganda', *East African*, 24 December 1999–02 January 2000: 1

Mugagga, R. 1999. 'Sabena Dumps Tortured Burundians at Entebbe', *Monitor*, 7 July: 6.

Mugeere, A. 2001. 'SPLA Recruits in Uganda Camps', *New Vision*, 16 August, from *In the News: a Compilation of Newspaper Cuttings on Refugees and Internally Displaced Persons from the Ugandan Press'*, Refugee Rights Advocacy Programme (RRAP), Sudan Human Rights Association: 37.

Mutumba, R. 1998a. 'ISO, ESO "Involved" in Rwanda Abductions', *New Vision*, 6 March: 1.

_____ . 1998b. 'Refugee Abductions Escalate – UHRC', *New Vision*, 19 May: 40.

Mwesige, P.G. 1995. 'Iraqis Held for 3 Weeks at Entebbe Airport', *Monitor*, 10–13 November.

Mwilinga, J. 1999a. 'Refugee Rights and Law', *Monitor*, 14 September: 29.

_____ . 1999b. 'The Time Is Now', *New Vision*, 10 August: 10.

_____ . 1999c. 'MPs Should Recall Their Days in Exile', *New Vision*, 17 September: 14.

_____ . 1999d. 'Refugee Jailed Without Trial', *Monitor*, 14 September: 4.

_____ . 1999e. 'Suad Begs for Circumcision', *Women's Vision*.

_____ . 1999f. 'Tears of a Congolese Asylum Seeker', *Monitor*, 30 August: 25.

Nabeta, L. 1995. 'Two Months Later, Iraqi Family Still Held at Entebbe', *Monitor*.

Newland, K. 1998. 'Such a Blast Does Real Damage to UNHCR', letter to the editor, *Financial Times*, 7 August.

New Vision. 2000. 'Arua Adopts New Strategy', 26 January: 11.

Ogata, S. 1999. 'The Goal Is to Make Refugee Camps Unnecessary', *Financial Times*, 20 May.

Ojera, C. 1998. 'Gulu Officials Deny Protecting "Defiler"', *Monitor*, 11 February: 6.

Oliver, M. 2000. 'Death of a Ghost', *Monitor*, 19 January: 28.

Olupot, M. and Osike, F. 2002. 'SPLA Refugees a Security Threat', *New Vision*, 20 July.

Omara, A./Uganda Human Rights Commission. 1998. 'Public Appeal', *New Vision*, 10 March.

Onyang, S. 1999. 'Refugees Resettled', *Monitor,* 22 February.

Oroma, L.S. 2000. 'UNHCR, InterAid a Disgrace', letter to the editor, *Monitor*, 20 January: 9.

Phillips, M. 1998. 'The UN says it wants safe birth control for refugees but risks killing the very women it aims to help', *Observer*, 5 April.

Reynell, P. 2000. 'UNHCR Starves Refugees', letter to the editor, *Monitor*, 13 January: 9.

RLP (Refugee Law Project). 2001b. 'New Policy Prohibits Sudanese Asylum Seekers from Registering in Kampala'. *Sudan Monitor* 6(1), 1 March.

Rutinwa, B. and Kathina, M.J. 1996. 'Refugees: MPs Demand for Repatriation Unacceptable', *Daily Nation*, 4 May.

Saidy, S. 2000. 'Prof. Harrell-Bond Hasn't Got UNHCR Right!', *New Vision*, 4 January: 9.

Skogmo, B. 1998. 'US Supportive but Concerned over UNHCR', letter to the editor, *Financial Times*, 31 July.

Sudan Monitor. 2000. 'Insecurity Reigns in the Refugee Camps in Northern Uganda', 5(3), 3 September.

_____ . 2001. 'The Security Situation in Kakuma Refugee Camp in Kenya', 6(1), 1 March.

Taft, J. 1998. 'US Supportive but Concerned over UNHCR', letter to the editor, *Financial Times*, 31 July.

Taylor, C. 1999a. 'The Travail of Being a Refugee', *New Vision*, 15 March.

_____ . 1999b. 'Paying the Price for Christian Boyfriend', *Monitor*, 21 December: 15.

Thoolen, H. 1999. 'Why Do You Share Harrell-Bond's View on Africa Refugee Day?', *New Vision,* 23 June: 15.

Tumusiime J. 1998. 'SPLA "Seen" with Ugandan Weapons', *Monitor,* 25 September: 14.

Twesigomwe, C. 1995. 'UNHCR Is Not Responsible', *Monitor*, 17 February.

_____ . 2000. 'Refugee Students', *New Vision*, 1 January.

UNHCR. 1999c. 'UNHCR Did Best for Prof. Banjo', *Monitor*, 9 April: 4.

UNHCR. 1999g. 'UNHCR Has Found No Persecution of Students in Rwanda," *New Vision*, 20 December: 15.

Veronese, P. 2001. 'La città fantasma dei profughi', *La Repubblica*, 2 August.

Warigi, G. 1998. 'Kenya Government's Move on Aliens Worries UNHCR', *East African*, 7–13 September: 28.

Weddi, D.J. 1998. 'ISO to Hunt Down Abductors', *New Vision*, 10 March.

Official Government Documents

DoR (Directorate of Refugees – Uganda). 1999. 'Unaccompanied Refugee Children', Memorandum from Carlos Twesigomwe to B.E. Harrell-Bond.

East African Community. 1997. *The East African Co-operation Development Strategy*.

GoU (Government of Uganda) – Ministry of Health. 1993. 'White Paper on Health Policy. Update and Review (1993)'. 18 October.

GoU-MoLG (Ministry of Local Government). 1993. 'Refugee Issue', letter to the Refugee Council, Kampala, 3 December (ref. 0.1985).

_____. 1997. 'Cessation of Refugee Status for the 1959/65 Rwandese Refugees Caseload in Uganda', Cabinet Memorandum. 14 May.

GoU-Moyo District. 1998. 'Development Plan 1998–2002', vol. I, Kampala. February.

GoU-OPM (Office of the Prime Minister) 1999a. 'Report of the Round Table on the Self-Reliance Strategy for Refugee Hosting Area in Arua and Adjumani Districts', Kampala. 11 June.

_____. 1999b. 'Disaster Preparedness and Management Policy for Uganda'. February.

_____. 1999c. 'Recommended Structure and Establishment: Disaster Management and Refugees'.

GoU-REC (Refugee Eligibility Committee). 1996. 'Minutes of the Meeting Held on 27/11/96 in the Office of the Director', Kampala.

_____. 1997a. 'Interview Notes', Kampala.

_____. 1997b. 'Minutes of the 2nd Meeting, held on 16th April 1997, in Ministry Board Room', Kampala.

_____. 1997c. 'Minutes of the 3rd Meeting, held on 21 May 1997', Kampala.

GoU-Refugee Secretariat, MoLG. 1997. 'The Refugee Settlement Population in Uganda'. 30 July.

GoU-UNHCR. 1998a. 'Minutes of the Education/Community Services Co-ordination Meeting', Kampala. 15–16 April.

_____. 1998b. 'Education and Community Services Coordination Meeting: Students' Views'. 13 April.

GoU-UNICEF (United Nations Children's Fund). 1997. *Implementing Universal Primary Education (UPE): Effects on Schools, Communities and Pupils*.

UK Government. 2003. 'New Vision for Refugees'. 7 March.

UN and UNHCR documents

'Arusha Conference on the Situation of Refugees in Africa'. 1979. UN doc. A/AC.96/INF.158.

EXCOM (Executive Committee of UNHCR). 1977. Conclusion no. 8: 'Determination of Refugee Status'.

_____. 1979. Conclusion no. 15: 'Refugees without an Asylum Country'.

_____. 1981. Conclusion no. 22: 'Protection of Asylum-Seekers in Situations of Large-Scale Influx'.

_____. 1985. Conclusion no. 36: 'General Conclusion on International Protection'.

_____. 1989. Conclusion no. 58: 'Problem of Refugees and Asylum-Seekers Who Move in an Irregular Manner from a Country in Which They Had Already Found Protection'.

_____. 1993. Conclusion no. 73: 'Refugee Protection and Sexual Violence'.

_____. 2002. Conclusion no. 94: 'Conclusion on the Civilian and Humanitarian Character of Asylum'.

ILC (International Law Commission). 2001a. 'First Report of the Special Rapporteur of the International Law Commission on Diplomatic Protection', UN doc. A/CN.4/506 and Corr.1 and Add. 1.

_____. 2001b. 'Articles on the Responsibility of States for Internationally Wrongful Acts. Adopted by the General Assembly in UNGA', res. 56/83.

International Conference on Population and Development, Cairo, 18 October 1994.

OCHA (Office for the Coordination of Humanitarian Affairs). 1999. *Humanitarian Update – Uganda*, vol. 1, issue 10. 21 December.

_____. 2000a. 'Gulu, Kitgum Paralysed by LRA,' *Humanitarian Update – Uganda*. 24 January.

_____. 2000b. 'LRA, ADF Attacks Increase Displacement', *Humanitarian Update – Uganda*. 24 January.

_____. 2000c. 'LRA Still Makes Presence Felt', *Humanitarian Update – Uganda*. 12 April.

_____. 2001. 'Refugees', 'LRA: Wreaking Havoc in South Sudan', and 'Security Still Eludes West Nile', *Humanitarian Update – Uganda*. May.

UN. 1997. 'Report of the Joint Mission Charged with Investigating Allegations of Massacres and Other Human Rights Violations Occurring in Eastern Zaire (now Democratic Republic of the Congo) since September 1996', UN doc. 51/942, New York. 2 July.

UNACC-SCN (United Nations Administrative Committee on Coordination/Sub-Committee on Nutrition). 1996. 'Report on the Nutrition Situation of Refugee and Displaced Populations', New York. December.

UNDP (United Nations Development Programme). 2000. *Human Development Report*. Oxford and New York.

_____. 2002. *Human Development Report*. Oxford and New York.

UNFPA (United Nations Fund for Population). 1997. 'Report on UNFPA/UNHCR Rapid Appraisal of Reproductive Health Services in Refugee Camps and Settlements', Kampala. April.

UNHCR. 1979. *Handbook for Procedures and Criteria for Determining Refugee Status*. Geneva.

_____. 1982. *Handbook for Emergencies*. Geneva.

UNHCR – Branch Office for Kenya. 1987a. 'Annual Protection Report', Nairobi.

UNHCR – Evaluation Unit. 1987b. 'Review of UNHCR Assistance to Refugees in Kenya', Geneva. July.

UNHCR – Branch Office for Uganda. 1988. 'Annual Protection Report', Kampala.

UNHCR. 1989. 'Determination of Refugee Status (RLD 2)', Geneva.

UNHCR – Branch Office for Uganda. 1991. 'Annual Protection Report', Kampala.

UNHCR. 1992a. *Handbook for Procedures and Criteria for Determining Refugee Status*. Geneva.

UNHCR – Branch Office for Kenya. 1992b. 'Annual Protection Report', Nairobi.

UNHCR. 1992c. 'Review of UNHCR's Emergency Operation in Kenya', Evaluation by David Kapya. Geneva. January.

UNHCR – Branch Office for Kenya. 1993a. 'Annual Protection Report', Nairobi.

UNHCR. 1993b. 'Interpreting in a Refugee Context (RLD 3)', Geneva.

UNHCR – Branch Office for Kenya. 1994a. 'Annual Protection Report', Nairobi.

UNHCR. 1994b. 'Review of UNHCR's Kenya-Somalia Cross-Border Operation', Geneva. December.

_____ . 1994c. 'Guidelines on the Protection and Care of Refugee Children', Geneva.

UNHCR – Branch Office for Uganda. 1994d. 'SitRep. No. 9: Uganda', Kampala. September.

UNHCR. 1995a. 'Interviewing Applicants for Refugee Status (RLD 4)', Geneva.

_____ . 1995b. 'Report on Mission in Kenya 27–31 March and 3 April 1995 by Mrs Anne Skatvedt, Senior Coordinator for Refugee Children', Geneva.

UNHCR – Branch Office for Uganda. 1995c. 'Education in Refugee-Affected Areas', Kampala.

_____ . 1995d. 'Community Based Rehabilitation in the Pakelle/Adjumani Refugee Areas of Uganda: A Feasibility Study and Plan of Action', Kampala. April–May.

UNHCR. 1995e. 'Mission to Uganda and Kenya by Blaise Cherif, Senior Legal Adviser for Africa, 12–19 March', Geneva. March.

_____ . 1995f. 'Kenya – Country Operation Plan', Geneva.

_____ . 1995g. 'Training Module 5: Human Rights and Refugee Protection', RLD 5, Geneva. October.

_____ . 1995h. 'Sexual Violence Against Women: Guidelines on Prevention and Response', Geneva.

UNHCR – Branch Office for Kenya. 1996a. 'Annual Protection Report for the Period 1995/96', Nairobi.

UNHCR. 1996b. 'Regional Workshop on Major Protection Issues in the Horn and Eastern Africa', Nairobi. 24–25 May.

_____ . 1996c. 'UNHCR Comprehensive Policy on Urban Refugees', Geneva.

UNHCR – Branch Office for Uganda. 1996d. 'Annual Protection Report', Kampala.

UNHCR – Inspection and Evaluation Service. 1996e. 'A Review of UNHCR's Women Victims of Violence Project in Kenya', Geneva. March.

UNHCR – Sub-Office Kakuma. 1996f. 'Non-Payment of March Incentives', Memorandum from the Officer in Charge to Refugees Working for NGOs in Kakuma, Kenya. 4 April.

UNHCR – Branch Office for Uganda. 1996g. 'Country Operations Plan for 1997–98', Kampala.

UNHCR. 1996h. 'Letter from Annika Linden, Senior Protection Officer, to Sr. Jane MacAndrews, People for Peace in Africa. Re: Procedures relating to Rejected Asylum-Seekers', 23 October (UNHCR Ref.: KEN/NRB/PT/96/IC/1109).

_____ . 1996i. 'Mission Report to Uganda and Kenya by K. Morjane, Director and O. Bajulaiye, Head of Desk II, Regional Bureau for Africa', Geneva. 6–17 February.

UNHCR – Branch Office Uganda. 1996j. 'Comments on the 1996 Refugee Bill of Uganda', Kampala. October.

_____ . 1996k. 'SitRep 23 October 1996', Kampala.

_____ . 1996l. 'SitRep 30 October 1996', Kampala.

UNHCR. 1996m. 'Project Delphi', CRP. 68, Geneva. May.

_____ . 1996n. 'Career Management System-Performance Appraisal and Objective Setting', Geneva. September.

_____ . 1997a. 'Country Operations Plan – Kenya, 1997 (revised) & 1998 (initial)', Nairobi.

_____ . 1997b. 'UNHCR Comprehensive Policy on Urban Refugees', Geneva. 25 March.

UNHCR – Branch Office for Kenya. 1997c. 'Annual Protection Report', Nairobi.

UNHCR – Branch Office for Uganda. 1997d. 'Annual Protection Report', Kampala.

UNHCR – Branch Office for Egypt. 1997e. 'Annual Protection Report', Cairo.

UNHCR – Inspection and Evaluation Service. 1997f. 'Review of UNHCR Implementing Arrangements and UNHCR Implementing Partners Selection Procedures', Geneva.

UNHCR – Sub-Office Dadaab. 1997g. 'Protection Unit Mission to Garissa Report', Kenya. 23–25 January.

UNHCR – Inspection and Evaluation Service. 1997h. 'Review of UNHCR Implementing Arrangements and Implementing Partner Selection Procedures', Geneva. November.

UNHCR. 1997i. 'Revised Internal Guidelines on Screening of Rwandans', Geneva. 2 December.

UNHCR – Sub-Office Dadaab. 1997j. 'Dadaab Monthly Protection Update', Kenya. November.

UNHCR. 1997k. 'Guidelines on Policies and Procedures in Dealing with Unaccompanied Children Seeking Asylum', Geneva. February.

_____. 1998a. *Resettlement Handbook* (revised). Geneva. April.

_____. 1998b. 'Kenya – Annual Protection Report', Nairobi.

UNHCR – Sub-Office Dadaab. 1998c. 'UNHCR Monthly Protection Update', Kenya. February.

UNHCR – Branch Office for Kenya. 1998d. 'Sub-Office Dadaab', Nairobi. 15 April.

_____. 1998e. 'Dadaab Firewood Project: Action Plan for the Project Pilot Phase and Proceedings of the Project Design Workshop Held in Dadaab, 12–14 January 1998', Nairobi. January.

UNHCR. 1998f. 'UNHCR Policy Regarding Refugees and Acquired Immuno-Deficiency Syndrome (AIDS)', Inter-Office Memorandum 78/98 from the Deputy High Commissioner to All Staff Members at Headquarters and in the Field, Geneva. 1 December.

_____. 1998g. 'UNHCR Response to Issues Raised by the Financial Times', document faxed to field offices, Geneva. August.

UNHCR – Branch Office for Uganda. 1998h. 'Newsletter', vol. 4, no. 2, July.

_____. 1998i. 'Uganda Refugee Bill 1998', paper presented by Zachary Kawi, senior protection officer, at the International Association of Refugee Law Judges Conference on the Realities of Refugee Determination on the Eve of a New Millennium: the Role of the Judiciary, Ottawa. 12–17 October.

UNHCR. 1998j. *UNHCR Manual*, Geneva.

_____. 1998k. *Operations Management System Draft Handbook*. Geneva. December.

UNHCR – Branch Office for Uganda. 1999a. Letter from Hans Thoolen, representative, to Carl Twesigomwe, deputy director for refugees in Uganda, 29 June.

UNHCR. 1999b. 'Global Asylum Application and Refugee Status Determination Statistics, 1998', Geneva.

_____. 1999d. *UNHCR Manual*, Geneva.

_____. 1999e. 'Uganda 1999 Annual Protection Report – Reporting Period November 1998–December 1999', Geneva.

_____. 1999f. 'Kenya 1999 Annual Protection Report – Reporting Period November 1998–December 1999', Geneva.

_____. 1999h. '1999 – Staffing for UNHCR Refugee Health Programme and Rate per 10,000 (Refugee and Nationals)', Kampala.

_____. 1999i. 'UNHCR Inter-Office Memorandum no. 91/1999' from Erika Feller, Director, Department of International Protection, to All Representatives and Chief of Missions/All Substantive Officers at Headquarters, Geneva. 23 September.

_____. 1999j. *Reproductive Health in Refugee Situations: An Interagency Field Manual*. Geneva.

UNHCR Burundi/UNHCR Headquarters, Burundi. 2000a. 'Repatriation and Reintegration Plan'. February.

UNHCR. 2000b. *The State of the World's Refugees*. Oxford.

_____. 2000c. 'Uganda 2000 Annual Protection Report – Reporting Period January 2000–December 2000', Geneva.

_____. 2000d. 'Summary of the Strategic Oral Presentation on UNHCR Operations in Africa', Standing Committee, 17th meeting, 29 February–2 March.

_____. 2000e. 'Islamic Republic of Iran 2000 Annual Protection Report', Geneva. January–December.

_____. 2000f *Handbook for Emergencies*, 2nd edn. Geneva.

_____. 2001a. 'Evaluation of the Implementation of UNHCR's Policy on Refugees in Urban Areas', Evaluation and Policy Analysis Unit, EPAU 2001/10, December (report prepared by Naoko Obi and Jeff Crisp), Geneva.

_____. 2001b. 'Evaluation of the Dadaab Firewood Project, Kenya', Evaluation and Policy Analysis Unit, EPAU/2001/08, June (report prepared by Virginia Thomas and Janni Jansen), Geneva.

_____. 2001c. 'Refugee Women and Mainstreaming: A Gender Equality Perspective', Executive Committee of the High Commissioner, UNHCR doc. EC/51/SC/CRP.17, 30 May.

_____. 2003a. 'Guidelines on International Protection No. 3: Cessation of Refugee Status', 10 February.

_____. 2003b. 'Guidelines on International Protection No. 5: The Application of the Exclusion Clauses', 4 September.

UNHCR New Stories. 2002. 'Refugees Killed, Aid Workers Kidnapped as Ugandan Rebels Raid Sudanese Settlement', 5 August. [Available from Helen Bishop, African Refugee Protection Network, Kampala, Uganda].

UNHCR. 2002a. 'Tragic Testimonies: Refugee Children in West Africa Allege Exploitation by Humanitarian Workers', in *Prima Facie*, the Newsletter of UNHCR's Department of International Protection, Geneva. April.

UNHCR/DFID. 1998. 'Review of DFID/UNHCR NGO Refugee Support Scheme by UNHCR/DFID', report on a visit to Uganda 30 November–4 December, Geneva.

UNHCR-ICVA (International Council of Voluntary Associations). 1994. 'Oslo Declaration and Plan of Action', Norway. 6–9 June.

UNHCR-OPM. 1998. 'From Local Settlement to Self-Sufficiency: A Long-Term Strategy for Assistance to Refugees in Uganda 1999–2002', draft joint paper, Kampala. 16 July.

_____. 1999. 'Self-Reliance Strategy', Kampala. May.

UNHCR-WFP (World Food Programme). 1998. 'Model Tripartite Agreement among UNHCR, WFP and the Implementing Partner', Rome. 13 March.

UNICEF. 1994. *Children of War: Wandering Alone in Southern Sudan*. New York.

_____. 1996. The Impact of Armed Conflict on Children. New York ('the Machel report').

_____. 2002. *Adult Wars, Child Soldiers*. New York.

WHO (World Health Organisation). 2001. *The World Health Report 2001*, Annex Table Five: 'Selected National Health Accounts Indicators for all Member States Estimates for 1997 and 1998', Geneva.

World Conference on Human Rights, Vienna Declaration and Programme of Action, 25 June 1993.

World Conference on Women (IV), Declaration and Platform for Action, Beijing, 15 September 1995.

National Legislation

Kenya

Aliens Restriction Act 1973 (cap. 173).
Citizenship Act 1963 (cap. 170).
Constitution 1963 (amended in 1964, 1969, 1991).
Constitution of Kenya Review Commission Act of 1997.
Draft Bill, Constitution of Kenya, 27 September 2002.
Immigration Act, no. 25, 1967 (cap. 172).
Immigration Act (Amendment) Act 1972, no. 6, 1976 (*see* section 6, classes of entry permits).
Judicature Act 1967.
Khadis Court Act 1967 (cap. 11).
Non-Governmental Organisations Coordination Act, no. 19, 1990.
Non-Governmental Organisations Coordination Regulations 1992.
Refugees Bill 2003 (published in the Kenya Gazette Supplement: Bills, 2003).

South Africa

Refugees Act 1998, act no. 130.

Sudan

Refugee Fund Act 1982.

Uganda

Adoption of Children Rules, 1998, Statutory Instrument Supplement no. 16, 25 August 1997.
Aliens Control Act 1984.
Citizenship and Immigration Control Act 1999.
Constitution 1995.
Control of Alien Refugees Act 1960.
Disaster Preparedness and Management Bill 1998.
Family and Children Court Rules, 1998, Statutory Instrument Supplement no. 17, 24 July 1998.
Human Rights Commission Act 1997.
Immigration Act of 1969 and subsequent modifications.
Non-Governmental Organisations Registration Statute 1989.
Non-Governmental Organisation Regulations 1990.
Penal Code Act, cap. 106 of 1950, *as amended* 24 October 1998.
Standing Orders and Parliamentary Procedures 1993.
Statute 16/1996 establishing the National Council for Children.

Treaties and other international instruments

African Charter on Human and Peoples' Rights (*adopted on* 17 June 1981, *entered into force on* 21 October 1986).
African Charter on the Rights and Welfare of the Child (*adopted in* July 1990, *entered into force on* 29 November 1999).
Convention Against Torture and Other Cruel, Inhuman or Degrading Treatment or Punishment (*adopted on* 10 December 1984, *entered into force on* 26 June 1987).
Convention Determining the State Responsible for Examining Applications for Asylum Lodged on One of the Members States of the European Communities (Dublin Convention) (*signed on* 15 June 1990, *entered into force on* 1 September 1997).

Convention on the Elimination of All Forms of Discrimination Against Women (*adopted on* 18 December 1979, *entered into force on* 3 September 1981).

Convention on the Rights of the Child (*adopted on* 20 November 1989, *entered into force on* 20 September 1990), *and* Optional Protocol on the Involvement of Children in Armed Conflict (*adopted on* 25 May 2000, entered into force on 12 February 2002).

Convention Relating to the Status of Refugees (*signed on* 28 July 1951, *entered into force on* 22 April 1954).

Declaration on Territorial Asylum (*adopted on* 14 December 1967).

Forced Labour Convention, International Labour Organisation Convention no. 29 (*adopted on* 28 June 1930, *entered into force on* 1 May 1932).

Geneva Convention (III) Relative to the Treatment of Prisoners of War (*adopted on* 12 August 1949, *entered into force on* 21 October 1950).

Geneva Convention (IV) Relative to the Protection of Civilian Persons in Time of War (*adopted on* 12 August 1949, *entered into force on* 21 October 1950).

International Covenant on Civil and Political Rights, *and* Optional Protocol (*adopted on* 16 December 1966, *entered into force on* 23 March 1976).

International Covenant on Economic, Social and Cultural Rights (*adopted on* 16 December 1966, *entered into force on* 3 January 1976).

International Convention on the Elimination of All Forms of Racial Discrimination (*adopted on* 21 December 1965, *entered into force on* 4 January 1969).

Lomé Convention (Fourth Convention between the African, Caribbean and Pacific Group of Countries (ACP) and the European Economic Community (EEC), (*signed on* 15 December 1989, *entered into force on* 1 March 1990).

Memorandum of Understanding, UNHCR-WFP, 1994 (*signed by* Catherine Bertini and Sadako Ogata).

Memorandum of Understanding, UNHCR-WFP (*entered into force on* 31 March 1997, *signed by* Catherine Bertini and Sadako Ogata).

Organisation of African Unity: Convention Governing the Specific Aspects of Refugee Problems in Africa (*adopted on* 10 September 1969, *entered into force on* 20 June 1974).

Protocol Additional to the Geneva Conventions of 12 August 1949, and Relating to the Protection of Victims of Non-International Armed Conflicts (Protocol II) (*signed on* 8 June 1977, *entered into force on* 7 December 1978).

Protocol to Prevent, Suppress and Punish Trafficking in Persons, Especially Women and Children, supplementing the United Nations Convention against Transnational Organized Crime (*adopted on* 15 November 2000, *entered into force on* 25 December 2003).

Protocol Relating to the Status of Refugees (*adopted on* 16 December 1966, *entered into force on* 4 October 1967).

Protocol against the Smuggling of Migrants by Land, Sea and Air, supplementing the United Nations Convention against Transnational Organized Crime (*adopted on* 15 November 2000, *entered into force on* 28 January 2004).

Schengen Agreement (Convention Applying the Schengen Agreement of 14 June 1985 between the Governments of the States of The Benelux Economic Union, The Federal Republic of Germany and the French Republic on the Gradual Abolition of Checks at their Common Borders, *signed on* 19 June 1990, *entered into force* 19 June 1990).

Slavery Convention (*signed on* 25 September 1926, *entered into force on* 9 March 1927, *modified by* the Protocol of 7 December 1953).

Statute of the Office of the United Nations High Commissioner for Refugees, UNGA res. 428 (V) of 14 December 1950.

Universal Declaration of Human Rights (UNGA res. 217 A (III) of 10 December 1948).

Vienna Convention on the Law of Treaties (*signed on* 22 May 1969, *entered into force* 27 January 1980).

Cases

1. National

Botswana

Unity Dow, [1991] Law Reports of the Commonwealth (Const) 574; [1992] Law Reports of the Commonwealth (Const) 623 (High Court and Supreme Court).

Kenya

Criminal case no. 648/94.
Kamau Kuria v. AG (15 Nairobi Law Monthly 33).
Maina Mbacha v. AG (1989, 17 Nairobi Law Monthly 38).
Republic v. Abdi Musa Said, case no. 1553/1997, Chief Magistrate's Court Nairobi.
Republic v. Aden Abdi Hussein, no cit.
Republic v. Bonaventure Ntamakemna, case no. 1537/1997, Chief Magistrate's Court Nairobi.
Republic v. Christine Niyitegeka, case no. 1483/1997, Chief Magistrate's Court Nairobi.
Republic v. Maurice Nsabimana, case no. 1527/1997, Chief Magistrate's Court Nairobi.
Republic v. Mohammed Abdi Noor Ahmed, no cit.

Uganda

Ahmed and Ahmed v. UNHCR, Complaint to the Uganda Human Rights Commission no. 44/97.
Kromah v. UNHCR, Complaint to the Uganda Human Rights Commission no. 297/97.
Uganda v. Daembu, Ngandru, Alimange, criminal case no. IMM/MN.32/96, Chief Magistrate's Court of Mengo at Nakawa.
Uganda v. Katanga and Kaseleka, criminal case no. IMM/MN.2/97, Chief Magistrate's Court of Mengo at Nakawa.
Uganda v. Katanga Mwendeluwa and four others, criminal case no. IMM/MN 3/97.
Uganda v. Lemi and Yopkwe, criminal case no. 32/96, Magistrate's Court of Arua.
Uganda v. Muhamed Abdul, criminal case no. IMM/MN/26/96.
Uganda v. Solomon Khemis Oliha, criminal case no. MM155/94, Magistrate's Court of Moyo.

UK

R v. Bow Street Metropolitan Stipendiary Magistrate ex parte Pinochet Uguarte [1999] 2 All E.R. 97.
R v. Secretary of State for the Home Deparment, ex parte Adan et al. [1999] 4 All E.R. 774 (Court of Appeal), noted in (1999) *International Journal of Refugee Law* 11: 702. [2001] 2 Weekly Law Reports 143 (House of Lords).
R v. Secretary of State for the Home Department ex parte Saadi and Others [2002] UKHL 41.

2. International

Committee Against Torture

Elmi v. Australia, Communication no. 120/1998.

European Court of Human Rights

Belilos v. UK, Application no. 100328/83.
Tyrer v. UK, Application no. 5856/72.
East African Asians v. UK, Application no. 4403/70.

International Court of Justice (*see* www.icj-cij.org)

Armed Activities on the Territory of the Congo (Democratic Republic of Congo v. Uganda) [2000] Order of 1 July.
Asylum (Columbia v. Peru) [1950] I.C.J. Rep. 266.
Military and Paramilitary Activities In and Against Nicaragua (Nicaragua v. United States of America) Judgment (Merits), [1986] I.C.J. Rep. 14.
North Sea Continental Shelf (Federal Republic of Germany v. Denmark; Federal Republic of Germany v. Netherlands) [1969] Judgment of 20 February.
Reservations to the Convention on Genocide [1951] I.C.J. Rep. 15.

ICCPR Committee (*see* www.unhchr.ch/tbs/doc.nsf)

1986. *General Comment 15: The Position of Aliens under the Covenant.* 11 April.
1994. *General Comment 24: Issues Relating to Reservations made upon Ratification or Acession to the Covenant or the Optional Protocols thereto, or in relation to Declaration under Article 41 of Covenant.* 4 November.
1999. *General Comment 27: Freedom of Movement (Art. 12).* CCPR/C/21/Rev. 1/Add. 9. 2 November. ICESCR Committee *see* www.unhchr.ch/tbs/doc.nsf)
1990. *General Comment 3: The Nature of States Obligations (Art. 2. para. 1).* 14 December.
1991. *General Comment 4: The Right to Adequate Housing (Art. 11.1).* 14 December.
1997. *General Comment 7: The Right to Adequate Housing (Art. 11.1): Forced Evictions.* 20 May.
1999. *General Comment 12: The Right to Adequate Food (Art. 11).* E/C.12/1999/5. 12 May.
2000. *General Comment 14: The Right to the Highest Attainable Standard of Health.* E/C.12/2000/4. 11 August.

International Criminal Tribunal for Rwanda

Prosecutor v. Akayesu, case no. ICTR-96-4-T, *in part reported at* 37 ILM (1998) 1399.

Index

A

abduction 165–67
  of children 160
  see also forced recruitment of
    children
abortion 254
access to courts *see* courts
action research 9–10, 13–15
admission of refugees 55
  airports, dumping at 63–65
  arrivals en masse 68
  documentation *see* documentation
  donor countries, influence of 55–57
  entry procedures 56, 68–69
  forged documents 57, 59–60, 63
  group recognition 57
  Kenya 58, 60, 62–65, 68–69, 70–72
  legal hurdles 59–63
  local people and 70–72
  ordeals of arrival 63–70
  point of arrival 68–70
  police and 60
  prosecutions 60–63
  'recyclers', identifying 69–70
  restrictionism 56
  standards and procedures 58–59
  Tingi Tingi refugees 65–68
  Uganda 70–72
  UNHCR 58–59
  'unlawful presence' xv, 60–63
advocacy 20–21
  status-determination procedures
    93–94
African Centre for Treatment and
    Rehabilitation of Torture Victims
    (ACTV) 134

African Charter on Human and
    Peoples' Rights 179, 182, 215, 306
African Commission on Human And
    Peoples' Rights 306
African Education Fund (AEF) 219
African Exodus xiii
African Network for the Protection
    and Prevention of Child Abuse
    and Neglect (ANPPCAN) 237–38
African Refugee Education
    Programme (AREP) 216
Agency for Cooperation and Research
    Development (ACORD) 220, 233
agriculture 44, 292–93, 296–97
Aideed, Muhammad 5
AIDS *see* HIV/AIDS
airports
  dumping refugees at 63–65
  refoulement at ('Air Refoulement') 64
Al-Nimeiry, Jaafar 2
Ali, Moses 52n.30, 177
Alliance of Democratic Forces for the
    Liberation of Congo (ADFL) 171
Amnesty International 6, 20, 67,
    76n.35, 112, 116n.34, 166, 167,
    169–70, 317–19
Anyanya war 2, 29
arbitrary arrest and detention 131,
    167–73, 334
  Kenya 32, 167–70
  Uganda 170–73
Arusha Conference on the Situation
    of Refugees in Africa 1979 79
assimilation 2
  forced 263
association, freedom of 200–1

Associazione Volontari per il Servizio Internazionale (AVSI) 219–20, 244–45
asylum-seeker, definition 22n.8
Auma, Alice 21n.4
Australia 56, 278, 282, 283

B
Balkans, 'safe havens' policy 326n.15
Belgium, deportations from 64–65
Bemba, Pierre 3
Bettelheim, Bruno 206n.55
'blaming the refugees' 248–49, 292–94
borders, porous 70–71
Britain *see* United Kingdom
Burundi 4
  civil war 4
  Hutu uprising 4
  refugees from 1, 2, 59, 101, 109–10, 135, 166, 167, 170, 188, 196, 200, 201, 224, 239, 254, 260, 276, 293
  refugees in 3

C
Canada
  gender discrimination 54n.52
  resettlement in 282–83
Canadian International Development Agency (CIDA) 149–50
capital punishment 130, 144
CARE 151–52, 220–21, 292
case studies 11–13
children
  abductions 159–60
  Convention on the Rights of the Child 173, 215, 253, 305
  Dinka youth 128–30
  female genital mutilation (FGM) 123, 148
  forced recruitment of 120, 122, 174–79, 261, 302, 334
  health, right to 247–48
  sexual violence against 145, 151
  Sudanese 'walking boys' 32, 68, 284–85
  see also education
Christian refugees 127, 128
citizenship, acquisition of, Uganda 28–29, 41
civil and political rights xv, 120–202
  access to courts and right to fair trial 182–94
  freedom of association 200–1

freedom of expression, thought, conscience and religion 198–200
freedom of movement 179–82
liberty and security of the person, right to 152–79
life, right to 130–33
non-discrimination 121–30
privacy and family life, respect for 195–97
slavery and forced labour, freedom from 151–52
torture, cruel, inhuman or degrading treatment or punishment, freedom from 133–51
civil society 312–25
clothing, provision of 238
Collectif contre les expulsions 64, 65
collective punishment 120, 193–94, 334
Committee on Economic, Social and Cultural Rights 265n.34
community self-management (CSM) 151–52
compliance with refugee law 305–7
confidentiality, status-determination procedures 91–92
Congolese Refugees Development Association (COREDA) 201
contraception 251
Convention against Torture and Other Cruel, Inhuman or Degrading Treatment or Punishment 50n.3, 50n.4, 133, 207
Convention on the Elimination of All Forms of Discrimination Against Women (CEDAW) xviii n.13, 50n.3–4, 121, 263, 267n.69,
Convention on Forced Labour 264n.1
Convention Governing the Specific Aspects of Refugee Problems in Africa 1969 (OAU Convention) xii, xiv, 24n.34, 30, 46, 47, 308, 309
  Article 1(2) xviiin.12, 57, 95, 96, 178
  Article 2(3) xvi, 57
  Article 2(6) 69, 152
  Article 3 198–99, 307
  definition of 'refugee' xvin.12, 95, 96
  facilitating entry 55
  freedom of expression 198–99
  group recognition 57
  Kenya and 26–27, 46, 49, 58, 81, 264n.4

reservations 50n.5
status-determination procedures 78, 79
Uganda and 28, 30–31, 47, 49
Convention Relating to the Status of Refugees 1951 xiii–xiv, xvi, xvii, 8, 17, 24n.34, 57 69, 104, 118n.60, 170
    Article 1(C)(2)(5) 110–13
    Article 1(F) 107–110
    Article 3 121
    Article 4 199
    Article 15 199
    Article 16 182
    Article 17 2, 3 48, 216
    Articles 17–19 215
    Article 20 216
    Article 22 xv, 253
    Article 23 216
    Article 24 264n.10
    Article 26 179
    Article 27 179
    Article 28 *see* convention travel document
    Article 31 xv, 60
    Article 32 308
    Article 38 305
    cessation clauses 110–13
    courts, access to 182
    definition of 'refugee' xviiin.12, 114n.3, 216
    dispute settlement under 305
    economic and social rights 215
    education xv, 255
    employment rights 215
    exclusion clauses 107–10
    freedom of movement 179
    identity papers 179
    Kenya and 26, 46, 49
    non-discrimination 121
    non-refoulement principle xii, 73n.8, 308
    penalties for illegal entry, prohibition of xv, 60
    status-determination procedures 78, 79
    Uganda and 28, 30–31, 47, 49, 54n.53
    United Kingdom and 50n.1
Convention on the Rights of the Child (CRC) xviii
    Article 38 174
    Article 39 174

enforcement 305
Kenya 215
recruitment of children 173–74
right to education 253
Uganda 215
convention travel documents (CTDs) xii, 59, 181, 196, 197, 211n.151, 226
Cook, Rebecca 207n.62
corporal punishment 134, 141, 184, 190
corruption
    Kenya 32, 273–74
    police 32, 135, 168–69
    resettlement 75n.27, 287
courts
    access to 182–94
    international courts 305–6
    international treaties and 48–49
    national judicial systems 183–85
    refugee cases tried in 185–86
    see also fair trial
Crescent of Hope 322, 323
cruel, inhuman or degrading treatment or punishment
    freedom from 133–50
    headcounts 139–41
    NGOs, acts by 137–41, 293–94
    other refugees, acts by 133, 141–42
    sexual violence 142–51
    State, acts by 134–37
    UNHCR, acts by 137–41, 293–94
    see also liberty and security of the person; torture
Cuban refugees xiii
cultural relativism 8
cultural rights 260–63
    Kenya 261
    Uganda 262
    UNHCR 263

D
DanChurchAid xx, 52n.23
death
    death penalty 130, 144
    extra-judicial killings 130–33
    morbidity rates 16, 266n.42
    in prison 132–33
Democratic Republic of the Congo (DRC)
    conflict in 3
    refugees from 1, 61, 65, 86, 96, 101, 110, 115n.20, 118n.67, 132, 133, 136, 165, 168, 171, 196, 244, 277, 284, 286, 293, 329n.67

torture, use of 133
see also Zaire
Department for International
    Development (DFID) 279–81
detention
    arbitrary 167–73
    death in 132–33
Deutsch-Afrikanische Frauen
    Initiative (DAFI) 256
Deutsche Entwicklungsdienst (DED)
    219
Dinka refugees 128–30, 153–54, 261
dirigisme 296–97
discrimination 16
    1951 Convention and xiv
    Dinka youth 128–30
    in employment 221–22
    gender discrimination 47, 121–23,
        264
    gender stereotyping 123–26, 264
    racial and ethnic 126–27
    religious 127–28
    right to non-discrimination 121–30
documentation 70, 81
    convention travel documents
        (CTDs) xii, 59, 181, 196, 197,
        211n.151, 226
    forged 57, 59, 60, 63
    identity papers xii, 8, 16, 47, 48, 168,
        179
    passports 57, 59–60, 168
    protection letters 33–34, 113, 168
    safe travel letters 180
    travel documents xii, 8, 48, 57,
        59–60, 226
    work permits 16, 216–18
domestic violence 122, 125, 186,
    190–91, 203n.16
donor countries
    admission, influence on 55–57
    'recyclers' and 101
    refugee protection and 278–84
    resettlement policy and 283–84
    UNHCR and 278–83
Dörner, Dietrich 324
Dublin Convention 75n.28, 99, 103,
    116n.40

E
'economic' migrants 19, 95
economic and social rights xv, 214–64
    adequate standard of living 225–40
    education 253–60

employment 215–25
    physical and mental health 241–53
education 16
    1951 Convention and xv, 255
    'education for repatriation' 260
    ICESCR and xv, 253
    Kenya 254–56, 256–57, 258–60
    peace education 258–60, 270n.104,
        300
    reproductive health programmes
        250–51
    right to 253–60
    scholarship programmes 31, 255
    Uganda 42, 48, 254, 256–58, 260
    UNCHR provision 256–60
eligibility determination *see* status-
    determination procedures
employment
    discrimination in 218–21
    dismissal 218
    incentives 218–21
    refugee teachers in Uganda 221–24
    rights 215–25
    UNHCR practices 218–21, 223–24
    work permits 16, 216–18
employment discrimination, Kenya
    221–22
encampment policy xv, xvii, 15–16,
    21n.6, 47, 271–72, 309, 333–34, 336
    cost-assessment 334
    donors and 278–79
    Kenya 18, 33, 335
    Uganda 36, 47, 335, 337
    UNHCR 17, 18, 51n.12, 287–89,
        297–99, 336–37
entry point *see* point of arrival
entry procedures *see* admission of
    refugees
Equatorian Civic Fund 280
Ethiopia, refugees from 1, 22n.11, 31,
    32, 33, 71, 85, 91, 104, 111–12,
    114n.6, 146, 154, 170, 191, 192,
    200, 225, 233, 236
ethnic discrimination 126–27
evictions *see* forced evictions
expression, freedom of *see* freedom of
    expression
extra-judicial killings 130–33

F
fair trial
    collective punishment 193–94

'justice' in refugee camps/
settlements
Kenya 191–92
Uganda 186–91
right to 182–94
see also courts
families
respect for family life 195–97
separation of 195–97
Farah, Nuruddin 204n.19, 328n.50
female genital mutilation (FGM) 123,
148
fertility rates 253
FIDA *see* International Federation of
Women Lawyers
field reports 299–303
'first country of asylum' rule 35, 64,
99–104, 106, 117n.42, 117n.54, 224
food 24n.43, 228–35
Kenya 232–33
malnutrition 228, 229–31, 235–39,
280, 294
nutritional surveys 229–31
'recyclers' and 69–70, 101, 228
right to 227–38
supplementary feeding 232, 262n.42
trade and barter 204n.28, 233–34,
293
Uganda 43–44
UNHCR and 228–29, 230–31, 233,
293
water supplies 236
withholding of 18, 43–44, 140,
228–29
WFP and 44, 161, 230–32, 233
forced deportations 64–65
forced evictions 239–40
Ogujebe transit centre, destruction
of 18, 128, 156, 161–64, 239–40,
297, 302
forced labour 2
see also employment
forced marriage 122, 123, 145, 150
forced recruitment of children 120,
122, 174–79, 261, 302, 334
forced relocations 164–65, 199, 200, 240
forged documents 60, 63
passports 57, 59–60
'Fortress Australia' 278
'Fortress Europe' 56, 278
Foucault, Michel 299, 328n.48
Foundation for Human Rights
Initiative (FHRI) 317

France 103–4
freedom of association 200–1
freedom of expression 198–200
UNHCR and 199–200
freedom of movement 16, 179–82
Kenya 32, 180–81
Uganda 28, 29, 47, 179–82
'full-belly' theory 289
funding
charity 332
of NGOs 17, 279–80
of UNHCR 17, 34, 35, 41
see also donor countries

G
Garang, John 2, 175–76, 277
Geldof, Sir Bob 324
gender discrimination 47, 121–26, 263
Canada 54n.52
Kenya 121
South Africa 54n.52
Uganda 47, 121
gender stereotyping 123–26, 264
gender-based violence 251–52
see also sexual violence
Geneva Convention III 266n.38, 316
Geneva Convention IV 140, 194
genital mutilation *see* female genital
mutilation
genocidaires, screening for 67, 107–10
genocide 206n.60
in Rwanda 3, 107, 108, 119n.73, 126,
131, 135
in Zaire 116n.34
Germany 103–4, 117n.55
Godfrey, Nancy 268n.73
Goodwin-Gill, G. 73n.8, 290, 303
Gramsci, Antonio 316
Great Britain *see* United Kingdom
group recognition 57
see also Convention Governing the
Specific Aspects of Refugee
Problems in Africa

H
Habyarimana, President of Rwanda 3
Haitian refugees xiii
headcounts 35, 101, 139–41, 193, 282
health, right to 241–53
children 247–48
individual violations 244–50
mental health 247–50
reproductive health 250–53

health services 16, 241, 242–43
  Kenya 241
  'over-utilisation' 248–49, 292
  preventive measures 242
  in prison 247
  triaging 249
  Uganda 241
  UNHCR parallel services 39, 241–44
helplessness, effects of 293
HIV/AIDS 232, 251–52
Holy Spirit Mobile Forces rebellion
  21n.4
Hope International School 201, 225,
  254
housing 238–39
Hugh Pilkington Charitable Trust 181,
  211n.135, 256
human rights
  awareness of law on 9, 14, 19
  nature of 8
  universality of 8
  see also civil and political rights;
    cultural rights; economic and
    social rights
human rights organisations 316–19
  international 316–18
  Kenya 21
  national 318–19
  Uganda 21
Human Rights Watch (HRW) 6, 20,
  138, 143, 144, 314, 317–18
human trafficking 56, 73n.1
humanitarian conscience 332
'humanitarian internationale' 26, 45
Hutus
  in Burundi 4
  discrimination against 126–27
  massacre of 3, 4
  Tingi Tingi refugees 65–67

I
identity papers xiv, 8, 16, 47, 48, 168,
  179
image management 299–305, 333
*Imposing Aid: Emergency Assistance to
  Refugees* xii–xiii, 313
'incentive' workers 218–21
infibulation *see* female genital
  mutilation
integration xviii, 2, 16, 100–1, 272, 278,
  288, 291, 334, 336–38
  Kenya 18, 25n.44, 32, 277, 336–37
  Uganda 29–30, 41, 44, 47, 337–38

Inter-African Organisation of Jurists
  201
InterAid 39–40, 52n.35, 83, 136, 137,
  145, 165, 167, 178, 197, 245, 246,
  293, 295
  status-determination procedures 86,
    89–90, 91, 93, 333
interception practices *see* admission
International Aid Sweden 22n.10, 70,
  326n.14
International Commission of Jurists
  (ICJ) 51n.16, 94, 290, 317–18
  PARinAC and 319–24
International Committee of the Red
  Cross (ICRC) 69, 195–96, 210n.39
International Conference on
  Assistance to Refugees in Africa
  (ICARA II) 42, 289
International Court of Justice 305
International Covenant on Civil and
  Political Rights (ICCPR)
  Article 2 121
  Article 7 205n.44
  Article 8(3)(c) 151
  Article 9 152
  Article 12 179, 195
  Article 14 182, 192
  Article 17 267n.64
  Article 18 198
  Article 19 198
  Article 20 198
  Article 23 195
  enforcement 305
  ICESCR compared with 214
International Covenant on Economic,
  Social and Cultural Rights
  (ICESCR) 215
adequate food, clothing and housing
  and improvement of living
  conditions 226, 239, 240
  Article 2(1) 215
  Article 6 215
  Article 7 151, 264n.10
  Article 11 225, 239, 240
  Article 12 241, 250
  Article 13 xvii, 253
  Article 15 241, 260
  Article 15(1)(a) 262
  benefits of scientific progress and
    applications 241
  ICCPR compared 214
  See also economic and social rights,
    and cultural rights

International Federation of Women
  Lawyers (FIDA) 123, 144, 145–46,
  147, 150, 197, 317
International Labour Organisation
  264n.1
International Monetary Fund (IMF)
  273
International Rescue Committee (IRC)
  234, 265n.36, 310
interpreters 92–93
'irregular movers' 100–1
Islamic African Relief Agency (IARA)
  322, 323

J
Jessen-Peterson, S. 304
Jesuit Refugee Service (JRS) 1, 24n.33,
  33–34, 42, 72–73, 83, 178–79
  partnership with UNHCR 313
  repatriation 42
  scholarship programme 254–56
  status-determination procedures 82,
    83, 87–89, 90, 98–99, 104, 333
  teachers' strike and 222–24
  training 217
Joint Voluntary Agency (JVA) 132,
  282, 326n.18

K
Kabila, Laurent 3
Kapuscinski, R. 265n.26
Kenya
  admission of refugees 58, 60, 62–65,
    68–69, 70–72
  airports, dumping at 63–65
  Anti-Corruption Authority 273
  arbitrary arrest and detention
    167–70
  arrivals en masse 68
  Bill of Rights 27
  capital punishment 130
  church organisations 31, 32
  closure of refugee camps 35
  collective punishment 193–95
  convention travel documents
    (CTDs) 226
  Conventions and 26–27, 49, 81, 121,
    216
  corruption 32, 274–75
  courts, access to 183, 184, 185
  cruel, inhuman or degrading
    treatment or punishment 134–35,
    136–37
  cultural rights 261–62
  death penalty 130
  draft refugee bills 45–46
  economic and social rights 216
  education, access to 254–55, 258–60
  employment discrimination 220–21
  encampment policy 18, 33, 335
  extra-judicial killings 130
  'first country of asylum' rule 99–104
  food distribution 231–32
  forced relocations of refugees
    164–65
  forged documents 60
  freedom of movement 32, 180–81
  gender discrimination 121
  gender stereotyping 123, 124
  government control of refugee
    policy 31–32
  health services 241, 242
  human rights organisations 21
  ICESCR and 215
  integration of refugees 18, 25n.44,
    32, 277, 336–37
  international law and 48–49
  international treaties 27, 49
  legal framework 26–27
  main movements into 1–5
  malnutrition 165, 199, 230, 231–32,
    234–38
  National Eligibility Committee
    (NEC) 83
  National Refugee Secretariat (NRS)
    31
  naturalisation 35, 121
  new constitution 27
  NGOs 21, 31, 33, 87–89, 90, 275, 313,
    314, 315
  numbers of refugees in 1
  open-door laissez-faire refugee
    policy 18, 26, 31, 70, 216
  Partners in Action (PARinAC)
    319–24
  physical safety in camps and
    settlements 152–56
  point of arrival 68–69
  prosecutions 62–63
  protection letters 33–34, 168
  reception centres 31, 32, 33, 68–69
  refoulement 32
  refugee policy 19, 26, 31–36
  refugees from 1
  safe travel letters 180
  SPLA and 276

status-determination procedures
31–32, 35, 36, 45–46
advocacy 93–94
cessation 110–13
confidentiality 91, 92
control of 80–83
credibility 104–7
decisions 96–107
exclusion 107–9
'first country of asylum' 99–104
interpreters 92–93
NGOs, role of 87–89, 90
standards 80
'stranger', role of 23n.20
Tingi Tingi refugees 65–68
UNCHR and 26, 31, 33, 34–36
work permits 216–17
Kenya Refugee Consortium (KRC) 10

L
Lakwena, Alice 21n.4, 142, 206n.59,
267n.63
Lawyers' Committee for Human
Rights (LCHR) 95, 108, 114n.5,
203n.17, 317
African Exodus xiii
PARinAC and 320, 321
Levi, Primo 206n.55
liberty and security of the person
arbitrary arrest and detention
167–73
forced recruitment of children 120,
122, 174–79, 261, 302, 334
housing 238–39
Ogujebe transit centre, destruction
of 18, 161–64, 240–41, 297, 302
physical safety in camps and
settlements 152–61
right to 152–79
Uganda 161–64
see also cruel, inhuman or
degrading treatment or
punishment; forced evictions;
sexual violence
life, right to 130–33
Live Aid 324
Lomé IV Convention 34
Lord's Resistance Army (LRA) 21n.4,
131, 156, 159–60
Lubbers, Ruud 287, 326n.25
Lutheran World Federation (LWF) 43,
137, 153, 164, 192, 204n.28,
238–39, 283, 314

M
malnutrition 228, 229–31, 235–39, 280,
294
Kenya 230, 235–38
Uganda 230, 235
Mandela, Nelson 4
marriage, forced 122, 123, 145, 150
Mau Mau rebellion 21n.4, 22n.11
Médecins san Frontières (MSF)
76n.37, 149, 248, 292, 313
Micombero, Michel 4
Moi, Daniel arap 32, 66, 169, 274, 276,
277
movement, freedom of *see* freedom of
movement
Movement for the Liberation of
Congo (MLC) 3
Museveni, Yoweri 2–3, 21n.4, 64, 86,
97, 126, 132, 159, 165, 211n.145,
254, 276
Muslim refugees 127–28

N
National Council of Churches of
Kenya (NCCK) 149, 250, 251
National Resistance Army (NRA) 3,
171
naturalisation
Kenya 35, 121
Tanzania 202n.2
Uganda 28–29, 30, 41
Ndadaye, Melchior 4, 119n.76
Ndayizeye, Domitien 4
Newland, Kathleen 305
1951 Convention *see* Convention
Relating to the Status of Refugees
1951
non-discrimination, right to 121–30
see also discrimination
non-governmental organisations
(NGOs) 1, 8, 17, 312–24
accountability 275
cruel, inhuman or degrading
treatment or punishment 137–41,
294
encampment policy and 18
food, right to 228
funding 17, 279–80
health services 241–42
human rights organisations 316–19
Kenya 21, 31, 33, 87–89, 90, 275, 313,
314, 315
performance measurement 316

refugee advocacy 20
regulation of 275
relationship with UNHCR 20, 313–15
repatriation and 18
status-determination procedures
    87–90
Uganda 21, 42, 43, 89–90, 276, 313,
    314
non-refoulement principle xii, 8, 57, 72,
    308
Uganda 30, 75n.23
see also refoulement
Ntaryamira, President of Burundi 3
Nyakagwa, Eroni 50n.10
Nyerere, Julius 4

O
OAU Convention *see* Convention
    Governing the Specific Aspects of
    Refugee Problems in Africa 1969
Ogaden war 4
Ogata, Sadako 287
Ogujebe transit centre 129
    destruction of 18, 128, 156, 161–64,
    239–40, 297, 302
Operation Lifeline Sudan (OLS) 73n.5,
    179, 326n.15, 339n.7
ostracism 122, 146, 202n.6
OXFAM 44, 253

P
Pacific Solution 56
participatory research 10–11, 15
Partners in Action (PARinAC) 319–24
passports 57, 59–60, 168
    forged 57, 59–60
    obtaining 59–60
peace education 258–59, 299–300
People for Peace in Africa 113
place of residence, choice of 16
    Uganda 28
Plato 330n.80
point of arrival 68–70
    Kenya 68–69
    Uganda 69–70
police
    corruption 32, 135, 168–69
    cruel, inhuman or degrading
    treatment or punishment 134–35
    deaths in custody 132–33
    knowledge of refugee law 14, 60
    status-determination procedures 19,
    60–61

see also arbitrary arrest and
    detention
Polish refugees 22n.11
political rights *see* civil and political
    rights
polygamy 203n.16
porous borders 70–71
privacy and family life, respect for
    195–97
prostitution 44, 125–26
protection *see* refugee protection
protection letters 33–34, 113, 168

Q
Quality of Mercy, The 313

R
racial discrimination 126–27
Rally for the Return of Refugees and
    Democracy in Rwanda (RDR) 107
rape *see* sexual violence
Rassemblement Congolais pour la
    Démocratie (RCD) 3, 133
recruitment of children, forced 120,
    122, 174–79, 261, 302, 334
'recyclers' 69–70, 101, 228, 238
refoulement 7, 115n.19, 302, 334
    at airport ('Air Refoulement') 63, 64
    Kenya 32
    rejection at frontier xiv, 57, 58
    Tanzania 66
    Uganda 30, 58
    see also non-refoulement principle
refugee, definitions xvin.12, 22n.8, 47
refugee advocacy 20–21, 93–94
Refugee-Affected Area (RAA) policy
    52n.23
refugee associations 200–1
Refugee Consortium of Kenya (RCK)
    94, 314
Refugee Eligibility Committee (REC)
    37, 64, 83–84, 109
refugee law
    awareness of 9, 14, 19
    UNHCR compliance 305–7
Refugee Law Project (RLP) 10, 14–15,
    50n.9, 85, 218, 314
refugee policy 18–19, 272, 325, 335–37
    government control 31–32, 36–37
    Kenya 19, 26, 31–36
    Sudan 34
    Uganda 19, 36–45, 48
    UNHCR control of 33–36, 37–44

refugee protection 7–8, 272–26, 306,
   333, 335
   diminution of 289–91
   donor countries 277–83
   encampment policy and 271–72
   foreign policy and 275–76
   Kenya 272–77
   resettlement 283–87
   Uganda 272–77
   UNHCR 287–312
refugee teachers, Uganda 221–24
religious discrimination 127–28
repatriation 2, 16, 35, 42, 240, 334–36
   'education for repatriation' 260
   UNHCR policy 18, 260, 272, 334–36
reproductive health 250–53
   fertility rates 253
   UNHCR policy 250–53
research
   action research 9–10, 13–15
   aims and objectives 5–7
   assumptions underlying 7–9
   case studies 11–13
   main findings 15–19
   methods 9–15
   participatory approach 10–11, 15
   reconstructing the practice of law 11
resettlement 16, 273, 283–87, 333
   buufis 286
   corruption 287
   donor countries and 282–83
   identifying cases for 282–85, 295–96
   as 'market opportunity' 285–86
   priority groups 284–85
   Somali Bantus 284
   Sudanese 'walking boys' 284
   UNHCR and 283–87, 295–96
residence *see* place of residence
return *see* non-refoulement principle;
   refoulement; repatriation
revalidation exercises 139–41
rights *see* civil and political rights;
   cultural rights; economic and
   social rights; human rights
Rwanda
   conflicts in 3
   genocidaires, screening for 68, 107–8
   genocide 3, 131
   massacres in 3
   passports 59
   refugees from 1, 2, 36, 65–68, 83, 86,
      101, 104, 107, 111, 254, 333
   screening for *genocidaires* 68

United States and 107, 275
   US support for 275
Rwandan Patriotic Army (RPA) 3
Rwandan Patriotic Front (RPF) 66, 67,
   107, 131

S
Sabena *see* Belgium
'safe havens' policy 326n.15
safe travel letters 180
safety *see* liberty and security of the
   person
sanitation, water supplies 236
Save the Children Fund (SCF) 229,
   237, 253
scholarship programmes 31, 254–56
segregation of refugees *see*
   encampment policy
'self-settled' refugees 3, 22n.9, 70
self-sufficiency, promotion of 21n.6,
   36, 37, 39, 41–44, 49, 296, 337
Sendashonga, Seth 130, 131
September 11, 2001 5
settlement policy *see* encampment
   policy
sexual exploitation 125–26
   prostitution 44, 125–26
sexual violence 120, 122, 142–51, 251,
   293
   children 145, 151
sexually transmitted diseases 126, 252
   HIV/AIDS 232, 251–52
shelter 238–39
Shermarke, Abdi Rashid Ali 4
Siad Barre, Muhammad 4–5
Slavery Convention 264n.1
slavery and forced labour, freedom
   from 151–52
social context 8
socio-economic rights *see* economic
   and social rights
Socrates 330n.80
soft power 333, 339n.2
Somali Bantus 128, 284
Somalia 4
   conflicts in 4, 32
   Ogaden war 4
   peacekeeping mission in 5
   refugees from 1, 4, 5, 32, 33, 68,
      71–72, 126, 127, 168, 216, 240
   UN intervention 5
Somaliland, declaration of
   independence 5

South Sudan Law Society (SSLS) 192,
201
South Sudan Relief Agency (SSRA) 69
Southern Sudan Relief Agency (SSRA)
97
Sphere Project 316
standard of living 225–40
clothing 238
food *see* food
measurement of 226
shelter 238–40
status-determination procedures
13–14, 78–114
1951 Convention 78, 79
advocacy 93–94
appeals 81
cessation 110–13
cessation en masse 111–12
confidentiality 91–92
control of 80–87
credibility 104–7
decisions 96–107
evidence, standards of 19, 94–96
exclusion 107–10
'first country of asylum' rule 35, 64,
99–104
genocidaires, screening for 68, 107–8
InterAid 86, 89–90, 91, 93, 333
interpreters 92–93
'irregular movers' 100–1
Jesuit Refugee Service (JRS) 82, 83,
87–89, 90, 98–99, 104, 333
Kenya *see* Kenya
NGOs, role of 87–90
OAU Convention 78, 79
'offshoring' of 56
police and 19, 60–61
reasons for decisions 97–98
recognition rates 79
'recyclers' 69–70
standards 79–80
Uganda *see* Uganda
UNHCR 17, 35, 36, 37, 78–79, 80–87,
91, 92, 93, 94–96, 99–113
'stranger', role of 23n.20
Sudan
Anyanya war 2, 29
conflicts in 2
refugee policy 34
refugees from 1, 36, 41, 85–86,
89–90, 97, 276
refugees in 3
'walking boys' 32, 68, 128, 284

Sudan Human Rights Association
(SHRA) 147, 201
Sudan People's Liberation Army
(SPLA) 2, 69, 97, 109, 122, 128,
133, 172, 175, 192, 261–62, 276,
278
forced recruitment of children 120,
122, 174–79, 261, 302, 334
refoulements 302
Sudan Women's Association in Nairobi
(SWAN) 169, 192, 201, 225
Sudanese Commission for Refugees
34, 54n.47
Sudanese Human Rights Association
317
Sweden 64
International Aid Sweden 22n.10,
70, 326n.14
Swedish International Development
Agency (SIDA) 278, 279
Switzerland 117n.56

T
Tanzania
destruction of infrastructure 53n.44
naturalisation 202n.2
refoulement from 66, 304, 310
refugees in 3, 4, 107, 206n.57, 329 n.
67, 333
Ted Turner Fund 150
Tingi Tingi refugees 65–68
torture
definition 133
freedom from 133–51
needs of victims 133–34
see also cruel, inhuman or
degrading treatment or
punishment
Torture Convention 133
Transcultural Psycho-social
Organisation (TPO) 163
travel documents 8, 48
convention travel documents
(CTDs) xii, 59, 181, 196, 197,
211n.151, 226
forged 57, 59–60, 63
passports 57, 59–60
Turkana nomads 125–26
Tutsis 4
discrimination against 105, 118n.67,
119, 126, 154
massacre of 3–4
refugees 2, 64

U
Uganda
abductions 165–67
administration of settlements 30, 36, 39
admission of refugees 60, 61–62, 63–65, 69–72
airports, dumping at 63–65
arbitrary arrest and detention 170–74
Bill of Rights 28
citizenship, acquisition of 28–29, 41
Constitution 28, 44
courts, access to 184, 185–86
cruel, inhuman or degrading treatment or punishment 135–36
cultural rights 262
Department of Refugees 48
Dinka refugees 128–30
Directorate of Refugees (DoR) 17, 30, 36–37, 38, 39, 84, 85, 168, 218, 256
disaster preparedness 44–45
dispossession of property 29
dispute settlement 187–91
draft refugee bill 10, 18, 45, 46–47
economic and social rights 216
education, right to 42, 48, 254, 256–58, 260
employment, right to seek 30, 48
encampment policy 36, 47, 335, 337
extra-judicial killings 131–32
'first country of asylum' 99–104
food rations, withdrawal of 43–44
forged documents 60
freedom of movement 28, 29, 47, 179–82
gender discrimination 47
government control of refugee policy 36–37
health services 241, 242
human rights organisations 21
ICESCR and 216
identity cards 47
integration of refugees 29–30, 41, 44, 47, 337–38
international law and 48–49
international treaties 28, 49
legal framework 26, 28–31, 218
liberty and security of the person 161–64, 165–67
main movements into 1–5
malnutrition 229, 235

National Resistance Movement (NRM) government 28–29, 31, 44
naturalisation 28–29, 30, 41
NGOs in 21, 42, 43, 89–90, 276, 313, 314
non-refoulement principle 30, 75n.23
numbers of refugees in 1
Ogujebe transit centre, destruction of 18, 128, 156, 161–64, 239–240, 297, 302
physical safety in camps and settlements 156–61
place of residence, choice of 28
point of arrival 69–70
Polish refugees 22n.11
powers of camp administrators 30
prosecutions 61–62
'recyclers', identifying 69–70
refoulement 30, 58
Refugee Eligibility Committee (REC) 37, 64, 83–84
refugee policy 19, 36–45, 48
refugee teachers 221–24
Refugee Welfare Committees (RWCs) 36, 129, 130, 141, 188, 258
refugees from 1, 32
segregation of refugees 30
'self-settled' populations 3
self-sufficiency, promotion of 21n.6, 36, 37, 39, 41–44, 49, 296, 337
SPLA and 276–77
status-determination procedures 19, 37, 46, 48
advocacy 94
cessation 110–13
confidentiality 91–92
control of 83–87
credibility 104–7
decisions 96–107
exclusion 109–10
'first country of asylum' 99–104
interpreters 92, 93
NGOs 89–90
standards 80
UNCHR and 26, 36, 37–44
urban refugee programme, Kampala 1
work permits 217–18
Uganda National Council for Children 14
Uganda National Rescue Front (UNRF II) 130

Uganda People's Defence Force
(UPDF) 172
Uganda Red Cross Society (URCS)
228, 307, 315
UN Relief and Works Agency
(UNRWA) 260
United Kingdom
1951 Convention and 50n.1
Department for International
Development (DFID) 279–81
'offshoring' of status determination
56
United Nations High Commissioner
for Refugees (UNHCR) xii, xiii,
xiv, 1, 8
accountability 273, 303–5, 329n.64,
330n.84
admission of refugees 58–59
bad publicity, dealing with 304–6
'blaming the refugees' 248–49,
292–94
bureaucratic interest in own
survival, precedence of 18, 26
community self-management
(CSM) 151–52
compliance with refugee law 305–7
conservatism of 311
cruel, inhuman or degrading
treatment or punishment 137–41,
293–94
cultural rights 263
cuts in expenditure 35
diminution in refugee protection
289–91
dirigisme 296–97
donor countries and 277–83
education, provision of 255–60
employment practices 218–21,
223–24
encampment policy 17, 18, 51n.12,
287–89, 297–99, 336–37
entry procedures 68–69
evaluation and policy analysis unit
303
'first country of asylum' rule 99–104
food distribution 228–29, 231–32,
232
forced evictions 239, 240
freedom of expression and 199–201
freedom of movement and 180,
181–82
funding 17, 34, 35, 41
handbooks 80, 93, 96, 291, 311

headcounts 139–41
health services, parallel systems
241–44
human rights and 18
ICJ and 291
image management 299–305, 333
'incentive' workers 218–21
individual incompetence 307–12
influence of 26
jurisdictional immunity 307
in Kenya 26, 31, 33, 34–36
nature of 9
negative publicity 303–5
Ogujebe transit centre, destruction
of 18, 128, 156, 161–64, 239–40,
297, 302
parallel services, provision of 39,
241–44
PARinAC and 319–24
peace education 258–60
refugee advocacy 20
refugee attitudes to 294–95
refugee policies, control of 33–36,
37–44
refugee protection 288–312
relationship with NGOs 20, 312–14
repatriation policy 18, 260, 272,
334–36
reports 84, 199, 299–305
reproductive health policy 250–53
resettlement and 283–87, 295–96
revalidation exercises 139–41
salary 'top-ups' 37–38
security, provision of 158–59, 160–61
staff appraisal system 310
status-determination procedures 17,
35, 36, 37, 78–79, 80–87, 113–14
advocacy 93, 94
cessation 110–13
confidentiality 91, 92
credibility 104–7
decisions 96–107
exclusion 107–10
'first country of asylum' rule
99–104
interpreters 92
NGOs, role of 87–90
standards of evidence 94–96
Uganda and 26, 36, 37–44
urban policy 44, 101, 288, 297–98,
335
as welfare agency 291–96
work permits 216, 217

United States, Rwanda and 107, 276
Universal Declaration of Human
    Rights (UDHR) xi, 195, 214, 225,
    260, 264n.10
urban policy, UNHCR 44, 101, 288,
    297–98, 335

V
violence
    domestic 122, 125, 186, 190–91,
        203n.16
    gender-based and sexual violence
        120, 122, 142–51, 251–52, 293

W
'walking boys', Sudanese 32, 68,
    284–85
Water Aid 43
water supplies 236
West Nile Bank Front (WNBF) 44,
    52n.32, 130
wife inheritance 122
women
    CEDAW xviii n.13, 50 n.3–4, 121,
        263, 267 n.69,
    discrimination against 47, 121–23,
        264
    female genital mutilation (FGM)
        123, 148
    forced marriage 122, 123, 145, 150
    gender stereotyping 123–26, 264
    prostitution 44, 125–26
    reproductive health 250–53
    sexual exploitation 125–26
    sexual violence 120, 122, 142–51,
        293
    wife inheritance 122
Women Lawyers' Association 123, 318
    see also International Federation of
        Women Lawyers
Women Victims of Violence (WVV)
    144, 149
work *see* employment
work permits 16, 216–18
    Kenya 216–17
    Uganda 217–18
    UNHCR and 217, 219
World Bank 272, 313, 318
World Food Programme (WFP) 33, 44,
    68
    donor countries and 281
    food distribution 44, 161, 227,
        230–32, 233

trade and barter of rations 233

Z
Zaire
    genocide in 116n.34
    refugees in 3, 66, 67, 107, 333
    see also Democratic Republic of the
        Congo